DATE DUE

PRINTED IN U.S.A.

D0557117

REGISTRATION CODE

2KXE-W9CU-AI85-FF9Z-4LT2

...ESS

...SOURCES.

For key premium o... ...de is entered, you will be...

If your course is us... ...ss the McGraw-Hill conten...

Access is provided... missing from this b... ...CT or Blackboard cou...

Registerin... ...ces

▽

TO gain a...
resources...

1. USE YOUR WEB BRO...
2. CLICK ON **FIRST T**...
3. ENTER THE REGISTRATION CODE* PRINTED ON THE TEAR-OFF BOOKMARK ON THE RIGHT.
4. AFTER YOU HAVE ENTERED YOUR REGISTRATION CODE, CLICK **REGISTER**.
5. FOLLOW THE INSTRUCTIONS TO SET-UP YOUR PERSONAL UserID AND PASSWORD.
6. WRITE YOUR UserID AND PASSWORD DOWN FOR FUTURE REFERENCE. KEEP IT IN A SAFE PLACE.

TO GAIN ACCESS to the McGraw-Hill content in your instructor's **WebCT** or **Blackboard** course simply log in to the course with the UserID and Password provided by your instructor. Enter the registration code exactly as it appears in the box to the right when prompted by the system. You will only need to use the code the first time you click on McGraw-Hill content.

Thank you, and welcome to your McGraw-Hill online Resources!

Higher Education

0-07-311125-2 T/A LANGAN: COLLEGE WRITING SKILLS WITH READINGS, 6E

THE FOUR BASES

Unity . . . *Seeing the whole as the sum of its parts*
Support . . . *The importance of evidence in writing*
Coherence . . . *The fundamentals of organization and transition*
Sentence Skills . . . *The craft of writing; its elements*

THE WRITING PROCESS:

1. **Prewriting.** Techniques such as freewriting, questioning, listing, and diagramming can help you identify your topic and your thesis.
2. **Writing a First Draft.** Once you've settled on a topic and thesis, write out a first draft of your essay. Make it your goal to state your thesis clearly and develop the content of your paper with plenty of specific details.
3. **Revising.** Revising means rewriting a paper in order to make it stronger. At this stage, focus on the style and content of your essay.
4. **Editing and Proofreading.** Editing involves reading over your paper closely, looking for errors in grammar, punctuation, and spelling. After proofreading for typographical and formatting errors, you are ready to hand in your essay!

Choosing the Right Word

- *accept* vs. *except*
  "I can accept those changes."
  [accept = welcome, admit]
  "I like all the cars except that one."
  [except = leaving out]

- *it's* vs. *its*
  "It's very hot in here." [it's = it is]
  "Never judge a book by its cover."
  [its = belonging to it]

- *affect* vs. *effect*
  "The death of my cat affected my day."
  [affect = influence]
  "The effect of the earthquake is still unclear."
  [effect = result]

- *than* vs. *then*
  "Coffee is better than vanilla."
  [than = comparison word]
  "Buy the cake, then come home."
  [then = at that time]

- *their* vs. *there* vs. *they're*
  "He lives in their basement."
  [their = belonging to them]
  "Don't go in there!"
  [there = at the place]
  "They're going to be angry."
  [they're = they are]

CORRECTION SYMBOLS

Agr: Correct the mistake in subject verb agreement or pronoun agreement.

Apos: Correct the apostrophe mistake.

Awk: Revise the awkward expression.

Cap: Correct the mistake in capital letters.

CS: Correct the comma splice.

DM: Correct the dangling modifier.

Det: Add more details.

Frag: Correct the sentence fragment.

Ic: Use a lowercase letter.

¶: Indent for a new paragraph.

Pro: Correct the pronoun mistake.

R-O: Fix the run-on sentence.

Sp: Correct the spelling error.

Trans: Supply a better transition.

Und: Underline.

WW: Replace the word marked with a more accurate one.

^: Add the omitted word or words.

√: Good point, detail, idea, etc.

Model Entries for a Works Cited List:

Book by One Author
Nuland, Sherwin B. *How We Die: Reflections on Life's Final Chapter.* New York:
Vintage, 1995.

Book by Two or More Authors
Baxandall, Rosalyn, and Elizabeth Ewen. *Picture Windows: How the Suburbs
Happened.* New York: Basic Books, 2000.

Magazine Article
Chin, Paula. "You Were a Good Man, Charlie Brown." *People* 28 June 2000: 52–59.

Newspaper Article
Zoroya, Gregg. "A Hunger for Heroes." *USA Today* 28 Feb. 2000: D1+.

Selection in an Edited Collection
Feist, Raymond E. "The Wood Boy." *Legends: Short Novels by the Masters of
Modern Fantasy.* Ed. Robert Silverberg. New York: Tor, 1998. 176–211.

Online Article
Bin, Thomas. "Texas Packaging Plant Burns out of Control." *CNN.Com.* 1 May 2002:
2 May 2002 <http://www.cnn.com/2002/US/05/01/texas.fire/index.html>.

USE WEBSITES:

College Writing Skills Online Learning
Center: www.mhhe.com/langan

Alta Vista: www.altavista.com

Google: www.google.com

Netscape: www.netscape.com

Yahoo!: www.yahoo.com

RefDesk: www.refdesk.com

INTERNET SEARCH TIPS:

- Use your search engine's "advanced search" option to narrow your search.

- Use " " to indicate phrases (words that should be grouped together).

- Be persistent – try different search terms if the first does not yield useful information.

- Try more than one search engine. Finding helpful sites on the Internet can take time.

FREQUENTLY MISSPELLED WORDS

accept	language	remember
all right	laugh	school
a lot	learn	sentence
although	led	several
another	leisure	should
attention	lesson	sight
awkward	loneliness	since
beautiful	measure	sometimes
because	minute	straight
been	necessary	studying
believe	neither	telephone
business	newspaper	though
can't	o'clock	through
careful	offer	together
choose	omit	tomorrow
different	only	understand
disease	opinion	until
doubt	opportunity	usual
education	original	variety
eight	ought	view
either	part	waist
except	peace	wear
foreign	pencil	weather
forward	people	weigh
general	possible	were
grammar	president	whether
great	psychology	which
having	quiet	without
head	quite	won't
however	raise	would
intelligence	really	written
interest	reason	year
interfere	receive	your
interrupt	recognize	you're
knowledge	refer	

College Writing Skills with Readings

ANNOTATED INSTRUCTOR'S EDITION

Praise for College Writing Skills with Readings

"The writing style, tone, and level of this text are perfect for my target student audience: the explanations are clear, the reading choices are varied and thought-provoking, and the amount of examples and exercises is just enough to help students but not so much that they feel overwhelmed."

—Marcie L. Sims, Green River Community College

"John Langan's pedagogical approach makes all kinds of sense to me. The emphasis on reading and structured writing provides students with a solid foundation in composition."

—Kristine R. Anderson, Riverside Community College

"The down-to-earth, believable student samples demonstrate the process of writing absolutely clearly, from a simple prewriting effort into a finished product. A student can identify not only with the content but see concrete examples of the process of writing."

—Gloria Jean Kirby, Lincoln Land Community College

"The structure of the book includes all of the essential content for teaching a freshman English class, and the organization is excellent."

—Julia L. Smith, Kennedy-King College

"The feature that I find the most appealing and useful is, first and foremost, the concept of the four bases. The supplements are also appealing because students can do work on their own, without having to listen too much to me."

—Christina Putney, Mott Community College

"I particularly like the emphasis on the 'traditional' (five-paragraph) essay. I view English as a skills course and I always stress tried-and-true approaches to writing that I know will prepare students for the types of essays they will be assigned in other college classes."

—J. Christian Tatu, Warren County Community College

"The text is organized for easy access. I don't feel like I'm lost or frustrated looking for the material I need when I need it."

—Midge Shaw, Rogue Community College

"I appreciate the concise and clear presentation of grammar and the grammar review tests. Students have ample examples, yet the grammar pages don't overtake the text."

—Lisa Windham, McLennan Community College

"I like the new edition's stronger emphasis on the writing process and the inclusion of professional essays."

—Judi Salsburg, Monroe Community College

"I'm especially pleased to see a stronger emphasis on prewriting and revision. As Donald Murray points out—good writing is essentially rewriting."

—Danielle True, Manatee Community College

College Writing Skills with Readings

Sixth Edition

ANNOTATED INSTRUCTOR'S EDITION

John Langan

Atlantic Cape Community College

Boston   Burr Ridge, IL   Dubuque, IA   Madison, WI   New York   San Francisco   St. Louis
Bangkok   Bogotá   Caracas   Kuala Lumpur   Lisbon   London   Madrid   Mexico City
Milan   Montreal   New Delhi   Santiago   Seoul   Singapore   Sydney   Taipei   Toronto

Higher Education

COLLEGE WRITING SKILLS WITH READINGS

This book is printed on acid-free paper.

2 3 4 5 6 7 8 9 0 VNH/VNH 0 9 8 7 6 5 4

ISBN 0-07-287132-6 (student edition)
ISBN 0-07-287136-9 (instructor's edition)

Publisher: *Lisa Moore*
Senior sponsoring editor: *Alexis Walker*
Director of development: *Carla K. Samodulski*
Marketing manager: *Lori DeShazo*
Senior project manager: *Christina Gimlin*
Production supervisor: *Tandra Jorgensen*
Photo researcher: *Alexandra Ambrose*
Senior designer: *Cassandra Chu*
Cover illustration: *Paul Turnbaugh*
Supplement producer: *Meghan Durko*
Media producer: *Todd Vaccaro*
Senior development editor, media: *Paul Banks*
Compositor: *Electronic Publishing Services, Inc., TN*
Typeface: *11/13 Times Roman*
Printer: *Von Hoffman Press*

Library of Congress Cataloging-in-Publication Data

Langan, John, 1942–
      College writing skills, with readings / John Langan.—6th ed., annotated instructor's ed.
         p.   cm.
      Includes index.
         ISBN 0-07-287132-6 (pbk. : acid-free paper)
         1. English language—Rhetoric. 2. English language—Grammar. 3. College readers.
      4. Report writing. I. Title.

      PE1408.L3178 2004
      808'.042'0711—dc22   2004052441

http://www.mhhe.com

About the Author

John Langan has taught reading and writing at Atlantic Cape Community College near Atlantic City, New Jersey, for over twenty-five years. The author of a popular series of college textbooks on both writing and reading, John enjoys the challenge of developing materials that teach skills in an especially clear and lively way. Before teaching, he earned advanced degrees in writing at Rutgers University and in reading at Rowan University. He also spent a year writing fiction that, he says, "is now at the back of a drawer waiting to be discovered and acclaimed posthumously." While in school, he supported himself by working as a truck driver, a machinist, a battery assembler, a hospital attendant, and an apple packer. John now lives with his wife, Judith Nadell, near Philadelphia. In addition to his wife and Philly sports teams, his passions include reading and turning on nonreaders to the pleasure and power of books. Through Townsend Press, his educational publishing company, he has developed the nonprofit "Townsend Library"—a collection of more than thirty new and classic stories that appeal to readers of any age.

The Langan Series

Contents

Readings Listed by Rhetorical Mode

Note: Some selections are cross-listed because they illustrate more than one rhetorical method of development.

Description

Narration

Examples

Process

Cause and Effect

Comparison and Contrast

To the Instructor

College Writing Skills with Readings is a rhetoric with readings that will help students master the traditional five-paragraph essay and variations of this essay. It is a very practical book with a number of unique features designed to aid instructors and their students.

Key Features of the Book

- *Four principles are presented as keys to effective writing.* These four principles — unity, support, coherence, and sentence skills—are highlighted on the inside front cover and reinforced throughout the book.

   Part One focuses on the first three principles and to some extent on sentence skills.

   Parts Two and Three show, respectively, how the four principles apply in the different patterns of essay development and in specialized types of writing.

   Part Four serves as a concise handbook of sentence skills.

   Finally, the professional readings in **Part Five** are followed by questions and assignments that encourage students to apply the four principles in a variety of well-developed essays.

   The ongoing success of *College Writing Skills with Readings* is evidence that the four principles are easily grasped, remembered, and followed by students.

- *Writing is treated as a process.* The first chapter introduces writing as both a skill and a process of discovery. The second chapter, "The Writing Process," explains and illustrates the sequence of steps in writing an effective essay. In particular, the chapter focuses on prewriting and revision as strategies to use with any writing assignment. Detailed suggestions for prewriting and revision then accompany many of the writing assignments in Part Two.

- *Activities and assignments are numerous and varied.* For example, in Part One there are more than 90 activities to help students apply and master the four principles, or bases, of effective writing. There are over 250 activities and tests in the entire book. A variety of writing assignments follow each pattern of essay development in Part Two and each reading in Part Five. Some topics are highly structured, for students who are still learning the steps in the writing process; others are open-ended. Instructors thus have the option of selecting those assignments most suited to the individual needs of their students.

- *Clear thinking is stressed throughout.* This emphasis on logic starts with the opening pages of the book. Students are introduced to the two principles that are the bedrock of clear thinking: *making a point* and *providing support to back up that point.* The focus on these principles then continues throughout the book, helping students learn that clear writing is inseparable from clear thinking.

- *The traditional essay is emphasized.* Students are asked to write formal essays with an introduction, three supporting paragraphs, and a conclusion. Anyone who has tried to write a solidly reasoned essay knows how much work is involved. A logical essay requires a great deal of mental discipline and close attention to a set of logical rules. Writing an essay in which there is an overall thesis statement and in which each of three supporting paragraphs begins with a topic sentence is more challenging for many students than writing a free-form or expressive essay. The demands are significant, but the rewards are great.

  At the same time that students learn and practice the rules of the five-paragraph essay, professional essays representing the nine patterns of development show them variations possible within the essay form. These essays provide models if instructors decide that their students will benefit from moving beyond the traditional essay form.

- *Lively teaching models are provided.* The book includes two high-interest student essays and one engaging professional essay with each chapter in Part Two. Students then read and evaluate these essays in terms of the four bases: unity, support, coherence, and sentence skills. Instructors can also refer their students to appropriate essays from the collection of professional readings in Part Five. After reading vigorous papers by other students as well as papers by professional authors and experiencing the power that good writing can have, students will be encouraged to aim for a similar honesty, realism, and detail in their own work.

- *The book is versatile.* Since no two people use an English text in exactly the same way, the material has been organized in a highly accessible manner. Each of the five parts of the book deals with a distinct area of writing. Instructors can therefore turn quickly and easily to the skills they want to present.

- *Nineteen professional essays appear in Part Five.* These essays, like the nine professional readings in Part Two, deal with both contemporary and timeless concerns. They will stimulate lively class discussions and individual thought as well as serve as a rich source of material for a wide range of writing assignments.

There are three special features of Part Five. First is the emphasis placed on helping students become stronger readers. An introductory section offers tips on effective reading, and questions after each selection help students practice skills in both reading comprehension and critical thinking. A second feature of Part Five is a set of questions about structure and technique so that students can analyze and learn from a writer's craft in developing an essay. Finally, a series of writing assignments include suggestions and guidelines that will help students think about and proceed with an assignment.

Changes in the Sixth Edition

Here is an overview of what is new in the sixth edition of the book:

- The most substantial change in the book is *its greater focus on purpose and audience.* The introductory chapter of the text signals this new emphasis with a segment titled "Writing as a Way to Communicate with Others." A new section, "Considering Purpose and Audience," has been added to each of the nine rhetorical pattern chapters in Part Two. This new section deepens students' understanding of the purpose of each mode and teaches them to adjust their writing to suit the needs and expectations of their audience. Finally, each mode chapter in Part Two now concludes with a special writing assignment titled "Writing for a Specific Audience and Purpose." This assignment encourages students' creativity and helps them connect their work in the classroom with writing needs in the outside world.

- Another addition is *an increased attention to writing thesis statements.* Four new practice activities have been added to Chapter 3, and the chapter also expands its coverage of common mistakes in thesis writing and helpful strategies for avoiding such mistakes. More examples of effective and ineffective thesis statements are now included.

- The book features *five new readings,* including new model essays for Chapter 12 (cause and effect) and Chapter 13 (comparison and contrast). Chosen for their appeal and relevance to today's students, these new essays address the widespread anger in our culture and what to do about it; the differences between the sexes that are so profound they may perhaps be hard-wired; the passions that give meaning to our lives; a child's experience of a defining moment in the lives of her parents; and the inspiring account of a mother who was a first-grade dropout but who goes on to dramatically change her life when her children are labeled as "slow learners" in school.

- The new edition includes an *expanded treatment of plagiarism.* Added cautions to students will help instructors deal with the widespread availability of information on the Internet. An activity is now provided to sharpen students' understanding of what is acceptable paraphrase and/or summary and what is plagiarism.

- Among a number of revisions to the library and research chapters are new model entries for electronic sources and added attention to the evaluation of Internet sources.

- Practice materials, example items, and activities have been revised and updated throughout the book, with special emphasis on Part Four. In particular, the chapter titled "ESL Pointers" has been expanded with four new activities to address common concerns of ESL Learners.

- A new full-color design adds visual appeal for students while highlighting key material for them and helping them make connections and find the information they need. In addition, one assignment in each of the modes chapters is now illustrated with a photograph to give today's visually oriented students even more help with choosing a topic. Photos of most of the authors of the readings have also been added to Part Five.

About the Media Links

The sixth edition of *College Writing Skills* includes icons that link the text and its class-tested media supplements: *College Writing Skills'* Student CD-ROM and Online Learning Center; *AllWrite!* 2.0, McGraw-Hill's acclaimed grammar tutorial software; and the new *Virtual Workbook,* which offers additional online activities. Each of the 45 chapters in this edition features marginal icons, that alert students to additional exercises, extended explanations, and supplemental resources for the topic at hand.

- **Learning Objectives/Chapter Outlines/Key Terms/Visuals:** A list of learning objectives, chapter outlines, definitions of key terms, and PowerPoint slides and other visuals supplement each chapter of the textbook.

- **Writing Online and Offline:** Online activities encourage students to activate new concepts in writing—for example, one exercise in Chapter 12 foregrounds cause and effect by asking students to relate the plot of a favorite movie.

- **Interactive Exercises:** Crossword puzzles, matching exercises, and true-false and multiple-choice questions reinforce comprehension of key concepts and grammar rules.

- **Additional Resources:** Offerings include a comprehensive glossary; guides to using the Internet, avoiding plagiarism, and doing electronic research; a study skills primer, links to further information on the readings in Part Five, and more.

- *AllWrite!* has more than 3,000 interactive exercises, complete with video clips and animations, to help students get grammar right. (The number tells you exactly which chapter and section of *AllWrite!* to consult; for instance, the icon at left refers to Chapter 15, Section 4.)

- **The *Virtual Workbook*** includes online activities and tests that supplement activities and tests in the book. (For more information on this new supplement, see below.)

New Technology: The *CWSwR Virtual Workbook* and *CWSwR, Online Edition*

With the Sixth Edition of *College Writing Skills with Readings*, we are pleased to introduce two new technology-based options that offer you an unprecedented opportunity to increase your students' motivation and engagement while simplifying your grading and course administration responsibilities: a *Virtual Workbook* to accompany *College Writing Skills with Readings*, and *College Writing Skills with Readings, Online Edition*.

The Virtual Workbook

The *Virtual Workbook* (ISBN 0-07-299415-0), an online supplement for students, offers brand-new activities that reinforce the skills students learn in Part Four of *College Writing Skills with Readings*. Authored by Donna Matsumoto, Leeward Community College, each interactive, Web-based activity in the *Virtual Workbook* specifically corresponds to a key section or chapter in Part Four, giving students additional opportunities for practice in grammar, punctuation, and mechanics. A *Virtual Workbook* icon in the margins of *College Writing Skills with Readings* makes the interactive activities easy for instructors to integrate into their courses and for motivated students to consult on their own. The *Virtual Workbook* is supported by a powerful array of Web-based instructor's tools, including an automated online gradebook, and assessment, analysis, and classroom management tools.

College Writing Skills with Readings, Online Edition

Ideal for distance learning or lab-based courses, *College Writing Skills with Readings, Online Edition* (ISBN 0-07-299413-4) represents an *alternative* to the traditional print textbook. Instructors opting to use the *Online Edition* in their courses give students online access to the contents of the printed textbook—over 2,500 activities, exercises, and writing assignments—in an interactive, Web-based format. To facilitate hybrid courses and ease the transition to Web-based courses and textbooks, each *Online Edition* is accompanied by a free copy of the *Offline Companion*, a printed supplement that contains activities and readings instructors have told us simply work better on the printed page. The *Online Edition* is accompanied by an array of Web-based features for instructors, including an automated online gradebook and assessment, analysis, and classroom management tools. To learn more about *College Writing Skills with Readings, Online Edition,* consult your local sales representative or send an e-mail to english@mcgraw-hill.com.

Helpful Learning Aids Accompany the Book

Supplements for Instructors

- *The Instructor's Edition* (ISBN 0-07-287136-9) consists of the student text complete with answers to all activities and tests, followed by an Instructor's Guide featuring teaching suggestions, a model syllabus, and suggested answers to the craft and discussion questions that follow the readings in Part Five. The Instructor's Edition of *College Writing Skills with Readings* also includes three new diagnostic/achievement tests: two 40-question tests (A and B), and, for added flexibility, a single 60-question test (C) derived from A and B. These tests, along with their scoring keys, are included in print form in the back of the book. The tests are also available via the *College Writing Skills with Readings* Online Learning Center (www.mhhe.com/langan). Instructors directing students to take the tests online can have students' scores and assessment e-mailed to them directly. (Students taking these tests will receive their final scores and an assessment, but not the correct answers to individual responses.)

- An *Online Learning Center* (**www.mhhe.com/langan**) offers a host of instructional aids and additional resources for instructors, including a comprehensive computerized test bank, the Instructor's Manual and Test Bank, online resources for writing instructors, and more.

- An *Instructor's CD-ROM* (0-07-287134-2) offers all of the above supplements in a convenient offline format.

- *PageOut!* helps instructors create graphically pleasing and professional Web pages for their courses, in addition to providing classroom management, collaborative learning, and content management tools. PageOut! is **FREE** to adopters of McGraw-Hill textbooks and learning materials. Learn more at **www.mhhe. com/pageout**.

Supplements for Students

- A free *Student CD-ROM* (ISBN 0-07-287137-7) offers a host of instructional aids and additional resources for students, in addition to all of the resources of the Students' Online Learning Center in a convenient offline format.

- An *Online Learning Center* (**www.mhhe.com/langan**) includes self-correcting exercises, writing activities for additional practice, a PowerPoint grammar tutorial, guides to doing research on the Internet and avoiding plagiarism, useful Weblinks, and more.

- *AllWrite!* is an interactive, browser-based tutorial program that provides an online handbook, comprehensive diagnostic pre-tests and post-tests, and extensive practice exercises in every area.

- The *Virtual Workbook* (ISBN 0-07-299415-0), which has been developed to accompany both the printed and online versions of the text, includes additional practices. Icons in the margin let students know when they can find an additional activity in the *Virtual Workbook.*

Dictionary and Vocabulary Resources

- *Random House Webster's College Dictionary* (ISBN 0-07-240011-0) This authoritative dictionary includes over 160,000 entries and 175,000 definitions. The most commonly used definitions are always listed first, so students can find what they need quickly.

- *The Merriam-Webster Dictionary* (ISBN 0-07-310057-9) Based on the best-selling *Merriam-Webster's Collegiate Dictionary,* the paperback dictionary contains over 70,000 definitions.

- *The Merriam-Webster Thesaurus* (ISBN 0-07-310067-6) This handy paperback thesaurus contains over 157,000 synonyms, antonyms, related and contrasted words, and idioms.

- *Merriam-Webster's Vocabulary Builder* (ISBN 0-07-310069-2) This handy paperback introduces 3,000 words, and includes quizzes to test progress.

- *Merriam-Webster's Notebook Dictionary* (ISBN 0-07-299091-0) An extremely concise reference to the words that form the core of English vocabulary, this popular dictionary, conveniently designed for 3-ring binders, provides words and information at students' fingertips.

- *Merriam-Webster's Notebook Thesaurus* (ISBN 0-07-310068-4) Conveniently designed for 3-ring binders, this thesaurus helps the student search for words they might need today. It provides concise, clear guidance for over 157,000 word choices.

- *Merriam-Webster's Collegiate Dictionary and Thesaurus, Electronic Edition* (ISBN 0-07-310070-6) Available on CD-ROM, this online dictionary contains thousands of new words and meanings from all areas of human endeavor, including electronic technology, the sciences, and popular culture.

You can contact your local McGraw-Hill representative or consult McGraw-Hill's Web site at **www.mhhe.com/english** for more information on the supplements that accompany *College Writing Skills with Readings, Sixth Edition.*

Acknowledgments

Reviewers who have contributed to this edition through their helpful comments include

Kristine R. Anderson, Riverside Community College

Ben DeSure, Pittsburgh Technical Institute

Carolyn E. Gordon, Cuyahoga Community College

Laura Hope-Aleman, Chaffey College

Teresa S. Irvin, Columbus State University

Gloria Jean Kirby, Lincoln Land Community College

Gail K. L. Levy, Leeward Community College

Donna Matsumoto, Leeward Community College

Christina Putney, Mott Community College

Judi Salsburg, Monroe Community College

Midge Shaw, Rogue Community College

Marcie L. Sims, Green River Community College

Julia L. Smith, Kennedy-King College

J. Christian Tatu, Warren County Community College

Eileen Thompson, Edison Community College

Dennielle True, Manatee Community College

Lisa Windham, McLennan Community College

I am also grateful for help provided by Janet M. Goldstein, Beth Johnson, Paul Langan, Eliza Comodromos, and Judith Nadell, as well as for the talented support of past and present McGraw-Hill editors: Susan Gamer, Carla Samodulski, and Alexis Walker.

John Langan

PART ONE

Essay Writing

1 An Introduction to Writing

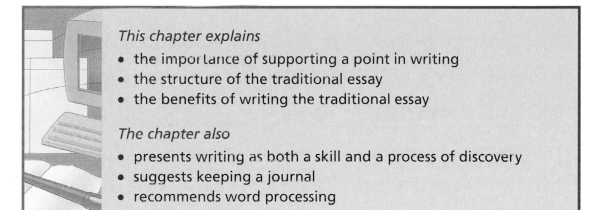

This chapter explains
- the importance of supporting a point in writing
- the structure of the traditional essay
- the benefits of writing the traditional essay

The chapter also
- presents writing as both a skill and a process of discovery
- suggests keeping a journal
- recommends word processing

The experience I had writing my first college essay helped shape this book. I received a C– for the essay. Scrawled beside the grade was the comment "Not badly written, but ill-conceived." I remember going to the instructor after class, asking about his comment as well as the word *Log* that he had added in the margin at various spots. "What are all these logs you put in my paper?" I asked, trying to make a joke of it. He looked at me a little wonderingly. "Logic, Mr. Langan," he answered, "logic." He went on to explain that I had not thought out my paper clearly. There were actually two ideas rather than one in my thesis, one supporting paragraph had nothing to do with either idea, another paragraph lacked a topic sentence, and so on. I've never forgotten his last words: "If you don't think clearly," he said, "you won't write clearly."

I was speechless, and I felt confused and angry. I didn't like being told that I didn't know how to think. I went back to my room and read over my paper several times. Eventually, I decided that my instructor was right. "No more logs," I said to myself. "I'm going to get these logs out of my papers."

My instructor's advice was invaluable. I learned that clear, disciplined thinking is the key to effective writing. *College Writing Skills with Readings* develops this idea by breaking down the writing process into a series of four logical, easily followed steps. These steps, combined with practical advice about prewriting and revision, will help you write strong papers.

Here are the four steps in a nutshell:

1   Discover a clearly stated point, or thesis.
2   Provide logical, detailed support for your thesis.
3   Organize and connect your supporting material.
4   Revise and edit so that your sentences are effective and error-free.

Part One of the book explains each of these steps in detail and provides many practice materials to help you master them.

Point and Support

An Important Difference between Writing and Talking

In everyday conversation, you make all kinds of points or assertions. You say, for example, "My boss is a hard person to work for"; "It's not safe to walk in our neighborhood after dark"; or "Poor study habits keep getting me into trouble." The points that you make concern personal matters as well as, at times, outside issues: "That trade will be a disaster for the team"; "Lots of TV commercials are degrading to women"; "Students are better off working for a year before attending college."

The people you are talking with do not always challenge you to give reasons for your statements. They may know why you feel as you do, or they may already agree with you, or they simply may not want to put you on the spot; and so they do not always ask, "Why?" But the people who read what you write may not know you, agree with you, or feel in any way obliged to you. If you want to communicate effectively with readers, you must provide solid evidence for any point you make. An important difference, then, between writing and talking is this: *In writing, any idea that you advance must be supported with specific reasons or details.*

Think of your readers as reasonable people. They will not take your views on faith, but they are willing to accept what you say as long as you support it. Therefore, remember to support with specific evidence any point that you make.

Point and Support in a Paragraph

In conversation, you might say to a friend who has suggested a movie, "No, thanks. Going to the movies is just too much of a hassle. Parking, people, everything." From shared past experiences, your friend may know what you are talking about so that you will not have to explain your statement. But in writing, your point would have to be backed up with specific reasons and details.

Below is a paragraph, written by a student named Diane Woods, on why moviegoing is a nuisance. A *paragraph* is a short paper of around 150 to 200 words. It usually consists of an opening point called a *topic sentence* followed by a series of sentences which support that point.

The Hazards of Moviegoing

Although I love movies, I've found that there are drawbacks to moviegoing. One problem is just the inconvenience of it all. To get to the theater, I have to drive for at least fifteen minutes, or more if traffic is bad. It can take forever to find a parking spot, and then I have to walk across a huge parking lot to the theater. There I encounter long lines, sold-out shows, and ever-increasing prices. And I hate sitting with my feet sticking to the floor because of other people's spilled snacks. Another problem is my lack of self-control at the theater. I often stuff myself with unhealthy calorie-laden snacks. My choices might include a bucket of popcorn, a box of Milk Duds, a giant soda, or all three. The worst problem is some of the other moviegoers. Kids run up and down the aisle. Teenagers laugh and shout at the screen. People of all ages drop soda cups and popcorn tubs, cough and burp, and talk to one another. All in all, I would rather stay home and wait to see the latest movie hits on cable TV in the comfort of my own living room.

Notice what the supporting evidence does here. It provides you, the reader, with a basis for understanding *why* the writer makes the point that is made. Through this specific evidence, the writer has explained and successfully communicated the idea that moviegoing can be a nuisance.

The evidence that supports the point in a paper often consists of a series of reasons followed by examples and details that support the reasons. That is true of the paragraph above: three reasons are provided, with examples and details that back up those reasons. Supporting evidence in a paper can also consist of anecdotes, personal experiences, facts, studies, statistics, and the opinions of experts.

ACTIVITY

The paragraph on moviegoing, like almost any piece of effective writing, has two essential parts: (1) a point is advanced, and (2) that point is then supported. Taking a minute to outline the paragraph will help you understand these basic parts clearly. Write in the following space the point that has been advanced in the paragraph. Then add the words needed to complete the outline of the paragraph.

Point   *There are drawbacks to moviegoing.*

Support

1. *Inconvenience*
   a. Fifteen-minute drive to theater
   b. *Long time to find parking spot, and long walk to theater*
   c. Long lines, sold-out shows, and increasing prices
   d. *Sticky floor*

2. Lack of self-control
   a. Often stuff myself with unhealthy snacks
   b. Might have popcorn, candy, soda, or all three

3. *Other moviegoers*
   a. *Running kids*
   b. *Laughing, shouting teenagers*
   c. People of all ages make noise.

Point and Support in an Essay

An excellent way to learn how to write clearly and logically is to practice the traditional college *essay*—a paper of about five hundred words that typically consists of an introductory paragraph, two to four supporting paragraphs (the norm in this book will be three), and a concluding paragraph. The central idea, or point, developed in any essay is called a *thesis statement* (rather than, as in a paragraph, a topic sentence). The thesis appears in the introductory paragraph, and the specific support for the thesis appears in the paragraphs that follow. The supporting paragraphs allow for a fuller treatment of the evidence that backs up the central point than would be possible in a single-paragraph paper.

Structure of the Traditional Essay

A Model Essay

The following model will help you understand the form of an essay. Diane Woods, the writer of the paragraph on moviegoing, later decided to develop her subject more fully. Here is the essay that resulted.

The Hazards of Moviegoing

Introductory
paragraph

I am a movie fanatic. My friends count on me to know movie trivia (who was the pigtailed little girl in <u>E.T.: The Extra-Terrestrial</u>? Drew Barrymore) and to remember every big Oscar awarded since I was in grade school (best picture 1994? <u>Forrest Gump</u>). My friends, though, have stopped asking me if I want to go out to the movies. While I love movies as much as ever, the inconvenience of going out, the temptations of the theater, and the behavior of some patrons are reasons for me to wait and rent the video.

First
supporting
paragraph

To begin with, I just don't enjoy the general hassle of the evening. Since small local movie theaters are a thing of the past, I have to drive for fifteen minutes to get to the nearest multiplex. The parking lot is shared with several restaurants and a supermarket, so it's always jammed. I have to drive around at a snail's pace until I spot another driver backing out. Then it's time to stand in an endless line, with the constant threat that tickets for the show I want will sell out. If we do get tickets, the theater will be so crowded that I won't be able to sit with my friends, or we'll have to sit in a front row gaping up at a giant screen. I have to shell out a ridiculous amount of money—up to $8—for a ticket. That entitles me to sit while my shoes seal themselves to a sticky floor coated with spilled soda, bubble gum, and crushed Raisinets.

Second
supporting
paragraph

Second, the theater offers tempting snacks that I really don't need. Like most of us, I have to battle an expanding waistline. At home I do pretty well by simply not buying stuff that is bad for me. I can make do with snacks like celery and carrot sticks because there is no ice cream in the freezer. Going to the theater, however, is like spending my evening in a Seven-Eleven that's been equipped with a movie screen and comfortable seats. As I try to persuade myself to just have a diet Coke, the smell of fresh popcorn dripping with butter soon overcomes me. Chocolate bars the size of small automobiles seem to jump into my hands. I risk pulling out my fillings as I chew enormous mouthfuls of Milk Duds. By the time I leave the theater, I feel disgusted with myself.

Third
supporting
paragraph

Many of the other patrons are even more of a problem than the concession stand. Little kids race up and down the aisles, usually in giggling packs. Teenagers try to impress their friends by talking back to the screen, whistling, and making what they consider to be hilarious noises. Adults act as if they were at home in their own living room. They comment loudly on the ages of the stars and reveal plot twists that are supposed to be a secret until the film's end. And people of all ages create distractions. They crinkle candy wrappers, stick gum on their seats, and drop popcorn tubs or cups of crushed ice and soda on the floor. They also cough and burp, squirm endlessly in their seats, file out for repeated trips to the rest rooms or concession stands, and elbow me out of the armrest on either side of my seat.

Concluding paragraph

After arriving home from the movies one night, I decided that I was not going to be a moviegoer anymore. I was tired of the problems involved in getting to the theater, resisting unhealthy snacks, and dealing with the patrons. The next day, I arranged to have premium movie channels installed as part of my cable TV service, and I also got a membership at my local video store. I may now see movies a bit later than other people, but I'll be more relaxed watching box office hits in the comfort of my own living room.

Parts of an Essay

"The Hazards of Moviegoing" is a good example of the standard short essay you will write in college English. It is a composition of over five hundred words that consists of a one-paragraph introduction, a three-paragraph body, and a one-paragraph conclusion. The roles of these paragraphs are described and illustrated below.

Introductory Paragraph

ALLWRITE!
8.1

The introductory paragraph of an essay should start with several sentences that attract the reader's interest. It should then advance the central idea, or *thesis*, that will be developed in the essay. The thesis often includes a *plan of development*—a "preview" of the major points that will support the thesis. These supporting points should be listed in the order in which they will appear in the essay. In some cases, the plan of development is presented in a sentence separate from the thesis; in other cases, it is omitted.

ACTIVITY

1. In "The Hazards of Moviegoing," which sentence or sentences are used to attract the reader's interest?

   a. First sentence

   b. First two sentences

   c. First three sentences

2. In which sentence is the thesis of the essay presented?

   a. Third sentence

   (b.) Fourth sentence

3. Does the thesis include a plan of development?

   (a.) Yes

   b. No

4. Write the words in the thesis that announce the three major supporting points in the essay:

   a. _inconvenience of going out_____

   b. _temptations of the theater_____

   c. _behavior of some patrons_____

Body: Supporting Paragraphs

Most essays have three supporting points, developed at length over three separate paragraphs. (Some essays have two supporting points, others four or more. For the purposes of this book, your goal will be three supporting points unless your instructor indicates otherwise.) Each of the supporting paragraphs should begin with a *topic sentence* that states the point to be detailed in that paragraph. Just as a thesis provides a focus for an entire essay, a topic sentence provides a focus for a supporting paragraph.

ACTIVITY

1. What is the topic sentence for the first supporting paragraph of the model essay?

   To begin with, I just don't enjoy the general hassle of the evening.

   _____

2. The first topic sentence is then supported by the following details (fill in the missing details):

   a. Have to drive fifteen minutes

   b. _Parking lot is always jammed._____

   c. Endless ticket line

   d. _Tickets may sell out, and theater is crowded._____

   e. _Tickets cost up to $8 each._____

   f. Sticky floor

3. What is the topic sentence for the second supporting paragraph of the essay?
   Second, the theater offers tempting snacks that I really don't need.

   _____

4. The second topic sentence is then supported by the following details:
   a. At home, only snacks are celery and carrot sticks.
   b. Theater is like a Seven-Eleven with seats.
      (1) fresh popcorn
      (2) chocolate bars
      (3) Milk Duds

5. What is the topic sentence for the third supporting paragraph of the essay?
   Many of the other patrons are even more of a problem than the concession stand.

6. The third topic sentence is then supported by the following details:
   a. Little kids race up and down the aisles.
   b. Teenagers talk back to the screen, whistle, make funny noises.
   c. Adults talk loudly and reveal plot twists.
   d. People of all ages create distractions.

Concluding Paragraph

ALLWRITE!
8.2

The concluding paragraph often summarizes the essay by briefly restating the thesis and, at times, the main supporting points. In addition, the writer often presents a concluding thought about the subject of the paper.

ACTIVITY

1. Which two sentences in the concluding paragraph restate the thesis and supporting points of the essay?
   (a.) First and second
   b. Second and third
   c. Third and fourth

2. Which sentence in the concluding paragraph contains the final thought of the essay?
   a. Second
   b. Third
   (c.) Fourth

Diagram of an Essay

The following diagram shows you at a glance the different parts of a standard college essay, also known as a *one-three-one essay*. This diagram will serve as a helpful guide when you are writing or evaluating essays.

Title of the Essay

Introduction

> Opening remarks to catch reader's interest
> Thesis statement
> Plan of development (optional)

Body

> Topic sentence 1 (supporting point 1)
> Specific evidence

> Topic sentence 2 (supporting point 2)
> Specific evidence

> Topic sentence 3 (supporting point 3)
> Specific evidence

Conclusion

> Summary (optional)
> General closing remarks
> (Or both)

You now have an overview of the traditional form of the essay. In Chapter 2, you will learn just how to go about writing an effective essay. First, though, it will be helpful to consider the following: the benefits of writing traditional essays; seeing writing as both a skill and a process of discovery; and the value of writing a journal and using a computer.

Benefits of Writing the Traditional Essay

Writing a traditional essay offers at least three benefits. First of all, mastering the traditional essay will help make you a better writer. For other courses, you'll often do papers that will be variations on the essay form—for example, examination essays, reports, and research papers. The basic structure of the traditional essay, with its emphasis on a clear point and well-organized, logical support, will help with almost every kind of writing that you have to do.

Second, the discipline of writing an essay will strengthen your skills as a reader and listener. As a reader, you'll become more critically aware of other writers' ideas and the evidence they provide (or fail to provide) to support those ideas. Essay writing will also help you become a better speaker. You'll be more prepared to develop the three basic parts of an effective speech—an appealing introduction, a solidly developed body, and a well-rounded conclusion—because of your experience writing three-part essays.

Most important, essay writing will make you a stronger thinker. Writing a solidly reasoned traditional essay requires mental discipline and close attention to a set of logical rules. Creating an essay in which there is an overall thesis statement and in which each of three supporting paragraphs begins with a topic sentence is more challenging than writing a free-form or expressive paper. Such an essay obliges you to carefully sort out, think through, and organize your ideas. You'll learn to discover and express just what your ideas are and to develop those ideas in a logical, reasoned way. Traditional essay writing, in short, will train your mind to think clearly, and that ability will prove to be of value in every phase of your life.

Writing as a Skill

A sure way to wreck your chances of learning how to write competently is to believe that writing is a "natural gift" rather than a learned skill. People with such an attitude think that they are the only ones for whom writing is unbearably difficult. They feel that everyone else finds writing easy or at least tolerable. Such people typically say, "I'm not any good at writing" or "English was not one of my good subjects." They imply that they simply do not have a talent for writing, while others do. The result of this attitude is that people try to avoid writing, and when they do write, they don't try their best. Their attitude becomes a self-fulfilling prophecy: their writing fails chiefly because they have brainwashed themselves into thinking that they don't have the "natural talent" needed to write. Unless their attitude changes, they probably will not learn how to write effectively.

A realistic attitude about writing must build on the idea that *writing is a skill*. It is a skill like driving, typing, or cooking; and, like any skill, it can be learned. If you have the determination to learn, this book will give you the extensive practice needed to develop your writing skills.

Many people find it difficult to do the intense, active thinking that clear writing demands. (Perhaps television has made us all so passive that the active thinking necessary in both writing and reading now seems harder than ever.) It is frightening to sit down before a blank sheet of paper and know that an hour later, nothing on it may be worth keeping. It is frustrating to discover how much of a challenge it is to transfer thoughts and feelings from one's head onto a sheet of paper. It is upsetting to find that an apparently simple subject often turns out to be complicated. But writing is not an automatic process: we will not get something for nothing—and we should not expect to. For almost everyone, competent writing comes from plain hard work—from determination, sweat, and head-on battle. The good news is that the skill of writing can be mastered, and if you are ready to work, you will learn what you need to know.

Writing as a Process of Discovery

In addition to believing that writing is a natural gift, many people falsely believe that writing should flow in a simple, straight line from the writer's head onto the written page. But writing is seldom an easy, one-step journey in which a finished paper comes out in a first draft. The truth is that *writing is a process of discovery* involving a series of steps, and those steps are very often a zigzag journey. Look at the following illustrations of the writing process:

Seldom the Case

Starting point ——————————————→ Finished paper

Usually the Case

Starting point ⌇⌇⌇⌇ Finished paper

Very often, writers do not discover just what they want to write about until they explore their thoughts in writing. For example, Diane Woods, the author of the paragraph and essay on moviegoing, had been assigned to write about some annoyance in everyday life. She did not know what annoyance she would choose; instead, she just began writing about annoyances in general, in order to discover a topic. One of those annoyances was traffic, which seemed promising, so she began putting down ideas and details that came to her about traffic. One detail was the traffic she had to deal with in going to the movies. That made her think of the traffic in the parking lot at the theater complex. At that point, she realized that moviegoing itself was an annoyance. She switched direction in midstream and began writing down ideas and details about moviegoing.

As Diane wrote, she realized how much other moviegoers annoyed her, and she began thinking that other movie patrons might be her main idea in a paper. But when she was writing about patrons who loudly drop popcorn tubs onto the floor, she realized how much all the snacks at the concession stand tempted her. She changed direction again, thinking now that maybe she could talk about patrons and tempting snacks. She kept writing, just putting down more and more details about her movie experiences, still not having figured out exactly how she would fit both patrons and snacks into the paper. Even though her paper had not quite jelled, she was not worried, because she knew that if she kept writing, it would eventually come together.

The point is that writing is often a process of continuing discovery; as you write, you may suddenly switch direction or double back. You may be working on a topic sentence and realize suddenly that it could be your concluding thought. Or you may be developing a supporting idea and then decide that it should be the main point of your paper. Chapter 2 will treat the writing process more directly. What is important to remember here is that writers frequently do not know their exact destination as they begin to write. Very often they discover the direction and shape of a paper during the process of writing.

Writing as a Way to Communicate with Others

When you talk, chances are you do not treat everyone the same. For example, you are unlikely to speak to your boss in the same way that you chat with a young child. Instead, you adjust what you say to suit the people who are listening to you—your *audience.* Similarly, you probably change your speech each day to suit whatever *purpose* you have in mind when you are speaking. For instance, if you wanted to tell someone how to get to your new apartment, you would speak differently than if you were describing your favorite movie.

To communicate effectively, people must constantly adjust their speech to suit their purpose and audience. This same idea is true for writing. When you write for others, it is crucial to know both your purpose for writing and the audience who will be reading your work. The ability to adjust your writing to suit your purpose and audience will serve you well not only in the classroom, but also in the workplace and beyond. Purpose and audience, further explained on pages 165–166, is a special focus of each of the nine patterns of essay development in Part Two.

Keeping a Journal

Because writing is a skill, it makes sense that the more you practice writing, the better you will write. One excellent way to get practice in writing, even before you begin composing essays, is to keep a daily or almost daily journal. Writing in a journal will help you develop the habit of thinking on paper and will show you how ideas can be discovered in the process of writing. A journal can make writing a familiar part of your life and can serve as a continuing source of ideas for papers.

At some point during the day—perhaps during a study period after your last class of the day, or right before dinner, or right before going to bed—spend fifteen minutes or so writing in your journal. Keep in mind that you do not have to plan what to write about, or be in the mood to write, or worry about making mistakes as you write; just write down whatever words come out. You should write at least one page in each session.

You may want to use a notebook that you can easily carry with you for on-the-spot writing. Or you may decide to write on loose-leaf paper that can be transferred later to a journal folder on your desk. No matter how you proceed, be sure to date all entries.

Your instructor may ask you to make journal entries a specific number of times a week, for a specific number of weeks. He or she may have you turn in your journal every so often for review and feedback. If you are keeping the journal on your own, try to make entries three to five times a week every week of the semester.

Using a Computer

Computers can be a real aid in all stages of the writing process. With powerful word-processing software, computers allow you to write, edit, format, and print anything from a single word to a lengthy essay. Once you type your work into a computer file, you can easily "cut" text and "paste" it elsewhere in seconds. Computers also make it possible to set margins, choose fonts, adjust line spacing, and insert page numbers—all with simple mouse clicks. In addition, computers can help you check your spelling, grammar, and (to some extent) your writing style.

In order to use a computer for writing, you must learn to use word-processing software. Fortunately, these programs are not difficult to learn and do not require you to be a computer expert. Chances are that with just a few minutes of instruction at your school computer center, you will be able to use a computer for all your college writing. If you have questions, just ask staff at your library or computer center to assist you.

Some Tips on Using a Computer

- If you are using your school's computer center, allow enough time. You may have to wait for a computer or printer to be free. In addition, you may need several sessions at the computer and printer to complete your paper.

- Every word-processing program allows you to "save" your writing by hitting one or more keys. Save your work frequently as you work on a draft. Work that is saved is preserved by the computer. Work that is not saved is lost when the file you are working on is closed, when the computer is turned off—or if there's a power or system failure.

- Keep your work in two places—the hard drive or disk you are working on and a backup disk. At the end of each session with the computer, copy your work onto the backup disk. Then, if the hard drive or working disk becomes damaged, you'll have the backup copy.

- Print out your work at least at the end of every session. Then not only will you have your most recent draft to work on away from the computer; you'll also have a copy in case something should happen to your disks.

- Work in single spacing so that you can see as much of your writing on the screen at one time as possible. Just before you print out your work, change to double spacing.

- Before making major changes in a paper, create a copy of your file. For example, if your file is titled "Worst Job," create a file called "Worst Job 2." Then make all your changes in that new file. If the changes don't work out, you can always go back to the original file.

Using a Computer at Each Stage of the Writing Process

Following are some ways to make word processing a part of your writing. Note that this section may be more meaningful *after* you have worked through Chapter 2 of the book.

Prewriting

If you're a fast typist, many kinds of prewriting will go well on the computer. With freewriting in particular, you can get ideas onto the screen almost as quickly as they occur to you. A passing thought that could be productive is not likely to get lost. You may even find it helpful, when freewriting, to dim the screen of your monitor so that you can't see what you're typing. If you temporarily can't see the screen, you won't have to worry about grammar or spelling or typing errors (all of which do not matter in prewriting); instead, you can concentrate on getting down as many ideas and details as possible about your subject.

After any initial freewriting, questioning, and list-making on a computer, it's often very helpful to print out a hard copy of what you've done. With a clean printout in front of you, you'll be able to see everything at once and revise and expand your work with handwritten comments in the margins of the paper.

If you have prepared a list of items, you may be able to turn that list into an outline right on the screen. Delete the ideas you feel should not be in your paper (saving them at the end of the file in case you change your mind), and add any new ideas that occur to you. Then use the cut and paste functions to shuffle the supporting ideas around until you find the best order for your paper.

Word processing also makes it easy for you to experiment with the wording of the point of your paper. You can try a number of versions in a short time. After you have decided on the version that works best, you can easily delete the other versions—or simply move them to a temporary "leftover" section at the end of the paper.

Writing Your First Draft

Like many writers, you may want to write out your first draft by hand and then type it into the computer for revision. Even as you type your handwritten draft, you may find yourself making some changes and improvements. And once you have a draft on the screen, or printed out, you will find it much easier to revise than a handwritten one.

If you feel comfortable composing directly on the screen, you can benefit from the computer's special features. For example, if you have written an anecdote in your freewriting that you plan to use in your paper, simply copy the story from your freewriting file and insert it where it fits in your paper. You can refine it then or later. Or, if you discover while typing that a sentence is out of place, cut it out from where it is and paste it wherever you wish. And, if while writing you realize that an earlier sentence can be expanded, just move your cursor back to that point and type in the added material.

Revising

It is during revision that the virtues of word processing really shine. All substituting, adding, deleting, and rearranging can be done easily within an existing file. All changes instantly take their proper places within the paper, not scribbled above the line or squeezed into the margin. You can concentrate on each change you want to make, because you never have to type from scratch or work on a messy draft. You can carefully go through your paper to check that all your supporting evidence is relevant and to add new support as needed here and there. Anything you decide to eliminate can be deleted in a keystroke. Anything you add can be inserted precisely where you choose. If you change your mind, all you have to do is delete or cut and paste. Then you can sweep through the paper, focusing on other changes, such as improving word choice, increasing sentence variety, and eliminating wordiness.

If you are like many students, you will find it convenient to print out a hard copy of your file at various points throughout the revision. You can then revise in longhand—adding, crossing out, and indicating changes—and later quickly make those changes in the document.

Editing and Proofreading

Editing and proofreading also benefit richly from word processing. Instead of crossing or whiting out mistakes, or rewriting an entire paper to correct numerous errors, you can make all necessary changes within the most recent draft. If you find editing or proofreading on the screen hard on your eyes, print out a copy. Mark any corrections on that copy, and then transfer them to the final draft.

If the word-processing package you're using includes spelling and grammar checks, by all means use them. The spell-check function tells you when a word is not in the computer's dictionary. Keep in mind, however, that the spell-check cannot tell you how to spell a name correctly or when you have mistakenly used, for example, *their* instead of *there*. To a spell-check, *Thank ewe four the complement* is as correct as *Thank you for the compliment*. Also, use the grammar check with caution. Any errors it doesn't uncover are still your responsibility.

A word-processed paper, with its clean appearance and handsome formatting, looks so good that you may feel it is in better shape than it really is. Do not be fooled. Take sufficient time to review your grammar, punctuation, and spelling carefully.

Even after you hand in your paper, save the computer file. Your teacher may ask you to do some revising, and then the file will save you from having to type the paper from scratch.

Review Activities

ACTIVITY 1

Answering the following questions will help you evaluate your attitude about writing.

Answers will vary.

1. How much practice were you given writing compositions in high school?

   _____ Much   _____ Some   _____ Little

2. How much feedback (positive or negative comments) from teachers were you given on your compositions?

   _____ Much   _____ Some   _____ Little

3. How did your teachers seem to regard your writing?

_____ Good   _____ Fair   _____ Poor

4. Do you feel that some people simply have a gift for writing and others do not?

_____ Yes   _____ Sometimes   _____ No

5. When do you start writing a paper?

_____ Several days before it is due

_____ About a day before it is due

_____ At the last possible minute

Many people who answer *Little* to questions 1 and 2 often answer *Poor, Yes,* and *At the last possible minute* to questions 3, 4, and 5. On the other hand, people who answer *Much* or *Some* to questions 1 and 2 also tend to have more favorable responses to the other questions. The point is that people with little practice in the skill of writing often have understandably negative feelings about their writing ability. They need not have such feelings, however, because writing is a skill that they can learn with practice.

6. Did you learn to write traditional essays (introductory paragraph, supporting paragraphs, concluding paragraph) in high school?

_____ Yes   _____ No

7. If so, did your teacher explain to you the benefits of writing such essays?

_____ Yes, very clearly

_____ Maybe, but not that I remember

_____ No

If you answered *Maybe* or *No* to question 7, you may not be looking forward to taking the course in which you are using this book. It will be worth your while to read and consider again (on page 12) the enormous benefits that can come from practice in writing traditional essays.

8. In your own words, explain what it means to say that writing is often a zigzag journey rather than a straight-line journey.

_____

_____

_____

_____

_____

ACTIVITY 2

Following is an excerpt from one student's journal. As you read, look for a general point and supporting material that could be the basis for an interesting paper.

September 6

My first sociology class was tonight. The parking lot was jammed when I got there. I thought I was going to be late for class. A guard had us park on a field next to the regular lot. When I got to the room, it had the usual painted-cinder-block construction. Every school I have ever been in since first grade seems to be made of cinder block. The students all sat there without saying anything, waiting for the instructor to arrive. I think they were all a bit nervous like me. I hoped there wasn't going to be a ton of work in the course. I think I was also afraid of looking foolish somehow. This goes back to grade school, when I wasn't a very good student and teachers sometimes embarrassed me in class. I didn't like grade school, and I hated high school. Now here I am six years later—in college, of all places. Who would have thought I would end up here? The instructor appeared—a woman who I think was a bit nervous herself. I think I like her. Her name is Barbara Hanlin. She says we should call her Barbara. We got right into it, but it was interesting stuff. I like the fact that she asks questions but then she lets you volunteer. I always hated it when teachers would call on you whether you wanted to answer or not. I also like the fact that she answers the questions and doesn't just leave you hanging. She takes the time to write important ideas on the board. I also like the way she laughs. This class may be OK.

1. If the writer of the journal entry above was looking for ideas for an essay, he could probably find several in this single entry. For example, he might write a story about the roundabout way he apparently wound up in college. See if you can find in the entry an idea that might be the basis for an interesting essay, and write your point in the space below.
   Answers will vary.
   _____

2. Take fifteen minutes now to write a journal entry on this day in your life. On a separate sheet of paper, just start writing about anything that you have seen, said, heard, thought, or felt today, and let your thoughts take you where they may.

Using This Text

Here is a suggested sequence for using this book if you are working on your own.

1   After completing this introduction, read Chapters 2 through 6 in Part One and work through as many of the activities as you need to master the ideas in these chapters. By the end of Part One, you will have covered all the basic theory needed to write effective papers.

2   Work through some of the chapters in Part Two, which describes a number of traditional patterns for organizing and developing essays. You may want to include "Examples," "Process," "Comparison and Contrast," and "Argumentation." Each chapter opens with a brief introduction to a specific pattern, followed by two student essays and one professional essay written in that pattern. Included are a series of questions so that you can evaluate the essays in terms of the basic principles of writing explained in Part One. Finally, a number of writing topics are presented, along with hints about prewriting and revising to help you plan and write an effective paper.

3   Turn to Part Three as needed for help with types of writing you will do in college: exam essays, summaries, reports, the résumé and job application letter, and the research paper. You will see that these kinds of writing are variations of the essay form you have already learned.

4   In addition, refer to Part Four as needed for review and practice in the skills needed to write effective, error-free sentences.

5   Finally, read some of the selections in Part Five and respond to the activities that follow the selections.

For your convenience, the book includes the following:

• On the inside front cover, there is a checklist of the four basic steps in effective writing.
• On the inside back cover, there is a list of commonly used correction symbols.

Get into the habit of referring to these guides on a regular basis; they'll help you produce clearly thought-out, well-written essays.

College Writing Skills with Readings will help you learn, practice, and apply the thinking and writing skills you need to communicate effectively. But the starting point must be your own determination to do the work needed to become a strong writer. The ability to express yourself clearly and logically can open doors of opportunity for you, both in school and in your career. If you decide—and only you can decide—that you want such language power, this book will help you reach that goal.

2 The Writing Process

This chapter explains and illustrates
- the sequence of steps in writing an effective essay
- prewriting
- revising
- editing

Chapter 1 introduced you to the essay form and to some basics of writing. This chapter explains and illustrates the sequence of steps in writing an effective essay. In particular, the chapter focuses on prewriting and revising—strategies that can help with every paper you write.

For many people, writing is a process that involves the following steps:

1   Discovering a thesis—often through prewriting.
2   Developing solid support for the thesis—often through more prewriting.
3   Organizing the thesis and supporting material and writing it out in a first draft.
4   Revising and then editing carefully to ensure an effective, error-free paper.

Learning this sequence will help give you confidence when the time comes to write. You'll know that you can use prewriting as a way to think on paper and to gradually discover just what ideas you want to develop. You'll understand that there are four clear-cut goals—unity, support, organization, and error-free sentences—to aim for in your writing. You'll realize that you can use revision to rework a paper until it is a strong and effective piece of writing. And you'll be able to edit a paper so that your sentences are clear and error-free.

Prewriting

1.1a

If you are like many people, you may have trouble getting started with writing. A mental block may develop when you sit down before a blank sheet of paper. You may not be able to think of an interesting topic or thesis. Or you may have trouble coming up with relevant details to support a possible thesis. And even after starting a paper, you may hit snags—moments when you wonder "What else can I say?" or "Where do I go next?"

The following pages describe five prewriting techniques that will help you think about and develop a topic and get words on paper: (1) freewriting, (2) questioning, (3) making a list, (4) diagramming, and (5) preparing a scratch outline. These techniques help you think about and create material, and they are a central part of the writing process.

Technique 1: Freewriting

2.3b

Freewriting means jotting down in rough sentences or phrases everything that comes to mind about a possible topic. See if you can write nonstop for ten minutes or more. Do not worry about spelling or punctuating correctly, about erasing mistakes, about organizing material, or about finding exact words. Instead, explore an idea by putting down whatever pops into your head. If you get stuck for words, repeat yourself until more words come. There is no need to feel inhibited, since mistakes *do not count* and you do not have to hand in your freewriting.

Freewriting will limber up your writing muscles and make you familiar with the act of writing. It is a way to break through mental blocks about writing. Since you do not have to worry about mistakes, you can focus on discovering what you want to say about a subject. Your initial ideas and impressions will often become clearer after you have gotten them down on paper, and they may lead to other impressions and ideas. Through continued practice in freewriting, you will develop the habit of thinking as you write. And you will learn a technique that is a helpful way to get started on almost any paper.

Freewriting: A Student Model

Diane Woods's essay "The Hazards of Moviegoing" on pages 7–8 was developed in response to an assignment to write about some annoyance in everyday life. Diane began by doing some general freewriting and thinking about things that annoy her. Here is her freewriting:

There are lots of things I get annoyed by. One of them that comes to mind is politishans, in fact I am so annoyed by them that I don't want to say anything about them the last thing I want is to write about them. Another thing that bothers me are people who keep complaining about everything. If you're having trouble, do something about it just don't keep complaining and just talking. I am really annoyed by traffic. There are too many cars in our block and its not surprising. Everyone has a car, the parents have cars and the parents are just too induljent and the kids have cars, and theyre all coming and going all the time and often driving too fast. Speeding up and down the street. We need a speed limit sign but here I am back with politiks again. I am really bothered when I have to drive to the movies all the congestion along the way plus there are just so many cars there at the mall. No space even though the parking lot is huge it just fills up with cars. Movies are a bother anyway because the people can be annoying who are sitting there in the theater with you, talking and dropping popcorn cups and acting like they're at home when they're not.

At this point, Diane read over her notes and, as she later commented, "I realized that I had several potential topics. I said to myself, 'What point can I make that I can cover in an essay? What do I have the most information about?' I decided that maybe I could narrow my topic down to the annoyances involved in going to the movies. I figured I would have more details for that topic." Diane then did more focused freewriting to accumulate details for a paper on problems with moviegoing:

I really find it annoying to go see movies anymore. Even though I love films. Traffic to Cinema Six is awful. I hate looking for a parking place, the lot isn't big enough for the theaters and other stores. You just keep driving to find a parking space and hoping someone will pull out and no one else will pull in ahead of you. Then you don't want there to be a long line and to wind up in one of the first rows with this huge screen right in front of you. Then I'm in the theater with the smell of popcorn all around. Sitting there smelling it trying to ignore it and just wanting to pour a whole bucket of popcorn with melted butter down my throat. I can't stop thinking about the choclate bars either. I love the stuff but I don't need it. The people who are there sometimes drive me nuts. Talking and laughing, kids running around, packs of teens hollaring, who can listen to the movie? And I might run into my old boyfriend—the last thing I need. Also sitting thru all the previews and commercals. If I arrive late enough to miss that junk the movie may be selled out.

Comment

Notice that there are errors in spelling, grammar, and punctuation in Diane's freewriting. Diane is not worried about such matters, nor should she be. At this stage, she just wants to do some thinking on paper and get some material down on the page. She knows that this is a good first step, a good way of getting started, and that she will then be able to go on and shape the material.

You should take the same approach when freewriting: explore your topic without worrying at all about being "correct." Figuring out what you want to say and getting raw material down on the page should have all of your attention at this early stage of the writing process.

ACTIVITY

To get a sense of the freewriting process, take a sheet of paper and freewrite about some of the everyday annoyances in your life. See how much material you can accumulate in ten minutes. And remember not to worry about "mistakes"; you're just thinking on paper.
Answers will vary.

Technique 2: Questioning

In *questioning,* you generate ideas and details by asking questions about your subject. Such questions include *Why? When? Where? Who?* and *How?* Ask as many questions as you can think of.

Here are some questions that Diane Woods might have asked while developing her paper.

Questioning: A Student Model

Questions	Answers
Why don't I like to go to a movie?	Just too many problems involved.
When is going to the movies a problem?	Could be any time—when a movie is popular, the theater is too crowded; when traffic is bad, the trip is a drag.
Where are problems with moviegoing?	On the highway, in the parking lot, at the concession stand, in the theater itself.
Who creates the problems?	I do by wanting to eat too much. The patrons do by creating disturbances. The theater owners do by not having enough parking space and showing too many commercials.
How can I deal with the problem?	I can stay home and watch movies on video or cable TV.

Comment

Asking questions can be an effective way of getting yourself to think about a topic from a number of different angles. The questions can really help you generate details about a topic.

ACTIVITY

To get a sense of the questioning process, use a sheet of paper to ask yourself a series of questions about a good or bad experience that you have had recently. See how many details you can accumulate in ten minutes. And remember again not to be concerned about "mistakes," because you are just thinking on paper.

Answers will vary.

Technique 3: Making a List

2.3a

In *making a list,* also known as *brainstorming,* you collect ideas and details that relate to your subject. Pile these items up, one after another, without trying to sort out major details from minor ones or trying to put the details in any special order. Your goal is just to make a list of everything about your subject that occurs to you.

After Diane did her freewriting about moviegoing, she made up the following list of details.

Making a List: A Student Model

> Traffic is bad between my house and theater
>
> Noisy patrons
>
> Don't want to run into Jeremy
>
> Hard to be on a diet
>
> Kids running in aisles
>
> I'm crowded into seats between strangers who push me off armrests
>
> Not enough parking
>
> Parking lot needs to be expanded
>
> Too many previews
>
> Can't pause or fast-forward as you can with a VCR
>
> Long lines
>
> *Continued*

High ticket prices

Too many temptatons at snack stand

Commercials for food on the screen

Can prepare healthy snacks for myself at home

Tubs of popcorn with butter

Huge choclate bars

Candy has always been my downfall

Movie may be sold out

People who've seen movie before talk along with actors and give away plot twists

People coughing and sneezing

Icky stuff on floor

Teenagers yelling and showing off

One detail led to another as Diane expanded her list. Slowly but surely, more details emerged, some of which she could use in developing her paper. By the time she was done with her list, she was ready to plan an outline of her paragraph and then to write her first draft.

ACTIVITY

To get a sense of list-making, list on a sheet of paper a series of realistic goals, major or minor, that you would like to accomplish between today and one year from today. Your goals can be personal, academic, and/or career-related.

Technique 4: Clustering

Clustering, also known as *diagramming* or *mapping,* is another strategy that can be used to generate material for a paper. This method is helpful for people who like to do their thinking in a visual way. In clustering, you use lines, boxes, arrows, and circles to show relationships among the ideas and details that occur to you.

Begin by stating your subject in a few words in the center of a blank sheet of paper. Then, as ideas and details come to you, put them in boxes or circles around the subject and draw lines to connect them to each other and to the subject. Put minor ideas or details in smaller boxes or circles, and use connecting lines to show how they relate as well.

Keep in mind that there is no right or wrong way of clustering or diagramming. It is a way to think on paper about how various ideas and details relate to one another. Below is an example of what Diane might have done to develop her ideas.

Clustering: A Student Model

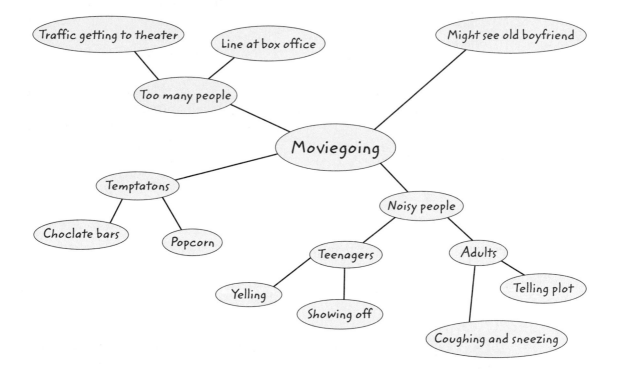

Comment

In addition to helping generate material, clustering can give you an early sense of how ideas and details relate to one another. For example, the cluster for Diane's essay suggests that different kinds of noisy people could be the focus of one paragraph and that different kinds of temptations could be the focus of another paragraph.

ACTIVITY

Use clustering (diagramming) to organize the list of year-ahead goals that you created for the previous activity (page 27).

Answers will vary.

Technique 5: Preparing a Scratch Outline

4.1a

A *scratch outline* is an excellent sequel to the first four prewriting techniques. A scratch outline often follows freewriting, questioning, list-making, or diagramming; or it may gradually emerge in the midst of these strategies. In fact, trying to make a scratch outline is a good way to see if you need to do more prewriting. If you cannot come up with a solid outline, then you know you need to do more prewriting to clarify your main point or its several kinds of support.

In a scratch outline, you think carefully about the point you are making, the supporting items for that point, and the order in which you will arrange those items. The scratch outline is a plan or blueprint to help you achieve a unified, supported, well-organized composition.

When you are planning a traditional essay consisting of an introduction, three supporting paragraphs, and a conclusion, a scratch outline is especially important. It may be only a few words, but it will be the framework on which your whole essay will be built.

Scratch Outline: A Student Model

As Diane was working on her list of details, she suddenly realized what the plan of her essay could be. She could organize many of her details into one of three supporting groups: (1) annoyances in going out; (2) too many tempting snacks; and (3) other people. She then went back to the list, crossed out items that she now saw did not fit, and numbered the items according to the group where they fit. Here is what Diane did with her list:

---

1 Traffic is bad between my house and the theater

3 Noisy patrons

~~Don't want to run into Jeremy~~

2 Hard to be on a diet

3 Kids running in aisles

3 I'm crowded into seats between strangers who push me off armrests

1 Not enough parking

1 Parking lot needs to be expanded

1 Too many previews

~~Can't pause or fast-forward as you can with a VCR~~

1 Long lines

Continued

---

1   High ticket prices
2   Too many temptatons at snack stand
    ~~Commercials for food on the screen~~
2   Can prepare healthy snacks for myself at home
2   Tubs of popcorn with butter
2   Huge choclate bars
    ~~Candy has always been my downfall~~
1   Movie may be sold out
3   People who've seen movie before talk along with actors and give away plot twists
3   People coughing and sneezing
1   Icky stuff on floor
3   Teenagers yelling and showing off

Under the list, Diane was now able to prepare her scratch outline:

Going to the movies offers some real problems.
1. Inconvenience of going out
2. Tempting snacks
3. Other moviegoers

Comment

After all her prewriting, Diane was pleased. She knew that she had a promising paper—one with a clear point and solid support. She saw that she could organize the material into a traditional essay consisting of an introduction, several supporting paragraphs, and a conclusion. She was now ready to write the first draft of her paper, using her outline as a guide. Chances are that if you do enough prewriting and thinking on paper, you will eventually discover the point and support of your essay.

ACTIVITY

Create a scratch outline that could serve as a guide if you were to write an essay about your year-ahead goals.

Answers will vary.

Writing a First Draft

1.1b

When you write a first draft, be prepared to put in additional thoughts and details that did not emerge during prewriting. And don't worry if you hit a snag. Just leave a blank space or add a comment such as "Do later" and press on to finish the paper. Also, don't worry yet about grammar, punctuation, or spelling. You don't want to take time correcting words or sentences that you may decide to remove later. Instead, make it your goal to state your thesis clearly and develop the content of your paper with plenty of specific details.

Writing a First Draft: A Student Model

Here is Diane's first draft:

> Even though I love movies, my friends have stopped asking me to go. There are just too many problems involved in going to the movies.
>
> There are no small theaters anymore, I have to drive fifteen minutes to a big multaplex. Because of a supermarket and restarants, the parking lot is filled. I have to keep driving around to find a space. Then I have to stand in a long line. Hoping that they do not run out of tickets. Finally, I have to pay too much money for a ticket. Putting out that much money, I should not have to deal with a floor that ~~is sticky~~ seems coated with rubber cement. By the end of a movie, my shoes are often sealed to a mix of spilled soda, bubble gum, and other stuff.
>
> The theater offers temptatons in the form of snacks I really don't need. Like most of us I have to worry about weight gain. At home I do pretty well by simply watching what I keep in the house and not buying stuff that is bad for me. I can make do with healthy snacks because there is nothing in the house. Going to the theater is like spending my evening in a ~~market~~ Seven-Eleven that's been equiped with a movie screen and there are seats which are comfortable. I try to persuade myself to just have a diet soda. The smell of popcorn soon overcomes me. My friends are as bad as I am. Choclate bars seem to jump into your hands, I am eating enormous mouthfuls of milk duds. By the time I leave the theater I feel sick and tired of myself.
>
> Some of the other moviegoers are the worst problem. There are teenagers who try to impress their friends in one way or another. Little kids

race up and down the aisles, gigling and laughing. Adults act as if they're watching the movie at home. They talk loudly about the ages of the stars and give away the plot. Other people are droping popcorn tubs or cups of ~~soda~~ crushed ice and soda on the floor. Also coughing a lot and doing other stuff—bs!

    I decided one night that I was not going to be a moviegoer anymore. I joined a local video store, and I'll watch movies comfortable in my own living room.

Comment

After Diane finished the first draft, she was able to put it aside until the next day. You will benefit as well if you can allow some time between finishing a draft and starting to revise. See if you can fill in the missing words in the following explanation of Diane's first draft.

ACTIVITY

1. Diane has a very brief introduction—no more than an opening sentence and a second sentence that states the _____thesis_____. She knows she can develop the introduction more fully in a later draft.

2. Of Diane's three supporting paragraphs, only the _____first_____ paragraph lacks a topic sentence. She realizes that this is something to work on in the next draft.

3. There are some misspellings—for example, _____equiped_____ *(answers may vary)*. Diane doesn't worry about spelling at this point. She just wants to get down as much of the substance of her paper as possible.

4. There are various punctuation errors, such as the run-ons in the ___second and third___ paragraphs. Again, Diane is focusing on content; she knows she can attend to punctuation and grammar later.

5. At several points in the essay, Diane revises on the spot to make images more _____specific_____: she changes "is sticky" to "seems coated with rubber cement," "market" to "Seven-Eleven," and "cups of soda" to "cups of crushed ice and soda."

6. Near the end of her essay, Diane can't think of added details to insert so she simply puts the letters "_____bs_____" at that point to remind herself to "be specific" in the next draft. She then goes on to finish her first draft.

7. Her _____conclusion_____ is as brief as her introduction. Diane knows she can round off her essay more fully during revision.

Revising

ALLWRITE!
4.3

Revising is as much a stage in the writing process as prewriting, outlining, and doing the first draft. *Revising* means rewriting a paper, building on what has already been done, in order to make it stronger. One writer has said about revision, "It's like cleaning house—getting rid of all the junk and putting things in the right order." But it is not just "straightening up"; instead, you must be ready to roll up your sleeves and do whatever is needed to create an effective paper. Too many students think that the first draft *is* the paper. They start to become writers when they realize that revising a rough draft three or four times is often at the heart of the writing process.

Here are some quick hints that can help make revision easier. First, set your first draft aside for a while. A few hours will do, but a day or two would be better. You can then come back to the draft with a fresh, more objective point of view. Second, work from typed or printed text. You'll be able to see the paper more impartially in this way than if you were just looking at your own familiar handwriting. Next, read your draft aloud. Hearing how your writing sounds will help you pick up problems with meaning as well as with style. Finally, as you do all these things, add your thoughts and changes above the lines or in the margins of your paper. Your written comments can serve as a guide when you work on the next draft.

There are three stages to the revising process:

- Revising content
- Revising sentences
- Editing

Revising Content

To revise the content of your essay, ask these questions:

1 Is my paper **unified?**
   - Do I have a thesis that is clearly stated or implied in the introductory paragraph of my essay?
   - Do all my supporting paragraphs truly support and back up my thesis?

2 Is my paper **supported?**
   - Are there three separate supporting points for the thesis?
   - Do I have *specific* evidence for each of the three supporting points?
   - Is there *plenty of* specific evidence for each supporting point?

3   Is my paper **organized?**

- Do I have an interesting introduction, a solid conclusion, and an accurate title?
- Do I have a clear method of organizing my paper?
- Do I use transitions and other connecting words?

Chapters 3 and 4 will give you practice in achieving **unity, support,** and **organization** in your writing.

Revising Sentences

To revise sentences in your essay, ask yourself:

1   Do I use parallelism to balance my words and ideas?

2   Do I have a consistent point of view?

3   Do I use specific words?

4   Do I use active verbs?

5   Do I use words effectively by avoiding slang, clichés, pretentious language, and wordiness?

6   Do I vary my sentences?

Chapter 5 will give you practice in revising sentences.

Editing

4.4

After you have revised your paper for content and style, you are ready to *edit*—check for and correct—errors in grammar, punctuation, and spelling. Students often find it hard to edit a paper carefully. They have put so much, or so little, work into their writing that it's almost painful for them to look at the paper one more time. You may simply have to *will* yourself to perform this important closing step in the writing process. Remember that eliminating sentence-skills mistakes will improve an average paper and help ensure a strong grade on a good paper. Further, as you get into the habit of checking your papers, you will also get into the habit of using the sentence skills consistently. They are an integral part of clear and effective writing.

Chapter 5 and Part Four of this book will serve as a guide while you are editing your paper for mistakes in **sentence skills.**

An Illustration of the Revising and Editing Processes

Revising with a Second Draft: A Student Model

Since Diane Woods was using a word-processing program on a computer, she was able to print out a double-spaced version of her essay about movies, leaving her plenty of room for revisions. Here is one of her revised paragraphs:

> *Second,*
> The theater offers ~~temptatons in the form of~~ *tempting* snacks I really don't need.
> Like most of us I have to ~~worry about weight gain.~~ *battle an expanding waistline.* At home I do pretty well
> by simply ~~watching what I keep in the house and~~ not buying stuff that is
> bad for me. I can make do with ~~healthy~~ *like celery and carrot sticks* snacks because there is ~~nothing~~ *no ice cream* in
> the freezer. *however* Going to the theater is like spending my evening in a Seven-
> Eleven that's been equiped with a movie screen and ~~there are~~ seats *comfortable* ~~which~~
> ~~are comfortable.~~ *As* I try to persuade myself to just have a diet soda*,* *+* The smell
> *dripping with butter*
> of fresh popcorn soon overcomes me. ~~My friends are as bad as I am.~~ Choclate
> bars seem to jump into ~~your~~ *my* hands. I ~~am eating~~ *risk pulling out my fillings as I chew* enormous mouthfuls of milk
> duds. By the time I leave the theater I feel ~~out of sorts~~ *disgusted* with myself.

Comment

Diane made her changes in longhand as she worked on the second draft. As you will see when you complete the activity below, her revision serves to make the paragraph more unified, better supported, and better organized.

ACTIVITY

Fill in the missing words.

1. To achieve better organization, Diane adds at the beginning of the paragraph the transitional phrase "_____*Second,*_____" making it very clear that her second supporting idea is tempting snacks.

2. Diane also adds the transition "____however____" to show clearly the difference between being at home and being in the theater.

3. In the interest of (*unity, support, organization*) ____unity____, Diane crosses out the sentence "____My friends are as bad as I am____." She realizes this sentence is not a relevant detail but really another topic.

4. To add more (*unity, support, organization*) ____support____, Diane changes "healthy snacks" to "____snacks like celery and carrot sticks____"; she changes "nothing in the freezer" to "____no ice cream in the freezer____"; she adds "____dripping with butter____" after "popcorn"; and she changes "am eating" to "____risk pulling out my fillings as I chew____."

5. In the interest of eliminating wordiness, she removes the words "____watching what I keep in the house____" from the third sentence.

6. In the interest of parallelism, Diane changes "and there are seats which are comfortable" to "____comfortable seats____."

7. For greater sentence variety, Diane combines two short sentences, beginning the first sentence with the subordinating word "____As____."

8. To create a consistent point of view, Diane changes "jump into your hands" to "____jump into my hands____."

9. Finally, Diane replaces the vague "out of sorts" with the more precise "____disgusted____."

Editing: A Student Model

After typing into her word-processing file all the changes in her second draft, Diane printed out another clean draft of the paper. The paragraph on tempting snacks required almost no more revision, so Diane turned her attention mostly to editing changes, illustrated below with her work on the second supporting paragraph:

Second, the theater offers tempting snacks I really don't need. Like most

of us, I have to battle an expanding waistline. At home I do pretty well by

simply not buying stuff that is bad for me. I can make do with snacks like

celery and carrot sticks because there is no ice cream in the freezer. Going to the theater, however, is like spending my evening in a Seven-Eleven that's

equipped

been ~~equiped~~ with a movie screen and comfortable seats. As I try to persuade

Coke

myself to just have a diet ~~soda~~, the smell of fresh popcorn dripping with

Chocolate   *the size of small automobiles*

butter soon overcomes me. ~~Choclate~~ bars seem to jump into my hands. I risk

M D

pulling out my fillings as I chew enormous mouthfuls of ~~milk duds~~. By the

time I leave the theater, I feel disgusted with myself.

Comment

Once again, Diane makes her changes in longhand right on the printout of her paper. To note these changes, complete the activity below.

ACTIVITY

Fill in the missing words.

1. As part of her editing, Diane checked and corrected the ___*spelling*___ of two words, *equipped* and *chocolate*.

2. She added ___*commas*___ to set off two introductory phrases ("Like most of us" in the second sentence and "By the time I leave the theater" in the final sentence) and also to set off the interrupting word *however* in the fifth sentence.

3. She realized that "milk duds" is a brand name and added ___*capital letters*___ to make it "Milk Duds."

4. And since revision can occur at any stage of the writing process, including editing, she makes one of her details more vivid by adding the descriptive words " ___*the size of small automobiles*___ ."

Review Activities

You now have a good overview of the writing process, from prewriting to first draft to revising to editing. The remaining chapters in Part One will deepen your sense of the four goals of effective writing: unity, support, organization or coherence, and sentence skills.

To reinforce the information about the writing process that you have learned in this chapter, you can now work through the following activities:

1 Taking a writing inventory
2 Prewriting
3 Outlining
4 Revising

1 Taking a Writing Inventory

ACTIVITY

Answer the questions below to evaluate your approach to the writing process. This activity is not a test, so try to be as honest as possible. Becoming aware of your writing habits will help you realize changes that may be helpful.

Answers will vary.

1. When you start work on a paper, do you typically do any prewriting?

    _____ Yes   _____ Sometimes   _____ No

2. If so, which prewriting techniques do you use?

    _____ Freewriting   _____ Diagramming

    _____ Questioning   _____ Scratch outline

    _____ List-making   _____ Other (please describe)

3. Which prewriting technique or techniques work best for you, or which do you think will work best for you?

4. Many students say they find it helpful to handwrite a first draft and then type that draft on a computer. They then print the draft out and revise it by hand. Describe the way you proceed in drafting and revising a paper.

5. After you write the first draft of a paper, do you have time to set it aside for a while so that you can come back to it with a fresh eye?

    _____ Yes   _____ No

6. How many drafts do you typically write when doing a paper? _____

7. When you revise, are you aware that you should be working toward a paper that is unified, solidly supported, and clearly organized? Has this chapter given you a better sense that unity, support, and organization are goals to aim for?

8. Do you revise a paper for the effectiveness of its sentences as well as for its content?

_____ Yes   _____ No

9. Do you typically do any editing of the almost-final draft of a paper, or do you tend to "hope for the best" and hand it in without careful checking?

_____ Edit   _____ Hope for the best

10. What (if any) information has this chapter given you about *prewriting* that you will try to apply in your writing?

11. What (if any) information has this chapter given you about *revising* that you will try to apply in your writing?

12. What (if any) information has this chapter given you about *editing* that you will try to apply in your writing?

2 Prewriting

ACTIVITY

On the following pages are examples of how the five prewriting techniques could be used to develop the topic "Problems of Combining Work and College." Identify each technique by writing F (for freewriting), Q (for questioning), L (for list-making), C (for clustering), or SO (for the scratch outline) in the answer space.

_____L_____

Never enough time
Miss campus parties
Had to study (only two free hours a night)
Give up activities with friends
No time to rewrite papers
Can't stay at school to play video games or talk to friends
Friends don't call me to go out anymore
Sunday no longer relaxed day—have to study
Missing sleep I should be getting
Grades aren't as good as they could be
Can't watch favorite TV shows
Really need the extra money
Tired when I sit down to study at nine o'clock

_____Q_____

<u>What</u> are some of the problems of combining work and school?

Schoolwork suffers because I don't have time to study or rewrite papers. I've had to give up things I enjoy, like sleep and touch football. I can't get into the social life at college, because I have to work right after class.

<u>How</u> have these problems changed my life?

My grades aren't as good as they were when I didn't work. Some of my friends have stopped calling me. My relationship with a girl I liked fell apart because I couldn't spend much time with her. I miss TV.

<u>What</u> do I do in a typical day?

I get up at 7 to make an 8 A.M. class. I have classes till 1:30, and then I drive to the supermarket where I work. I work till 7 P.M., and then I drive home and eat dinner. After I take a shower and relax for a half hour, it's about 9. This gives me only a couple of hours to study—read textbooks, do math exercises, write essays. My eyes start to close well before I go to bed at 11.

<u>Why</u> do I keep up this schedule?

I can't afford to go to school without working, and I need a degree to get the accounting job I want. If I invest my time now, I'll have a better future.

_____SO_____   Juggling a job and college has created major difficulties in my life.
  1. Little time for studying
      a. Not reading textbooks
      b. No rewriting papers
      c. Little studying for tests
  2. Little time for enjoying social side of college
      a. During school
      b. After school
  3. No time for personal pleasures
      a. Favorite TV shows
      b. Sunday football games
      c. Sleeping late

_____C_____

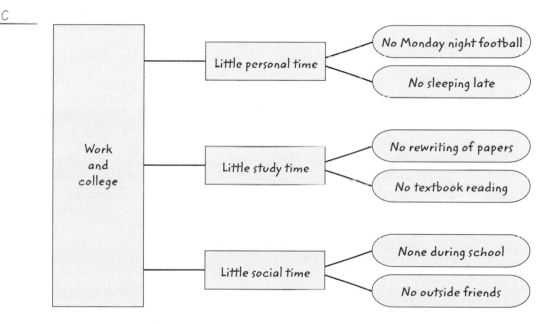

_____F_____   It's hard working and going to school at the same time. I never realized how much I'd have to give up. I won't be quitting my job because I need the money. And the people are friendly at the place where I work. I've had to give up a lot more than I thought. We used to play touch football games every Sunday. They were fun and we'd go out for drinks afterwards. Sundays now are for catch-up work with my courses. I have to catch up because I don't get home every day until 7, I have to eat dinner first before studying. Sometimes I'm so hungry I just eat cookies or chips. Anyway, by the time I take a shower it's 9 P.M. or later and I'm already feeling tired. I've been up since 7 A.M. Sometimes I write an English paper in twenty minutes and don't even read it over. I feel that I'm missing out on a lot in college. The other day some people I like were sitting in the cafeteria listening to music and talking. I would have given anything to stay and not have to go to work. I almost called in sick. I used to get invited to parties, I don't much anymore. My friends know I'm not going to be able to make it, so they don't bother. I can't sleep late on weekends or watch TV during the week.

3 Outlining

4.1

As already mentioned (see page 29), outlining is central to writing a good paper. An outline lets you see, and work on, the bare bones of a paper, without the distraction of a clutter of words and sentences. It develops your ability to think clearly and logically. Outlining provides a quick check on whether your paper will be *unified*. It also suggests right at the start whether your paper will be adequately *supported*. And it shows you how to plan a paper that is *well organized*.

The following two exercises will help you develop the outlining skills so important to planning and writing a solid essay.

ACTIVITY 1

One key to effective outlining is the ability to distinguish between major ideas and details that fit under those ideas. In each of the four lists below, major and supporting items are mixed together. Put the items into logical order by filling in the outline that follows each list. In items 3 and 4, one of the three major ideas is missing and must be added.

1. Thesis: My high school had three problem areas.

Involved with drugs
Leaky ceilings
Students
Unwilling to help after class
Formed cliques
Teachers
Buildings
Ill-equipped gym
Much too strict

a. Students
   (1) Involved with drugs
   (2) Formed cliques

b. Teachers
   (1) Much too strict
   (2) Unwilling to help after class

c. Buildings
   (1) Leaky ceilings
   (2) Ill-equipped gym

2. Thesis: Working as a dishwasher in a restaurant was my worst job.

Ten-hour shifts
Heat in kitchen
Working conditions
Minimum wage
Hours changed every week
No bonus for overtime
Hours
Pay
Noisy work area

a. Working conditions
  (1) Heat in kitchen
  (2) Noisy work area
b. Hours
  (1) Ten-hour shifts
  (2) Hours changed every week
c. Pay
  (1) Minimum wage
  (2) No bonus for overtime

3. Thesis: Joining an aerobics class has many benefits.

Make new friends
Reduces mental stress
Social benefits
Strengthens heart
Improves self-image
Mental benefits
Tones muscles
Meet interesting instructors

a. Physical benefits
  (1) Strengthens heart
  (2) Tones muscles
b. Mental benefits
  (1) Reduces mental stress
  (2) Improves self-image
c. Social benefits
  (1) Make new friends
  (2) Meet interesting instructors

4. Thesis: My favorite times in school were the days before holiday vacations.

Lighter workload
Teachers more relaxed
Pep rallies
Less work in class
Friendlier atmosphere
Less homework
Holiday concerts
Students happy about vacation

a. Lighter workload
  (1) Less work in class
  (2) Less homework
b. Friendlier atmosphere
  (1) Teachers more relaxed
  (2) Students happy about vacation
c. Appealing activities
  (1) Pep rallies
  (2) Holiday concerts

ACTIVITY 2

Read the following essay and outline it in the spaces provided. Write out the central point and topic sentences, and summarize in a few words the supporting material that fits under each topic sentence. One item is summarized for you as an example.

Losing Touch

Steve, a typical American, stays home on workdays. He plugs into a computer terminal in order to hook up with the office, and he sends and receives work during the day by electronic mail and a fax-modem. Evenings, he puts on his stereo headphones, watches a movie on his VCR, or logs back onto the computer to visit the Internet. On many days, Steve doesn't talk to any other human beings, and he doesn't see any people except those on television. Steve is imaginary, but his lifestyle is very common. More and more, the inventions of modern technology seem to be cutting us off from contact with our fellow human beings.

Thesis: _More and more, the inventions of modern technology seem to be cutting us off from contact with our fellow human beings._

The world of business is one area in which technology is isolating us. Many people now work alone at home. With access to a large central computer, employees such as secretaries, insurance agents, and accountants do their jobs at display terminals in their own homes. They no longer actually have to see the people they're dealing with. In addition, employees are often paid in an impersonal way. Workers' salaries are automatically credited to their bank accounts, eliminating the need for paychecks. Fewer people stand in line with their coworkers to receive their pay or cash their checks. Finally, personal banking is becoming a detached process. Customers interact with machines rather than people to deposit or withdraw money from their accounts. Even some bank loans are approved or rejected, not in an interview with a loan officer, but through a display on a computer screen.

First topic sentence: _The world of business is one area in which technology is isolating us._

Support: 1. Many people now work alone at home.
         2. _Workers' salaries are automatically credited to their bank accounts._

3. _Personal banking is becoming a detached process._

   a. _Customers interact with machines to make deposits and withdrawals._

   b. _Some loans are accepted or rejected by computers, not loan officers._

Another area that technology is changing is entertainment. Music, for instance, was once a group experience. People listened to music in concert halls or at small social gatherings. For many people now, however, music is a solitary experience. Walking along the street or sitting in their living rooms, they wear headphones to build a wall of music around them. Movie entertainment is changing, too. Movies used to be social events. Now, some people are not going out to see a movie. Some are choosing to wait for a film to appear on cable television. Instead of being involved with the laughter, applause, or hisses of the audience, viewers watch movies in the isolation of their own living rooms.

Second topic sentence: _Another area that technology is changing is entertainment._

Support: 1. _Music is a solitary experience._

          2. _Fewer people go out to see movies._

Education is a third important area in which technology is separating us from others. From elementary schools to colleges, students spend more and more time sitting by themselves in front of computers. The computers give them feedback, while teachers spend more time tending the computers and less time interacting with their classes. A similar problem occurs in homes. As more families buy computers, increasing numbers of students practice their math and reading skills with software programs instead of with their friends, brothers and sisters, and parents. Last, alienation is occurring as a result of another high-tech invention, DVDs. People are buying DVDs on subjects such as cooking, real estate investment, speaking, and speed-reading. They then practice their skills at home rather than by taking group classes in which a rich human interaction can occur.

Third topic sentence: <u>Education is a third important area in which technology is</u>
<u>separating us from others.</u>

Support: 1. <u>Students sit alone in front of computers at school.</u>

_____

2. <u>Students use software at home instead of interacting with</u>
<u>others.</u>

3. <u>DVDs are replacing class instruction.</u>

_____

Technology, then, seems to be driving human beings apart. Soon, we may no longer need to communicate with other human beings in order to do our work, entertain ourselves, or pursue an education. Machines will be the coworkers and companions of the future.

4 Revising

ACTIVITY

Following is the second supporting paragraph from an essay called "Problems of Combining School and Work." The paragraph is shown in four different stages of development: (1) first full draft, (2) revised second draft, (3) edited next-to-final draft, (4) final draft. The four stages appear in scrambled order. Write the number 1 in the answer blank for the first full draft, and number the remaining stages in sequence.

_____2_____   I have also given up some personal pleasures in my life. On sundays for example I used to play softball or football, now I use the entire day to study. Good old-fashioned sleep is another lost pleasure for me now. I never get as much as I like because their just isn't time. Finally I miss having the chance to just sit in front of the TV, on weeknights. In order to watch the whole lineup of movies and sports that I used to watch regularly. These sound like small pleasures, but you realize how important they are when you have to give them up.

_____1_____   I've had to give up pleasures in my life. I use to spend sundays playing games, now I have to study. Im the sort of person who needs a lot of sleep, but I dont have the time for that either. Sleeping nine or ten hours a night woul'dnt be unusual for me. Psycologists say that each individual need a different amount of sleep, some people need as little as five hours, some need as much as nine or ten. So I'm not unusual in that. But Ive given up that pleasure too. And I can't watch the TV shows I use to enjoy. This is another personal pleasure Ive lost because of doing work and school. These may seem like small things, but you realize how good they are when you give them up.

4

Besides missing the social side of college life, I've also had to give up some of my special personal pleasures. I used to spend Sunday afternoons, for example, playing lob-pitch softball or touch football depending on the season. Now I use Sunday as a catch-up day for my studies. Another pleasure I've lost is sleeping late on days off and weekends. I once loved mornings when I could check the clock, bury my head in the pillow, and drift off for another hour. These days I'm forced to crawl out of bed the minute the alarm lets out its piercing ring. Finally, I no longer have the chance to just sit watching the movies and sports programs that I enjoy. A leisurely night of <u>Monday Night Football</u> or a network premiere of a Tom Cruise movie is a pleasure of the past for me now.

3

Besides missing the social side of college life, I've also had to give up some of my special personal pleasures. I used to spend sunday afternoons, for example playing lob-pitch softball or touch football depending on the season. Now I use the day as a catch-up day for my studies. Another pleasure I've lost is sleeping late on days off and weekends. I once loved mornings when I could check the clock, then burying my head in the pillow, and you drift off to sleep for another hour. These days I'm forced to get out of bed the minute the alarm lets out it's ring. Finally I no longer have the chance to just sit watching the movies and also programs with sports that I enjoy. A leisurely night of Monday Night Football or a network premiere of a Tom Cruise movie is a pleasure of the past for me now.

3 The First and Second Steps in Essay Writing

This chapter shows you how to
- start an essay with a point, or thesis
- support that point, or thesis, with specific evidence

Chapter 2 emphasized how prewriting and revising can help you become an effective writer. This chapter focuses on the first two steps in writing an effective essay:

1   Begin with a point, or thesis.
2   Support the thesis with specific evidence.

The chapters that follow will focus on the third and fourth steps in writing:

3   Organize and connect the specific evidence (pages 76–100);
4   Write clear, error-free sentences (pages 101–134).

Step 1: Begin with a Point, or Thesis

ALLWRITE!
3

Your first step in writing is to discover what point you want to make and to write that point out as a single sentence. There are two reasons for doing this. You want to know right from the start if you have a clear and workable thesis. Also, you will be able to use the thesis as a guide while writing your essay. At any stage you can ask yourself, "Does this support my thesis?" With the thesis as a guide, the danger of drifting away from the point of the essay is greatly reduced.

Understanding Thesis Statements

3.2

In Chapter 1, you learned that effective essays center around a thesis, or main point, that a writer wishes to express. This central idea is usually presented as a *thesis statement* in an essay's introductory paragraph.

A good thesis statement does two things. First, it tells readers an essay's *topic*. Second, it presents the writer's *attitude, opinion, idea,* or *point* about that topic. For example, look at the following thesis statement:

Owning a pet has several important benefits.

In this thesis statement, the topic is *owning a pet;* the writer's main point is that owning a pet *has several important benefits.*

ACTIVITY

For each thesis statement below, single-underline the topic and double-underline the main point that the writer wishes to express about the topic.

EXAMPLES   Our company president should be fired for three main reasons.

The Internet has led to new kinds of frustration in everyday life.

1. Our cafeteria would be greatly improved if several changes were made.
2. Celebrities are often poor role models because of the way they dress, talk, and behave.
3. My first night as a security guard turned out to be one of the most frightening experiences of my life.
4. SUVs are inferior to cars because they are harder to control, more expensive, and dangerous to the environment.
5. The twentieth century produced three inventions that dramatically changed the lives of all Americans.
6. Stress in the fast-food workplace has led to serious physical, psychological, and emotional problems for employees.
7. Advertisers target young people in order to market cigarettes, alcohol, and adult movies.
8. Living in the city has certain advantages over living in the suburbs.

9. Before moving away from home, every person should have mastered certain key skills.

10. Independent "mom and pop" stores are superior to larger chain stores for a number of reasons.

Writing a Good Thesis I

3.2

Now that you know how thesis statements work, you can prepare to begin writing your own. To start, you need a topic that is neither too broad nor too narrow. Suppose, for example, that an instructor asks you to write a paper on marriage. Such a subject is too broad to cover in a five-hundred-word essay. You would have to write a book to support adequately any point you might make about the general subject of marriage. What you need to do, then, is limit your subject. Narrow it down until you have a thesis that you can deal with specifically in about five hundred words. In the box that follows are (1) several general subjects, (2) a limited version of each general subject, and (3) a thesis statement about each limited subject.

General Subject	Limited Subject	Thesis
Marriage	Honeymoon	A honeymoon is perhaps the worst way to begin a marriage.
Family	Older sister	My older sister helped me overcome my shyness.
Television	TV preachers	TV evangelists use sales techniques to promote their messages.
Children	Disciplining of children	My husband and I have several effective ways of disciplining our children.
Sports	Players' salaries	Players' high salaries are bad for the game, for the fans, and for the values our children are developing.

ACTIVITY

Sometimes a subject must go through several stages of limiting before it is narrow enough to write about. Below are four lists reflecting several stages that writers went through in moving from a general subject to a narrow thesis statement. Number the stages in each list from 1 to 5, with 1 marking the broadest stage and 5 marking the thesis.

List 1

<u>2</u> Teachers

<u>1</u> Education

<u>3</u> Math teacher

<u>5</u> My high school math teacher was incompetent.

<u>4</u> High school math teacher

List 3

<u>1</u> Retail companies

<u>2</u> Supermarkets

<u>4</u> Dealing with customers

<u>3</u> Working in a supermarket

<u>5</u> I've learned how to handle unpleasant supermarket customers.

List 2

<u>3</u> Bicycles

<u>4</u> Dangers of bike riding

<u>1</u> Recreation

<u>2</u> Recreational vehicles

<u>5</u> Bike riding in the city is a dangerous activity.

List 4

<u>3</u> Camping

<u>4</u> First camping trip

<u>2</u> Summer vacation

<u>5</u> My first camping trip was a disastrous experience.

<u>1</u> Vacations

Later in this chapter, you will get more practice in narrowing general subjects to thesis statements.

Writing a Good Thesis II

When writing thesis statements, people often make mistakes that undermine their chances of producing an effective essay. One mistake is to simply announce the subject rather than state a true thesis. A second mistake is to write a thesis that is too broad, and a third is to write a thesis that is too narrow. A fourth error is to write a thesis containing more than one idea. Here are tips for avoiding such mistakes and writing good thesis statements.

1 Write Statements, Not Announcements

The subject of this paper will be my parents.

I want to talk about the crime wave in our country.

The "baby boom" generation is the concern of this essay.

In this first group, the sentences are not thesis statements but just announcements of a topic. For instance, "The subject of this paper will be my parents" does not make a point about the parents but merely tells, in a rather weak and unimaginative way, the writer's general subject. Remember, a thesis statement must make a point about a limited subject. Effective thesis statements based on the above sentences could be as follows:

My parents each struggled with personal demons.

The recent crime wave in our city has several apparent causes.

The "baby boom" generation has changed American society in key ways.

2 Avoid Statements That Are Too Broad

3.3a

Disease has shaped human history.

Insects are fascinating creatures.

Men and women are very different.

In the above examples, each statement is too broad to be supported adequately in a student essay. For instance, "Disease has shaped human history" would require far more than a five-hundred-word essay. In fact, there are many lengthy books written on the exact same topic. Remember, your thesis statement should be focused enough that it can be effectively supported in a five-paragraph essay. Revised thesis statements based on the topics in the above sentences could be as follows:

In the mid-1980s, AIDS changed people's attitudes about dating.

Strength, organization, and communication make ants one of nature's most successful insects.

Men and women are often treated very differently in the workplace.

3 Avoid Statements That Are Too Narrow

Here are three statements that are too narrow:

The speed limit near my home is sixty-five miles per hour.

A hurricane hit southern Florida last summer.

A person must be at least thirty-five years old in order to be elected president of the United States.

In this third group, there is no room in any of the three statements for support to be given. For instance, "The speed limit near my home is sixty-five miles per hour" is too narrow to be expanded into a paper. It is a simple fact that does not require any support. Such a statement is sometimes called a *dead-end statement:* there is no place to go with it. Remember, a thesis statement must be broad enough to require support in an essay. Successful thesis statements based on the sentences above are as follows:

> The speed limit near my home should be lowered to fifty-five miles per hour for several reasons.
>
> Federal officials made a number of mistakes in their response to the recent Florida hurricane.
>
> The requirement that a U.S. president must be at least thirty-five years old is unfair and unreasonable.

4 Make Sure Statements Develop Only One Idea

Here are three statements that contain more than one idea:

> One of the most serious problems affecting young people today is bullying, and it is time more kids learned the value of helping others.
>
> Studying with others has several benefits, but it also has drawbacks and can be difficult to schedule.
>
> Teachers have played an important role in my life, but they were not as important as my parents.

In this fourth group, each statement contains more than one idea. For instance, "One of the most serious problems affecting young people today is bullying, and it is time more kids learned the value of helping others" clearly has two separate ideas ("One of the most serious problems affecting young people today is bullying" *and* "it is time more kids learned the value of helping others"). The reader is asked to focus on two separate points, each of which more logically belongs in an essay of its own. Remember, the point of an essay is to communicate a *single* main idea to readers. To be as clear as possible, then, try to limit your thesis statement to the single key idea you want your readers to know. Revised thesis statements based on each of the examples above are as follows:

> One of the most serious problems affecting young people today is bullying.
>
> Studying with others has several benefits.
>
> Teachers have played an important role in my life.

ACTIVITY

Write TN in the space next to the two statements that are too narrow to be developed in an essay. Write TB beside the two statements that are too broad to be covered in an essay. Then, in the spaces provided, revise one of the too-narrow statements and one of the too-broad statements to make them each an effective thesis.
Wording of answers may vary.

___TB___   1. The way our society treats elderly people is unbelievable.
            Our society discriminates against elderly people in a number of ways.

___TN___   2. Up to 70 percent of teenage marriages end in divorce.
            Teenage marriages often end in divorce for several reasons.

___TB___   3. Action must be taken against drugs.
            Several steps should be taken to reduce the use of drugs in schools.

___TN___   4. I failed my biology course.
            I am doing poorly in school because of three major distractions in my life.

Step 2: Support the Thesis with Specific Evidence

The first essential step in writing a successful essay is to formulate a clearly stated thesis. The second basic step is to support the thesis with specific reasons or details.

To ensure that your essay will have adequate support, you may find an informal outline very helpful. Write down a brief version of your thesis idea, and then work out and jot down the three points that will support the thesis.

Here is the scratch outline that was prepared by the author of the earlier essay on moviegoing:

> Moviegoing is a problem.
> 1. Inconvenience of going out
> 2. Tempting snacks
> 3. Other moviegoers

A scratch outline like this one looks simple, but developing it often requires a great deal of careful thinking. The time spent on developing a logical outline is invaluable, though. Once you have planned the steps that logically support your thesis, you will be in an excellent position to go on to write an effective essay.

Activities in this section will give you practice in the crucial skill of planning an essay clearly.

ACTIVITY

Following are ten informal outlines. Complete any five of them by adding a third logical supporting point (*c*) that will parallel the two already provided (*a* and *b*).
Answers will vary; examples are shown.

1. The first day on a new job can be nerve-racking.
   a. Meeting new people
   b. Finding your way around a new place
   c. Learning new rules and procedures _____

2. My stepmother has three qualities I admire.
   a. Patience
   b. Thoughtfulness
   c. Sense of humor _____

3. The neighborhood grocery store is poorly managed.
   a. The checkout lines are always long.
   b. The aisles are dirty and understocked.
   c. The employees are unhelpful and even rude. _____

4. College students should live at home.
   a. Stay in touch with family
   b. Avoid distractions of dorm or apartment life
   c. Save money _____

5. _____ is the worst job I've ever had.
   a. Difficult boss
   b. Poor pay
   c. Long hours _____

6. College is stressful for many people.
   a. Worry about grades
   b. Worry about being accepted
   c. Worry about finances _____

7. My landlord adds to the stress in my life.
   a. Neglects repairs
   b. Ignores phone calls
   c. Raises rent frequently _____

8. Our neighborhood park is an unsafe place to visit.
   a. Aggressive dogs
   b. Broken glass
   c. _Strangers/Gangs/Teens_____

9. Buying a used car is better than buying a new one.
   a. Used cars are less likely to be stolen than new cars.
   b. Used cars don't lose their value as quickly as most new cars.
   c. _Used cars are cheaper/easier to repair/easier to insure._____

10. Many companies use annoying practices to increase sales.
    a. Junk mail
    b. Spam e-mail
    c. _Telemarketers/Rebates/Infomercials_____

The Importance of *Specific* Details

Just as a thesis must be developed with three supporting points, each supporting point must be developed with specific details. Specific details are valuable in two key ways. First, details excite the reader's interest. They make writing a pleasure to read, for we all enjoy learning particulars about people, places, and things. Second, details serve to explain a writer's points. They give the evidence needed for us to see and understand general ideas.

All too often, the body paragraphs in essays contain only vague generalities, rather than the specific supporting details that are needed to engage and convince a reader. Here is what one of the paragraphs in "The Hazards of Moviegoing" would have looked like if the writer had not detailed her supporting evidence vividly:

> Some of the other patrons are even more of a problem than the theater itself. Many people in the theater often show themselves to be inconsiderate. They make noises and create disturbances at their seats. Included are people in every age group, from the young to the old. Some act as if they were at home in their own living room watching the TV set. And people are often messy, so that you're constantly aware of all the food they're eating. People are also always moving around near you, creating a disturbance and interrupting your enjoyment of the movie.

The following box contrasts the vague support in the preceding paragraph with the specific support in the essay.

Vague Support	Specific Support
1. Many people in the theater show themselves to be inconsiderate. They make noises and create disturbances at their seats. Included are people in every age group, from the young to the old. Some act as if they were at home in their own living room watching the TV set.	1. Little kids race up and down the aisles, usually in giggling packs. Teenagers try to impress their friends by talking back to the screen, whistling, and making what they consider to be hilarious noises. Adults act as if they were at home in their own living room and comment loudly on the ages of the stars or why movies aren't as good anymore.
2. And people are often messy, so that you're constantly aware of all the food they're eating.	2. And people of all ages crinkle candy wrappers, stick gum on their seats, and drop popcorn tubs or cups of crushed ice and soda on the floor.
3. People are also always moving around near you, creating a disturbance and interrupting your enjoyment of the movie.	3. They also cough and burp, squirm endlessly in their seats, file out for repeated trips to the rest rooms or concession stand, and elbow you out of the armrest on either side of your seat.

The effective paragraph from the essay provides details that make vividly clear the statement that patrons are a problem in the theater. The writer specifies the exact age groups (little kids, teenagers, and adults) and the offenses of each (giggling, talking and whistling, and loud comments). She specifies the various food excesses (crinkled wrappers, gum on seats, dropped popcorn and soda containers). Finally, she provides concrete details that enable us to see and hear other disturbances (coughs and burps, squirming, constant trips to rest rooms, jostling for elbow room). The ineffective paragraph asks us to guess about these details; the effective paragraph describes the details in a specific and lively way.

In the strong paragraph, then, sharp details capture our interest and enable us to share the writer's experience. They provide pictures that make each of us feel, "I am there." The particulars also enable us to understand clearly the writer's point that patrons are a problem. Aim to make your own writing equally convincing by providing detailed support.

ACTIVITY

Write S in front of the two selections below that provide specific evidence to support the opening point. Write X in front of the two selections in which the opening point is followed by vague, general, wordy sentences.

_____S_____ 1. The people who have moved in beside us are unpleasant neighbors.

They barely say "Hi" when we're in our neighboring yards. When we invited them to a neighborhood barbecue, they said they were going to be busy. They sometimes turn loud music on late at night, and we have to close our window to shut out the noise. To top it off, they own a dog, which they let roam free in our street.

_____X_____ 2. My mother was a harsh disciplinarian.

When I did something wrong, no matter how small, she would inflict serious punishment. She had expectations that I was to live up to, and she never changed her attitude. When I did not behave as I should, I was dealt with severely. There were no exceptions as far as my mother was concerned.

_____S_____ 3. Some things are worse when they're "improved."

A good cheesecake, for one thing, is perfect. It doesn't need pineapple, cherries, blueberries, or whipped cream smeared all over it. Plain old American blue jeans, the ones with five pockets and copper rivets, are perfect too. Manufacturers only made them worse when they added flared legs, took away the pockets, tightened the fit, and plastered white logos and designers' names all over them.

_____X_____ 4. Pets can be more trouble than children.

My dog, unlike my children, has never been completely housebroken. When he's excited or nervous, he still has an occasional problem. My dog, unlike my children, has never learned how to take care of himself when we're away, despite the fact that we've given him plenty of time to do so. We don't have to worry about our grown children anymore. However, we still have to hire a dog-sitter.

The Importance of *Adequate* Details

One of the most common and most serious problems in students' writing is inadequate development. You must provide *enough* specific details to fully support the point in a body paragraph of an essay. You could not, for example, include a paragraph about a friend's unreliability and provide only a one- or two-sentence example. You would have to extend the example or add several other examples showing your friend as an unreliable person. Without such additional support, your paragraph would be underdeveloped.

Students may try to disguise unsupported paragraphs through repetition and generalities. Do not fall into this "wordiness trap." Be prepared to do the plain hard work needed to ensure that each paragraph has solid support.

ACTIVITY 1

Both of the following body paragraphs were written on the same topic, and each has a clear opening point. Which paragraph is adequately developed? Which one has only several particulars and uses mostly vague, general, wordy sentences to conceal the fact that it is starved for specific details?

First paragraph is adequately developed.

Eternal Youth?—No, Thanks

I wouldn't want to be a teenager again, first of all, because I wouldn't want to worry about talking to girls. I still remember how scary it was to call up a girl and ask her out. My heart would race, my pulse would pound, and perspiration would trickle down my face, adding to my acne by the second. I never knew whether my voice would come out deep and masculine, like a television anchorman's, or squeaky, like a little boy's. Then there were the questions: Would she be at home? If she was, would she want to talk to me? And if she did, what would I say? The one time I did get up the nerve to take a girl in my homeroom to a movie, I was so tongue-tied that I stared silently at the box of popcorn in my lap until the feature finally started. Needless to say, I wasn't very interesting company.

Terrors of My Teenage Years

I wouldn't want to be a teenager again, first of all, because I wouldn't want to worry about talking to girls. Calling up a girl to ask her out was something that I completely dreaded. I didn't know what words to express or how to express them. I would have all the symptoms of nervousness when

I got on the phone. I worried a great deal about how I would sound, and I had a lot of doubts about the girl's reaction. Once, I managed to call up a girl to go out, but the evening turned out to be a disaster. I was too unsure of myself to act in a confident way. I couldn't think of anything to say and just kept quiet. Now that I look back on it, I really made a fool of myself. Agonizing over my attempts at relationships with the opposite sex made adolescence a very uncomfortable time.

The first paragraph offers a series of well-detailed examples of the author's nerve-racking experiences, as a teenager, with girls. The second paragraph, on the other hand, is underdeveloped. For instance, the second paragraph makes only the general observation "I would have all the symptoms of nervousness when I got on the phone"; but the first paragraph states, "My heart would race, my pulse would pound, and perspiration would trickle down my face."

The second paragraph makes the general statement "I worried a great deal about how I would sound," but in the first paragraph the author wonders if his voice will "come out deep and masculine, like a television anchorman's, or squeaky, like a little boy's." And in the second paragraph, there is no specific description of the evening that turned into a disaster. In summary, the second paragraph lacks the full, detailed support needed to develop its opening point convincingly.

ACTIVITY 2

Take a few minutes to write a paragraph supporting the point "My room is a mess." Afterward, you and your classmates, perhaps working in small groups, should read your paragraphs aloud. The best-received paragraphs are almost sure to be those with plenty of specific details.

Answers will vary.

Practice in Advancing and Supporting a Thesis

You now know the two most important steps in competent essay writing: (1) advancing a point, or thesis, and (2) supporting that thesis. The purpose of this section is to expand and strengthen your understanding of these two basic steps. You will first work through a series of activities on *developing* a thesis:

1 Identifying the parts of an essay
2 Evaluating thesis statements
3 Completing thesis statements

4 Writing a thesis statement

5 Limiting a topic and writing a thesis

You will then sharpen your understanding of how to *support* a thesis effectively by working through the following activities:

6 Providing specific evidence

7 Identifying adequate supporting evidence

8 Adding details to complete an essay

1 Identifying the Parts of an Essay

ACTIVITY 1

Each cluster below contains one topic, one thesis statement, and two supporting sentences. In the space provided, label each item as follows:

T—topic
TH—thesis statement
S—supporting sentence

Group 1

_S_ a. TV has forced politicians to focus more on appearance than substance.

_TH_ b. Television has had a massive impact on politics in the United States.

_S_ c. The expense of producing and airing ads has made politicians worry more about fund-raising than serving their public.

_T_ d. Television

Group 2

_S_ a. Community colleges are much more affordable than most four-year colleges.

_TH_ b. There are several advantages to attending a community college instead of a four-year school.

_T_ c. Community colleges

_S_ d. Community colleges typically offer more convenient and more flexible scheduling than traditional schools.

Group 3

_T_ a. Medicine

_S_ b. Antibiotics have enabled doctors to control many diseases that were once fatal.

_S_ c. Organ transplants have prolonged the lives of tens of thousands of people.

_TH_ d. Advances in modern medicine have had great success in helping people.

Group 4

_T_ a. Reading

_TH_ b. There are steps parents can take to encourage their children to enjoy reading.

_S_ c. The adults' own behavior can influence children to become readers.

_S_ d. Parents can make sure the physical environment of the home encourages reading.

Group 5

_TH_ a. Insects perform many helpful functions for human beings.

_S_ b. Insects are essential to the growth of many important crops.

_T_ c. Insects

_S_ d. Insects protect the environment by removing wastes and controlling disease-causing germs.

ACTIVITY 2

This activity will sharpen your sense of the parts of an essay. "Coping with Old Age" has no indentations starting new paragraphs. Read this essay carefully, and then double-underline the thesis and single-underline the topic sentence for each of the three supporting paragraphs and the first sentence of the conclusion. Write the numbers of those sentences in the spaces provided at the end.

Coping with Old Age

[1]I recently read about an area of the former Soviet Union where many people live to be well over a hundred years old. [2]Being 115 or even 125 isn't considered unusual there, and these old people continue to do productive work right up until they die. [3]The United States, however, isn't such a healthy place for older people. [4]Since I retired from my job, I've had to cope with the physical, mental, and emotional stresses of being "old." [5]For one thing, I've had to adjust to physical changes. [6]Now that I'm over sixty, the trusty body that carried me around for years has turned traitor. [7]Aside from the deepening wrinkles on my face and neck, and the wiry gray hairs that have replaced my brown hair, I face more frightening changes. [8]I don't have the energy I used to. [9]My eyes get tired. [10]Once in a while, I miss something that's said to me. [11]My once faithful feet seem to have lost their comfortable soles, and I sometimes feel I'm walking on marbles. [12]In order to fight against this slow decay, I exercise whenever I can. [13]I walk, I stretch, and I climb stairs. [14]I battle constantly to keep as fit as possible. [15]I'm also trying to cope with mental changes. [16]My mind was once as quick and sure as a champion gymnast. [17]I never found it difficult to memorize answers in school or to remember the names of people I met. [18]Now, I occasionally have to search my mind for the name of a close neighbor or favorite television show. [19]Because my mind needs exercise, too, I challenge it as much as I can. [20]Taking a college course like this English class, for example, forces me to concentrate. [21]The mental gymnast may be a little slow and out of shape, but he can still do a back flip or turn a somersault when he has to. [22]Finally, I must deal with the emotional impact of being old. [23]Our society typecasts old people. [24]We're supposed to be unattractive, senile, useless leftovers. [25]We're supposed to be the crazy drivers and the cranky customers. [26]At first, I was angry and frustrated that I was considered old at all. [27]And I knew that people were wrong to stereotype me. [28]Then I got depressed. [29]I even started to think that maybe I was a cast-off, one of those old animals that slow down the rest of the herd. [30]But I have now decided to rebel against these negative feelings. [31]I try to have friends of all ages and to keep up with what's going on in the world. [32]I try to remember that I'm still the same person who sat at a first-grade desk, who fell in love, who comforted a child, who got a raise at work. [33]I'm not "just" an old person. [34]Coping with the changes of old age has become my latest full-time job. [35]Even though it's a job I never applied for, and one for which I had no experience, I'm trying to do the best I can.

Thesis statement in "Coping with Old Age": ___4___

Topic sentence of first supporting paragraph: ___5___

Topic sentence of second supporting paragraph: __15__

Topic sentence of third supporting paragraph: __22__

First sentence of the conclusion: __34__

2 Evaluating Thesis Statements

As was explained on pages 51–52, some writers announce a subject instead of stating a true thesis idea. Others write a dead-end thesis statement that is too narrow to need support or development. Contrasting with such a dead-end statement is the statement that is wide open—too broad to be adequately supported in the limited space of a five-hundred-word essay. Other thesis statements are vague or contain more than one idea. They suggest that the writer has not thought out the main point sufficiently.

ACTIVITY 1

Write A beside each sentence that is an announcement rather than a thesis statement. Write OK beside the statement in each pair that is a clear, limited point which could be developed in an essay.

1. __A__ a. This essay will discuss the people you meet in exercise class.

   __OK__ b. The kinds of workout clothes worn in my aerobics class identify "jocks," "strugglers," and "princesses."

2. __OK__ a. I made several mistakes in the process of trying to win the respect and affection of my teenage stepson.

   __A__ b. My thesis in this paper is relationships between stepparents and stepchildren.

3. __OK__ a. A period of loneliness can teach you to use your creativity, sort out your values, and feel empathy for others.

   __A__ b. Loneliness is the subject of this paper.

4. __A__ a. This paper will be about sharing housework.

   __OK__ b. Deciding who will perform certain unpleasant household chores can be the crisis that makes or breaks a marriage.

5. __A__ a. My concern here is to discuss "near-death" experiences reported by some patients.

   __OK__ b. There are several possible explanations for the similar "near-death" experiences reported by some patients.

ACTIVITY 2

Write TN beside each statement that is too narrow to be developed in an essay. Write OK beside the statement in each pair that is a clear, limited point.

1. __TN__ a. I had squash, tomatoes, and corn in my garden last summer.

   __OK__ b. Vegetable gardening can be a frustrating hobby.

2. __TN__ a. The main road into our town is lined with billboards.

   __OK__ b. For several reasons, billboards should be abolished.

3. __TN__ a. There are now more single-parent households in our country than ever before.

   __OK__ b. Organization is the key to being a successful single parent.

4. __OK__ a. My first job taught me that I had several bad work habits.

   __TN__ b. Because I was late for work yesterday, I lost an hour's pay and was called in to see the boss.

5. __OK__ a. Americans abuse alcohol because it has become such an important part of our personal and public celebrations.

   __TN__ b. Consumption of wine, beer, and hard liquor increases in the United States every year.

ACTIVITY 3

Write TB beside each statement that is too broad to be developed in an essay. Write OK beside the statement in each pair that is a clear, limited point.

1. __TB__ a. In many ways, sports are an important part of American life.

   __OK__ b. Widespread gambling has changed professional football for the worse.

2. __TB__ a. Modern life makes people suspicious and unfriendly.

   __OK__ b. A frightening experience in my neighborhood has caused me to be a much more cautious person in several ways.

3. __OK__ a. Toy ads on television teach children to be greedy, competitive, and snobbish.

   __TB__ b. Advertising has bad effects on all of society.

4. __TB__ a. Learning new skills can be difficult and frustrating.

   __OK__ b. Learning to write takes work, patience, and a sense of humor.

5. __TB__ a. I didn't get along with my family, so I did many foolish things.

__OK__ b. Running away from home taught me that my parents weren't as terrible as I thought.

ACTIVITY 4

For each pair, write 2 beside the statement that contains more than one idea. Write OK beside the statement that is a clear, limited point.

1. __OK__ a. Working with old people changed my stereotyped ideas about the elderly.

__2__ b. My life has moved in new directions since the rewarding job I had working with older people last summer.

2. __2__ a. The new architecture on this campus is very unpleasant, although the expansion was desperately needed.

__OK__ b. Our new college library building is ugly, intimidating, and inefficient.

3. __OK__ a. Among the most entertaining ads on TV today are those for mail-order products.

__2__ b. Although ads on TV for mail-order products are often misleading, they can still be very entertaining.

4. __2__ a. My roommate and I are compatible in most ways, but we still have conflicts at times.

__OK__ b. My roommate has his own unique systems for studying, writing term papers, and cleaning our room.

5. __2__ a. Although some good movies have come out lately, I prefer to watch old movies because they're more interesting.

__OK__ b. Movies of the 1930s and 1940s have better plots, sets, and actors than movies made today.

3 Completing Thesis Statements

ACTIVITY

Complete the following thesis statements by adding a third supporting point that will parallel the two already provided. You might first want to check the section on parallelism in Chapter 5 (page 101) to make sure you understand parallel form.

Answers will vary; examples are given.

1. Because I never took college preparatory courses in high school, I entered college deficient in mathematics, study skills, and _____science_____.

2. A good salesperson needs to like people, to be aggressive, and ____to be enthusiastic_____.

3. Rather than blame myself for failing the course, I blamed the instructor, my adviser, and even _____my boyfriend_____.

4. Anyone who buys an old house planning to fix it up should be prepared to put in a lot of time, hard work, and _____money_____.

5. Our old car eats gas, makes funny noises, and ____fails to start on cold mornings_____.

6. My mother, my boss, and my _____coach_____ are three people who are very important in my life right now.

7. Getting married too young was a mistake because we hadn't finished our education, we weren't ready for children, and ____we weren't able to commit ourselves to each other_____.

8. Some restaurant patrons seem to leave their honesty, their cleanliness, and their _____manners_____ at home.

9. During my first semester at college, I had to learn how to manage my time, my diet, and ____my relationships with others_____.

10. Three experiences I wish I could forget are the time I fell off a ladder, the time I tried to fix my parents' lawn mower, and ____the time I performed in a piano recital_____.

4 Writing a Thesis Statement

ACTIVITY

Write a thesis for each group of supporting statements. This activity will give you practice in writing an effective essay thesis—one that is neither too broad nor too narrow. It will also help you understand the logical relationship between a thesis and its supporting details.

Wording of thesis may vary.

1. Thesis: __My cars have reflected stages in my life.__

    a. My first car was a rebellious-looking one that matched the way I felt and acted as a teenager.

    b. My next car reflected my more mature and practical adult self.

    c. My latest car seems to tell me that I'm aging; it shows my growing concern with comfort and safety.

2. Thesis: __A two-year college has certain advantages.__

    a. All the course credits that are accumulated can be transferred to a four-year school.

    b. Going to a two-year college can save a great deal of money in tuition and other fees.

    c. If the college is nearby, there are also significant savings in everyday living expenses.

3. Thesis: __I have tried several ways to give up snacks.__

    a. First, I tried simply avoiding the snacks aisle of the supermarket.

    b. Then I started limiting myself to only five units of any given snack.

    c. Finally, in desperation, I began keeping the cellophane bags of snacks in a padlocked cupboard.

4. Thesis: __Halloween is not all fun.__

    a. The holiday can be very frightening for little children.

    b. Children can be struck by cars while wearing vision-obstructing masks and dark costumes.

    c. There are always incidents involving deadly treats: fruits, cookies, and candies that contain razor blades or even poison.

5. Thesis: __Three factors contributed to my heart attack.__

    a. First of all, I was a typical "type A" personality: anxious, impatient, and hard-driving.

    b. I also had a family history of relatives with heart trouble.

    c. My unhealthy lifestyle, though, was probably the major factor.

5 Limiting a Topic and Writing a Thesis Statement

The following two activities will give you practice in distinguishing general from limited subjects and in writing a thesis.

ACTIVITY 1

Look carefully at the ten general subjects and ten limited subjects below. Then write a thesis statement for any five of them.

Hint   To create a thesis statement for a limited subject, ask yourself, "What point do I want to make about _____ (*my limited subject*)?"

General Subject	Limited Subject
1. Apartment	1. Sharing an apartment with a roommate
2. Self-improvement	2. Behavior toward others
3. Family	3. My mother
4. Eating	4. Fast-food restaurants
5. Automobiles	5. Bad driving habits
6. Health	6. Regular exercise
7. Owning a house	7. Do-it-yourself home repairs
8. Baseball	8. Free-agent system
9. Parenthood	9. Being a single parent
10. Pollution	10. Noise pollution

Thesis statements for five of the limited subjects:

Answers will vary; examples are given.

1. Sharing an apartment with a roommate calls for goodwill, a sense of give-and-take, and plenty of intelligence.

2. To improve your behavior toward others, learn to listen, to sympathize, and to share.

5. Three potentially deadly driving habits are inattention, a "tough guy" attitude, and a short temper.

6. Regular exercise is a good way to reduce stress, worry, and your waistline.

10. Interestingly, sources of noise pollution can be loud, moderate, or even very faint.

ACTIVITY 2

Here is a list of ten general subjects. Limit five of the subjects. Then write a thesis statement about each of the five limited subjects.

General Subject	Limited Subject
	Answers will vary; examples are given.
1. Pets	Beagles
2. Teenagers	Teenage motherhood
3. Television	Sports announcers on television
4. Work	Working at home
5. College	Your first week at college
6. Doctors	Our family doctor
7. Vacations	Disastrous vacations
8. Cooking	Cooking for one
9. Money	Unusual things used as money
10. Shopping	Shopping for a wedding gown

Thesis statements for five of the limited subjects:

Answers will vary; examples are given.

1. Beagles make great pets because they are loving, cheerful, and sturdy.

2. Teenage motherhood can be harmful to the mother herself, to her child, and to society.

4. Working at home is a sensible alternative for many people, including parents of young children, older people, and technology wizards.

5. A few simple tips will help you survive your first week at college.

8. Cooking for one person—yourself—can be remarkably pleasant.

6 Providing Specific Evidence

ACTIVITY

Provide three details that logically support each of the following points. Your details can be drawn from your own experience, or they can be invented. In each case, the details should show *specifically* what the point expresses only generally. State your details briefly in several words rather than in complete sentences.

EXAMPLE   We quickly spruced up the apartment before our guest arrived.

1. Hid toys and newspapers in spare closet
2. Vacuumed pet hairs off sofa
3. Sprayed air freshener around living room

Answers will vary; examples are given.

1. The dinner was a disaster.

   Guests arrived two hours late

   Roast was burned

   Host and hostess got into a huge fight

2. My seven-year-old nephew has some disgusting habits.

   Collects dead frogs, birds, and worms

   Loves to dunk pizza in his chocolate milk

   Combs his hair with his toothbrush

3. There are several reasons why I put off studying.

   Too tired.

   Too hungry.

   Too disorganized.

4. My parents never allowed me to think for myself.

   Chose my friends for me

   Chose my clothes for me

   Chose my college for me

5. I have several ways in which I can earn extra cash.

   Baby-sitting

   Gardening

   Baking cookies

6. My car needs repairs.

New ignition
_____

New brakes
_____

New heater
_____

7. Friday evening, I didn't sit still for a minute.

Cat got sick
_____

Kids got sick
_____

Roof started to leak
_____

8. Mr. (or Ms.) _____ was the worst teacher I ever had.

Slept at his desk
_____

Gave six hours of homework per night
_____

Had a terrible temper
_____

7 Identifying Adequate Supporting Evidence

ACTIVITY

The following body paragraphs were taken from student essays. Two of the paragraphs provide sufficient details to support their topic sentences convincingly. Write AD for *adequate development* beside those paragraphs. Three paragraphs use vague, wordy, general, or irrelevant sentences instead of real supporting details. Write U for *underdeveloped* beside those paragraphs.

____AD____   1.   Another consideration in adopting a dog is the cost. Initial fees for shots and a license might add up to $40. Annual visits to the vet for heartworm pills, rabies or distemper shots, and general checkups could cost $50 or more. Then there is the cost of food. A twenty-five-pound bag of dry food (the cheapest kind) costs around $10. A large dog can eat that much in a couple of weeks.

____U____   2.   People can be cruel to pets simply by being thoughtless. They don't think about a pet's needs, or they simply ignore those needs. It never occurs to them that their pet can be experiencing a great deal of discomfort as a result of their failure to be sensitive. The cruelty is a result of the basic lack of attention and concern—qualities that should be there, but aren't.

____U____   3.   If I were in charge of the nighttime programming on a TV network, I would make changes. I would completely eliminate some shows. In fact, all the shows that proved to be of little interest would be canceled. Commercials would also change so that it would be possible to watch them without wanting to turn off the TV set. I would expand the good shows so that people would come away with an even better experience. My ideal network would be a great improvement over the average lineup we see today on any of the major networks.

_____AD_____ 4.   A friend's rudeness is much more damaging than a stranger's. When a friend says sharply, "I don't have time to talk to you just now," you feel hurt instead of angry. When a friend shows up late for lunch or a shopping trip, with no good reason, you feel that you're being taken for granted. Worst, though, is when a friend pretends to be listening to you but his or her wandering eyes show a lack of attention. Then you feel betrayed. Friends, after all, are supposed to make up for the thoughtless cruelties of strangers.

_____U_____ 5.   Giving my first shampoo and set to a real person, after weeks of practicing on wigs, was a nerve-racking experience. The customer was a woman who acted very sure about what she came for. She tried to describe what she wanted, and I tried without much success to understand what she had in mind. Every time I did something, she seemed to be indicating in one way or another that it was not what she wanted. I got more and more nervous as I worked on her hair, and the nervousness showed. The worst part of the ordeal happened at the very end, when I added the final touches. Nothing, to this woman, had turned out right.

8 Adding Details to Complete an Essay

ACTIVITY

The following essay needs specific details to back up the ideas in the supporting paragraphs. Using the spaces provided, add a sentence or two of clear, convincing details for each supporting idea. This activity will give you practice at supplying specific details and an initial feel for writing an essay.

Answers will vary.

Life Without Television

Introduction   When my family's only television set went to the repair shop the other day, my parents, my sister, and I thought we would have a terrible week. How could we get through the long evenings in such a quiet house? What would it be like without all the shows to keep us company? We soon realized, though, that living without television for a while was a stroke of good fortune. It became easy for each of us to enjoy some activities alone, to complete some postponed chores, and to spend rewarding time with each other and friends.

First
supporting
paragraph

First of all, with no television to compete for our time, we found plenty of hours for personal interests. We all read more that week than we had read during the six months before. _____

_____

_____

We each also enjoyed some hobbies we had ignored for ages. _____

_____

_____

_____

In addition, my sister and I both stopped procrastinating with our homework. _____

_____

_____

_____

_____

Second
supporting
paragraph

Second, we did chores that had been hanging over our heads for too long. There were many jobs around the house that had needed attention for some time. _____

_____

_____

We also had a chance to do some long-postponed shopping. _____

_____

_____

And each of us also did some letter writing or other paperwork that was long overdue. _____

_____

_____

Third supporting paragraph

      Finally, and probably most important, we spent time with each other. Instead of just being in the same room together while we stared at a screen, we actually talked for many pleasant hours. _____ _____

_____ _____ _____

_____ _____

Moreover, for the first time in years my family played some games together. _____ _____ _ _____

_____ _____

___ _____ _____ ___ _____ _____ _____ _

And because we didn't have to worry about missing this or that show, we had some family friends over on a couple of evenings and spent an enjoyable time with them. ____ _____ _____ _____ _____

___ _____ _____ _____ _____ _____ _

_____ _____ _____ _____ _____ _____ ___

Conclusion

      Once our television set returned, we were not prepared to put it in the attic. But we had a sense of how it can take over our lives if we are not careful. We are now more selective. We turn on the set for our favorite shows, certain sports events, and the news, but we don't leave it running all night. As a result, we find we can enjoy television and still have time left over for other activities and interests.

4 The Third Step in Essay Writing

This chapter shows you how to

- organize and connect specific evidence in the body paragraphs of an essay
- begin and end an essay with effective introductory and concluding paragraphs

You know from Chapter 3 that the first two steps in writing an effective essay are advancing a thesis and supporting it with specific evidence. This chapter deals with the third step. You'll learn the chief ways to organize and connect the supporting information in a paper. You'll then see how to start an essay with a suitable introductory paragraph and how to finish it with a well-rounded concluding paragraph.

Step 3: Organize and Connect the Specific Evidence

As you are generating the specific details needed to support a thesis, you should be thinking about ways to organize and connect those details. All the details in your essay must *cohere,* or stick together, so that your reader will be able to move smoothly from one bit of supporting information to the next. This section shows you how to organize and connect supporting details by using (1) common methods of organization, (2) transitions, and (3) other connecting words.

Common Methods of Organization

ALLWRITE!
7.5

Two common methods used to organize the supporting material in an essay are time order and emphatic order. (You will learn more specific methods of development in Part Two of this book.)

Time, or *chronological*, *order* simply means that details are listed as they occur in time. *First* this is done; *next* this; *then* this; *after* that, this; and so on. Here is an outline of an essay in this book in which time order is used:

Thesis

To exercise successfully, you should follow a simple plan consisting of arranging the time, making preparations, and warming up properly.

1. To begin with, set aside a regular hour for exercise.
2. Next, prepare for your exercise session.
3. Finally, do a series of warm-up activities.

Fill in the missing words: The topic sentences in the essay use the words _____To begin with_____, _____Next_____, and _____Finally_____ to help show time order.

Here is one supporting paragraph from the essay:

Next, prepare for your exercise session. You do this, first, by not eating or drinking anything for an hour before the session. Why risk an upset stomach? Then, dress comfortably in something that allows you to move freely. Because you'll be in your own home, there's no need to invest in a high-fashion dance costume. A loose T-shirt and shorts are good. A bathing suit is great in summer, and in winter long underwear is warm and comfortable. If your hair tends to flop in your eyes, pin it back or wear a headband or scarf. After dressing, prepare the exercise area. Turn off the phone and lock the door to prevent interruptions. Shove the coffee table out of the way so that you won't bruise yourself on it. Finally, get out the simple materials you'll need to exercise on.

Fill in the missing words: The paragraph uses the following words to help show time order: _____Next_____, _____first_____, _____Then_____, _____After_____, and _____Finally_____.

7.5d

Emphatic order is sometimes described as "saving the best till last." It is a way to put *emphasis* on the most interesting or important detail by placing it in the last part of a paragraph or in the final supporting paragraph of an essay. (In cases where all the details seem equal in importance, the writer should impose a personal order that seems logical or appropriate.) The last position in a paper is the most emphatic position because the reader is most likely to remember the last thing read. *Finally, last of all,* and *most important* are typical words or phrases showing emphasis. Here is an outline of an essay in this book that uses emphatic order:

Thesis

Celebrities lead very stressful lives.

1. For one thing, celebrities don't have the privacy an ordinary person does.
2. In addition, celebrities are under constant pressure.
3. Most important, celebrities must deal with the stress of being in constant danger.

Fill in the missing words: The topic sentences in the essay use the words _____For one thing_____, _____In addition_____, and _____Most important_____ to help show emphatic order.

Here is the third supporting paragraph from the essay:

Most important, celebrities must deal with the stress of being in constant danger. The friendly grabs, hugs, and kisses of enthusiastic fans can quickly turn into uncontrolled assaults on a celebrity's hair, clothes, and car. Celebrities often get strange letters from people who become obsessed with their idols or from people who threaten to harm them. Worst of all, threats can turn into deeds. The attempt to kill Ronald Reagan and the murder of John Lennon came about because two unbalanced people tried to transfer the celebrity's fame to themselves. Famous people must live with the fact that they are always fair game—and never out of season.

Fill in the missing words: The words _____Worst of all_____ are used to mark the most emphatic detail in the paragraph.

Some essays use a combination of time order and emphatic order. For example, the essay on moviegoing in Chapter 1 includes time order: the writer first describes getting to the theater, then the theater itself, and finally the behavior of patrons during the movie. At the same time, the writer uses emphatic order, ending with the most important reason for her dislike of moviegoing: "Some of the other patrons are even more of a problem than the theater itself."

ACTIVITY

Part A   Read the essays listed below and identify their method of organizing details—time order, emphatic order, or a combination of both.

1. "Adopting a Handicap" (page 191)
   time order

2. "A Vote for McDonald's (page 266)
   emphatic order

3. "Everyday Cruelty" (page 207)
   combination

Part B   Now see if you can complete the explanations that follow.

The essay titled "Adopting a Handicap" uses (*add the missing word*) _____time_____ order. The author begins with the challenge of learning to sit properly in the wheelchair, then moves on to learning to move in the wheelchair, and ends with several problems that occurred next, during the church service. "A Vote for McDonald's" uses (*add the missing word*) _____emphatic_____ order. The writer presents three advantages of eating at McDonald's and ends with the most important one: reasonable prices. "Everyday Cruelty" uses a combination of (*add the missing words*) _____time_____ and _____emphatic_____ order. It moves from the beginning to the end of a particular workday. It also ends with the "worst incident of mean-spiritedness" that the writer witnessed that day.

Transitions

Transitional Words

6.1

Transitions signal the direction of a writer's thought. They are like the road signs that guide travelers. In the box on the following page are some common transitions, grouped according to the kind of signal they give to readers. Note that certain words provide more than one kind of signal.

Addition signals: one, first of all, second, the third reason, also, next, another, and, in addition, moreover, furthermore, finally, last of all

Time signals: first, then, next, after, as, before, while, meanwhile, soon, now, during, finally

Space signals: next to, across, on the opposite side, to the left, to the right, above, below, near, nearby

Change-of-direction signals: but, however, yet, in contrast, although, otherwise, still, on the contrary, on the other hand

Illustration signals: for example, for instance, specifically, as an illustration, once, such as

Conclusion signals: therefore, consequently, thus, then, as a result, in summary, to conclude, last of all, finally

ACTIVITY

1. Underline the three *addition* signals in the following selection:

    To create the time you need to pass difficult courses, find some easy courses. These are the ones that combine the least amount of work with the fewest tests and the most lenient professors. One way to find such courses is to ask friends and classmates about courses in which they received A's after attending only 25 percent of the classes. Also, inquire around to see which instructors lecture with the same notes every year and give the same tests. Photocopies of the class notes are usually cheap and widely available. Another great way of finding simple courses is to pick up a copy of the master schedule and study it carefully. Find the telltale course titles that signal an easy glide through a painless subject. Look for titles like "History of the Animated Cartoon," "Arts and Crafts for Beginners," and "Rock Music of the 1950s."

2. Underline the four *time* signals in the following selection:

    After you've snagged the job of TV sports reporter, you have to begin working on the details of your image. First, invest in two or three truly loud sports jackets. Look for gigantic plaid patterns in odd color combinations like purple and green or orange and blue. These should become familiar enough to viewers so that they will associate that crazy jacket with that dynamic sportscaster. Next, try to cultivate a distinctive voice that will be just annoying enough to be memorable. A nasal whine or a gravelly growl will do it. Be sure to speak only in tough, punchy sentences that seem to be punctuated with imaginary exclamation points. <u>Finally,</u> you must share lots of pompous, obnoxious opinions with your viewers. Your tone of voice must convey the hidden message "I dare anyone to disagree with me." If the home teams lose, call them bums. If players strike, talk sarcastically about the good old days. If a sports franchise leaves town, say, "Good riddance."

3. Underline the three *space* signals in the following selection:

The vegetable bin of my refrigerator contained an assortment of weird-looking items. <u>Next</u> to a shriveled, white-coated lemon were two oranges covered with blue fuzz. <u>To the right</u> of the oranges was a bunch of carrots that had begun to sprout points, spikes, knobs, and tendrils. The carrots drooped into U shapes as I picked them up with the tips of my fingers. <u>Near</u> the carrots was a net bag of onions; each onion had sent curling shoots through the net until the whole thing resembled a mass of green spaghetti. The most horrible item, though, was a head of lettuce that had turned into a pool of brown goo. It had seeped out of its bag and coated the bin with a sticky, evil-smelling liquid.

4. Underline the two *change-of-direction* signals in the following selection:

Taking small children on vacation, for instance, sounds like a wonderful experience for the entire family. <u>But</u> vacations can be scary or emotionally overwhelming times for children. When children are taken away from their usual routine and brought to an unfamiliar place, they can become very frightened. That strange bed in the motel room or the unusual noises in Grandma's spare bedroom may cause nightmares. On vacations, too, children usually clamor to do as many things in one day as they can and to stay up past their usual bedtime. And, since it is vacation time, parents may decide to give in to the children's demands. A parental attitude like this, <u>however,</u> can lead to problems. After a sixteen-hour day of touring the amusement park, eating in a restaurant, and seeing a movie, children can experience sensory and emotional overload. They become cranky, unhappy, or even rebellious and angry.

5. Underline the two *illustration* signals in the following selection:

Supermarkets also use psychology to encourage you to buy. <u>For example,</u> in most supermarkets, the milk and the bread are either at opposite ends of the store or located far away from the first aisle. Even if you've stopped at the market only for staples like these, you must pass hundreds of items in order to reach them. The odds are that instead of leaving with just a quart of milk, you'll leave with additional purchases as well. Special displays, <u>such as</u> a pyramid of canned green beans in an aisle and a large end display of cartons of paper towels, also increase sales. Because you assume that these items are a good buy, you may pick them up. However, they may not even be on sale! Store managers know that the customer is automatically attracted to a display like this, and they will use it to move an overstocked product.

6. Underline the two *conclusion* signals in the following selection:

<u>Finally,</u> my grandmother was extremely thrifty. She was one of those people who hoard pieces of used aluminum foil after carefully scraping off the cake icing or beef gravy. She had a drawer full of old eyeglasses that dated back at least thirty years. The lens prescriptions were no longer accurate, but Gran couldn't bear to throw away "a good pair of glasses." She kept them "just in case," but we could never figure out what situation would involve a desperate need for a dozen pairs of old eyeglasses. We never realized the true extent of Gran's thriftiness, though, until after she died. Her house was to be sold, and <u>therefore</u> we cleaned out its dusty attic. In one corner was a cardboard box filled with two- and three-inch pieces of string. The box was labeled, in Gran's spidery hand, "String too short to be saved."

Transitional Sentences

Transitional, or *linking, sentences* are used between paragraphs to help tie together the supporting paragraphs in an essay. They enable the reader to move smoothly from the idea in one paragraph to the idea in the next paragraph.

Here is the linking sentence used in the essay on moviegoing:

Many of the other patrons are even more of a problem than the concession stand.

The words *concession stand* remind us of the point of the first supporting paragraph, while *Many of the other patrons* presents the point to be developed in the second supporting paragraph.

ACTIVITY

Following is a brief sentence outline of an essay. The second and third topic sentences serve as transitional, or linking, sentences. Each reminds us of the point in the preceding paragraph and announces the point to be developed in the current or by the box, these baked goods will satisfyingly fill both the stomach and the pocketbook.

ACTIVITY

Read the selection below and then answer the questions about it that follow.

¹When I think about my childhood in the 1930s, life today seems like the greatest of luxuries. ²In our house, we had only a wood-burning cookstove in the kitchen to keep us warm. ³In the morning, my father would get up in the icy cold, go downstairs, and light a fire in the black iron range. ⁴When he called us, I would put off leaving my warm bed until the last possible minute and then quickly grab my school clothes. ⁵The water pitcher and washing basin in my room would be layered with ice, and my breath would come out as white puffs as I ran downstairs. ⁶My sisters and I would all dress—as quickly as possible—in the chilly but bearable air of the kitchen. ⁷Our schoolroom, once we had arrived, didn't provide much relief from the cold. ⁸Students wore woolen mitts which left their fingers free but covered their palms and wrists. ⁹Even with these, we occasionally suffered chilblains. ¹⁰The throbbing swellings on our hands made writing a painful process. ¹¹When we returned home in the afternoon, we spent all our indoor hours in the warm kitchen. ¹²We hated to leave it at bedtime in order to make the return trip to those cold bedrooms and frigid sheets. ¹³My mother made up hot-water bottles and gave us hot bricks to tuck under the covers, but nothing could eliminate the agony of that penetrating cold when we first slid under the bedclothes.

1. How many times is the key word *cold* used? _____4_____

2. Write here the pronoun that is used for *father* (sentence 4): _____he_____

3. Write here the words in sentence 3 that are used as a synonym for *cookstove:* ___iron range___; write in the words in sentence 10 that are used as a synonym for *chilblains:* ___throbbing swellings___; write in the word in sentence 12 that is used as a synonym for *cold:* _____frigid_____.

Introductions, Conclusions, and Titles

So far, this chapter has discussed ways to organize and connect the supporting paragraphs of an essay. A well-organized essay, however, also needs a strong introductory paragraph, an effective concluding paragraph, and a good title.

---

paragraph. In the spaces provided, add the words needed to complete the second and third topic sentences.

Thesis

The most helpful values I learned from my parents are the importance of family support, of hard work, and of a good education.

First supporting paragraph

First, my parents taught me that family members should stick together, especially in time of trouble. . . .

Second supporting paragraph

In addition to teaching me about the importance of ___family support___ _____,

my parents taught me the value of _____hard work_____
_____ . . . .

Third supporting paragraph

Along with the value of _____hard work_____,

my parents emphasized the benefits of _____a good education_____
_____ . . . .

Other Connecting Words

6.2

In addition to transitions, there are three other kinds of connecting words that help tie together the specific evidence in a paper: *repeated words, pronouns,* and *synonyms.* Each will be discussed in turn.

Repeated Words

Many of us have been taught—correctly—not to repeat ourselves in writing. However, repeating *key* words helps tie together the flow of thought in a paper. Below, repeated words remind readers of the selection's central idea.

One reason for studying psychology is to help you deal with your children. Perhaps your young daughter refuses to go to bed when you want her to and bursts into tears at the least mention of "lights out." A little knowledge of <u>psychology</u> comes in handy. Offer her a choice of staying up until 7:30 with you or going upstairs and playing until 8:00. Since she gets to make the choice, she does not feel so powerless and will not resist. <u>Psychology</u> is also useful in rewarding a child for a job well done. Instead of telling your ten-year-old son what a good boy he is when he makes his own bed, tell him how neat it looks, how happy you are to see it, and how proud of him you are for doing it by himself. The <u>psychology</u> books will tell you that being a good boy is much harder to live up to than doing one job well.

Pronouns

Pronouns (*he, she, it, you, they, this, that,* and others) are another way to connect ideas. Also, using pronouns in place of other words can help you avoid needless repetition. (Note, however, that pronouns should be used with care to avoid the problems described on pages 463–465.) Here is a selection that makes good use of pronouns:

> Another way for people to economize at an amusement park is to bring <u>their</u> own food. If <u>they</u> pack a nourishing, well-balanced lunch of cold chicken, carrot sticks, and fruit, <u>they</u> will avoid having to pay high prices for hamburgers and hot dogs. <u>They</u> will also save on calories. Also, instead of filling up on soft drinks, <u>they</u> should bring a thermos of iced tea. Iced tea is more refreshing than soda, and <u>it</u> is a great deal cheaper. Every dollar that is not spent at a refreshment stand is <u>one</u> that can be spent on another ride.

Synonyms

Synonyms are words alike in meaning. Using synonyms can also help move the reader easily from one thought to the next. In addition, the use of synonyms increases variety and interest by avoiding needless repetition.

Note the synonyms for *method* in the following selection:

> There are several methods of fund-raising that work well with small organizations. One <u>technique</u> is to hold an auction, with everyone either contributing an item from home or obtaining a donation from a sympathetic local merchant. Because all the merchandise and the services of the auctioneer have been donated, the entire proceeds can be placed in the organization's treasury. A second fund-raising <u>procedure</u> is a car wash. Club members and their children get together on a Saturday and wash all the cars in the neighborhood for a few dollars apiece. A third, time-tested <u>way</u> to raise money is to hold a bake sale, with each family contributing homemade cookies, brownies, layer cakes, or cupcakes. Sold by the piece

Introductory Paragraph

Functions of the Introduction

8.1

A well-written introductory paragraph performs four important roles:

1   It attracts the reader's interest, encouraging him or her to continue reading the essay.

2   It supplies any background information that the reader may need to understand the essay.

3   It presents a thesis statement. This clear, direct statement of the main idea of the paper usually appears near the end of the introductory paragraph.

4   It indicates a plan of development. In this "preview," the major supporting points for the thesis are listed in the order in which they will be presented. In some cases, the thesis and plan of development appear in the same sentence. However, writers sometimes choose not to describe the plan of development.

Common Methods of Introduction

Here are some common methods of introduction. Use any one method, or a combination of methods, to introduce your subject to the reader in an interesting way.

1   ***Begin with a broad, general statement of your topic and narrow it down to your thesis statement.*** Broad, general statements ease the reader into your thesis statement by first introducing the topic. In the example below, the writer talks generally about diets and then narrows down to comments on a specific diet.

> Bookstore shelves today are crammed with dozens of different diet books. The American public seems willing to try any sort of diet, especially the ones that promise instant, miraculous results. And authors are more than willing to invent new fad diets to cash in on this craze. Unfortunately, some of these fad diets are ineffective or even unsafe. One of the worst fad diets is the "Palm Beach" plan. It is impractical, doesn't achieve the results it claims, and is a sure route to poor nutrition.

2   ***Start with an idea or a situation that is the opposite of the one you will develop.*** This approach works because your readers will be surprised, and then intrigued, by the contrast between the opening idea and the thesis that follows it.

> When I decided to return to school at age thirty-five, I wasn't at all worried about my ability to do the work. After all, I was a grown woman who had raised a family, not a confused teenager fresh out of high school.

But when I started classes, I realized that those "confused teenagers" sitting around me were in much better shape for college than I was. They still had all their classroom skills in bright, shiny condition, while mine had grown rusty from disuse. I had to learn how to locate information in a library, how to write a report, and even how to speak up in class discussions.

3   *Explain the importance of your topic to the reader.* If you can convince your readers that the subject in some way applies to them, or is something they should know more about, they will want to keep reading.

Diseases like scarlet fever and whooping cough used to kill more young children than any other cause. Today, however, child mortality due to disease has been almost completely eliminated by medical science. Instead, car accidents are the number-one killer of our children. And most of the children fatally injured in car accidents were not protected by car seats, belts, or restraints of any kind. Several steps must be taken to reduce the serious dangers car accidents pose to our children.

4   *Use an incident or a brief story.* Stories are naturally interesting. They appeal to a reader's curiosity. In your introduction, an anecdote will grab the reader's attention right away. The story should be brief and should be related to your main idea. The incident in the story can be something that happened to you, something you have heard about, or something you have read about in a newspaper or magazine.

Early Sunday morning the young mother dressed her little girl warmly and gave her a candy bar, a picture book, and a well-worn stuffed rabbit. Together, they drove downtown to a Methodist church. There the mother told the little girl to wait on the stone steps until children began arriving for Sunday school. Then the young mother drove off, abandoning her five-year-old because she couldn't cope with being a parent anymore. This incident is one of thousands of cases of child neglect and abuse that occur annually. Perhaps the automatic right to become a parent should no longer exist. Would-be parents should be forced to apply for parental licenses for which they would have to meet three important conditions.

5   *Ask one or more questions.* You may simply want the reader to think about possible answers, or you may plan to answer the questions yourself later in the paper.

What is love? How do we know that we are really in love? When we meet that special person, how can we tell that our feelings are genuine and not merely infatuation? And, if they are genuine, will these feelings last? Love, as we all know, is difficult to define. But most people agree that true and lasting love involves far more than mere physical attraction. Love involves mutual respect, the desire to give rather than take, and the feeling of being wholly at ease.

6   *Use a quotation.* A quotation can be something you have read in a book or an article. It can also be something that you have heard: a popular saying or proverb ("Never give advice to a friend"), a current or recent advertising slogan ("Reach out and touch someone"), or a favorite expression used by friends or family ("My father always says . . ."). Using a quotation in your introductory paragraph lets you add someone else's voice to your own.

"Fish and visitors," wrote Benjamin Franklin, "begin to smell after three days." Last summer, when my sister and her family came to spend their two-week vacation with us, I became convinced that Franklin was right. After only three days of my family's visit, I was thoroughly sick of my brother-in-law's corny jokes, my sister's endless complaints about her boss, and their children's constant invasions of our privacy.

ACTIVITY

The box below summarizes the six kinds of introduction. Read the introductions that follow it and, in the space provided, write the letter of the kind of introduction used in each case.

A. General to narrow	D. Incident or story
B. Starting with an opposite	E. Questions
C. Stating importance of topic	F. Quotation

_____B_____   1. The ad, in full color on a glossy magazine page, shows a beautiful kitchen with gleaming counters. In the foreground, on one of the counters, stands a shiny new food processor. Usually, a feminine hand is touching it lovingly. Around the main picture are other, smaller shots. They show mounds of perfectly sliced onion rings, thin rounds of juicy tomatoes, heaps of matchstick-sized potatoes, and piles of golden, evenly grated cheese. The ad copy tells you how wonderful, how easy, food preparation will be with a processor. Don't believe it. My processor turned out to be expensive, difficult to operate, and very limited in its use.

_____F_____ 2. My father stubbornly says, "You <u>can</u> often tell a book by its cover," and when it comes to certain paperbacks, he's right. When you're browsing in the drugstore or supermarket and you see a paperback featuring an attractive young woman in a low-cut dress fleeing from a handsome dark figure in a shadowy castle, you know exactly what you're getting. Every romance novel has the same elements: an innocent heroine, an exotic setting, and a cruel but fascinating hero.

_____A_____ 3. We Americans are incredibly lazy. Instead of cooking a simple, nourishing meal, we pop a frozen dinner into the oven. Instead of studying a daily newspaper, we are contented with the capsule summaries on the network news. Worst of all, instead of walking even a few blocks to the local convenience store, we jump into our cars. This dependence on the automobile, even for short trips, has robbed us of a valuable experience—walking. If we drove less and walked more, we would save money, become healthier, and discover fascinating things about our surroundings.

Concluding Paragraph

8.2

A concluding paragraph is your chance to remind the reader of your thesis idea and bring the paper to a natural and graceful end.

Common Methods of Conclusion

You may use any one of the methods below, or a combination of methods, to round off your paper.

1 ***End with a summary and final thought.*** When army instructors train new recruits, each of their lessons follows a three-step formula:

   a Tell them what you're going to tell them.

   b Tell them.

   c Tell them what you've told them.

An essay that ends with a summary is not very different. After you have stated your thesis ("Tell them what you're going to tell them") and supported it ("Tell them"), you restate the thesis and supporting points ("Tell them what you've told them"). However, don't use the exact wording you used before. Here is a summary conclusion:

   Catalog shopping at home, then, has several advantages. Such shopping is convenient, saves you money, and saves you time. It is not surprising that growing numbers of devoted catalog shoppers are welcoming those full-color mail brochures that offer everything from turnip seeds to televisions.

Note that the summary is accompanied by a final comment that "rounds off" the paper and brings the discussion to a close. This combination of a summary and a final thought is the most common method of concluding an essay.

2   *Include a thought-provoking question or short series of questions.* A question grabs the reader's attention. It is a direct appeal to your reader to think further about what you have written. A question should follow logically from the points you have already made in the paper. A question must deal with one of these areas:

a Why the subject of your paper is important

b What might happen in the future

c What should be done about this subject

d Which choice should be made

In your conclusion, you may provide an answer to your question. Be sure, though, that the question is closely related to your thesis. Here is an example:

> What, then, will happen in the twenty-first century when most of the population will be over sixty years old? Retirement policies could change dramatically, with the age-sixty-five testimonial dinner and gold watch postponed for five or ten years. Even television would change as the Metamucil generation replaces the Pepsi generation. Glamorous gray-haired models would sell everything from toilet paper to televisions. New soap operas and situation comedies would reveal the secrets of the "sunset years." It will be a different world indeed when the young find themselves outnumbered.

3   *End with a prediction or recommendation.* Like questions, predictions and recommendations also involve your readers. A prediction states what may happen in the future:

> If people stopped to think before acquiring pets, there would be fewer instances of cruelty to animals. Many times, it is the people who adopt pets without considering the expense and responsibility involved who mistreat and neglect their animals. Pets are living creatures. They do not deserve to be treated as carelessly as one would treat a stuffed toy.

A recommendation suggests what should be done about a situation or problem:

Stereotypes such as the helpless homemaker, harried executive, and dotty grandparent are insulting enough to begin with. In magazine ads or television commercials, they become even more insulting. Now these unfortunate characters are not just being laughed at; they are being turned into hucksters to sell products to an unsuspecting public. Consumers should boycott companies whose advertising continues to use such stereotypes.

ACTIVITY

In the space provided, note how each concluding paragraph ends: with a summary and final thought (write S in the space), with a prediction or recommendation (write P/R), or with a question (write Q).

_P/R_   1. Disappointments are unwelcome, but regular, visitors in everyone's life. We can feel depressed about them, or we can try to escape from them. The best thing, though, is to accept a disappointment and then try to use it somehow: step over the unwelcome visitor and then get on with life.

_Q_   2. Holidays, it is clear, are often not the fulfilling experience they are supposed to be. They can, in fact, be very stressful. But would we rather have a holiday-free calendar?

_S_   3. Some people dream of starring roles, their names in lights, and their pictures on the cover of People magazine. I'm not one of them, though. A famous person gives up private life, feels pressured all the time, and is never completely safe. So let someone else have that cover story. I'd rather lead an ordinary, but calm, life than a stress-filled one.

Titles

A title is usually a very brief summary of what your paper is about. It is often no more than several words. You may find it easier to write the title *after* you have completed your paper.

Following are the introductory paragraphs for two of the essays in this text, along with the titles of the essays.

Introductory paragraph

I'm not just a consumer—I'm a victim. If I order a product, it is sure to arrive in the wrong color, size, or quantity. If I hire people to do repairs, they never arrive on the day scheduled. If I owe a bill, the computer is bound to overcharge me. Therefore, in self-defense, I have developed the following consumer's guide to complaining effectively.

Title: How to Complain

Schools divide people into categories. From first grade on up, students are labeled "advanced" or "deprived" or "remedial" or "antisocial." Students pigeonhole their fellow students, too. We've all known the "brain," the "jock," the "dummy," and the "teacher's pet." In most cases, these narrow labels are misleading and inaccurate. But there is one label for a certain type of college student that says it all: "zombie."

Title: **Student Zombies**

Note that you should not underline the title. Nor should you put quotation marks around it. On the other hand, you should capitalize all but small connecting words in the title. Also, you should skip a space between the title and the first line of the text. (See "Manuscript Form," page 488.)

ACTIVITY

Write an appropriate title for each of the introductory paragraphs that follow.
Answers may vary.

1. For my birthday this month, my wife has offered to treat me to dinner at the restaurant of my choice. I think she expects me to ask for a meal at the Chalet, the classiest, most expensive restaurant in town. However, I'm going to eat my birthday dinner at McDonald's. When I compare the two restaurants, the advantages of eating at McDonald's are clear.

   Title: Advantages of McDonald's

2. I've been in lots of diners, and they've always seemed to be warm, busy, friendly, happy places. That's why, on a recent Monday night, I stopped at a diner for a cup of coffee. I was returning home after an all-day car trip and needed something to help me make the last forty-five miles. A diner at midnight, however, was not the place I had expected. It was different—and lonely.

   Title: A Lonely Diner

3. If you see rock-concert audiences only on television or in newspaper photos, the people at these events may all seem to be excited teenagers. However, if you attended a few rock shows, you would see that several kinds of people make up the crowd. At any concert, you would find the typical fan, the out-of-place person, and the troublemaker.

   Title: Audiences at Rock Concerts

Practice in Organizing and Connecting Specific Evidence

 You now know the third step in effective writing: organizing the specific evidence used to support the thesis of a paper. This closing section will expand and strengthen your understanding of the third step in writing. You will work through the following series of activities:

1 Organizing through time or emphatic order
2 Providing transitions
3 Identifying transitions and other connecting words
4 Completing transitional sentences
5 Identifying introductions and conclusions

1 Organizing through Time or Emphatic Order

ACTIVITY 1

Use time order to organize the scrambled lists of supporting ideas below. Write 1 beside the supporting idea that should come first in time, 2 beside the idea that logically follows, and 3 beside the idea that comes last in time.

1. Thesis: When I was a child, Disney movies frightened me more than any other kind.

____1____   As a five-year-old, I was terrified by the movie *Pinocchio,* about a puppet transformed into a boy.

____3____   Although I saw *Bambi* when I was old enough to begin poking fun at "baby movies," the scene during which Bambi's mother is killed has stayed with me to this day.

____2____   About a year after *Pinocchio,* I gripped my seat in fear as the witches and goblins of *Fantasia* flew across the screen.

2. Thesis: There are techniques to help you overcome three common pitfalls in making a cheesecake.

____3____   There's only one way to remove the cake cleanly and easily from its pan.

___1___ Plan in advance to have your equipment ready and the ingredients at room temperature.

___2___ Remember to time the baking process and regulate the oven temperature while the cake is baking.

3. Thesis: Applying for unemployment benefits was a confusing, frustrating experience.

___1___ It was difficult to find both the office and a place to park.

___3___ When I finally reached the head of the line after four hours of waiting, the clerk had problems processing my claim.

___2___ There was no one to direct or help me when I entered the large office, which was packed with people.

ACTIVITY 2

Use emphatic order (order of importance) to arrange the following scrambled lists of supporting ideas. For each thesis, write 1 in the blank beside the point that is perhaps less important or interesting than the other two, 2 beside the point that appears more important or interesting, and 3 beside the point that should be most emphasized.

1. Thesis: My after-school job has been an invaluable part of my life this year.

___2___ Better yet, it has taught me how to get along with many kinds of people.

___1___ Since it's in the morning, it usually keeps me from staying up too late.

___3___ Without it, I would have had to drop out of school.

2. Thesis: We received some odd gifts for our wedding.

___3___ The winner in the odd-gift category was a large wooden box with no apparent purpose or function.

___1___ Someone gave us a gift certificate for a massage.

___2___ Even stranger, my uncle gave me his favorite bowling ball.

3. Thesis: Donna is my most loyal friend.

___2___ She has taken time to do special favors for me.

___3___ She's always there in real emergencies or emotional crises.

___1___ She once lent me her favorite necklace to wear on a date.

2 Providing Transitions

ACTIVITY

In the spaces provided, add appropriate transitions to tie together the sentences and ideas in the following essay. Draw from the words given in the boxes above the paragraphs. Use each word only once.

Annoying People

President Richard Nixon used to keep an "enemies list" of all the people he didn't especially like. I'm ashamed to confess it, but I, too, have an enemies list—a mental one. On this list are all the people I would gladly live without, the ones who cause my blood pressure to rise to the boiling point. The top three places on the list go to people with annoying nervous habits, people who talk in movie theaters, and people who talk on car phones while driving.

For example	First of all	Another	However

_____First of all_____, there are the people with annoying nervous habits. _____For example_____, there are the ones who make faces. When in deep thought, they twitch, squint, and frown, and they can be a real distraction when I'm trying to concentrate during an exam. _____Another_____ type of nervous character makes useless designs. These people bend paper clips into abstract sculptures or string the clips into necklaces as they talk. _____However_____, neither of these groups is as bad as the people who make noises. These individuals, when they are feeling uncomfortable, bite their fingernails or crack their knuckles. If they have a pencil in their hands, they tap it rhythmically against whatever surface is handy—a desk, a book, a head. Lacking a pencil to play with, they jingle the loose change or keys in their pockets. These people make me wish I were hard of hearing.

On the contrary	Then	As a result	After	second

A _____second_____ category of people I would gladly do away with is the ones who talk in movie theaters. These people are not content to sit back, relax, and enjoy the film they have paid to see. _____On the contrary_____, they feel compelled to comment loudly on everything from the hero's hairstyle to the appropriateness of the background music. _____As a result_____, no one hears a word of any dialog except theirs. _____After_____ they have been in the theater for a while, their interest in the movie may fade. _____Then_____ they will start discussing other things, and the people around them will be treated to an instant replay of the latest family scandal or soap-opera episode. These stories may be entertaining, but they don't belong in a movie theater.

In addition	But	Last of all

_____Last of all_____, there are the people who talk on the phone while they're driving. One of the things that irritate me about them is the way they seem to be showing off. They're saying, "Look at me! I'm so important I have to make phone calls in my car." _____In addition_____, such behavior is just plain dangerous. Instead of concentrating on adjusting carefully to ever-changing traffic conditions, they're weaving all over the road or getting much too close to the car in front of them as they gossip with a friend, make an appointment with a doctor, or order a pizza.

So long as murder remains illegal, the nervous twitchers, movie talkers, and car-phone users of the world are safe from me. _____But_____ if ever I am granted the power of life or death, these people had better think twice about annoying me. They might not have long to live.

3 Identifying Transitions and Other Connecting Words

ACTIVITY

The following items use connecting words to help tie ideas together. The connecting words you are to identify are set off in italics. In the space, write T for *transition*, RW for *repeated word*, S for *synonym*, or P for *pronoun*.

S 1. Kate wears a puffy, quilted, down-filled jacket. In this *garment,* she resembles a stack of inflated inner tubes.

P 2. Plants like poinsettias and mistletoe are pretty. *They* are also poisonous.

T 3. A strip of strong cloth can be used as an emergency fan-belt replacement. *In addition,* a roll of duct tape can be used to patch a leaky hose temporarily.

S 4. Newspapers may someday be brought to your home, not by paper carriers, but by computers. Subscribers will simply punch in a code, and the *machines* will display the desired pages.

P 5. I'm always losing my soft contact lenses, which resemble little circles of thick Saran Wrap. One day I dropped both of *them* into a cup of hot tea.

RW 6. The molded plastic chairs in the classrooms are hard and uncomfortable. When I sit in one of these *chairs,* I feel as if I were sitting in a bucket.

P 7. One way to tell if your skin is aging is to pinch a fold of skin on the back of your hand. If *it* doesn't smooth out quickly, your skin is losing its youthful tone.

P 8. I never eat sloppy joes. *They* look as if they've already been eaten.

T 9. Clothing intended just for children seems to have vanished. *Instead,* children wear scaled-down versions of everything adults wear.

RW 10. Some successful salespeople use voice tones and hand gestures that are almost hypnotic. Customers are not conscious of this *hypnotic* effect but merely feel an urge to buy.

S 11. The giant cockroaches in Florida are the subject of local legends. A visitor, according to one tale, saw one of the *insects,* thought it was a Volkswagen, and tried to drive it away.

T 12. Some thieves scour garbage cans for credit-card receipts. *Then* they use the owner's name and card number to order merchandise by phone.

P 13. When the phone rang, I dropped the garden hose. *It* whipped around crazily and squirted water through the kitchen screen door.

RW 14. There are many phobias other than the ones described in psychology textbooks. I have *phobias,* for instance, about toasters and lawn mowers.

T 15. My mother believes that food is love. *Therefore,* when she offers homemade cookies or cupcakes, I hate to hurt her feelings by refusing them.

4 Completing Transitional Sentences

ACTIVITY

Following are brief sentence outlines from two essays. In each outline, the second and third topic sentences serve as transitional, or linking, sentences. Each reminds us of the point in the preceding paragraph and announces the point to be developed in the current paragraph. In the spaces provided, add the words needed to complete the second and third topic sentences.

Thesis 1

In order to set up a day-care center in your home, you must make sure your house conforms to state regulations, obtain the necessary legal permits, and advertise your service in the right places.

First supporting paragraph

First of all, as a potential operator of a home day-care center, you must make sure your house conforms to state regulations. . . .

Second supporting paragraph

After making certain that _your house conforms to regulations_

_____,

you must obtain _____legal permits_____ . . . .

Third supporting paragraph

Finally, once you have the necessary _____legal permits_____,

you can begin to _____advertise_____.

Thesis 2

Cheaper cost, greater comfort, and superior electronic technology make watching football at home more enjoyable than attending a game at the stadium.

First supporting paragraph

For one thing, watching the game on TV eliminates the cost of attending the game. . . .

Second supporting paragraph	In addition to saving me money, watching the game at home is more _____comfortable_____ than sitting in a stadium. . . .

Third supporting paragraph	Even more important than _____cost_____ and _____comfort_____, though, is the _____technology_____ that makes a televised game better than the "real thing." . . .

5 Identifying Introductions and Conclusions

ACTIVITY

The following box lists six common kinds of introductions and three common kinds of conclusions. Read the three pairs of introductory and concluding paragraphs that follow. Then, in the space provided, write the letter of the kind of introduction and conclusion used in each paragraph.

Introductions

A. General to narrow
B. Starting with an opposite
C. Stating importance of topic
D. Incident or story
E. Question(s)
F. Quotation

Conclusions

G. Summary and final thought
H. Question(s)
I. Prediction or recommendation

Pair 1

_____D_____

Shortly before Easter, our local elementary school sponsored a fund-raising event at which classroom pets and their babies—hamsters, guinea pigs, and chicks—were available for adoption. Afterward, as I was driving home, I saw a hand drop a baby hamster out of the car ahead of me. I couldn't avoid running over the tiny creature. One of the parents had taken the pet, regretted the decision, and decided to get rid of it. Such people have never stopped to consider the several real obligations involved in owning a pet.

_____I_____

A pet cannot be thrown onto a trash heap when it is no longer wanted or tossed into a closet if it begins to bore its owner. A pet, like us, is a living thing that needs attention and care. Would-be owners, therefore, should think seriously about their responsibilities before they acquire a pet.

Pair 2

_____E_____

What would life be like if we could read each other's minds? Would communications be instantaneous and perfectly clear? These questions will never be answered unless mental telepathy becomes a fact of life. Until then, we will have to make do with less perfect means of communication. Letters, telephone calls, and e-mail messages do have serious drawbacks.

_____G_____

Neither letters, phone calls, nor e-mails guarantee perfect communication. With all our sophisticated skills, we human beings often communicate less effectively than howling wolves or chattering monkeys. We always seem to find some way to foul up the message.

Pair 3

_____F_____

"Few things are harder to put up with," said Mark Twain, "than the annoyance of a good example." Twain obviously knew the problems faced by siblings cursed with older brothers or sisters who are models of perfection. All our lives, my older sister Shelley and I have been compared. Unfortunately, in competition with my sister's virtues, my looks, talents, and accomplishments always ended up on the losing side.

_____G_____

Although I always lost in the sibling contests of looks, talents, and accomplishments, Shelley and I have somehow managed not to turn into deadly enemies. Feeling like the "dud" of the family, in fact, helped me to develop a drive to succeed and a sense of humor. In our sibling rivalry, we both managed to win.

5 The Fourth Step in Essay Writing

> *This chapter shows you how to*
> - revise so that your sentences flow smoothly and clearly
> - edit so that your sentences are error-free

Up to now this book has emphasized the first three goals in effective writing: unity, support, and coherence. This chapter focuses on the fourth goal of writing effectively: sentence skills. You'll learn how to revise an essay so that your sentences flow smoothly and clearly. Then you'll review how to edit a paper for mistakes in grammar, punctuation, and spelling.

Revising Sentences

These strategies will help you to revise your sentences effectively:

- Use parallelism.
- Use a consistent point of view.
- Use specific words.
- Use active verbs.
- Use concise words.
- Vary your sentences.

Use Parallelism

ALLWRITE!
16.5

Words in a pair or a series should have parallel structure. By balancing the items in a pair or a series so that they have the same kind of structure, you will make the sentence clearer and easier to read. Notice how the parallel sentences that follow read more smoothly than the nonparallel ones.

101

Nonparallel (Not Balanced)	Parallel (Balanced)
My job includes checking the inventory, initiating the orders, and *to call* the suppliers.	My job includes checking the inventory, initiating the orders, and calling the suppliers (A balanced series of *-ing* words: *checking, initiating, calling*)
The game-show contestant was told to be cheerful, charming, and *with enthusiasm.*	The game-show contestant was told to be cheerful, charming, and enthusiastic. (A balanced series of descriptive words: *cheerful, charming, enthusiastic*)
Grandmother likes to read mystery novels, to do needlepoint, and *browsing* the Internet on her home computer.	Grandmother likes to read mystery novels, to do needlepoint, and to browse the Internet on her home computer. (A balanced series of *to* verbs: *to read, to do, to browse*)
We painted the trim in the living room; *the wallpaper was put up by a professional.*	We painted the trim in the living room; a professional put up the wallpaper. (Balanced verbs and word order: *We painted . . . ; a professional put up . . .*)

Balanced sentences are not a skill you need worry about when writing first drafts. But when you rewrite, you should try to put matching words and ideas into matching structures. Such parallelism will improve your writing style.

ACTIVITY

Cross out and revise the unbalanced part of each of the following sentences.

EXAMPLE   Chocolate makes me gain weight, lose my appetite, and ~~breaking~~ out
     break
in hives.

1. The novelty store sells hand buzzers, plastic fangs, and insects ~~that are fake~~.
             fake

2. Many people share the same three intense fears: being in high places, working
with numbers, and *making* speeches.

3. To decide on a career, students should think closely about their interests,
hobbies, and ~~what they are skilled at~~.
       skills

4. At the body shop, the car was sanded down to the bare metal, painted with
    sprayed with
    primer, and red enamel ~~was sprayed on.~~
                      ^

5. In order to become a dancer, Lola is taking lessons, working in amateur shows,
    auditioning
    and ~~auditioned~~ for professional companies.
                                  his new job offers
6. Juan's last job offered security; a better chance for advancement ~~is offered by~~
                                              ^
    ~~his new job.~~

7. People in today's world often try to avoid silence, whether on the job, in school,

    or ~~when relaxing~~ at home.

                                                    courageous
8. Because the dying woman was dignified and ~~with courage~~, she won everyone's

    respect.
                                                        depended
9. The politician trusted no one, rewarded loyalty, and ~~was dependent~~ only on his

    own instincts.

10. If we're not careful, we'll leave the next generation polluted air, contaminated
                              dying
    water, and forests ~~that are dying.~~
                    ^

Use a Consistent Point of View

Consistency with Verbs

ALLWRITE!
18.5

Do not shift verb tenses unnecessarily. If you begin writing a paper in the present tense, do not shift suddenly to the past. If you begin in the past, do not shift without reason to the present. Notice the inconsistent verb tenses in the following example:

> Jean *punched* down the risen yeast dough in the bowl. Then she *dumps* it onto the floured worktable and *kneaded* it into a smooth, shiny ball.

The verbs must be consistently in the present tense:

> Jean *punches* down the risen yeast dough in the bowl. Then she *dumps* it onto the floured worktable and *kneads* it into a smooth, shiny ball.

Or the verbs must be consistently in the past tense:

> Jean *punched* down the risen yeast dough in the bowl. Then she *dumped* it onto the floured worktable and *kneaded* it into a smooth, shiny ball.

ACTIVITY

Make the verbs in each sentence consistent with the *first* verb used. Cross out the incorrect verb and write the correct form in the space at the left.

ran **EXAMPLE** Aunt Flo tried to kiss her little nephew, but he ~~runs~~ out of the room.

arrived 1. An aggressive news photographer knocked a reporter to the ground as the movie stars ~~arrive~~ for the Academy Awards.

asked 2. The winning wheelchair racer in the marathon slumped back in exhaustion and ~~asks~~ for some ice to soothe his blistered hands.

slices 3. On the TV commercial for mail-order kitchen knives, an actor cuts a tree branch in half and ~~sliced~~ an aluminum can into ribbons.

goes 4. "My husband is so dumb," said Martha, "that when he ~~went~~ to Las Vegas, he tries to play the soda machines."

tipped 5. The jeep swerved around the corner, went up on two wheels, and ~~tips~~ over on its side.

floats 6. In a zero-gravity atmosphere, water breaks up into droplets and ~~floated~~ around in space.

grabbed 7. Ralph ripped open the bag of cheese puffs with his teeth, ~~grabs~~ handfuls of the salty orange squiggles, and stuffed them into his mouth.

swoops 8. From his perch high up on the rocky cliff, the eagle spots a white-tailed rabbit and ~~swooped~~ down toward his victim.

recharge 9. Several times a year, I like to take a day off, go away by myself, and ~~recharged~~ my mental batteries.

burned 10. When the great earthquake struck San Francisco in 1906, the entire city ~~burns~~ to the ground in less than twenty-four hours.

Consistency with Pronouns

When writing a paper, you should not shift your point of view unnecessarily. Be consistent in your use of first-, second-, or third-person pronouns.

	Singular	**Plural**
First-person pronouns	I (my, mine, me)	we (our, us)
Second-person pronouns	you (your)	you (your)
Third-person pronouns	he (his, him)	they (their, them)
	she (her)	
	it (its)	

Note   Any person, place, or thing, as well as any indefinite pronoun such as *one, anyone, someone,* and so on (page 464), is a third-person word.

For instance, if you start writing in the first person, *I,* do not jump suddenly to the second person, *you.* Or if you are writing in the third person, *they,* do not shift unexpectedly to *you.* Look at the examples.

Inconsistent

One of the fringe benefits of my job is that *you* can use a company credit card for gasoline.

(The most common mistake people make is to let *you* slip into their writing after they start with another pronoun.)

Though *we* like most of *our* neighbors, there are a few *you* can't get along with.

(The writer begins with the first-person pronouns *we* and *our,* but then shifts to the second-person *you.*)

Consistent

One of the fringe benefits of my job is that *I* can use a company credit card for gasoline.

Though *we* like most of *our* neighbors, there are a few *we* can't get along with.

ACTIVITY

Cross out inconsistent pronouns in the following sentences, and revise with the correct form of the pronoun above each crossed out word.

EXAMPLE   When I examined the used car, ~~you~~ could see that one of the front
fenders had been replaced.

1. Many people are ignorant of side effects that diets can have on ~~your~~ *their* health.

2. When I buy lipstick or nail polish, ~~you~~ *I* never know how the color will actually look.

3. It is expensive for us to take public transportation to work every day, but what choice do ~~you~~ *we* have if ~~you~~ *we* can't afford a car?

4. During the border crisis, each country refused to change ~~their~~ *its* aggressive stance.

5. If you want to do well in this course, ~~one~~ *you* should plan on attending every day.

6. One of the things I love about my new apartment is that ~~you~~ *I* can own a pet.

7. Toni refuses to eat pepperoni pizza because she says it gives ~~you~~ *her* indigestion.

8. It's hard for us to pay for health insurance, but ~~you~~ *we* don't dare go without it.

9. People often take a first-aid course so that ~~we~~ *they* can learn how to help choking and heart attack victims.

10. There are several ways you can impress your new boss. For example, ~~one~~ *you* should dress well, arrive at work on time, and complete tasks efficiently.

Use Specific Words

To be an effective writer, you must use specific words rather than general words. Specific words create pictures in the reader's mind. They help capture interest and make your meaning clear. Compare the following sentences:

General

She walked down the street.
Animals came into the place.
The man signed the paper.

Specific

Anne wandered slowly along Rogers Lane.

Hungry lions padded silently into the sawdust-covered arena.

The biology teacher hastily scribbled his name on the course withdrawal slip.

The specific sentences create clear pictures in our minds. The details *show* us exactly what has happened.

Here are four ways to make your sentences specific.

1   Use exact names.

    He sold his *camper.*

    Luke sold his *Winnebago.*

2   Use lively verbs.

    The flag *moved* in the breeze.

    The flag *fluttered* in the breeze.

3   Use descriptive words (modifiers) before nouns.

    A man strained to lift the crate.

    A *heavyset, perspiring* man strained to lift the *heavy wooden* crate.

4   Use words that relate to the senses—sight, hearing, taste, smell, touch.

    That woman jogs five miles a day.

    That *fragile-looking, gray-haired* woman jogs five miles a day. (*sight*)

    A noise told the crowd that there were two minutes left to play.

    A *piercing whistle* told the *cheering* crowd that there were two minutes left to play. (*hearing*)

    When he returned, all he found in the refrigerator was bread and milk.

    When he returned, all he found in the refrigerator was *stale* bread and *sour* milk. (*taste*)

    Neil stroked the kitten's fur until he felt its tiny claws on his hand.

    Neil stroked the kitten's *velvety* fur until he felt its tiny, *needle-sharp* claws on his hand. (*touch*)

    Fran placed a sachet in her bureau drawer.

    Fran placed a *lilac-scented* sachet in her bureau drawer. (*smell*)

ACTIVITY 1

Revise the following sentences, changing vague, indefinite words into sharp, specific ones.

EXAMPLE   *Several of our appliances* broke down at the same time.

Our washer, refrigerator, and television broke . . .

Answers will vary; examples are shown.

1. *Salty snacks* are my diet downfall.

    Potato chips, pretzels, and salted peanuts . . .

    _____

    _____

2. I swept aside the *things* on my desk in order to spread out the road map.

    . . . papers, books, and magazines . . .

    _____

    _____

3. Our neighbor's family room has *a lot of electronic equipment.*

    . . . a TV, a CD player, and a computer.

    _____

    _____

4. *Several sections* of the newspaper were missing.

    The comics, the sports pages, the obituaries, and the society page . . .

    _____

    _____

5. The doctor examined *various parts of my body* before diagnosing my illness as bronchitis.

    . . . my throat, my ears, and my lungs . . .

    _____

    _____

ACTIVITY 2

Again, you will practice changing vague, indefinite writing into lively, image-filled writing that helps capture the reader's interest and makes your meaning clear. With the help of the methods described above, add specific details to the five sentences that follow. Note the two examples.

EXAMPLES   The person got off the bus.

The teenage boy bounded down the steps of the shiny yellow

school bus.

She worked hard all summer.

All summer, Eva sorted peaches and blueberries in the hot, noisy

canning factory.

Answers will vary; examples are shown.

1. The car would not start.

    The rusty old Buick sputtered, whined, and refused to start.

2. The test was difficult.

    The mathematics final was filled with tricky, baffling problems.

3. The boy was tired.

    Little Robbie was so exhausted that he could scarcely keep his eyes open.

4. My room needs cleaning.

    My cluttered, jumbled, dusty bedroom needs to be swept out, scrubbed,

    and reorganized.

5. A vehicle blocked traffic.

    A broken-down city bus blocked Main Street and stopped traffic for an

    hour.

Use Active Verbs

When the subject of a sentence performs the action of the verb, the verb is in the *active voice.* When the subject of a sentence receives the action of a verb, the verb is in the *passive voice.*

The passive form of a verb consists of a form of the verb *to be* (*am, is, are, was, were*) plus the past participle of the main verb (which is usually the same as its past tense form). Look at the following active and passive forms.

Passive

The computer *was turned on* by Hakim.

The car's air conditioner *was fixed* by the mechanic.

Active

Hakim *turned on* the computer.

The mechanic *fixed* the car's air conditioner.

In general, active verbs are more effective than passive verbs. Active verbs give your writing a simpler and more vigorous style.

ACTIVITY

Revise the following sentences, changing verbs from the passive to the active voice and making any other word changes necessary.

EXAMPLE   Fruits and vegetables are painted often by artists.
          Artists often paint fruits and vegetables.

1. Many unhealthy foods are included in the typical American diet.
   The typical American diet includes many unhealthy foods.

2. The family picnic was invaded by hundreds of biting ants.
   Hundreds of biting ants invaded the family picnic.

3. Antibiotics are used by doctors to treat many infections.
   Doctors use antibiotics to treat many infections.

4. The fatal traffic accident was caused by a drunk driver.
   A drunk driver caused the fatal traffic accident.

5. Final grades will be determined by the instructor on the basis of class performance.
   The instructor will determine final grades . . .

Use Concise Words

Wordiness—using more words than necessary to express a meaning—is often a sign of lazy or careless writing. Your readers may resent the extra time and energy they must spend when you have not done the work needed to make your writing direct and concise.

Here are two examples of wordy sentences:

In this paper, I am planning to describe the hobby that I enjoy of collecting old comic books.

In Ben's opinion, he thinks that cable television will change and alter our lives in the future.

Omitting needless words improves these sentences:

I enjoy collecting old comic books.

Ben thinks that cable television will change our lives.

Following is a list of some wordy expressions that could be reduced to single words.

Wordy Form	Short Form
at the present time	now
in the event that	if
in the near future	soon
due to the fact that	because
for the reason that	because
is able to	can
in every instance	always
in this day and age	today
during the time that	while
a large number of	many
big in size	big
red in color	red
five in number	five
return back	return
good benefit	benefit
commute back and forth	commute
postponed until later	postponed

ACTIVITY

Revise the following sentences, omitting needless words.

Answers will vary.

1. In conclusion, I would like to end my essay by summarizing each of the major points that were covered within my paper.

     I will conclude by summarizing my major points.

2. Controlling the quality and level of the television shows that children watch is a continuing challenge to parents that they must meet on a daily basis.

     Every day, parents must control their children's television watching.

3. In general, I am the sort of person who tends to be shy, especially in large crowds or with strangers I don't know well.

     I am shy.

4. Someone who is analyzing magazine advertising can find hidden messages that, once uncovered, are seen to be clever and persuasive.

     Magazine advertising contains clever hidden messages.

5. My greatest mistake that I made last week was to hurt my brother's feelings and then not to have the nerve to apologize and say how sorry I was.

     My worst mistake last week was to hurt my brother's feelings and not

     apologize.

6. In today's uncertain economic climate, it is clear that people, namely, average middle-class working people, have great difficulty saving much money or putting anything aside for emergencies.

     In today's uncertain economy, the middle class finds it hard to save.

7. We thought the television program that was on last night was enjoyable, whereas our parents reacted with dislike to the content of the show.

     We liked last night's television show, but our parents didn't.

8. Because of the bad weather, the school district felt it would be safer to cancel classes and let everyone stay home than risk people having accidents on the way to school.

   The school district canceled classes because of the bad weather.

   _____

9. Out of all the regrets in my life so far, one of my greatest ones to the present time is that I did not take additional art classes when I was still in high school and had a chance to do so.

   I regret not having taken additional art classes in high school.

   _____

10. It seems obvious to me, and it should be to everyone else too, that people can be harmed as much by emotional abuse as by physical abuse, even if you don't lay a hand on them.

   People are harmed by emotional as well as physical abuse.

   _____

Vary Your Sentences

One part of effective writing is to vary the kinds of sentences you write. If every sentence follows the same pattern, writing may become monotonous to read. This section explains four ways you can create variety and interest in your writing style. It also describes coordination and subordination—two important techniques for achieving different kinds of emphasis in writing.

The following are four methods you can use to revise simple sentences, making them more complex and sophisticated:

1   Add a second complete thought (coordination).

2   Add a dependent thought (subordination).

3   Begin with a special opening word or phrase.

4   Place adjectives or verbs in a series.

Revise by Adding a Second Complete Thought

15.5

When you add a second complete thought to a simple sentence, the result is a *compound* (or double) sentence. The two complete statements in a compound sentence are usually connected by a comma plus a joining or coordinating word (*and, but, for, or, nor, so, yet*).

A compound sentence is used to give equal weight to two closely related ideas. The technique of showing that ideas have equal importance is called *coordination*. Following are some compound sentences. In each case, the sentence contains two ideas that the writer considers equal in importance.

Greg worked on the engine for three hours, but the car still wouldn't start.

Bananas were on sale this week, so I bought a bunch for the children's lunches.

We laced up our roller blades, and then we moved cautiously onto the rink.

ACTIVITY

Combine the following pairs of simple sentences into compound sentences. Use a comma and a logical joining word (*and, but, for, so*) to connect each pair of statements.

Note   If you are not sure what *and, but, for,* and *so* mean, review pages 433–434.

EXAMPLE   The weather was cold and windy.
Al brought a thick blanket to the football game.

The weather was cold and windy, so Al brought a thick blanket to

the football game.

1. My son can't eat peanut butter snacks or sandwiches.
   He is allergic to peanuts.
   . . . sandwiches, for he is allergic . . .

   _____

2. I tried to sleep.
   The thought of tomorrow's math exam kept me awake.
   . . . sleep, but the thought . . .

   _____

3. This diner has its own bakery.
   It has take-out service as well.
   . . . bakery, and it has . . .

   _____

4. The cardboard storage boxes were soggy.

   Rainwater had seeped into the basement during the storm.

   ... soggy, for rainwater had ...

   _____

   _____

5. I didn't have enough money to buy my parents an anniversary present.

   I offered to mow their lawn for the whole summer.

   ... present, so I offered ...

   _____

   _____

Revise by Adding a Dependent Thought

ALLWRITE!

155

When you add a dependent thought to a simple sentence, the result is a *complex* sentence.* A dependent thought begins with one of the following subordinating words:

after	if, even if	when, whenever
although, though	in order that	where, wherever
as	since	whether
because	that, so that	which, whichever
before	unless	while
even though	until	who
how	what, whatever	whose

A complex sentence is used to emphasize one idea over another. Look at the following complex sentence:

Although the exam room was very quiet, I still couldn't concentrate.

---

*The two parts of a complex sentence are sometimes called an *independent clause* and a *dependent clause*. A *clause* is simply a word group that contains a subject and a verb. An independent clause expresses a complete thought and can stand alone. A dependent clause does not express a complete thought in itself and "depends on" the independent clause to complete its meaning. Dependent clauses always begin with a dependent or subordinating word.

The idea that the writer wishes to emphasize here—*I still couldn't concentrate*—is expressed as a complete thought. The less important idea—*Although the exam room was very quiet*—is subordinated to the complete thought. The technique of giving one idea less emphasis than another is called *subordination*.

Following are other examples of complex sentences. In each case, the part starting with the dependent word is the less emphasized part of the sentence.

Even though I was tired, I stayed up to watch the horror movie.

Before I take a bath, I check for spiders in the tub.

When Ivy feels nervous, she pulls on her earlobe.

ACTIVITY

Use logical subordinating words to combine the following pairs of simple sentences into sentences that contain a dependent thought. Place a comma after a dependent statement when it starts the sentence.

EXAMPLE   Rita bit into the hard taffy.
　　　　　　　She broke a filling.

　　　　　When Rita bit into the hard taffy, she broke a filling.
　　　　　――――――――――――――――――――――――――――――――――――――

Answers may vary.

1. I had forgotten to lock the front door.
   I had to drive back to the house.

   Because I had forgotten to lock the front door, I . . .
   ―――

2. The bear turned over the rotten log.
   Fat white grubs crawled in every direction.

   When the bear turned over the rotten log, fat . . .
   ―――

3. Kevin had sent away for a set of tools.
   He changed his mind about spending the money.

   After Kevin had sent away for a set of tools, he . . .
   ―――

4. Some people are allergic to wool.
   They buy only sweaters made from synthetic fibers.

   Because some people are allergic to wool, they . . .
   ―――

5. An older woman in my typing class can type almost one hundred words a minute.
   She is having trouble landing a secretarial job.
   Even though an . . . minute, she is . . .

Revise by Beginning with a Special Opening Word or Phrase

Among the special openers that can be used to start sentences are *-ed* words, *-ing* words, *-ly* words, *to* word groups, and prepositional phrases. Here are examples of all five kinds of openers:

-ed word

Concerned about his son's fever, Paul called a doctor.

-ing word

Humming softly, the woman browsed through the rack of dresses.

-ly word

Hesitantly, Sue approached the instructor's desk.

to word group

To protect her hair, Eva uses the lowest setting on her blow dryer.

Prepositional phrase

During the exam, drops of water fell from the ceiling.

ACTIVITY

Combine each of the following pairs of simple sentences into one sentence by using the opener shown at the left and omitting repeated words. Use a comma to set off the opener from the rest of the sentence.

EXAMPLE   *-ing* word   The pelican scooped small fish into its baggy bill. It dipped into the waves.

Dipping into the waves, the pelican scooped small fish into its baggy bill.

-ly word

1. Shirley signed the repair contract.

   She was reluctant.

   Reluctantly, Shirley signed the repair contract.

   _____

to word
group

2. The interns volunteered to work overtime.

   They wanted to improve their chances of promotion.

   To improve their chances of promotion, the interns . . .

   _____

Prepositional
phrase

3. The accused murderer grinned at the witnesses.

   He did this during the trial.

   During the trial, the accused murderer . . .

   _____

-ed word

4. The vet's office was noisy and confusing.

   It was crowded with nervous pets.

   Crowded with nervous pets, the vet's office . . .

   _____

-ing word

5. Barry tried to find something worth watching.

   He flipped from channel to channel.

   Trying to find something worth watching, Barry flipped from channel to channel.

   _____

Revise by Placing Adjectives or Verbs in a Series

Various parts of a sentence may be placed in a series. Among these parts are adjectives (descriptive words) and verbs. Here are examples of both in a series:

Adjectives

I gently applied a *sticky new* Band-Aid to the *deep, ragged* cut on my finger.

Verbs

The truck *bounced* off a guardrail, *sideswiped* a tree, and *plunged* down the embankment.

ACTIVITY

Combine the simple sentences into one sentence by using adjectives or verbs in a series and by omitting repeated words. Use a comma when necessary between adjectives or verbs in a series.

EXAMPLE Jesse spun the basketball on one finger.
He rolled it along his arms.
He dribbled it between his legs.

Jesse spun the basketball on one finger, rolled it along his arms, and dribbled it between his legs.

Answers may vary.

1. The baby toddled across the rug.
He picked up a button.
He put the button in his mouth.

The baby toddled across the rug, picked up a button, and put the button in his mouth.

2. Water dribbled out of the tap.
The water was brown.
The water was foul-tasting.
The tap was rusty.
The tap was metal.

Brown, foul-tasting water dribbled out of the rusty metal tap.

3. By 6 A.M. I had read the textbook chapter.
I had taken notes on it.
I had studied the notes.
I had drunk eight cups of coffee.

By 6 A.M. I had read the textbook chapter, taken notes on it, studied the notes, and drunk eight cups of coffee.

4. The exterminator approached the wasps' nests hanging under the eaves.
The nests were large.
The nests were papery.
The eaves were old.
The eaves were wooden.

. . . approached the large, papery wasps' nests hanging under the old wooden eaves.

5. Reeds bordered the pond.
The reeds were slim.
The reeds were brown.
The pond was green.
The pond was stagnant.

Slim brown reeds bordered the stagnant green pond.

Editing Sentences

After revising sentences in a paper so that they flow smoothly and clearly, you need to edit the paper for mistakes in grammar, punctuation, mechanics, usage, and spelling. Even if a paper is otherwise well-written, it will make an unfavorable impression on readers if it contains such mistakes. To edit a paper, check it against the agreed-upon rules or conventions of written English—simply called *sentence skills* in this book. Here are the most common of these conventions:

1 Write complete sentences rather than fragments.

2 Do not write run-ons.

3 Use verb forms correctly.

4 Make sure that subject, verbs, and pronouns agree.

5 Eliminate faulty modifiers.

6 Use pronoun forms correctly.

7 Use capital letters where needed.

8 Use the following marks of punctuation correctly: apostrophe, quotation marks, comma, semicolon, colon, hyphen, dash, parentheses.

9 Use correct manuscript form.

10 Eliminate slang, clichés, and pretentious words.

11 Check for possible spelling errors.

12 Eliminate careless errors.

These sentence skills are treated in detail in Part Four of this book, and they can be referred to easily as needed. Both the list of sentence skills on the inside front cover of this book and the correction symbols on the inside back cover include page references so that you can turn quickly to any skill you want to check.

Hints about Editing

These hints can help you edit the next-to-final draft of a paper for sentence-skills mistakes:

1   Have at hand two essential tools: a good dictionary and a grammar handbook (you can use the one in this book beginning on page 411).

2   Use a sheet of paper to cover your essay so that you will expose only one sentence at a time. Look for errors in grammar, spelling, and typing. It may help to read each sentence out loud. If a sentence does not read clearly and smoothly, chances are something is wrong.

3   Pay special attention to the kinds of errors you tend to make. For example, if you tend to write run-ons or fragments, be especially on the lookout for those errors.

4   Try to work on a typewritten or word-processed draft, where you'll be able to see your writing more objectively than you can on a handwritten page; use a pen with colored ink so that your corrections will stand out.

Note   A series of editing tests appears on pages 553–565. You will probably find it most helpful to take these tests after reviewing the sentence skills in Part Four.

Proofreading

Proofreading means checking the final, edited draft of your paper closely for typos and other careless errors. A helpful strategy is to read your paper backward, from the last sentence to the first. This helps keep you from getting caught up in the flow of the paper and missing small mistakes. Here are six helpful proofing symbols:

Proofing Symbol	Meaning	Example
^	insert missing letter or word	achéve
⎯ℓ	omit	draw two ~~two~~ conclusions
∽	reverse order of words or letters	lived happily after ever
#	add space	allright
⌣	close up space	base ball
cap, lc	Add a capital (or a lowercase) letter	cap My english Class lc

If you make many corrections, retype the page or enter corrections into your word-processor file and reprint the page.

ACTIVITY

In the spaces at the bottom, write the numbers of the ten word groups that contain fragments or run-ons. Then, in the spaces between the lines, edit by making the necessary corrections. One is done for you as an example.

Corrections may vary.

¹A unique object in my family's living room is an ashtray. ²Which I made in second grade. ³I can still remember the pride I felt. ⁴When I presented it to my mother. ⁵Now, I'm amazed that my parents didn't hide it away at the back of a shelf it is a remarkably ugly object. ⁶The ashtray is made out of brown clay which I had tried to mold into a perfect circle, unfortunately, my class was only forty-five minutes long. ⁷The best I could do was to shape it into a lopsided oval. ⁸Its most distinctive feature, though, was the grooves carved into its rim. ⁹I had theorized that each groove could hold a cigarette or cigar, I made at least fifty of them. ¹⁰I somehow failed to consider that the only person who smoked in my family was my father, ¹¹Who smoked about five cigars a year. ¹²Further, although our living room is decorated in sedate tans and blues, my ashtray is bright purple, ¹³My favorite color at the time. ¹⁴For variety, it has stripes around its rim they are colored neon green. ¹⁵My parents have proudly displayed my little masterpiece on their coffee table for the past ten years. ¹⁶If I ever wonder if my parents love me, ¹⁷I look at that ugly ashtray, the answer is plain to see.

1. __2__   3. __5__   5. __9__   7. __13__   9. __16__

2. __4__   4. __6__   6. __11__   8. __14__   10. __17__

Practice in Revising Sentences

You now know the fourth step in effective writing: revising and editing sentences. You also know that practice in *editing* sentences is best undertaken after you have worked through the sentence skills in Part Four. The focus in this section, then, will be on *revising* sentences—using a variety of methods to ensure that your sentences flow smoothly and are clear and interesting. You will work through the following series of Review Tests:

1   Using parallelism
2   Using a consistent point of view
3   Using specific words
4   Using active verbs
5   Using concise words
6   Varying your sentences

Using Parallelism

■ Review Test 1

Cross out the unbalanced part of each sentence. In the space provided, revise the unbalanced part so that it matches the other item or items in the sentence.

    EXAMPLE   Cigarette smoking is expensive, disgusting, and ~~a health risk~~. *unhealthy*

1. Jesse prefers books that are short, scary, and ~~filled with suspense~~.
   suspenseful

2. A sale on electrical appliances, ~~furniture for the office~~, and stereo equipment begins this Friday.
   office furniture

3. To escape the stresses of everyday life, I rely upon watching television, reading books, and ~~my kitchen~~.
   working in my kitchen

4. The keys to improving grades are to take effective notes in class, to plan study time, and ~~preparing~~ carefully for exams.
   to prepare

5. Qualities that I look for in friends are a sense of humor, ~~being kind~~, and dependability.
   kindness

6. My three favorite jobs were veterinary assistant, gardener, and ~~selling toys~~.
   toy salesperson

7. Housekeeping shortcuts will help you speed up doing laundry, cleaning rooms, and ~~food on the table~~.
   putting food on the table

8. Studying a little every day is more effective than ~~to cram~~.
   cramming

9. The chickens travel on a conveyor belt, where they are plucked, washed, rinsed, and ~~bags are put on them~~.
   bagged (or: put into bags)

10. The speaker impressed the audience because of his clear, reasonable presentation ~~with friendliness as well~~.
    and his friendliness

Using Parallelism

■ **Review Test 2**

Cross out the unbalanced part of each sentence. In the space provided, revise the unbalanced part so that it matches the other item or items in the sentence.

1. Paying college tuition and not studying is as sensible as ~~to buy~~ tickets to a movie and not watching it. _____buying_____

2. The best programming on television includes news coverage, ~~shows on science~~, and children's series. _____science shows_____

3. Curling overgrown vines, ~~porch furniture that was rotted~~, and sagging steps were my first impressions of the neglected house. _rotting porch furniture_

4. The little girl came home from school with a tear-streaked face, a black eye, and ~~her shirt was torn~~. _____a torn shirt_____

5. There are two ways to the top floor: climb the stairs or ~~taking~~ the elevator.
   take (or: climbing . . . taking)

6. While waiting for the exam to start, small groups of nervous students glanced over their notes, drank coffee, and ~~were whispering~~ to each other.
   _____whispered_____

7. In many ways, starting college at forty is harder than ~~to start~~ at eighteen.
   starting

8. Interesting work is as important to me as ~~pay that is good~~.
   _____ good pay _____

9. The homeless woman shuffled along the street, bent over to pick something
   up, and ~~was putting~~ it in her shopping bag. _____ put _____

10. A teamsters' strike now would mean interruptions in food deliveries, a slowdown
    in the economy, and ~~losing~~ wages for workers. _____ lost _____

Using a Consistent Point of View

■ Review Test 1

Change verbs as needed in the following selection so that they are consistently in the past tense. Cross out each incorrect verb and write the correct form above it, as shown in the example. You will need to make ten corrections.

   My uncle's shopping trip last Thursday was discouraging to him. First
of all, he had to drive around for fifteen minutes until he ~~finds~~ ^{found} a parking
space. There was a half-price special on paper products in the supermarket,
and every spot ~~is~~ ^{was} taken. Then, when he finally got inside, many of the items
on his list were not where he expected. For example, the pickles he wanted
~~are~~ ^{were} not on the same shelf as all the other pickles. Instead, they were in a
refrigerated case next to the bacon. And the granola was not on the cereal
shelves but in the health-food section. Shopping thus ~~proceeds~~ ^{proceeded} slowly.
About halfway through his list, he knew there would not be time to cook
dinner and ~~decides~~ ^{decided} to pick up a barbecued chicken. The chicken, he learned,
was available at the end of the store he had already passed. So he ~~parks~~ ^{parked} his
shopping cart in an aisle, ~~gets~~ ^{got} the chicken, and came back. After adding half
a dozen more items to his cart, he suddenly ~~realizes~~ ^{realized} it contained someone
else's food. So he retraced his steps, found his own cart, ~~transfers~~ ^{transferred} the
groceries, and continued to shop. Later, when he began loading items onto
the checkout counter, he ~~notices~~ ^{noticed} that the barbecued chicken was missing.
He must have left it in the other cart, certainly gone by now. Feeling totally

said
defeated, he returned to the deli counter and ~~says~~ to the clerk, "Give me another chicken. I lost the first one." My uncle told me that when he saw the look on the clerk's face, he felt as if he'd flunked Food Shopping.

Using a Consistent Point of View

■ Review Test 2

Cross out inconsistent pronouns in the following sentences, and revise with the correct form of the pronoun above each crossed-out word.

they
EXAMPLE   Dog owners should put tags on their dogs in case ~~you~~ lose their pets.

1. These days people never seem to get the recognition they deserve no matter
   they
   how hard ~~you~~ work.
2. All ~~you~~ could hear was the maddening rattle of the heating register, even though I buried my face in the pillow.
3. When we answer the telephone at work, *we* ~~you~~ are supposed to say the company's name.
4. Each year I pay more money for my college tuition. But, despite the cost, ~~one~~ must complete college in order to get a better, more meaningful job.
5. Gary bought the used car from a local dealership. The car was so clean and
   he
   shiny that ~~you~~ could not tell that the engine needed to be replaced.
6. I would like to go to a school where ~~one~~ can meet many people who are different from me.
7. When I first began to work as a waitress, I was surprised at how rude some
   me
   customers were to ~~you~~.
8. When ~~you~~ drive on the highway, I get disgusted at the amount of trash I see.
9. Students may not leave the exam room unless *they* ~~you~~ have turned in the exam.
10. Nina wanted to just browse through the store, but in every department a
    her
    salesperson came up and asked to help ~~you~~.

Using Specific Words

■ **Review Test 1**

Revise the following sentences, changing vague, indefinite words into sharp, specific ones.

Answers will vary; examples are shown.

1. When my marriage broke up, I felt *various emotions.*

   . . . I felt sad, angry, and worried. _____

   _____

2. The *food choices* in the cafeteria were unappetizing.

   The lukewarm soup, stale sandwiches, and limp salads . . . ____

   _____

3. *Bugs* invaded our kitchen and pantry this summer.

   Ants, moths, and spiders . . . _____

   _____

4. All last week, *the weather was terrible.*

   . . . it rained nonstop, with a bone-chilling wind. _____

   _____

5. In the car accident, our teacher suffered *a number of injuries.*

   . . . a broken arm, two broken ribs, and a concussion. _____

   _____

Using Specific Words

■ **Review Test 2**

With the help of the methods described on page 107, add specific details to the sentences that follow.

Answers will vary; examples are given.

1. The salesperson was obnoxious.

   The haughty, scowling salesman told us not to waste his time with stupid

   questions.

   _____

2. The child started to cry.

   Betty dug her fists into her eyes and shook with sobs.

   _____

   _____

3. The game was exciting.

   The third game of the World Series was a tense pitchers' duel.

   _____

   _____

4. The lounge area was busy.

   The airport lounge was thronged with holiday travelers.

   _____

   _____

5. A passenger on the bus was acting strangely.

   The woman in the front seat was muttering to herself and trembling.

   _____

   _____

Using Active Verbs

■ **Review Test**

Revise the following sentences, changing verbs from the passive to the active voice and making any other necessary word changes.

EXAMPLE   Soccer is played by children all over the world.

Children all over the world play soccer.

1. The pizza restaurant was closed by the health inspector.
   The health inspector closed the pizza restaurant.

2. Huge stacks of donated books were sorted by the workers in the library.
   The workers in the library sorted huge stacks of donated books.

3. My computer was infected by a virus.
   A virus infected my computer.

4. Gasoline prices will not be increased by oil companies this winter.
   Oil companies will not increase gasoline prices this winter.

5. High-powered bombs were dropped by our airplanes onto enemy bases.
   Our airplanes dropped high-powered bombs onto enemy bases.

6. An additional charge was placed on our phone bill by the telephone company.
   The telephone company placed an additional charge on our phone bill.

7. The community center was damaged by a group of vandals.
   A group of vandals damaged the community center.

8. Stress is relieved by physical activity, meditation, and relaxation.
   Physical activity, meditation, and relaxation relieve stress.

9. Taxes will be raised by the federal government to pay for highway improvements.
   The federal government will raise taxes to pay . . .

10. Studies show that violent behavior among young children is increased by watching violent TV programs.
    Studies show that watching violent TV programs increases violent behavior.

Using Concise Words

■ **Review Test 1**

Revise the following sentences, omitting needless words.

Answers may vary; examples are given.

1. I finally made up my mind and decided to look for a new job.

    <u>I finally decided to look for a new job.</u>

    _____

2. Due to the fact that the printer was out of paper, Renee went to the store for the purpose of buying some.

    <u>Because her printer was out of paper, Renee went to buy some.</u>

    _____

3. Tamika realized suddenly that her date had stood her up and was not going to show up.

    <u>Tamika realized suddenly that her date had stood her up.</u>

    _____

4. Our teacher does not know at this point in time if she will return to our school next year.

    <u>Our teacher does not yet know if she will return next year.</u>

    _____

5. The salesperson advised us not to buy the computer at this time because it was going to have a drop in price in the very near future.

    <u>The salesperson advised us to wait until the price dropped before buying</u>

    <u>our computer.</u>

Using Concise Words

■ **Review Test 2**

Revise the following sentences, omitting needless words.

Answers may vary; examples are given.

1. The policy at our company at the present time is that there are two coffee breaks, with each of them being fifteen minutes long.

   Our company allows two fifteen-minute coffee breaks.

2. Permit us to take this opportunity to inform you that your line of credit has been increased.

   Your line of credit has been increased.

3. I have a strong preference for candy over fruit, which, in my opinion, doesn't taste as good as candy does.

   I prefer candy to fruit.

   Or: I think candy tastes better than fruit.

4. Lynn is one of those people who rarely admit being wrong, and it is very unusual to hear her acknowledge that she has made a mistake.

   Lynn rarely admits that she has made a mistake.

5. Many people are of the opinion that children should be required by law to attend school until they reach the age of sixteen years old.

   Many people think that children should, by law, attend school until age

   sixteen.

Varying Your Sentences

■ **Review Test 1**

Combine each of the following groups of simple sentences into one longer sentence. Omit repeated words. Various combinations are often possible, so try to find a combination in each group that flows most smoothly and clearly.

Answers will vary; examples are shown.

1. Sophie had repaired her broken watchband with a paper clip.
   The clip snapped.
   The watch slid off her wrist.

   . . . with a paper clip, but the clip snapped and the watch slid . . .

2. The physical therapist watched.
   Julie tried to stand on her weakened legs.
   They crumpled under her.

   . . . watched as Julie tried to stand on her weakened legs and they crumpled
   under her.

3. There were parking spaces on the street.
   Richie pulled into an expensive garage.
   He did not want to risk damage to his new car.

   Although there were parking spaces on the street, Richie pulled . . . garage
   because he did not want . . .

4. The truck was speeding.
   The truck was brown.
   The truck skidded on some ice.
   The truck almost hit a police officer.
   The police officer was startled.
   The police officer was young.

   Speeding, the brown truck skidded on some ice and almost hit a startled
   young police officer.

5. The rainstorm flooded our basement.
   The rainstorm was sudden.
   The rainstorm was terrible.
   It knocked slates off the roof.
   It uprooted a young tree.

   A sudden terrible rainstorm flooded our basement, knocked slates off the
   roof, and uprooted a young tree.

Varying Your Sentences

■ **Review Test 2**

Combine each of the following groups of simple sentences into two longer sentences. Omit repeated words. Various combinations are often possible, so try to find combinations in each group that flow most smoothly and clearly.

Answers will vary; examples are shown.

1. A sudden cold front hit the area.
   Temperatures dropped thirty degrees in less than an hour.
   My teeth began to chatter.
   I was not wearing a warm jacket.

   When a sudden . . . area, temperatures dropped . . . hour. I was not wearing

   a warm jacket, so my teeth . . .

2. Vern works as a model.
   He has to look his best.
   He gained ten pounds recently.
   He had to take off the extra weight.
   He would have lost his job.

   Vern works as a model, so he has to look his best. When he gained ten

   pounds recently, he had to take off the extra weight, since he would have

   lost his job.

3. The ball game was about to begin.
   A dog ran onto the field.
   The dog began nipping the infielders' ankles.
   The game had to be delayed.
   The dog was chased away.

   As the ball game was about to begin, a dog ran onto the field and began

   nipping the infielders' ankles. The game had to be delayed until the dog was

   chased away.

4. The lion was hungry.
   It watched the herd of gazelle closely.
   A young or sick animal wandered away from the group.
   The lion would move in for the kill.

   The hungry lion watched the herd of gazelle closely. If a young . . . group, the

   lion would move in for the kill.

5. My aunt decided to find a helpful form of exercise.
   She was suffering from arthritis.
   She learned that swimming is very healthful.
   It works every muscle group in the body without straining the muscles.

   My aunt, suffering from arthritis, decided . . . exercise. She learned that

   swimming is very helpful because it works . . .

Varying Your Sentences

■ **Review Test 3**

Combine the sentences in the following paragraph into four sentences. Omit repeated words. Try to find combinations in each case that flow as smoothly and clearly as possible.

Lena and Miles wanted a vacation. They wanted a vacation that was nice. They wanted one that was quiet. They wanted one that was relaxing. They rented a small lakeside cabin. Their first day there was very peaceful. The situation quickly changed. A large family moved into a nearby cabin. They played music at top volume. They raced around in a speedboat with a loud whining engine. Lena and Miles were no longer very relaxed. They packed up their things. They drove off. They returned to their quiet apartment.

Answers will vary. An example is shown.

Lena and Miles wanted a nice, quiet, relaxing vacation, so they rented

a small lakeside cabin. Their first day there was very peaceful, but the

situation quickly changed when a large family moved into a nearby cabin.

They played music at top volume and raced around in a speedboat with a

large whining engine. Lena and Miles, no longer very relaxed, packed up their

things, drove off, and returned to their quiet apartment.

6 Four Bases for Revising Essays

This chapter shows you how to evaluate an essay for

- unity
- support
- coherence
- sentence skills

In the preceding chapters, you learned four essential steps in writing an effective paper. The box below shows how the steps lead to four standards, or bases, you can use in revising an essay.

Four Steps ⟶	*Four Bases*
1 If you advance a single point and stick to that point,	your paper will have *unity*.
2 If you support the point with specific evidence,	your paper will have *support*.
3 If you organize and connect the specific evidence,	your paper will have *coherence*.
4 If you write clear, error-free sentences,	your paper will demonstrate effective *sentence skills*.

This chapter discusses these four bases—unity, support, coherence, and sentence skills—and shows how the four bases can be used to evaluate and revise a paper.

135

Base 1: Unity

Understanding Unity

5

The following student essays are on the topic "Problems or Pleasures of My Teenage Years." Which one makes its point more clearly and effectively, and why?

Essay 1

Teenage Pranks

Looking back at some of the things I did as a teenager makes me break   1
out in a sweat. The purpose of each adventure was fun, but occasionally
things got out of hand. In my search for good times, I was involved in three
notable pranks, ranging from fairly harmless to fairly serious.

The first prank proved that good, clean fun does not have to be dull. As   2
a high school student, I was credited with making the world's largest dessert.
With several friends, I spent an entire year collecting boxes of Jell-O. Entering
our school's indoor pool one night, we turned the water temperature up as
high as it would go and poured in box after box of the strawberry powder.
The next morning, school officials arrived to find the pool filled with thirteen
thousand gallons of the quivering, rubbery stuff. No one was hurt by the
prank, but we did suffer through three days of a massive cleanup.

Not all my pranks were harmless, and one involved risking my life.   3
As soon as I got my driver's license, I wanted to join the "Fliers' Club."
Membership in this club was limited to those who could make their cars fly
a distance of at least ten feet. The qualifying site was an old quarry field
where friends and I had built a ramp made of dirt. I drove my battered Ford
Pinto up this ramp as fast as it would go. The Pinto flew ten feet, but one
of the tires exploded when I landed. The car rolled on its side, and I luckily
escaped with only a bruised arm.

Risking my own life was bad enough, but there was another prank   4
where other people could have been hurt, too. On this occasion, I
accidentally set a valley on fire. Two of my friends and I were sitting on
a hill sharing a few beers. It was a warm summer night, and there was
absolutely nothing to do. The idea came like a thunderclap. We collected
a supply of large plastic trash bags, emergency highway flares, and a half
tank of helium left over from a science-fair experiment. Then we began to
construct a fleet of UFOs. Filling the bags with helium, we tied them closed
with wire and suspended several burning flares below each bag. Our UFOs
leaped into the air like an army of invading Martians. Rising and darting in
the blackness, they convinced even us. Our fun turned into horror, though,
as we watched the balloons begin to drop onto the wooded valley of
expensive homes below. Soon, a brushfire started and, quickly sobered, we
hurried off to call the fire department anonymously.

Every so often, I think back on the things that I did as a teenager. I   5
chuckle at the innocent pranks and feel lucky that I didn't harm myself or
others with the not-so-innocent ones. Those years were filled with wild
times. Today I'm older, wiser—and maybe just a little more boring.

Essay 2

Problems of My Adolescence

In the unreal world of television situation comedies, teenagers are   1
carefree, smart, funny, wisecracking, secure kids. In fact, most of them are
more "together" than the adults on the shows. This, however, isn't how I
recall my teenage years at all. As a teen, I suffered. Every day, I battled the
terrible physical, family, and social troubles of adolescence.

For one thing, I had to deal with a demoralizing physical problem—   2
acne. Some days, I would wake up in the morning with a red bump the size
of a taillight on my nose. Since I worried constantly about my appearance
anyway, acne outbreaks could turn me into a crying, screaming maniac.
Plastering on a layer of (at the time) orange-colored Clearasil, which didn't
fool anybody, I would slink into school, hoping that the boy I had a crush on
would be absent that day. ~~Within the last few years, however, treatments
for acne have improved. Now, skin doctors prescribe special drugs that clear
up pimples almost immediately.~~ An acne attack could shatter whatever
small amount of self-esteem I had managed to build up.

In addition to fighting acne, I felt compelled to fight my family. As a   3
teenager, I needed to be independent. At that time, the most important
thing in life was to be close to my friends and to try out new, more adult
experiences. Unfortunately, my family seemed to get in the way. My little
brother, for instance, turned into my enemy. ~~We are close now, though. In
fact, Eddie recently painted my new apartment for me.~~ Eddie used to barge
into my room, listen to my phone conversations, and read my secret letters.
I would threaten to tie him up and leave him in a garbage dumpster. He
would scream, my mother would yell, and all hell would break loose. My
parents, too, were enemies. They wouldn't let me stay out late, wear the
clothes I wanted to wear, or hang around with the friends I liked. So I tried
to get revenge on them by being miserable, sulky, and sarcastic at home.

Worst of all, I had to face the social traumas of being a teenager. Things   4
that were supposed to be fun, like dates and dances, were actually horrible.
On the few occasions when I had a real date, I agonized over everything—
my hair, my weight, my pimples. After a date, I would come home, raid
the kitchen, and drown my insecurities in a sea of junk food. Dances were
also stressful events. My friends and I would sneak a couple of beers
just to get up the nerve to walk into the school gym. ~~Now I realize that
teenage drinking is dangerous. I read recently that the number one killer of
teenagers is drunk driving.~~ At dances, I never relaxed. It was too important
to look exactly right, to act really cool, and to pretend I was having fun.

I'm glad I'm not a teenager anymore. I wouldn't ever want to feel   5
so unattractive, so confused, and so insecure again. I'll gladly accept the
crow's-feet and stomach bulge of adulthood in exchange for a little peace
of mind.

ACTIVITY

Fill in the blanks.

Essay __1__ makes its point more clearly and effectively because _____
it is more unified.

_____

_____

Comment   Essay 1 is more effective because it is unified. All the details in this
essay are on target; they support and develop each of its three topic sentences
("The first prank proved that good, clean fun does not have to be dull"; "Not all
my pranks were harmless, and one involved risking my life"; and "Risking my own
life was bad enough, but there was another prank where other people could have
been hurt, too").

On the other hand, essay 2 contains some details irrelevant to its topic sentences.
In the first supporting paragraph (paragraph 2), for example, the sentences "Within
the last few years, however, treatments for acne have improved. Now, skin doctors
prescribe special drugs that clear up pimples almost immediately" do not support
the writer's topic statement that she had to deal with the physical problem of acne.
Such details should be left out in the interest of unity.

The difference between these first two essays leads us to the first base or
standard of effective writing: *unity.* To achieve unity is to have all the details in
your paper related to your thesis and to your three supporting topic sentences. Each
time you think of something to put into your paper, ask yourself whether it relates
to your thesis and your supporting points. If it does not, leave it out. For example,
if you were writing a paper about the problems of being unemployed and then spent
a couple of sentences talking about the pleasures of having a lot of free time, you
would be missing the first and most essential base of good writing.

Revising for Unity

ACTIVITY

Go back to essay 2 and cross out the two sentences in the second supporting
paragraph (paragraph 3) and the two sentences in the third supporting paragraph
(paragraph 4) that are off target and do not help support their topic sentences.

Base 2: Support

Understanding Support

The following essays were written on "Dealing with Disappointment." Both are unified, but one communicates more clearly and effectively. Which one, and why?

Essay 1

Dealing with Disappointment

One way to look at life is as a series of disappointments. Life can certainly appear that way because disappointment crops up in the life of everyone more often, it seems, than satisfaction. How disappointments are handled can have a great bearing on how life is viewed. People can react negatively by sulking or by blaming others, or they can try to understand the reasons behind the disappointment.   1

Sulking is one way to deal with disappointment. This attitude—"Why does everything always happen to me?"—is common because it is easy to adopt, but it is not very productive. Everyone has had the experience of meeting people who specialize in feeling sorry for themselves. A sulky manner will often discourage others from wanting to lend support, and it prevents the sulker from making positive moves toward self-help. It becomes easier just to sit back and sulk. Unfortunately, feeling sorry for oneself does nothing to lessen the pain of disappointment. It may, in fact, increase the pain. It certainly does not make future disappointments easier to bear.   2

Blaming others is another negative and unproductive way to cope with disappointment. This all-too-common response of pointing the finger at someone else doesn't help one's situation. This posture will lead only to anger, resentment, and, therefore, further unhappiness. Disappointment in another's performance does not necessarily indicate that the performer is at fault. Perhaps expectations were too high, or there could have been a misunderstanding as to what the performer actually intended to accomplish.   3

A positive way to handle disappointment is to try to understand the reasons behind the disappointment. An analysis of the causes of disappointment can have an excellent chance of producing desirable results. Often understanding alone can help alleviate the pain of disappointment and can help prevent future disappointments. Also, it is wise to try to remember that what would be ideal is not necessarily what is reasonable to expect in any given situation. The ability to look disappointment squarely in the face and then go on from there is the first step on the road back.   4

Continuous handling of disappointment in a negative manner can lead to a negative view of life itself. Chances for personal happiness in such a   5 state of being are understandably slim. Learning not to expect perfection in an imperfect world and keeping in mind those times when expectations were actually surpassed are positive steps toward allowing the joys of life to prevail.

Reactions to Disappointment

Ben Franklin said that the only sure things in life are death and taxes. He left something out, however: disappointment. No one gets through life without experiencing many disappointments. Strangely, though, most people seem unprepared for disappointment and react to it in negative ways. They feel depressed or try to escape their troubles instead of using disappointment as an opportunity for growth.   1

One negative reaction to disappointment is depression. For example, Helen, a woman trying to win a promotion, works hard for over a year in her department. Helen is so sure she will get the promotion, in fact, that she has already picked out the car she will buy when her salary increase comes through. However, the boss names one of Helen's coworkers to the spot. The fact that all the other department employees tell Helen that she is the one who really deserved the promotion doesn't help her deal with the crushing disappointment. Deeply depressed, Helen decides that all her goals are doomed to defeat. She loses her enthusiasm for her job and can barely force herself to show up every day. Helen tells herself that she is a failure and that doing a good job just isn't worth the work.   2

Another negative reaction to disappointment, and one that often follows depression, is the desire to escape. Jamal fails to get into the college his brother is attending, the college that was the focus of all his dreams, and decides to escape his disappointment. Why worry about college at all? Instead, he covers up his real feelings by giving up on his schoolwork and getting completely involved with friends, parties, and "good times." Or Carla doesn't make the varsity basketball team—something she wanted very badly—and so refuses to play sports at all. She decides to hang around with a new set of friends who get high every day; then she won't have to confront her disappointment and learn to live with it.   3

The positive way to react to disappointment is to use it as a chance for growth. This isn't easy, but it's the only useful way to deal with an inevitable part of life. Helen, the woman who wasn't promoted, could have handled her disappointment by looking at other options. If her boss doesn't recognize her talent and hard work, perhaps she could transfer to another department. Or she could ask the boss how to improve her performance so that she would be a shoo-in for the next promotion. Jamal, the boy who didn't get into the college of his choice, should look into other schools. Going to another college may encourage him to be his own person,   4 step out of his brother's shadow, and realize that being turned down by one college isn't a final judgment on his abilities or potential. Rather than escape into drugs, Carla could improve her basketball skills for a year or pick up another sport—like swimming or tennis—that would probably turn out to be more useful to her as an adult.

Disappointments are unwelcome but regular visitors to everyone's life.   5
We can feel depressed about them, or we can try to escape from them. The best thing, though, is to accept a disappointment and then try to use it somehow: step over the unwelcome visitor on the doorstep and get on with life.

ACTIVITY

Fill in the blanks.

Essay ___2___ makes its point more clearly and effectively because _____ it has better support for its thesis. _____

_____   _____

Comment   Here, essay 2 is more effective, for it offers specific examples of the ways people deal with disappointment. We see for ourselves the kinds of reactions people have to disappointment.

Essay 1, on the other hand, gives us no specific evidence. The writer tells us repeatedly that sulking, blaming others, and trying to understand the reasons behind a disappointment are the reactions people have to a letdown. However, the writer never *shows* us any of these responses in action. Exactly what kinds of disappointments is the writer talking about? And how, for instance, does someone analyze the causes of disappointment? Would a person write a list of causes on a piece of paper, or review the causes with a concerned friend, or speak to a professional therapist? In an essay like this, we would want to see *examples* of how sulking and blaming others are negative ways of dealing with disappointment.

Consideration of these two essays leads us to the second base of effective writing: *support*. After realizing the importance of specific supporting details, one student writer revised a paper she had done on being lost in the woods as the worst experience of her childhood. In the revised paper, instead of talking about "the terror of being separated from my parents," she referred to such specifics as "tears streamed down my cheeks as I pictured the faces I would never see again" and "I clutched the locket my parents had given me as if it were a lucky charm that could help me find my way back to the campsite." All your papers should include such vivid details!

Revising for Support

ACTIVITY

On a separate sheet of paper, revise one of the three supporting paragraphs in "Dealing with Disappointment" by providing specific supporting examples.

Answers will vary.

Base 3: Coherence

Understanding Coherence

The following two essays were written on the topic "Positive or Negative Effects of Television." Both are unified, and both are supported. However, one communicates more clearly and effectively. Which one, and why?

Essay 1

Harmful Effects of Watching Television

In a recent cartoon, one character said to another, "When you think of   1
the awesome power of television to educate, aren't you glad it doesn't?"
It's true that television has the power to educate and to entertain, but
unfortunately, these benefits are outweighed by the harm it does to
dedicated viewers. Television is harmful because it creates passivity,
discourages communication, and presents a false picture of reality.

Television makes viewers passive. Children who have an electronic   2
baby-sitter spend most of their waking hours in a semiconscious state.
Older viewers watch tennis matches and basketball games with none
of the excitement of being in the stands. Even if children are watching
Sesame Street or Barney & Friends, they are being educated passively. The
child actors are going on nature walks, building crafts projects, playing
with animals, and participating in games, but the little viewers are simply
watching. Older viewers watch guests discuss issues with Oprah Winfrey,
but no one will turn to the home viewers to ask their opinion.

Worst of all, TV presents a false picture of reality that leaves viewers   3
frustrated because they don't have the beauty or wealth of the characters
on television. Viewers absorb the idea that everyone else in the United
States owns a lavish apartment, a suburban house, a sleek car, and an
expensive wardrobe. Every detective, police officer, oil baron, and lawyer,
male or female, is suitable for a pinup poster. The material possessions
on TV shows and commercials contribute to the false image of reality.
News anchors and reporters, with their perfect hair and makeup, must
fit television's standard of beauty. From their modest homes or cramped

apartments, many viewers tune in daily to the upper-middle-class world that TV glorifies.

Television discourages communication. Families watching television do very little talking except for brief exchanges during commercials. If Uncle Bernie or the next-door neighbors drop in for a visit, the most comfortable activity for everyone may be not conversation but watching ESPN. The family may not even be watching the same set; instead, in some households, all the family members head for their own rooms to watch their own sets. At dinner, plates are plopped on the coffee table in front of the set, and the meal is wolfed down during NBC Nightly News. During commercials, the only communication a family has all night may consist of questions like "Do we have any popcorn?" and "Where's TV Guide?"   4

Television, like cigarettes or saccharin, is harmful to our health. We are becoming isolated, passive, and frustrated. And, most frightening, the average viewer now spends more time watching television than ever before.   5

Essay 2

The Benefits of Television

We hear a lot about the negative effects of television on the viewer. Obviously, television can be harmful if it is watched constantly to the exclusion of other activities. It would be just as harmful to listen to CDs all the time or to eat constantly. However, when television is watched in moderation, it is extremely valuable, as it provides relaxation, entertainment, and education.   1

First of all, watching TV has the value of sheer relaxation. Watching television can be soothing and restful after an eight-hour day of pressure, challenges, or concentration. After working hard all day, people look forward to a new episode of a favorite show or yet another showing of Casablanca or Sleepless in Seattle. This period of relaxation leaves viewers refreshed and ready to take on the world again. Watching TV also seems to reduce stress in some people. This benefit of television is just beginning to be recognized. One doctor, for example, advises his patients with high blood pressure to relax in the evening with a few hours of television.   2

In addition to being relaxing, television is entertaining. Along with the standard comedies, dramas, and game shows that provide enjoyment to viewers, television offers a variety of movies and sports events. Moreover, in many areas, viewers can pay a monthly fee and receive special cable programming. With this service, viewers can watch first-run movies, rock and classical music concerts, and specialized sports events, like international soccer and Grand Prix racing. Viewers can also buy or rent movies to show on their television sets through DVD players or VCRs. Still another growing area of TV entertainment is video games. Cartridges are available for everything from electronic baseball to Mortal Kombat, allowing the owner to have a video game arcade in the living room.   3

Most important, television is educational. Preschoolers learn colors,   4
numbers, and letters from public television programs, like <u>Sesame Street</u>,
that use animation and puppets to make learning fun. Science shows for
older children, like <u>Fun with Nature</u>, go on location to analyze everything
from volcanoes to rocket launches. Adults, too, can get an education
(college credits included) from courses given on television. Also, television
widens our knowledge by covering important events and current news.
Viewers can see and hear presidents' speeches, state funerals, natural
disasters, and election results as they are happening. Finally, with a phone
line and a special terminal, television allows any member of the family to
access and learn from all the information resources on the Internet.

Perhaps because television is such a powerful force, we like to criticize   5
it and search for its flaws. However, the benefits of television should not be
ignored. We can use television to relax, to have fun, and to make ourselves
smarter. This electronic wonder, then, is a servant, not a master.

ACTIVITY

Fill in the blanks.

Essay __2__ makes its point more clearly and effectively because _____
<u>it is more clearly organized.</u>

_____

Comment   In this case, essay 2 is more effective because the material is organized
clearly and logically. Using emphatic order, the writer develops three positive uses
of television, ending with the most important use: television as an educational tool.
The writer includes transitional words that act as signposts, making movement from
one idea to the next easy to follow. The major transitions include *First of all, In
addition,* and *Most important;* transitions within paragraphs include such words as
Moreover, Still another, too, Also, and *Finally.* And this writer also uses a linking
sentence ("In addition to being relaxing, television is entertaining") to tie the first
and second supporting paragraphs together clearly.

Although essay 1 is unified and supported, the writer does not have any clear
and consistent way of organizing the material. The most important idea (signaled
by the phrase *Worst of all*) is discussed in the second supporting paragraph instead
of being saved for last. None of the supporting paragraphs organizes its details
in a logical fashion. The first supporting paragraph, for example, discusses older
viewers, then goes to younger viewers, then jumps back to older people again. The
third supporting paragraph, like the first, leaps from an opening idea (families
talking only during commercials) to several intervening ideas and then back to the
original idea (talking during commercials). In addition, essay 1 uses practically no
transitional devices to guide the reader.

These two essays lead us to the third base of effective writing: *coherence*. All the supporting ideas and sentences in a paper must be organized so that they cohere, or "stick together." As has been discussed in Chapter 3, key techniques for tying together the material in a paper include a clear method of organization (such as time order or emphatic order), transitions, and other connecting words.

Revising for Coherence

ACTIVITY

On a separate sheet of paper, revise one of the three supporting paragraphs in "Harmful Effects of Watching Television" by providing a clear method of organizing the material and transitional words.

Answers will vary.

Base 4: Sentence Skills

Understanding Sentence Skills

Following are the opening paragraphs from two essays. Both are unified, supported, and organized, but one version communicates more clearly and effectively. Which one, and why?

Essay 1,
First Part

"revenge"

[1]Revenge is one of those things that everyone enjoy. [2]People don't like   1
to talk about it, though. [3]Just the same, there is nothing more tempting,
more satisfying, or with the reward of a bit of revenge. [4]The purpose is
not to harm your victims. [5]But to let them know that you are upset about
something they are doing. [6]Careful plotting can provide you with relief
from bothersom coworkers, gossiping friends, or nagging family members.

[7]Coworkers who make comments about the fact that you are always   2
fifteen minutes late for work can be taken care of very simply. [8]The first
thing that you should do is to get up extra early one day. [9]Before the sun
comes up, drive to each coworker's house, reach under the hood of his car,
and disconnected the center wire that leads to the distrib. cap. [10]The car
will be unharmed, but it will not start, and your friends at work will all be
late for work on the same day. [11]If your lucky, your boss might notice that
you are the only one there and will give you a raise. [12]Later if you feel guilty
about your actions you can call each person anonymously and tell them
how to get the car running. . . .

A Bit of Revenge

Revenge is one of those things that everyone enjoys. People don't like   1
to talk about it, though. Just the same, there is nothing more tempting,
more satisfying, or more rewarding than a bit of revenge. The purpose is
not to harm your victims but to let them know that you are upset about
something they are doing to you. Careful plotting can provide you with
relief from bothersome coworkers, gossiping friends, or nagging family
members.

Coworkers who make comments about the fact that you are always   2
fifteen minutes late for work can be taken care of very simply. The first
thing that you should do is to get up extra early one day. Before the sun
comes up, drive to each coworker's house. Reach under the hood of your
coworker's car and disconnect the center wire that leads to the distributor
cap. The car will be unharmed, but it will not start, and your friends at
work will all be late for work on the same day. If you're lucky, your boss
might notice that you are the only one there and will give you a raise.
Later, if you feel guilty about your actions, you can call your coworkers
anonymously and tell them how to get their cars running again. . . .

ACTIVITY

Fill in the blanks.

Essay ___2___ makes its point more clearly and effectively because _____
it is free of errors in grammar, spelling, and punctuation. It shows good use

of sentence skills.

Comment   Essay 2 is more effective because it uses *sentence skills,* the fourth
base of competent writing. Here are the sentence-skills mistakes in essay 1:

- The title should not be set off in quotation marks.
- The first letter of the title should be capitalized.
- The singular subject *everyone* in sentence 1 should have a singular verb: *enjoy* should be *enjoys.*
- There is a lack of parallelism in sentence 3: *with the reward of* should be *more rewarding.*
- Word group 5 is a fragment; it can be corrected by attaching it to the previous sentence.
- The word *bothersom* in sentence 6 is misspelled; it should be *bothersome.*
- The word *disconnected* in sentence 9 should be *disconnect* to be consistent in tense with *reach,* the other verb in the sentence.

- The word *distrib.* in sentence 9 should be spelled out in full: *distributor.*
- The first *your* in sentence 11 stands for *you are;* an apostrophe and an *e* must be added: *you're.*
- Commas must be added in sentence 12 to set off the interrupting words.
- The words *each person* and *the car* in sentence 12 need to be changed to plural forms to agree with *them.*

Revising for Sentence Skills

ACTIVITY

Here are the final three paragraphs from the two essays. Edit the sentences in the first essay to make the corrections needed. Note that comparing essays 1 and 2 will help you locate the mistakes. This activity will also help you identify some of the sentence skills you may want to review in Part Four.
Editing may vary slightly.

Essay 1, Last Part

3 ...¹³Gossiping friends at school are also perfect targets for a simple act of revenge. ¹⁴A way to trap either male or female friends ~~are~~ *is* to leave phony messages on their lockers. ¹⁵If the friend that you want to get is male, leave a message that a certain girl would like him to stop by her house later that day. ¹⁶With any luck, her boyfriend will be there. ¹⁷The girl won't know what's going on, and the victim will be so embarrassed that he probably won't leave his home for a month. ¹⁸The plan works just as well for female friends, too.

4 ¹⁹When Mom and Dad and your sisters and brothers really begin to annoy you, harmless revenge may be just the way to make them ~~quite~~ *quiet* down for a while. ²⁰The dinner table, where most of the nagging probably happens, is a likely place. ²¹Just before the meal begins, throw a handful of raisins into the food. ²²Wait about ~~5~~ *five* minutes and, after everyone has ~~began~~ *begun* to eat, clamp your hand over your mouth and begin to make odd noises. ²³When they ask you what the matter is, point to a raisin and yell,"Bugs!" ²⁴~~Dumping the~~ *They'll all dump their* food in the disposal, *jump into* the car, ~~will~~ *and* head quickly for ~~mcdonald's~~ *McDonald's.* ²⁵That night, you'll have your first quiet, peaceful meal in a long time.

5 ²⁶Well-planned revenge does not have to hurt anyone. ²⁷The object is simply to let other people know that they are beginning to bother you.

²⁸You should remember, though, to stay on your guard after completing your revenge. ²⁹The reason for this is simple, ~~coworkers~~, *Coworkers,* friends, and family can also plan revenge on you.

Essay 2,
Last Part

. . . Gossiping friends at school are also perfect targets for a simple act   3
of revenge. A way to trap either male or female friends is to leave phony messages on their lockers. If the friend that you want to get is male, leave a message that a certain girl would like him to stop by her house later that day. With any luck, her boyfriend will be there. The girl won't know what's going on, and the victim will be so embarrassed that he probably won't leave his home for a month. The plan works just as well for female friends, too.

When Mom and Dad and your sisters and brothers really begin to annoy   4
you, harmless revenge may be just the way to make them quiet down for a while. The dinner table, where most of the nagging probably happens, is a likely place. Just before the meal begins, throw a handful of raisins into the food. Wait about five minutes and, after everyone has begun to eat, clamp your hand over your mouth and begin to make odd noises. When they ask you what the matter is, point to a raisin and yell, "Bugs!" They'll all dump their food in the disposal, jump into the car, and head quickly for McDonald's. That night, you'll have your first quiet, peaceful meal in a long time.

Well-planned revenge does not have to hurt anyone. The object is   5
simply to let other people know that they are beginning to bother you. You should remember, though, to stay on your guard after completing your revenge. The reason for this is simple. Coworkers, friends, and family can also plan revenge on you.

Practice in Using the Four Bases

You are now familiar with four standards, or bases, of effective writing: *unity, support, coherence,* and *sentence skills.* In this section you will expand and strengthen your understanding of the four bases as you evaluate and revise essays for each of them.

1 Revising Essays for Unity

ACTIVITY

Both of the following essays contain irrelevant sentences that do not relate to the thesis of the essay or support the topic sentence of the paragraph in which they appear. Cross out the irrelevant sentences and write the numbers of those sentences in the spaces provided.

Essay 1

Playing on the Browns

[1]For the past three summers, I have played first base on a softball team known as the Browns. [2]We play a long schedule, including playoffs, and everybody takes the games pretty seriously. [3]In that respect, we're no different from any other of the thousand or so teams in our city. [4]But in one respect, we <u>are</u> different. [5]In an all-male league, we have a woman on the team—me. [6]Thus I've had a chance to observe something about human nature by seeing how the men have treated me. [7]Some have been disbelieving; some have been patronizing; and, fortunately, some have simply accepted me.

1

[8]One new team in the league was particularly flabbergasted to see me start the game at first base. [9]Nobody on the Comets had commented one way or the other when he saw me warming up, but playing in the actual game was another story. [10]The Comets' first-base coach leaned over to me with a disbelieving grin and said, "You mean, you're starting, and those three guys are on the bench?" [11]I nodded and he shrugged, still amazed. [12]He probably thought I was the manager's wife. [13]When I came up to bat, the Comet pitcher smiled and called to his outfielders to move way in on me. [14]Now, I don't have a lot of power, but I'm not exactly feeble. [15]~~I used to work out on the exercise machines at a local health club until it closed, and now I lift weights at home a couple of times a week.~~ [16]I wiped the smirks off their faces with a line drive double over the left fielder's head.

2

The number of the irrelevant sentence: ___15___

[17]The next game, we played another new team, the Argyles, and their attitude was patronizing. [18]The Argyles had seen me take batting practice, so they didn't do anything so rash as to draw their outfield way in. [19]They had respect for my ability as a player. [20]However, they tried to annoy me with phony concern. [21]For example, a redheaded Argyle got on base in the first inning and said to me, "You'd better be careful, Hon. [22]When you have your foot on the bag, somebody might step on it. [23]You can get hurt in this game." [24]~~I was mad, but I have worked out several mental techniques to control my anger because it interferes with my playing ability.~~ [25]Well, this delicate little girl survived the season without injury, which is more than I can say for some of the "he-men" on the Argyles.

3

The number of the irrelevant sentence: ___24___

[26]Happily, most of the teams in the league have accepted me, just as the Browns did. [27]The men on the Browns coached and criticized me (and occasionally cursed me) just like anyone else. [28]~~Because I'm a religious person, I don't approve of cursing, but I don't say anything about it to my teammates.~~ [29]They are not amazed when I get a hit or stretch for a wide

4

throw. ³⁰My average this year was higher than the averages of several of my teammates, yet none of them acted resentful or threatened. ³¹On several occasions I was taken out late in a game for a pinch runner, but other slow players on the team were also lifted at times for pinch runners. ³²Every woman should have a team like the Browns!

The number of the irrelevant sentence: ___28___

³³Because I really had problems only with the new teams, I've concluded   5
that it's when people are faced with an unfamiliar situation that they react defensively. ³⁴Once a rival team has gotten used to seeing me on the field, I'm no big deal. ³⁵Still, I suspect that the Browns secretly feel we're a little special. ³⁶After all, we won the championship with a woman on the team.

Essay 2   **How to Con an Instructor**

¹Enter college, and you'll soon be reminded of an old saying: "The pen   1
is mightier than the sword." ²That person behind the instructor's desk holds your future in his or her ink-stained hands. ³So your first important assignment in college has nothing to do with required readings, examinations, or even the hazards of registration. ⁴It is, instead, how to con an instructor.
⁵The first step in conning an instructor is to use body language. ⁶You   2
may be able to convince your instructor that you are special without even saying a word. ⁷When you enter the classroom, be sure to sit in the front row. ⁸That way, the instructor can't possibly miss you. ⁹Then, as the instructor lectures, take notes frantically. ¹⁰The instructor will be flattered that you think so much of his or her words that you want to write them all down. ¹¹A felt-tip pen is superior to a pen or pencil; it will help you write faster and prevent aching wrists. ¹²While you are writing, be sure to smile at the instructor's jokes and nod violently in agreement with every major point. ¹³Most important, as class continues, sit with your body pitched forward and your eyes wide open, fixed firmly, as if hypnotized, on your instructor's face. ¹⁴Make your whole body suggest that you are watching a star.

The number of the irrelevant sentence: ___11___

¹⁵Once you have mastered body language, it is time to move on to   3
the second phase of conning the instructor: class participation. ¹⁶Everyone knows that the student who is most eager to learn is the one who responds to the questions that are asked and even comes up with a few more. ¹⁷Therefore, be sure to be responsive. ¹⁸Questions such as "How does this affect the future of the United States?" or "Don't you think that someday all this will be done by computer?" can be used in any class without prior knowledge of the subject matter. ¹⁹Many students, especially in large

classes, get lost in the crowd and never do anything to make themselves stand out. [20]Another good participation technique is to wait until the instructor has said something that sounds profound and then ask him or her to repeat it slowly so you can get it down word for word in your notes. [21]No instructor can resist this kind of flattery.

The number of the irrelevant sentence: ___19___

[22]However, the most advanced form of conning an instructor happens after class. [23]Don't be like the others who slap their notebooks closed, snatch up their books, and rush out the door before the echoes of the final bell have died away. [24]Did you ever notice how students begin to get restless about five minutes before class ends, even if there's no clock on the wall? [25]Instead, be reluctant to leave. [26]Approach the instructor's desk hesitantly, almost reverently. [27]Say that you want to find out more about the topic. [28]Is there any extra reading you can do? [29]Even better, ask if the instructor has written anything on the topic—and whether you could borrow it. [30]Finally, compliment your instructor by saying that this is the most interesting course you've ever taken. [31]Nothing beats the personal approach for making an instructor think you care.

4

The number of the irrelevant sentence: ___24___

[32]Body language, questions, after-class discussions—these are the secrets of conning an instructor that every college student should know. [33]These kinds of things go on in high school, too, and they're just as effective on that level. [34]Once you master these methods, you won't have to worry about a thing—until the final exam.

5

The number of the irrelevant sentence: ___33___

2 Revising Essays for Support

ACTIVITY

Both of the essays below lack supporting details at certain key points. In each essay, identify the spots where details are needed.

Essay 1

Formula for Happiness

[1]Everyone has his or her own formula for happiness. [2]As we go through life, we discover the activities that make us feel best. [3]I've already discovered three keys to happiness. [4]I depend on karate, music, and self-hypnosis.

1

⁵Karate helps me feel good physically. ⁶Before taking karate lessons, I was tired most of the time, my muscles felt like foam rubber, and I was twenty pounds overweight. ⁷After three months of these lessons, I saw an improvement in my physical condition. ⁸Also, my endurance has increased. ⁹At the end of my workday, I used to drag myself home to eat and watch television all night. ¹⁰Now, I have enough energy to play with my children, shop, or see a movie. ¹¹Karate has made me feel healthy, strong, and happy.

2

The spot where supporting details are needed occurs after sentence ____7____.

¹²Singing with a chorus has helped me achieve emotional well-being by expressing my feelings. ¹³In situations where other people would reveal their feelings, I would remain quiet. ¹⁴Since joining the chorus, however, I have an outlet for joy, anger, or sadness. ¹⁵When I sing, I pour my emotions into the music and don't have to feel shy. ¹⁶For this reason, I most enjoy singing certain kinds of music, since they demand real depth of feeling.

3

The first spot where supporting details are needed occurs after sentence ___13___.
The second spot occurs after sentence ___16___.

¹⁷Self-hypnosis gives me peace of mind. ¹⁸This is a total relaxation technique, which I learned several years ago. ¹⁹Essentially I breathe deeply and concentrate on relaxing all my muscles. ²⁰I then repeat a key suggestion to myself. ²¹Through self-hypnosis, I have gained control over several bad habits that have long been haunting me. ²²I have also learned to reduce the stress that goes along with my secretarial job. ²³Now I can handle the boss's demands or unexpected work without feeling tense.

4

The first spot where supporting details are needed occurs after sentence ___20___.
The second spot occurs after sentence ___21___.

²⁴In short, my physical, emotional, and mental well-being have been greatly increased through karate, music, and self-hypnosis. ²⁵These activities have become important elements in my formula for happiness.

5

Essay 2

Problems of a Foreign Student

¹About ten months ago I decided to leave my native country and come to the United States to study. ²When I got here, I suddenly turned into someone labeled "foreign student." ³A foreign student, I discovered, has problems. ⁴Whether from Japan, like me, or from some other country, a foreign student has to work twice as hard as Americans do to succeed in college.

1

⁵First of all, there is the language problem. ⁶American students have the advantage of comprehending English without working at it. ⁷But even they complain that some professors talk too fast, mumble, or use big words. ⁸As a result, they can't take notes fast enough to keep up, or they misunderstand what was said. ⁹Now consider my situation. ¹⁰I'm trying to cope with a language that is probably one of the hardest in the world to learn. ¹¹Dozens of English slang phrases—"mess around," "hassle," "get into"—were totally new to me. ¹²Other language problems gave me trouble, too.   2

The spot where supporting details are needed occurs after sentence ___12___.

¹³Another problem I face has to do with being a stranger to American culture. ¹⁴For instance, the academic world is much different in Japan. ¹⁵In the United States, instructors seem to treat students as equals. ¹⁶Many classes are informal, and the relationship between instructor and student is friendly; in fact, students call some instructors by their first names. ¹⁷In Japan, however, the instructor-student relationship is different. ¹⁸Lectures, too, are more formal, and students show respect by listening quietly and paying attention at all times. ¹⁹This more casual atmosphere occasionally makes me feel uncomfortable in class.   3

The spot where supporting details are needed occurs after sentence ___17___.

²⁰Perhaps the most difficult problem I face is social. ²¹American students may have some trouble making new friends or may feel lonely at times. ²²However, they usually manage to find other people with the same background, interests, or goals. ²³It is twice as hard to make friends, though, if a person has trouble making the small talk that can lead to a relationship. ²⁴I find it difficult to become friends with other students because I don't understand some aspects of American life. ²⁵Students would rather talk to someone who is familiar with these things.   4

The spot where supporting details are needed occurs after sentence ___24___.

²⁶Despite all the handicaps that I, as a foreign student, have to overcome, I wouldn't give up this chance to go to school in the United States. ²⁷Each day, the problems seem a little bit less overwhelming. ²⁸Like a little child who is finally learning to read, write, and make sense of things, I am starting to enjoy my experience of discovering a brand-new world.   5

3 Revising Essays for Coherence

ACTIVITY

Both of the essays that follow could be revised to improve their coherence. Answer the questions about coherence that come after each essay.

Essay 1

Noise Pollution

[1]Natural sounds—waves, wind, birdsong—are so soothing that companies   1
sell recordings of them to anxious people seeking a relaxing atmosphere at home or in the car. [2]One reason why "environmental sounds" are big business is the fact that ordinary citizens, especially city dwellers, are bombarded by noise pollution. [3]On the way to work, on the job, and on the way home, the typical urban resident must cope with a continuing barrage of unpleasant sounds.

[4]The noise level in an office can be unbearable. [5]From nine to five   2
o'clock, phones and fax machines ring, computer keyboards chatter, intercoms buzz, and copy machines thump back and forth. [6]Every time the receptionists can't find people, they resort to a nerve-shattering public address system. [7]And because the managers worry about the employees' morale, they graciously provide the endless droning of canned music. [8]This effectively eliminates any possibility of a moment of blessed silence.

[9]Traveling home from work provides no relief from the noisiness of the   3
office. [10]The ordinary sounds of blaring taxi horns and rumbling buses are occasionally punctuated by the ear-piercing screech of car brakes. [11]Taking a shortcut through the park will bring the weary worker face to face with chanting religious cults, freelance musicians, screaming children, and barking dogs. [12]None of these sounds can compare with the large radios many park visitors carry. [13]Each radio blasts out something different, from heavy-metal rock to baseball, at decibel levels so strong that they make eardrums throb in pain. [14]If there are birds singing or wind in the trees, the harried commuter will never hear them.

[15]Even a trip to work at 6 or 7 A.M. isn't quiet. [16]No matter which route   4
a worker takes, there is bound to be a noisy construction site somewhere along the way. [17]Hard hats will shout from third-story windows to warn their coworkers below before heaving debris out and sending it crashing to earth. [18]Huge front-end loaders will crunch into these piles of rubble and back up, their warning signals letting out loud, jarring beeps. [19]Air hammers begin an earsplitting chorus of rat-a-tat-tat sounds guaranteed to shatter sanity as well as concrete. [20]Before reaching the office, the worker is already completely frazzled.

[21]Noise pollution is as dangerous as any other kind of pollution. [22]The   5
endless pressure of noise probably triggers countless nervous breakdowns,

vicious arguments, and bouts of depression. [23]And imagine the world problems we could solve, if only the noise stopped long enough to let us think.

1. In "Noise Pollution," what is the number of the sentence to which the transition word *Also* could be added in paragraph 2? ___6___

2. In the last sentence of paragraph 2, to what does the pronoun *This* refer?
   ___endless droning of canned music___

3. What is the number of the sentence to which the transition word *But* could be added in paragraph 3? ___12___

4. What is the number of the sentence to which the transition word *Then* could be added in paragraph 4? ___18___

5. What is the number of the sentence to which the transition word *Meanwhile* could be added in paragraph 4? ___19___

6. What word is used as a synonym for *debris* in paragraph 4? ___rubble___

7. How many times is the key word *sounds* used in the essay? ___six times___

8. The time order of the three supporting paragraphs is confused. What is the number of the supporting paragraph that should come first? ___4___ Second? ___2___ Third? ___3___

Essay 2

Weight Loss

[1]The big fraternity party turned out to be the low point of my first year   1 at college. [2]I was in heaven until I discovered that my date with handsome Greg, the fraternity vice president, was a hoax: he had used me to win the "ugliest date" contest. [3]I ran sobbing back to the dorm, wanting to resign from the human race. [4]Then I realized that it was time to stop kidding myself about my weight. [5]Within the next two years, I lost forty-two pounds and turned my life around. [6]Losing weight gave me self-confidence socially, emotionally, and professionally.

[7]I am more outgoing socially. [8]Just being able to abandon dark colors,   2 baggy sweaters, and tent dresses in favor of bright colors, T-shirts, and designer jeans made me feel better in social situations. [9]I am able to do more things. [10]I once turned down an invitation for a great camping trip with my best friend's family, making up excuses about sun poisoning and allergies. [11]Really, I was too embarrassed to tell them that I couldn't fit into the bathroom in their Winnebago! [12]I made up for it last summer when I was one of the organizers of a college backpacking trip through the Rockies.

¹³Most important, losing weight helped me seek new professional goals.   3
¹⁴When I was obese, I organized my whole life around my weight, as if it were a defect I could do nothing about. ¹⁵With my good grades, I could have chosen almost any major the college offered, but I had limited my goal to teaching kindergarten because I felt that little children wouldn't judge how I looked. ¹⁶Once I was no longer fat, I realized that I love working with all sorts of people. ¹⁷I became a campus guide and even had small parts in college theater productions. ¹⁸As a result, last year I changed my major to public relations. ¹⁹The area fascinates me, and I now have good job prospects there.

²⁰I have also become more emotionally honest. ²¹Rose, at the college   4
counseling center, helped me see that my "fat and jolly" personality had been false. ²²I was afraid others would reject me if I didn't always go along with their suggestions. ²³I eventually put Rose's advice to the test. ²⁴My roommates were planning an evening at a Greek restaurant. ²⁵I loved the restaurant's atmosphere, but there wasn't much I liked on the menu. ²⁶Finally, in a shaky voice I said, "Actually, I'm not crazy about lamb. ²⁷How about Chinese food?" ²⁸They scolded me for not mentioning it before, and we had dinner at a Chinese restaurant. ²⁹We all agreed it was one of our best evenings out.

³⁰Fortunately, the low point of my first year turned out to be the   5
turning point leading to what promises to be an exciting senior year. ³¹Greg's cruel joke became a strange sort of favor, and I've gone from wanting to resign from the human race to welcoming each day as a source of fresh adventure and self-discovery.

1. In "Weight Loss," what is the number of the sentence to which the transition words *For one thing* could be added in paragraph 2? __8__

2. What is the number of the sentence to which the transition word *Also* could be added in paragraph 2? __9__

3. What is the number of the sentence to which the transition word *But* could be added in paragraph 2? __12__

4. In sentence 11, to what does the pronoun *them* refer? __my best friend's family__

5. What is the number of the sentence to which the transition word *However* could be added in paragraph 3? __16__

6. What word is used as a synonym for *obese* in paragraph 3? __fat__

7. How many times is the key word *weight* used in the essay? __four times__

8. What is the number of the supporting paragraph that should be placed in the emphatic final position? __3__

4 Revising Essays for All Four Bases: Unity, Support, Coherence, and Sentence Skills

ACTIVITY

In this activity, you will evaluate and revise two essays in terms of all four bases: unity, support, coherence, and sentence skills. Comments follow each supporting paragraph. Circle the letter of the *one* statement that applies in each case.

Essay 1

Chiggers

I had lived my whole life not knowing what chiggers are. I thought   1
they were probably a type of insect Humphrey Bogart encountered in
The African Queen. I never had any real reason to care, until one day last
summer. Within twenty-four hours, I had vividly experienced what chigger
bites are, learned how to treat them, and learned how to prevent them.

First of all, I learned that chiggers are the larvae of tiny mites found   2
in the woods and that their bites are always multiple and cause intense
itching. A beautiful summer day seemed perfect for a walk in the woods.
I am definitely not a city person, for I couldn't stand to be surrounded by
people, noise, and concrete. As I walked through the ferns and pines, I
noticed what appeared to be a dusting of reddish seeds or pollen on my
slacks. Looking more closely, I realized that each speck was a tiny insect.
I casually brushed off a few and gave them no further thought. I woke up
the next morning feeling like a victim staked to an anthill by an enemy
wise in the ways of torture. Most of my body was speckled with measlelike
bumps that at the slightest touch burned and itched like a mosquito bite
raised to the twentieth power. When antiseptics and calamine lotion failed
to help, I raced to my doctor for emergency aid.

a. Paragraph 2 contains an irrelevant sentence.

b. Paragraph 2 lacks supporting details at one key spot.

c. Time order in paragraph 2 is confused.

d. Paragraph 2 contains two run-ons.

Healing the bites of chiggers, as the doctor diagnosed them to be,   3
is not a simple procedure. It seems that there is really no wonder drug or
commercial product to help. The victim must rely on a harsh and primitive
home remedy and mostly wait out the course of the painful bites. First,
the doctor explained, the skin must be bathed carefully in alcohol. An
antihistamine spray applied several hours later will soothe the intense
itching and help prevent infection. Before using the spray, I had to saturate

each bite with gasoline or nail polish to kill any remaining chiggers. A few days after the treatment, the bites finally healed. Although I was still in pain, and desperate for relief, I followed the doctor's instructions. I carefully applied gasoline to the bites and walked around for an hour smelling like a filling station.

a. Paragraph 3 contains an irrelevant sentence.
b. Paragraph 3 lacks supporting details at one key spot.
c. Time order in paragraph 3 is confused.
d. Paragraph 3 contains one fragment.

4   Most important of all, I learned what to do to prevent getting chigger bites in the future. Mainly, of course, stay out of the woods in the summertime. But if the temptation is too great on an especially beautiful day, I'll be sure to wear the right type of clothing, like a long-sleeved shirt, long pants, knee socks, and closed shoes. In addition, I'll cover myself with clouds of superstrength insect repellent. I will then shower thoroughly as soon as I get home, I also will probably burn all my clothes if I notice even one suspicious red speck.

a. Paragraph 4 contains an irrelevant sentence.
b. Paragraph 4 lacks supporting details at one key spot.
c. Paragraph 4 lacks transitional words.
d. Paragraph 4 contains a run-on and a fragment.

5   I will never forget my lessons on the cause, cure, and prevention of chigger bites. I'd gladly accept the challenge of rattlesnakes and scorpions in the wilds of the West but will never again confront a siege of chiggers in the pinewoods.

Essay 2

The Hazards of Being an Only Child

1   Many people who have grown up in multichild families think that being an only child is the best of all possible worlds. They point to such benefits as the only child's annual new wardrobe and the lack of competition for parental love. But single-child status isn't as good as people say it is. Instead of having everything they want, only children are sometimes denied certain basic human needs.

2   Only children lack companionship. An only child can have trouble making friends, since he or she isn't used to being around other children. Often, the only child comes home to an empty house; both parents are

working, and there are no brothers or sisters to play with or to talk to about the day. At dinner, the single child can't tell jokes, giggle, or throw food while the adults discuss boring adult subjects. An only child always has his or her own room but never has anyone to whisper to half the night when sleep doesn't come. Some only children thrive on this isolation and channel their energies into creative activities like writing or drawing. Owing to this lack of companionship, an only child sometimes lacks the social ease and self-confidence that come from being part of a close-knit group of contemporaries.

a. Paragraph 2 contains an irrelevant sentence.
b. Paragraph 2 lacks supporting details at one key spot.
c. Paragraph 2 lacks transitional words.
d. Paragraph 2 contains one fragment and one run-on.

Second, only children lack privacy. An only child is automatically the center of parental concern. There's never any doubt about which child tried to sneak in after midnight on a weekday. And who will get the lecture the next morning. Also, whenever an only child gives in to a bad mood, runs into his or her room, and slams the door, the door will open thirty seconds later, revealing an anxious parent. Parents of only children sometimes don't even understand the child's need for privacy. For example, they may not understand why a teenager wants a lock on the door or a personal telephone. After all, the parents think, there are only the three of us, there's no need for secrets.

a. Paragraph 3 contains an irrelevant sentence.
b. Paragraph 3 lacks supporting details at one key spot.
c. Paragraph 3 lacks transitional words.
d. Paragraph 3 contains one fragment and one run-on.

Most important, only children lack power. They get all the love; but if something goes wrong, they also get all the punishment. When a bottle of perfume is knocked to the floor or the television is left on all night, there's no little sister or brother to blame it on. Moreover, an only child has no recourse when asking for a privilege of some kind, such as permission to stay out late or to take an overnight trip with friends. There are no other siblings to point to and say, "You let them do it. Why won't you let me?" With no allies their own age, only children are always outnumbered, two to one. An only child hasn't a chance of influencing any major family decisions, either.

a. Paragraph 4 contains an irrelevant sentence.

b. Paragraph 4 lacks supporting details at one key spot.

c. Paragraph 4 lacks transitional words.

d. Paragraph 4 contains one fragment and one run-on.

Being an only child isn't as special as some people think. It's no fun being without friends, without privacy, and without power in one's own home. But the child who can triumph over these hardships grows up self-reliant and strong. Perhaps for this reason alone, the hazards are worth it.   5

Patterns of Essay Development

7 Introduction to Essay Development

7.1

Traditionally, essay writing has been divided into the following patterns of development:

- Description
- Narration
- Exposition

Examples	Comparison and contrast
Process	Definition
Cause and effect	Division and classification

- Argumentation

A *description* is a verbal picture of a person, place, or thing. In *narration,* a writer tells the story of something that happened.

In *exposition,* the writer provides information about and explains a particular subject. Patterns of development within exposition include giving *examples,* detailing a *process* of doing or making something, analyzing *causes and effects, comparing and contrasting, defining* a term or concept, and *dividing* something into parts or *classifying* it into categories.

Finally, in *argumentation,* a writer attempts to support a controversial point or to defend a position on which there is a difference of opinion.

The pages ahead present individual chapters on each pattern. You will have a chance, then, to learn nine different patterns or methods for organizing material in your papers. Each pattern has its own internal logic and provides its own special strategies for imposing order on your ideas. As you practice each pattern, keep these two points in mind:

- *Point 1:* While each essay that you write will involve one predominant pattern, very often one or more additional patterns may be involved. For example, consider the two student essays in Chapter 10, "Examples." The first essay there, "Everyday Cruelty" (page 207), is developed through a series of *examples.* But there is also an element of *narration,* because the writer presents examples that then support it in a variety of ways. To some extent, also, you will write papers to inform—to provide readers with information about a particular subject. And since, in practice, writing often combines purposes, you might also find yourself at times providing vivid or humorous details in order to entertain your readers.

Your audience will be primarily your instructor and sometimes other students. Your instructor is really a symbol of the larger audience you should see yourself writing for—educated adult readers who expect you to present your ideas in a clear, direct, organized way. If you can learn to write to persuade or inform such a general audience, you will have accomplished a great deal.

It will also be helpful for you to write some papers for a more specific audience. By doing so, you will develop an ability to choose words and adopt a tone and point of view that are just right for a given audience. This part of the book includes assignments asking you to write with very specific purposes in mind, and for very specific audiences.

Determining Your Point of View

When you write, you can take any of three approaches, or points of view: first person, second person, or third person.

First-Person Approach

In the first-person approach—a strongly individualized point of view—you draw on your own experience and speak to your audience in your own voice, using pronouns like *I, me, mine, we, our,* and *us.*

The first-person approach is most common in narrative essays based on personal experience. It also suits other essays where most of the evidence presented consists of personal observation.

Here is a first-person supporting paragraph from an essay on camping:

> First of all, I like comfort when I'm camping. My Airstream motor home, with its completely equipped kitchen, shower stall, toilet, double bed, and color television, resembles a mobile motel room. I can sleep on a real mattress, clean sheets, and fluffy pillows. Next to my bed are devices that make me feel at home: a radio, an alarm clock, and a TV remote-control unit. Unlike the poor campers huddled in tents, I don't have to worry about cold, rain, heat, or annoying insects. After a hot shower, I can slide into my best nightgown, sit comfortably on my down-filled quilt, and read the latest best-seller while a thunderstorm booms outside.

Second-Person Approach

In the second-person approach, the writer speaks directly to the reader, using the pronoun *you*. The second-person approach is considered appropriate for giving direct instructions and explanations to the reader. That is why *you* is used throughout this book.

You should plan to use the second-person approach only when writing a process essay. Otherwise, as a general rule, *never* use the word *you* in writing. (If doing so has been a common mistake in your writing, you should review the rule about pronoun point of view on pages 104–105.)

Third-Person Approach

The third-person approach is by far the most common point of view in academic writing. In the third person, the writer includes no direct references to the reader (*you*) or the self (*I, me*). Third person gets its name from the stance it suggests—that of an outsider or "third person" observing and reporting on matters of public rather than private importance. In this approach, you draw on information that you have gotten through observation, thinking, or reading.

Here is the paragraph on camping, recast in the third person. Note the third-person pronouns *their, them,* and *they,* which all refer to *campers* in the first sentence.

> First of all, modern campers bring complete bedrooms with them. Winnebagos, Airstream motor homes, and Fleetwood recreational vehicles lumber into America's campgrounds every summer like mobile motel rooms. All the comforts of home are provided inside. Campers sleep on real mattresses with clean sheets and fluffy pillows. Next to their beds are the same gadgets that litter their night tables at home—radios, alarm clocks, and TV remote-control units. It's not necessary for them to worry about annoyances like cold, heat, rain, or buzzing insects, either. They can sit comfortably in bed and read the latest best-sellers while a thunderstorm booms outside.

Using Peer Review

In addition to having your instructor as an audience for your writing, you will benefit from having another student in your class as an audience. On the day a paper is due, or on a day when you are writing papers in class, your instructor may ask you to pair up with another student. That student will read your paper, and you will read his or her paper.

Ideally, read the other paper aloud while your peer listens. If that is not practical, read it in a whisper while your peer looks on. As you read, both you and your peer should look and listen for spots where the paper does not read smoothly and clearly. Check or circle the trouble spots where your reading snags.

Your peer should then read your paper, marking possible trouble spots. Then each of you should do three things.

1 Identification

At the top of a separate sheet of paper, write the title and author of the paper you have read. Under it, write your name as the reader of the paper.

2 Scratch Outline

"X-ray" the paper for its inner logic by making up a scratch outline. The scratch outline need be no more than twenty words or so, but it should show clearly the logical foundation on which the essay is built. It should identify and summarize the overall point of the paper and the three areas of support for the point.

Your outline can look like this:

Point: _____

Support:

(1) _____

(2) _____

(3) _____

For example, here is a scratch outline of the essay on moviegoing on pages 7–8:

Point: Moviegoing is a problem. _____

Support:

(1) Inconvenience of going out _____

(2) Tempting snacks _____

(3) Other patrons _____

3 Comments

Under the outline, write a heading: "Comments." Here is what you should comment on:

- Look at the spots where your reading of the paper snagged. Are words missing or misspelled? Is there a lack of parallel structure? Are there mistakes with punctuation? Is the meaning of a sentence confused? Try to figure out what the problems are and suggest ways to fix them.
- Are there spots in the paper where you see problems with *unity, support,* or *organization?* (You'll find it helpful to refer to the checklist on the inside front cover of this book.) If so, offer comments. For example, you might say, "More details are needed in the first supporting paragraph," or, "Some of the details in the last supporting paragraph don't really back up your point."
- Finally, note something you really liked about the paper, such as good use of transitions or an especially realistic or vivid specific detail.

After you have completed your evaluation of the paper, give it to your peer. Your instructor may give you the option of rewriting a paper in light of the feedback you get. Whether or not you rewrite, be sure to hand in the peer-evaluation form with your paper.

Doing a Personal Review

1 While you're writing and revising an essay, you should be constantly evaluating it in terms of *unity, support,* and *organization.* Use as a guide the detailed checklist on the inside front cover of the book.

2 After you've finished the next-to-final draft of an essay, check it for the *sentence skills* listed on the inside front cover. It may also help to read the paper out loud. If a given sentence does not sound right—that is, if it does not read clearly and smoothly—chances are something is wrong. Then revise or edit as needed until your paper is error-free.

8 Description

When you describe someone or something, you give your readers a picture in words. To make the word picture as vivid and real as possible, you must observe and record specific details that appeal to your readers' senses (sight, hearing, taste, smell, and touch). More than any other type of essay, a descriptive paper needs sharp, colorful details.

Here is a sentence in which there is almost no appeal to the senses: "In the window was a fan." In contrast, here is a description rich in sense impressions: "The blades of the rusty window fan clattered and whirled as they blew out a stream of warm, soggy air." Sense impressions in this second example include sight (*rusty window fan, whirled*), hearing (*clattered*), and touch (*warm, soggy air*). The vividness and sharpness provided by the sensory details give us a clear picture of the fan and enable us to share the writer's experience.

In this chapter, you will be asked to describe a person, place, or thing sharply, by using words rich in sensory details. To prepare for this assignment, first read the student essays and the professional essay that follow and work through the questions that accompany the essays.

Student Essays to Consider

Family Portrait

My mother, who is seventy years old, recently sent me a photograph 1
of herself that I had never seen before. While cleaning out the attic of her
Florida home, she came across a studio portrait she had had taken about a
year before she married my father. This picture of my mother as a twenty-
year-old girl and the story behind it have fascinated me from the moment
I began to consider it.

The young woman in the picture has a face that resembles my own 2
in many ways. Her face is a bit more oval than mine, but the softly waving
brown hair around it is identical. The small, straight nose is the same model
I was born with. My mother's mouth is closed, yet there is just the slightest
hint of a smile on her full lips. I know that if she had smiled, she would have
shown the same wide grin and down-curving "smile lines" that appear

in my own snapshots. The most haunting feature in the photo, however, is my mother's eyes. They are an exact duplicate of my own large, dark-brown ones. Her brows are plucked into thin lines, which are like two pencil strokes added to highlight those fine, luminous eyes.

I've also carefully studied the clothing and jewelry in the photograph. Although the photo was taken fifty years ago, my mother is wearing a blouse and skirt that could easily be worn today. The blouse is made of heavy eggshell-colored satin and reflects the light in its folds and hollows. It has a turned-down cowl collar and smocking on the shoulders and below the collar. The smocking (tiny rows of gathered material) looks hand-done. The skirt, which covers my mother's calves, is straight and made of light wool or flannel. My mother is wearing silver drop earrings. They are about two inches long and roughly shield-shaped. On her left wrist is a matching bracelet. My mother can't find this bracelet now, despite the fact that we spent hours searching through the attic for it. On the third finger of her left hand is a ring with a large, square-cut stone. 3

The story behind the picture is as interesting to me as the young woman it captures. Mom, who was earning twenty-five dollars a week as a file clerk, decided to give her boyfriend (my father) a picture of herself. She spent almost two weeks' salary on the skirt and blouse, which she bought at a fancy department store downtown. She borrowed the earrings and bracelet from her older sister, my Aunt Dorothy. The ring she wore was a present from another young man she was dating at the time. Mom spent another chunk of her salary to pay the portrait photographer for the hand-tinted print in old-fashioned tones of brown and tan. Just before giving the picture to my father, she scrawled at the lower left, "Sincerely, Beatrice." 4

When I study this picture, I react in many ways. I think about the trouble that Mom went to in order to impress the young man who was to be my father. I laugh when I look at the ring, which was probably worn to make my father jealous. I smile at the serious, formal inscription my mother used at this stage of the budding relationship. Sometimes, I am filled with a mixture of pleasure and sadness when I look at this frozen long-ago moment. It is a moment of beauty, of love, and—in a way—of my own past. 5

The Diner at Midnight

I've been in lots of diners, and they've always seemed to be warm, busy, friendly, happy places. That's why, on a recent Monday night, I stopped in a diner for a cup of coffee. I was returning home after an all-day car trip and needed something to help me get through the last forty-five miles. I'd been visiting my cousins, whom I try to get together with at least twice a year. A diner at midnight, however, was not the place I had expected—it was different, and lonely. 1

Even the outside of the diner was uninviting. My Focus pulled to a halt in front of the dreary gray aluminum building, which looked like an old 2 railroad car. A half-lit neon sign sputtered the message "Fresh baked goods daily," reflected on the surface of the rain-slick parking lot. Only half a dozen cars and a battered pickup were scattered around the lot. An empty paper coffee cup made a hollow scraping sound as it rolled in small circles on one cement step close to the entrance. I pulled hard at the balky glass door, and it banged shut behind me.

The diner was quiet when I entered. As there was no hostess on duty,   3 only the faint odor of stale grease and the dull hum of an empty refrigerated pastry case greeted me. The outside walls were lined with vacant booths which squatted back to back in their black vinyl upholstery. On each black-and-white checkerboard-patterned table were the usual accessories—glass salt and pepper shakers, ketchup bottle, sugar packets—silently waiting for the next morning's breakfast crowd. I glanced through the round windows on the two swinging metal doors leading to the kitchen. I could see only part of the large, apparently deserted cooking area, with a shiny stainless-steel range and blackened pans of various sizes and shapes hanging along a ledge.

I slid onto one of the cracked vinyl seats at the Formica counter. Two   4 men in rumpled work shirts also sat at the counter, on stools several feet apart, smoking cigarettes and staring wearily into cups of coffee. Their faces sprouted what looked like a daylong stubble of beard. I figured they were probably shift workers who, for some reason, didn't want to go home. Three stools down from the workers, I spotted a thin young man with a mop of curly black hair. He was dressed in new-looking jeans with a black Gap polo shirt, unbuttoned at the neck. He wore a blank expression as he picked at a plate of limp french fries. I wondered if he had just returned from a disappointing date. At the one occupied booth sat a middle-aged couple. They hadn't gotten any food yet. He was staring off into space, idly tapping his spoon against the table, while she drew aimless parallel lines on her paper napkin with a bent dinner fork. Neither said a word to the other. The people in the diner seemed as lonely as the place itself.

Finally, a tired-looking waitress approached me with her thick order   5 pad. I ordered the coffee, but I wanted to drink it fast and get out of there. My car, and the solitary miles ahead of me, would be lonely. But they wouldn't be as lonely as that diner at midnight.

QUESTIONS

About Unity

1. In which supporting paragraph of "The Diner at Midnight" does the topic sentence appear at the paragraph's end, rather than the beginning?

   a. paragraph 2

   b. paragraph 3

   c. paragraph 4

2. Which sentence in paragraph 1 of "The Diner at Midnight" should be eliminated in the interest of paragraph unity? (*Write the opening words.*)

   I'd been visiting my cousins . . .

3. Which of the following sentences from paragraph 3 of "Family Portrait" should be omitted in the interest of paragraph unity?

   a. Although the photo was taken fifty years ago, my mother is wearing a blouse and skirt that could easily be worn today.

   b. It has a turned-down cowl collar and smocking on the shoulders and below the collar.

   (c.) My mother can't find this bracelet now, despite the fact that we spent hours searching the attic for it.

   d. On the third finger of her left hand is a ring with a large, square-cut stone.

About Support

4. How many separate items of clothing and jewelry are described in paragraph 3 of "Family Portrait"?

   a. four

   (b.) five

   c. seven

5. Label as sight, touch, hearing, or smell all the sensory details in the following sentences taken from the two essays. The first one is done for you as an example.

   a. "As there was no hostess on duty, only the faint odor of stale grease and the [*smell*] [*sight*] dull hum of an empty refrigerated pastry case greeted me." [*hearing* *sight*]

   b. "He was staring off into space, idly tapping his spoon against the table, [*sight*] [*hearing*] while she drew aimless parallel lines on her paper napkin with a bent [*sight*] dinner fork."

   c. "The blouse is made of heavy eggshell-colored satin and reflects the light [*touch* *sight* *sight*] in its folds and hollows." [*sight*]

   d. Her brows are plucked into thin lines, which are like two pencil strokes [*touch* *sight* *sight*] added to highlight those fine, luminous eyes. [*sight*]

6. What are three details in paragraph 3 of "The Diner at Midnight" that reinforce the idea of "quiet" expressed in the topic sentence?

... dull hum ...

... silently waiting ...

... deserted cooking area ...

About Coherence

6

7. Which method of organization does paragraph 2 of "Family Portrait" use?
    a. Time order
    b. Emphatic order

8. Which sentence in paragraph 2 of "Family Portrait" suggests the method of organization? *(Write the opening words.)*
    The most haunting feature in the photo, ...

9. The last paragraph of "The Diner at Midnight" begins with a word that serves as which type of signal?
    a. time
    b. addition
    c. contrast
    d. illustration

About the Introduction and Conclusion

8

10. Which statement best describes the introduction to "The Diner at Midnight"?
    a. It starts with an idea that is the opposite of the one then developed.
    b. It explains the importance of the topic to its readers.
    c. It begins with a general statement of the topic and narrows it down to a thesis statement.
    d. It begins with an anecdote.

Developing a Descriptive Essay

Considering Purpose and Audience

The main purpose of a descriptive essay is to make readers see—or hear, taste, smell, or feel—what you are writing about. Vivid details are the key to descriptive essays, enabling your audience to picture and, in a way, experience what you describe.

As you start to think about your own descriptive essay, choose a topic that appeals strongly to at least one of your senses. It's possible to write a descriptive essay, maybe even a good one, about a boiled potato. But it would be easier (not to mention more fun) to describe a bowl of potato salad, with its contrasting textures of soft potato, crisp celery, and spongy hard-boiled egg: the crunch of the diced onion; the biting taste of the bits of pickle; the salad's creamy dressing and its tangy seasonings. The more senses you involve, the more likely your audience is to enjoy your paper.

Also, when selecting your topic, consider how much your audience already knows about it. If your topic is a familiar one— for instance, potato salad—you can assume your audience already understands the general idea. However, if you are presenting something new or unfamiliar to your readers—perhaps a description of one of your relatives or a place where you've lived—you must provide background information.

Once you have selected your topic, focus on the goal or purpose of your essay. What message do you hope to convey to your audience? For instance, if you chose as your topic a playground you used to visit as a child, decide what dominant impression you want to communicate. Is your goal to make readers see the park as a pleasant play area, or do you want them to see it as a dangerous place? If you choose the second option, focus on conveying that sense of danger to your audience. Then jot down any details which support that idea. You might describe broken beer bottles on the asphalt, graffiti sprayed on the metal jungle gym, or a pack of loud teenagers gathered on a nearby street corner. In this case, the details support your overall purpose, creating a threatening picture that your audience can see and understand.

Development through Prewriting

When Cindy, the author of "Family Portrait," sat down to think about a topic for her essay, she looked around her apartment for inspiration. First she thought about describing her own bedroom. But she had moved into the apartment only recently and hadn't done much in the way of decorating, so the room struck her as too bare and sterile. Then she looked out her window, thinking of describing the view. That seemed much more promising: she noticed the sights and sounds of children playing on the sidewalks and a group of older men playing cards, as well as smells—neighbors' cooking and exhaust from passing traffic. She was jotting down some details for such an essay when she glanced up at the framed portrait of her mother on her desk. "I stopped and stared at it, as I often do, wondering again about this twenty-year-old girl who became my mother," she said. "While I sat there studying it, I realized that the best topic of all was right under my nose."

As she looked at the photograph, Cindy began to freewrite. This is what she wrote:

Mom is twenty in the picture. She's wearing a beautiful skirt and blouse and jewelry she borrowed from Dorothy. Looks a lot like me—nose, eyes, mouth. She's shorter than I am but you really can't tell in picture. Looks a lot like old photos I've seen of Grandma too—all the Diaz women resemble each other. Earrings and bracelet are of silver and they match. Ring might be amber or topaz? We've laughed about the "other man" who gave it to her. Her brown hair is down loose on her shoulders. She's smiling a little. That doesn't really look like her—her usual smile is bigger and opens her mouth. Looking at the photo makes me a little sad even though I really like it. Makes me realize how much older she's getting and I wonder how long she'll be with us. It's funny to see a picture of your parent at a younger age than you are now—stirs up all kinds of weird feelings. Picture was taken at a studio in Houston to give to Dad. Signed "Sincerely, Beatrice." So serious! Hard to imagine them being so formal with each other.

Cindy looked over her notes and thought about how she might organize her essay. First she thought only of describing how the photograph *looked*. With that in mind, she thought her main points might be (1) what her mother's face looked like and (2) what her mother was wearing. But she was stuck for a third main point.

Studying her notes again, Cindy noticed two other possible main points. One was her own emotional reaction to the photo—how it made her feel. The other was the story of the photo—how and why it was taken. Not sure which of those two she would use as her third main point, she began to write. Her first draft follows.

First Draft

Family Portrait

I have a photograph of my mother that was taken fifty years ago, when she was only twenty. She sent it to me only recently, and I find it very interesting.

In the photo, I see a girl who looks a good deal like I do, even though it's been a long time since I was twenty. Like most of the women in her family, including me, the girl in the picture has a short, straight nose, waving brown hair, and large brown eyes. Her mouth is closed and she is smiling slightly. That isn't my mother's usual big grin that shows her teeth and her "smile lines."

In the photo, Mom is wearing a very pretty skirt and blouse. They look like something that would be fashionable today. The blouse is made of heavy satin. The satin falls in lines and hollows that reflect the light. It has a turned-down cowl collar and smocking on the shoulders and under the collar. Her skirt is below her knees and looks like it is made of light wool. She is wearing jewelry. Her silver earrings and bracelet match. She had borrowed them from her sister. Dorothy eventually gave them both to her, but the bracelet has disappeared. On her left hand is a ring with a big yellow stone.

When I look at this photo, I feel conflicting emotions. It gives me pleasure to see Mom as a pretty young woman. It makes me sad, too, to think how quickly time passes and realize how old she is getting. It amuses me to read the inscription to my father, her boyfriend at the time. She wrote, "Sincerely, Beatrice." It's hard for me to imagine Mom and Dad ever being so formal with each other.

Mom had the photograph taken at a studio near where she worked in Houston. She spent nearly two weeks' salary on the outfit she wore for it. She must have really wanted to impress my father to go to all that trouble and expense.

Development through Revising

4.3

Cindy showed this first draft to her classmate Elena, who read it and returned it with these notes jotted in the margin:

Reader's Comments

Was this the first time you'd seen it? Where's it been? And "very interesting" doesn't really say anything. Be more specific about why it interests you.

The "Diaz family nose" isn't helpful for someone who doesn't know the Diaz family—describe it!

Nice beginning, but I still can't quite picture her. Can you add more specific detail? Does anything about her face really stand out?

Color?

This is nice—I can picture the material.

What is smocking?

How—what are they like?

Family Portrait

I have a photograph of my mother that was taken fifty years ago, when she was only twenty. She sent it to me only recently, and I find it very interesting.

In the photo, I see a girl who looks a good deal like I do, even though it's been a long time since I was twenty. Like most of the women in her family, including me, the girl in the picture has a short, straight nose, waving brown hair, and large brown eyes. Her mouth is closed and she is smiling slightly. That isn't my mother's usual big grin that shows her teeth and her "smile lines."

In the photo, Mom is wearing a very pretty skirt and blouse. They look like something that would be fashionable today. The blouse is made of heavy satin. The satin falls in lines and hollows that reflect the light. It has a turned-down cowl collar and smocking on the shoulders and under the collar. Her skirt is below her knees and looks like it is made of light wool. She is wearing jewelry. Her silver earrings and bracelet match. She had borrowed them from her sister. Dorothy eventually gave them both to her, but the bracelet

It'd make more sense for the main points of the essay to be about your mom and the photo. How about making this—your reaction—the conclusion of the essay?

has disappeared. On her left hand is a ring with a big yellow stone.

When I look at this photo, I feel conflicting emotions. It gives me pleasure to see Mom as a pretty young woman. It makes me sad, too, to think how quickly time passes and realize how old she is getting. It amuses me to read the inscription to my father, her boyfriend at the time. She wrote, "Sincerely, Beatrice." It's hard for me to imagine Mom and Dad ever being so formal with each other.

This is interesting stuff—she really did go to a lot of trouble to have the photo taken. I think the story of the photograph deserves to be a main point.

Mom had the photograph taken at a studio near where she worked in Houston. She spent nearly two weeks' salary on the outfit she wore for it. She must have really wanted to impress my father to go to all that trouble and expense.

Making use of Elena's comments and her own reactions upon rereading her essay, Cindy wrote the final draft that appears on page 170.

A Professional Essay to Consider

Read the following professional essay. Then answer the questions and read the comments that follow.

Lou's Place

by Beth Johnson

(Activity 3)

Imagine a restaurant where your every whim is catered to, your every 1 want satisfied, your every request granted without hesitation. The people on the staff live to please you. They hover anxiously as you sample your selection, waiting for your judgment. Your pleasure is their delight, your dissatisfaction their dismay.

Lou's isn't that kind of place.   2

At Lou's Kosy Korner Koffee Shop, the mock abuse flows like a cup of 3 spilled Folgers. Customers are yelled at, lectured, blamed, mocked, teased, and ignored. They pay for the privilege of pouring their own coffee and scrambling their own eggs. As in a fond but dysfunctional family, Lou displays his affection through criticism and insults, and his customers respond in kind. If Lou's had a slogan, it might be, "If I'm polite to you, ask yourself what's wrong."

Lou's is one of three breakfast joints located in the business district of a 4 small mid-Atlantic town. The county courthouse is nearby, supplying a steady stream of lawyers, jurors, and office workers looking for a bite to eat. A local trucking firm also provides Lou with customers as its drivers come and go in town. Lou's is on the corner. Beside it is a jewelry shop ("In Business Since 1946—Watch Repairs Our Speciality") and an upscale home accessories store that features bonsai trees and hand-painted birdhouses in its window. There's a bus stop in front of Lou's. Lou himself has been known to storm out onto the sidewalk to shoo away people who've dismounted from the bus and lingered too long on the corner.

The sign on Lou's front door says "Open 7 A.M.–3 P.M." But by 6:40 on a 5 brisk spring morning, the restaurant's lights are on, the door is unlocked, and Lou is settled in the booth nearest the door, with the *Philadelphia Inquirer* spread over the table. Lou is sunk deep into the booth's brown vinyl seat, its rips neatly mended with silver duct tape. He is studying the box scores from the night before as a would-be customer pauses on the sidewalk, unsure whether to believe the sign or her own eyes. She opens the door enough to stick her head in.

"Are you open?" she asks.   6

Without lifting his eyes from the paper, Lou answers. "I'm here, aren't I?"   7

Unsure how to interpret this remark, the woman enters and sits at a 8 booth. Lou keeps studying the paper. He begins to hum under his breath. The woman starts tracing a pattern on the glass-topped table with her fingernail. She pulls out her checkbook and pretends to balance it. After a few long minutes, Lou apparently reaches a stopping point in his reading. He rises, his eyes still on the folded newspaper he carries with him. His humming breaks into low-volume song as he trudges behind the counter. "Maaaaaaaake someone happy . . . Make-make-maaaaaake someone happy," he croons as he lifts the steaming pot that has infused the room with the rich aroma of freshly brewed coffee. He carries it to the woman's table, fills her cup, and drops two single-serving containers of half-and-half nearby. He then peers over the tops of his reading glasses at his customer. "You want anything else, dear?" he asks, his bushy gray eyebrows rising with the question.

She shakes her head. "I'm meeting someone. I'll order when he gets 9 here."

Lou nods absently, his eyes back on his paper. As he shuffles back to his 10 seat, he mutters over his shoulder, "Hope he shows up before three. I close then."

Lou reads his paper; the woman drinks her coffee and gazes around the   11
room. It's a small restaurant: just an eight-seat counter and seven padded
booths. A grill, coffeepots, and a huge stainless-steel refrigerator line the
wall behind the counter. Under the glass top of the tables is the breakfast
menu: it offers eggs, pancakes, home fries, bacon, and sausage. A wall rack
holds Kellogg's Jumbo Packs of single-serving cereals: smiling toucans and
cheerful tigers offer Froot Loops and Frosted Flakes.

Two poster-size photographs hang side by side at the far wall. One is   12
of Lou and his wife on their wedding day. They appear to be in their mid-
twenties. He is slim, dark-haired, beaming; his arm circles the shoulders of
his fair-haired bride. The other photo shows the same couple in an identical
pose—only in this one, Lou looks much as he is today. His short white hair
is parted at the side; a cropped white beard emphasizes his prominent
red mouth. His formerly slim figure now expands to take up much of the
photograph. But the smile is the same as he embraces his silver-haired wife.

The bell at the door tinkles; two sleepy-eyed men in flannel shirts, work   13
boots, and oil-company caps walk in. Lou glances up and grunts at them; they
nod. One picks up an *Inquirer* from the display stand and leaves two quarters
on the cash register. They drop onto seats at the counter, simultaneously
swivel to look at the woman in the booth behind them, and then turn back.
For a few minutes, they flip through the sports section. Lou doesn't move.
One man rises from his seat and wanders behind the counter to find cups and
the coffeepot. He fills the cups, returns to his seat, and immerses himself in
the paper. There is no noise but the occasional slurping of men sipping hot
coffee.

Minutes pass. Finally one of the men speaks. "Lou," he says. "Can I   14
maybe get some breakfast?"

"I'm reading the paper," says Lou. "Eggs are in the refrigerator."   15

The man sighs and lumbers behind the counter again. "In some   16
restaurants, they actually cook for ya," he says, selecting eggs from the
carton.

Lou doesn't raise his eyes. "In some restaurants, they wouldn't let a guy   17
with a face like yours in."

The room falls silent again, except for the splatter of grease on the grill   18
and the scrape of the spatula as the customer scrambles his eggs. He heaps
them onto his plate, prepares some toast, and returns to his seat. The bell at
the door begins tinkling as the breakfast rush begins—men, mostly, about
half in work clothes and the rest in suits. They pour in on a wave of talk
and laughter. Lou reluctantly rises and goes to work behind the counter,
volleying comments with the regulars:

"Three eggs, Lou," says one.   19

"Three eggs. One heart attack wasn't enough for you? You want some   20
bacon grease on top of that?"

A large red-haired man in blue jeans and a faded denim shirt walks in 21 with a newspaper, which he reads as he waits for his cup of takeout coffee. "Anything good in the paper, Dan?" Lou asks.

"Not a thing," drawls Dan. "Not a *damn* thing. The only good thing is 22 that the machine down the street got my fifty cents instead of you."

Lou flips pancakes as the restaurant fills to capacity. The hum of voices 23 fills the room as the aromas of coffee, bacon, eggs, and toasting bread mingle in the air. A group of suits[1] from the nearby courthouse slide into the final empty booth. After a moment one rises, goes behind the counter, and rummages in a drawer.

"Whatcha need, Ben?" Lou asks, pouring more batter. 24

"Rag," Ben answers. He finds one, returns to the booth, and wipes 25 crumbs off the tabletop. A minute later he is back to drop a slice of ham on the hot grill. He and Lou stand side by side attending to their cooking, as comfortable in their silence as an old married couple. When the ham is sizzling and its rich fragrance reaches the far corners of the room, Ben slides it onto a plate and returns to his booth.

Filled plate in hand, Lou approaches a woman sitting at the counter. Her 26 golden hair contrasts with her sunken cheeks and her wrinkled lips sucking an unfiltered Camel. "You wanna I put this food in your ashtray, or are you gonna move it?" Lou growls. The woman moves the ashtray aside.

"Sorry, Lou," she says. 27

"I'm not really yelling at you, dear," he answers. 28

"I know," says the woman. "I'm glad *you're* here this morning." She 29 lowers her voice. "That girl you've got working here sometimes, Lou—she doesn't *like* me." Lou rolls his eyes, apparently at the poor taste of the waitress, and moves down to the cash register. As he rings up a bill, a teenage girl enters and walks by silently. Lou glares after her. "Start the day with a 'Good morning,' please," he instructs.

"Good morning, Lou," she replies obediently. 30

"*Very* nice," he mutters, still punching the cash-register buttons. "Thank 31 you *so* much for your concern. I get up at the crack of dawn to make your breakfast, but don't bother saying 'good morning' to *me*."

The day's earliest arrival, the woman in the booth, has been joined by a 32 companion. They order eggs and hash browns. As Lou slides the filled plates before them, he reverts briefly to the conventional manners he saves for first-timers. "Enjoy your meal," he says.

"Thank you," says the woman. "May I have some hot sauce?" 33

Lou's reserve of politeness is instantly exhausted. "Hot sauce. Jeez. She 34 wants *hot sauce*!" he announces to the room at large. "Anything else? Some caviar on the side, maybe?" He disappears behind the counter, reemerging with an enormous red bottle. "Here you are. It's a new bottle. Don't use it all,

[1]*suits:* business executives or professionals (people wearing business suits).

please. I'd like to save a little for other customers. Hey, on second thought, use it all if you want. Then I'll know you'll like my chili." Laughing loudly at his own joke, he refills the woman's coffee cup without being asked. Golden-brown coffee splashes into her saucer. Lou ignores it.

Lou's waitress, Stacy, has arrived, and begins taking orders and delivering 35 meals. Lou alternates between working the grill and clearing tables. Mid-stride, he halts before the golden-haired woman at the counter, who has pushed her plate aside and is lighting another cigarette. "What? What is this?" he demands.

"Looouuu . . . " she begins soothingly, a stream of smoke jetting from 36 her mouth with the word.

"Don't 'Lou' me," he retorts. "You don't eat your toast, you don't eat your 37 potatoes, you barely touch your eggs. Whatcha gonna live on? Camels?"

"Awww, Lou," she says, but she pulls her plate back and eats a few more 38 bites.

As the rush of customers slows to a trickle, Lou returns to the register, 39 making change and conversation, talking Phillies and the weather. One of the flannel-shirted men rises from his counter seat and heads for the door, dropping his money on the counter. "'Bye, Stacy," he says to the waitress. "Have a nice day."

"'Bye, Mel," she replies. "You too."   40

"What about me?" Lou calls after Mel.   41

Mel doesn't pause. "Who cares what kind of a day *you* have?"   42

Mel disappears into the morning sunshine; the Camel lady pulls a 43 crossword puzzle out of her purse and taps an unlit cigarette rapidly against the counter. Stacy wipes the tables and empties a wastebasket of its load of dark, wet coffee grounds. Lou butters a piece of toast and returns to his favorite booth. He spreads out his newspaper again, then glances up to catch the eye of the hot-sauce woman. "Where's your friend?" he asks.

"He left," she replies.   44

"He left you, eh?" Lou asks.   45

"No, he didn't *leave* me. He just had to go to work . . . "   46

"Dump him," Lou responds automatically. "And now, if you don't mind 47 *very* much, I would like to finish my newspaper."

QUESTIONS

About Unity

1. What is the thesis of Johnson's essay? If it is stated directly, locate the relevant sentence or sentences. If it is implied, state the thesis in your own words.

   Lou's coffee shop is like "a fond but dysfunctional family." (Wording may vary.)

2. Which statement would best serve as a topic sentence for paragraph 13?

   a. Many of Lou's customers are, like him, interested in the Philadelphia sports teams.

   b. Lou doesn't mind if customers serve themselves coffee.

   c. Lou apparently disliked the two men in oil-company caps who came into the restaurant.

   d. Regular customers at Lou's are used to taking care of themselves while Lou reads his paper.

About Support

3. In paragraph 3, Johnson claims that Lou and his customers are fond of one another. How does she support that claim in the case of the golden-haired woman who is first mentioned in paragraph 26?

   Lou is concerned that she is smoking rather than eating.

4. Which of these sentences from "Lou's Place" best supports the idea that customers enjoy the unusual atmosphere at the coffee shop?

   a. "The bell at the door tinkles; two sleepy-eyed men in flannel shirts, work boots, and oil-company caps walk in."

   b. "He and Lou stand side by side attending to their cooking, as comfortable in their silence as an old married couple."

   c. "As [Lou] rings up a bill, a teenage girl enters and walks by silently."

   d. "Mid-stride, [Lou] halts before the golden-haired lady at the counter, who has pushed her plate aside and is lighting another cigarette."

5. Check each sense appealed to in the passage below from "Lou's Place."

   "Maaaaaaaake someone happy . . . Make-make-maaaaaaake someone happy," he croons as he lifts the steaming pot that has infused the room with the rich aroma of freshly brewed coffee. He carries it to the woman's table, fills her cup, and drops two single-serving containers of half-and-half nearby.

   Sight ___✓___ Hearing ___✓___ Taste _____ Smell ___✓___ Touch _____

About Coherence

6. Which of the following sentences contains a change-of-direction signal?

   a. "'You want anything else, dear?' he asks, his bushy gray eyebrows rising with the question."

    b. "In some restaurants, they wouldn't let a guy with a face like yours in."

    c. "After a moment one rises, goes behind the counter, and rummages in a drawer."

    (d.) "I get up at the crack of dawn to make your breakfast, but don't bother saying 'good morning' to *me*."

7. Which sentence in paragraph 23 begins with a time signal? (*Write the opening words of that sentence.*)

    <u>After a moment . . .</u>

8. The sentence that makes up paragraph 38 includes which of the following types of transition?

    a. time

    b. addition

    (c.) change of direction

    d. conclusion

About the Introduction and Conclusion

9. Which statement describes the style of Johnson's introduction?

    (a.) It presents a situation that is the opposite of the one that will be developed.

    b. It explains the importance of the topic to the reader.

    c. It asks a question.

10. Which statement describes the conclusion of "Lou's Place"?

    a. It summarizes its description of the coffee shop.

    (b.) It ends with a comment of Lou's that characterizes the mood of his shop.

    c. It ends with a prediction of the future of the coffee shop.

Writing a Descriptive Essay

WRITING ASSIGNMENT 1

Write an essay about a particular place that you can observe carefully or that you already know well. You might choose one of the following or another place that you think of:

Pet shop

Doctor's waiting room

Laundromat

Bar or nightclub

Video arcade

Library study area

Your bedroom or the bedroom of someone you know

Locker room after the winning or loss of an important game

Waiting room at train station, bus terminal, or airport

Antique shop or some other small shop

Prewriting

a Remember that, like all essays, a descriptive paper must have a thesis. Your thesis should state a dominant impression about the place you are describing. Write a short single sentence in which you name the place you want to describe and the dominant impression you want to make. Don't worry if your sentence doesn't seem quite right as a thesis—you can refine it later. For now, you just want to find and express a workable topic. Here are some examples of such sentences:

The study area was noisy.

The bedroom was well-organized.

The pet shop was crowded.

The restaurant was noisy.

The bus terminal was frightening.

The locker room was glum.

The exam room was tense.

b Once you have written your sentence, make a list of as many details as you can to support that general impression. For example, this is the list made by the writer of "The Diner at Midnight":

Tired workers at counter

Rainy parking lot

Vacant booths

Quiet

Few cars in lot

Dreary gray building

Lonely young man

Silent middle-aged couple

Out-of-order neon sign

No hostess

Couldn't see anyone in kitchen

Tired-looking waitress

c   Organize your paper according to one or a combination of the following:

Physical order—move from left to right or from far to near, or follow some other consistent order.

Size—Begin with large features or objects and work down to smaller ones.

A special order—Use an order that is appropriate to your subject.

For example, the writer of "The Diner at Midnight" builds his essay around the dominant impression of loneliness. The paper is organized in terms of physical order (from the parking lot to the entrance to the interior); a secondary method of organization is size (large parking lot to smaller diner to still smaller people).

d   Use as many senses as possible in describing a scene. Chiefly you will use sight, but to an extent you may be able to use touch, hearing, smell, and perhaps even taste as well. Remember that it is through the richness of your sense impressions that the reader will gain a picture of the scene.

e   Proceed to write the first draft of your essay.

Revising

ALLWRITE!
4.3

After you have completed the first draft of the paper, set it aside for a while—if possible, until the next day. When you review the draft, try to do so as critically as you would if it were not your own work. Ask yourself these questions:

- Does my paper have a clearly stated thesis, including a dominant impression?
- Have I provided rich, specific details that appeal to a variety of senses (sight, hearing, smell, taste, touch)?
- Is there any irrelevant material that should be eliminated or rewritten?
- Have I organized my essay in some consistent manner—physical order, size, time progression, or another way that is appropriate to my subject?

- Have I used transition words to help readers follow my train of thought?
- Do I have a concluding paragraph that provides a summary, a final thought, or both?

As you revise your essay through one or more additional drafts, continue to refer to this list until you can answer "yes" to each question. Then be sure to check the next-to-final draft of the paper for the sentence skills listed on the inside front cover.

WRITING ASSIGNMENT 2

Write an essay about a family portrait. (The picture may be of an individual or a group.)

Prewriting

a   Decide how you will organize your essay. Your decision will depend on what seems appropriate for the photograph. Two possibilities are these:

> As in "Family Portrait," you might use the first supporting paragraph to describe the subjects' faces, the second to describe their clothing and jewelry, and the third to describe the story behind the picture.

> Another possible order might be, first, the people in the photograph (and how they look); second, the relationships among the people (and what they are doing in the photo); and third, the story behind the picture (time, place, occasion, other circumstances).

b   Make a scratch outline for your essay, based on the organization you have chosen.

c   Using your scratch outline as a guide, make a list of details that support each of your main points. As practice in doing this, complete this list of details based on "Family Portrait":

A.   Mother's face

Small, straight nose
Slight smile on her full lips
Large, dark eyes

Plucked eyebrows
_____

Oval face
_____

Wavy brown hair
_____

Continued

B.   Mother's clothing and jewelry

Blouse of heavy satin
Blouse is eggshell-colored
Cowl collar
Smocking on blouse
Light wool skirt

Silver earrings

Bracelet

Ring

C.   Story behind the photo

Mother spent two weeks' salary on clothing
Borrowed jewelry from sister
Ring from another man

Signature ("Sincerely . . .")

d   Use your scratch outline and list of details to write your first draft.

Revising

Refer to the guidelines for revising provided on page 186 with Writing Assignment 1.

WRITING ASSIGNMENT 3

Write an essay describing a person. First, decide on your dominant impression of the person, and then use only those details that will add to it. Here are some examples of interesting types of people you might want to write about:

Campus character	Competitor	Drunk
Dentist	Clergyman	Employer
Bus driver	Clergywoman	TV or movie personality
Close friend	Teacher	Street person
Rival	Child	Older person
White-collar crook	Bum	Hero

WRITING ASSIGNMENT 4

Writing for a Specific Purpose and Audience

In this descriptive essay, you will write with a specific purpose and for a specific audience. Imagine that you have subscribed to a video dating service. Clients of the service are asked to make a five-minute presentation that will be recorded on videotape. Write a paper in which you describe yourself. Your goal is to give interested members of the dating service a good sense of what you are like.

Prewriting

a   Decide how you will organize your presentation. What aspects of yourself will you describe? Remember, your presentation will be recorded on videotape, so viewers of the tape will see for themselves what you look like. Therefore it won't be necessary to describe your appearance.

You might organize your presentation in terms of describing your attitudes and beliefs, your interests, and your personal habits. Other ideas you might use as main points could be your hopes for the future, how you spend a typical day, or your imaginary perfect date.

b   Focus on each of the main points you've decided to write on, and ask yourself questions to generate details to support each one. For example, if you were going to write about your perfect date, you would ask questions like these:

Where would I go?

What would I do?

What time of day would the date occur?

Why would I enjoy this date so much?

How would I travel to my destination?

Continue questioning until you have a number of rich, specific, sensory details to support each of your main points.

c   Plan a brief introductory paragraph that will indicate to your viewer how you'll organize your presentation. For instance, one student might write, "I'm Terry Jefferson. I'm going to tell you something about what I believe, what I enjoy doing, and what I hope to accomplish in the future."

d   Write the first draft of your presentation.

Revising

Once you have the first draft of your paper completed, review it with these questions in mind:

- Does my introduction indicate a clear plan of development?
- Is my presentation clearly organized according to three main points?
- Have I filled each of my supporting paragraphs with rich, descriptive details that help the viewer vividly imagine me?
- Have I rounded off my presentation with an appropriate concluding paragraph?
- Have I proofread my presentation, referring to the list of sentence skills on the inside front cover?

9 Narration

7.2

Children beg to hear a beloved story read again and again. Over dinner, tired adults tell each other about their day. A restless class is hushed when a teacher says, "Let me tell you something strange that happened to me once." Whatever our age, we never outgrow our hunger for stories. Just as our ancestors entertained and instructed each other with tales of great hunts and battles, of angry gods and foolish humans, we still love to share our lives and learn about others through storytelling.

Narration is storytelling, whether we are relating a single story or several related ones. Through narration, we make a statement clear by relating in detail something that has happened to us. In the story we tell, we present the details in the order in which they happened. A person might say, for example, "I was really embarrassed the day I took my driver's test," and then go on to develop that statement with an account of the experience. If the story is sharply detailed, we will be able to see and understand just why the speaker felt that way.

In this chapter, you'll be asked to tell a story that illustrates some point. To prepare for this assignment, first read the student essays and the professional essay that follow and work through the questions that accompany the essays. All three essays use narratives to develop their points.

Student Essays to Consider

Adopting a Handicap

My church recently staged a "Sensitivity Sunday" to make our congregation more aware of the problems faced by people with physical disabilities. We were asked to "adopt a disability" for several hours one Sunday morning. Some members, like me, chose to use wheelchairs. Others wore sound-blocking earplugs, hobbled around on crutches, or wore blindfolds.

Just sitting in the wheelchair was instructive. I had never considered before how awkward it would be to use one. As soon as I sat down, my weight made the chair begin to roll. Its wheels were not locked, and I fumbled clumsily to correct that. Another awkward moment occurred when I realized I had no place to put my feet. I fumbled some more to turn the

1

2

metal footrest into place. I felt psychologically awkward as well, as I took my first uneasy look at what was to be my only means of transportation for several hours. I realized that for many people, "adopting a wheelchair" is not a temporary experiment. That was a sobering thought as I sank back into my seat.

Once I sat down, I had to learn how to cope with the wheelchair. I   3
shifted around, trying to find a comfortable position. I thought it might be restful, even kind of nice, to be pushed around for a while. I glanced around to see who would be pushing me and then realized I would have to navigate the contraption by myself! My palms reddened and my wrist and forearm muscles started to ache as I tugged at the heavy metal wheels. I realized, as I veered this way and that, that steering and turning were not going to be easy tasks. Trying to make a right-angle turn from one aisle to another, I steered straight into a pew. I felt as though everyone was staring at me and commenting on my clumsiness.

When the service started, other problems cropped up to frustrate   4
me further. Every time the congregation stood up, my view was blocked. I could not see the minister, the choir, or the altar. Also, as the church's aisles were narrow, I seemed to be in the way no matter where I parked myself. For instance, the ushers had to squeeze by me to pass the collection plate. This made me feel like a nuisance. Thanks to a new building program, however, our church will soon have the wide aisles and well-spaced pews that will make life easier for the disabled. After the service ended, when people stopped to talk to me, I had to strain my neck and look up at them. This made me feel like a little child being talked down to and added to my sense of powerlessness.

My wheelchair experiment was soon over. It's true that it made an   5
impression on me. I no longer resent large tax expenditures for ramp-equipped buses, and I wouldn't dream of parking my car in a space marked "Handicapped Only." But I also realize how little I know about the daily life of a truly disabled person. A few hours of voluntary "disability" gave me only a hint of the challenges, both physical and emotional, that people with handicaps must overcome.

A Night of Violence

According to my history instructor, Adolf Hitler once said that he   1
wanted to sign up "brutal youths" to help him achieve his goals. If Hitler were still alive, he wouldn't have any trouble recruiting the brutal youths he wanted; he could get them right here in the United States. I know, because I was one of them. As a teenager, I ran with a gang. And it took a frightening incident for me to see how violent I had become.

The incident was planned one Thursday night when I was out with my   2
friends. I was still going to school once in a while, but most of my friends

weren't. We spent our days on the streets, talking, showing off, sometimes shoplifting a little or shaking people down for a few dollars. My friends and I were close, maybe because life hadn't been very good to any of us. On this night, we were drinking wine and vodka on the corner. For some reason, we all felt tense and restless. One of us came up with the idea of robbing one of the old people who lived in the high-rise close by. We would just knock him or her over, grab the money, and party with it.

The robbery did not go as planned. After about an hour, and after more wine and vodka, we spotted an old man. He came out of the glass door of the building and started up the street. Pine Street had a lot of antique stores as well as apartment buildings. Stuffing our bottles in our jacket pockets, we closed in behind him. Suddenly, the old man whipped out a homemade wooden club from under his jacket and began swinging. The club thudded loudly against Victor's shoulder, making him yelp with pain. When we heard that, we went crazy. We smashed our bottles over the old man's head. Not content with that, Victor kicked him savagely, knocking him to the ground. As we ran, I kept seeing him sprawled on the ground, blood from our beating trickling into his eyes. Victor, the biggest of us, had said, "We want your money, old man. Hand it over."   3

Later, at home, I had a strong reaction to the incident. My head would not stop pounding, and I threw up. I wasn't afraid of getting caught; in fact, we never did get caught. I just knew I had gone over some kind of line. I didn't know if I could step back, now that I had gone so far. But I knew I had to. I had seen plenty of people in my neighborhood turn into the kind of people who hated their lives, people who didn't care about anything, people who wound up penned in jail or ruled by drugs. I didn't want to become one of them.   4

That night, I realize now, I decided not to become one of Hitler's "brutal youths." I'm proud of myself for that, even though life didn't get any easier and no one came along to pin a medal on me. I just decided, quietly, to step off the path I was on. I hope my parents and I will get along better now, too. Maybe the old man's pain, in some terrible way, had a purpose.   5

QUESTIONS

About Unity

1. Which essay lacks an opening thesis statement?

   "Adopting a Handicap"

2. Which sentence in paragraph 4 of "Adopting a Handicap" should be omitted in the interest of paragraph unity? *(Write the opening words.)*

   Thanks to a new building program . . .

ALLWRITE!

5

3. What sentence in paragraph 3 of "A Night of Violence" should be omitted in the interest of paragraph unity? *(Write the opening words.)*

   Pine Street had a lot of antique stores . . .

4. What sentence in the final paragraph of "A Night of Violence" makes the mistake of introducing a new topic and so should be eliminated? *(Write the opening words.)*

   I hope my parents and I . . .

About Support

5. Label as *sight, touch, hearing,* or *smell* all the sensory details in the following sentences taken from the essays.

   a. "My palms reddened and my wrist and forearm muscles started to ache as
   sight   touch
   sight   touch
   I tugged at the heavy metal wheels."

   b. "I could not see the minister, the choir, or the altar."
   (sight)

   c. "The club thudded loudly against Victor's shoulder, making him yelp
   (hearing   hearing)

   with pain."

   d. "As we ran, I kept seeing him sprawled on the ground, blood from our
   (sight)

   beating trickling into his eyes."

6. In a narrative, the main method of organization is time order. Which sentence in paragraph 3 of "A Night of Violence" is placed out of order? *(Write the opening words.)*

   "Victor, the biggest of us . . .

7. In "Adopting a Handicap," how many examples support the topic sentence of paragraph 4, "When the service started, other problems cropped up to frustrate me further"? _____three_____

About Coherence

8. The first stage of the writer's experience in "Adopting a Handicap" might be called *sitting down in the wheelchair.* What are the other two stages of the experience?

   Coping with the wheelchair

   Dealing with additional problems in the wheelchair

9. List three time transitions used in the third paragraph of "A Night of Violence."

<u>_____After_____</u>   <u>_____When_____</u>   <u>_____As_____</u>

About the Introduction and Conclusion

10. What method of introduction forms the first paragraph of "A Night of Violence"? Circle the appropriate letter.

    a. Broad, general statement narrowing to a thesis

    b. Idea that is the opposite of the one to be developed

    c. Questions

Developing a Narrative Essay

Considering Purpose and Audience

The main purpose of a narrative essay is to make a point by telling your audience a story. Colorful details and interesting events that build up to a point of some kind make narrative essays enjoyable for readers and writers alike.

At one time or another, you have probably listened to someone tell a rambling story that didn't seem to go anywhere. You might have impatiently wondered, "Where is this story going?" or "Is there a point here?" Keep such questions in mind as you think about your own narrative essay. To satisfy your audience, your story must have some overall purpose and point.

Also keep in mind that your story should deal with an event or a topic that will appeal to your audience. A group of young children, for example, would probably be bored by a narrative essay about your first job interview. They might, however, be very interested if you wrote about a time you were chased by a pack of mean dogs or when you stood up to a bully in your school. In general, narrative essays that involve human conflict—internal or external—are entertaining to readers of all ages.

Development through Prewriting

Freewriting is a particularly helpful prewriting technique as you're planning your narrative essay. (For more about freewriting, see pages 23–25.) As you think about the story you want to relate, many ideas will crowd into your mind. Simply writing them down in free-form style will jog loose details you may have forgotten and also help you determine what the central point of your story really is.

Lisa, the writer of "Adopting a Handicap," spent a half-hour freewriting before she wrote the first draft of her essay. Here is what she came up with:

Our church was planning a building renovation to make the church more accessible to handicapped people. Some people thought it was a waste of money and that the disabled could get along all right in the church the way it was. Not many disabled people come to our church anyway. Pastor Henry gave a sermon about disabilities. He suggested that we spend one Sunday pretending to be disabled ourselves. We got to choose our disability. Some people pretended to be blind or deaf or in need of crutches. I chose to use a wheelchair. I thought it might be fun to have someone push me around. It was a lot scarier and more disturbing than I expected. We borrowed wheelchairs and crutches from the local nursing home. I didn't like sitting down in the wheelchair. I didn't know how to work it right. It rolled when I didn't want it to. I felt clumsy trying to make it move. I even ran into a pew. I felt silly pretending to be disabled and also sort of disrespectful because for most people sitting in a wheelchair isn't a choice. It also bothered me to think what it'd be like if I couldn't get up again. It turned out that nobody was going to push me around. I thought Paula would, but instead she put on a blindfold and pretended to be blind. She knocked over a cup of coffee before the morning was over. She told me later she felt really panicky when that happened. Sitting down so low in the wheelchair was weird. I couldn't see much of anything. People ignored me or talked to me like I was a little kid. I was glad when the morning was over. Making the wheels turn hurt my hands and arms.

As Lisa read over her freewriting passage, she decided that the central point of her story was her new realization of how challenging it would be to be truly disabled. In order to support that central point, she realized, she would need to concentrate on details that demonstrated the frustrations she felt. She created a scratch outline for the first draft of her essay:

Thesis statement: A church experiment led to my spending the morning in a wheelchair.

1. Sitting in the wheelchair
   a. Awkward because it rolled
   b. Awkward because footrest was out of place
   c. Psychologically awkward

2. Moving the wheelchair
   a. I thought someone would push me.
   b. It was hard to make the chair move and it hurt my hands.
   c. It was difficult to steer.

3.   Ways the wheelchair affected me
    a.   I couldn't see.
    b.   I felt in the way.
    c.   I felt funny talking to people as they bent down over me.

Lisa based her first draft on her scratch outline. Here is the draft:

First Draft

Adopting a Handicap

The pastor at our church suggested that we each "adopt a disability" for a few hours on Sunday morning. Some members, like me, chose to use wheelchairs. Others wore earplugs, used crutches, or wore blindfolds.

It surprised me that I felt nervous about sitting down in my wheelchair. I'm not sure why I felt scared about it. I guess I realized that most people who use wheelchairs don't do it by choice—they have to.

When I sat down, I thought my friend Paula would push me around. We had talked about her doing that earlier. But she decided instead to "adopt" her own disability and she pretended to be blind. I saw her with a blindfold on, trying to fix herself a cup of coffee and knocking it off the table as she stirred it. So I had to figure out how to make the chair move by myself. It wasn't so easy. Pushing the wheels made my hands and arms sore. I also kept bumping into things. I felt really awkward. I even had trouble locking the wheels and finding the footrest.

I couldn't see well as I sat down low in my chair. When the rest of the congregation stood up, I could forget about seeing entirely. People would nod or chuckle at something that had happened up at the front of the church and I could only guess what was going on. Instead of sitting in the pew with everyone else, I was parked out in the aisle, which was really too narrow for the chair. The new building program our church is planning will make that problem better by widening the aisles and making the pews farther apart. It's going to be expensive, but it's a worthwhile thing. Another thing I disliked was how I felt when people talked to me. They had to lean down as though I was a kid, and I had to stare up at them as though I was too. One person I talked to who seemed to understand what I was experiencing was Don Henderson, who mentioned that his brother-in-law uses a wheelchair.

Development through Revising

ALLWRITE!

4.3

Lisa read over her first draft. Then she showed it to her roommate. After hearing her roommate's comments, Lisa read the essay again. This time she made a list of comments about how she thought it could be improved:

- The introduction should explain <u>why</u> the pastor wanted us to adopt disabilities.
- The second paragraph is sort of weak. Instead of saying "I'm not sure why I felt scared," I should try put into specific words what was scary about the experience.
- The stuff about Paula doesn't really add to my main point. The story is about me, not Paula.
- Maybe I shouldn't talk so much about the new building program. It's related to people with disabilities, but it doesn't really support the idea that my morning in a wheelchair was frustrating.
- Eliminate the part about Don Henderson. It doesn't contribute to my feeling frustrated.
- The essay ends too abruptly. I need to wrap it up with some sort of conclusion.

With that list of comments in hand, Lisa returned to her essay. She then wrote the version that appears on page 191.

A Professional Essay to Consider

Read the following professional essay. Then answer the questions and read the comments that follow.

The Yellow Ribbon

by Pete Hamill

(Activity 3)

They were going to Fort Lauderdale, the girl remembered later. There were six of them, three boys and three girls, and they picked up the bus at the old terminal on 34th Street, carrying sandwiches and wine in paper bags, dreaming of golden beaches and the tides of the sea as the gray cold spring of New York vanished behind them. Vingo was on board from the beginning. 1

As the bus passed through Jersey and into Philly, they began to notice that Vingo never moved. He sat in front of the young people, his dusty face masking his age, dressed in a plain brown ill-fitting suit. His fingers were stained from cigarettes and he chewed the inside of his lip a lot, frozen into some personal cocoon of silence. 2

Somewhere outside of Washington, deep into the night, the bus pulled into a Howard Johnson's, and everybody got off except Vingo. He sat rooted in his seat, and the young people began to wonder about him, trying to imagine his life: Perhaps he was a sea captain, maybe he had run away from 3 his wife, he could be an old soldier going home. When they went back to the bus, the girl sat beside him and introduced herself.

"We're going to Florida," the girl said brightly. "You going that far?"   4

"I don't know," Vingo said.   5

"I've never been there," she said. "I hear it's beautiful."   6

"It is," he said quietly, as if remembering something he had tried to   7
forget.

"You live there?"   8

"I did some time there in the Navy. Jacksonville."   9

"Want some wine?" she said. He smiled and took the bottle of Chianti   10
and took a swig. He thanked her and retreated again into silence. After a
while, she went back to the others, as Vingo nodded into sleep.

In the morning they awoke outside another Howard Johnson's, and   11
this time Vingo went in. The girl insisted that he join them. He seemed very
shy and ordered black coffee and smoked nervously, as the young people
chattered about sleeping on the beaches. When they went back on the bus,
the girl sat with Vingo again, and after a while, slowly and painfully and with
great hesitation, he began to tell his story. He had been in jail in New York
for the last four years, and now he was going home.

"Four years!" the girl said. "What did you do?"   12

"It doesn't matter," he said with quiet bluntness. "I did it and I went to   13
jail. If you can't do the time, don't do the crime. That's what they say and
they're right."

"Are you married?"   14

"I don't know."   15

"You don't know?" she said.   16

"Well, when I was in the can I wrote to my wife," he said. "I told her, I   17
said, Martha, I understand if you can't stay married to me. I told her that.
I said I was gonna be away a long time, and that if she couldn't stand it, if
the kids kept askin' questions, if it hurt her too much, well, she could just
forget me. Get a new guy—she's a wonderful woman, really something—
and forget about me. I told her she didn't have to write me or nothing. And
she didn't. Not for three and a half years."

"And you're going home now, not knowing?"   18

"Yeah," he said shyly. "Well, last week, when I was sure the parole was   19
coming through I wrote her. I told her that if she had a new guy, I understood.
But if she didn't, if she would take me back she should let me know. We used
to live in this town, Brunswick, just before Jacksonville, and there's a great
big oak tree just as you come into town, a very famous tree, huge. I told
her if she would take me back, she should put a yellow handkerchief on the
tree, and I would get off and come home. If she didn't want me, forget it, no
handkerchief, and I'd keep going on through."

"Wow," the girl said. "Wow."   20

She told the others, and soon all of them were in it, caught up in the   21
approach of Brunswick, looking at the pictures Vingo showed them of his
wife and three children, the woman handsome in a plain way, the children
still unformed in a cracked, much-handled snapshot. Now they were twenty
miles from Brunswick and the young people took over window seats on the
right side, waiting for the approach of the great oak tree. Vingo stopped
looking, tightening his face into the ex-con's mask, as if fortifying himself
against still another disappointment. Then it was ten miles, and then five
and the bus acquired a dark hushed mood, full of silence, of absence, of lost
years, of the woman's plain face, of the sudden letter on the breakfast table,
of the wonder of children, of the iron bars of solitude.

Then suddenly all of the young people were up out of their seats,   22
screaming and shouting and crying, doing small dances, shaking clenched
fists in triumph and exaltation. All except Vingo.

Vingo sat there stunned, looking at the oak tree. It was covered with   23
yellow handkerchiefs, twenty of them, thirty of them, maybe hundreds, a
tree that stood like a banner of welcome blowing and billowing in the wind,
turned into a gorgeous yellow blur by the passing bus. As the young people
shouted, the old con slowly rose from his seat, holding himself tightly, and
made his way to the front of the bus to go home.

QUESTIONS

About Unity

1. The thesis of Hamill's essay is implied rather than stated directly. See if you
   can state the thesis in your own words.

   Answers will vary. On a very simple level, the theme could be stated: Vingo

   returned from prison to find that his wife still loved him.

2. Which statement best expresses the implied point of paragraph 2?
   a. Vingo sat very still in his seat.
   (b.) Something about Vingo made the young people curious.
   c. Vingo appeared to be a nervous person.
   d. Vingo was the most unusual person the young people had ever seen.

3. Which statement would best serve as a topic sentence for paragraph 11?
   (a.) The girl's friendliness finally caused Vingo to confide in her.
   b. The group woke up outside of a Howard Johnson's.
   c. Vingo had been in jail for four years.
   d. The girl persisted in being friendly to Vingo.

About Support

4. "His fingers were stained from cigarettes and he chewed the inside of his lip a lot, frozen in some personal cocoon of silence." This line from paragraph 2 supports the idea that

    a. Vingo had been drinking.

    (b.) Vingo was nervous.

    c. Vingo was a hostile person.

    d. Vingo knew the young people were watching him.

5. Hamill writes in paragraph 11 that Vingo "seemed very shy." Find at least two pieces of evidence in the essay to support the idea that Vingo was shy.

    Answers may vary; examples are given.

    1. He tells his story "slowly and painfully and with great hesitation."

    2. He asks his wife to leave a signal (the handkerchief), rather than

    confront her directly.

6. Hamill implies that despite his crime, Vingo was an honorable man. Find evidence that supports that point.

    Doesn't express any self-pity about being in jail; owns up to his crime.

    Offers his wife her freedom.

About Coherence

7. The story in this essay takes place on a trip, so it's especially appropriate that Hamill uses geographical and place names to signal the passing of time and miles. List at least four of the specific places named.   *Any four answers:*

    Fort Lauderdale,   New Jersey,   *Washington,   Jacksonville,*

    34th Street terminal in New York,   *Philadelphia,   Brunswick*

8. What sentence in paragraph 19 begins with a transition word that indicates contrast? *(Write the opening words.)*

    But if she didn't . . .

About the Introduction and Conclusion

9. The introductory paragraph indicates that Hamill

    a. was one of the young people on the bus.

    b. heard the story from Vingo years later.

    c. was a friend of Vingo's wife.

    (d.) interviewed one of the young girls who'd been on the bus.

10. Hamill has concluded his narrative with

    a. a summary.

    b. a thought-provoking question.

    c. a recommendation.

    d. the last event of his narrative.

Writing a Narrative Essay

WRITING ASSIGNMENT 1

Write an essay narrating an experience in which a certain emotion was predominant. The emotion might be disappointment, embarrassment, happiness, frustration, any of the following, or some other:

Fear	Shock	Nervousness	Loss
Pride	Love	Hate	Sympathy
Jealousy	Anger	Surprise	Violence
Sadness	Nostalgia	Shyness	Bitterness
Terror	Relief	Silliness	Envy
Regret	Greed	Disgust	Loneliness

The experience should be limited in time. Note that each of the three essays presented in this chapter describes an experience that occurred within a relatively short period. One writer described her frustration in acting like a disabled person at a morning church service; another detailed the terror of a minute's mugging that had lifelong consequences; Pete Hamill described an overnight bus trip and its thrilling conclusion.

ALLWRITE!

2.3

Prewriting

a   Think of an experience or event in your life in which you felt a certain emotion. Then spend at least ten minutes freewriting about that experience. Do not worry at this point about such matters as spelling or grammar or putting things in the right order; instead, just try to get down as many details as you can think of that seem related to the experience.

b   This preliminary writing will help you decide whether your topic is promising enough to continue working on. If it is not, choose another emotion. If it is, do three things:

   First, write out your thesis in a single sentence, underlining the emotion you will focus on. For example, "My first day in kindergarten was one of the scariest days of my life."

Second, think about just what creates the conflict—the source of tension— in your story. What details can you add that will build up enough tension to "hook" readers and keep them interested?

Third, make up a long list of all the details involved in the experience. Then arrange those details in chronological (time) order.

c   Using your list as a guide, prepare a rough draft of your paper.

Revising

4.3

Once you have a first draft of your essay completed, consider the following as you work on a second draft:

a   *To achieve unity:* Do you state the thesis of your narrative in the introductory paragraph? If it is not stated, have you clearly implied it somewhere in the essay? Ask yourself if there are any portions of the essay that do not support the thesis and therefore should be eliminated or rewritten.

b   *To achieve support:* Do you have enough details, including dialogue? Notice how dialogue in Pete Hamill's essay adds drama and immediacy and helps a situation come alive. See if during this revision you can add more vivid, exact details that will help your readers experience the event as it actually happened.

c   *To achieve coherence:* See if you can add time signals such as *first, then, next, after, while, during,* and *finally* to help connect details as you move from the beginning to the middle to the end of the narrative.

Also, see if you can divide the story into separate stages (what happened first, what happened next, what finally happened). Put each stage into a separate paragraph. In narratives, it is sometimes difficult to write a topic sentence for each supporting paragraph. You may, therefore, want to start new paragraphs at points where natural shifts or logical breaks in the story seem to occur.

d   *To achieve sentence skills:* Use the checklist on the inside front cover to edit and proofread your next-to-final draft for sentence-skills mistakes, including spelling.

WRITING ASSIGNMENT 2

Think of an experience in your life that supports one of the statements below:

If you never have a dream, you'll never have a dream come true.—popular saying

For fools rush in where angels fear to tread.—Alexander Pope

Before I got married I had six theories about bringing up children; now I have six children and no theories.—John Wilmot, Earl of Rochester

There are some things you learn best in calm, and some in storm.—Willa Cather

Success is 99 percent perspiration and 1 percent inspiration.—Thomas Edison

Lying is an indispensable part of making life tolerable.—Bergen Evans

What a tangled web we weave / When first we practice to deceive.—Walter Scott

There's a sucker born every minute.—P. T. Barnum

We lie loudest when we lie to ourselves.—Eric Hoffer

All marriages are happy. It's the living together afterward that causes all the trouble.—Raymond Hull

Hoping and praying are easier but do not produce as good results as hard work.—Andy Rooney

A little learning is a dangerous thing.—Alexander Pope

Nothing is as good as it seems beforehand.—George Eliot

You don't like weak women / You get bored too quick / And you don't like strong women / 'Cause they're hip to your tricks.—Joni Mitchell

Give a pig a finger, and he'll take the whole hand.—folk saying

Life shrinks or expands in proportion to one's courage.—Anaïs Nin

When I got to the end of my long journey in life / I realized I was the architect of my own destiny.—Amado Nervo

A fool and his money are soon parted.—popular saying

From what we get, we can make a living; what we give, however, makes a life.—Arthur Ashe

No matter how lovesick a woman is, she shouldn't take the first pill that comes along.—Dr. Joyce Brothers

Fear not those who argue but those who dodge.—Marie von Ebner-Eschenback

Trust in Allah, but tie your camel.—old Muslim proverb

Think of an experience you have had that demonstrates the truth of one of the above statements or another noteworthy saying—perhaps one that has been a guidepost for your life. Then, using one of these statements as your thesis, write a narrative essay about that experience. As you develop your essay, refer to the suggestions in the following prewriting strategies and rewriting strategies.

Prewriting

The key to the success of your essay will be your choice of an incident from your life that illustrates the truth of the statement you have chosen. Here are some guidelines to consider as you choose such an incident:

- The incident should include a *conflict,* or a source of tension. That conflict does not need to be dramatic, such as a fistfight between two characters. Equally effective is a quieter conflict, such as a conflict between a person's conscience and desires, or a decision that must be made, or a difficult situation that has no clear resolution.
- The incident should be limited in time. It would be difficult to do justice in such a brief essay to an experience that continued over several weeks or months.
- The incident should evoke a definite emotional response in you so that it might draw a similar response from your reader.
- The incident must *fully support* the statement you have chosen, not merely be linked by some of the same ideas. Do not, for example, take the statement "We lie loudest when we lie to ourselves" and then write about an incident in which someone just told a lie. The essay should demonstrate the cost of being untruthful to oneself.

     Here is how one adult student tested whether her plan for her narrative essay was a good one:

- What statement have I chosen as my thesis?

     The chains of habit are too weak to be felt until they are too strong to be broken.—Samuel Johnson

- Does the incident I have chosen include some kind of tension?

     Yes. I am going to write about a day when I overheard my little daughter make a remark that made me realize she was aware of my alcohol abuse. The tension is between my fantasy, which was that my drinking was a secret, and the truth, which was that even a little child knew about it.

- Is the incident limited in time?

     Yes. I am going to write about events that happened in one afternoon.

- Does the incident evoke an emotional response in me?

     Yes. I was ashamed, embarrassed, and angry at myself.

- Does the incident support the statement I have chosen?

     Yes. My "habit" was drinking, and I did not realize I was caught in its "chains" until I was unable to stop without help.

Revising

Once you have completed a first draft of your essay, you should review it with these questions in mind:

- Have I included the essay's thesis (my chosen statement) in my introductory paragraph, or is it clearly implied?
- Does each paragraph, and each sentence within that paragraph, help either to keep the action moving or to reveal important things about the characters?
- Do transitional words and phrases, and linking sentences between paragraphs, help make the sequence of events clear?
- Should I break up the essay by using bits of interesting dialogue instead of narration?
- Are there portions of the essay that do not support my thesis and therefore should be eliminated or rewritten?

WRITING ASSIGNMENT 3

Writing for a Specific Purpose and Audience

In this narrative essay, you will write with a specific purpose and for a specific audience.

Option 1   Imagine that you are in a town fifty miles from home, that your car has broken down several miles from a gas station, and that you are carrying no money. You're afraid you are going to have a terrible time, but the friendly people who help you turn your experience into a positive one. It is such a good day, in fact, that you don't want to forget what happened.

Write a narrative of the day's events in your diary so that you can read it ten years from now and remember exactly what happened. Begin with the moment you realize your car has broken down and continue until you're safely back home. Include a thesis at either the beginning or the end of your narration.

Option 2   Imagine that a friend or sister or brother has to make a difficult decision of some kind. Perhaps he or she must decide how to deal with a troubled love affair, or a problem with living at home, or a conflict with a boss or coworker. Write a narrative from your own experience that will teach him or her something about the decision that must be made.

10 Examples

In our daily conversations, we often provide examples—details, particulars, and specific instances—to explain statements that we make. Here are several statements and supporting examples:

The first day of school was frustrating.	My sociology course was canceled. Then, I couldn't find the biology lab. And the lines at the bookstore were so long that I went home without buying my textbooks.
That washing machine is unreliable.	The water temperature can't be predicted; it stops in midcycle; and it sometimes shreds my clothing.
My grandfather is a thrifty person.	He washes and reuses aluminum foil. He wraps gifts in newspaper. And he's worn the same Sunday suit for twenty years.

In each case, the examples help us see for ourselves the truth of the statement that has been made. In essays, too, explanatory examples help your audience fully understand your point. Lively, specific examples also add interest to your paper.

In this chapter, you will be asked to provide a series of examples to support your thesis. First read the student essays and the professional essay that follow and work through the questions that accompany the essays. All three essays use examples to develop their points.

Student Essays to Consider

Everyday Cruelty

Last week, I found myself worrying less about problems of world politics and national crime and more about smaller evils. I came home one day with a bad taste in my mouth, the kind I get whenever I witness the

1

little cruelties that people inflict on each other. On this particular day, I had seen too much of the cruelty of the world.

Every day I walk from the bus stop to the office where I work. This walk is my first step away from the comforts of home and into the tensions of the city. For me, a landmark on the route is a tiny patch of ground that was once strewn with rubbish and broken glass. The city is trying to make a "pocket park" out of it by planting trees and flowers. Every day this spring, I watched the skinny saplings put out tiny leaves. When I walked past, I always noted how big the tulips were getting and made bets with myself on when they would bloom. To pass time as I walk, I often make silly little bets with myself, such as predicting that the next man I see will be wearing a blue tie. But last Wednesday, as I reached the park, I felt sick. Someone had knocked the trees to the ground and trampled the budding tulips into the dirt. Someone had destroyed a bit of beauty for no reason.

At lunchtime on Wednesday, I witnessed more meanness. Along with dozens of other hungry, hurried people, I was waiting in line at McDonald's. Also in line was a young mother with two tired, impatient children clinging to her legs. The mother was trying to calm the children, but it was obvious that their whining was about to give way to full-fledged tantrums. The lines barely moved, and the lunchtime tension was building. Then, one of the children began to cry and scream. As people stared angrily at the helpless mother, the little boy's bloodcurdling yells resounded through the restaurant. Finally, one man turned to her and said, "Lady, you shouldn't bring your kids to a public place if you can't control them." A young woman chimed in with another piece of cruel criticism. The mother was exhausted and hungry. Someone in line could have helped her by kneeling down to interact on eye level with one of the kids. Instead, even though many of the customers in the restaurant were parents themselves, they treated her like a criminal.

The worst incident of mean-spiritedness that I saw that day happened after I left work. As I walked to the bus stop, I approached an old woman huddled in a doorway. She was wrapped in a dirty blanket and clutched a cheap vinyl bag packed with her belongings. She was one of the "street people" our society leaves to fend for themselves. Approaching the woman from the opposite direction were three teenagers who were laughing and talking in loud voices. When they saw the old woman, they began to shout crude remarks at her. Then they did even more cruel things to torment her. The woman stared helplessly at them, like a wounded animal surrounded by hunters. Then, having had their fun, the teenagers went on their way.

I had seen enough of the world's coldness that day and wanted to leave it all behind. At home, I huddled in the warmth of my family. I wondered why we all contribute to the supply of petty cruelty. There's enough of it already.

Altered States

Most Americans are not alcoholics. Most do not cruise seedy city streets looking to score crack cocaine or heroin. Relatively few try to con their doctors into prescribing unneeded mood-altering medications. And yet, many Americans are traveling through life with their minds slightly out of kilter. In its attempt to cope with modern life, the human mind seems to have evolved some defense strategies. Confronted with inventions like television, the shopping center, and the Internet, the mind will slip—all by itself—into an altered state.

Never in the history of humanity have people been expected to sit passively for hours, staring at moving pictures emanating from an electronic box. Since too much exposure to flickering images of police officers, detectives, and talk-show hosts can be dangerous to human sanity, the mind automatically goes into a state of TV hypnosis. The eyes see the sitcom or the dog-food commercial, but the mind goes into a holding pattern. None of the televised images or sounds actually enters the brain. This is why, when questioned, people cannot remember commercials they have seen five seconds before or why the TV cops are chasing a certain suspect. In this hypnotic, trancelike state, the mind resembles an armored armadillo. It rolls up in self-defense, letting the stream of televised information pass by harmlessly.

If the TV watcher arises from the couch and goes to a shopping mall, he or she will again cope by slipping into an altered state. In the mall, the mind is bombarded with the sights, smells, and sounds of dozens of stores, restaurants, and movie theaters competing for its attention. There are hundreds of questions to be answered. Should I start with the upper or lower mall level? Which stores should I look in? Should I bother with the sweater sale at J. C. Penney? Should I eat fried chicken or try the healthier-sounding Pita Wrap? Where is my car parked? To combat this mental overload, the mind goes into a state resembling the whiteout experienced by mountain climbers trapped in a blinding snowstorm. Suddenly, everything looks the same. The shopper is unsure where to go next and cannot remember what he or she came for in the first place. The mind enters this state deliberately so that the shopper has no choice but to leave. Some kids can be in a shopping mall for hours, but they are exceptions to the rule.

But no part of everyday life so quickly triggers the mind's protective shutdown mode as that favorite pastime of the new millennium: cruising the Internet. A computer user sits down with the intention of briefly checking his or her e-mail or looking up a fact for a research paper. But once tapped into the immense storehouse of information, entertainment, and seemingly intimate personal connections that the Internet offers, the

1

2

3

4

user loses all sense of time and priorities. Prospects flood the mind: Should I explore the rise of Nazi Germany? Play a trivia game? Hear the life story of a lonely stranger in Duluth? With a mind dazed with information overload, the user numbly hits one key after another, leaping from topic to topic, from distraction to distraction. Hours fly by as he or she sits hunched over the terminal, unable to account for the time that has passed.

Therefore, the next time you see TV viewers, shoppers, or Internet 5
surfers with eyes as glazed and empty as polished doorknobs, you'll know these people are in a protective altered state. Be gentle with them. They are merely trying to cope with the mind-numbing inventions of modern life.

QUESTIONS

About Unity

1. Which sentence in paragraph 3 of "Altered States" should be omitted in the interest of paragraph unity? (*Write the opening words.*)
   Some kids can be . . .

2. Which supporting paragraph in one of the essays lacks a topic sentence?
   Paragraph 2 in "Everyday Cruelty"

3. Which sentence in paragraph 2 of "Everyday Cruelty" should be omitted in the interest of paragraph unity? (*Write the opening words.*)
   To pass time as I walk . . .

About Support

4. Which sentence in paragraph 4 of "Everyday Cruelty" needs to be followed by more supporting details? (*Write the opening words.*)
   Then they did even more cruel things . . .

5. In paragraph 3 of "Everyday Cruelty," what sentence should be followed by supporting details? (*Write the opening words.*)
   A young woman chimed in . . .

6. What three pieces of evidence does the writer of "Altered States" offer to support the statement that the Internet is an "immense storehouse of information, entertainment, and seemingly intimate personal connections"?
   . . . explore the rise of Nazi Germany . . .

   . . . Play a trivia game . . .

   . . . Hear the life story of a lonely stranger . . .

6

About Coherence

7. In paragraph 3 of "Everyday Cruelty," which four *time* signals does the author begin sentences with? (*Write the four signals here.*)

   At lunchtime on Wednesday _____   Then _____   As people stared _____   Finally _____

8. What sentence in "Altered States" indicates that the author has used emphatic order, saving his most important point for last? (*Write the opening words.*)

   But no part of everyday life . . . _____

8

About the Introduction and Conclusion

9. Of the two student essays, which indicates in its introduction the essay's plan of development? (*Write the title of the essay and the opening words of the sentence that indicates the plan.*)

   "Altered States": Confronted with inventions . . . _____

10. Which statement best describes the concluding paragraph of "Altered States"?

    a. It contains a prediction.

    b. It combines a summary with a recommendation of how to treat people in an altered state.

    c. It refers to the point made in the introduction about alcohol and drugs.

    d. It contains thought-provoking questions about altered states.

Developing an Examples Essay

Considering Purpose and Audience

If you make a statement and someone says to you, "Prove it," what do you do? Most likely, if you can, you will provide an example or two to support your claim. An examples essay has the same purpose: to use specific instances or actual cases to convince an audience that a particular point is true.

In an examples essay, you support your point by *illustrating* it with examples. If, for instance, you decide to write an essay that claims capital punishment is immoral, you might cite several cases in which an innocent person was executed. Keep in mind that your examples should connect clearly to your main point so that readers will see the truth of your claim.

The number of examples you choose to include in your essay may vary depending, in part, on your audience. For a group already opposed to the death penalty, you would not need detailed examples to support your belief that capital punishment is immoral.

However, if you were writing to a group undecided about capital punishment, you would need more instances to get your point across—and even then, some would not believe you. Still, when used well, examples make writing more persuasive, increasing the chances readers will understand and believe your point.

Development through Prewriting

2.3

When Cedric, the student author of "Altered States," was considering a topic for his example essay, he looked around his dorm for inspiration. He first considered writing about examples of different types of people: jocks, brains, spaceheads. Then he thought about examples of housekeeping in dorm rooms: the Slob Kingdom, the Neat Freak Room, and the Packrat's Place.

"But that evening I was noticing how my roommate acted as he was cruising the Internet," Cedric said. "He sat down to write his brother a brief e-mail, and three hours later he was still there, cruising from website to website. His eyes were glassy and he seemed out of touch with reality. It reminded me of how spaced out I get when I go to a busy shopping mall. I began to think about how our minds have to adjust to challenges that our grandparents didn't know anything about. I added 'watching television' as the third category, and I had a pretty good idea what my essay would be about."

Cedric had his three categories, but he needed to do some more work in order to generate supporting details for each. He used the technique of clustering, or diagramming, to help inspire his thinking. Here is what his diagram looked like.

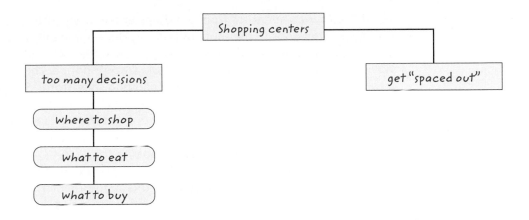

Looking at his diagram, Cedric saw that he would have no trouble supporting the thesis that people's minds go into an "altered state" when they watch TV, go to shopping centers, or use the Internet. As he quickly jotted down details in cluster form, he had easily come up with enough ideas for his essay. He started writing and produced this first draft.

First Draft

Altered States

Modern life makes demands on the human mind that no other period of history has made. As society becomes more and more complex, the mind has developed some defense mechanisms. Confronted with inventions like the Internet, television, and the shopping center, the mind will slip—all by itself—into an altered state.

Cruising the Internet can quickly make the mind slip into a strange state. A computer user sits down to check his e-mail or look up something. But once tapped into the Internet, the user loses all sense of time. He can chat with strangers, research any topic, play a game, or shop for any product. Some people begin to think of the online world and online friends as more real than the people in their own homes. While my roommate is absorbed in the Internet, he can even have brief conversations with people who come into our room, yet not be able to remember the conversations later. He sits there in a daze from information overload. He seems numb as he hits key after key, going from website to website.

Then there's TV. Our grandparents could not have imagined the idea of sitting passively for hours, staring at moving pictures emanating from a box. It's not a normal state of affairs, so the mind goes into something like a hypnotic trance. You see the sitcom or the dog-food commercial, but your mind goes into a holding pattern. You don't really absorb the pictures or sounds. Five minutes after I watch a show I can't remember commercials I've seen or why the TV cops are chasing a certain suspect.

If the TV watcher arises from the couch and journeys into the real world, he often goes to the shopping center. Here, the mind is bombarded with the sights, smells, and sounds of dozens of stores, restaurants, and movie theaters competing for its attention. Dazed shoppers begin to feel like mountain climbers trapped in a blinding snowstorm. Suddenly, everything looks the same. My father is the worst of all when it comes to shopping in an altered state. He comes back from the mall looking like he'd been through a war. After about fifteen minutes of shopping, he can't concentrate enough to know what he's looking for.

Internet surfers, TV viewers, and shoppers all have one thing in common. They're just trying to cope with the mind-numbing inventions of modern life. Hopefully someday we'll turn away from such inventions and return to a simpler and more healthy way of life.

Development through Revising

4.3

Cedric showed his first-draft essay to a classmate for her critique. She returned his essay with these comments:

Altered States

Modern life makes demands on the human mind that no other period of history has made. As society becomes more and more complex, the mind has developed some defense mechanisms. Confronted with inventions like the Internet, television, and the shopping center, the mind will slip—all by itself—into an altered state.

Cruising the Internet can quickly make the mind slip into a strange state. A computer user sits down to check his e-mail or look up something. But once tapped into the Internet, the user loses all sense of time. He can chat with strangers, research any topic, play a game, or shop for any product. Some people begin to think of the online world and online friends as more real than the

Reader's Comments

This seems to me like a separate topic—people's relationships with people they meet on the Internet.

Sometimes you write about "a user," other times about "you," and then about "my

roommate." It's confusing. Also, is the paragraph about your roommate on the Internet or what people in general are like?

These last two sentences are good. I'd like to read more about this "altered state" you think people go into.

The idea of the "hypnotic trance" is interesting, but you need more details to back it up.

The point of view is a problem again. You skip from "you" to "I."

Good image!

I don't think this works. The essay isn't about your father. It should be about modern shoppers, not just one man.

This final sentence seems to introduce a new topic—that we shouldn't get caught up in TV and the Internet, etc.

people in their own homes. While my roommate is absorbed in the Internet, he can even have brief conversations with people who come into our room, yet not be able to remember the conversations later. He sits there in a daze from information overload. He seems numb as he hits key after key, going from website to website.

Then there's TV. Our grandparents could not have imagined the idea of sitting passively for hours, staring at moving pictures emanating from a box. It's not a normal state of affairs, so the mind goes into something like a hypnotic trance. You see the sitcom or the dog-food commercial, but your mind goes into a holding pattern. You don't really absorb the pictures or sounds. Five minutes after I watch a show I can't remember commercials I've seen or why the TV cops are chasing a certain suspect.

If the TV watcher arises from the couch and journeys into the real world, he often goes to the shopping center. Here, the mind is bombarded with the sights, smells, and sounds of dozens of stores, restaurants, and movie theaters competing for its attention. Dazed shoppers begin to feel like mountain climbers trapped in a blinding snowstorm. Suddenly, everything looks the same. My father is the worst of all when it comes to shopping in an altered state. He comes back from the mall looking like he'd been through a war. After about fifteen minutes of shopping, he can't concentrate enough to know what he's looking for.

Internet surfers, TV viewers, and shoppers all have one thing in common. They're just trying to cope with the mind-numbing inventions of modern life. Hopefully someday we'll turn away from such inventions and return to a simpler and more healthy way of life.

Cedric read his classmate's comments and reviewed the essay himself. He agreed with her criticisms about point of view and the need for stronger supporting details. He also decided that the Internet was his strongest supporting point and should be saved for the last paragraph. He then wrote the final version of his essay, the version that appears on page 209.

A Professional Essay to Consider

Read the following professional essay. Then answer the questions and read the comments that follow.

Dad

by Andrew H. Malcolm

(Activity 3)

The first memory I have of him—of anything, really—is his strength. 1 It was in the late afternoon in a house under construction near ours. The unfinished wood floors had large, terrifying holes whose yawning darkness I knew led to nowhere good. His powerful hands, then age thirty-three, wrapped all the way around my tiny arms, then age four, and easily swung me up to his shoulders to command all I surveyed.

The relationship between a son and his father changes over time. It may 2 grow and flourish in mutual maturity. It may sour in resented dependence or independence. With many children living in single-parent homes today, it may not even exist.

But to a little boy right after World War II, a father seemed a god with 3 strange strengths and uncanny powers enabling him to do and know things that no mortal could do or know. Amazing things, like putting a bicycle chain back on, just like that. Or building a hamster cage. Or guiding a jigsaw so it formed the letter F; I learned the alphabet that way in those pretelevision days, one letter or number every other evening plus a review of the collection. (The vowels we painted red because they were special somehow.)

He seemed to know what I thought before I did. "You look like you 4 could use a cheeseburger and a chocolate shake," he would say on hot Sunday afternoons. When, at the age of five, I broke a neighbor's garage window with a wild curveball and waited in fear for ten days to make the announcement, he seemed to know about it already and to have been waiting for something.

There were, of course, rules to learn. First came the handshake. None 5 of those fishy little finger grips, but a good firm squeeze accompanied by an equally strong gaze into the other's eyes. "The first thing anyone knows about you is your handshake," he would say. And we'd practice it each night on his return from work, the serious toddler in the battered Cleveland Indians cap running up to the giant father to shake hands again and again until it was firm enough.

When my cat killed a bird, he defused the anger of a nine-year-old with 6 a little chat about something called "instinked." The next year, when my dog got run over and the weight of sorrow was just too immense to stand, he was there, too, with his big arms and his own tears and some thoughts on the natural order of life and death, although what was natural about a speeding car that didn't stop always escaped me.

As time passed, there were other rules to learn. "Always do your best." 7 "Do it now." "NEVER LIE!" And, most important, "You can do whatever you have to do." By my teens, he wasn't telling me what to do anymore, which was scary and heady at the same time. He provided perspective, not telling me what was around the great corner of life but letting me know there was a lot more than just today and the next, which I hadn't thought of.

When the most important girl in the world—I forget her name now— 8 turned down a movie date, he just happened to walk by the kitchen phone. "This may be hard to believe right now," he said, "but someday you won't even remember her name."

One day, I realize now, there was a change. I wasn't trying to please 9 him so much as I was trying to impress him. I never asked him to come to my football games. He had a high-pressure career, and it meant driving through most of Friday night. But for all the big games, when I looked over at the sideline, there was that familiar fedora. And, by God, did the opposing team captain ever get a firm handshake and a gaze he would remember.

Then, a school fact contradicted something he said. Impossible that he 10 could be wrong, but there it was in the book. These accumulated over time, along with personal experiences, to buttress[1] my own developing sense of values. And I could tell we had each taken our own, perfectly normal paths.

I began to see, too, his blind spots, his prejudices, and his weaknesses. 11 I never threw these up at him. He hadn't to me, and, anyway, he seemed to need protection. I stopped asking his advice; the experiences he drew from no longer seemed relevant to the decisions I had to make. On the phone, he would go on about politics at times, why he would vote the way he did or why some incumbent was a jerk. And I would roll my eyes to the ceiling and smile a little, though I hid it in my voice.

He volunteered advice for a while. But then, in more recent years, politics 12 and issues gave way to talk of empty errands and, always, to ailments—his friends', my mother's, and his own, which were serious and included heart disease. He had a bedside oxygen tank, and he would ostentatiously[2] retire there during my visits, asking my help in easing his body onto the mattress. "You have very strong arms," he once noted.

[1]*buttress:* strengthen and support.
[2]*ostentatiously:* dramatically.

From his bed, he showed me the many sores and scars on his misshapen 13
body and all the bottles of medicine. He talked of the pain and craved much
sympathy. He got some. But the scene was not attractive. He told me, as
the doctor had, that his condition would only deteriorate. "Sometimes," he
confided, "I would just like to lie down and go to sleep and not wake up."

After much thought and practice ("You can do whatever you have to 14
do"), one night last winter, I sat down by his bed and remembered for an
instant those terrifying dark holes in another house thirty-five years before.
I told my father how much I loved him. I described all the things people were
doing for him. But, I said, he kept eating poorly, hiding in his room, and
violating other doctors' orders. No amount of love could make someone else
care about life, I said: it was a two-way street. He wasn't doing his best. The
decision was his.

He said he knew how hard my words had been to say and how proud he 15
was of me. "I had the best teacher," I said. "You can do whatever you have to
do." He smiled a little. and we shook hands, firmly, for the last time.

Several days later, at about 4 A.M., my mother heard Dad shuffling about 16
their dark room. "I have some things I have to do," he said. He paid a bundle
of bills. He composed for my mother a long list of legal and financial what-
to-do's "in case of emergency." And he wrote me a note.

Then he walked back to his bed and laid himself down. He went to sleep, 17
naturally. And he did not wake up.

QUESTIONS

About Unity

1. In the story about Malcolm and his father, which sentence expresses Malcolm's thesis?

   a. The last sentence of paragraph 1

   (b.) The first sentence of paragraph 2

   c. The last sentence of paragraph 2

   d. The first sentence of paragraph 3

2. Which statement would best serve as a topic sentence for paragraph 6?

   a. My dad loved my dog as much as I did.

   b. Pets were a subject that drew my dad and me together.

   (c.) My dad helped me make sense of life's tragedies.

   d. I was angry at my cat for killing a bird.

3. Which statement would best serve as a topic sentence for paragraph 10?

   a. School set the author against his father.

   b. The author came to see more and more that his father was usually wrong.

c. It is best for father and son to see eye to eye.

(d) Some of the author's ideas gradually came to differ from those of his father.

About Support

4. How many details does the author use in paragraph 3 to support the idea that his father "seemed a god with strange strengths and uncanny powers"?

   a. one

   b. two

   (c) three

5. With which sentence does Malcolm support his statement in paragraph 14 that his father "wasn't doing his best"? *(Write the opening words.)*
   But, I said, he kept . . .

6. Which of these points is supported by the anecdote in paragraph 8?

   a. "As time passed, there were other rules to learn."

   (b) "He provided perspective . . . letting me know there was a lot more than just today and the next . . ."

   c. "One day, I realize now, there was a change."

   d. "I wasn't trying to please him so much as I was trying to impress him."

About Coherence

7. Initially, Malcolm saw his father as all-wise and all-powerful. Which paragraph in the essay signals the turning point at which he began seeing his father in more realistic, less idealized terms? ___10___

8. In paragraph 6, find each of the following:

   a. two time transition signals
      ____When____   ____The next year____

   b. one addition transition signal
      ____too____

   c. one change-of-direction transition signal
      ____although____

9. Which method of organization does Malcolm use in his essay?

   (a) Time

   b. Emphatic

About the Conclusion

10. The conclusion of "Dad" is made up of

 a. a summary of the narrative and a final thought.

 b. a question about fatherhood.

 c. the last event of the story about Malcolm and his father.

 d. a prediction of what kind of father Malcolm hopes to be himself.

Writing an Examples Essay

WRITING ASSIGNMENT 1

For this assignment, you will complete an unfinished essay by adding appropriate supporting examples. Here is the incomplete essay:

Problems with My Apartment

> When I was younger, I fantasized about how wonderful life would be when I moved into my own apartment. Now I'm a bit older and wiser, and my dreams have turned into nightmares. My apartment has given me nothing but headaches. From the day I signed the lease, I've had to deal with an uncooperative landlord, an incompetent janitor, and inconsiderate neighbors.

> First of all, my landlord has been uncooperative. . . .

> I've had a problem not only with my landlord but also with an incompetent janitor. . . .

> Perhaps the worst problem has been with the inconsiderate neighbors who live in the apartment above me. . . .

Sometimes, my apartment seems like a small, friendly oasis surrounded by hostile enemies. I never know what side trouble is going to come from next: the landlord, the janitor, or the neighbors. Home may be where the heart is, but my sanity is thinking about moving out.

Note   If you do not have experience with living in an apartment, write instead about problems of living in a dormitory or problems of living at home. Revise the introduction and conclusion so that they fit your topic. Problems of living in a dorm might include these:

Restrictive dorm regulations

Inconsiderate students on your floor

A difficult roommate

Problems of living at home might be these:

Lack of space

Inconsiderate brothers and sisters

Conflict with your parent or parents

Prewriting

ALLWRITE!

2.3

a   Generate details for your paper by using questioning as a prewriting technique. Write answers to the following questions. *(Use separate paper.)*
Answers will vary.

How has the landlord been uncooperative?

In what ways have you been inconvenienced?

Has he (or she) been uncooperative more than once?

How have you reacted to the landlord's lack of cooperation?

What has been the landlord's reaction?

What kinds of things have you said to each other?

What is the most uncooperative thing the landlord has done?

Who is the janitor?

What has he (or she) tried to fix in the apartment?

In what ways has the janitor been incompetent?

How has the janitor inconvenienced you?

Has the janitor's incompetence cost you money?

What is the worst example of the janitor's incompetence?

Who are the neighbors?

How long have they lived upstairs?

What kind of problems have you had with them?

Have these problems occurred more than once?

If you have spoken to the neighbors about the problems, how did they respond?

What is the worst problem with these neighbors?

b   Use the details generated by your questioning to flesh out the three paragraphs with details and examples. Remember that you may use one extended example in each paragraph (as in "Everyday Cruelty") or several brief examples (as in "Altered States").

c   As you write your first draft, keep asking yourself these questions:

Do my examples truly show my landlord as *uncooperative?*

Do my examples truly show the janitor as *incompetent?*

Do my examples truly show my neighbors as *inconsiderate?*

d   Proceed to write the first draft of your essay.

Revising

ALLWRITE!

4.3

After you have completed the first draft of the paper, set it aside for a while if you can. When you review it, try to do so as critically as you would if it were not your own work. Ask yourself these questions:

- Do I have a clearly stated (or implied) thesis?
- Have I provided *relevant* specific details for the landlord's uncooperativeness, the janitor's incompetence, and the neighbors' inconsiderateness?
- Have I provided *enough* specific details to support each of the three qualities?
- Have I used transitions, including transitions between paragraphs, to help readers follow my train of thought?
- Do I have a concluding paragraph that provides a summary or final thought or both?

As you revise your essay through one or more additional drafts, continue to refer to this list until you can answer "yes" to each question. Then be sure to check the next-to-final draft of the paper for the sentence skills listed on the inside front cover.

WRITING ASSIGNMENT 2

Write an examples essay on the outstanding qualities (good or bad) of a person you know well. This person might be a member of your family, a friend, a roommate, a boss, a neighbor, an instructor, or someone else.

You may approach this assignment in one of two ways. You may choose to write about three related qualities of one person. For example, "My brother is stubborn, bad-tempered, and suspicious." Or you may write about one quality that is apparent in three different aspects of a person's life. For example, "My sister's patience is apparent in her relationships with her students, her husband, and her teenage son."

Just to jog your thinking, here are some descriptive words that can be applied to people. You are *not* restricted to writing about these qualities. Write about whatever qualities the person you choose possesses.

Honest	Persistent	Flirtatious	Spineless
Bad-tempered	Shy	Irresponsible	Good-humored
Ambitious	Sloppy	Stingy	Cooperative
Prejudiced	Hardworking	Aggressive	Disciplined
Considerate	Outgoing	Trustworthy	Sentimental
Argumentative	Supportive	Courageous	Defensive
Softhearted	Suspicious	Compulsive	Dishonest
Energetic	Lazy	Jealous	Insensitive
Patient	Cynical	Modest	Neat
Reliable	Independent	Sarcastic	
Generous	Stubborn	Self-centered	

Prewriting

a   Ask yourself questions to come up with supporting details for your thesis. For instance, if you are writing about your sentimental father, you would ask questions like these:

Why do I think of Dad as being sentimental?

When have I seen him be sentimental?

What sort of occasions make him sentimental?

Where are some places he's become sentimental about?

Whom does Dad become sentimental about?

What are some memorable examples of Dad's acting sentimental?

b   Look over the material generated by your questioning, and decide what your three main points will be.

c   Decide on the order of your supporting paragraphs. If one of your main points seems stronger than the others, consider making it the final point in the body of the essay.

d   Decide whether to use one extended example or two or three brief examples to support each main point.

e   Prepare a scratch outline for your essay. To find your main points and supporting examples, draw on details generated by your questioning.

f   Write the first draft of your essay.

Revising

Refer to the guidelines for rewriting provided on page 222.

WRITING ASSIGNMENT 3

Write an examples essay based on an outside reading. It might be a selection recommended by your instructor, or it might be a piece by one of the following authors, all of whom have written books of essays that should be available in your college library.

Annie Dillard	Amy Tan
Ellen Goodman	Deborah Tannen
Molly Ivins	Henry David Thoreau
Maxine Hong Kingston	Calvin Trillin
George Orwell	Alice Walker
Richard Rodriguez	E. B. White
Andy Rooney	Marie Winn

Base your essay on some idea in the selection you have chosen, and provide a series of examples to back up your idea. A student model follows.

Paying Attention to a Death

In "A Hanging," George Orwell describes the execution of a man in a Burmese prison. The prisoner, a Hindu, is marched from his cell, led to a gallows, and killed when the drop opens and the noose tightens. The entire procedure takes eight minutes. As he depicts this incident, Orwell uses a   1 series of details that make us sharply aware of the enormity of killing a human being.

The moments leading up to the hanging are filled with tension. Six tall guards, two of them armed with rifles, surround the prisoner, "a puny wisp of a man." The guards not only handcuff the man but also chain his handcuffs to their belts and lash his arms to his sides. The guards, nervous about fulfilling their duty, treat the Hindu like "a fish which is still alive and may jump back into the water." Meanwhile, the jail superintendent prods the head jailer to get on with the execution. The superintendent's irritability is a mask for his discomfort. Then, the procession toward the gallows is interrupted by the appearance of a friendly dog, "wagging its whole body, wild with glee at finding so many human beings together." This does not ease the tension but increases it. The contrast of the lively dog licking the doomed man's face momentarily stuns the guards and arouses in the superintendent a sense of angry urgency.   2

Next, in the gallows scene, Orwell uses vivid details that emphasize the life within the man who is about to die. The condemned prisoner, who has been walking steadily up to this point, moves "clumsily" up the ladder. And until now, he has been utterly silent. But, after the noose is placed around his neck, he begins "crying out to his god." The repeated cry of "Ram! Ram! Ram!" is "like the tolling of a bell," a death knell. The dog begins to whine at the sound, and the guards go "grey," their bayonets trembling. It is as if the hooded, faceless man on the wooden platform has suddenly become a human being, a soul seeking aid and comfort. The superintendent, who has been hiding his emotions behind a stern face, gives the execution order "fiercely." The living man of moments ago simply ceases to be.   3

After the hanging, Orwell underscores the relief people feel when the momentous event is over. The jail superintendent checks to be sure that the prisoner is dead and then blows out "a deep breath" and loses his "moody look." "One felt an impulse," Orwell says, "to sing, to break into a run, to snigger." Suddenly, people are talking and chattering, even laughing. The head jailer's story about a condemned prisoner who clung to the bars of his cell so tightly that it took six men to move him sets off a gale of laughter. On the road outside the prison, everyone who participated in the execution has a whiskey. The men, having been so close to death, need to reassure themselves of the fact that they are alive. They must laugh and drink, not because they are insensitive, but because they are shaken. They must try to forget that the dead man is only a hundred yards away.   4

"A Hanging" sets out to create a picture of death in the midst of life. Orwell tries to make us see, through the details he chooses, that killing a person results in "one mind less, one world less." Such an act—"cutting a life short when it is in full tide"—violates the laws of life and nature.   5

WRITING ASSIGNMENT 4

Writing for a Specific Purpose and Audience

In this examples essay, you will write with a specific purpose and for a specific audience. Imagine that you have completed a year of college and have agreed to take part in your college's summer orientation program for incoming students. You will be meeting with a small group of new students to help them get ready for college life.

Prepare a presentation to the new students in which you make the point that college is more demanding than high school. Make vividly clear—using several hypothetical students as examples—just what the consequences of being unprepared for those demands can be. Focus on three areas of college and the demands of each. Some areas you might consider are these: instructors, class attendance, time control, class note-taking, studying a textbook, work habits, balancing work and social life, and getting help when it is needed. Each of the areas you choose should be developed in a separate paragraph. Each paragraph should have its own detailed examples.

11 Process

Every day we perform many activities that are *processes*, that is, series of steps carried out in a definite order. Many of these processes are familiar and automatic: for example, loading film into a camera, diapering a baby, or making an omelet. We are thus seldom aware of the sequence of steps making up each activity. In other cases—for example, when someone asks us for directions to a particular place, or when we try to read and follow directions for a new table game that someone has given us—we may be painfully conscious of the whole series of steps involved in the process.

In this chapter, you will be asked to write a process essay—one that explains clearly how to do or make something. To prepare for this assignment, you should first read the student process papers and the professional essay and then answer the questions that follow them.

Student Essays to Consider

Successful Exercise

Regular exercise is something like the weather—we all talk about it, but we tend not to do anything about it. Exercise classes on television and exercise programs on videos and CDs—as well as instructions in books, magazines, and pamphlets—now make it easy to have a low-cost personal exercise program without leaving home. However, for success in exercise, you should follow a simple plan consisting of arranging time, making preparations, and starting off at a sensible pace.

Everyone has an excuse for not exercising: a heavy schedule at work or school; being rushed in the morning and exhausted at night; too many other responsibilities. However, one solution is simply to get up half an hour earlier in the morning. Look at it this way: if you're already getting up too early, what's an extra half hour? Of course, that time could be cut to fifteen minutes earlier if you could lay out your clothes, set the breakfast table, fill the coffee maker, and gather your books and materials for the next day before you go to bed.

1

2

Next, prepare for your exercise session. To begin with, get yourself   3
ready by not eating or drinking anything before exercising. Why risk an
upset stomach? Then, dress comfortably in something that allows you to
move freely. Since you'll be in your own home, there's no need to invest
in a high-fashion dance costume. A loose T-shirt and shorts are good. A
bathing suit is great in summer, and in winter long underwear is warm and
comfortable. If your hair tends to flop in your eyes, pin it back or wear a
headband or scarf. Prepare the exercise area, too. Turn off the phone and
lock the door to prevent interruptions. Shove the coffee table out of the
way so you won't bruise yourself on it or other furniture. Then get out the
simple materials you'll need to exercise with.

Finally, use common sense in getting started. Common sense isn't so   4
common, as anyone who reads the newspapers and watches the world can
tell you. If this is your first attempt at exercising, begin slowly. You do not
need to do each movement the full number of times at first, but you should
<u>try</u> each one. After five or six sessions, you should be able to do each one
the full number of times. Try to move in a smooth, rhythmic way; this will
help prevent injuries and pulled muscles. Pretend you're a dancer and make
each move graceful, even if it's just getting up off the floor. After the last
exercise, give yourself five minutes to relax and cool off—you have earned
it. Finally, put those sore muscles under a hot shower and get ready for a
great day.

Establishing an exercise program isn't difficult, but it can't be achieved   5
by reading about it, talking about it, or watching models exercise on
television. It happens only when you get off that couch and do something
about it. As my doctor likes to say, "If you don't use it, you'll lose it."

How to Complain

I'm not just a consumer—I'm a victim. If I order a product, it is sure to   1
arrive in the wrong color, size, or quantity. If I hire people to do repairs,
they never arrive on the day scheduled. If I owe a bill, the computer is
bound to overcharge me. Therefore, in self-defense, I have developed the
following consumer's guide to complaining effectively.

The first step is getting organized. I save all sales slips and original   2
boxes. Also, I keep a special file for warranty cards and appliance
guarantees. This file does not prevent a product from falling apart the
day after the guarantee runs out. One of the problems in our country is
the shoddy workmanship that goes into many products. However, these
facts give me the ammunition I need to make a complaint. I know the date
of the purchase, the correct price (or service charge), where the item was
purchased, and an exact description of the product, including model and
serial numbers. When I compose my letter of complaint, I find it is not
necessary to exaggerate. I just stick to the facts.

The next step is to send the complaint to the person who will get   3
results quickly. My experience has shown that the president of the company
is the best person to contact. I call the company to find out the president's
name and make sure I note the proper spelling. Then I write directly to that
person, and I usually get prompt action. For example, the head of AMF
arranged to replace my son's ten-speed "lemon" when it fell apart piece
by piece in less than a year. Another time, the president of a Philadelphia
department store finally had a twenty-dollar overcharge on my bill
corrected after I had spent three months arguing uselessly with a computer.

If I get no response to a written complaint within ten days, I follow   4
through with a personal telephone call. When I had a new bathtub
installed a few years ago, the plumber left a gritty black substance on the
bottom of the tub. No amount of scrubbing could remove it. I tried every
cleanser on the supermarket shelf, but I still had a dirty tub. The plumber
shrugged off my complaints and said to try Comet. The manufacturer never
answered my letter. Finally, I made a personal phone call to the president
of the firm. Within days a well-dressed executive showed up at my door. In
a business suit, white shirt, striped tie, and rubber gloves, he cleaned the
tub. Before he left, he scolded me in an angry voice: "You didn't have to
call the president." The point is, I did have to call the president. No one else
cared enough to solve the problem.

Therefore, my advice to consumers is to keep accurate records, and   5
when you have to complain, go right to the top. It has always worked for me.

QUESTIONS

About Unity

1. The (*fill in the correct answer:* first, second, third) _____first_____
   supporting paragraph of "Successful Exercise" lacks a topic sentence. Write a
   topic sentence that expresses its main point: Wording of answers may vary.
   First, arrange time for exercise.

   _____

2. Which of the following sentences from paragraph 4 of "Successful Exercise"
   should be omitted in the interest of paragraph unity?
   a. "Finally, use common sense in getting started."
   b. "Common sense isn't so common, as anyone who reads newspapers and
      watches the world can tell you."
   c. "If this is your first attempt at exercising, begin slowly."
   d. "You do not need to do each movement the full number of times at first, but
      you should *try* each one."

3. Which sentence in paragraph 2 of "How to Complain" should be omitted in the interest of paragraph unity? *(Write the opening words.)*

   One of the problems . . .

About Support

4. Which sentence in paragraph 3 of "Successful Exercise" needs to be followed by more supporting details? *(Write the opening words.)*

   Then get out the simple materials . . .

5. Which supporting paragraph in "How to Complain" uses one extended example? Write the number of that paragraph and tell (in just a few words) what the example was about.   Wording of answers may vary.

   Paragraph 4 describes an incident with a plumber who left a bathtub dirty.

6. Which supporting paragraph in "How to Complain" depends on two short examples? Write the number of that paragraph and tell (in just a few words) what each example was about.   Wording of answers may vary.

   Paragraph 3 describes an incident with a "lemon" bicycle and an incident

   about an overcharge by a department store.

About Coherence

6

7. Read paragraph 3 of "Successful Exercise" and find the four sentences that begin with time signals. Write those four signals here.

Next	Then
To begin with	Then

8. "In How to Complain," which time transition word is used in the topic sentence of paragraph 2? _____first_____ In the topic sentence of paragraph 3?

   _____next_____

About the Introduction and Conclusion

8

9. Which statement best describes the introduction of "Successful Exercise"?

   a. It begins with a couple of general points about the topic and then narrows down to the thesis.

   b. It explains the importance of daily exercise to the reader.

    c. It uses a brief story about the author's experience with exercise.

    d. It asks a question about the role of exercise in life.

10. Which method of conclusion is used in both "Successful Exercise" and "How to Complain"?

    a. Summary

    b. Thought-provoking question

    c. Prediction

    (d.) Recommendation

Developing a Process Essay

Considering Purpose and Audience

Glance at a newsstand and you'll see magazine cover stories with titles such as "How to Impress Your Boss," "How to Add Romance to Your Life," or "How to Dress Like a Movie Star." These articles promise to give readers directions or information they can follow, and they are popular versions of process essays.

In general, the purpose of a process essay is to explain the steps involved in a particular action, process, or event. Some process essays focus on giving readers actual instructions, while others concentrate on giving readers information. The type of essay you write depends on the specific topic and purpose you choose.

As you prepare to write your process essay, begin by asking yourself what you want your readers to know. If, for example, you want your audience to know how to make the ultimate chocolate chip cookie, your process essay would include directions telling readers exactly what to do and how to do it. On the other hand, if you want your audience to know the steps involved in the process of digesting a chocolate chip cookie, you would instead detail the events that happen in the body as it turns food into energy. In this second instance, you would not be giving directions; you would be giving information.

No matter what your main point, keep your audience in mind as you work. As with any essay, select a topic that will interest readers. A group of college students, for example, might be interested in reading an essay on how to get financial aid but bored by an essay on how to prepare for retirement. In addition, consider how much your readers already know about your topic. An audience unfamiliar with financial aid may need background information in order to understand the process you have chosen to describe. Also, be sure to follow a clear sequence in your essay, putting events or steps in an order that readers can easily follow. Typically, steps in a process essay should be presented in time order, though not always. (For more information about words that signal time, see page 80.)

A final consideration for writing a process essay is point of view. If you are writing specific directions to readers (something done in this book), it is acceptable to write in *second person,* directly addressing your audience as "you." However, if you are presenting information, as in the example about digestion above, it is better to write in the more formal *third person.* (For more information about point of view, see pages 166–167.) In all cases, the goal is to choose the point of view that best suits your audience of readers and increases the likelihood that they will understand your main point.

Development through Prewriting

A process essay requires the writer to think through the steps involved in an activity. As Marian, the author of "How to Complain," thought about possible topics for her essay, she asked herself, "What are some things I do methodically, step by step?" A number of possibilities occurred to her, including getting herself and her children ready for school in the morning, shopping for groceries (from preparing a shopping list to organizing her coupons), and the one she finally settled on: effective complaining. "People tell me I'm 'so organized' when it comes to getting satisfaction on things I buy," Marian said. "I realized that I do usually get results when I complain because I go about complaining in an organized way. In order to write my essay, I just needed to put those steps into words."

Marian began by making a list of the steps she follows when she makes a complaint. This is what she wrote:

Save sales slips and original boxes

Engrave items with ID number in case of burglary

Write letter of complaint

Make photocopy of letter

Create file of warranties and guarantees

Send complaint letter directly to president

Call company for president's name

Follow through with telephone call if no response

Make thank-you call after action is taken

Next, she numbered those steps in the order in which she performs them. She struck out some items she realized weren't really necessary to the process of complaining:

1   Save sales slips and original boxes

~~Engrave items with ID number in case of burglary~~

4   Write letter of complaint

~~Make photocopy of letter~~

2   Create file of warranties and guarantees

5   Send complaint letter directly to president

3   Call company for president's name

6   Follow through with telephone call if no response

~~Make thank-you call after action is taken~~

Next, she decided to group her items into three steps: (1) getting organized, (2) sending the complaint to the president, and (3) following up with further action.

With that preparation done, Marian wrote her first draft.

First Draft

How to Complain

Because I find that a consumer has to watch out for herself and be ready to speak up if a product or service isn't satisfactory, I have developed the following consumer's guide to complaining effectively.

The first step is getting organized. I save all sales slips, original boxes, warranty cards, and appliance guarantees. This file does not prevent a product from falling apart the day after the guarantee runs out. One of the problems in our country is the shoddy workmanship that goes into many products. That way I know the date of the purchase, the correct price, where the item was purchased, and an exact description of the product.

The next step is to send the complaint to the person who will get results quickly. I call the company to find out the president's name and then I write directly to that person. For example, the head of AMF arranged to replace my son's bike. Another time, the president of a Philadelphia department store finally had a twenty-dollar overcharge on my bill corrected.

If I get no response to a written complaint within ten days, I follow through with a personal telephone call. When I had a new bathtub installed a few years ago, the plumber left a gritty black substance on the bottom of the tub. I tried everything to get it off. Finally, I made a personal phone call to the president of the firm. Within days a well-dressed executive showed up at my door. In a business suit, white shirt, striped tie, and rubber gloves, he cleaned the tub. Before he left, he said, "You didn't have to call the president."

Therefore, my advice to consumers is to keep accurate records, and when you have to complain, go right to the top. It has always worked for me.

Development through Revising

After she had written the first draft, Marian set it aside for several days. When she reread it, she was able to look at it more critically. These are her comments:

> I think this first draft is OK as the "bare bones" of an essay, but it needs to be fleshed out everywhere. For instance, in paragraph 2, I need to explain <u>why</u> it's important to know the date of purchase etc. And in paragraph 3, I need to explain more about <u>what happened</u> with the bike and the department store overcharge. In paragraph 4, especially, I need to explain <u>how</u> I tried to solve the problem with the bathtub before I called the president. I want to make it clear that I don't immediately go to the top as soon as I have a problem—I give the people at a lower level a chance to fix it first. All in all, my first draft looks as if I just rushed to get the basic ideas down on paper. Now I need to take the time to back up my main points with better support.

With that self-critique in mind, Marian wrote the version of "How to Complain" that appears on page 228.

A Professional Essay to Consider

Read the following professional essay. Then answer the questions and read the comments that follow.

How to Do Well on a Job Interview

by Glenda Davis

(Activity 3)

Ask a random selection of people for a listing of their least favorite activities, and right up there with "getting my teeth drilled" is likely to be "going to a job interview." The job interview is often regarded as a confusing, humiliating, and nerve-racking experience. First of all, you have to wait for your appointment in an outer room, often trapped there with other people applying for the same job. You sit nervously, trying not to think about the fact that only one of you may be hired. Then you are called into the interviewer's

1

office. Faced with a complete stranger, you have to try to act both cool and friendly as you are asked all sorts of questions. Some questions are personal: "What is your greatest weakness?" Others are confusing: "Why should we hire you?" The interview probably takes about twenty minutes but seems like two hours. Finally, you go home and wait for days and even weeks. If you get the job, great. But if you don't, you're rarely given any reason why.

2   The job-interview "game" may not be much fun, but it is a game you can win if you play it right. The name of the game is standing out of the crowd—in a positive way. If you go to the interview in a Bozo the Clown suit, you'll stand out of the crowd, all right, but not in a way that is likely to get you hired.

3   Here are guidelines to help you play the interview game to win:

4   **Present yourself as a winner.** Instantly, the way you dress, speak, and move gives the interviewer more information about you than you would think possible. You doubt that this is true? Consider this: a professional job recruiter, meeting a series of job applicants, was asked to signal the moment he decided *not* to hire each applicant. The thumbs-down decision was often made *in less than forty-five seconds—even before the applicant thought the interview had begun.*

5   How can you keep from becoming a victim of an instant "no" decision?

- *Dress appropriately.* This means business clothing: usually a suit and tie or a conservative dress or skirt suit. Don't wear casual student clothing. On the other hand, don't overdress: you're going to a job interview, not a party. If you're not sure what's considered appropriate business attire, do some spying before the interview. Walk past your prospective place of employment at lunch or quitting time and check out how the employees are dressed. Your goal is to look as though you would fit in with that group of people.

- *Pay attention to your grooming.* Untidy hair, body odor, dandruff, unshined shoes, a hanging hem, stains on your tie, excessive makeup or cologne, a sloppy job of shaving—if the interviewer notices any of these, your prospect of being hired takes a probably fatal hit.

- *Look alert, poised, and friendly.* When that interviewer looks into the waiting room and calls your name, he or she is getting a first impression of your behavior. If you're slouched in your chair, dozing or lost in the pages of a magazine; if you look up with an annoyed "Huh?"; if you get up slowly and wander over with your hands in your pockets, he or she will not be favorably impressed. What *will* earn you points is rising promptly and walking briskly toward the interviewer. Smiling and looking directly at that person, extend your hand to shake his or hers, saying, "I'm Lesley Brown. Thank you for seeing me today."

- *Expect to make a little small talk.* This is not a waste of time; it is the interviewer's way of checking your ability to be politely sociable, and it is your opportunity to cement the good impression you've already made. The key is to follow the interviewer's lead. If he or she wants to chat about the weather for a few minutes, do so. But don't drag it out; as soon as you get a signal that it's time to talk about the job, be ready to get down to business.

   Be ready for the interviewer's questions. The same questions come up   6
again and again in many job interviews. *You should plan ahead for all these questions!* Think carefully about each question, outline your answer, and memorize each outline. Then practice reciting the answers to yourself. Only in this way are you going to be prepared. Here are common questions, what they really mean, and how to answer them:

- *"Tell me about yourself."* This question is raised to see how organized you are. The *wrong* way to answer it is to launch into a wandering, disjointed response or—worse yet—to demand defensively, "What do you want to know?" or "What do you mean?" When this question comes up, you should be prepared to give a brief summary of your life and work experience—where you grew up, where your family lives now, where you went to school, what jobs you've had, and how you happen to be here now looking for the challenge of a new job.
- *"What are your strengths and weaknesses?"* In talking about your strong points, mention traits that will serve you well in this particular job. If you are well-organized, a creative problem-solver, a good team member, or a quick learner, be ready to describe specific ways those strengths have served you in the past. Don't make the mistake of saying, "I don't have any real weaknesses." You'll come across as more believable if you admit a flaw—but make it one that an employer might actually like. For instance, admit that you are a workaholic or a perfectionist.
- *"Why should we hire you?"* Remember that it is up to *you* to convince the interviewer that you're the man or woman for this job. If you just sit there and hope that the interviewer will magically discern your good qualities, you are likely to be disappointed. Don't be afraid to sell yourself. Tell the recruiter that from your research you have learned that the interviewer's company is one you would like to work for, and that you believe the company's needs and your skills are a great match.
- *"Why did you leave your last job?"* This may seem like a great opportunity to cry on the interviewer's shoulder about what a jerk your last boss was or how unappreciated you were. It is not. The experts agree: never bad-mouth *anyone* when you are asked this question. Say that you left in order to seek greater responsibilities or challenges. Be positive, not negative. No matter how justified you may feel about hating your last job or boss, if

you give voice to those feelings in an interview, you're going to make the interviewer suspect that you're a whiner and hard to work with.

- *"Do you have any questions?"* This is the time to stress one last time how interested you are in this particular job. Ask a question or two about specific aspects of the job, pointing out again how well your talents and the company's needs are matched. Even if you're dying to know how much the job pays and how much vacation you get, don't ask. There will be time enough to cover those questions after you've been offered the job. Today, your task is to demonstrate what a good employee you would be.

Send a thank-you note. Once you've gotten past the interview, there is 7 one more chance for you to make a fine impression. As soon as you can— certainly no more than one or two days after the interview— write a note of thanks to your interviewer. In it, briefly remind him or her of when you came in and what job you applied for. As well as thanking the interviewer for seeing you, reaffirm your interest in the job and mention again why you think you are the best candidate for it. Make the note courteous, businesslike, and brief—just a paragraph or two. If the interviewer is wavering between several equally qualified candidates, such a note could tip the scales in your favor.

No amount of preparation is going to make interviewing for a job your 8 favorite activity. But if you go in well-prepared and with a positive attitude, your potential employer can't help thinking highly of you. And the day will come when you are the one who wins the job.

QUESTIONS

About Unity

1. Either of two sentences in "How to Do Well on a Job Interview" might serve as the thesis. Write the opening words of either of these sentences:

   The job-interview "game" may not be much fun, but . . . you can win if you

   play it right.

   Here are guidelines to help you play the interview game to win.

2. Which statement would make the best topic sentence for paragraph 4?
   a. Beauty is only skin-deep.
   b. Interviewers care only about how applicants dress.
   c. Professional job recruiters meet many applicants for a single job.
   d. You should present yourself as a winner because first impressions count a lot.

3. In paragraph 6, which statement would best serve as a topic sentence for the list item about strengths and weaknesses?

  a. A quality such as perfectionism or workaholism can be seen as both a strength and a weakness.

  (b) As you talk about your strengths and weaknesses, tailor what you say to the job you're applying for.

  c. Claiming to be a "creative problem-solver" is a good idea as you apply for almost any position.

  d. The interviewer is not likely to be impressed if you claim to have no major weaknesses.

About Support

4. In paragraph 5, the supporting details for the list item "dress appropriately" are

  a. reasons for dressing appropriately.

  b. quotations of experts on how to dress for job interviews.

  (c) ideas on how to dress appropriately.

  d. statistics on how people who are interviewed dress and how well they succeed.

5. Which sentence from paragraph 7 best provides a *reason* for the author's suggestion about "sending a thank-you note?

  a. "As soon as you can—certainly no more than one or two days after the interview—write a note of thanks to your interviewer."

  b. "In it, briefly remind him or her of when you came in and what job you applied for."

  c. "Make the note courteous, businesslike, and brief—just a paragraph or two."

  (d) "If the interviewer is wavering between several equally qualified candidates, such a note could tip the scales in your favor."

About Coherence

6. In paragraph 1, what three transitional words or phrases are used to begin sentences as the author describes the process of interviewing?

  _____First of all_____   _____Then_____   _____Finally_____

7. The main method of organization of paragraph 1 is

  (a) time order.

  b. emphatic order.

8. In paragraph 5, find the "change of direction" signal that begins a sentence in the first list item. Write the opening words of that sentence here.

On the other hand

About the Introduction and Conclusion

9. Which statement best describes the introductory paragraph of "How to Do Well on a Job Interview"?

   a. It begins with a broad, general statement about job interviews and narrows it down to the thesis statement.

   b. It describes a typical job interview and its aftermath.

   c. It explains the importance of doing well on a job interview.

   d. It asks a series of questions that encourage readers to think about how they prepare for a job interview.

10. Which statement best describes the concluding paragraph of "How to Do Well on a Job Interview"?

    a. It ends with a summary of the article.

    b. It ends with a prediction of what will happen if advice in the article is followed.

    c. It ends with a series of questions that prompt the reader to think further about what's been written.

Writing a Process Essay

WRITING ASSIGNMENT 1

Choose a topic from the list below to use as the basis for a process essay.

How to shop for groceries in a minimum of time

How to shop for a car, rent an apartment, or buy a house

How to do household cleaning efficiently

How to gain or lose weight

How to get over a broken heart

How to plan an event (party, wedding, garage sale, etc.)

How to choose a pet

How to quit smoking (or another bad habit)

How to cook a favorite dish

Prewriting

a   Freewrite for ten minutes on the topic you have tentatively chosen. Don't worry about spelling, grammar, organization, or anything other than getting your thoughts down on the page. If ideas are still flowing at the end of ten minutes, keep on writing. This freewriting will give you a base of raw material that you can draw on in the next phase of your work. Judging from your freewriting, do you think you have enough material to support a process essay? If so, keep following the steps below. If not, choose another topic and freewrite about *it* for ten minutes.

b   Develop a single clear sentence that will serve as your thesis. Your thesis can either (1) say it is important that your readers know about this process ("Knowing how to choose a pet wisely can ensure that the two of you have a happy relationship") or (2) state your opinion of this process ("Quitting smoking is the most important single thing you can do for your health").

c   Make a list of the steps you are describing. Here, for example, is the list prepared by the author of "Successful Exercise."

Wear comfortable, loose clothing
Clear an area for exercise
Lock the door and turn off the phone
Tie hair back
Move smoothly and gracefully
Start slowly
Take hot shower afterward
Make time—get up early, give up a TV show
Get out weights or other equipment
Turn on music
Cool down

d   Number your items in time order. Strike out items that do not fit in the list; add others as they occur to you. Thus:

2 Wear comfortable, loose clothing

4 Clear an area for exercise

6 Lock the door and turn off the phone

3 Tie hair back

8 Move smoothly and gracefully

7 Start slowly

10 Take hot shower afterward

1 Make time—get up early, give up a TV show

5 Get out weights or other equipment

~~Turn on music~~

9 Cool down

e   After making the list, decide how the items can be grouped into a minimum of three steps. For example, with "Successful Exercise," you might divide the process into (1) setting a regular time, (2) preparing for exercise, and (3) doing the exercise. With a topic like "How to Quit Smoking," you might divide the process into (1) keeping a journal of your smoking, (2) preparing mentally and physically, and (3) getting through the first days.

f   Use your list as a guide to write the first rough draft of your paper. Do not expect to finish your paper in one draft. You should be ready to write a series of drafts as you work toward the goals of unity, support, and coherence.

Revising

ALLWRITE!

4.3

After you have completed the first draft of the paper, set it aside for a while if you can. Then read the paper out loud to a friend or classmate whose judgment you respect. Keep these points in mind as you hear your own words, and ask your friend to respond to them as well.

- It's essential for a process paper to describe a series of activities in a way that is easy to follow. Does this paper describe the steps in a clear, logical way? Have I used transitions such as *first, next, also, then, after, now, during,* and *finally* to make the paper move smoothly and clearly from one step to another?

- Does the paper describe the necessary steps so that a reader could perform the task described, or is essential information missing?

- Do I have a concluding paragraph that provides a summary or final thought or both?
- Is the paper free of sentence-skills mistakes?

As you revise your essay through one or more additional drafts, continue to refer to this list until you can answer "yes" to each question. Then be sure to proofread the next-to-final draft of the paper for the sentence skills listed on the inside front cover.

WRITING ASSIGNMENT 2

Everyone is an expert at something. Write a process essay on some skill that you can perform very well. Write from the point of view that "This is how _____ *should* be done." Remember that your skill need not be unusual. It can be anything from "making a perfect pie crust" to "hooking up a car stereo" to "dealing with unpleasant customers" to "using a digital camcorder."

Prewriting

a   If possible, perform the task and, as you go along, take notes on what you're doing. If that's not possible (as in "dealing with unpleasant customers"), think through a particular time you had to deal with such a task and make notes about just what you did.

b   Look over your notes and make a list of the steps you followed.

c   Considering your list, decide how you can divide the items listed into at least three steps. For instance, look at the following list of items for the process of "Cooking a Pot Roast." Then fill in the blanks in the scratch outline that follows:

---

1   Marinate the roast for thirty minutes with Adolph's Marinade.

2   Sprinkle the roast with seasoned flour.

3   Heat oil in a heavy pot.

4   Brown roast on all sides in the hot oil.

5   Cover the roast with one-third water, one-third beef broth, and one-third red wine.

6   Bring roast and liquid to boil.

7   Cover pot.

8   Turn down heat and simmer for an hour.

9 Taste broth and add seasonings as desired—salt, pepper, Worcestershire sauce.

10 Peel potatoes and carrots and cut into chunks.

11 Cut onions into chunks.

12 Add vegetables to pot for the last half hour of cooking.

13 Cook until meat flakes easily when you stick a fork in it.

14 Remove meat and vegetables from broth.

15 Dissolve two tablespoons of flour in half-cup cold water.

16 Stir flour mixture into boiling broth to thicken into gravy.

17 Serve gravy with the meat and vegetables.

Step 1:   Preparing and cooking the meat
           Items ___1___ through ___9___
Step 2:   Preparing and cooking the vegetables
           Items ___10___ through ___12___
Step 3:   Preparing the gravy and serving
           Items ___13___ through ___17___

d Prepare such a scratch outline of your main points. Use it as your guide as you write the rough draft of your paper.

Revising

As you read through your first draft and subsequent drafts, ask yourself these questions:

- Have I introduced my essay with either a statement of the importance of the process or my opinion of the process?
- Have I provided a clear step-by-step description of the process?
- Have I divided the items in the process into at least three logical steps (main points of the essay)?
- Have I used transition words such as *first, next, then, during,* and *finally* to help readers follow my train of thought?

As you revise your essay through one or more additional drafts, continue to refer to this list until you can answer "yes" to each question. Then be sure to check the next-to-final draft of the paper for the sentence skills listed on the inside front cover.

WRITING ASSIGNMENT 3

Any one of the topics below can be written as a process paper. Follow the steps suggested for Writing Assignment 1. Note that some of these topics invite a humorous point of view.

How to break a bad habit

How to live with a two-year-old, a teenager, or a parent

How to make someone like you

How to make excuses

How to fall out of love

How to improve your reading skills

How to care for an aging relative

How to improve a school or a place of work

WRITING ASSIGNMENT 4

Writing for a Specific Purpose and Audience

In this process essay, you will write with a specific purpose and for a specific audience. Imagine that you have a younger brother or sister who has asked you to be a guest editor of his or her high school paper. Prepare an informal essay in which you summarize, in your own words, the steps involved in successfully managing your time in college or in preparing for and taking an essay exam.

12 Cause and Effect

7.4e

Why did Gail decide to move out of her parents' house? What made you quit a well-paying job? Why are horror movies so popular? Why has Ben acted so depressed lately? Why did our team fail to make the league play-offs?

Every day we ask questions like these and look for answers. We realize that many actions do not occur without causes, and we realize also that a given action can have a series of effects—good or bad. By examining the causes or effects of an action, we seek to understand and explain things that happen in our lives.

You will be asked in this chapter to do some detective work by examining the cause of something or the effects of something. First read the student essays and the professional essay that follow and work through the questions that accompany the essays. All three essays support their thesis statements by explaining a series of causes or a series of effects.

Student Essays to Consider

The Joys of an Old Car

Some of my friends can't believe that my car still runs. Others laugh when they see it parked outside the house and ask if it's an antique. But they aren't being fair to my twenty-year-old Toyota Corolla. In fact, my "antique" has opened my eyes to the rewards of owning an old car.

1

One obvious reward of owning my old Toyota is economy. Twenty years ago, when my husband and I were newly married and nearly broke, we bought the car—a shiny red year-old leftover—for a mere $4,200. Today it would cost four times as much. We save money on insurance, since it's no longer worthwhile for us to have collision coverage. Old age has even been kind to the Toyota's engine, which has required only three major repairs in the last several years. And it still delivers twenty-eight miles per gallon in the city and forty-one on the highway—not bad for a senior citizen.

2

I've heard that when a Toyota passes the twenty-thousand-mile mark with no problems, it will probably go on forever. I wouldn't disagree. Our Toyota breezed past that mark many years ago. Since then, I've been able

3

245

to count on it to sputter to life and make its way down the driveway on the coldest, snowiest mornings. When my boss got stuck with his brand-new BMW in the worst snowstorm of the year, I sauntered into work on time. The single time my Toyota didn't start, unfortunately, was the day I had a final exam. The Toyota may have the body of an old car, but beneath its elderly hood hums the engine of a teenager.

Last of all, having the same car for many years offers the advantage of familiarity. When I open the door and slide into the driver's seat, the soft vinyl surrounds me like a well-worn glove. I know to the millimeter exactly how much room I have when I turn a corner or back into a curbside parking space. When my gas gauge points to "empty," I know that 1.3 gallons are still in reserve, and I can plan accordingly. The front wheels invariably begin to shake when I go more than fifty-five miles an hour, reminding me that I am exceeding the speed limit. With the Toyota, the only surprises I face come from other drivers.   4

I prize my twenty-year-old Toyota's economy and dependability, and most of all, its familiarity. It is faded, predictable, and comfortable, like a well-worn pair of jeans. And, like a well-worn pair of jeans, it will be difficult to throw away.   5

Stresses of Being a Celebrity

A woman signing herself "Wants the Truth in Westport" wrote to Ann Landers with a question she just had to have answered. "Please find out for sure," she begged the columnist, "whether or not Oprah Winfrey has had a face-lift." Fortunately for Ms. Winfrey's privacy, Ann Landers refused to answer the question. But the incident was disturbing. How awful it would be to be a celebrity, always in the public eye. Celebrities lead very stressful lives, for no matter how glamorous or powerful they are, they have too little privacy, too much pressure, and no safety.   1

For one thing, celebrities don't have the privacy an ordinary person has. The most personal details of their lives are splashed all over the front pages of the National Enquirer and the Globe so that bored supermarket shoppers can read about "Leonardo DiCaprio's Awful Secret" or "The Heartbreak Behind Winona Ryder's Smile." Even a celebrity's family is hauled into the spotlight. A teenage son's arrest for pot possession or a wife's drinking problem becomes the subject of glaring headlines. Photographers hound celebrities at their homes, in restaurants, and on the street, hoping to get a picture of Halle Berry in curlers or Jim Carrey guzzling a beer. When celebrities try to do the things that normal people do, like eat out or attend a football game, they run the risk of being interrupted by thoughtless autograph hounds or mobbed by aggressive fans.   2

In addition to the loss of privacy, celebrities must cope with the constant pressure of having to look great and act right. Their physical appearance is always under observation. Famous women, especially, suffer from the spotlight, drawing remarks like "She really looks old" or "Boy, has she put on weight." Unflattering pictures of celebrities are photographers' prizes to be sold to the highest bidder; this increases the pressure on celebrities to look good at all times. Famous people are also under pressure to act calm and collected under any circumstances. Because they are constantly observed, they have no freedom to blow off steam or to do something just a little crazy.

Most important, celebrities must deal with the stress of being in constant danger. The friendly grabs, hugs, and kisses of enthusiastic fans can quickly turn into uncontrolled assaults on a celebrity's hair, clothes, and car. Most people agree that photographers bear some responsibility for the death of one of the leading celebrities of the 1990s—Princess Diana. Whether or not their pursuit caused the crash that took her life, it's clear she was chased as aggressively as any escaped convict by bloodhounds. And celebrity can even lead to deliberately lethal attacks. The attempt to kill Ronald Reagan and the murder of John Lennon came about because two unbalanced people became obsessed with these world-famous figures. Famous people must live with the fact that they are always fair game—and never out of season.

Some people dream of starring roles, their name in lights, and their picture on the cover of People magazine. But the cost is far too high. A famous person gives up private life, feels pressured to look and act certain ways all the time, and is never completely safe. An ordinary, calm life is far safer and saner than a life of fame.

QUESTIONS

About Unity

1. Which supporting paragraph in "The Joys of an Old Car" lacks a topic sentence?
   a. 2
   b. 3
   c. 4

2. Which sentence in paragraph 3 of "The Joys of an Old Car" should be omitted in the interest of paragraph unity? (Write the opening words.)

   The single time . . .

3. Rewrite the thesis statement of "The Joys of an Old Car" to include a plan of development.   Wording of answers may vary.

In fact, my "antique" has opened my eyes to the advantages of owning an

old car: economy, reliability, and familiarity.

About Support

4. In paragraph 4 of "Stresses of Being a Celebrity," the author supports the idea that "celebrities must deal with the stress of being in constant danger" with (circle the letters of the two answers that apply)

a. statistics.

b. an explanation.

c. a quotation by an expert.

d. examples.

5. After which sentence in paragraph 3 of "Stresses of Being a Celebrity" are more specific details needed? (Write the opening words.)

Because they are constantly observed . . .

6. In "The Joys of an Old Car," how many examples are given to support the topic sentence "One obvious reward . . . is economy"?

a. two

b. three

c. four

d. five

About Coherence

7. Which topic sentence in "Stresses of Being a Celebrity" functions as a linking sentence between paragraphs? (Write the opening words.)

In addition to the loss of privacy . . .

8. Paragraph 3 of "Stresses of Being a Celebrity" includes two main transition words or phrases. List those words or phrases.

In addition   also

9. What are the two transition words or phrases in "The Joys of an Old Car" that signal two major points of support for the thesis?

One   Last of all

8

About the Introduction and Conclusion

10. Which method is used in the conclusion of "The Joys of an Old Car"?
   a. Summary and final thought
   b. Thought-provoking question
   c. Recommendation

Developing a Cause-and-Effect Essay

Considering Purpose and Audience

The main purpose of a cause-and-effect essay is to explain to your audience (1) the causes of a particular event or situation; (2) the effects of an event or a situation; or, more rarely, (3) a combination of both.

The type of cause-effect essay you write will depend on the topic you choose and the main point you wish to communicate. If, for example, your purpose is to tell readers about the impact a special person had on your life, your essay would focus mainly on the *effects* of that person. However, if your purpose is to explain why you moved out of your family home, your essay would focus on the *causes* of your decision.

As with all essays, try to pick a topic that will appeal to your audience of readers. An essay on the negative effects of steroids and other drugs on professional athletes may be especially interesting to an audience of sports fans. On the other hand, this same topic might *not be as appealing* to people who dislike sports. In addition to selecting a lively topic, be sure to make your main point clear so that your audience can follow the cause-effect relationship you've chosen to develop. In the above instance, you might even announce specific causes or effects by signaling them to readers: "One effect drug use has on athletes is to . . . ."

Development through Prewriting

2.3

The best essays are often those written about a topic that the author genuinely cares about. When Janine, the author of "The Joys of an Old Car," was assigned a cause-effect essay, she welcomed the assignment. She explains: "My husband and I believe in enjoying what we have and living simply, rather than 'keeping up with the Joneses.' Our beat-up old car is an example of that way of life. People often say to me, 'Surely you could buy a nicer car!' I enjoy explaining to them why we keep our old 'clunker.' So when I heard 'cause-effect essay,' I immediately thought of the car as a topic. Writing this essay was just an extension of a conversation I've had many times."

Although Janine had often praised the virtues of her old car to friends, she wasn't sure how to divide what she had to say into three main points. In order to get started, she made a list of all the good things about her car. Here is what she wrote:

Starts reliably

Has needed few major repairs

Reminder of Bill's and my first days of marriage

Gets good gas mileage

Don't need to worry about scratches and scrapes

I know exactly how much room I need to turn and park

Saves money on insurance

I'm very comfortable in it

No car payments

Cold weather doesn't seem to bother it

Don't worry about its being stolen

Uses regular gas

Can haul anything in it—dog, plants—and not worry about dirt

Know all its little tics and shimmies and don't worry about them

---

When Janine reviewed her list, she saw that the items fell into three major categories. There was (1) the car's economy, (2) its familiarity, and (3) its dependability. She went back and noted which category each of the items best fit. Then she crossed out those items that didn't seem to belong in any of the categories.

---

3   Starts reliably

1   Has needed few major repairs

~~Reminder of Bill's and my first days of marriage~~

1   Gets good gas mileage

~~Don't need to worry about scratches and scrapes~~

2   I know exactly how much room I need to turn and park

1   Saves money on insurance

> 2 I'm very comfortable in it
>
> 1 No car payments
>
> 3 Cold weather doesn't seem to bother it
>
> ~~Don't worry about its being stolen~~
>
> 1 Uses regular gas
>
> ~~Can haul anything in it—dog, plants—and not worry about dirt~~
>
> 2 Know all its little tics and shimmies and don't worry about them

Now Janine had three main points and several items to support each point. She produced this as a first draft:

First Draft

The Joys of an Old Car

When people see my beat-up old car, they sometimes laugh at it. But I tell them that owning a twenty-year-old Toyota has its good points.

One obvious reward is economy. My husband and I bought the car when we were newly married. We paid $4,200 for it. That seemed like a lot of money then, but today we'd spend four times that much for a similar car. We also save money on insurance. In the twenty years we've had it, the Toyota has needed only a few major repairs. It even gets good gas mileage.

I like the familiar feel of the car. I'm so used to it that driving anything else feels very strange. When I visited my sister recently, I drove her new Plymouth to the grocery store. Everything was so unfamiliar! I couldn't even figure out how to turn on the radio. I was relieved to get back to my own car.

Finally, my car is very dependable. No matter how cold and snowy it is, I know the Toyota will start quickly and get me where I need to go. Unfortunately, one day it didn't start, and naturally that day I had a final exam. But otherwise it just keeps on going and going.

My Toyota reminds me of a favorite piece of clothing that you wear forever and can't bear to throw away.

Development through Revising

4.3

Janine traded first drafts with a classmate, Sharon, and each critiqued the other's work before it was revised. Here is Janine's first draft again, with Sharon's comments in the margins.

The Joys of an Old Car

When people see my beat-up old car, they sometimes laugh at it. But I tell them that owning a twenty-year-old Toyota has its good points.

One obvious reward is economy. My husband and I bought the car when we were newly married. We paid $4,200 for it. That seemed like a lot of money then, but today we'd spend four times that much for a similar car. We also save money on insurance. In the twenty years we've had it, the Toyota has needed only a few major repairs. It even gets good gas mileage.

I like the familiar feel of the car. I'm so used to it that driving anything else feels very strange. When I visited my sister recently, I drove her new Plymouth to the grocery store. Everything was so unfamiliar! I couldn't even figure out how to turn on the radio. I was relieved to get back to my own car.

Finally, my car is very dependable. No matter how cold and snowy it is, I know the Toyota will start quickly and get me where I need to go. Unfortunately, one day it didn't start, and naturally that day I had a final exam. But otherwise it just keeps on going and going.

My Toyota reminds me of a favorite piece of clothing that you wear forever and can't bear to throw away.

Reader's Comments

How? Is the insurance less expensive just because the car is old?

Here would be a good place for a specific detail—how good is the mileage?

This topic sentence doesn't tie in with the others—shouldn't it say "Second," or "Another reason I like the car . . ."?

This is too much about your sister's car and not enough about yours.

This is a good comparison. But draw it out more—how is the car like comfortable old clothes?

Making use of Sharon's comments, Janine wrote the final version of "The Joys of an Old Car" that appears on page 245.

A Professional Essay to Consider

Read the following professional essay. Then answer the questions and read the comments that follow.

Taming the Anger Monster

by Anne Davidson

(Activity 3)

Laura Houser remembers the day with embarrassment. 1

"My mother was visiting from Illinois," she says. "We'd gone out to lunch 2 and done some shopping. On our way home, we stopped at an intersection. When the light changed, the guy ahead of us was looking at a map or something and didn't move right away. I leaned on my horn and automatically yelled—well, what I generally yell at people who make me wait. I didn't even think about what I was doing. One moment I was talking and laughing with my mother, and the next I was shouting curses at a stranger. Mom's jaw just dropped. She said, 'Well, I guess *you've* been living in the city too long.' That's when I realized that my anger was out of control."

Laura has plenty of company. Here are a few examples plucked from the 3 headlines of recent newspapers:

- Amtrak's Washington–New York train: When a woman begins to use her cell phone in a designated "quiet car," her seatmate grabs the phone and smashes it against the wall.
- Reading, Mass.: Arguing over rough play at their ten-year-old sons' hockey practice, two fathers begin throwing punches. One of the dads beats the other to death.
- Westport, Conn.: Two supermarket shoppers get into a fistfight over who should be first in a just-opened checkout line.

Reading these stories and countless others like them which happen daily, it's hard to escape the conclusion that we are one angry society. An entire vocabulary has grown up to describe situations of out-of-control fury: road rage, sideline rage, computer rage, biker rage, air rage. Bookstore shelves are filled with authors' advice on how to deal with our anger. Court-ordered anger management classes have become commonplace, and anger-management workshops are advertised in local newspapers.

Human beings have always experienced anger, of course. But in earlier, 4 more civil decades, public displays of anger were unusual to the point of being aberrant. Today, however, whether in petty or deadly forms, episodes of unrepressed rage have become part of our daily landscape.

What has happened to us? Are we that much angrier than we used to 5 be? Have we lost all inhibitions about expressing our anger? Are we, as a society, literally losing our ability to control our tempers?

Why Are We So Angry?

According to Sybil Evans, a conflict-resolution expert in New York City, 6 there are three components to blame for our societal bad behavior: time, technology and tension.

What's eating up our time? To begin with, Americans work longer hours 7
and are rewarded with less vacation time than people in any other industrial
society. Over an average year, for example, most British employees work
250 hours less than most Americans; most Germans work a full 500 hours
less. And most Europeans are given four to six weeks vacation every year,
compared to the average American's two weeks. To make matters worse,
many Americans face long stressful commutes at the beginning and end of
each long workday.

Once we Americans finally get home from work, our busy day is rarely 8
done. We are involved in community activities; our children participate in
sports, school programs, and extra-curricular activities; and our houses, yards
and cars cry out for maintenance. To make matters worse, we are reluctant to
use the little bit of leisure time we do have to catch up on our sleep. Compared
with Americans of the nineteenth and early twentieth centuries, most of us are
chronically sleep-deprived. While our ancestors typically slept nine-and-a-half
hours a night, many of us feel lucky to get seven. We're critical of "lazy" people
who sleep longer, and we associate naps with toddlerhood. (In doing so, we
ignore the example of successful people including Winston Churchill, Albert
Einstein, and Napoleon, all of whom were devoted to their afternoon naps.)

The bottom line: we are time-challenged and just plain tired—and tired 9
people are cranky people. We're ready to blow—to snap at the slow-moving
cashier, to tap the bumper of the slowpoke ahead of us, or to do something
far worse.

Technology is also to blame for the bad behavior so widespread in our 10
culture. Amazing gadgets were supposed to make our lives easier—but have
they? Sure, technology has its positive aspects. It is a blessing, for instance,
to have a cell phone on hand when your car breaks down far from home
or to be able to "instant message" a friend on the other side of the globe.
But the downsides are many. Cell phones, pagers, fax machines, handheld
computers and the like have robbed many of us of what was once valuable
downtime. Now we're *always* available to take that urgent call or act on
that last-minute demand. Then there is the endless pressure of feeling we
need to keep up with our gadgets' latest technological developments. For
example, it's not sufficient to use your cell phone for phone calls. Now you
must learn to use the phone for text-messaging and downloading games. It's
not enough to take still photos with your digital camera. You should know
how to shoot ultra high-speed fast-action clips. It's not enough to have an
enviable CD collection. You should be downloading new songs in MP3 format.
The computers in your house should be connected by a wireless router, and
online via high-speed DSL service. In other words, if it's been more than ten
minutes since you've updated your technology, you're probably behind.

In fact, you're not only behind; you're a stupid loser. At least, that's 11
how most of us end up feeling as we're confronted with more and more

unexpected technologies: the do-it-yourself checkout at the supermarket, the telephone "help center" that offers a recorded series of messages, but no human help. And feeling like losers makes us frustrated and, you guessed it, angry. "It's not any one thing but lots of little things that make people feel like they don't have control of their lives," says Jane Middleton-Moz, an author and therapist. "A sense of helplessness is what triggers rage. It's why people end up kicking ATM machines."

Her example is not far-fetched. According to a survey of computer users   12
in Great Britain, a quarter of those under age 25 admitted to having kicked or punched their computers on at least one occasion. Others confessed to yanking out cables in a rage, forcing the computer to crash. On this side of the Atlantic, a Wisconsin man, after repeated attempts to get his daughter's malfunctioning computer repaired, took It to the store where he had bought it, placed it in the foyer, and attacked it with a sledgehammer. Arrested and awaiting a court appearance, he told local reporters, "It feels good, in a way." He had put into action a fantasy many of us have had—that of taking out our feelings of rage on the machines that so frustrate us.

Tension, the third major culprit behind our epidemic of anger, is intimately   13
connected with our lack of time and the pressures of technology. Merely our chronic exhaustion and our frustration in the face of a bewildering array of technologies would be enough to cause our stress levels to skyrocket, but we are dealing with much more. Our tension is often fueled by a reserve of anger that might be the result of a critical boss, marital discord, or (something that many of today's men and women experience, if few will admit it) a general sense of being stupid and inadequate in the face of the demands of modern life. And along with the challenges of everyday life, we now live with a widespread fear of such horrors as terrorist acts, global warming, and antibiotic-resistant diseases. Our sense of dread may be out of proportion to actual threats because of technology's ability to so constantly bombard us with worrisome information. Twenty-four hours a day news stations bring a stream of horror into our living rooms. As we work on our computers, headlines and graphic images are never more than a mouseclick away.

The Result of Our Anger

Add it all together—our feeling of never having enough time; the   14
chronic aggravation caused by technology; and our endless, diffuse sense of stress—and we become time bombs waiting to explode. Our angry outbursts may be briefly satisfying, but afterwards we are left feeling—well, like jerks. Worse, flying off the handle is a self-perpetuating behavior. Brad Bushman, a psychology professor at Iowa State University, says, "Catharsis is worse than useless." Bushman's research has shown that when people vent their anger, they actually become more, not less, aggressive. "Many people think

of anger as the psychological equivalent of the steam in a pressure cooker. It has to be released, or it will explode. That's not true. The people who react by hitting, kicking, screaming, and swearing just feel more angry."

Furthermore, the unharnessed venting of anger may actually do us physical harm. The vigorous expression of anger pumps adrenaline into our system and raises our blood pressure, setting the stage for heart attack and strokes. Frequently-angry people have even been shown to have higher cholesterol levels than even-tempered individuals.   15

How to Deal with Our Anger

Unfortunately, the culprits behind much of our anger—lack of time, frustrating technology, and mega-levels of stress—are not likely to resolve themselves anytime soon. So what are we to do with the anger that arises as a result?   16

According to Carol Tavris, author of *Anger: The Misunderstood Emotion*, the keys to dealing with anger are common sense and patience. She points out that almost no situation is improved by an angry outburst. A traffic jam, a frozen computer, or a misplaced set of car keys are annoying. To act upon the angry feelings those situations provoke, however, is an exercise in futility. Shouting, fuming, or leaning on the car horn won't make traffic begin to flow, the screen unlock, or keys materialize.   17

Patience, on the other hand, is a highly practical virtue. People who take the time to cool down before responding to an anger-producing situation are far less likely to say or do something they will regret later. "It is as true of the body as of arrows," Tavris says, "that what goes up must come down. Any emotional arousal will simmer down if you just wait long enough." When you are stuck in traffic, in other words, turn on some soothing music, breathe deeply, and count to ten—or thirty or forty, if need be.   18

Anger-management therapist Doris Wild Helmering agrees. "Like any feeling, anger lasts only about three seconds," she says. "What keeps it going is your own negative thinking." As long as you focus on the idiot who cut you off on the expressway, you'll stay angry. But if you let the incident go, your anger will go with it. "Once you come to understand that you're driving your own anger with your thoughts," adds Helmering, "you can stop it."   19

Experts who have studied anger also encourage people to cultivate activities that effectively vent their anger. For some people, it's reading the newspaper or watching TV, while others need more active outlets, such as using a treadmill, taking a walk, hitting golf balls, or working out with a punching bag. People who succeed in calming their anger can also enjoy the satisfaction of having dealt positively with their frustrations.   20

For Laura Houser, the episode in the car with her mother was a wake-up call. "I saw myself through her eyes," she said, "and I realized I had become a chronically angry, impatient jerk. My response to stressful situations had   21 become habitual—I automatically flew off the handle. Once I saw what I was doing, it really wasn't that hard to develop different habits. I simply decided I was going to treat other people the way I would want to be treated." The changes in Laura's life haven't benefited only her former victims. "I'm a calmer, happier person now," she reports. "I don't lie in bed at night fuming over stupid things other people have done and my own enraged responses." Laura has discovered the satisfaction of having a sense of control over her own behavior—which ultimately is all any of us can control.

QUESTIONS

About Unity

1. Which of the following statements best represents the implied thesis of "Taming the Anger Monster"?

    a. People today have lost their ability to control their anger and to behave in a civil fashion.

    b. Anger would last only a few seconds if we didn't keep it going with negative thinking.

    c. While technology has its positive aspects, it has made us constantly available to others and frustrates us with the need to master its endless new developments.

    d. Our out-of-control anger has understandable causes, but common sense and patience are more satisfying than outbursts of rage.

2. Which statement would best serve as a topic sentence for paragraphs 3 and 4?

    a. Anger has become an increasingly common problem in our society.

    b. People should be more thoughtful and tolerant of those around them.

    c. Displays of anger frequently lead to physical violence and even death.

    d. Anger is a natural response to irritating situations.

3. Which statement is the best topic sentence for paragraphs 16–18?

    a. "Unfortunately, the culprits behind much of our anger—lack of time, frustrating technology, and mega-levels of stress—are not likely to resolve themselves anytime soon."

    b. "According to Carol Tavris, author of *Anger: The Misunderstood Emotion*, the keys to dealing with anger are common sense and patience."

    c. "Patience, on the other hand, is a highly practical virtue."

    d. "People who take the time to cool down before responding to an anger-producing situation are far less likely to say or do something they will regret later."

About Support

4. The essay is about one main effect and three possible causes. What is the one main effect? What are the three causes?

Effect: _An epidemic of anger_

Three causes: _Lack of time, technology, tension_

5. What are some examples cited to support the idea that technology has contributed to America's anger problem? _Answers may vary._
Cell phones, faxes, pagers, digital cameras, computers, the do-it-yourself

checkout at the supermarket, the telephone "help center."

About Coherence

6. What is the best description of the organization of this essay?

   a. Introduction, Thesis, Three Supporting Parts, Conclusion

   (b.) Introduction, Thesis, Four Supporting Parts, Conclusion

   c. Introduction, Thesis, Five Supporting Parts

   d. Thesis, Six Supporting Parts, Conclusion

7. As shown by the outline below, "Taming the Anger Monster" bears a general resemblance to the traditional one-three-one essay model. Fill in the missing paragraph numbers.

   Introduction: Paragraphs: _1–5_

   Supporting Point 1:   Paragraph(s)   _6–9_

   Supporting Point 2:   Paragraph(s)   _10–12_

   Supporting Point 3:   Paragraph(s)   _13_

   Supporting Point 4:   Paragraphs   _14–15_

   Supporting Point 5:   Paragraphs   _16–20_

   Conclusion: Paragraph: _21_

8. What are the three addition signals used to introduce the three causes of anger?

   To begin with   _Technology is also_   _Tension, the third major culprit_

About the Introduction and Conclusion

9. What method best describes the introduction to "Taming the Anger Monster"?

   a. Quotation

   b. Broad, general statement narrowing to thesis

c. Idea that is the opposite of the one to be developed

(d.) Anecdote and questions

10. What is the relationship between the essay's first paragraph and its concluding paragraph?   Wording of answers may vary.

The first paragraph presents a story about a person with anger problems.

The last paragraph shows how that story was successfully resolved.

Writing a Cause-and-Effect Essay

WRITING ASSIGNMENT 1

In scratch-outline form, on a separate piece of paper, provide brief causes *or* effects for at least *four* of the ten statements below. The first item is done for you as an example. Make sure that you have three *separate* and *distinct* items for each statement—don't provide two rewordings that say essentially the same thing. Also, indicate whether the items you have listed are causes or effects.

When you have finished your four scratch outlines, decide which of them would provide the best basis for a cause-and-effect essay that you will write.

1. Many youngsters are terrified of school.

   Causes:

   a. _Afraid of not being liked by other students_

   b. _Afraid of failing tests_

   c. _Intimidated by teachers_

   Answers will vary.

2. Having more mothers in the workforce has changed the way many kids grow up.

3. Society would benefit if nonviolent criminals were punished in ways other than jail time.

4. Americans tend to get married later in life than they used to.

5. Among winners of prestigious academic awards, a high percentage are children of immigrant families recently arrived in this country.

6. It is easy to fall into an unhealthy diet in our society.

7. Growing up in my family has influenced my life in significant ways.

8. A bad (or good) teacher can have long-lasting impact on a student.

9. The average workweek should be no more than thirty hours.

10. My relationship with (*name a relative or friend*) _____ has changed over time.

Prewriting

2.3

a Look at the outline you produced in the previous step. You will now use it as the basis for a cause-and-effect essay. The statement will serve as your thesis, and the three causes or effects will function as your main points. Make sure that each of your main points is a *separate* and *distinct* point, not a restatement of one of the other points.

b Decide whether you will support each of your main points with several short examples or with one extended example. You may want to freewrite about each of these examples for a few minutes, or you may want to make up a list of as many details as you think of that would go with each of the examples.

c Write a first draft of an introduction that attracts the reader's interest, states your thesis, and presents a plan of development.

Revising

2.3

After you have completed the first draft of the paper, set it aside for a while (if possible). When you reread what you have written, prepare for rewriting by asking yourself these questions:

4.3

- Does the paper have a clearly stated thesis?
- Have I backed up each main point with one extended example or several shorter examples? Do I have enough detailed support?
- Is there any irrelevant material that should be eliminated or rewritten?
- Have I used transition words to help readers follow my train of thought?
- Have I provided a concluding paragraph to wrap up the essay?

As you revise your essay through one or more additional drafts, continue to refer to this list until you can answer "yes" to each question. Then be sure to check the next-to-final draft of the paper for the sentence skills listed on the inside front cover.

WRITING ASSIGNMENT 2

If friendly aliens from a highly developed civilization decided to visit our planet, they would encounter a contradictory race of beings—us. We humans would have reasons to feel both proud and ashamed of the kind of society the aliens would encounter. Write an essay explaining whether you would be proud or ashamed of the state of the human race today. Give reasons for your feelings.

Prewriting

a   You will probably have an instant gut reaction to the question "Am I more proud of or ashamed of the human race?" Go with that reaction; you will find it easier to come up with supporting points for the thesis that occurred to you immediately.

b   Generate supporting details for your thesis by making a list. Title it "Reasons I am proud of the human race" or "Reasons I am ashamed of the human race." Then list as many items as you can think of. Don't worry about whether the reasons are important or silly, significant or trivial. Just write down as many as possible.

c   Review your list and ask yourself if some of the items could be grouped into one category. For instance, a list of reasons to be proud of humanity might include items such as "We've come up with cures for major diseases," "We've developed the computer," and "We've invented wonderful communication devices like the telephone, radio, movies, and TV." All of these could be grouped into a category called "Important inventions." That category, in turn, could serve as a main supporting point in your essay.

d   As described in step *c,* decide on three supporting points. Write a scratch outline that includes those points and the examples (one extended example or several shorter ones). The point described in step *c* would be outlined like this:

Point: The human race has come up with wonderful inventions that benefit all society.

(1) Cures for diseases

(2) Computers

(3) Communication devices, including radio and TV

e   Using your scratch outline, write a first draft of the paper. Include an introduction that states your thesis and plan of development, and a conclusion that reminds readers of your thesis and leaves them with a final point to consider.

Revising

As you work through subsequent drafts, ask yourself these questions:

- Have I introduced my essay with a clearly stated thesis and plan of development?
- Is each of my main points supported by solid, specific details?
- Have I used transition words such as *first, another, in addition,* and *also?*
- Have I checked my writing for the sentence skills listed on the inside front cover?

Write a cause-and-effect essay in which you advance an idea about a poem, story, play, film, literary essay, or novel. The work you choose may be assigned by your instructor or may require your instructor's approval. To develop your idea, use a series of two or more reasons and specific supporting evidence for each reason. A student model follows.

Paul's Suicide

Paul, the main character in Willa Cather's short story "Paul's Case,"   1
is a young man on a collision course with death. As Cather reveals Paul's story, we learn about elements of Paul's personality that inevitably come together and cause his suicide. Paul takes his own life as a result of his inability to conform to his society, his passive nature, and his emotional isolation.

First of all, Paul cannot conform to the standards of his own society.   2
At school, Paul advertises his desire to be part of another, more glamorous world by wearing fancy clothes that set him apart from the other students. At home on Cordelia Street, Paul despises everything about his middle-class neighborhood. He hates the houses "permeated by kitchen odors," the "ugliness and commonness of his own home," and the respectable neighbors sitting on their front stoops every Sunday, "their stomachs comfortably protruding." Paul's father hopes that Paul will settle down and become like the young man next door, a nearsighted clerk who works for a corporate steel magnate. Paul, however, is repelled by the young man and all he represents. It seems inevitable, then, that Paul will not be able to cope with the office job his father obtains for him at the firm of Denny & Carson; and this inability to conform will, in turn, lead to Paul's theft of $1,000.

Paul's suicide is also due, in part, to his passive nature. Throughout his   3
life, Paul has been an observer and an onlooker. Paul's only escape from the prison of his daily life comes from his job as an usher at Pittsburgh's Carnegie Hall; he lives for the moments when he can watch the actors, singers, and musicians. However, Paul has no desire to <u>be</u> an actor or musician. As Cather says, "What he wanted was to see, to be in the atmosphere, float on the wave of it, to be carried out . . . away from everything." Although Paul steals the money and flees to New York, these uncharacteristic actions underscore the desperation he feels. Once at the Waldorf in New York, Paul is again content to observe the glamorous world he has craved for so long: "He had no especial desire to meet or to know any of these people; all he demanded was the right to look on and conjecture, to watch the pageant." During his brief stay in the city, Paul enjoys simply sitting in his luxurious rooms, glimpsing the show of city life

through a magical curtain of snow. At the end, when the forces of ordinary life begin to close in again, Paul kills himself. But it is typical that he does not use the gun he has bought. Rather, more in keeping with his passive nature, Paul lets himself fall under the wheels of a train.

Finally, Paul ends his life because he is emotionally isolated. Throughout   4
the story, not one person makes any real contact with Paul. His teachers do not understand him and merely resent the attitude of false bravado that he uses as a defense. Paul's mother is dead; he cannot even remember her. Paul is completely alienated from his father, who obviously cares for him but who cannot feel close to this withdrawn, unhappy son. To Paul, his father is only the man waiting at the top of the stairs, "his hairy legs sticking out of his nightshirt," who will greet him with "inquiries and reproaches." When Paul meets a college boy in New York, they share a night on the town. But the "champagne friendship" ends with a "singularly cool" parting. Paul is not the kind of person who can let himself go or confide in one of his peers. For the most part, Paul's isolation is self-imposed. He has drifted so far into his fantasy life that people in the "real" world are treated like invaders. As he allows no one to enter his dream, there is no one Paul can turn to for understanding.

The combination of these personality factors—inability to conform,   5
passivity, and emotional isolation—makes Paul's tragic suicide inevitable. Before he jumps in front of the train, Paul scoops a hole in the snow and buries the carnation that he has been wearing in his buttonhole. Like a hothouse flower in the winter, Paul has a fragile nature that cannot survive in its hostile environment.

WRITING ASSIGNMENT 4

Writing for a Specific Purpose and Audience

In this cause-and-effect essay, you will write with a specific purpose and for a specific audience. Imagine that several friends of yours say they are having a hard time learning anything in a class taught by Professor X. You volunteer to attend the class and see for yourself. You also get information from your friends about the course requirements.

Afterward, you write a letter to Professor X, politely calling attention to what you see as causes of the learning problems that students are having in the class. To organize your essay, you might develop each of these causes in a separate supporting paragraph. In the second part of each supporting paragraph, you might suggest changes that Professor X could make to deal with each problem.

13 Comparison and Contrast

ALLWRITE!
7.4b

Comparison and contrast are two thought processes we go through constantly in everyday life. When we *compare* two things, we show how they are similar; when we *contrast* two things, we show how they are different. We may compare or contrast two brand-name products (for example, Pepsi and Coca-Cola), two television shows, two cars, two teachers, two jobs, two friends, or two possible solutions to a problem we are facing. The purpose of comparing or contrasting is to understand each of the two things more clearly and, at times, to make judgments about them.

You will be asked in this chapter to write a paper of comparison or contrast. To prepare for this assignment, first read about the two methods of development you can use in writing your paper. Then read the student essays and the professional essay that follow and work through the questions that accompany the essays.

Methods of Development

A comparison or contrast essay calls for one of two types of development. Details can be presented *one side at a time* or *point by point*. Each format is illustrated below.

One Side at a Time

Look at the following supporting paragraph from "A Vote for McDonald's," one of the model essays that will follow.

> For one thing, going to the Chalet is more difficult than going to McDonald's. The Chalet has a jacket-and-tie rule, which means I have to dig a sport coat and tie out of the back of my closet, make sure they're semiclean, and try to steam out the wrinkles somehow. The Chalet also requires reservations. Since it is downtown, I have to leave an hour early to give myself time to find a parking space within six blocks of the restaurant. The Chalet cancels reservations if a party is more than ten minutes late. Going to McDonald's, on the other hand, is easy. I can feel comfortable wearing my jeans or warm-up suit. I don't have to do any advance planning. I can leave my house whenever I'm ready and pull into a doorside parking space within fifteen minutes.

The first half of this paragraph fully explains one side of the contrast (the difficulty of going to the Chalet). The second half of the paragraph deals entirely with the other side (the ease of going to McDonald's). When you use this method, be sure to follow the same order of points of contrast (or comparison) for each side. An outline of the paragraph shows how the points for each side are developed in a consistent sequence.

Outline

One Side at a Time

Thesis: Going to the Chalet is more difficult than going to McDonald's.

1. Chalet
   a. Dress code
   b. Advance reservations
   c. Leave an hour early
   d. Find parking space
2. McDonald's
   a. Casual dress
   b. No reservations
   c. Leave only fifteen minutes ahead of time
   d. Plenty of free parking

Point by Point

Now look at the supporting paragraph below, which is taken from another essay you will read, "Studying: Then and Now":

> Ordinary studying during the term is another area where I've made changes. In high school, I let reading assignments go. I told myself that I'd have no trouble catching up on two hundred pages during a fifteen-minute ride to school. College courses have taught me to keep pace with the work. Otherwise, I feel as though I'm sinking into a quicksand of unread material. When I finally read the high school assignment, my eyes would run over the words but my brain would be plotting how to get the car for Saturday night. Now, I use several techniques that force me to really concentrate on my reading.

The paragraph contrasts two styles of studying point by point. The following outline illustrates the point-by-point method.

Outline   **Point by Point**

Thesis: Studying is something I do differently in college than in high school.

1.   Keeping up with reading assignments

    a.   High school

    b.   College

2.   Concentration while reading

    a.   High school

    b.   College

When you begin writing a comparison or contrast paper, you should decide right away which format you will use: one side at a time or point by point. Use that format as you create the outline for your paper. Remember that an outline is an essential step in planning and writing a clearly organized paper.

Student Essays to Consider

A Vote for McDonald's

For my birthday this month, my wife has offered to treat me to dinner at the restaurant of my choice. I think she expects me to ask for a meal at the Chalet, the classiest, most expensive restaurant in town. However, I'm going to eat my birthday dinner at McDonald's. When I compare the two restaurants, the advantages of eating at McDonald's are clear.

For one thing, going to the Chalet is more difficult than going to McDonald's. The Chalet has a jacket-and-tie rule, which means I have to dig a sport coat and tie out of the back of my closet, make sure they're semiclean, and try to steam out the wrinkles somehow. The Chalet also requires reservations. Since it is downtown, I have to leave an hour early to give myself time to find a parking space within six blocks of the restaurant. The Chalet cancels reservations if a party is more than ten minutes late. Going to McDonald's, on the other hand, is easy. I can feel comfortable wearing my jeans or warm-up suit. I don't have to do any advance planning. I can leave my house whenever I'm ready and pull into a doorside parking space within fifteen minutes.

The Chalet is a dimly lit, formal place. While I'm struggling to see what's 3 on my plate, I worry that I'll knock one of the fragile glasses off the table. The waiters at the Chalet can be uncomfortably formal, too. As I awkwardly pronounce the French words on the menu, I get the feeling that I don't quite live up to their standards. Even the other diners can make me feel uncomfortable. And though the food at the Chalet is gourmet, I prefer simpler meals. I don't like unfamiliar food swimming in a pasty white sauce. Eating at the Chalet is, to me, less enjoyable than eating at McDonald's. McDonald's is a pleasant place where I feel at ease. It is well lighted, and the bright-colored decor is informal. The employees serve with a smile, and the food is easy to pronounce and identify. I know what I'm going to get when I order a certain type of sandwich.

The most important difference between the Chalet and McDonald's, 4 though, is price. Dinner for two at the Chalet, even without appetizers or desserts, would easily cost $50. And the $50 doesn't include the cost of parking the car and tipping the waiter, which can come to an additional $10. Once, I forgot to bring enough money. At McDonald's, a filling meal for two will cost around $10. With the extra $50, my wife and I can eat at McDonald's five more times, or go to the movies three times, or buy tickets to a football game.

So, for my birthday dinner, or any other time, I prefer to eat at 5 McDonald's. It is convenient, friendly, and cheap. And with the money my wife saves by taking me to McDonald's, she can buy me what I really want for my birthday—a new Sears power saw.

Studying: Then and Now

One June day, I staggered into a high school classroom to take my final 1 exam in United States History IV. I had made my usual desperate effort to cram the night before, with the usual dismal results—I had gotten only to page seventy-five of a four-hundred-page textbook. My study habits in high school, obviously, were a mess. But in college, I've made an attempt to reform my note-taking, studying, and test-taking skills.

As I took notes in high school classes, I often lost interest and began 2 doodling, drawing Martians, or seeing what my signature would look like if I married the cute guy in the second row. Now, however, I try not to let my mind wander, and I pull my thoughts back into focus when they begin to go fuzzy. In high school, my notes often looked like something written in Arabic. In college, I've learned to use a semiprint writing style that makes my notes understandable. When I would look over my high school notes, I couldn't understand them. There would be a word like "Reconstruction," then a big blank, then the word "important." Weeks later, I had no idea what Reconstruction was or why it was important. I've since learned to write down connecting ideas, even if I have to take the time to do it after class. Taking notes is one thing I've really learned to do better since high school days.

Ordinary studying during the term is another area where I've made changes. In high school, I let reading assignments go. I told myself that I'd have no trouble catching up on two hundred pages during a fifteen-minute ride to school. College courses have taught me to keep pace with the work. Otherwise, I feel as though I'm sinking into a quicksand of unread material. When I finally read the high school assignment, my eyes would run over the words but my brain would be plotting how to get the car for Saturday night. Now, I use several techniques that force me to really concentrate on my reading.

In addition to learning how to cope with daily work, I've also learned to handle study sessions for big tests. My all-night study sessions in high school were experiments in self-torture. Around 2:00 A.M., my mind, like a soaked sponge, simply stopped absorbing things. Now, I space out exam study sessions over several days. That way, the night before can be devoted to an overall review rather than raw memorizing. Most important, though, I've changed my attitude toward tests. In high school, I thought tests were mysterious things with completely unpredictable questions. Now, I ask instructors about the kinds of questions that will be on the exam, and I try to "psych out" which areas or facts instructors are likely to ask about. These practices really work, and for me they've taken much of the fear and mystery out of tests.

Since I've reformed, note-taking and studying are not as tough as they once were. And I am beginning to reap the benefits. As time goes on, my college test sheets are going to look much different from the red-marked tests of my high school days.

QUESTIONS

About Unity

1. Which supporting paragraph in "A Vote for McDonald's" has its topic sentence within the paragraph, rather than at the beginning? (*Write the paragraph number and the opening words of the topic sentence.*)
   Paragraph 3: Eating at the Chalet is . . .

2. Which sentence in paragraph 4 of "A Vote for McDonald's" should be omitted in the interest of paragraph unity? (*Write the opening words.*)
   Once, I forgot . . .

3. In which supporting paragraph in "Studying: Then and Now" is the topic sentence at the end rather than at the beginning, where it generally belongs in student essays? _2 (the first supporting paragraph)_

About Support

4. In paragraph 3 of "A Vote for McDonald's," what three points does the writer make to support his statement that, for him, dining at McDonald's is a more pleasant experience than dining at the Chalet? _Wording of answers may vary._

   (1) Chalet is dimly lit; McDonald's is bright.

   (2) Waiters at the Chalet are formal; employees at McDonald's are friendly.

   (3) Food is unfamiliar at the Chalet; food is familiar at McDonald's.

5. In paragraph 3 of "A Vote for McDonald's," what sentence should be followed up by supporting details? *(Write the opening words of that sentence.)*
   Even the other diners . . .

6. Which sentence in paragraph 3 of "Studying: Then and Now" needs to be followed by more supporting details? *(Write the opening words.)*
   Now, I use several techniques . . .

About Coherence

7. In paragraph 2 of "A Vote for McDonald's," what "change of direction" signal does the author use to indicate that he has finished discussing the Chalet and is now going to discuss McDonald's? _on the other hand_

8. Write the words in paragraph 4 of "A Vote for McDonald's" that indicate the writer has used emphatic order in organizing his supporting points.
   most important

About the Introduction and Conclusion

9. Which sentence best describes the opening paragraph of "Studying: Then and Now"?
   a. It begins with a broad statement that narrows down to the thesis.
   b. It explains the importance of the topic to the reader.
   c. It uses an incident or a brief story.
   d. It asks a question.

10. The conclusion of "Studying: Then and Now" falls into which category?
   a. Some observations and a prediction
   (b.) Summary and final thought
   c. Question or series of questions

Developing a Comparison or Contrast Essay

Considering Purpose and Audience

The purpose of a comparison or contrast essay is to make a point by showing readers that two distinct items are either similar or different. Whether you choose to compare or contrast two items depends on the specific point you want to convey to readers. Suppose, for instance, the main point of your essay is that home-cooked hamburgers are superior to fast-food burgers. To convince your audience of your claim, you might contrast the two items, pointing out those differences—price, taste, and nutrition—that make the homemade dish better. If, however, your main point is that tap water is just as good as store-bought bottled water, you could compare the two, pointing out the similarities that support your main point. Tap water and bottled water, for example, might be equally clean, fresh, and mineral-rich. In both examples above, comparing or contrasting is used to convince readers of a larger main point.

As you think about your own essay, ask yourself what two things you wish to discuss. Then determine whether you want to focus on the differences between the two items or their similarities. You may even decide that you want to do both. If, say, you choose as your topic Macintosh and PC computers, you may write paragraphs on the similarities and differences between the two computer systems. But remember, no matter what topic you select, be sure that your comparison and/or contrast is connected to a main point that readers can see and understand.

Be sure to keep your audience in mind when planning your essay. If you were writing about Macs and PCs for computer majors, for example, you could assume your readers were familiar with the two systems. On the other hand, if your audience was made up of liberal arts majors, you could not make such an assumption, and it would be up to you to provide background information. Thinking about your audience will help you determine the tone of your essay as well. Once again, if you are writing for an audience of programmers, it is appropriate to write in an objective, technical tone. But if you are writing for a more general audience, you should assume a friendly, informal tone.

Development through Prewriting

When Jesse, one of the student writers featured earlier, had to choose two things to compare or contrast, the Chalet and McDonald's quickly came to mind: "My wife and I had been talking that morning about where I wanted to go for my birthday," he said. "I'd been thinking how I would explain to her that I'd really prefer McDonald's. So the comparisons and contrasts between the two restaurants were fresh in my mind."

To generate ideas for his paper, Jesse turned to the technique of freewriting. Without concerning himself with organization, finding the perfect word, or even spelling, he simply wrote whatever came into his mind as he asked himself, "Why would I rather eat at McDonald's than at the Chalet?" Here is what Jesse came up with:

> The Chalet is a beautiful restaurant and it's sweet of Lilly to want to take me there. But I honestly like McDonald's better. To me, food is food, and a meal at the Chalet is not five times better than a meal at McDonald's but that's what it costs. I like a plain cheeseburger better than something I can't pronounce or identify. The waiters at the Chalet are snooty and make me feel awkward—how can you enjoy eating when you're tensed up like that? Have to wear jacket and tie to the Chalet and I've gained weight; not sure jacket will even fit. Sweats or jeans are great at McDonald's. Desserts at Chalet are great, better than McCookies or whatever they're called. Parking is a hassle at the Chalet and easy at McD's. No tipping at McD's, either. I don't know why they keep it so dark at the Chalet—guess it's supposed to be relaxing, but seems creepy to me. McD's is bright and cheerful.

As Jesse looked over his freewriting, he saw that most of what he had written fell into three categories that he could use as the three supporting points of his essay. Using these three points, he prepared this first scratch outline for the essay:

I'd rather eat my special dinner at McDonald's than at the Chalet.
1. Can wear anything I want to McD's.
2. Waiters, lighting, menu at Chalet make me feel awkward.
3. Chalet is <u>much</u> more expensive than McD's.

Next, Jesse went back and inserted some supporting details that fit in with his three main points.

I'd rather eat my special dinner at McDonald's than at the Chalet.

1. Going to the Chalet is a hassle.
    a. Have to wear jacket, tie to Chalet
    b. Have to make reservations
    c. Long drive; trouble parking
2. Waiters, lighting, menu at Chalet make me feel awkward.
    a. Waiters are snooty
    b. Lighting is dim
    c. French names on menu don't mean anything to me
3. Chalet is <u>much</u> more expensive than McD's.
    a. Meal costs five times as much
    b. Parking, tips on top of that
    c. Rather spend that money on other things

Working from this scratch outline, Jesse wrote the following first draft of his essay.

First Draft

A Vote for McDonald's

Lilly has offered to take me anywhere I want for my birthday dinner. She thinks I'll choose the Chalet, but instead I want to eat at McDonald's.

The Chalet has a jacket-and-tie rule, and I hate wearing a jacket and tie, and the jacket's probably too tight for me anyway. I have to dig them out of the closet and get them cleaned. I can wear any old thing to McDonald's. We'd also have to leave the house early, since the Chalet requires reservations. Since it is downtown, I have to leave an hour early so I'm sure to have time to park. The Chalet cancels reservations if a party is more than ten minutes late. Going to McDonald's, on the other hand, is easy. I don't have to do any advance planning. I can leave my house whenever I'm ready.

McDonald's is a pleasant place where I feel at ease. It is bright and well lighted. The employees serve with a smile, and the food is easy to pronounce and identify. I know what I'm going to get when I order a certain type of sandwich. I like simple meals more than gourmet ones. The Chalet is dimly lit. While I'm struggling to see what's on my plate, I worry that I'll knock one of the glasses off the table. The waiters at the Chalet can be uncomfortably formal, too. I get the feeling that I don't quite live up to their standards. Even the other diners can make me feel uncomfortable.

There's a big price difference between the Chalet and McDonald's. Dinner for two at the Chalet can easily cost $50, even without any "extras" like appetizers and dessert. And the $50 doesn't include the cost of parking the car and tipping the waiter. Once, I forgot to bring enough money. At McDonald's, a meal for two will cost around $10.

So, for my birthday dinner, or any other time, I prefer to eat at McDonald's. It is convenient, friendly, and cheap.

Development through Revising

4.3

Jesse put the first draft of his essay aside and took it to his writing class the next day. His instructor asked Jesse and the other students to work in small groups reading their drafts aloud and making suggestions for revision to one another. Here are the notes Jesse made on his group's comments:

- I need to explain that Lilly is my wife.
- I'm not consistent in developing my paragraphs. I forgot to do a "one side at a time" or "point by point" comparison. I think I'll try "one side at a time." I'll describe in each paragraph what the Chalet is like, then what McDonald's is like.
- I could use more support for some of my points, like when I say that the waiters at the Chalet make me uncomfortable. I should give some examples of what I mean by that.
- I want to say something about what I'd rather do with the money we save by going to McDonald's. For me that's important—we can "eat" that money at the Chalet, or do other things with it that we both enjoy.

After making these observations about his first draft, Jesse proceeded to write the version of his essay that appears on page 266.

A Professional Essay to Consider

Read the following professional essay. Then answer the questions and read the comments that follow.

Born to Be Different?

by Camille Lewis

(Activity 3)

Some years ago, when my children were very young, I cut a cartoon out 1 of a magazine and taped it to my refrigerator. It showed a young couple welcoming friends over for Christmas. The hosts rather proudly announce that instead of dolls, they have given their little daughter her own set of tools. And sure enough, the second panel shows their little girl playing in her room, a wrench in one hand and a hammer in the other. But she's making the wrench say, "Would you like to go to the prom, Barbie?" and the hammer answer, "Oh, Ken! I'd love to!"

Oh my, did that cartoon strike a chord. I grew up with *Ms.* magazine 2 and the National Organization of Women and a firm belief that gender differences were *learned,* not inborn. Other parents may have believed that pink and baby dolls and kindergarten teaching were for girls, and blue and trucks and engineering were for boys, but by golly, *my* kids were going to be different. They were going to be raised free of all that harmful gender indoctrination. They were just going to be *people.*

I don't remember exactly when I began to suspect I was wrong. Maybe 3 it was when my three-year-old son, raised in a "no weapons" household, bit his toast into a gun shape and tried to shoot the cat. Maybe it was when his younger brother nearly levitated out of his car seat, joyously crowing "backhoe!" upon spotting his first piece of earth-moving equipment. Maybe it was when my little daughter first lined up her stuffed animals and began teaching them their ABC's and bandaging their boo-boos.

It wasn't that my sons couldn't be sweet and sensitive, or that my daughter 4 wasn't sometimes rowdy and boisterous. But I had to rethink my earlier assumptions. Despite my best efforts not to impose gender-specific expectations on them, my boys and my girl were, well, different. *Really* different.

Slowly and hesitantly, medical and psychological researchers have begun 5 confirming my observations. The notion that the differences between the sexes (beyond the obvious anatomical ones) are biologically based is fraught with controversy. Such beliefs can easily be misinterpreted and used as the basis for harmful, oppressive stereotypes. They can be overstated and exaggerated into blanket statements about what men and women "can" and "can't" do; about what the genders are "good" and "bad" at. And yet, the unavoidable fact is that studies are making it ever clearer that, as groups, men and women differ in almost every measurable aspect. Learning about those differences helps us understand why men and women are simultaneously so attracted and fascinated, and yet so frequently stymied and frustrated, by the opposite sex. To dig into what it really means to be masculine and feminine helps to depersonalize our responses to one another's behavior— to avoid the "*My* perceptions and behaviors are normal; *your's* don't make sense" trap. Our differences are deep-rooted, hard-wired, and present from the moment of conception.

To begin with, let's look at something as basic as the anatomy of the brain. 6 Typically, men have larger skulls and brains than women. But the sexes score equally well on intelligence tests. This apparent contradiction is explained by the fact that our brains are apportioned differently. Women have about 15 percent more "gray matter" than men. Gray matter, made up of nerve cells and the branches that connect them, allows the quick transference of thought from one part of the brain to another. This high concentration of gray matter helps explain women's ability to look at many sides of an argument at once, and to do several tasks (or hold several conversations) simultaneously.

Men's brains, on the other hand, have a more generous portion of 7 "white matter." White matter, which is made up of neurons, actually inhibits the spread of information. It allows men to concentrate very narrowly on a specific task, without being distracted by thoughts that might conflict with the job at hand. In addition, men's larger skulls contain more cerebrospinal fluid, which cushions the brain. Scientists theorize that this reflects men's history of engaging in warfare and rough sports, activities which bring with them a high likelihood of having one's head banged about.

Our brains' very different makeup leads to our very different methods 8 of interacting with the world around us. Simon Baron-Cohen, author of *The Essential Difference: Men, Women and the Extreme Male Brain,* has labeled the classic female mental process as "empathizing." He defines empathizing as "the drive to identify another person's emotions and thoughts, and to respond to these with an appropriate emotion." Empathizers are constantly measuring and responding to the surrounding emotional temperature. They are concerned about showing sensitivity to the people around them. This empathetic quality can be observed in virtually all aspects of women's lives: from the choice of typically female-dominated careers (nursing, elementary school teaching, social work) to reading matter popular mainly with women (romantic fiction, articles about relationships, advice columns about how people can get along better) to women's interaction with one another (which typically involves intimate discussion of relationships with friends and family, and sympathy for each others' concerns). So powerful is the empathizing mindset that it even affects how the typical female memory works. Ask a woman when a particular event happened, and she often pinpoints it in terms of an occurrence that had emotional content: "That was the summer my sister broke her leg," or "That was around the time Gene and Mary got into such an awful argument." Likewise, she is likely to bring her empathetic mind to bear on geography. She'll remember a particular address not as 11th and Market Streets but being "near the restaurant where we went on our anniversary," or "around the corner from Liz's old apartment."

In contrast, Baron-Cohen calls the typical male mindset "systemizing," 9 which he defines as "the drive to analyze and explore a system, to extract underlying rules that govern the behavior of a system." A systemizer is less interested in how people feel than in how things work. Again, the systematic brain influences virtually all aspects of the typical man's life. Male-dominated professions (such as engineering, computer programming, auto repair, and mathematics) rely heavily on systems, formulas, and patterns, and very little on the ability to intuit another person's thoughts or emotions. Reading material most popular with men includes science fiction and history, as well as factual "how-to" magazines on such topics as computers, photography, home repair, and woodworking. When they get together with male friends, men are far less likely to engage in intimate conversation than they are to share an activity: watching or playing sports, working on a car, bowling, golfing, or fishing. Men's conversation is peppered with dates and addresses, illustrating their comfort with systems: "Back in 1996 when I was living in Boston . . ." or "The best way to the new stadium is to go all the way out Walnut Street to 33rd and then get on the bypass . . . ."

One final way that men and women differ is in their typical responses   10 to problem-solving. Ironically, it may be this very activity—intended on both sides to eliminate problems—that creates the most conflict between partners of the opposite sex. To a woman, the *process* of solving a problem is all-important. Talking about a problem is a means of deepening the intimacy between her and her partner. The very anatomy of her brain, as well as her accompanying empathetic mindset, makes her want to consider all sides of a question and to explore various possible solutions. To have a partner who is willing to explore a problem with her is deeply satisfying. She interprets that willingness as an expression of the other's love and concern.

But men have an almost completely opposite approach when it comes   11 to dealing with a problem. Everything in their mental makeup tells them to focus narrowly on the issue, solve it, and get it out of the way. The ability to fix a problem quickly and efficiently is, to them, a demonstration of their power and competence. When a man hears his female partner begin to describe a problem, his strongest impulse is to listen briefly and then tell her what to do about it. From his perspective, he has made a helpful and loving gesture; from hers, he's short-circuited a conversation that could have deepened and strengthened their relationship.

The challenge that confronts men and women is to put aside ideas of   12 "better" and "worse" when it come to their many differences. Our diverse brain development, our ways of interacting with the world, and our modes of dealing with problems all have their strong points. In some circumstances, a typically feminine approach may be more effective; in others, a classically masculine mode may have the advantage. Our differences aren't going to disappear: my daughter, now a middle-schooler, regularly tells me she loves me, while her teenage brothers express their affection by grabbing me in a headlock. Learning to understand and appreciate one another's gender-specific qualities is the key to more rich and rewarding lives together.

Born

QUESTIONS

About Unity

1. Which of the following statements best represents the implied thesis of "Born to Be Different"?
   a. Although the author believed that gender differences were learned rather than inborn, experience with her own children convinced her otherwise.
   b. Researchers have classified the typical female mental process as "empathizing" and the typical male process as "systemizing."
   c. Many of the differences in the ways men and women think and behave may be due to their biological makeup.
   d. In order to live together happily, men and women need to appreciate and understand their gender-based differences.

2. Which statement would best serve as a topic sentence for paragraphs 6 and 7?
   a. Because of their different construction, men's and women's brains function differently.
   b. Women are skilled at doing several tasks or holding several conversations simultaneously.
   c. Although men's brains are larger than women's, men and women score equally on tests of intelligence.
   d. Men's brains have a larger allocation of white matter, which contributes to the ability to focus narrowly on a particular task.

3. What statement below would best serve as the topic sentence of paragraph 11?
   a. Men solve problems quickly to demonstrate power and competence.
   b. Men's approach to solving problems usually involves giving instructions.
   c. Men's gestures of love are often unhelpful to women.
   d. Men's approach to problem solving is the opposite of women's.

About Support

4. Paragraph 8 states that the "empathizing" mindset "can be observed in virtually all aspects of women's lives." What evidence does Lewis provide to support that claim?   Wording of answers may vary.
   She lists a series of examples where the "empathizing" mindset is evident: female-dominated careers, female reading matter, and female relationships.

5. According to the author, what are the three major differences between men and women?

(1) _Brain anatomy_

(2) _Ways of interacting with the world_

(3) _Ways of problem solving._

About Coherence

6. Has the author presented her evidence one side at a time or point by point? Explain your answer. _Wording of answers may vary._

Lewis presents her essay point by point. The first point is about brain anatomy, the second is about interacting with the world, and the third is about problem solving. For each point, she discusses women and then men.

7. As shown by the outline below, the organization of "Born to Be Different?" resembles the traditional one-three-one essay model. Fill in the missing paragraph numbers.

Introduction: Paragraphs   _1–5_

Supporting Point 1:   Paragraph(s)   _6–7_

Supporting Point 2:   Paragraph(s)   _8–9_

Supporting Point 3:   Paragraph(s)   _10–11_

Conclusion: Paragraph   _12_

8. What are the three contrast signals used to introduce the main supporting paragraphs in the essay? Where do they occur? *(Write the paragraph number after the signal.)*

On the other hand (7)   _In contrast (9)_   _But (11)_

About the Introduction and Conclusion

9. What method best describes the introductory paragraph to the essay?
   a. Broad, general statement narrowing to a thesis
   b. Questions
   c. Idea that is the opposite of the one to be developed
   (d.) Anecdote

10. With which common method of conclusion does the essay end?
    (a.) A summary and final thought
    b. Questions that prompt the reader to think further about what's been written
    c. A prediction

Writing a Comparison or Contrast Essay

WRITING ASSIGNMENT 1

Write an essay of comparison or contrast on one of these topics:

Two teachers you've had

Two jobs you'd held

Two bosses you've worked for

Two restaurants you've eaten in

Two parenting styles you've observed

Two friends you've had

Two pets you've had or seen

Two sports you're acquainted with

Two singers or bands you've heard

Two dates you've been on

Two places you've lived

Prewriting

a   As you select your topic, keep in mind that you won't merely be *describing* the two things you're writing about—you will be emphasizing the ways they are alike or different.

b   Make two columns on a sheet of paper, one for each of the two things you'll write about. In the left-hand column, jot down words or phrases that describe the first of the two. Write anything that comes into your head about that half of your topic. Then go back and write a corresponding word or phrase about the item in the right-hand column. For example, here is one student's list of characteristics about two games. He began brainstorming for words and phrases to describe Scrabble.

Scrabble	Volleyball
quiet	
involves words	
played sitting down	
involves small group of people	

continued

ALLWRITE!
2.3

can let mind wander when it's not your turn

mental concentration, not physical

part chance—don't know what letters you'll get

part strategy and skill

some see as boring, nerdy game

Then he wrote a corresponding list of characteristics for volleyball, which helped him modify and add to his first list:

Scrabble	Volleyball
quiet	noisy, talking and yelling
involves words	involves ball and a net
played sitting down	played standing up, jumping
involves as few as two players	involves twelve players
can let mind wander when it's not your turn	have to stay alert every minute
mental concentration, not physical	mental and physical concentration required
part chance (what letters you get), part strategy and skill	mostly skill, strategy; little chance
some see as boring, nerdy game	seen as glamorous—stars get advertising contracts
players' size doesn' t matter	being tall helps

c   Your list of characteristics will help you decide if the two things you are writing about are more alike (in which case you'll write an essay *comparing* them) or different (in which case you'll emphasize how they *contrast*).

d   As you look over your lists, think how the characteristics you've written down (and others that occur to you) could fit into three categories that can serve as your supporting points. Prepare a scratch outline for your essay based on these three supporting points.

For instance, the student writing about Scrabble and volleyball came up with these three groupings of characteristics. Fill in the blanks in his outline to indicate the supporting points.

Wording of answers may vary.

Thesis: Although they are two of my favorite activities, Scrabble and volleyball could hardly be more different.

Point _Different playing requirements_

Scrabble requires a board and letter tiles.

Volleyball needs a ball and net.

Scrabble can be played by two people.

Twelve people are needed for a volleyball game.

Scrabble can be played anywhere there's room for two people to sit down.

Volleyball needs a large room and high ceilings or an outdoor playing area.

Point _Different traits and skills involved_

You have to concentrate mentally to play Scrabble.

You need mental and physical concentration to play volleyball.

It doesn't matter what size you are to play Scrabble.

It helps to be tall to play volleyball.

There's some chance involved in playing Scrabble.

Chance is not a big part of volleyball.

Point _Different images_

Scrabble players are seen as "nerdy" by the general public.

Star volleyball players are seen as glamorous by the public.

Volleyball players get contracts to endorse athletic shoes.

Scrabble players don't endorse anything, even dictionaries.

Volleyball players are admired for the power of their spike.

Scrabble players are admired for the number of unusual two-letter words they know.

e   Decide which method of development you will use to design your essay: one side at a time or point by point. Be consistent in your use of one method or the other in each of your paragraphs.

f   Proceed to write the first draft of your essay.

4.3

Revising

As you review the first draft of your essay, ask yourself these questions:

- Have I made it clear in my opening paragraph what two things I am writing about, and whether I will compare or contrast them?
- Do my supporting points offer three areas in which I will compare or contrast my two subjects?
- Have I consistently used a single method of development—one side at a time or point by point—in each supporting paragraph?
- Have I used transition words to help readers follow my train of thought?
- If one area of comparison or contrast is stronger than the others, am I using emphatic order and saving that area for my final supporting paragraph?
- Have I rounded off my essay with an appropriate concluding paragraph?

As you revise your essay through one or more additional drafts, continue to refer to this list until you can answer "yes" to each question. Then be sure to check the next-to-final draft of the paper for the sentence skills listed on the inside front cover.

WRITING ASSIGNMENT 2

Write a paper in which you contrast two attitudes on a controversial subject. You may want to contrast your views with those of someone else, or contrast the way you felt about the subject in the past with the way you feel now. You might consider writing about one of these subjects:

Legalization of narcotics

Abortion

Men and women serving together in military units

Prayer in public schools

Nuclear power plants

Gay couples adopting children

Fertility methods that allow older women to have children

Welfare reform

The death penalty

Euthanasia

Prostitution

The public's right to know about elected officials' private lives

Prewriting

a   To gather information for the point of view that contrasts with your own, you will need to do some research. You'll find useful material if you go to the library and search through article indexes for recent newsmagazines. (If you need help, ask your instructor or the research librarian.) Or interview friends and acquaintances whose attitude on the subject is different from yours.

b   To generate ideas for your paper, try the following two-part exercise.

- Part 1: Pretend that a visitor from Mars who has never heard of the topic of your paper has asked you to explain it, as well as why you take the attitude you do toward it. Using the technique of freewriting—not worrying about sentence structure, organization, spelling, repetition, etc.— write an answer for the Martian. Throw in every reason you can think of for your attitude.

- Part 2: Now the Martian asks you to do the same, taking the opposing point of view. Remember that it's up to you to make this interplanetary visitor understand both sides of the issue, so really try to put yourself in the other guy's shoes as you represent the contrasting attitude.

c   As you look over the writing on both sides of the issue you've done for the Martian, note the strongest points on both sides. From them, select your three main supporting points. Are there other thoughts in your writing that can be used as supporting details for those points?

d   Write your three supporting paragraphs. Decide whether it is more effective to contrast your attitude and the opposing attitude point by point within each paragraph, or by devoting the first half of each paragraph to one side's attitude and then contrasting it with the other's.

e   In your concluding paragraph, summarize the contrast between your attitude and the other point of view. Consider closing with a final comment that makes it clear why you stand where you do.

Revising

Refer to the guidelines for rewriting provided on page 282.

WRITING ASSIGNMENT 3

Write an essay that contrasts two characters or two points of view in one or more poems, stories, plays, or novels. The work you choose may be assigned by your instructor, or it may require your instructor's approval. For this assignment, your essay may have two supporting paragraphs, with each paragraph representing one side of the contrast. A student model follows.

Warren and Mary

In "Death of the Hired Man," Robert Frost uses a brief incident—the   1
return of Silas, an aging farmhand—to dramatize the differences between
a husband and wife. As Warren and Mary talk about Silas and reveal his
story, the reader learns their story, too. By the end of the poem, Warren
and Mary emerge as contrasting personalities; one is wary and reserved,
while the other is open and giving.

Warren is a kindly man, but his basic decency is tempered by practicality   2
and emotional reserve. Warren is upset with Mary for sheltering Silas,
who is barely useful and sometimes unreliable: "What use he is there's no
depending on." Warren feels that he has already done his duty toward
Silas by hiring him the previous summer and is under no obligation to care
for him now. "Home," says Warren, "is the place where, when you have
to go there / They have to take you in." Warren's home is not Silas's home,
so Warren does not have a legal or moral duty to keep the shiftless old
man. Warren's temperament, in turn, influences his attitude toward Silas's
arrival. Warren hints to Mary—through a condescending smile—that Silas
is somehow playing on her emotions or faking his illness. Warren considers
Silas's supposed purpose in coming to the farm—to ditch the meadow—
nothing but a flimsy excuse for a free meal. The best that Warren can find
to say about Silas is that he does have one practical skill: the ability to build
a good load of hay.

Mary, in contrast, is distinguished by her giving nature and her   3
concentration on the workings of human emotion. In caring for Silas, Mary
sees not his lack of ability or his laziness but the fact that he is "worn out"
and needs help. To Mary, home represents not obligation ("They have to
take you in") but unconditional love: "I should have called it / Something
you somehow haven't to deserve." Mary is observant, not only of outer
appearances but also of the inner person; this is why she thinks not that
Silas is trying to trick them but that he is a desperate man trying to salvage
a little self-respect. She realizes, too, that he will never ditch the meadow,
and she knows that Silas's insecurity prompted his arguments with the
college boy who helped with the haying. Mary is also perceptive enough
to see that Silas could never humble himself before his estranged brother.
Mary's attitude is more sympathetic than Warren's; whereas Warren
wonders why Silas and his brother don't get along. Mary thinks about how
Silas "hurt my heart the way he lay / And rolled his old head on that sharp-
edged chairback."

In describing Silas, Warren and Mary describe themselves. We see   4
a basically good man whose spirit has been toughened by a hard life.
Warren, we learn, would have liked to pay Silas a fixed wage but simply
couldn't afford to. Life has taught Warren to be practical and to rein in his

emotions. In contrast, we see a nurturing woman, alert to human feelings, who could never refuse to care for a lonely, dying man. Warren and Mary are both decent people. This is the reason why, as Mary instinctively feels, Silas chooses their home for his final refuge.

WRITING ASSIGNMENT 4

Writing for a Specific Purpose and Audience

In this comparison-contrast essay, you will write with a specific purpose and for a specific audience.

Option 1   Your niece or nephew is finishing high school soon and is thinking about getting a job instead of going to college. You would prefer to see him or her give college a try. Write him or her a letter in which you compare and contrast the advantages and disadvantages of each course of action. Use the one-side-at-a-time method in making your analysis.

Option 2   Write a letter to your boss in which you compare your abilities with those of the ideal candidate for a position to which you'd like to be promoted. Use the point-by-point method, discussing each desired qualification and then describing how well you measure up to it. Use the requirements of a job you are familiar with, ideally a job you would really like to apply for some day.

14 Definition

ALL WRITE!
7.4c

In talking with other people, we sometimes offer informal definitions to explain just what we mean by a particular term. Suppose, for example, we say to a friend, "Larry is really an inconsiderate person." We might then explain what we mean by "inconsiderate" by saying, "He borrowed my accounting book 'overnight' but didn't return it for a week. And when I got it back, it was covered with coffee stains." In a written definition, we make clear in a more complete and formal way our own personal understanding of a term. Such a definition typically starts with one meaning of a term. The meaning is then illustrated with a series of details.

In this chapter, you will be asked to write an essay in which you define and illustrate a term. To prepare for this assignment, first read the student essays and the professional essay that follow and work through the questions that accompany the essays.

Student Essays to Consider

Definition of a Football Fan

What is a football fan? The word "fan" is an abbreviation of "fanatic," meaning "an insane or crazy person." In the case of football fans, the term is appropriate. They behave insanely, they are insane about the past, and they are insanely loyal. 1

Football fans wear their official team T-shirts and warm-up jackets to the mall, the supermarket, the classroom, and even—if they can get away with it—to work. If the team offers a giveaway item, the fans rush to the stadium to claim the hat or sports bag or water bottle that is being handed out that day. Baseball fans go similarly nuts when their favorite teams give away some attractive freebie. Football fans just plain behave insanely. Even the fact that fans spend the coldest months of the year huddling on icy metal benches in places like Chicago proves it. In addition, football fans decorate their houses with football-related items of every kind. To them, team bumper stickers belong not only on car bumpers, but also on fireplace 2 mantels and front doors. When they go to a game, which they do as often as possible, they also decorate their bodies. True football fans not only put on their team jackets and grab their pennants but also paint their heads to look like helmets or wear glow-in-the-dark cheeseheads. At the game, these fans devote enormous energy to trying to get a "wave" going.

Football fans are insanely fascinated by the past. They talk about   3
William "Refrigerator" Perry's 1985 Super Bowl touchdown as though it had happened last week. They describe the "Fog Bowl" as if dense fog blanketed yesterday's game, not 1988's playoff match between the Philadelphia Eagles and the Chicago Bears. They excitedly discuss John Elway's final game before retiring—when he won the 1999 Superbowl and received MVP honors—as if it were current news. And if you can't manage to get excited about such ancient history, they look at you as though you were the insane one.

Last of all, football fans are insanely loyal to the team of their choice,   4
often dangerously so. Should their beloved team lose three in a row, fans may begin to react negatively as a way to hide their broken hearts. They still obsessively watch each game and spend the entire day afterward reading and listening to the postgame commentary in newspapers, on TV sports segments, and on sports radio. Further, this intense loyalty makes fans dangerous. To anyone who dares to say to a loyal fan that another team has better players or coaches, or, God forbid, to anyone wandering near the home cheering section wearing the jacket of the opposing team, physical damage is a real possibility. Bloody noses, black eyes, and broken bones are just some of the injuries inflicted on people cheering the wrong team when fans are around. In 1997, one man suffered a concussion at a game in Philadelphia when Eagles fans beat him up for wearing a jacket with another team's insignia.

From February through August, football fans act like any other human   5
beings. They pay their taxes, take out the garbage, and complain about the high cost of living. But when September rolls around, the colors and radios go on, the record books come off the shelves, and the devotion returns. For the true football fan, another season of insanity has begun.

Student Zombies

Schools divide people into categories. From first grade on up, students   1
are labeled "advanced" or "deprived" or "remedial" or "antisocial." Students pigeonhole their fellow students, too. We've all known the "brain," the "jock," the "dummy," and the "teacher's pet." In most cases, these narrow labels are misleading and inaccurate. But there is one label for a certain type of college student that says it all: "zombie."

Zombies are the living dead. Most of us haven't known a lot of real   2
zombies personally, but we do know how they act. We have horror movies
to guide us. The special effects in horror movies are much better these
days. Over the years, we've learned from the movies that zombies stalk
around graveyards, their eyes glued open by Hollywood makeup artists,
bumping like cheap toy robots into living people. Zombie students in
college do just about the same thing. They stalk around campus, eyes
glazed, staring off into space. When they do manage to wander into a
classroom, they sit down mechanically and contemplate the ceiling. Zombie
students rarely eat, dance, talk, laugh, or toss Frisbees on campus lawns.
Instead, they vanish when class is dismissed and return only when some
mysterious zombie signal summons them back into a classroom. The signal
may not occur for weeks.

Zombies are controlled by some mysterious force. According to legend,   3
real zombies are corpses that have been brought back to life to do the
bidding of a voodoo master. Student zombies, too, seem directed by a
strange power. They continue to attend school although they have no
apparent desire to do so. They show no interest in college-related activities
like tests, grades, papers, and projects. And yet some inner force compels
them to wander through the halls of higher education.

An awful fate awaits all zombies unless something happens to break   4
the spell they're under. In the movies, zombies are often shot, stabbed,
drowned, electrocuted, and run over by large vehicles, all to no avail.
Finally the hero or heroine realizes that a counterspell is needed. Once that
spell is cast, with the appropriate props of chicken feet, human hair, and
bats' eyeballs, the zombie-corpse can return peacefully to its coffin. The
only hope for a student zombie to change is for him or her to undergo a
similarly traumatic experience. Sometimes the evil spell can be broken by a
grade transcript decorated with large red "F's." At other times a professor
will succeed through a private, intensive exorcism session. But in other cases
zombies blunder around for years until they are gently persuaded by the
college administration to head for another institution. Then they enroll in a
new college or get a job in the family business.

Every college student knows that it's not necessary to see Night of the   5
Living Dead or The Dead Don't Die in order to see zombies in action—or
nonaction. Forget the campus film series or the late-late show. Just sit in
a classroom and wait. You know what you're looking for—the students
who walk in without books or papers and sit in the very last row of seats.
The ones with personal stereos plugged into their ears don't count as
zombies—that's a whole different category of "student." Day of the Living
Dead is showing every day at a college near you.

QUESTIONS

About Unity

1. Which supporting paragraph in "Definition of a Football Fan" has a topic sentence buried within the paragraph, rather than at the paragraph's beginning? (*Write the paragraph number and the opening words of the topic sentence.*)

   Paragraph 2: Football fans just plain . . .

2. What sentence in paragraph 2 of "Definition of a Football Fan" should be omitted in the interest of paragraph unity? (*Write the opening words.*)

   Baseball fans go . . .

3. Which sentence in paragraph 2 of "Student Zombies" should be omitted in the interest of paragraph unity? (*Write the opening words.*)

   The special effects . . .

4. What sentence in the final paragraph of "Student Zombies" introduces a new topic and so should be eliminated? (*Write the opening words.*)

   The ones with personal stereos . . .

About Support

5. Which essay develops its definitions through a series of comparisons?

   "Student Zombies"

6. After which sentence in paragraph 4 of "Definition of a Football Fan" is more support needed? (*Write the opening words.*)

   Should their beloved team . . .

7. In the second paragraph of "Definition of a Football Fan," how many examples are given of fans' "insane" behavior? (*Circle the letter of the answer.*)

   a. two

   b. four

   c. six

About Coherence

8. Which paragraph in "Definition of a Football Fan" begins with a transitional phrase? _____4_____

9. Which sentence in paragraph 2 of "Student Zombies" begins with a change-of-direction transitional word? (*Write the opening words.*)

   Instead, they vanish . . .

8

About the Introduction and Conclusion

10. Which method of introduction is used in the opening paragraph of "Student Zombies"? *(Circle the letter of the answer.)*

    a. Anecdote

    b. Idea that is the opposite of the one to be developed

    c. Quotation

    d. Broad, general statement narrowing to a thesis

    e. Questions

Developing a Definition Essay

Considering Purpose and Audience

When you write a definition essay, your main purpose is to explain to readers your understanding of a key term or concept, while your secondary purpose is to persuade them that your definition is a legitimate one. Keep in mind that a definition essay *does not* simply repeat a word's dictionary meaning. Instead, it conveys what a particular term means *to you*. For example, if you were to write about the term "patriotism," you might begin by presenting your definition of the word. You might say patriotism means turning out for Fourth of July parades, displaying the flag, or supporting the government. Or perhaps you think patriotism is about becoming politically active and questioning government policy. Whatever definition you choose, be sure to provide specific instances so that readers can fully understand your meaning of the term. For example, in writing an essay on patriotism, you might describe three people who you see as truly patriotic. Writing about each person will help ensure that readers see and understand the term as you do.

As with other essay forms, keep your audience in mind. If, for instance, you were proposing a new definition of patriotism, an audience of war veterans might require different examples than would an audience of college students.

Development through Prewriting

2.3

Brian, the author of "Definition of a Football Fan," spent a few minutes jotting down a number of possible essay topics, keeping in mind the question "What do I know a good deal about, or at least have an interest in exploring?" Here is his list of topic ideas. Notice how they reflect Brian's interest in outdoor activities, sports, and history:

Definition of . . .

A person who fishes

A soccer goalie

A reenactor of Civil War battles

People who vacation at Gettysburg

A bodybuilder

A Green Bay Packers fan

A history buff

A Little League coach

After looking over his list, Brian selected "A Green Bay Packers fan" as the topic that interested him most. He thought it would lend itself well to a lighthearted essay that defined the sometimes nutty fans of the Wisconsin football team. After giving it further thought, however, Brian decided to broaden his topic to include all football fans. "I realized I just didn't know enough specifically about Green Bay fans to support an entire essay," he said.

A person who likes to think in visual terms, Brian decided to develop ideas and details about his topic by clustering his thoughts.

Football fans

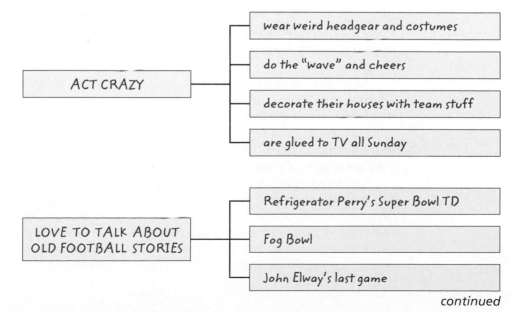

ACT CRAZY
- wear weird headgear and costumes
- do the "wave" and cheers
- decorate their houses with team stuff
- are glued to TV all Sunday

LOVE TO TALK ABOUT OLD FOOTBALL STORIES
- Refrigerator Perry's Super Bowl TD
- Fog Bowl
- John Elway's last game

continued

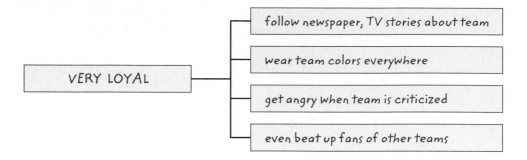

When he looked over his diagram, Brian realized that he could characterize each of his three main topics as a kind of "insanity." He decided on a thesis (he would define football fans as insane) that would indicate his essay's plan of development ("they behave insanely, they are insane about the past, and they are insanely loyal").

With that thesis and plan of development in mind, Brian wrote the first draft of his essay.

First Draft

Definition of a Football Fan

Football fans are by definition crazy. They behave insanely, they are insane about the past, and they are insanely loyal.

If their team gives away something free, the fans rush to the stadium to get the hat or whatever. Football fans just plain behave insanely. Baseball fans go similarly nuts when their favorite teams give away some attractive freebie. But football fans are even worse. Football fans freeze themselves in order to watch their favorite game. In addition, football fans decorate their houses with football-related items of every kind. When they go to a game, which they do as often as possible, the true football fans make themselves look ridiculous by decorating themselves in weird team-related ways. At the game, these fans do the "wave" more than they watch the game.

Football fans love to talk about the past. They talk about William "Refrigerator" Perry's 1985 Super Bowl touchdown as though it had happened last week. They still get all excited about 1988's "Fog Bowl." They talk about John Elway's final game as though it's today's news, though it happened in 1999. They think everyone should be as excited as they are about such old stories.

Last of all, football fans are insanely loyal to the team of their choice. Football fans wear their team T-shirts and warm-up jackets everywhere, even to work. Of course, if they have to dress up in business clothes, they can't do that. Should their beloved team lose three in a row, their fans may begin to criticize their team. But these reactions only hide their broken hearts. They still obsessively watch each game and read all the newspaper stories about it. This intense loyalty makes fans dangerous. To anyone who dares to say to a loyal fan that another team is better, or, God forbid, to anyone wandering near the home cheering section wearing the jacket of the opposing team, physical damage is a real possibility. Incidents of violence in football stadiums have increased in recent years and are a matter of growing concern.

Football fans really act as if they're crazy. They behave insanely, they are crazy about the past, and they're too loyal.

Development through Revising

ALLWRITE!
4.3

The next day, Brian showed his first draft to a study partner from his composition class. She returned it with comments noted in the margins.

Reader's Comments

Huh? I guess this is about the weather—make it clearer.

Like what? Details here.

Details needed. How do they decorate themselves?

I'm not a football fan, so I don't understand these references. Can you briefly explain them?

Definition of a Football Fan

Football fans are by definition crazy. They behave insanely, they are insane about the past, and they are insanely loyal.

If their team gives away something free, the fans rush to the stadium to get the hat or whatever. Football fans just plain behave insanely. Baseball fans go similarly nuts when their favorite teams give away some attractive freebie. But football fans are even worse. Football fans freeze themselves in order to watch their favorite game. In addition, football fans decorate their houses with football-related items of every kind. When they go to a game, which they do as often as possible, the true football fans make themselves look ridiculous by decorating themselves in weird team-related ways. At the game, these fans do the "wave" more than they watch the game.

Football fans love to talk about the past. They talk about William "Refrigerator" Perry's 1985 Super Bowl touchdown as though it had happened last week. They still get all excited about 1988's "Fog Bowl." They talk about John Elway's final game as though it's today's news, though it happened in 1999. They think everyone should be as excited as they are about such old stories.

continued

Shouldn't this be in the second paragraph? It seems to belong to "they behave insanely," not "loyalty."

This doesn't support your topic statement, so take it out.

Last of all, football fans are insanely loyal to the team of their choice. Football fans wear their team T-shirts and warm-up jackets everywhere, even to work. Of course, if they have to dress up in business clothes, they can't do that. Should their beloved team lose three in a row, their fans may begin to criticize their team. But these reactions only hide their broken hearts. They still obsessively watch each game and read all the newspaper stories about it. This intense loyalty makes fans dangerous. To anyone who dares to say to a loyal fan that another team is better, or, God forbid, to anyone wandering near the home cheering section wearing the jacket of the opposing team, physical damage is a real possibility. Incidents of violence in football stadiums have increased in recent years and are a matter of growing concern.

Kind of a boring way to end it. You're just repeating your thesis.

Football fans really act as if they're crazy. They behave insanely, they are crazy about the past, and they're too loyal.

After reading his classmate's comments, Brian went to work on his next draft. As he worked, he read his essay aloud several times and noticed places where his wording sounded awkward or too informal. (Example: "If their team gives away a freebie, the fans rush to the stadium to get the hat or whatever.") A few drafts later, he produced the version of "Definition of a Football Fan" that appears on page 286.

A Professional Essay to Consider

Read the following professional essay. Then answer the questions and read the comments that follow.

(Activity 3)

Television Addiction

by Marie Winn

The word "addiction" is often used loosely and wryly in conversation. 1
People will refer to themselves as "mystery book addicts" or "cookie addicts." E. B. White writes of his annual surge of interest in gardening, "We are hooked and are making an attempt to kick the habit." Yet nobody really

believes that reading mysteries or ordering seeds by catalogue is serious enough to be compared to an addiction to heroin or alcohol. The word "addiction" is here used jokingly to denote a tendency to overindulge in some pleasurable activity.

People often refer to being "hooked on TV." Does this, too, fall into 2 the lighthearted category of eating cookies and other pleasures that people pursue with unusual intensity, or is there a kind of television viewing that falls into the more serious category of destructive addiction?

When we think about addiction to drugs or alcohol, we frequently focus 3 on negative aspects, ignoring the pleasures that accompany drinking or taking drugs. And yet the essence of any serious addiction is a pursuit of pleasure, a search for a "high" that normal life does not supply. It is only the inability to function without the addictive substance that is dismaying, the dependence of the organism upon a certain experience and an increasing inability to function without it. Thus a person will take two or three drinks at the end of the day not merely for the pleasure drinking provides, but also because he "doesn't feel normal" without them.

An addict does not merely pursue a pleasurable experience and need 4 to experience it in order to function normally. He needs to repeat it again and again. Something about that particular experience makes life without it less than complete. Other potentially pleasurable experiences are no longer possible, for under the spell of the addictive experience, his life is peculiarly distorted. The addict craves an experience, and yet he is never really satisfied. The organism may be temporarily sated, but soon it begins to crave again.

Finally, a serious addiction is distinguished from a harmless pursuit of 5 pleasure by its distinctly destructive elements. A heroin addict, for instance, leads a damaged life: his increasing need for heroin in increasing doses prevents him from working, from maintaining relationships, from developing in human ways. Similarly, an alcoholic's life is narrowed and dehumanized by his dependence on alcohol.

Let us consider television viewing in the light of the conditions that define 6 serious addictions.

Not unlike drugs and alcohol, the television experience allows the 7 participant to blot out the real world and enter into a pleasurable and passive mental state. The worries and anxieties of reality are as effectively deferred by becoming absorbed in a television program as by going on a "trip" induced by drugs or alcohol. And just as alcoholics are only vaguely aware of their addiction, feeling that they control their drinking more than they really do ("I can cut it out any time I want—I just like to have three or four drinks before dinner"), people similarly overestimate their control over watching television. Even as they put off other activities to spend hour after hour watching television, they feel they could easily resume living in a different, less passive style. But somehow or other while the television set is present in their homes, the click doesn't sound. With television pleasures available, those other experiences seem less attractive, more difficult somehow.

A heavy viewer (a college English instructor) observes: "I find television 8 almost irresistible. When the set is on, I cannot ignore it. I can't turn it off. I feel sapped, will-less, enervated. As I reach out to turn off the set, the strength goes out of my arms. I sit there for hours and hours."

The self-confessed television addict often feels he "ought" to do other 9 things—but the fact that he doesn't read and doesn't plant his garden or sew or crochet or play games or have conversations means that those activities are no longer as desirable as television. In a way the heavy viewer's life is as imbalanced by his television "habit" as a drug addict's or an alcoholic's. He is living in a holding pattern, as it were, passing up the activities that lead to growth or development or a sense of accomplishment. This is one reason people talk about their television viewing so ruefully, so apologetically. They are aware that it is an unproductive experience, that almost any other endeavor is more worthwhile by any human measure.

Finally, it is the adverse effect of television viewing on the lives of so 10 many people that defines it as a serious addiction. The television habit distorts the sense of time. It renders other experiences vague and curiously unreal while taking on a greater reality for itself. It weakens relationships by reducing and sometimes eliminating normal opportunities for talking, for communicating.

And yet television does not satisfy, else why would the viewer continue 11 to watch hour after hour, day after day? "The measure of health," writes Lawrence Kubie, "is flexibility . . . and especially the freedom to cease when sated." But the television viewer can never be sated with his television experiences—they do not provide the true nourishment that satiation requires—and thus he finds that he cannot stop watching.

QUESTIONS

About Unity

1. Winn's thesis is not presented directly in the essay. See if you can state it in your own words.

   Answers will vary. Example: Addiction to TV resembles addiction to alcohol

   or drugs in several ways.

2. Which statement would best serve as a topic sentence for paragraph 4?

   a. Addicts enjoy pleasurable experiences more than nonaddicts.

   b. Addicts feel that their lives are not really complete.

c. Addicts would give up their addiction if other pleasurable experiences were available.

(d.) Addicts need to endlessly repeat the experience on which they are dependent.

3. Which statement would best serve as a topic sentence for paragraph 7?

a. People become television addicts because they have more troubled lives than most other people.

(b.) Television addicts develop a distorted perception of reality and lose self-control.

c. Few experiences in life are as pleasurable as watching television.

d. Alcoholics often believe they have more control over their drinking than they really do.

About Support

4. The author defines TV as an addiction by first defining

a. being hooked on TV.

(b.) serious addiction.

c. a heavy viewer.

d. the real world.

5. The topic sentence of paragraph 5 states, "Finally, a serious addiction is distinguished from a harmless pursuit of pleasure by its distinctly destructive elements." What details does the author use to support this point?

heroin addict's damaged life

alcoholic's narrowed and dehumanized life

6. Paragraph 8

(a.) supports the idea in paragraph 7 that TV addicts overestimate their control over TV watching.

b. raises a point not dealt with elsewhere.

c. supports the idea in paragraph 9 that TV addicts are stuck in a living holding pattern.

About Coherence

7. Which paragraph fully signals the author's switch from discussing addiction in general terms to talking specifically about addiction to television? __6__

8. What key transitional word is used twice in the essay? ___Finally___

About the Introduction and Conclusion

9. Which statement best describes the introductory paragraph of Winn's essay?

    a. It explains the importance of the topic of television addiction.

    b. It tells an anecdote that illustrates the nature of television addiction.

    c. It presents a type of "addiction" very different from the one discussed in the essay.

10. Which statement best describes the conclusion of "Television Addiction"?

    a. Winn recommends that the television addict try to "kick the habit."

    b. Winn summarizes the points made in the body of the essay.

    c. Winn comments on the damage television does to society at large.

Writing a Definition Essay

WRITING ASSIGNMENT 1

Below are an introduction, a thesis, and supporting points for an essay that defines the word *maturity*. Using a separate sheet of paper, plan out and write the supporting paragraphs and a conclusion for the essay.

The Meaning of Maturity

> Being a mature student does not mean being an old-timer. Maturity is not measured by the number of years a person has lived. Instead, the yardstick of maturity is marked by the qualities of self-denial, determination, and dependability.

> Self-denial is an important quality in the mature student. . . .

> Determination is another characteristic of a mature student. . . .

> Although self-denial and determination are both vital, probably the most important measure of maturity is dependability. . . .

> In conclusion, . . .

Prewriting

2.3

a Prepare examples for the three qualities of maturity. For each quality, you should have one extended example that takes up an entire paragraph *or* two or three shorter examples that together form enough material for a paragraph.

b To generate these details, ask yourself questions like these, based on the topic sentence of the first supporting paragraph:

What could I do, or what have I done, that would be an example of self-denial?

What has someone I know ever done that could be described as self-denial?

What kind of behavior on the part of a student could be considered self-denial?

Write down quickly whatever answers occur to you. As when you freewrite, don't worry about grammar, punctuation, or spelling. Instead, concentrate on getting down as many details relating to self-denial as you can think of. Then repeat the questioning and writing process, substituting "determination" and "dependability" for "self-denial."

c Now go through the material you have compiled. If you think of other details as you read, jot them down. Next, decide just what information you will use in each supporting paragraph. List the details in the order in which you will present them.

d Now write the first draft of your paper.

Revising

4.3

After you have completed the first draft of the paper, set it aside for a while (if possible). When you reread what you have written, prepare for rewriting by asking yourself these questions:

- Have I provided enough details to support each of the three characteristics of maturity?
- Have I eliminated or rewritten any irrelevant material?
- Have I used transition words to help readers follow my train of thought?
- Does my concluding paragraph provide a summary or a final thought or both?

As you revise your essay through one or more additional drafts, continue to refer to this list until you can answer "yes" to each question. Then be sure to check the next-to-final draft of the paper for the sentence skills listed on the inside front cover.

WRITING ASSIGNMENT 2

Choose one of the terms below as the subject of a definition essay. Each term refers to a certain kind of person.

Slob	Optimist	Snob
Cheapskate	Pessimist	Tease
Loser	Team player	Practical joker
Good neighbor	Bully	Procrastinator
Busybody	Scapegoat	Loner
Whiner	Religious person	Straight arrow
Con artist	Hypocrite	

Prewriting

a   As you devise your opening paragraph, you may want to refer to the dictionary definition of the term. If so, be sure to use only one meaning of the term. (Dictionaries often provide several different meanings for a term.) *Don't* begin your paper with the overused phrase "According to Webster. . . . "

b   Remember that the thesis of a definition essay is a version of "What _____ means to me." The thesis presents what *your* experience has made *you* think the term actually means.

c   As you plan your supporting paragraphs, think of different parts or qualities of your term. Here, for example, are the three-part divisions of the student essays considered in this chapter:

Football fans are crazy in terms of their behavior, their fascination with the past, and their loyalty.

Student zombies are the "living dead," are controlled by a "mysterious force," and are likely to suffer an "awful fate."

d   Support each part of your division with either a series of examples or a single extended example.

e   You may find outlining to be the most helpful prewriting strategy for your definition essay. As a guide, write your thesis and three supporting points in the spaces below. *Answers will vary.*

Thesis: _____

Support: 1. _____

2. _____

3. _____

Revising

Once you have the first draft of your essay completed, review it with these questions in mind:

- Does my thesis statement indicate how I define the term, and does it indicate my plan of development for the essay?
- Does each of my supporting paragraphs have a clear topic sentence?
- Have I supported each of my three topic sentences with one extended example or a series of examples?
- Have I rounded off my essay with an appropriate concluding paragraph?
- Have I proofread my essay, referring to the list of sentence skills on the inside front cover?

WRITING ASSIGNMENT 3

In this definition essay, you will write with a specific purpose and for a specific audience.

Option 1   You work in a doctor's office and have been asked to write a brochure that will be placed in the waiting room. The brochure is intended to tell patients what a healthy lifestyle is. Write a definition of *healthy lifestyle* for your readers, using examples wherever appropriate. Your definition might focus on both mental and physical health and might include eating, sleeping, exercise, and recreational habits.

Alternatively, you might decide to take a playful point of view and write a brochure defining an *unhealthy lifestyle*.

Option 2   Your Spanish class is host to some students from Mexico. The class is preparing a "dictionary of slang" for the visitors. Your job is to write a paragraph in which you define the term *to gross out*.

In your introduction, consider including the nonslang definition of *gross,* which led to the slang usage. To find that definition, consult a dictionary. Your thesis should reflect your understanding of the slang usage of *to gross out*. Each of your supporting paragraphs can be based on an example of how the term is used, or a circumstance in which the term is appropriate.

Alternatively, you may write about any other slang term. If necessary, first get the approval of your instructor.

WRITING ASSIGNMENT 4

Writing for a Specific Purpose and Audience

Write an essay that defines one of these terms:

Persistence	Responsibility	Fear
Rebellion	Insecurity	Arrogance
Sense of humor	Assertiveness	Conscience
Escape	Jealousy	Class
Laziness	Practicality	Innocence
Danger	Nostalgia	Freedom
Curiosity	Gentleness	Violence
Common sense	Depression	Shyness
Soul	Obsession	Idealism
Family	Christianity	Spirituality

15 Division and Classification

7.4d

When you return home from your weekly trip to the supermarket with five bags packed with your purchases, how do you sort them out? You might separate food items from nonfood items (like toothpaste, paper towels, and detergent). Or you might divide and classify the items into groups intended for the freezer compartment, the refrigerator, and the kitchen cupboards. You might even put the items into groups like "to be used tonight," "to be used soon," and "to be used last." Sorting supermarket items in such ways is just one simple example of how we spend a great deal of our time organizing our environment in one manner or another.

In this chapter, you will be asked to write an essay in which you divide or classify a subject according to a single principle. To prepare for this assignment, first read the student essays and the professional essay that follow and work through the questions that accompany the essays.

Student Essays to Consider

Mall People

Just what goes into "having fun"? For many people, "fun" involves getting out of the house, seeing other people, having something interesting to look at, and enjoying a choice of activities, all at a reasonable price. Going out to dinner or to the movies may satisfy some of those desires, but often not all. But an attractive alternative does exist in the form of the free-admission shopping mall. Teenagers, couples on dates, and the nuclear family can all be observed having a good time at the mall.

Teenagers are drawn to the mall to pass time with pals and to see and be seen by other teens. The guys saunter by in sneakers, T-shirts, and blue jeans, complete with a package of cigarettes sticking out of a pocket. The girls stumble along in midriff-baring tank tops, with a cellphone tucked snugly in the rear pocket of their low-waisted jeans. Traveling in a gang that resembles a wolf pack, the teenagers make the shopping mall their hunting ground. Mall managers have obviously made a decision to attract all this teenage activity. The kids' raised voices, loud laughter, and occasional shouted obscenities can be heard from as far as half a mall away. They come to "pick up girls," to "meet guys," and just to "hang out."

Couples find fun of another sort at shopping malls. The young lovers 3 are easy to spot because they walk hand in hand, stopping to sneak a quick kiss after every few steps. They first pause at a jewelry store window so that they can gaze at diamond engagement rings and gold wedding bands. Then, they wander into furniture departments in the large mall stores. Finally, they drift away, their arms wrapped around each other's waist.

Mom, Dad, little Jenny, and Fred, Jr., visit the mall on Friday and 4 Saturday evenings for inexpensive recreation. Hearing the music of the antique carousel housed there, Jenny begs to ride her favorite pony with its shining golden mane. Shouting "I'm starving!" Fred, Jr., drags the family toward the food court, where he detects the seductive odor of pizza. Mom walks through a fabric store, running her hand over the soft velvets and slippery silks. Meanwhile, Dad has wandered into an electronics store and is admiring the sound system he'd love to buy someday. The mall provides something special for every member of the family.

Sure, some people visit the mall in a brief, businesslike way, just to pick 5 up a specific purchase or two. But many more are shopping for inexpensive recreation. The teenagers, the dating couples, and the nuclear families all find cheap entertainment at the mall.

Genuine Draft

The other night, my six-year-old son turned to me and asked for a 1 light beer. My husband and I sat there for a moment, stunned, and then explained to him that beer was only for grown-ups. I suddenly realized how many beer ads appear on television, and how often they appear. To my little boy, it must seem that every American drinks beer after work, or after playing softball, or while watching a football game. Brewers have pounded audiences with all kinds of campaigns to sell beer. There seems to be an ad to appeal to the self-image of every beer drinker.

One type of ad attracts people who think of themselves as grown-up 2 kids. Budweiser's animated frogs, squatting on lily pads and croaking "Bud," "Weis," "Er," are a perfect example of this type. The frogs are an example of the wonders of computer animation, which is being increasingly mixed in with real-life action in advertisements. The campaign was an immediate hit with the underage set as well as with adult beer-drinkers. Within weeks, the frogs were as recognizable to children as Tony the Tiger or Big Bird. They became so popular that the new Bud ads were a feverishly anticipated part of the Super Bowl—as much a part of the entertainment as the game itself or the halftime show. These humorous ads suggest that beer is part of a lighthearted approach to life.

A second kind of ad is aimed not at wanna-be kids but at macho men, guys who think of themselves as "men's men," doing "guy things" together. One campaign features men who see themselves as victims of their nagging wives. Ads in this series show men howling with laughter about how they've fooled their wives into thinking they're home doing chores (by leaving dummy-stuffed pants lying under leaky sinks or broken furnaces) while they're really out drinking. Beer is a man's drink, the ads seem to say, and women are a nuisance to be gotten around.

European and European-sounding beers such as Löwenbräu and Heineken like to show handsome, wealthy-looking adults enjoying their money and leisure time. A typical scene shows such people enjoying an expensive hobby in a luxurious location. Beer, these ads tell us, is an essential part of the "good life." This type of ad appeals to people who want to see themselves as successful and upper-class.

To a little boy, it may well seem that beer is necessary to every adult's life. After all, we need it to make us laugh, to bond with our friends, and to celebrate our financial success. At least, that's what advertisers tell him—and us.

3

4

5

QUESTIONS

About Unity

1. In which supporting paragraph in "Genuine Draft" is the topic sentence at the end rather than, as is more appropriate for student essays, at the beginning?

   _____4_____

2. Which sentence in paragraph 2 of "Mall People" should be omitted in the interest of paragraph unity? (*Write the opening words.*)

   Mall managers have obviously . . .

3. What sentence in paragraph 2 of "Genuine Draft" should be omitted in the interest of paragraph unity? (*Write the opening words.*)

   The frogs are an example . . .

About Support

4. After which sentence in paragraph 3 of "Mall People" are more supporting details needed? (*Write the opening words.*)

   Then, they wander . . .

ALLWRITE!

5

5. Which paragraph in "Genuine Draft" lacks sufficient specific details? ___4___

6. Label as *sight, touch, hearing,* or *smell* all the sensory details in the following sentences taken from "Mall People."

        hearing
  a. "Hearing the music of the antique carousel housed there, Jenny begs to ride
                               sight
     her favorite pony with its shining golden mane."
        hearing   *sight*
  b. "Shouting 'I'm starving!' Fred, Jr., drags the family toward the food court,
                            smell
     where he detects the seductive odor of pizza."
         sight   *touch*
  c. "Mom walks through a fabric store, running her hand over the soft velvets
         touch
     and slippery silks."

About Coherence

7. What are the time transition words used in paragraph 3 of "Mall People"?
        first   *Then*   *Finally*

8. Which topic sentence in "Genuine Draft" functions as a linking sentence between paragraphs? *(Write the opening words.)*

   A second kind of ad . . .

About the Introduction and Conclusion

9. What kind of introduction is used in "Genuine Draft"? *(Circle the appropriate letter.)*

  a. Broad, general statement narrowing to a thesis
  b. Idea that is the opposite of the one to be developed
  c. Quotation
  (d.) Anecdote
  e. Questions

10. What conclusion technique is used in "Mall People"? *(Circle the appropriate letter.)*

  (a.) Summary
  b. Prediction or recommendation
  c. Question

Developing a Division or Classification Essay

Considering Purpose and Audience

When writing a division or classification essay, your purpose is to present your audience with your own unique way of dividing and classifying a particular topic. In order to write a successful essay, you will need to first choose a topic that interests readers and lends itself to being divided and classified. Once you pick your topic, you will then have to come up with your own unique sorting system—one that readers will be able to understand.

For example, if you choose clothing, there are a number of ways to sort this topic into categories. You could divide clothing by the function it serves: shirts and jackets (to cover the upper body), pants and skirts (for the lower body), and shoes and socks (for the feet). Or you could divide clothes according to the materials they are made from: animal products, plant products, and synthetic materials. A more interesting, and potentially humorous, way to divide clothes is by fashion: clothes that are stylish, clothes that are going out of style, and clothes that are so unattractive that they never were in style. Notice that in all three of these cases, the broad topic of clothing has been divided into categories according to a particular principle (function, materials, and fashion). When you divide your topic for your essay, be sure to come up with your own division principle, and make it clear to your readers.

Once you've selected your topic and figured out how to divide it, you will need to provide specific details so that readers fully understand the categories you made. For the example about fashion above, you might classify plaid bell-bottom pants as part of the "going out of style" category, while blue jeans might belong in the "clothes that are stylish" group and a mustard-yellow velour jacket might fit in the "never stylish" group. Whatever divisions you make, be sure to include enough details to make your division-classification method—your main point—clear to your readers. Equally important, keep your audience in mind. An audience of fashion-conscious young people, for instance, would probably have very different opinions about what is and isn't stylish than an audience of middle-aged bankers. Or an audience made up of the parents of middle-school students who are clamoring for "cool" clothes would have much more interest in clothing styles than the parents of students about to enter college.

Development through Prewriting

Julia, the writer of "Mall People," believed from her observations that "people at malls" would make a good topic for a division or classification essay. But she did not immediately know how she wanted to group those people or what she wanted to say about them. She decided to begin her prewriting by making a list of observations about mall shoppers. Here is what she came up with:

Families with kids

Lots of snacking

Crowds around special displays—automobiles, kiddie rides

Older people walking in mall for exercise

Groups of teenagers

Women getting made over at makeup counter

Dating couples

Blind woman with Seeing Eye dog

Lots of people talking and laughing rather than shopping

Interviewers stopping shoppers to fill out questionnaires

Kids hanging out, meeting each other

As Julia reviewed her list, she concluded that the three largest groups of "mall people" were families with children, groups of teens, and dating couples. She decided to organize her essay around those three groups. To further flesh out her idea, she created a scratch outline that her essay would follow. Here is the scratch outline Julia prepared:

Thesis statement: Mall offers inexpensive fun for several groups.

1   Teens

    a.   Roam in packs

    b.   Dress alike

    c.   Meet new people

2   Dating couples

    a.   Act romantic

    b.   Window-shop for future home

    c.   Have lovers' quarrels

3   Families

    a.   Kids' activities

    b.   Cheap food

    c.   Adults shop

Julia's list and outline prepared her to write the first draft of her essay.

First Draft

Mall People

Malls aren't only places to go shopping. They also offer free or at least cheap fun and activities for lots of people. Teenagers, dating couples, and families all like to visit the mall.

Teenagers love to roam the mall in packs, like wolves. They often dress alike, depending on the latest fashion. They're noisy and sometimes rude, and mall security officers sometimes kick them out of the building. Then they find somewhere else to go, maybe one of the warehouse-sized amusement and video-game arcades that are springing up everywhere. Those places are fun, but they tend to be more expensive than just "hanging out" at the mall. Teens are usually not as interested in shopping at the mall as they are in picking up members of the opposite sex and seeing their friends.

Dating couples also enjoy wandering around the mall. They are easy to spot because they walk along holding hands and sometimes kissing. They stare at diamond rings and wedding bands and shop for furniture together. Sometimes they have spats and one of them stamps off to sulk on a bench for a while.

Little kids and their parents make up a big group of mall-goers. There is something for every member of the family there. There are usually some special displays that interest the kids, and Mom and Dad can always find things they like to window-shop for. Another plus for the family is that there is inexpensive food, like burgers and pizza, available at the mall's food court.

Development through Revising

4.3

After Julia completed her first draft, she put it aside. She knew from previous experience that she was a better critic of her own writing after she took a break from it. The following morning, when Julia read over her first draft, she noticed several places where it could be improved. Here are the observations she put in her writing journal:

- My first paragraph does present a thesis (malls offer inexpensive entertainment), and it tells how I'm going to develop that thesis (by discussing three groups of people). But it isn't very interesting. I think I could do a better job of drawing readers in by describing what is fun about malls.
- Some of the details in the essay aren't necessary; they don't support my main idea. For instance, the stuff about teens being kicked out of the mall and about dating couples having fights doesn't have anything to do with the entertainment malls provide. I'll eliminate this.

- Some of my statements that do support the main idea need more support. For example, when I say there are "special displays that interest the kids" in paragraph 4, I should give an example of such a display. I should also back up the idea that many teens dress alike.

With these observations in mind, Julia returned to her essay and revised it, producing the version that appears on page 303.

A Professional Essay to Consider

Now read the following professional essay. Then answer the questions and read the comments that follow.

Wait Divisions

by Tom Bodett

(Activity 3)

I read somewhere that we spend a full third of our lives waiting. I've also 1 read that we spend a third of our lives sleeping, a third working, and a third at our leisure. Now either somebody's lying, or we're spending all our leisure time waiting to go to work or sleep. That can't be true or league softball and Winnebagos never would have caught on.

So where are we doing all of this waiting, and what does it mean to an 2 impatient society like ours? Could this unseen waiting be the source of all our problems? A shrinking economy? The staggering deficit? Declining mental health and moral apathy? Probably not, but let's take a look at some of the more classic "waits" anyway.

The very purest form of waiting is what we'll call the *Watched-Pot Wait.* 3 This type of wait is without a doubt the most annoying of all. Take filling up the kitchen sink. There is absolutely nothing you can do while this is going on but keep both eyes glued to the sink until it's full. If you try to cram in some extracurricular activity, you're asking for it. So you stand there, your hands on the faucets, and wait. A temporary suspension of duties. During these waits it's common for your eyes to lapse out of focus. The brain disengages from the body and wanders around the imagination in search of distraction. It finds none and springs back into action only when the water runs over the edge of the counter and onto your socks.

The phrase "a watched pot never boils" comes of this experience. Pots 4 don't care whether they are watched or not; the problem is that nobody has ever seen a pot actually come to a boil. While people are waiting, their brains turn off.

Other forms of the Watched-Pot Wait would include waiting for your 5 dryer to quit at the laundromat, waiting for your toast to pop out of the toaster, or waiting for a decent idea to come to mind at a typewriter.

What they all have in common is that they render the waiter helpless and mindless.

A cousin to the Watched-Pot Wait is the *Forced Wait*. Not for the weak   6
of will, this one requires a bit of discipline. The classic Forced Wait is starting your car in the winter and letting it slowly idle up to temperature before engaging the clutch. This is every bit as uninteresting as watching a pot, but with one big difference. You have a choice. There is nothing keeping you from racing to work behind a stone-cold engine save[1] the thought of the early demise of several thousand dollars' worth of equipment you haven't paid for yet. Thoughts like that will help you get through a Forced Wait.

Properly preparing packaged soup mixes also requires a Forced Wait.   7
Directions are very specific on these mixes. "Bring three cups of water to boil, add mix, simmer three minutes, remove from heat, let stand five minutes." I have my doubts that anyone has actually done this. I'm fairly spineless when it comes to instant soups and usually just boil the bejeezus out of them until the noodles sink. Some things just aren't worth a Forced Wait.

All in all Forced Waiting requires a lot of a thing called patience, which is   8
a virtue. Once we get into virtues I'm out of my element and can't expound on the virtues of virtue, or even lie about them. So let's move on to some of the more far-reaching varieties of waiting.

The *Payday Wait* is certainly a leader in the long-term anticipation field.   9
The problem with waits that last more than a few minutes is that you have to actually do other things in the meantime. Like go to work. By far the most aggravating feature of the Payday Wait is that even though you must keep functioning in the interludes,[2] there is less and less you are able to do as the big day draws near. For some of us the last few days are best spent alone in a dark room for fear we'll accidentally do something that costs money. With the Payday Wait comes a certain amount of hope that we'll make it, and faith that everything will be all right once we do.

With the introduction of faith and hope, I've ushered in the most potent   10
wait class of all, the *Lucky-Break Wait,* or the *Wait for One's Ship to Come In.* This type of wait is unusual in that it is for the most part voluntary. Unlike the Forced Wait, which is also voluntary, waiting for your lucky break does not necessarily mean that it will happen.

Turning one's life into a waiting game of these proportions requires   11
gobs of the aforementioned faith and hope, and is strictly for the optimists among us. For these people life is the thing that happens to them while they're waiting for something to happen to them. On the surface it seems as ridiculous as following the directions on soup mixes, but the Lucky-Break Wait performs an outstanding service to those who take it upon themselves to do it. As long as one doesn't come to rely on it, wishing for a few good things to happen never hurt anybody.

[1]*save:* except
[2]*interludes:* times in between

In the end it is obvious that we certainly do spend a good deal of our   12
time waiting. The person who said we do it a third of the time may have
been going easy on us. It makes a guy wonder how anything at all gets done
around here. But things do get done, people grow old, and time boils on
whether you watch it or not.

The next time you're standing at the sink waiting for it to fill while   13
cooking soup mix that you'll have to eat until payday or until a large bag of
cash falls out of the sky, don't despair. You're probably just as busy as the
next guy.

QUESTIONS

About Unity

1. The thesis of Bodett's essay is not presented directly. See if you can state it in
   your own words. *Answers will vary. An example is given.*
   Various kinds of waiting interrupt everyone's life.

2. In paragraph 2, Bodett introduces several possible effects of waiting, then
   dismisses them with a "probably not." Is it a sign of careless writing that
   Bodett mentions irrelevant topics and then dismisses them? Or does he intend a
   particular effect by introducing unnecessary topics? If he does intend an effect,
   how would you describe it? *Answers will vary. An example is given.*
   This is intentional; it is done for a humorous effect.

About Support

3. Bodett writes of four "classic waits": the Watched-Pot Wait, the Forced Wait,
   the Payday Wait, and the Lucky-Break Wait. For which two "waits" does he
   provide several examples?
   Watched-Pot Wait   Forced Wait

4. Bodett refers to the first two waits as cousins. How does he differentiate
   between them?
   "You have a choice" in the Forced Wait.

5. How does Bodett support his claim that the Forced Wait "requires a bit of
   discipline"?
   He gives examples: protecting your car by not running it cold, and preparing
   soup properly.

About Coherence

6. Bodett's essay does not follow the strict one-three-one model (introduction, three supporting paragraphs, conclusion) often used in student essays. Instead, its form is a looser one that includes an introduction, four topics for development (the four "waits"), and a conclusion. Indicate in the following outline how the paragraphs of Bodett's essay are broken up:

Introduction: Paragraph(s)   _1–2_

Topic 1:   Paragraph(s)   _3–5_

Topic 2:   Paragraph(s)   _6–8_

Topic 3:   Paragraph(s)   _9_

Topic 4:   Paragraph(s)   _10–11_

Conclusion: Paragraph(s)   _12–13_

7. Which words in the first sentence of paragraph 6 link that sentence to the preceding three paragraphs?

   A cousin to the Watched-Pot Wait is . . .

8. Bodett organizes the waits

   a. from the most harmful to the least harmful.

   (b) from the shortest waits to the longest.

   c. from the most difficult wait to the easiest one.

   d. in no particular order.

About the Introduction and Conclusion

9. Which method best describes the introduction to "Wait Divisions"?

   a. Quotation

   b. Idea that is the opposite of the one to be developed

   c. Anecdote

   (d) Broad, general statement narrowing to thesis

10. In what way does the first sentence in paragraph 13 serve as a summary of Bodett's main points?   Wording of answer may vary. An example is given.

   He uses an image in which all the waits are involved.

Writing a Division or Classification Essay

WRITING ASSIGNMENT 1

Shown below are an introduction, a thesis, and supporting details for a classification essay on stress in college. Using separate paper, plan out and write the supporting paragraphs and a conclusion for the essay.

College Stress

Jack's heart pounds as he casts panicky looks around the classroom. He doesn't recognize the professor, he doesn't know any of the students, and he can't even figure out what the subject is. In front of him is a test. At the last minute his roommate awakens him. It's only another anxiety dream. The very fact that dreams like Jack's are common suggests that college is a stressful situation for young people. The causes of this stress can be academic, financial, and personal.

Academic stress is common. . . .

In addition to academic stress, the student often feels financial pressure. . . .

Along with academic and financial worries, the student faces personal pressures. . . .

In conclusion, . . .

Prewriting

a   To develop some ideas for the division-classification essay in Writing Assignment 1, freewrite for five minutes apiece on (1) *academic,* (2) *financial,* and (3) *personal* problems of college students.

b   Then add to the material you have written by asking yourself these questions:

> What are some examples of academic problems that are stressful for students?
>
> What are some examples of financial problems that students must contend with?
>
> What are some examples of personal problems that create stress in students?

Write down quickly whatever answers occur to you. As with freewriting, do not worry at this stage about writing correct sentences. Instead, concentrate on getting down as much information as you can think of that supports each of the three points.

c   Now go through all the material you have accumulated. Perhaps some of the details you have written down may help you think of even better details that would fit. If so, write down these additional details. Then make decisions about the exact information that you will use in each supporting paragraph. List the details in the order in which you will present them (1, 2, 3, and so on).

d   Now write the first draft of your paper.

Revising

After you have completed the first draft of the paper (and ideally set it aside for a while), you should prepare yourself to rewrite by asking the following questions:

- Have I provided relevant examples for each of the three kinds of stress?
- Have I provided enough details to support each of the three kinds of stress?
- Have I used transition words to help readers follow my train of thought?
- Have I added a concluding paragraph that rounds out and completes the essay?
- Have I checked the paper carefully for the sentence skills listed on the inside front cover?

As you revise your essay, continue to refer to this list until you can answer "yes" to each question.

WRITING ASSIGNMENT 2

Choose one of the following subjects as the basis for a division-classification essay:

Music	Pet owners
Videos	Junk food
TV shows	College courses
Fiction	Dating couples
Comic strips	Shoppers
Vacations	Bosses
Answering-machine messages	Parties
Breakfast foods	Advertisements
Pets	Catalogs
Attitudes toward exercise	

Prewriting

a   For a division-classification essay, the prewriting strategy that may be especially helpful is outlining. The success of your essay will depend on your division of your topic into three well-balanced parts. In order to create those three parts, you must use the same rule, or principle, of division for each. Most topics can be divided in several ways according to several principles. For example, the topic "Hit movies" could be divided in the following ways:

> By *film categories:* Action, comedy, romance
>
> By *intended audience:* Families, dating couples, teens

The topic "My favorite books" could be divided like this:

> By *book categories:* Novels, how-to books, biographies
>
> By *purpose they serve for me:* Escape, self-improvement, amusement

The topic "Places to eat" could be divided in these ways:

> By *cost:* Cheap, moderate, expensive
>
> By *type of food:* American, Italian, Chinese

If you look back at the essays that appear earlier in this chapter, you'll see that the topics are divided according to the following principles:

"Mall People" is divided by *groups of shoppers:* Teens, dating couples, families

"Genuine Draft" is divided by *beer-drinkers' self-images:* Grown-up kids, men's men, upper-class

"Wait Divisions" is divided by *types of waits:* Watched-Pot Wait, Forced Wait, Payday Wait, Lucky-Break Wait

The important point to remember is to divide your topic consistently, according to a single principle. It would be illogical, for example, to divide the topic "Places to eat" into "American" (type of food served), "Italian" (type of food served), and "Expensive" (cost). In order for the essay to be balanced and consistent, choose one principle of division and stick to it.

b As you consider a topic for your own paper, think of principles of division you might use. Test them by filling out this outline and answering the question. Answers will vary.

Topic: _____

Principle of division: _____

Three-part division of topic:

1. _____

2. _____

3. _____

Have I used the same principle of division for each of the three parts?

When you are confident that you have chosen a topic of interest to you that you can divide into three parts according to one principle, you are ready to begin writing.

c Before writing your first draft, you may want to freewrite on each of the three parts, make lists, or ask and answer questions to generate the supporting details you will need to develop your ideas.

Revising

Once you have completed a first draft of your essay, you should review it with these questions in mind:

- Have I included the essay's thesis in my introductory paragraph?
- Does my thesis state my topic and the principle of division I have chosen?

- Is each of the paragraphs in the body of my essay based on one division of my topic?
- Have I backed up statements in my essay with relevant examples or illustrations?
- Have I eliminated irrelevant material that does not support my thesis?
- Have I used transition words within the paragraphs to help readers follow my train of thought?
- Have I used linking sentences between paragraphs to help tie those paragraphs together?
- Have I included a concluding paragraph that provides a sense of completion to the essay?

As you revise your essay, continue to refer to this list until you can answer "yes" to each question.

WRITING ASSIGNMENT 3

Writing for a Specific Purpose and Audience

In this division-classification essay, you will write with a specific purpose and for a specific audience.

Option 1   Your younger sister or brother has moved to another city and is about to choose a roommate. Write her or him a letter about what to expect from different types of roommates. Label each type of roommate ("The Messy Type," "The Neatnik," "The Loud-Music Lover," etc.) and explain what it would be like to live with each.

Option 2   Unsure about your career direction, you have gone to a vocational counseling service. To help you select the type of work you are best suited for, a counselor has asked you to write a detailed description of your "ideal job." You will present this description to three other people who are also seeking to choose a career.
    To describe your ideal job, divide work life into three or more elements, such as

Activities done on the job
Skills used on the job
Physical environment
People you work with and under
How the job affects society

In your paper, explain your ideals for each element. Use specific examples where possible to illustrate your points.

16 Argumentation

Do you know someone who enjoys a good argument? Such a person likes to challenge any sweeping statement we might make. For example, when we say something like "Ms. Lucci doesn't grade fairly," he or she comes back with "Why do you say that? What are your reasons?"

Our questioner then listens carefully as we state our case, judging if we really do have solid evidence to support our point of view. We realize that saying, "Ms. Lucci just doesn't, that's all," sounds weak and unconvincing, so we try to come up with stronger evidence to back up our statement. Such a questioner may make us feel uncomfortable, but we may also feel grateful to him or her for helping us clarify our opinions.

The ability to put forth sound and compelling arguments is an important skill in everyday life. You can use argumentation to make a point in a class discussion, persuade a friend to lend you money, or talk an employer into giving you a day off. Becoming skilled in clear, logical reasoning can also help you see through faulty arguments that others may make. You'll become a better critic of advertisements, newspaper articles, political speeches, and the other persuasive appeals you see and hear every day.

In this chapter, you will be asked to write an essay in which you defend a position with a series of solid reasons. In a general way, you have done the same thing—making a point and then supporting it—with all the essays in this book. The difference here is that argumentation advances a *controversial* point, a point that at least some of your readers will not be inclined to accept. To prepare for this assignment, first read about five strategies you can use in advancing an argument. Then read the student essays and the professional essay that follow and work through the questions that accompany the essays.

Strategies for Argumentation

Because argumentation assumes controversy, you have to work especially hard to convince readers of the validity of your position. Here are five strategies you can use to help win over readers whose viewpoint may differ from yours.

319

1 Use Tactful, Courteous Language

In an argumentation essay, you are attempting to persuade readers to accept your viewpoint. It is important, therefore, not to anger them by referring to them or their opinions in rude or belittling terms. Stay away from sweeping statements like "Everybody knows that . . ." or "People with any intelligence agree that . . . ." Also, keep the focus on the issue you are discussing, not on the people involved in the debate. Don't write, "*My opponents* say that orphanages cost less than foster care." Instead, write, "*Supporters of orphanages* say that orphanages cost less than foster care." Terms like *my opponents* imply that the argument is between you and anyone who disagrees with you. By contrast, a term such as *supporters of orphanages* suggests that those who don't agree with you are nevertheless reasonable people who are willing to consider differing opinions.

2 Point Out Common Ground

Another way to persuade readers to consider your opinion is to point out common ground—opinions that you share. Find points on which people on all sides of the argument can agree. Perhaps you are arguing that there should be an 11 P.M. curfew for juveniles in your town. Before going into detail about your proposal, remind readers who oppose such a curfew that you and they share certain goals: a safer city, a lower crime rate, and fewer gang-related tragedies. Readers will be more receptive to your idea once they have considered the ways in which you and they think alike.

3 Acknowledge Differing Viewpoints

10.5

It is a mistake to simply ignore points of view that conflict with yours. Acknowledging other viewpoints strengthens your position in several ways. First, it helps you spot flaws in the opposing position—as well as in your own argument. Second, and equally important, it gives the impression that you are a reasonable person, willing to look at an issue from all sides. Readers will be more likely to consider your point of view if you indicate a willingness to consider theirs.

At what point in your essay should you acknowledge opposing arguments? The earlier the better—ideally, in the introduction. By quickly establishing that you recognize the other side's position, you get your readers "on board" with you, ready to hear what else you have to say.

One effective technique is to *cite the opposing viewpoint in your thesis statement.* You do this by dividing your thesis into two parts. In the first part, you acknowledge the other side's point of view; in the second, you state your opinion, suggesting that yours is the stronger viewpoint. In the following example, the opposing viewpoint is underlined once; the writer's own position is underlined twice:

> Although some students believe that studying a foreign language is a waste of time, two years of foreign-language study should be required of all college graduates.

For another example of a thesis that acknowledges an opposing viewpoint, look at this thesis statement, taken from the essay titled "Once Over Lightly: Local TV News" (page 323):

> While local TV newscasts can provide a valuable community resource, too often such programs provide mere entertainment at the expense of solid news.

Another effective technique is to use one or two sentences (separate from the thesis) in the introduction to acknowledge the alternative position. Such sentences briefly state the "other side's" argument. To see this technique at work, look at the introduction to the essay "Teenagers and Jobs" (page 322), noting the sentence "Many people argue that working can be a valuable experience for the young."

A third technique is to *use a paragraph within the body of your essay to summarize opposing opinions in greater detail*. To do this successfully, you must spend some time researching those opposing arguments. A fair, evenhanded summary of the other side's ideas will help convince readers that you have looked at the issue from all angles before deciding where you stand. Imagine, for instance, that you are writing an essay arguing that the manufacture and sale of handguns should be outlawed. You would begin by doing some library research to find information on both sides of the issue, making sure to pay attention to material that argues against your viewpoint. You might also talk with local representatives of the National Rifle Association or other organizations that support gun ownership. Having done your research, you would be in a good position to write a paragraph summarizing the opposing viewpoints. In this paragraph, you might mention that many citizens believe that gun ownership is a right guaranteed by the Constitution and that gun owners fear that outlawing handguns would deprive law-abiding people of protection against gun-toting criminals. Once you had demonstrated that you understood opposing views, you would be in a stronger position to present your own point of view.

4 When Appropriate, Grant the Merits of Differing Viewpoints

Sometimes an opposing argument contains a point whose validity you cannot deny. What should you do then? The strongest strategy is to admit that the point is a good one. You will lose credibility if you argue against something that clearly makes sense. Admit the merit of one aspect of the other argument while making it clear that you still believe your argument to be stronger overall. Suppose that you were arguing against the use of computers in writing classrooms. You might say,

"Granted, students who are already accustomed to computers can use them to write papers more quickly and efficiently"—admitting that the other side has a valid point. But you could quickly follow this admission with a statement making your own viewpoint clear: "But for students like me who write and think in longhand, a computer in the classroom is more a hindrance than a help; it would require too great a learning curve to be of any value to me."

5 Rebut Differing Viewpoints

Sometimes it may not be enough simply to acknowledge other points of view and present your own argument. When you are dealing with an issue that your readers feel strongly about, you may need to *rebut* the opposing arguments. To *rebut* means to point out problems with an opposing view, to show where an opponent's argument breaks down.

Imagine that you are writing an essay arguing that your college should use money intended to build a campus health and fitness center to upgrade the library instead. From reading the school paper, you know that supporters of the center say it will help attract new students to the college. You rebut that point by citing a study conducted by the admissions office which shows that most students choose a college because they can afford it and because they like its academic programs and facilities. You also emphasize that many students, already financially strapped, would have trouble paying the proposed fee for using the center.

A rebuttal can take two forms. (1) You can first mention all the points raised by the other side and then present your counterargument to each of those points. (2) You can present the first point raised by the opposition and rebut that point, then move on to the second opposing point and rebut that, and so on.

Student Essays to Consider

Teenagers and Jobs

"The pressure for teenagers to work is great, and not just because of the economic plight in the world today. Much of it is peer pressure to have a little bit of freedom and independence, and to have their own spending money. The concern we have is when the part-time work becomes the primary focus." These are the words of Roxanne Bradshaw, educator and officer of the National Education Association. Many people argue that working can be a valuable experience for the young. However, working more than about fifteen hours a week is harmful to adolescents because it reduces their involvement with school, encourages a materialistic and expensive lifestyle, and increases the chance of having problems with drugs and alcohol.

1

Schoolwork and the benefits of extracurricular activities tend to go by   2
the wayside when adolescents work long hours. As more and more teens
have filled the numerous part-time jobs offered by fast-food restaurants
and malls, teachers have faced increasing difficulties. They must both
keep the attention of tired pupils and give homework to students who
simply don't have time to do it. In addition, educators have noticed less
involvement in the extracurricular activities that many consider a healthy
influence on young people. School bands and athletic teams are losing
players to work, and sports events are poorly attended by working
students. Those teens who try to do it all—homework, extracurricular
activities, and work—may find themselves exhausted and prone to illness.
A recent newspaper story, for example, described a girl in Pennsylvania
who came down with mononucleosis as a result of aiming for good grades,
playing on two school athletic teams, and working thirty hours a week.

Another drawback of too much work is that it may promote   3
materialism and an unrealistic lifestyle. Some parents claim that working
helps teach adolescents the value of a dollar. Undoubtedly that can be true.
It's also true that some teens work to help out with the family budget or to
save for college. However, surveys have shown that the majority of working
teens use their earnings to buy luxuries—computers, video-game systems,
clothing, even cars. These young people, some of whom earn $400 or more
a month, don't worry about spending wisely—they can just about have it
all. In many cases, experts point out, they are becoming accustomed to a
lifestyle they won't be able to afford several years down the road, when
they no longer have parents paying for car insurance, food, lodging, and
so on. At that point, they'll be hard-pressed to pay for necessities as well as
luxuries.

Finally, teenagers who work a lot are more likely than others to get   4
involved with alcohol and drugs. Teens who put in long hours may seek a
quick release from stress, just like the adults who need to drink a couple of
martinis after a hard day at work. Stress is probably greater in our society
today than it has been at any time in the past. Also, teens who have money
are more likely to get involved with drugs.

Teenagers can enjoy the benefits of work while avoiding its drawbacks,   5
simply by limiting their work hours during the school year. As is often the
case, a moderate approach will be the most healthy and rewarding.

Once Over Lightly: Local TV News

Are local television newscasts a reliable source of news? Do they provide   1
in-depth coverage and analysis of important local issues? Unfortunately,
all too often they do not. While local TV newscasts can provide a valuable
community resource, too often such programs provide mere entertainment

at the expense of solid news. In their battle for high ratings, local programs emphasize news personalities at the expense of stories. Visual appeal has a higher priority than actual news. And stories and reports are too brief and shallow.

Local TV newscasters are as much the subject of the news as are   2
the stories they present. Nowhere is this more obvious than in weather reports. Weatherpersons spend valuable news time joking, drawing cartoons, chatting about weather fronts as "good guys" and "bad guys," and dispensing weather trivia such as statistics about relative humidity and record highs and lows for the date. Reporters, too, draw attention to themselves. Rather than just getting the story, the reporters are shown jumping into or getting out of helicopters to get the story. When reporters interview crime victims or the residents of poor neighborhoods, the camera angle typically includes them and their reaction as well as their subjects. When they report on a storm, they stand outside in the storm, their styled hair blowing, so we can admire how they "brave the elements." Then there are the anchorpersons, who are chosen as much for their looks as their skills. They too dilute the news by putting their personalities at center stage.

Often the selection of stories and the way they are presented are based   3
on visual impact rather than news value. If a story is not accompanied by an interesting film clip, it is not likely to be shown on the local news. The result is an overemphasis on fires and car crashes and little attention to such important issues as the economy. A tractor-trailer spill on the highway slightly injures one person and inconveniences motorists for only an hour. But because it provides dramatic pictures—the big truck on its side, its load spilled, emergency personnel running around, lots of flashing lights—it is given greater emphasis in the local newscast than a rise in local taxes, which has far more lasting effect on the viewer. "If it bleeds, it leads" is the unofficial motto of many local news programs. A story that includes pictures of death and destruction, no matter how meaningless, is preferable on the local news to a solid, important story without flashy visuals. The mania for visuals is so strong that local news programs will even slap irrelevant visuals onto an otherwise strong story. A recent story on falling oil prices, for example, was accompanied by footage of a working oil well that drew attention away from the important economic information in the report.

On the average, about half a minute is devoted to a story. Clearly,   4
stories that take less than half a minute are superficial. Even the longest stories, which can take up to several minutes, are not accompanied by meaningful analysis. Instead, the camera jumps from one location to another, and the newscaster simplifies and trivializes the issues. For instance, one recent "in-depth" story about the homeless consisted of a glamorous reporter talking to a homeless person and asking him what should be done about the problem. The poor man was in no condition

to respond intelligently. The story then cut to an interview with a city bureaucrat who mechanically rambled on about the need for more government funding. Is raising taxes the answer to every social problem? There were also shots of homeless people sleeping in doorways and on top of heating vents, and there were interviews with people in the street, all of whom said that something should be done about the terrible problem of homelessness. There was, in all of this, no real exploration of the issue and no proposed solution. It was also apparent that the homeless were just the issue of the week. After the week's coverage was over, the topic was not mentioned again.

Because of the emphasis on newscasters' personalities and on the visual impact of stories and the short time span for stories, local news shows provide little more than diversion. What viewers need instead is news that has real significance. Rather than being amused and entertained, we need to deal with complex issues and learn uncomfortable truths that will help us become more responsible consumers and citizens.

5

QUESTIONS

ALLWRITE!

5

About Unity

1. Which paragraph in "Once Over Lightly" lacks a topic sentence? _____4_____
   Write a topic sentence for the paragraph: _Answers may vary; an example is given: Local news is often lacking in depth._

2. What sentence in paragraph 4 of "Once Over Lightly" should be omitted in the interest of paragraph unity? *(Write the opening words.)*
   Is raising taxes . . .

3. Which sentence in paragraph 4 of "Teenagers and Jobs" should be omitted in the interest of paragraph unity? *(Write the opening words.)*
   Stress is probably greater . . .

About Support

4. Which sentence in paragraph 4 of "Teenagers and Jobs" needs to be followed by more supporting details? Which sentence in paragraph 2 of "Once Over Lightly" needs to be followed by supporting details? *(Write the opening words of each sentence.)*
   "Teenagers and Jobs": Also, teens who have money . . .
   "Once Over Lightly": They too dilute the news . . .

5. In "Teenagers and Jobs," which supporting paragraph raises an opposing idea and then argues against that idea? ___3___ What transition word is used to signal the author's change of direction? _____However_____

6. In paragraph 2 of "Once Over Lightly," the topic sentence is supported by details about three types of newscasters. What are those three types?

_____weatherpersons_____   _____reporters_____   _____anchorpersons_____

About Coherence

7. Which two paragraphs of "Teenagers and Jobs" begin with an addition transition, and what are those words?

_____3: Another_____   _____4: Finally_____

8. Write the change-of-direction transition and the illustration transition in paragraph 3 of "Once Over Lightly."

Change of direction: _____But_____   *Illustration:* _____for example_____

About the Introduction and Conclusion

9. Two methods of introduction are used in "Teenagers and Jobs." Circle the letters of these two methods.
   a. Broad, general statement narrowing to thesis
   b. Idea that is the opposite of the one to be developed
   c. Quotation
   d. Anecdote
   e. Questions

10. Both essays end with the same type of conclusion. What method do they use?
   a. Summary only
   b. Summary and recommendation
   c. Prediction

Developing an Argumentation Essay

Considering Purpose and Audience

When you write an argumentation essay, your main purpose is to convince readers that your particular view or opinion on a *controversial* issue is correct. In addition, at times, you may have a second purpose for your argumentation essay: to persuade your audience to take some sort of action.

In order to convince readers in an argumentation essay, it is important to provide them with a clear main point and plenty of logical evidence to back it up. Say, for example, you want to argue that public schools should require students to wear uniforms. In this case, you might do research to gather as much evidence as possible to support your point. You may check to see, for instance, if uniforms are cheaper than the alternative. Perhaps you could find out if schools with uniforms have a lower rate of violence than those without them. You may even look for studies to see if students' academic performance improves when school uniforms are adopted. As you search for evidence, be sure that it clearly links to your topic and supports the main point you are trying to get across to your audience.

While consideration of your audience is important for all essay forms, it is absolutely critical to the success of your argumentation essay. Depending on the main point you choose, your audience may be firmly opposed to your view or somewhat supportive of it. As you begin planning your own argumentation essay, then, consider what your audience already knows, and how it feels, about the main point of your argument. Using the example above, for instance, ask yourself what opinion your audience holds about school uniforms. What are likely to be their objections to your argument? Why would people *not* support your main point? What, if anything, are the merits of the opposing point of view? In order to "get inside the head" of your opposition, you might even want to interview a few people you're sure will disagree with you: say, for instance, a student with a very funky personal style who you know would dislike wearing a uniform. By becoming aware of the points of view your audience might have, you will know how to proceed in researching your rebuttal to their arguments. (For more information on how to deal with opposing views in your essay, see pages 320–322.) By directly addressing your opposition, you add credibility to your argument and increase the chances that others will be convinced that your main point is valid.

Development through Prewriting

ALLWRITE!
2.3

Before choosing a topic for her essay, Anna, the writer of "Teenagers and Jobs," asked herself what controversial subject she was particularly well qualified to argue. She wanted to select something she cared about, something she could "sink her teeth into." As a person who had been an active member of her high school community—she had worked on the newspaper, played basketball, and sung in a chorus—Anna first thought of writing about "student apathy." It had always bothered her to see few students taking advantage of the opportunities available to them in school. But as she thought more about individual students she knew and their reasons for not getting more involved in school and extracurricular activities, she changed her opinion. "I realized that 'apathy' was not really the problem," she explained. "Many of them worked so much that they literally didn't have time for school life."

After narrowing her thesis to the idea of "teenagers and work," Anna made a list of what she perceived as the bad points of students' working too much:

> No time for real involvement in school and school activities
>
> Students leave right after school—can't stay for clubs, practices
>
> Don't have time to attend games, other school functions
>
> Students sleep in class and skip homework
>
> Stress, extra money contribute to drug and alcohol use
>
> Teachers frustrated trying to teach tired students
>
> Having extra money makes teens materialistic
>
> Some get so greedy they drop out of school to work full-time
>
> Students miss the fun of being young, developing talents and social abilities
>
> Students burn out, even get sick
>
> Hanging around older coworkers can contribute to drug, alcohol use
>
> Buying luxuries gives teens unrealistic idea of standard of living

As she reviewed and revised her list of points, Anna identified three main points to develop in her essay. Those she identified as points 1, 2, and 3. She realized that some of the other items she had jotted down were related ideas that might be used to support her main topics. She marked those with the number of the main idea they supported, in parentheses, like this: (1). She also crossed out points that did not fit.

> 1 No time for real involvement in school and school activities
>
> (1) Students leave right after school—can't stay for clubs, practices
>
> (1) Don't have time to attend games, other school functions
>
> ~~Students sleep in class and skip homework~~
>
> 2 Stress, extra money contribute to drug and alcohol use
>
> (1) Teachers frustrated trying to teach tired students
>
> 3 Having extra money makes teens materialistic
>
> (3) Some get so greedy for money they drop out of school to work full-time

~~Students miss the fun of being young, developing talents and social abilities~~

~~Students burn out, even get sick~~

(2) Hanging around older coworkers can contribute to drug, alcohol use

(3) Buying luxuries gives teens unrealistic idea of standard of living

Referring to this list, Anna wrote the following first draft of her essay.

First Draft

Teenagers and Jobs

Many people think that working is a valuable experience for young people. But when teenagers have jobs, they are too likely to neglect their schoolwork, become overly materialistic, and get into trouble with drugs and alcohol.

Schoolwork and the benefits of extracurricular activities tend to go by the wayside when adolescents work long hours. As more and more teens have taken jobs, teachers have faced increasing difficulties. They must both keep the attention of tired pupils and give homework to students who simply don't have time to do it. In addition, educators have noticed less involvement in extracurricular activities. School bands and athletic teams are losing players to work, and sports events are poorly attended by working students. Those teens who try to do it all—homework, extracurricular activities, and work—may find themselves exhausted and burned out.

Another drawback of too much work is that it may promote materialism and an unrealistic lifestyle. Most working teens use their earnings to buy luxuries. These young people don't worry about spending wisely—they can just about have it all. They are becoming accustomed to a lifestyle they won't be able to afford several years down the road, when they have to support themselves.

Finally, teenagers who work are more likely than others to get involved with alcohol and drugs. Teens who put in long hours may seek a quick release from stress, just like the adults who need to drink a couple of martinis after a hard day at work. Also, teens who have money are more likely to get involved with drugs.

In short, teens and work just don't mix.

Development through Revising

Anna's instructor had offered to look over students' first drafts and suggest improvements for revision. Here is the note she wrote at the end of Anna's work:

Anna — Good beginning. While I think your thesis is overstated, it and each of your main topics are on the right track. Here are some points to consider as you write your next draft:

- Many teenagers find working a <u>limited</u> number of hours a week to be a good experience. I think it's a mistake to state flatly that it's <u>always</u> a negative thing for teenagers to have jobs. Think about acknowledging that there can be good points to students' working part-time.

- You do a pretty good job of supporting your first main point ("Schoolwork and the benefits of extracurricular activities tend to go by the wayside when adolescents work long hours") by noting the effect of too much work on scholastic achievement and extracurricular activities. You <u>less</u> effectively support points 2 and 3 ("Another drawback of too much work is that it may promote materialism and an unrealistic lifestyle" and "Finally, teenagers who work are more likely than others to get involved with alcohol and drugs"). <u>Show</u> how teens become too materialistic; don't just state that they do. And what evidence do you have that working teens use drugs and alcohol more than others?

- Throughout the essay, can you come up with evidence beyond your own observations to support the idea that too much working is detrimental to teens? Look into the magazine indexes in the library and on the Internet for studies or stories that might support your thesis.

I'll look forward to seeing your final draft.

After considering her instructor's comments, Anna wrote the version of "Teenagers and Jobs" that appears on page 322.

A Professional Essay to Consider

Read the following professional essay. Then answer the questions and read the comments that follow.

(Activity 3)

Ban the Things. Ban Them All.

by Molly Ivins

Guns. Everywhere guns.   1

Let me start this discussion by pointing out that I am not anti-gun. I'm   2
pro-knife. Consider the merits of the knife.

In the first place, you have to catch up with someone to stab him. A 3 general substitution of knives for guns would promote physical fitness. We'd turn into a whole nation of great runners. Plus, knives don't ricochet. And people are seldom killed while cleaning their knives.

As a civil libertarian,[1] I of course support the Second Amendment. 4 And I believe it means exactly what it says: "A well-regulated militia being necessary to the security of a free state, the right of the people to keep and bear arms shall not be infringed[2]." Fourteen-year-old boys are not part of a well-regulated militia. Members of wacky religious cults are not part of a well-regulated militia. Permitting unregulated citizens to have guns is destroying the security of this free state.

I am intrigued by the arguments of those who claim to follow the judicial 5 doctrine of original intent. How do they know it was the dearest wish of Thomas Jefferson's heart that teenage drug dealers should cruise the cities of this nation perforating their fellow citizens with assault rifles? Channeling[3]?

There is more hooey spread about the Second Amendment. It says quite 6 clearly that guns are for those who form part of a well-regulated militia, i.e., the armed forces including the National Guard. The reasons for keeping them away from everyone else get clearer by the day.

The comparison most often used is that of the automobile, another 7 lethal object that is regularly used to wreak great carnage. Obviously, this society is full of people who haven't got enough common sense to use an automobile properly. But we haven't outlawed cars yet.

We do, however, license them and their owners, restrict their use to 8 presumably sane and sober adults and keep track of who sells them to whom. At a minimum, we should do the same with guns.

In truth, there is no rational argument for guns in this society. This is no 9 longer a frontier nation in which people hunt their own food. It is a crowded, overwhelmingly urban country in which letting people have access to guns is a continuing disaster. Those who want guns—whether for target shooting, hunting or potting[4] rattlesnakes (get a hoe)—should be subjected to the same restrictions placed on gun owners in England, a nation in which liberty has survived nicely without an armed populace.

The argument that "guns don't kill people" is patent nonsense. Anyone 10 who has ever worked in a cop shop knows how many family arguments end in murder because there was a gun in the house. Did the gun kill someone? No. But if there had been no gun, no one would have died. At least not without a good footrace first. Guns do kill. Unlike cars, that is all they do.

Michael Crichton makes an interesting argument about technology in his 11 thriller *Jurassic Park.* He points out that power without discipline is making

---

[1]*civil libertarian:* someone actively concerned with protecting rights guaranteed to the individual by law.
[2]*infringed:* violated.
[3]*channeling:* serving as a medium in order to communicate with spirits.
[4]*potting:* shooting with a potshot (an easy shot).

this society into wreckage. By the time someone who studies the martial arts becomes a master—literally able to kill with bare hands—that person has also undergone years of training and discipline. But any fool can pick up a gun and kill with it.

"A well-regulated militia" surely implies both long training and long   12
discipline. That is the least, the very least, that should be required of those who are permitted to have guns, because a gun is literally the power to kill. For years, I used to enjoy taunting my gun-nut friends about their psychosexual hangups—always in a spirit of good cheer, you understand. But letting the noisy minority in the National Rifle Association force us to allow this carnage to continue is just plain insane.

I do think gun nuts have a power hangup. I don't know what is missing   13
in their psyches that they need to feel they have the power to kill. But no sane society would allow this to continue.

Ban the damn things. Ban them all.   14

You want protection? Get a dog.   15

QUESTIONS

About Unity

1. Which of the following statements best represents the implied thesis of the essay?

    a. The author is pro-knife.

    b. The Second Amendment is poorly understood.

    (c.) Despite arguments to the contrary, people without long training and discipline should not be allowed to have guns.

    d. In his novel *Jurassic Park,* Michael Crichton argues that power without discipline is wrecking society.

2. Which statement would best serve as a topic sentence for paragraphs 5 and 6?

    a. Drug dealers should not be allowed to purchase assault rifles.

    b. Ivins is interested in other people's points of view concerning gun ownership.

    c. Thomas Jefferson was opposed to the idea of a "well-regulated militia."

    (d.) Applying the original intent of the Second Amendment to modern circumstances is not clear-cut and must be done with common sense.

3. Which is the topic sentence of paragraph 9?

    (a.) "In truth, there is no rational argument for guns in this society."

    b. "This is no longer a frontier nation in which people hunt their own food."

c. "It is a crowded, overwhelmingly urban country in which letting people have access to guns is a continuing disaster."

d. "Those who want guns . . . should be subjected to the same restrictions placed on gun owners in England . . . ."

About Support

4. Why does Ivins contrast the use of martial arts with the use of guns?

   a. To support the idea that gun owners should be required to study the martial arts

   b. To support the idea that a martial arts master can kill with his bare hands

   c. To support the idea that power without discipline is dangerous

   d. To support the idea that guns are more practical than the martial arts

5. Which statement best expresses the implied point of paragraph 10?

   a. Guns kill people.

   b. Many family arguments are surprisingly violent.

   c. Many arguments end in death only because a gun was handy.

   d. Guns and cars are similar.

6. In what ways, according to Ivins, is the knife preferable to the gun? Is Ivins really "pro-knife," or is she making some other point in her discussion of knives versus guns?   Answers may vary.

   Knives promote physical fitness, don't ricochet, don't kill people cleaning them.

   No, she is not really pro-knife; her point is that guns are even more

   dangerous than knives.

About Coherence

7. In paragraph 3, Ivins uses three addition signals—one to introduce each of her three reasons for being pro-knife. What are those three signals? (Two are *not* in the list of addition signals on page 80.)

   In the first place   Plus   And

8. In paragraph 7, Ivins acknowledges an opposing point of view when she mentions that automobiles, like guns, "wreak great carnage." In paragraph 8, what sentence includes a "change of direction" signal indicating that Ivins will present her argument against that point of view? *(Write the first few words of that sentence.)*

   We do, however, license . . .

About the Introduction and Conclusion

9. Ivins's introduction consists of three very brief paragraphs. Which statement best describes the style of her introduction?

  a. It presents an anecdote that is related to the topic of unregulated gun ownership.

  b. It presents a provocative question that grabs the reader's attention.

  c. It makes a startling point that at first seems unrelated to the topic.

  d. It presents a quotation that puts the topic in some sort of historical context.

10. Which of these best describes the conclusion of "Ban the Things"?

  a. It makes a blunt recommendation.

  b. It asks a thought-provoking question.

  c. It narrates an anecdote about guns.

  d. It predicts what will happen if guns are not banned.

Writing an Argumentation Essay

WRITING ASSIGNMENT 1

Write a paper in which you argue *for* or *against* any one of the three comments below (options 1–3). Support and defend your argument by drawing on your reasoning ability and general experience.

Option 1   In many ways, television has proved to be one of the worst inventions of modern times. All too often, television is harmful because of the shows it broadcasts and the way it is used in the home.

Option 2   Many of society's worst problems with drugs result from the fact that they are illegal. During Prohibition, Americans discovered that making popular substances unlawful causes more problems than it solves. Like alcohol and tobacco, drugs should be legal in this country.

Option 3   Statistics show that newly licensed teenage boys cause a higher number of serious automobile accidents than any other group. It is evident that many young men are too reckless and impulsive to be good drivers. In order to protect the larger society, the age at which a boy can earn his license should be raised to eighteen.

Prewriting

a   Take a few minutes to think about the three options. Which one in particular are you for or against, and *why?*

b On a sheet of paper, make a brief outline of support for your position on one of the options. (Remember, you may choose to argue *against* one of the three comments, as well as for it.) Preparing the outline will give you a chance to think further about your position. And the outline will show whether you have enough support for your position. (If you find that you don't, choose another position and prepare another outline.)

c Next, decide how you will develop each of your three supporting points. Make up brief outlines of the three supporting paragraphs. In addition to preparing brief outlines, you may want to use other prewriting techniques. You may want to freewrite or ask questions or make up lists.

d Decide in which order you want to present your paragraphs. *Emphatic order* (in which you *end* with your most important reason) is often the most effective way to organize an argument. Your reader is most likely to remember your final reason.

e As you write, think of your audience as a jury that will ultimately believe or disbelieve your argument. Have you presented a convincing case? Do you need more details? If *you* were on the jury, would you be favorably impressed with this argument?

f Proceed to write the first draft of your essay.

Revising

After you have completed the first draft of the paper, set it aside for a while (if possible). When you review it, try to do so as critically as you would if it were not your own work. Ask yourself these questions:

- Have I provided persuasive details to support my argument?
- Have I acknowledged the opposing point of view, showing that I am a reasonable person willing to consider other arguments?
- Is my language tactful and courteous? Have I avoided insulting anyone who doesn't agree with me?
- Have I used transition words to help readers follow my train of thought?
- Does my final supporting paragraph include a strong argument for my position?
- Have I provided a concluding paragraph to summarize my argument or add a final persuasive touch?

As you revise your essay through added drafts, continue to refer to this list until you can answer "yes" to each question. Then be sure to check the next-to-final draft of the paper for the sentence skills listed on the inside front cover.

ALLWRITE!
4.3

Writing Assignment 2

Write a paper in which you argue *for* or *against* any one of the three comments below. Support and defend your argument by drawing on your reasoning ability and general experience.

Option 1   Giving students grades does more harm than good. Schools should replace grades with written evaluations of the student's strengths and weaknesses. These would benefit both students and parents.

Option 2   Jails are overcrowded. Furthermore, jails often function as "schools for crime" in which petty lawbreakers learn to become hardened criminals. Of course, it is necessary to put violent criminals in jail in order to protect others. But society would benefit if nonviolent criminals received punishments other than jail sentences.

Option 3   Physical punishment "works" in the sense that it may stop a child from misbehaving, but adults who frequently spank and hit are also teaching children that violence is a good method of accomplishing a goal. Nonviolent methods are a more effective way of training children.

Prewriting

a   As you write your opening paragraph, acknowledge the opposing point of view before stating your thesis. If you have trouble figuring out what the "other side" would argue, completing this exercise will give you practice in acknowledging another way of looking at the question.

In each item, you will see a statement and then a question related to that statement. Write *two* answers to each question. Your first will answer "yes" to the question and briefly explain why. The other will answer "no" to the question, and also state why. The first item is done for you as an example:

1. Smoking has been proved to be bad for health. Should it therefore be made illegal?

   "Yes": *Because smoking has been shown to have so many negative effects on health, the sale of tobacco should be made illegal.*

   "No": *Although smoking has been linked to various health problems, adults should have the right to make their own decision about whether or not to smoke. Smoking should not be made illegal.*

Answers will vary.

2. Animals feel pain when they are killed for food. Is eating animals therefore immoral?

"Yes": _____

_____

"No": _____

_____

3. Professional boxing often leads to serious injury. Should it be outlawed?

"Yes": _____

_____

"No": _____

_____

4. Some high school students are sexually active. Should birth control devices and information be given out by high schools to their students?

"Yes": _____

_____

"No": _____

_____

b   Make a list of the thoughts that support your argument. Don't worry about repetition, spelling, or grammar at this point. Just write down everything that occurs to you.

c   Once you have written down all the thoughts that occur to you, identify what you see as your strongest points. Select your three main supporting points. Are there other thoughts in your list that you can use as supporting details for those points?

d   Write your three supporting paragraphs. Keep in mind that you are writing for an audience of people who, initially, will not all agree with you. It isn't enough to state your opinion. You must show *why* you feel as you do, persuading your reader that your point of view is valid.

e   Your concluding paragraph is your final chance to persuade your readers to accept your argument. Consider ending with a prediction of what will happen if your point of view does not prevail. Will an existing situation grow worse? Will a new problem arise?

Revising

Follow the suggestions for revising provided on page 335.

WRITING ASSIGNMENT 3

Write a paper in which you argue *for* or *against* any one of the three comments below. Support and defend your argument by drawing on your reasoning ability and general experience.

Option 1   Junk food is available in school cafeterias and school vending machines, and the cafeteria menus do not encourage the best eating habits. But good education should include good examples as well as classwork. Schools should practice what they preach about a healthy diet and stop providing junk food.

Option 2   By the time many students reach high school, they have learned the basics in most subjects. Some still have much to gain from the education that high schools offer, but others might be better off spending the next four years in other ways. For their benefit, high school attendance should be voluntary.

Option 3   Many of today's young people are mainly concerned with prestigious careers, making money, and owning things. It seems we no longer teach the benefits of spending time and money to help the community, the country, or the world. Our country can strengthen these human values and improve the world by requiring young people to spend a year working in some type of community service.

WRITING ASSIGNMENT 4

Writing for a Specific Purpose and Audience

In this argument essay, you will write with a specific purpose and for a specific audience.

Option 1   You'd like to live in a big city, but your parent or spouse refuses to budge from the suburbs. Write him or her a letter in which you argue the advantages of city life. Since the success of your argument will depend to some degree on how well you overcome the other person's objections to city life, be sure to address those as well. Use specific, colorful examples wherever possible.

Option 2   Find an editorial in your local newspaper that you either strongly agree with or strongly disagree with. Write a letter to the editor responding to that editorial. State why you agree or disagree with the position taken by the paper. Provide several short paragraphs of supporting evidence for your position. Actually send your letter to the newspaper. When you turn in a copy of your letter to your instructor, also turn in the editorial that you are responding to.

PART THREE

Special Skills

17 Taking Essay Exams

Essay exams are perhaps the most common type of writing you will do in school. They include one or more questions to which you must respond in detail, writing your answers in a clear, well-organized manner. Many students have trouble with essay exams because they do not realize there is a sequence to follow that will help them do well on such tests. This chapter describes five basic steps needed to prepare adequately for an essay test and to take the test. It is assumed, however, that you are already doing two essential things: first, attending class regularly and taking notes on what happens in class; second, reading your textbook and other assignments and taking notes on them. If you are *not* consistently going to class, reading your text, and taking notes in both cases, you are likely to have trouble with essay exams and other tests as well.

To write an effective exam essay, follow these five steps:

Step 1: Anticipate ten probable questions.
Step 2: Prepare and memorize an informal outline answer for each question.
Step 3: Look at the exam carefully and do several things.
Step 4: Prepare a brief, informal outline before writing your essay answer.
Step 5: Write a clear, well-organized essay.

The following pages explain and illustrate these steps.

Step 1: Anticipate Ten Probable Questions

Because exam time is limited, the instructor can give you only several questions to answer. He or she will, reasonably, focus on questions dealing with the most important areas of the subject. You can probably guess most of them.

Go through your class notes with a colored pen and mark off those areas where your instructor has spent a good deal of time. The more time spent on any one area, the better the chance you will get an essay question on it. If the instructor spent a week talking about present-day changes in the traditional family structure, or the importance of the carbon molecule, or the advantages of capitalism, or key early figures in the development of psychology as a science, you can reasonably expect that you will get a question about the emphasized area.

In both your class notes and your textbooks, pay special attention to definitions and examples and to basic lists of items (enumerations). Enumerations in particular are often a key to essay questions. For instance, if your instructor spoke at length about causes of the Great Depression, effects of water pollution, or advantages of capitalism, you should probably expect a question such as "What were the causes of the Great Depression?" or "What are the effects of water pollution?" or "What are the advantages of capitalism?"

If your instructor has given you a study guide, look there for probable essay questions. (Some instructors choose essay questions from those listed in study guides.) Look for clues to essay questions on any short quizzes that you may have been given. Finally, consider very carefully any review that the instructor provides. Always write down such reviews—your instructor has often made up the test or is making it up at the time of the review and is likely to give you valuable hints about it. Take advantage of them! Note also that if the instructor does not offer to provide a review, do not hesitate to *ask* for one in a friendly way. Essay questions are likely to come from areas the instructor may mention.

An Illustration of Step 1

A psychology class was given one day to prepare for an essay exam on stress—a subject that had been covered in class and comprised a chapter in the textbook for the course. One student, Mark, read carefully through his class notes and the textbook chapter. On the basis of the headings, major enumerations, and definitions he noted, he decided that there were five likely essay questions:

1. What are the common sources of stress?
2. What are the types of conflict?
3. What are the defense mechanisms that people use to cope with stress?
4. What effects can stress have on people?
5. What are the characteristics of a well-adjusted person?

Step 2: Prepare and Memorize an Informal Outline Answer for Each Question

Write out each question you have made up and, under it, list the main points that need to be discussed. Put important supporting information in parentheses after each main point. You now have an informal outline that you can memorize.

Pick out a *key word* in each part, and then create a *catchphrase* to help you remember the key words.

Note   If you have spelling problems, make up a list of words you might have to spell in writing your answers. For example, if you are having a psychology test on the principles of learning, you might want to study such terms as *conditioning, reinforcement, Pavlov, reflex, stimulus,* and so on.

An Illustration of Step 2

After identifying the likely questions on the exam, Mark made up an outline answer for each of the questions. For example, here is the outline answer that he made up for the first question:

Common sources of stress:

1. (Pressure)(internal and external)
2. (Anxiety)(sign of internal conflict)
3. (Frustration)(can't reach desired goal)
4. (Conflict)(three types of approach-avoidance)

    P A F C (People are funny creatures.)

ACTIVITY

See whether you can complete the following explanation of what Mark has done in preparing for the essay question.

First, Mark wrote down the heading and then numbered the sources of stress under it. Also, in parentheses beside each point he added _____ an explanation _____. Then he circled the four key words, and he wrote down the first _____letter_____ of each word underneath his outline. Mark then used the first letter in each key word to make up a catchphrase that he could easily remember. Finally, he _____tested_____ himself over and over until he could recall all four of the sources of stress that the first letters stood for. He also made sure that he recalled the supporting material that went with each idea.

Step 3: Look at the Exam Carefully and Do Several Things

1 Get an overview of the exam by reading *all* the questions on the test.

2 Note *direction words* (*compare, illustrate, list,* and so on) for each question. Be sure to write the kind of answer that each question requires. For example, if a question says "illustrate," do not "compare." The list on the opposite page will help clarify the distinctions among various direction words.

3 Budget your time. Write in the margin the number of minutes you should spend for each essay. For example, if you have three essays worth an equal number of points and a one-hour time limit, figure twenty minutes for each essay. Make sure you are not left with only a couple of minutes to do a high-point essay.

4 Start with the easiest question. Getting a good answer down on paper will help build up your confidence and momentum. Number your answers plainly so that your instructor knows what question you are answering first.

An Illustration of Step 3

When Mark received the exam, the question was "Describe the four common sources of stress in our lives." Mark circled the direction word *describe,* which meant he should explain in detail each of the four causes of stress. He also jotted a "30" in the margin when the instructor said that students would have a half hour to write the answer.

ACTIVITY

Complete the short matching quiz below. It will help you review the meanings of some of the direction words listed on the following page.

1. List ___b___

2. Contrast ___d___

3. Define ___e___

4. Summarize ___c___

5. Describe ___a___

a. Tell in detail about something.

b. Give a series of points and number them 1, 2, 3, etc.

c. Give a condensed account of the main points.

d. Show differences between two things.

e. Give the normal meaning of a term.

Direction Words

Term	Meaning
Compare	Show similarities between things.
Contrast	Show differences between things.
Criticize	Give the positive and negative points of a subject as well as evidence for those positions.
Define	Give the formal meaning of a term.
Describe	Tell in detail about something.
Diagram	Make a drawing and label it.
Discuss	Give details and, if relevant, the positive and negative points of a subject as well as evidence for those positions.
Enumerate	List points and number them 1, 2, 3, etc.
Evaluate	Give the positive and negative points of a subject as well as your judgment about which outweighs the other and why.
Illustrate	Explain by giving examples.
Interpret	Explain the meaning of something.
Justify	Give reasons for something.
List	Give a series of points and number them 1, 2, 3, etc.
Outline	Give the main points and important secondary points. Put main points at the margin and indent secondary points under the main points. Relationships may also be described with logical symbols, as follows:

    1. _____

        a. _____

        b. _____

    2. _____

Term	Meaning
Prove	Show to be true by giving facts or reasons.
Relate	Show connections among things.
State	Give the main points.
Summarize	Give a condensed account of the main points.
Trace	Describe the development or history of a subject.

Step 4: Prepare a Brief, Informal Outline before Writing Your Essay Answer

4.1a

Use the margin of the exam or a separate piece of scratch paper to jot down quickly, as they occur to you, the main points you want to discuss in each answer. Then decide in what order you want to present these points in your response. Write 1 in front of the first item, 2 beside the second, and so on. You now have an informal outline to guide you as you answer your essay question.

If there is a question on the exam that is similar to the questions you anticipated and outlined at home, quickly write down the catchphrase that calls back the content of the outline. Below the catchphrase, write the key words represented by each letter in the catchphrase. The key words, in turn, will remind you of the concepts they represent. If you have prepared properly, this step will take only a minute or so, and you will have before you the guide you need to write a focused, supported, organized answer.

An Illustration of Step 4

Mark immediately wrote down his catchphrase, "People are funny creatures." He next jotted down the first letters in his catchphrase and then the key words that went with each letter. He then filled in several key details and was ready to write his essay answer. Here is what his brief outline looked like:

People are funny creatures.

P   Pressure (internal and external)

A   Anxiety (internal conflict)

F   Frustration (prevented from reaching goal)

C   Conflict (approach-avoidance)

Step 5: Write a Clear, Well-Organized Essay

If you have followed steps 1 through 4, you have done all the preliminary work needed to write an effective essay. Now, be sure not to ruin your chance of getting a good grade by writing carelessly. Keep in mind the principles of good writing: unity, support, coherence, and clear, error-free sentences.

First, start your essay with a sentence that clearly states what your answer will be about. Then make sure that everything in your paper relates to your opening statement.

Second, though you must obviously take time limitations into account, provide as much support as possible for each of your main points.

Third, use transitions to guide your reader through your answer. Words such as *first, next, then, however,* and *finally* make it easy to follow your thought.

Last, leave time to proofread your essay for sentence-skills mistakes you may have made while you concentrated on writing your answer. Look for words omitted, miswritten, or misspelled (if it is possible, bring a dictionary with you); look for awkward phrasings or misplaced punctuation marks; and look for whatever else may prevent the reader from understanding your thought. Cross out any mistakes and make your corrections neatly above the errors. If you want to change or add to some point, insert an asterisk at the appropriate spot, put another asterisk at the bottom of the page, and add the corrected material there.

An Illustration of Step 5

Read Mark's answer, reproduced below, and then do the activity that follows.

There are four common sources of stress in our lives. The first one is pressure, which can be internal or external. Internal pressure occurs when a person tries to live up to his or her own goals and standards. This kind of pressure can help (when a person strives to be a better musician, for instance) or hurt (as when someone tries to reach impossible standards of beauty). External pressure occurs when people must compete, deal with rapid change, or cope with outside demands. Another source of stress is anxiety. People who are ~~anxous~~ anxious often don't know why they feel this way. Some psychologists think anxiety comes from some internal conflict, like feeling angry and trying hard to repress this ~~angry feeling~~ anger. A third source of stress is frustration, which occurs when people are prevented from reaching goals or obtaining certain needs. For example, a woman may do poorly on an important exam because she has a bad cold. She feels angry and frustrated because she could not reach her goal of an A or B grade. The most common source of stress is conflict. Conflict results when a person is faced with two incompatible ~~goals.~~ desires. The person may want both goals (a demanding career and motherhood, for instance). This is called approach-approach. Or a person may want to avoid both choices (avoidance-avoidance). Or a person may be both attracted to and repelled by a desire (as a woman who wants to marry a gambler). This is approach-avoidance.

ACTIVITY 1

The following sentences comment on Mark's essay. Fill in the missing word or words in each case.

1. Mark begins with a sentence that clearly states what his paper ___is about___

   _____. Always begin with such a clear statement!

2. Notice the ___corrections___ that Mark made when writing and proofreading his paper. He neatly crossed out miswritten or unwanted words, and he used insertion signs (^) to add omitted words.

3. The four signal words that Mark used to guide his readers, and himself, through the main points of his answer are ___first___, ___Another___, ___third___, and ___most common___.

ACTIVITY 2

1. Make up five questions you might be expected to answer on an essay exam for a course in a social or physical science (such as sociology, psychology, or biology).

2. For each of the five questions, make up an outline answer comparable to the one on anxiety.

3. Finally, write a full essay answer, in complete sentences, to one of the questions. Your outline will serve as your guide.

Answers will vary.

Be sure to begin your essay with a statement that makes clear the direction of your answer. An example might be "The six major defense mechanisms are defined and illustrated below." If you are explaining in detail the different causes of, reasons for, or characteristics of something, you may want to develop each point in a separate paragraph. For example, if you were answering a question in sociology about the primary functions of the family unit, you could start with the statement "The family unit has three primary functions" and go on to develop and describe each function in a separate paragraph.

You will submit the essay answer to your English instructor, who will evaluate it using the standards for effective writing applied to your other written assignments.

18 Writing a Summary

(Summarizing & Paraphrasing)

At some point in a course, your instructor may ask you to write a summary of a book, an article, a TV show, or the like. In a *summary* (also referred to as a *précis* or an *abstract*), you reduce material in an original work to its main points and key supporting details. Unlike an outline, however, a summary does not use symbols such as 1, A, 1, 2, etc., to indicate the relations among parts of the original material.

A summary may consist of a single word, a phrase, several sentences, or one or more paragraphs. The length of any summary you prepare will depend on your instructor's expectations and the length of the original work. Most often, you will be asked to write a summary consisting of one or more paragraphs.

Writing a summary brings together a number of important reading, study, and writing skills. To condense the original assigned material, you must preview, read, evaluate, organize, and perhaps outline it. Summarizing, then, can be a real aid to understanding; you must "get inside" the material and realize fully what is being said before you can reduce its meaning to a few words.

How to Summarize an Article

ALLWRITE!
12.1b

To write a summary of an article, follow the steps described below. If the assigned material is a TV show or film, adapt the suggestions accordingly.

1   Take a few minutes to preview the work. You can preview an article in a magazine by taking a quick look at the following:

   a   *Title.* A title often summarizes what an article is about. Think about the title for a minute, and about how it may condense the meaning of the article.

   b   *Subtitle.* A subtitle, if given, is a short summary appearing under or next to the title. For example, in a *Newsweek* article titled "Growing Old, Feeling Young," the following caption appeared: "Not only are Americans living longer, they are staying active longer—and their worst enemy is not nature, but the myths and prejudices about growing old." In short, the subtitle, the caption, or any other words in large print under or next to the title often provide a quick insight into the meaning of an article.

349

c *First and last several paragraphs.* In the first several paragraphs, the author may introduce you to the subject and state the purpose of the article. In the last several paragraphs, the writer may present conclusions or a summary. The previews or summaries can give you a quick overview of what the entire article is about.

d *Other items.* Note any heads or subheads that appear in the article. They often provide clues to the article's main points and give an immediate sense of what each section is about. Look carefully at any pictures, charts, or diagrams that accompany the article. Page space in a magazine or journal is limited, and such visual aids are generally used only to illustrate important points in the article. Note any words or phrases set off in *italic type* or **bold-face type;** such words have probably been emphasized because they deal with important points in the article.

2 Read the article for all you can understand the first time through. Do not slow down or turn back. Check or otherwise mark main points and key supporting details. Pay special attention to all the items noted in the preview. Also, look for definitions, examples, and enumerations (lists of items), which often indicate key ideas. You can also identify important points by turning any heads into questions and reading to find the answers to the questions.

3 Go back and reread more carefully the areas you have identified as most important. Also, focus on other key points you may have missed in your first reading.

4 Take notes on the material. Concentrate on getting down the main ideas and the key supporting points.

5 Prepare the first draft of your summary, keeping these points in mind:

a Identify at the start of the summary the title and author of the work. Include in parentheses the date of publication. For example, "In 'Leaking with a Vengeance' (*Time,* October 13, 2003), Michael Duffy states . . . ."

b Do not write an overly detailed summary. Remember that the purpose of a summary is to reduce the original work to its main points and essential supporting details.

c Express the main points and key supporting details in your own words. Do not imitate the style of the original work.

d Quote from the material only to illustrate key points. Also, limit your quotations. A one-paragraph summary should not contain more than one or two quoted sentences.

e Preserve the balance and proportion of the original work. If the original devoted 70 percent of its space to one idea and only 30 percent to another, your summary should reflect that emphasis.

f Revise your first draft, paying attention to the principles of effective writing (*unity, support, coherence,* and *clear, error-free sentences*) explained in Part One.

g Write the final draft of the paper.

A Model Summary of an Article

Here is a model summary of a magazine article:

> In "How to Heal a Hypochondriac" (<u>Time</u>, September 30, 2003), Michael Lemonick reports on research into ways of dealing with hypochondria, a thinking disorder that makes healthy people believe that they are suffering from one or more serious diseases. Not only do hypochondriacs genuinely suffer from their disorder, but they create a significant burden on the health-care system. Research suggests that hypochondriacs fall into three categories: those who have a variant of obsessive-compulsive disorder, those whose hypochondria was triggered by a stressful life event, and those who are hypersensitive to any physical symptoms. Cognitive therapy, in which patients are trained to direct their attention away from their symptoms, and antidepressant medication both seem helpful in treating hypochondria. The most difficult part of treatment is suggesting that a patient suffers from hypochondria without angering or embarrassing him or her.

ACTIVITY 1

Answers will vary.

Write an essay-length summary of the following article. Include a short introductory paragraph that states the thesis of the article. Then summarize in your three supporting paragraphs the three important areas in which study skills can be useful. Your conclusion might be a single sentence restating the thesis.

Power Learning

(Study Skills)

1   Jill had not done as well in high school as she had hoped. Since college involved even more work, it was no surprise that she didn't do better there.

2   The reason for her so-so performance was not a lack of effort. She attended most of her classes and read her textbooks. And she never missed handing in any assignment, even though it often meant staying up late the night before homework was due. Still, she just got by in her classes. Before long, she came to the conclusion that she simply couldn't do any better.

3   Then one day, one of her instructors said something to make her think otherwise. "You can probably build some sort of house by banging a few boards together," he said. "But if you want a sturdy home, you'll have to

use the right techniques and tools. Building carefully takes work, but it gets better results. The same can be said of your education. There are no shortcuts, but there are some proven study skills that can really help. If you don't use them, you may end up with a pretty flimsy education."

Jill signed up for a study-skills course and found out a crucial fact— that learning how to learn is the key to success in school. There are certain dependable skills that have made the difference between disappointment and success for generations of students. These techniques won't free you from work, but they will make your work far more productive. They include three important areas: time control, classroom note-taking, and textbook study.   4

Time Control

Success in college depends on time control. *Time control* means that you deliberately organize and plan your time, instead of letting it drift by. Planning means that you should never be faced with an overdue term paper or a cram session the night before a test.   5

There are three steps involved in time control. *First,* you should prepare a large monthly calendar. Buy a calendar with a large white block around each date, or make one yourself. At the beginning of the college semester, circle important dates on this calendar. Circle the days on which tests are scheduled; circle the days when papers are due. This calendar can also be used to schedule study plans. At the beginning of the week, you can jot down your plans for each day. An alternative method would be to make plans for each day the night before. On Tuesday night, for example, you might write down "Read Chapter 5 in psychology" in the Wednesday block. Hang this calendar where you will see it every day—your kitchen, bedroom, even your bathroom!   6

The *second step* in time control is to have a weekly study schedule for the semester—a chart that covers all the days of the week and all the waking hours in each day. Below is part of one student's schedule: 7

Time	Mon.	Tues.	Wed.	Thurs.	Fri.	Sat.	Sun.
6:00 A.M.							
7:00	Breakfast	Breakfast	Breakfast	Breakfast	Breakfast		
8:00	Math	STUDY	Math	STUDY	Math	Breakfast	
9:00	STUDY	Biology	STUDY	Biology	STUDY	Job	
10:00	Psychology	↓	Psychology	↓	Psychology		
11:00	STUDY	English		English			
12:00	Lunch		Lunch	↓	Lunch	↓	

On your own schedule, fill in all the fixed hours in each day—hours for meals, classes, job (if any), and travel time. Next, mark time blocks that you can *realistically* use for study each day. Depending on the number of courses you are taking and the demands of these courses, you may want to block off five, ten, or even twenty or more hours of study time a week. Keep in mind that you should not block off time that you do not truly intend to use for study. Otherwise, your schedule will be a meaningless gimmick. Also, remember that you should allow time for "rest and relaxation." You will be happiest, and able to accomplish the most, when you have time for both work and play.

The *third step* in time control is to make a daily or weekly "to do" list. 8 This may be the most valuable time-control method you ever use. On this list, write down the things you need to do for the following day or the following week. If you choose to write a weekly list, do it on Sunday night. If you choose to write a daily list, do it the night before. Here is part of one student's daily list:

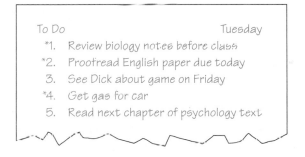

To Do   Tuesday
  *1.   Review biology notes before class
  *2.   Proofread English paper due today
   3.   See Dick about game on Friday
  *4.   Get gas for car
   5.   Read next chapter of psychology text

You may use a three- by five-inch notepad or a small spiral-bound notebook for this list. Carry the list around with you during the day. Always concentrate on doing the most important items first. To make the best use of your time, mark high-priority items with an asterisk and give them precedence over low-priority items. For instance, you may find yourself wondering what to do after dinner on Thursday evening. Among the items on your list are "Clean inside of car" and "Review chapter for math quiz." It is obviously more important for you to review your notes at this point; you can clean out the car some other time. As you complete items on your "to do" list, cross them out. Do not worry about unfinished items. They can be rescheduled. You will still be accomplishing a great deal and making more effective use of your time.

Classroom Note-Taking

One of the most important single things you can do to perform well in a 9 college course is to take effective class notes. The following hints should help you become a better note-taker.

First, attend class faithfully. Your alternatives—reading the text, reading   10
someone else's notes, or both—cannot substitute for the class experience of
hearing ideas in person as someone presents them to you. Also, in class lectures
and discussions, your instructor typically presents and develops the main ideas
and facts of the course—the ones you will be expected to know on exams.

Another valuable hint is to make use of abbreviations while taking notes.   11
Using abbreviations saves time when you are trying to get down a great deal
of information. Abbreviate terms that recur frequently in a lecture and put a
key to your abbreviations at the top of your notes. For example, in sociology
class, *eth* could stand for *ethnocentrism;* in a psychology class, *STM* could
stand for *short-term memory.* (When a lecture is over, you may want to go
back and write out the terms you have abbreviated.) Also, use *e* for *example;*
def for *definition; info* for *information;* + for *and;* and so on. If you use the
same abbreviations all the time, you will soon develop a kind of personal
shorthand that makes taking notes much easier.

A third hint for taking notes is to be on the lookout for signals of   12
importance. Write down whatever your instructor puts on the board. If he
or she takes the time to put material on the board, it is probably important,
and the chances are good that it will come up later on exams. Always write
down definitions and enumerations. Enumerations are lists of items. They
are signaled in such ways as "The four steps in the process are . . ."; "There
were three reasons for . . ."; "The two effects were . . ."; "Five characteristics
of . . ."; and so on. In your notes, always number such enumerations (1, 2, 3,
etc.). They will help you understand relationships among ideas and organize
the material of the lecture. Watch for emphasis words—words your instructor
may use to indicate that something is important. Examples of such words
are "This is an important reason . . ."; "A point that will keep coming up
later . . ."; "The chief cause was . . ."; "The basic idea here is . . ."; and so on.
Always write down the important statements announced by these and other
emphasis words. Finally, if your instructor repeats a point, you can assume
that it is important. You might put an *R* for *repeated* in the margin so that
later you will know that your instructor stressed it.

Next, be sure to write down the instructor's examples and mark them   13
with an *e.* The examples help you understand abstract points. If you do not
write them down, you are likely to forget them later, when they are needed
to help make sense of an idea.

Also, be sure to write down the connections between ideas. Too many   14
students merely copy terms the instructor puts on the board. They forget
that, as time passes, the details that serve as connecting bridges between
ideas quickly fade. You should, then, write down the relationships and
connections in class. That way you'll have them to help tie together your
notes later on.

Review your notes as soon as possible after class. You must make them   15
as clear as possible while they are fresh in your mind. A day later may be too

late, because forgetting sets in very quickly. Make sure that punctuation is clear, that all words are readable and correctly spelled, and that unfinished sentences are completed (or at least marked off so that you can check your notes with another student's). Add clarifying or connecting comments wherever necessary. Make sure that important ideas are clearly marked. Improve the organization if necessary so that you can see at a glance main points and relationships among them.

Finally, try in general to get down a written record of each class. You must   16
do this because forgetting begins almost immediately. Studies have shown that within two weeks you are likely to have forgotten 80 percent or more of what you have heard. And in four weeks you are lucky if 5 percent remains! This is so crucial that it bears repeating: To guard against the relentlessness of forgetting, it is absolutely essential that you write down what you hear in class. Later you can concentrate on working to understand fully and to remember the ideas that have been presented in class. And then, the more complete your notes are, the more you are likely to learn.

Textbook Study

In many college courses, success means being able to read and study a   17
textbook skillfully. For many students, unfortunately, textbooks are heavy going. After an hour or two of study, the textbook material is as formless and as hard to understand as ever. But there is a way to attack even the most difficult textbook and make sense of it. Use a sequence in which you preview a chapter, mark it, take notes on it, and then study the notes.

Previewing

Previewing a selection is an important first step to understanding. Taking   18
the time to preview a section or chapter can give you a bird's-eye view of the way the material is organized. You will have a sense of where you are beginning, what you will cover, and where you will end.

There are several steps in previewing a selection. First, study the title.   19
The title is the shortest possible summary of a selection and will often tell you the limits of the material you will cover. For example, the title "FDR and the Supreme Court" tells you to expect a discussion of President Roosevelt's dealings with the Court. You know that you will probably not encounter any material dealing with FDR's foreign policies or personal life. Next, quickly read over the first and last paragraphs of the selection; these may contain important introductions to, and summaries of, the main ideas. Then briefly examine the headings and subheadings in the selection. Together, the headings and subheadings are a mini-outline of what you are reading. Headings are often main ideas or important concepts in capsule form; subheadings are breakdowns of ideas within main areas. Finally, read the first sentence of some paragraphs, look for words set off in **boldface** or *italics*,

and look at pictures or diagrams. After you have previewed a selection in this way, you should have a good general sense of the material to be read.

Marking

You should mark a textbook selection at the same time that you read   20
it through carefully. Use a felt-tip highlighter to shade material that seems important, or use a ballpoint pen and put symbols in the margin next to the material: stars, checks, or NB (*nota bene,* Latin for "note well"). What to mark is not as mysterious as some students believe. You should try to find main ideas by looking for clues: definitions and examples, enumerations, and emphasis words.

1   *Definitions and examples:* Definitions are often among the most impor-   21
    tant ideas in a selection. They are particularly significant in introductory courses in almost any subject area, where much of your learning involves mastering the specialized vocabulary of that subject. In a sense, you are learning the "language" of psychology or business or whatever the subject might be.

    Most definitions are abstract, and so they usually are followed by   22
    one or more examples to help clarify their meaning. Always mark off definitions and at least one example that makes a definition clear to you. In a psychology text, for example, we are told that "rationalization is an attempt to reduce anxiety by deciding that you have not really been frustrated." Several examples follow, among them: "A young man, frustrated because he was rejected when he asked for a date, convinces himself that the girl is not very attractive or interesting."

2   *Enumerations:* Enumerations are lists of items (causes, reasons, types, and   23
    so on) that are numbered 1, 2, 3, . . . or that could easily be numbered. They are often signaled by addition words. Many of the paragraphs in this book, for instance, use words like *First of all, Another, In addition,* and *Finally* to signal items in a series. Other textbooks also use this very common and effective organizational method.

3   *Emphasis words:* Emphasis words tell you that an idea is important.   24
    Common emphasis words include phrases such as *a major event, a key feature, the chief factor, important to note, above all,* and *most of all.* Here is an example: "The most significant contemporary use of marketing is its application to nonbusiness areas, such as political parties."

Note-Taking

Next, you should take notes. Go through the chapter a second time,   25
rereading the most important parts. Try to write down the main ideas in a simple outline form. For example, in taking notes on a psychology selection, you might write down the heading "Defense Mechanisms." Below the heading you would define them, number and describe each kind, and give an example of each.

Defense Mechanisms

a. Definition: unconscious attempts to reduce anxiety

b. Kinds:

  (1) Rationalization: An attempt to reduce anxiety by deciding that you have not really been frustrated.
       Example: A man turned down for a date decides that the woman was not worth going out with anyway.

  (2) Projection: Projecting onto other people motives or thoughts of one's own.
       Example: A wife who wants to have an affair accuses her husband of having one.

Studying Notes

To study your notes, use repeated self-testing. For example, look at the heading "Defense Mechanisms" and say to yourself, "What are the kinds of defense mechanisms?" When you can recite them, then say to yourself, "What is rationalization?" "What is an example of rationalization?" Then ask yourself, "What is projection?" "What is an example of projection?" After you learn each section, review it, and then go on to the next section.   26

Do not simply read your notes; keep looking away and seeing if you can recite them to yourself. This self-testing is the key to effective learning.   27

Summary: Textbook Study

In summary, remember this sequence for dealing with a textbook: preview, mark, take notes, study the notes. Approaching a textbook in this methodical way will give you very positive results. You will no longer feel bogged down in a swamp of words, unable to figure out what you are supposed to know. Instead, you will understand exactly what you have to do, and how to go about doing it.   28

Take a minute now to evaluate your own study habits. Do you practice many of the above skills in order to take effective classroom notes, control your time, and learn from your textbooks? If not, perhaps you should. The skills are not magic, but they are too valuable to ignore. Use them carefully and consistently, and they will make academic success possible for you. Try them, and you won't need convincing.   29

ACTIVITY 2

Answers will vary.

Write an essay-length summary of a broadcast of the CBS television show *60 Minutes*. In your first sentence, include the date of the show. For example, "The December 17, 2004, broadcast of CBS's *60 Minutes* dealt with three subjects most people would find of interest. The first segment of the show centered on . . . ; the second segment examined . . . ; the final segment discussed . . . ." Be sure to use parallel form in describing the three segments of the show. Then summarize each segment in the three supporting paragraphs that follow.

Answers
will vary.

Write an essay-length summary of a cover story of interest to you in a recent issue of *Time, Newsweek,* or *U.S. News & World Report.*

How to Summarize a Book

To write a summary of a book, first preview the book by briefly looking at:

1 *Title.* A title is often the shortest possible summary of what a book is about. Think about the title and how it may summarize the whole book.

2 *Table of contents.* The contents will tell you the number of chapters in the book and the subject of each chapter. Use the contents to get a general sense of how the book is organized. You should also note the number of pages in each chapter. If thirty pages are devoted to one episode or idea and an average of fifteen pages to other episodes or ideas, you should probably give more space in your summary to the contents of the longer chapter .

3 *Preface.* Here you will probably find out why the author wrote the book. Also, the preface may summarize the main ideas developed in the book and may describe briefly how the book is organized.

4 *First and last chapters.* In these chapters, the author may preview or review important ideas and themes developed in the book.

5 *Other items.* Note how the author has used headings and subheadings to organize information in the book. Check the opening and closing paragraphs of each chapter to see if these paragraphs contain introductions or summaries. Look quickly at charts, diagrams, and pictures in the book, since they are probably there to illustrate key points. Note any special features (index, glossary, appendixes) that may appear at the end of the book.

Next, adapt steps 2 through 5 for summarizing an article on page 351.

Answers
will vary.

Write an essay-length summary of a book you have read.

19 Writing a Report

Each semester, you will probably be asked by at least one instructor to read a book or an article and write a paper recording your response to the material. In these reports or reaction papers, your instructor will most likely expect you to do two things: *summarize the material* and *detail your reaction to it*. The following pages explain both parts of a report.

Part 1 of a Report: A Summary of the Work

To develop the first part of a report, do the following. (An example follows, on page 361.)

1   Identify the author and title of the work, and include in parentheses the publisher and publication date. With magazines, give the date of publication.

2   Write an informative summary of the material. Condense the content of the work by highlighting its main points and key supporting points. (See pages 349–358 for a complete discussion of summarizing techniques.) Use direct quotations from the work to illustrate important ideas.

   Do *not* discuss in great detail any single aspect of the work while neglecting to mention other equally important points. Summarize the material so that the reader gets a general sense of *all* key aspects of the original work. Also, keep the summary objective and factual. Do not include in the first part of the paper your personal reaction to the work; your subjective impression will form the basis of the second part of the paper.

Part 2 of a Report: Your Reaction to the Work

To develop the second part of a report, do the following:

1   Focus on any or all of the questions below. (Check with your instructors to see if they want you to emphasize specific points.)

a How is the assigned work related to ideas and concerns discussed in the course? For example, what points made in the course textbook, class discussions, or lectures are treated more fully in the work?

b How is the work related to problems in our present-day world?

c How is the work related to your life, experiences, feelings, and ideas? For instance, what emotions did it arouse in you? Did it increase your understanding of an issue or change your perspective?

2 Evaluate the merit of the work: the importance of its points; its accuracy, completeness, and organization; and so on. You should also indicate here whether you would recommend the work to others, and why.

Points to Keep in Mind When Writing a Report

Here are some important matters to consider as you prepare a report:

1 Apply the four basic standards of effective writing (unity, support, coherence, and clear, error-free sentences).

a Make sure each major paragraph presents and then develops a single main point. For example, in the model report that follows, a paragraph summarizes the book, and the three paragraphs that follow detail three separate reactions that the student writer had. The student then closes the report with a short concluding paragraph.

b Support with specific reasons and details any general points or attitudes you express. Statements such as "I agreed with many ideas in this article" and "I found the book very interesting" are meaningless without specific evidence that shows why you feel as you do. Look at the model report to see how the main point or topic sentence of each paragraph is developed by specific supporting evidence.

c Organize the material in the paper. Follow the basic *plan of organization* already described: an introduction, a summary consisting of one or more paragraphs, a reaction consisting of two or more paragraphs, and a conclusion. Use *transitions* to connect the parts of the paper.

d Proofread the paper for grammar, mechanics, punctuation, and word use.

2 Document quotations from all works by giving the page number in parentheses after the quoted material (see the model report). You may use quotations in the summary and reaction parts of the paper, but do not rely too much on them. Use them only to emphasize key ideas.

A Model Report

Here is a report written by a student in an introductory sociology source. Look at the paper closely to see how it follows the guidelines for report writing described in this chapter.

A Report on I Know Why the Caged Bird Sings

Introductory paragraph

In I Know Why the Caged Bird Sings (New York: Bantam Books, 1971), Maya Angelou tells the story of her earliest years. Angelou, a dancer, poet, and television producer as well as a writer, has continued her life story in three more volumes of autobiography. I Know Why the Caged Bird Sings is the start of Maya Angelou's story; in this book, she writes with crystal clarity about the pains and joys of being black in America.   1

PART 1: SUMMARY
Topic sentence for summary paragraph

I Know Why the Caged Bird Sings covers Maya Angelou's life from age three to age sixteen. We first meet her as a gawky little girl in a white woman's cut-down lavender silk dress. She has forgotten the poem she had memorized for the Easter service, and all she can do is rush out of the church. At this point, Angelou is living in Stamps, Arkansas, with her grandmother and uncle. The town is rigidly segregated: "People in Stamps used to say that the whites in our town were so prejudiced that a Negro couldn't buy vanilla ice cream" (40). Yet Angelou has some good things in her life: her adored older brother Bailey, her success in school, and her pride in her grandmother's quiet strength and importance in the black community. There is laughter, too, as when a preacher is interrupted in midsermon by an overly enthusiastic woman shouting, "Preach it, I say preach it!" The woman, in a frenzied rush of excitement, hits the preacher with her purse; his false teeth fly out of his mouth and land at Angelou's feet. Shortly after this incident, Angelou and her brother are taken by her father to live in California with their mother. Here, at age eight, she is raped by her mother's boyfriend, who is mysteriously murdered after receiving only a suspended sentence for his crime. She returns, silent and withdrawn, to Stamps, where the gloom is broken when a friend of her mother introduces her to the magic of great books. Later, at age thirteen, Angelou returns to California. She learns how to dance. She runs away after a violent family fight and lives for a month in a junkyard. She becomes the first black female to get a job on the San Francisco streetcars. She graduates from high school eight months pregnant. And she survives.   2

PART 2: REACTION
Topic sentence for first reaction paragraph

I was impressed with the vividness of Maya Angelou's writing style. For example, she describes the lazy dullness of her life in Stamps: "Weekdays revolved in a sameness wheel. They turned into themselves so steadily and inevitably that each seemed to be the original of yesterday's rough draft" (93). She also knows how to bring a scene to life, as when she describes   3 her eighth-grade graduation. For months, she has been looking forward to this event, knowing she will be honored for her academic successes. She is even happy with her appearance: her hair has become pretty, and her yellow dress is a miracle of hand-sewing. But the ceremony is spoiled when the speaker—a white man—implies that the only success available to blacks is in athletics. Angelou remembers: "The man's dead words fell like bricks around the auditorium and too many settled in my belly. . . . The proud graduating class of 1940 had dropped their heads" (152). Later, Angelou uses a crystal-clear image to describe her father's mistress sewing: "She worked the thread through the flowered cloth as if she were sewing the torn ends of her life together" (208). With such vivid details and figures of speech, Maya Angelou re-creates her life for her readers.

Topic sentence for second reaction paragraph →   I also reacted strongly to the descriptions of injustices suffered by   4
blacks two generations ago. I was as horrified as the seven-year-old Maya when some "powhitetrash" girls torment her dignified grandmother, calling her "Annie" and mimicking her mannerisms. In another incident, Mrs. Cullinan, Angelou's white employer, decides that Marguerite (Angelou's real name) is too difficult to pronounce and so renames her Mary. This loss of her name—a "hellish horror" (91)—is another humiliation suffered at white hands, and Angelou leaves Mrs. Cullinan's employ soon afterward. Later, Angelou encounters overt discrimination when a white dentist tells her grandmother, "Annie, my policy is I'd rather stick my hand in a dog's mouth than in a nigger's" (160)—and only slightly less obvious prejudice when the streetcar company refuses to accept her application for a conductor's job. We see Angelou over and over as the victim of a white society.

Topic sentence for third reaction paragraph →   Although I was saddened to read about the injustices, I rejoiced in   5
Angelou's triumphs. Angelou is thrilled when she hears the radio broadcast of Joe Louis's victory over Primo Carnera: "A Black boy. Some Black mother's son. He was the strongest man in the world" (114). She weeps with pride when the class valedictorian leads her and her fellow eighth-graders in singing the Negro National Anthem. And there are personal victories, too. One of these comes after her father has gotten drunk in a small Mexican town. Though she has never driven before, she manages to get her father into the car and drives fifty miles through the night as he lies intoxicated in the backseat. Finally, she rejoices in the birth of her son: "He was beautiful and mine. Totally mine. No one had bought him for me" (245). Angelou shows us, through these examples, that she is proud of her race—and of herself.

Concluding paragraph →   I Know Why the Caged Bird Sings is a remarkable book. Angelou   6
could have been just another casualty of race prejudice. Yet by using her intelligence, sensitivity, and determination, she succeeds in spite of the odds against her. And by writing with such power, she lets us share her defeats and joys. She also teaches us a vital lesson: with strength and persistence, we can all escape our cages—and sing our songs.

ACTIVITY 1

Read a magazine article that interests you. Then write a report on the article. Include an introduction, a one-paragraph summary, a reaction (consisting of one or more paragraphs), and a brief conclusion. You may, if you like, quote briefly from the article. Be sure to enclose the words that you take from the article in quotation marks and put the page number in parentheses at the end of the quoted material.

ACTIVITY 2

Read a book suggested by your instructor. Then write a report on the book. Include an introduction, a one-paragraph summary, a reaction consisting of one or more paragraphs, and a brief conclusion. Make sure that each major paragraph in your report develops a single main point. You may quote some sentences from the book, but they should be only a small part of your report. When you quote material, follow the directions in Activity 1.

20 Writing a Résumé and Job Application Letter

(Career Considerations)

When applying for a job through the mail, you should ordinarily send (1) a résumé and (2) a letter of application.

Résumé

9.3a

A résumé is a summary of your personal background and your qualifications for a job. It helps your potential employer see at a glance whether you are suited for a job opening. A sample job résumé follows.

ERIC KURLAND
27 Hawkins Road
Clarksboro, New Jersey 08020
609-723-2166

Professional objective	A challenging position in the computer technology field.
Education	2001 to present: Rowan University, Glassboro, New Jersey 08028
	Degree: B.S. (in June)
Major courses:	Introduction to Computer Science I and II Data Structures and Algorithms I and II Programming Languages Programming in Pascal Assembly Language Operating Systems I and II

Related courses:	Introduction to Discrete Mathematics I and II Calculus I and II Logic Entrepreneurship and Small Business Management Business Law Organizational Behavior
Special school project	As part of a class project, I chaired a study group that advised a local business about the advantages of installing a computerized payroll system. We projected comparative cost figures, developed a time-sharing purchase plan, and prepared a budget. The fifteen-page report received the highest grade in the class.
Work experience	2001 to present: As a salesperson at Radio Shack, I am involved in sales, inventory control, repairs, and customer relations. I have designed a computer program that our store uses to demonstrate the multimedia aspects of a personal computer. This program, written in Visual Basic, demonstrates ways the Compaq Presario 5062 can be used in the home and small businesses. 1998–2001: My temporary jobs included word-processing secretary, theater usher, and child-care aide.
Skills	I am experienced in the following computer languages: C++, Visual Basic, Pascal, and COBOL. I have sales experience, am good with figures, am detail-oriented, relate easily to people, have initiative, and am dependable.
References	My references are available on request from Rowan University Placement Office, Glassboro, New Jersey 08028.

Points to Note about the Résumé

1   Your résumé, along with your letter of application, is your introduction to a potential employer. First impressions count, so *make the résumé neat!*

a Type the résumé on good-quality letter paper (8½ by 11 inches). If possible, prepare your résumé on a computer; if you don't have access to a computer, you can use a résumé service listed in the yellow pages of the telephone directory.

b Proofread *very carefully* for sentence-skills and spelling mistakes. A potential employer may regard such mistakes as signs of carelessness in your character. You might even want to get someone else to proofread the résumé for you. If you are using word-processing software, see if it has a "spell-check" feature.

c Be brief and to the point: use only one page if possible.

d Use a format like that of the model résumé (see also the variations described ahead). Balance your résumé on the page so that you have roughly the same margin on all sides.

e Note that you should start with your most recent education or employment and work backward in time.

2 Your résumé should point up strengths, not weaknesses. Don't include "Special Training" if you have had none. Don't refer to your grade-point average if it's a low C.

On the other hand, include a main heading like "Extracurricular Activities" if the activities or awards seem relevant. For example, if Eric Kurland had been a member of the Management Club or vice president of the Computer Club in high school or college, he should have mentioned those facts.

If you have no work experience related to the job for which you're applying, then list the jobs you have had. Any job that shows a period of responsible employment may favorably impress a potential employer.

3 You can list the names of your references directly on the résumé. Be sure to get the permission of people you cite before listing their names.

You can also give the address of a placement office file that holds references, as shown on the model résumé.

(Activity 1, 3)

Or you can simply say that you will provide references on request.

Job Application Letter

ALLWRITE!

9.3b

The purpose of the letter of application that goes with your résumé is to introduce yourself briefly and to try to make an employer interested in you. You should include only the high points of the information in your résumé.

Following is the letter of application that Eric Kurland sent with his résumé.

27 Hawkins Road
Clarksboro, New Jersey 08020
May 13, 2004

Mr. George C. Arline
Personnel Manager, Indesco Associates
301 Sharptown Road
White Plains, New York 10019

Dear Mr. Arline:

I would like to be considered as a candidate for the assistant computer programmer position advertised in the Philadelphia Inquirer on April 28, 2004.

I am currently finishing my degree in Computer Science at Rowan University. I have taken every required computer course offered at Rowan and have a solid background in the following computer languages: C++, Visual Basic, Pascal, and COBOL. In addition to my computer background, I have supplemented my education with business and mathematics courses.

My knowledge of computers and the business field goes beyond my formal classroom education. For the past two years I have worked part-time at Radio Shack, where I have gained experience in sales and inventory control. Also, on my own initiative, I designed a demonstration program for the Compaq Presario 5062 and developed promotional fliers about the program.

In short, I believe I have the up-to-date computer background and professional drive needed to contribute to your organization. I have enclosed a copy of my résumé to give you further details about my experience. Sometime next week, I'll give you a call to see whether I can come in for an interview at your convenience. I look forward to speaking with you then.

Sincerely,

Eric Kurland

Eric Kurland

Points to Note about the Job Application Letter

1   Your letter should do the following:

a   In the first paragraph, state that you are an applicant for a job and identify the source through which you learned about the job.

Here is how Eric Kurland's letter might have opened if his source had been the college placement office. "I learned through the placement office at Rowan University of the assistant computer programmer position at your company. I would like to be considered as a candidate for the job."

Sometimes an ad will list only a box number (such as Y 172) to reply to. Your inside address should then be:

Y 172
Philadelphia Inquirer
Philadelphia, Pennsylvania 19101

Dear Sir or Madam:

b In the second paragraph, briefly state your qualifications for the job and refer the reader to your résumé.

c In the last paragraph, state your willingness to come for an interview. If you can be available for an interview only at certain times, indicate this.

2 As with your résumé, neatness is crucial. Follow the same hints for the letter that you did for the résumé.

a Type the letter on good paper.

b Proofread *very carefully* for sentence-skills mistakes and spelling mistakes. Use the checklist of sentence skills on the inside front cover.

c Be brief and to the point: use no more than one page.

d Use a format like the model letter. Keep roughly the same margin on all sides.

e Use punctuation and spelling in the model letter as a guide. For example:

(1) Skip two spaces between the inside address and the salutation ("Dear Mr. Arline").

(2) Use a colon after the salutation.

(3) Sign your name at the bottom, in addition to typing it.

(Activity 2, 4)

ACTIVITY

Answers will vary.

Clip a job listing from a newspaper or copy a job description posted in your school placement office. The job should be one that you feel you are qualified for or that you would one day like to have.

Write a résumé and a letter of application for the job. Use the models already considered as guides.

Use the checklist of the four steps on the inside front cover as a guide in your writing.

21 Using the Library and the Internet

11

This chapter provides the basic information you need to use your college library and the Internet with confidence. You will learn that for most research topics there are two basic steps you should take:

1   Find books on your topic.
2   Find articles on your topic.

You will learn, too, that while the library is the traditional way of doing such research, a home computer with an online service and Internet access now enables you to thoroughly investigate any topic.

Using the Library

Most students know that libraries provide study space, computer workstations, and copying machines. They are also aware of a library's reading area, which contains recent copies of magazines and newspapers. But the true heart of a library consists of a *main desk, the library's catalog(s) of holdings, book stacks,* and *the periodicals storage area.* Each of these will be discussed in the pages that follow.

Main Desk

The main desk is usually located in a central spot. Check with the main desk to see if there is a brochure that describes the layout and services of the library. You might also ask if the library staff provides tours. If not, explore your library to find each of the areas in the activity below.

ACTIVITY

Answers
will vary.

Make up a floor plan of your college library. Label the main desk, catalog(s), book stacks, and periodicals storage area.

369

Library Catalog

The library catalog will be your starting point for almost any research project. The catalog is a list of all the holdings of the library. It may be an actual card catalog: a file of cards alphabetically arranged in drawers. More likely, the catalog is computerized and can be accessed on computer terminals located at different spots in the library. And increasingly, local and college libraries can be accessed online, so you may be able to check their book holdings on your computer.

Finding a Book: Author, Title, and Subject

ALL**WRITE!**

11.1

Whether you use an actual file of cards or a computer terminal or visit your library's holdings online, it is important for you to know that there are three ways to look up a book: according to *author, title,* or *subject*. For example, suppose you wanted to see if the library had the book *A Tribe Apart*, by Patricia Hersch. You could check for the book in any of three ways:

1   You could do an *author* search and look it up under *Hersch, Patricia*. An author is always listed under his or her last name.

2   You could do a *title* search and look it up under *Tribe Apart, A*. Note that you always look up a book under the first word in the title, excluding the words *A, An,* or *The*.

3   If you know the subject that the book deals with—in this case the subject is "teenagers"—you could do a *subject* search and look it up under *Teenagers*.

Here is the author entry in a computerized card catalog for Hersch's book *A Tribe Apart:*

Author:	Hersch, Patricia
Title:	A tribe apart: a journey into the heart of American adolescence
Publisher:	New York: Ballantine, 1998
LC Subjects:	Teenagers—United States
Call Number:	HQ796/H43
Location:	Gibbsboro
Status:	Available

Note that in addition to giving you the publisher (Ballantine) and year of publication (1998), the entry also tells you the *call number*—where to find the book in the library. If the computerized catalog is part of a network of libraries, you may also learn at what branch or location the book is available. If the book is not at your library, you can probably arrange for an interlibrary loan.

Using Subject Headings to Research a Topic

Generally, if you are looking for a particular book, it is easier to search by *author* or *title*. On the other hand, if you are researching a topic, then you should search by *subject*.

The subject section performs three valuable functions:

- It will give you a list of books on a given topic.
- It will often provide related topics that might have information on your subject.
- It will suggest more-limited topics, helping you narrow your general topic.

Chances are you will be asked to do a research paper of about five to fifteen pages. You do not want to choose a topic so broad that it could be covered only by an entire book or more. Instead, you want to come up with a limited topic that can be adequately supported in a relatively short paper. As you search the subject section, take advantage of ideas that it might offer on how you can narrow your topic.

ACTIVITY

Part A   Answer the following questions about your library's catalog.

1. Is your library's catalog an actual file of cards in drawers, or is it computerized? _Answers will vary._

2. Which type of catalog search will help you research and limit a topic?
   subject section

Part B   Use your library's catalog to answer the following questions.

1. What is the title of one book by Anna Quindlen?
   Answers will vary. Example: A Short Guide to a Happy Life.

2. What is the title of one book by Bill Geist?
   Answers will vary. Example: The Big Five-Oh!

3. Who is the author of *A Tree Grows in Brooklyn?* (Remember to look up the title under *Tree*, not *A*.)

   Betty Smith

4. Who is the author of *Seven Habits of Highly Effective People?*

   Stephen R. Covey

5. List two books and their authors dealing with the subject of adoption.

   a. Answers will vary. Examples: The Adoption Resource Book, Fourth Edition,

   b. by Lois Gilman; Adopting After Infertility by Patricia Johnston

6. Look up a book titled *When Bad Things Happen to Good People* or *Silent Spring* and give the following information: Answers to some items may vary.

   a. Author   Bad Things - Harold S. Kushner   Silent Spring - Rachel Carlson

   b. Publisher   Schocken Books   Houghton Mifflin

   c. Date of publication   1989   1994

   d. Call number   296.3/11 20   632.95 Car

   e. One subject heading   Pastoral counseling   Pesticides—Environment

7. Look up a book written by Deborah Tannen or Garrison Keillor and give the following information: Answers to some items may vary.

   a. Title   You Just Don't Understand   Love Me

   b. Publisher   St. Martin's   Random House

   c. Date of publication   *Example for Dewey Tan* 1982   *Example for Garrison Keillor* 2003

   d. Call number   302 Tan   Fiction Keillor

   e. One subject heading   Conversation   Married people

   Note: Dewey Decimal call numbers are shown.

Book Stacks

The book stacks are the library shelves where books are arranged according to their call numbers. The call number, as distinctive as a social security number, always appears on the catalog entry for any book. It is also printed on the spine of every book in the library.

If your library has open stacks (ones that you are permitted to enter), here is how to find a book. Suppose you are looking for *A Tribe Apart,* which has the call number HQ796/H43 in the Library of Congress system. (Libraries using the Dewey decimal system have call letters made up entirely of numbers rather than letters and numbers. However, you use the same basic method to locate a book.) First, you go to the section of the stacks that holds the *H*'s. When you locate the *H*'s, you look for the *HQ*'s. After that, you look for *HQ796*. Finally, you look for *HQ796/H43*, and you have the book.

If your library has closed stacks (ones you are not permitted to enter), you will have to write down the title, author, and call number on a request form. (Such forms will be available near the card catalog or computer terminals.) You'll then give the form to a library staff person, who will locate the book and bring it to you.

ACTIVITY

Use the book stacks to answer one of the following sets of questions. Choose the questions that relate to the system of classifying books used by your library.

Option 1: Library of Congress System (letters and numbers)

1. Books in the E184.6—E185.9 area deal with
   - a. Benjamin Franklin.
   - b. American Indians.
   - c. American presidents.
   - d. African Americans.
2. Books in the HM–HN65 area deal with
   - a. sociology.
   - b. history.
   - c. economics.
   - d. psychology.
3. Books in the M1–M220 area deal with
   - a. painting.
   - b. sculpture.
   - c. music.
   - d. architecture.

Option 2: Dewey Decimal System (numbers)

1. Books in the 200–299 area deal with
   - a. language.
   - b. philosophy.
   - c. religion.
   - d. sports.
2. Books in the 370–372 area deal with
   - a. education.
   - b. death.
   - c. the military.
   - d. waste disposal.
3. Books in the 613 area deal with
   - a. wildflowers.
   - b. health.
   - c. drugs.
   - d. the solar system.

Periodicals

11.2

The first step in researching a topic is to check for relevant books; the second step is to locate relevant periodicals. *Periodicals* (from the word *periodic,* which means "at regular periods") are magazines, journals, and newspapers. Periodicals often contain recent or very specialized information about a subject, which may not be available in a book.

The library's catalog lists the periodicals that it holds, just as it lists its book holdings. To find articles in these periodicals, however, you will need to consult a *periodicals index.* Following are three indexes that are widely used in libraries.

Readers' Guide to Periodical Literature

11.2a

The old-fashioned way to do research is to use the familiar green volumes of the *Readers' Guide,* found in just about every library. They list articles published in more than one hundred popular magazines, such as *Newsweek, Health, People, Ebony, Redbook,* and *Popular Science.* Articles appear alphabetically under both subject and author. For example, if you wanted to learn the titles of articles published on the subject of child abuse within a certain time span, you would look under the heading "Child abuse."

Following is a typical entry from the *Guide.*

Subject heading   Title of article   Author of article   Illustrated

Parenting
The Case for Staying Home C. Wallis il *Time*
51–59 Mar 22, '04

Page numbers   Date   Name of magazine

Note the sequence in which information is given about the article:

1   Subject heading.

2   Title of the article. In some cases, there will be bracketed words [ ] after the title that help make clear just what the article is about.

3   Author (if it is a signed article). The author's first name is always abbreviated.

4   Whether the article has a bibliography (*bibl*) or is illustrated with pictures (*il*). Other abbreviations sometimes used are shown in the front of the *Readers' Guide.*

5   Name of the magazine. A short title like *Time* is not abbreviated, but longer titles are. For example, the magazine *Popular Science* is abbreviated *Pop Sci.* Refer to the list of magazines in the front of the index to identify abbreviations.

6   Page numbers on which the article appears.

7   Date when the article appeared. Dates are abbreviated: for example, *Mr* stands for *March, Ag* for *August, O* for *October.* Other abbreviations are shown in the front of the *Guide.*

The *Readers' Guide* is published in monthly supplements. At the end of a year, a volume is published covering the entire year. You will see in your library large green volumes that say, for instance, *Readers' Guide 2000* or *Readers' Guide 2002.* You will also see the small monthly supplements for the current year.

The drawback of the *Readers' Guide* is that it gives you only a list of articles; you must then go to your library's catalog to see if the library actually has copies of the magazines that contain those articles. If you're lucky and it does, you must take the time to locate the relevant issue and then to read and take notes on the articles or to make copies of them.

The *Readers' Guide* may also be available at your library online. If so, you can quickly search for articles on a given subject simply by typing in a keyword or key phrase.

EBSCOhost

Many libraries now provide an online computer search service such as *InfoTrac* or *EBSCOhost.* Sitting at a terminal and using EBSCOhost, for instance, you will be able to use key words to quickly search many hundreds of periodicals for full-text articles on your subject. When you find relevant articles, you can either print them out using a library printer (libraries may charge you about ten cents a page) or e-mail those articles to your home computer and run them off on your own printer. Obviously, if an online resource is available, that is the way you should conduct your research.

ACTIVITY 1

At this point in the chapter, you now know the two basic steps in researching a topic in the library. What are the steps?

1. Find books on your topic.

2. Find articles on your topic.

ACTIVITY 2

1. Look up a recent article on nursing home costs using one of your library's periodicals indexes, and fill in the following information: Answers will vary.

   a. Name of the index you used _____

   b. Article title _____

   c. Author (if given) _____

   d. Name of magazine _____

   e. Pages _____   f. Date _____

2. Look up a recent article on organ donation using one of your library's periodicals indexes, and fill in the following information: Answers will vary.

   a. Name of the index you used _____

   b. Article title _____

   c. Author (if given) _____

   d. Name of magazine _____

   e. Pages _____   f. Date _____

Using the Internet

11.7

(Using the Internet)

The *Internet* is dramatic proof of the computer revolution that has occurred in our lives. It is a giant network that connects computers at tens of thousands of educational, scientific, government, and commercial agencies around the world. Within the Internet is the World Wide Web, a global information system that got its name because countless individual websites contain *links* to other sites, forming a kind of web.

To use the Internet, you need a personal computer with a *modem*—a device that sends or receives electronic data over a telephone or cable line. You also need to subscribe to an online service provider such as America Online or Earthlink. If you have an online service as well as a printer for your computer, you can do a good deal of your research for a paper at home. As you would in a library, you should proceed by searching for books and articles on your topic.

Before you begin searching the Internet on your own, though, take the time to learn if your local or school library is online. If it is, visit its online address to find out exactly what sources and databases it has available. You may be able to do all your research using the online resources available through your library. On the other hand, if your library's resources are limited, you can turn on your own to the Internet to search for material on any topic, as explained here.

Finding Books on Your Topic

To find current books on your topic, go online and type in the address of one of the large commercial online booksellers:

Amazon at *www.amazon.com*

Barnes and Noble at *www.bn.com*

The easy-to-use search facilities of both Amazon and Barnes and Noble are free, and you are under no obligation to buy books from them.

The "Browse Subjects" Box

After you arrive at the Amazon or Barnes and Noble website (or the online library site of your choice), go to the "Browse Subjects" or "Keyword" box. You'll then get a list of categories where you might locate books on your general subject. For example, if your assignment was to report on personal obstacles faced by an American president, you would notice that one of the subject listings is "Biography." Upon choosing "Biography," you would get several subcategories, one of which is "Presidents." When you click on that, you would get a list of recent books on American presidents. You could then click on each title for information about each book. All this browsing and searching could be done very quickly and would help you decide on a specific president as your topic.

The "Keyword" Box

If your assignment is, for instance, to prepare a paper on some aspect of adoption, type the word "adoption" in the keyword search box provided. You'll then get a list of books on that subject. Just looking at the list may help you narrow your subject and decide on a specific topic you might want to develop. For instance, one student typed in "adoption" as her keyword on Barnes and Noble's site and got back a list of six hundred books. Considering just part of that list helped her realize that she wanted to write on some aspect of international adoption. She typed "international adoption" and got back a list of nineteen titles. After looking at information about those books, she was able to decide on a limited topic for her paper.

A Note on the Library of Congress

The commercial bookstore sites described are especially quick and easy to use. But you should know that to find additional books on your topic, you can also visit the Library of Congress website (*www.loc.gov*). The Library of Congress, in Washington, D.C., has copies of all books published in the United States. Its online catalog contains about twelve million entries. You can browse this catalog by subject or search by keywords. The search form permits you to check just those books that interest you. After you find a given book, click on the "Full Record" option to view publication information and call number. You can then try to find the book in your college library or through an interlibrary loan.

Other Points to Note

Remember that at any time, you can use your printer to quickly print out information presented on the screen. (For example, the student planning a paper on adoption could print out a list of the nineteen books on international adoption, along with sheets of information about individual books.) You could then go to your library knowing just what books you want to borrow. Indeed, if your own local or school library is accessible online, you can visit in advance to find out whether it has the books you want. Also, if you have time and money and if some of the books are in paperback, you may want to purchase them from the online bookstore such as Amazon. Used books are often available at greatly reduced prices, and they often ship out in just a couple of days.

Finding Articles on Your Topic

Online Magazines and Newspaper Articles

As already mentioned, your library may have an online search service such as EBSCOhost or InfoTrac that you can use to find and access relevant articles on your subject. Another online research service, one that you can subscribe to individually on a home computer, is *elibrary*. You may be able to get a free seven-day trial subscription or enroll on a monthly basis at a limited cost. Elibrary contains millions of newspaper and magazine articles as well as many thousands of book chapters and television and radio transcripts. After typing in one or more keywords, you'll get long lists of articles that may relate to your subject. When you then click on a given title, the full text of the article appears. If it fits your needs, you can print it out right away on your printer. Very easily, then, you can research a full range of magazine and newspaper articles.

Search Engines

ALLWRITE!
11.7b

An Internet search engine will help you quickly go through a vast amount of information on the Web to find articles about almost any topic. One extremely helpful search engine is Google; you can access it by typing

www.google.com

A screen will then appear with a box in which you can type one or more keywords. For example, if you are thinking of doing a paper on road rage, you simply enter the words *road rage*. Within a second or so you will get a list of over one million articles and sites on the Web about road rage!

Results from a keyword search on Google using "educational programs for preventing road rage" in the search box.

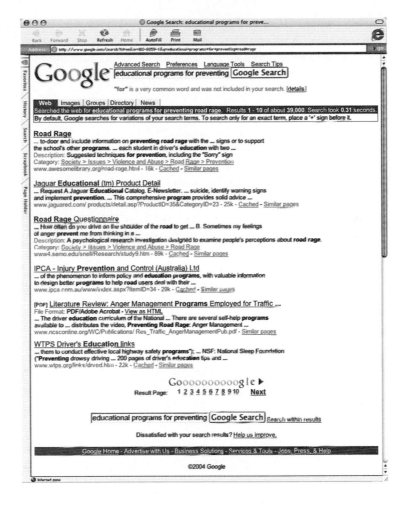

You should then try to narrow your topic by adding other keywords. For instance, if you typed "preventing road rage," you would get a list of over fifty thousand articles and sites. If you narrowed your potential topic further by typing "educational programs for preventing road rage," you would get a list of about four thousand items. Google does a superior job of returning "hits" that are genuinely relevant to your search, so just scanning the early part of a list may be enough to provide you with the information you need.

Very often your challenge with searches will be getting too much information rather than too little. Try making your keywords more specific, or use different combinations of keywords. You might also try another search engine, such as *www.yahoo.com*. In addition, consult the search engine's built-in "Advanced Search" feature for tips on successful searching.

Finally, remember while you search to save the addresses of relevant websites that you may want to visit again. The service provider that you are using (for example, AOL or Earthlink) will probably have a "Bookmark" or "Favorite Places" option. With the click of a mouse, you can "bookmark" a site. You will then be able to return to it simply by clicking on its name (which will automatically be in a bookmark list), rather than having to remember and type its address.

Evaluating Internet Sources

11.8

Keep in mind that the quality and reliability of information you find on the Internet may vary widely. Anyone with a bit of computer know-how can create a website and post information there. That person may a Nobel Prize winner, a leading authority in a specialized field, a high school student, or a crackpot. Be careful, then, to look closely at your electronic source in the following ways:

1   **Internet address**   Who is sponsoring the website? Look first at the address's extension—the part that follows the "dot." The accompanying box provides a guide to extensions.

Reliability of Internet Sponsors

Extension	What It Indicates	Example	Reliability
.com	Commercial or business organization	*www.newsweek. com (Newsweek* magazine)	Varies. How well established is the organization? What kind of local or national reputation does it have?
.edu	Educational institution	*www.harvard.edu* (Harvard University)	Usually reliable
.gov	Government agency	*www.census.gov* (U.S. Census Bureau)	Reliable
.net	Commercial or business organization or personal site	*www.streisand.net* (Barbra Streisand)	Varies. What kind of reputation does the organization or person have?
.org	Nonprofit organization	*www.consumer reports.org* (*Consumer Reports* magazine)	Usually reliable

2   **Author**   What credentials does the author have (if any)? Has the author published other material on the topic?

3   **Internal evidence**   Does the author seem to proceed objectively—presenting all sides of a topic fairly before arguing his or her own views? Does the author produce solid, adequate support for his or her views?

4   **Date**   Is the information up-to-date? Check at the top or bottom of the document for copyright, publication, or revision dates. Knowing such dates will help you decide whether the material is current enough for your purposes.

ACTIVITY

Part A   Go on the Internet to *www.google.com* and perform a search for the word "education." Then complete the items below.

1. How many items did your search yield? _____over 3 million_____

2. In the early listings, you will probably find each of the following extensions: *edu, gov, org,* and *com.* Pick one site with each extension and write its full address. Answers will vary.

   a. Address of one *.com* site you found: ____www.education.com____

   b. Address of one *.gov* site: ____www.ed.gov____

   c. Address of one *.org* site: ____www.edweek.org____

   d. Address of one *.edu* site: ____www.acenet.edu____

Part B   Circle *one* of the sites you identified above and use it to complete the following evaluation. Answers will vary.

3. Name of site's author or authoring institution: ____U.S. Dept. of Education____

4. Is site's information current (within two years)? _____Yes_____

5. Does the site serve obvious business purposes (with advertising or attempts to sell products)? ___No___

6. Does the site have an obvious connection to a governmental, commercial, business, or religious organization? If so, which one?
   Yes—federal government

7. Does the site's information seem fair and objective?
   For the most part, though the site supports the policies of the current
   administration.

8. Based on the information above, would you say the site appears reliable? ___Yes___

Practice in Using the Library and the Internet

11.5

(Activity 2)

ACTIVITY

Use your library or the Internet to research a subject that interests you. Select one of the following areas or (with your teacher's permission) an area of your own choice:

Assisted suicide

Interracial adoption

Ritalin and children

Sexual harassment

Gay marriage

Greenhouse effect

Nursing-home costs

Pro-choice movement today

Pro-life movement today

Health insurance reform

Pollution of drinking water

Problems of retirement

Cremation

Capital punishment

Prenatal care

Acid rain

New aid for people with disabilities

New remedies for allergies

Censorship on the Internet

Prison reform

Drug treatment programs

Sudden infant death syndrome

New treatments for insomnia

Organ donation

Child abuse

Voucher system in schools

Food poisoning (salmonella)

Computer use and carpal tunnel syndrome

Noise control

Animals nearing extinction

Animal rights movement

Anti-gay violence

Drug treatment programs for adolescents

Fertility drugs

Witchcraft today

New treatments for AIDS

Mind-body medicine

Origins of Kwanzaa

Hazardous substances in the home

Airbags

Gambling and youth

Nongraded schools

Forecasting earthquakes

Ethical aspects of hunting

Ethics of cloning

Recent consumer frauds

Stress reduction in the workplace

Sex on television

Everyday addictions

Toxic waste disposal

Self-help groups

Telephone crimes

Date rape

Alzheimer's disease   Steroids

Holistic healing   Surrogate mothers

Best job prospects today   Vegetarianism

Heroes for today

Research the topic first through a subject search in your library's catalog or that of an online bookstore. Then research the topic through a periodicals index (print or online). On a separate sheet of paper, provide the following information. Answers will vary.

1. Topic

2. Three books that either cover the topic directly or at least touch on the topic in some way. Include

   Author

   Title

   Place of publication

   Publisher

   Date of publication

3. Three articles on the topic published in 2001 or later. Include:

   Title of article

   Author (if given)

   Title of magazine

   Date

   Page(s) (if given)

4. Finally, write a paragraph describing just how you went about researching your topic. In addition, include a photocopy or printout of one of the three articles.

22 Writing a Research Paper

The process of writing a research paper has six steps:

1   Select a topic that you can readily research.
2   Limit your topic and make the purpose of your paper clear.
3   Gather information on your limited topic.
4   Plan your paper and take notes on your limited topic.
5   Write the paper.
6   Use an acceptable format and method of documentation.

This chapter explains and illustrates each of these steps and then provides a model research paper.

Step 1: Select a Topic That You Can Readily Research

Researching at a Local Library

First of all, do a subject search of your library's catalog (as described on page 371) and see whether there are several books on your general topic. For example, if you initially choose the broad topic "parenting," try to find at least three books on being a parent. Make sure that the books are actually available on the library shelves.

Next, go to a *periodicals index* in your library (see pages 374–375) to see if there are a fair number of magazine, newspaper, or journal articles on your subject. You can use the *Readers' Guide to Periodical Literature* (described on page 374) to find articles that appear in the back issues of periodicals that your library may keep. But you may find that your library subscribes to an electronic database such as EBSCOhost, which will allow you access to articles published in a far greater range of publications. For instance, when Sonya Philips, author of the model research paper "Successful Families," visited her local library, she typed the search term "parenting" into a computer that connected her to EBSCOhost. In seconds, EBSCOhost came back with hundreds of "hits"—titles, publication information, and the complete text of articles about parenting.

Researching on the Internet

ALLWRITE!

11.7

If you have access to the Internet on a home or library computer, you can use it to determine if resources are available for your topic.

The first step is to go to the subjects section of a library catalog or large online bookseller to find relevant books. (Don't worry—you don't have to buy any books; you're just browsing for information.) As mentioned in Chapter 21, two of the largest online booksellers are Barnes and Noble and Amazon.

"I checked out both Barnes and Noble and Amazon as I began my research," said Sonya Philips. "When I went to their websites, I saw that I could search for books by subject, and I knew that I was in business. All I had to do was click on a box titled 'Browse Subjects.'

"Barnes and Noble has a category called 'Parenting and Family,' and when I clicked on that, I got a bunch of subcategories, including one for 'Teenagers.' I clicked on 'Teenagers' and that brought up a list of hundreds of books! I went through the list, and when I got to a book that sounded promising, I just clicked on that title and up like magic came reviews of the book—and sometimes a table of contents and a summary as well! All of this information helped me decide on the dozen or so books I eventually picked out that seemed relevant to my paper. I then went to my local library and found five of those titles on the shelves. Another title was a recent paperback, so I went to a nearby bookstore and bought it." (If you find relevant books in your online search that your local library does not own, ask your research librarian if he or she can obtain them from another library through an interlibrary loan program.)

Next, determine if magazine or newspaper articles on your topic are available online. The simplest way is to use the Internet search engine Google (see pages 378–380), which allows you to search the Internet for information on any topic you like. Sonya relates her experience using Google in this way:

"First I typed in the word 'parenting' in the keyword box," she said. "I got more than eight million hits! So I tried more specific search terms. I tried 'parenting and teenagers' first, but that was still too general. I got several hundred thousand hits and I didn't know where to start reading. So I narrowed my topics even more: 'parenting and teenagers and television' and 'parenting and teenagers and home-schooling.' Those reduced the number of hits a lot. I was still getting thousands, but I could see that some of the very first ones looked really promising. Better yet, I found some useful sites, like 'The Television Project,' which is an online resource that doesn't exist anywhere else.

"In order to look just for magazine and newspaper articles, I went directly to the site of some popular publications, such as *Time* (*time.com*), *Newsweek* (*newsweek.*

com), and *USA Today* (*usatoday.com*). I was able to search each one for recent articles about parenting. I saw that I would have to use a credit card and pay a fee of about two dollars to read each article online. So I noted down the date and page number of the articles I was interested in and looked up the ones that were available in the back-issue section of my library's reading room. Between doing that and using EBSCOhost, I found plenty of recent material related to my subject."

In summary, then, the first step in doing a research paper is to find out if both books and articles are available on the topic in which you are interested. If they are, pursue your topic. Otherwise, you may have to explore another topic. You cannot write a paper on a topic for which research materials are not available.

Step 2: Limit Your Topic and Make the Purpose of Your Paper Clear

A research paper should *thoroughly* develop a *limited* topic. The paper should be narrow and deep rather than broad and shallow. Therefore, as you read through books and articles, look for ways to limit your general topic.

For instance, as Sonya read through materials on the general topic "parenting," she chose to limit her topic to the particular problems of parents raising children in today's culture. Furthermore, she decided to limit it even more by focusing on what successful parents do to deal with those challenges. To take some other examples, the general topic "drug abuse" might be narrowed to successful drug treatment programs for adolescents. After doing some reading on the worldwide problem of overpopulation, you might decide to limit your paper to the birth-control policies enforced by the Chinese government. The broad subject "death" could be reduced to euthanasia or the unfair pricing practices in some funeral homes. "Divorce" might be limited to its most damaging effects on the children of divorced parents; "stress in everyday life" could be narrowed to methods of reducing stress in the workplace.

The subject headings in your library's catalog and periodicals indexes will give you helpful ideas about how to limit your subject. For example, under the subject heading "Parenting" in the book file were several related headings, such as "moral and ethical considerations of parenting" and "stepparenting." In addition, there was a list of seventy-eight books, including several titles that suggested limited directions for research: parents and discipline, parenting and adolescent girls, how parents can protect their kids from violence, parents' questions about teenagers' development. Under the subject heading "Parenting" in the library's periodicals index were subheadings and titles of many articles which suggested additional limited topics that a research paper might explore: how parents can limit the impact of TV on kids, keeping the lines of communication open between parents and teenagers, how much influence parents can have on kids, secrets to raising a successful teen. The point is that *subject headings and related headings, as well as book and article titles, may be of great help to you in narrowing your topic.* Take advantage of them.

Do not expect to limit your topic and make your purpose clear all at once. You may have to do quite a bit of reading as you work out the limited focus of your paper. Note that many research papers have one of two general purposes. Your purpose might be to make and defend a point of some kind. (For example, your purpose in a paper might be to provide evidence that elected officials should be limited to serving a single term in office.) Or, depending on the course and the instructor, your purpose might simply be to present information about a particular subject. (For instance, you might be asked to write a paper describing the most recent scientific findings about the effect of diet on heart disease.)

Step 3: Gather Information on Your Limited Topic

After you have a good sense of your limited topic, you can begin gathering relevant information. A helpful way to proceed is to sign out the books that you need from your library. In addition, make copies of all relevant articles from magazines, newspapers, or journals. If your library has an online periodicals database, you may be able to print those articles right out.

In other words, take the steps needed to get all your key source materials together in one place. You can then sit and work on these materials in a quiet, unhurried way in your home or some other place of study.

Step 4: Plan Your Paper and Take Notes on Your Limited Topic

Preparing a Scratch Outline

ALLWRITE!

4.1a

As you carefully read through the material you have gathered, think constantly about the specific content and organization of your paper. Begin making decisions about exactly what information you will present and how you will arrange it. Prepare a scratch outline for your paper that shows both its thesis and the areas of support for the thesis. Try to plan at least three areas of support.

Thesis: _____

Support: (1) _____

          (2) _____

          (3) _____

Following, for example, is the brief outline that Sonya Philips prepared for her paper on successful parenting.

Thesis: There are things parents can do to overcome the negative influences hurting their families.

Support: (1) Create quality time with families

(2) Increase families' sense of community

(3) Minimize the impact of media and technology

Note-Taking

12.1

(Summarizing & Paraphrasing)

With a tentative outline in mind, you can begin taking notes on the information that you expect to include in your paper. Write your notes on four-by-six-inch or five-by-eight-inch cards, on sheets of loose-leaf paper, or in a computer file. The notes you take should be in the form of *direct quotations, summaries in your own words,* or both. At times, you may also *paraphrase*—use an equal number of your own words in place of someone else's words. Since most research involves condensing information, you will summarize much more than you will paraphrase. (For more information on summarizing, see pages 349–358.)

A *direct quotation* must be written *exactly* as it appears in the original work. But as long as you don't change the meaning, you may omit words from a quotation if they are not relevant to your point. To show such an omission, use three spaced periods (known as *ellipses*) in place of the deleted words:

Original passage

We cannot guarantee that bad things will happen, but we can argue that good things are not happening. It is the contention of this report that increasing numbers of young people are left to their own devices at a critical time in their development.

Direct quotation with ellipses

"We cannot guarantee that bad things will happen, but we can argue that good things are not happening. . . . [I]ncreasing numbers of young people are left to their own devices at a critical time in their development."

(Note that there are four dots in the above example; the first dot indicates the period at the end of the sentence. The capital letter in brackets shows that the word was capitalized by the student but did not begin the sentence in the original source.)

In a *summary,* you condense the original material by expressing it in your own words. Summaries may be written as lists, as brief paragraphs, or both. On the next page is one of Sonya Philips's summary note cards.

Keep in mind the following points about your research notes:

- Write on only one side of each card or sheet of paper.

> Movie content
>
> Study conducted in 1996 showed that of PG-13 movies, 91 percent had crude language, 89 percent had obscene language, 45 percent had actual or suggested sex. Worrisome because most parents assume PG-13 movies are OK for their kids.
>
> Medved and Medved, 62

- Write only one kind of information, from one source, on any one card or sheet. For example, the sample card above has information on only one idea (movie content) from one source (Medved and Medved).
- At the top of each card or sheet, write a heading that summarizes its content. This will help you organize the different kinds of information that you gather.
- Identify the source and page number at the bottom.

Whether you quote or summarize, be sure to record the exact source and page from which you take each piece of information. In a research paper, you must document all information that is not common knowledge or not a matter of historical record. For example, the birth and death dates of Dr. Martin Luther King, Jr., are established facts and do not need documenting. On the other hand, the average number of hours worked annually today compared with the 1980s is a specialized fact that should be documented. As you read several sources on a subject, you will develop a sense of what authors regard as generally shared or common information and what is more specialized information that must be documented.

A Caution about Plagiarism

(Plagiarism
&
the Internet)

If you fail to document information that is not your own, you will be stealing. The formal term is *plagiarizing*—using someone else's work as your own, whether you borrow a single idea, a sentence, or an entire essay.

One example of plagiarism is turning in a friend's paper as if it is one's own. Another example is copying an article found in a magazine, newspaper, journal, or on the Internet and turning it in as one's own. By copying someone else's work, you may risk being failed or even expelled. Equally, plagiarism deprives you of what can be a most helpful learning and organizational experience—researching and writing about a selected topic in detail.

Keep in mind, too, that while the Internet has made it easier for students to plagiarize, it has also made it riskier. Teachers can easily discover that a student has taken material from an Internet source by typing a sentence or two from the student's paper into a powerful search engine like Google; that source is then often quickly identified.

With the possibility of plagiarism in mind, then, be sure to take careful, documented notes during your research. Remember that if you use another person's material, *you must acknowledge your source.* When you cite a source properly, you give credit where it is due, you provide your readers with a way to locate the original material on their own, and you demonstrate that your work has been carefully researched.

ACTIVITY

Here are three sets of passages. Each set begins with an original passage followed by notes on the passage. Both notes include a parenthetical citation (24) crediting the original source. But while one note is an acceptable paraphrase/summary, the other is an unacceptable paraphrase/summary in which the sentences and ideas too closely follow the original, using some of the same structure and the same words as the original. Identify the acceptable note with an *A* and the unacceptable note with a *U*.

Set 1: Original Passage

The self-confessed television addict often feels he "ought" to do other things—but the fact that he doesn't read and doesn't plant his garden or sew or crochet or play games or have conversations means that those activities are no longer as desirable as television. In a way the heavy viewer's life is as imbalanced by his television "habit" as a drug addict's or an alcoholic's. He is living in a holding pattern, as it were, passing up the activities that lead to growth or development or a sense of accomplishment. This is one reason people talk about their television viewing so ruefully, so apologetically. They are aware that it is an unproductive experience, that almost any other endeavor is more worthwhile by any human measure.

—Marie Winn, from "Television Addiction,"
in *The Plug-In Drug* (Viking Penguin, 2002)

___U___ a. Television addicts may feel they should do other things like play games or have conversations. But they pass up activities that might lead to a sense of accomplishment. Their lives are as imbalanced by their television watching as a drug addict's or alcoholic's. Aware of how unproductive television viewing is, they talk about it apologetically (24).

___A___ b. TV addicts feel that they ought to spend their time doing more worthwhile activities. But like alcohol or drugs, TV has taken over their lives. The addicts' apologetic tone when they talk about their TV watching indicates that they know they're wasting time on a completely unproductive activity (24).

Set 2: Original Passage

Now, however, there is growing evidence that restorative naps are making a comeback. Recognizing that most of their employees are chronically sleep-deprived, some companies have set up nap rooms with reclining chairs, blankets and alarm clocks. If unions are truly interested in worker welfare, they should make such accommodations a standard item in contract negotiations. Workers who take advantage of the opportunity to sleep for twenty minutes or so during the workday report that they can go back to work with renewed enthusiasm and energy. My college roommate, Dr. Linda Himot, a psychiatrist in Pittsburgh, who has a talent for ten-minute catnaps between patients, says these respites help her focus better on each patient's problems, which are not always scintillating. And companies that encourage napping report that it reduces accidents and errors and increases productivity, even if it shortens the workday a bit. Studies have shown that sleepy workers make more mistakes and cause more accidents, and are more susceptible to heart attacks and gastrointestinal disorders.

—Jane Brody, from "New Respect for the Nap"
(*New York Times,* 2001)

___A___ a. As employers realize that many workers are short on sleep, they are becoming more open to the idea of napping on the job. Some even provide places for workers to stretch out and nap briefly. Companies that allow napping find their employees are more alert and productive, and even suffer fewer physical ailments.

___U___ b. Naps are becoming more acceptable. Some companies have done such things as set up nap rooms with reclining chairs and blankets. Naps provide workers with renewed enthusiasm and energy. Although naps shorten the workday a bit, they reduce accidents and increase productivity. Sleep-deprived workers are prone to heart attacks and gastrointestinal disorders.

Set 3: Original Passage

Chances are, you are going to go to work after you complete college. How would you like to earn an extra $950,000 on your job? If this sounds appealing, read on. I'm going to reveal how you can make an extra $2,000 a month between the ages of 25 and 65. Is this hard to do? Actually, it is simple for some, but impossible for others. All you have to do is be born a male and graduate from college. If we compare full-time workers, this is how much more the average male college graduate earns over the course of his career. Hardly any single factor pinpoints gender discrimination better than this total. The pay gap, which shows up at all levels of education, is so great that women who work full-time average only two-thirds (67 percent) of what men are paid. This gap does not occur only in the United States. All industrialized nations have it, although only in Japan is the gap larger than in the United States.

—James Henslin, from *Essentials of Sociology,*
Fourth Edition (Allyn and Bacon, 2002)

U a. In order to make an extra $2,000 a month between the ages of 25 and 65, you need to be born male and graduate from college. This adds up to an additional $950,000. The pay gap between genders shows up at all levels of education. It is so great that women who work full-time make only two-thirds what men make. The gender gap occurs in all industrialized nations, although only in Japan is it greater than in the U.S.

A b. The effect of gender on salary is significant. At all levels of education, a woman who works full-time earns about two-thirds as much as a man who works full-time. For college graduates, this adds up to a difference of $950,000 over the course of a 40-year working life. The gender gap exists in all industrialized nations, but it is greatest in Japan and the U.S.

Step 5: Write the Paper

After you have finished your reading and note-taking, you should have a fairly clear idea of the plan of your paper. Make a *final outline* and use it as a guide to write your first full draft. If your instructor requires an outline as part of your paper, you should prepare either a *topic outline,* which contains your thesis plus supporting words and phrases; or a *sentence outline,* which consists of complete sentences. In the model paper shown on pages 398–408, a topic outline appears on page 399. You will note that roman numerals are used for first-level headings, capital letters for second-level headings, and arabic numbers for third-level headings.

In an *introduction,* include a thesis statement expressing the purpose of your paper and indicate the plan of development that you will follow. The section on writing introductions for an essay (pages 86–88) is also appropriate for the introductory section of the research paper. Notice that the model research paper uses a two-paragraph introduction (page 400).

As you move from introduction to *main body* to *conclusion,* strive for unity, support, and coherence so that your paper will be clear and effective. Repeatedly ask, "Does each of my supporting paragraphs develop the thesis of my paper?" Use the checklist on the inside front cover of this book to make sure that your paper follows all four steps of effective writing.

Step 6: Use an Acceptable Format and Method of Documentation

Format

The model paper shows acceptable formats for a research paper, including the style recommended by the Modern Language Association (MLA). Be sure to note carefully the comments and directions that are set in small print in the margins of each page.

Documentation of Sources

You must tell the reader the sources (books, articles, and so on) of borrowed material in your paper. Whether you quote directly or summarize ideas in your own words, you must acknowledge your sources. In the past, you may have used footnotes and a bibliography to cite your sources. Here you will learn a simplified and widely accepted documentation style used by the MLA.

Citations within a Paper

When citing a source, you must mention the author's name and the relevant page number. The author's name may be given either in the sentence you are writing or in parentheses following the sentence. Here are two examples:

> In The Way We Really Are, Stephanie Coontz writes, "Right up through the 1940s, ties of work, friendship, neighborhood, ethnicity, extended kin, and voluntary organizations were as important a source of identity for

most Americans, and sometimes a <u>more</u> important source of obligation, than marriage and the nuclear family" (37).

"Some . . . are looking for a way to reclaim family closeness in an increasingly fast-paced society . . . . Still others worry about unsavory influences in school—drugs, alcohol, sex, violence" (Kantrowitz and Wingert 66).

There are several points to note about citations within the paper:

- When the author's name is provided in parentheses, only the last name is given.
- There is no punctuation between the author's name and the page number.
- The parenthetical citation is placed after the borrowed material but before the period at the end of the sentence.
- If you are using more than one work by the same author, include a shortened version of the title within the parenthetical citation. For example, suppose you were using two books by Stephanie Coontz, and you included a second quotation from her book *The Way We Really Are.* Your citation within the text would be

(Coontz, <u>Really Are</u> 39).

Note that a comma separates the author's last name from the abbreviated title and page number.

Citations at the End of a Paper

13.2

Your paper should end with a list of "Works Cited" that includes all the sources actually used in the paper. (Don't list any other sources, no matter how many you have read.) Look at the "Works Cited" page in the model research paper (page 408) and note the following points:

- The list is organized alphabetically according to the authors' last names. Entries are not numbered.
- Entries are double-spaced, with no extra space between entries.
- After the first line of each entry, there is a half-inch indentation for each additional line in the entry.
- Use the abbreviation *qtd. in* when citing a quotation from another source. For example, a quotation from Edward Wolff on page 2 of the paper is from a book not by Wolff but by Sylvia Ann Hewlett and Cornel West. The citation is therefore handled as follows:

The economist Edward Wolff explains the loss of time:

> Over a thirty-year time span, parental time has declined 13 percent. The time parents have available for their children has been squeezed by the rapid shift of mothers into the paid labor force, by escalating divorce rates and the subsequent abandonment of children by their fathers, and by an increase in the number of hours required on the job. The average worker is now at work 163 hours a year more than in 1969, which adds up to an extra month of work annually (qtd. in Hewlett and West 48).

Model Entries for a List of "Works Cited"

Model entries of "Works Cited" are given below. Use these entries as a guide when you prepare your own list.

Book by One Author

Bryson, Bill. <u>A Short History of Nearly Everything</u>. New York: Broadway Books, 2003.

Note that the author's last name is written first.

Two or More Entries by the Same Author

---. <u>I'm a Stranger Here Myself</u>. New York: Broadway Books, 1999.

If you cite two or more entries by the same author (in the example above, a second book by Bill Bryson is cited), do not repeat the author's name. Instead, begin the line with three hyphens followed by a period. Then give the remaining information as usual. Arrange works by the same author alphabetically by title. The words *A*, *An*, and *The* are ignored in alphabetizing by title.

Book by Two or More Authors

Simon, David, and Edward Burns. <u>The Corner</u>. New York: Broadway Books, 1997.

For a book with two or more authors, give all the authors' names but reverse only the first name.

Magazine Article

Kalb, Claudia. "Brave New Babies." <u>Newsweek</u> 26 Jan. 2004: 45–52.

Newspaper Article

Farrell, Greg. "Online Time Soars at Office." <u>USA Today</u> 18 Feb. 2000: A1–2.

The final letter and numbers refer to pages 1 and 2 of section A.

If the article is not printed on consecutive pages, simply list the first page followed by a plus sign "+" (in that case, the above example would read "A1+").

Editorial

"Fouling the Air." Editorial. <u>New York Times</u> 23 Aug. 2003: A12.

List an editorial as you would any signed or unsigned article, but indicate the nature of the piece by adding *Editorial* after the article's title.

Selection in an Edited Collection

Paige, Satchel. "Rules for Staying Young." Baseball: A Literary Anthology. Ed. Nicholas Dawidoff. New York: Library of America, 2002. 318.

Revised or Later Edition

Henslin, James M. Essentials of Sociology. 5th ed. Boston: Allyn and Bacon, 2004.

The abbreviations *Rev. ed., 2nd ed., 3rd ed.,* and so on, are placed right after the title.

Chapter or Section in a Book by One Author

Krugman, Paul. "The Angry People." The Great Unraveling. New York: Norton, 2003. 272–74.

Pamphlet

Funding Your Education 2003–2004. Washington: Dept. of Education Office of Federal Student Aid, 2003.

Television Program

"Musically Speaking." 60 Minutes. Report. Lesley Stahl. CBS. 28 Sept. 2003.

Film

The Lord of the Rings: The Return of the King. Dir. Peter Jackson. New Line Cinema, 2003.

Sound Recording

Springsteen, Bruce. "Empty Sky." The Rising. Sony Music, 2002.

Videocassette

"Cedric's Journey." Nightline. Narr. Ted Koppel, ABC, WABC, New York. 24 June 1998. Videocassette. ABC/FDCH, 1998.

Personal Interview

McClintock, Ann. Personal interview. 23 June 2004.

Article in an Online Magazine

Hobson, Katherine. "Cancer: The Best Tests to Find a Killer." USnews.com 1 Sept. 2003. 9 Oct. 2004 <http://www.usnews.com/usnews/issue/archive/030901/20030901041310.php>.

The first date (1 Sept. 2003) refers to the issue of the publication in which the article appeared; the second date (9 Oct. 2004) refers to the day when the student researcher accessed the source.

Article in an Online Website

"Being Chased." Dreams and Nightmares. Internet Resources. 2003. 17 Mar. 2004 <http://www.dreamnightmares.com/chasedindreams.html>.

No author is given, so the article is cited first, followed by the title of the website (*Dreams and Nightmares*) and the sponsor of the website (Internet Resources). The first date (2003) refers to when the material was electronically published, updated, or posted; the second date (17 Mar. 2004) refers to when the student researcher accessed the source.

Article in a Reference Database

"Dreams." Encyclopaedia Britannica. 2003. Encyclopaedia Britannica
        Premium Service. 8 Oct. 2004 <http://www.britannica.com/eb/
        article?eu=117531>.

The first date (2003) refers to when the material was electronically published, updated, or posted; the second date (8 Oct. 2004) refers to when the student researcher accessed the source.

Electronic Mail (E-mail) Posting

Graham, Vanessa. "Teenager Problems." E-mail to Sonya Philips. 12 Apr. 2004.

ACTIVITY

On a separate sheet of paper, convert the information in each of the following references into the correct form for a list of "Works Cited." Use the appropriate model above as a guide.

1. A book by David Anderegg called *Worried All the Time* and published in New York by Free Press in 2003.
2. An article by Susan Page titled "No Experience Necessary" on pages 1A–2A of the September 29, 2003, issue of *USA Today*.
3. A book by Michael W. Passner and Ronald E. Smith titled *Psychology: The Science of Mind and Behavior* and published in a second edition by McGraw-Hill in New York in 2004.
4. An article by Mark Miller titled "Parting with a Pet" found on May 16, 2004, at <http://www.msnbc.com/news/977726.asp?Ocv-KB20> in the October 8, 2003, issue of *Newsweek Online*.
5. An article titled "Depression in Teenagers" found on April 24, 2004, on the website titled *Troubled Teens* at <http://www.4troubledteens.com> and sponsored by the Aspen Education Group.

1. Anderegg, David. Worried All the Time. New York: Free Press, 2003.
2. Page, Susan. "No Experience Necessary." USA Today 29 Sept. 2003. 1A–2A.
3. Passner, Michael W., and Ronald E. Smith. The Science of Mind and Behavior. 2nd ed. New York: McGraw-Hill, 2004.
4. Miller, Mark. "Parting with a Pet." Newsweek Online 8 Oct. 2003. 16 May 2004 <http://www. msnbc.com/news/977726.asp?Ocv-KB20>.
5. "Depression in Teenagers." Troubled Teens. Aspen Education Group. 24 Apr. 2004 <http:// www.4troubledteens.com>.

Model Paper

Model Title Page

While the *MLA Handbook* does not require a title page or an outline for a paper, your instructor may ask you to include one or both. Here is a model title page.

The title should begin about one-third of the way down the page. Center the title. Double-space between lines of the title and your name. Also center and double-space the instructor's name and the date.

Successful Families:

Fighting for Their Kids

by

Sonya Philips

English 101

Professor Lessig

5 May 2004

Model First Page of MLA-Style Paper

Papers written in MLA style use the simple format shown below. There is no title page or outline.

1 inch

1/2 inch

Philips 1

Sonya Philips
Professor Lessig
English 101
5 May 2004

Successful Families: Fighting for Their Kids

Double-space between lines. Leave a one-inch margin on all sides.

It's a terrible time to be a teenager, or even a teenager's parent. That message is everywhere. Television, magazines, and newspapers are all full of frightening stories about teenagers and families. They say that America's families are falling apart, that kids don't care about anything, and that parents have trouble doing anything. . . .

Model Outline Page

After the title page, number all pages in upper-right corner, a half-inch from the top. Place your name before the page number. Use small roman numerals on outline pages. Use arabic numerals on pages following the outline.

The word *Outline* (without underlining or quotation marks) is centered one inch from the top. Double-space between lines. Leave a one-inch margin on all sides.

Use this format if your instructor asks you to submit an outline of your paper.

Philips i

Outline

Thesis: Although these are difficult times to be raising teenagers, successful families are finding ways to cope with the challenges.

I. Meeting the challenge of spending quality time together

    A. Barriers to spending quality time

        1. Increased working hours

        2. Rising divorce rates

        3. Women in workforce

    B. Danger of lack of quality time

    C. Ways found to spend time together

        1. Working less and scaling back lifestyle

        2. Home schooling

II. Meeting the challenge of creating sense of community

    A. Lack of traditional community ties

    B. Ways found to create sense of community

        1. Intentional communities

        2. Religious ties

III. Meeting the challenge of limiting the negative impact of media and technology

    A. Negative impact of media and technology

        1. Creation of environment without protection

        2. Flood of uncontrolled, inappropriate information

    B. Ways of controlling media and technology

        1. Banning TV

        2. Using technology in beneficial ways

Here is a full model paper. It assumes the writer has included a title page.

Philips 1

Successful Families: Fighting for Their Kids

It's a terrible time to be a teenager, or even a teenager's parent. That message is everywhere. Television, magazines, and newspapers are all full of frightening stories about teenagers and families. They say that America's families are falling apart, that kids don't care about anything, and that parents have trouble doing anything about it. Bookstores are full of disturbing titles like these: Parenting Your Out-of-Control Teenager, Teenage Wasteland, Unhappy Teenagers, and Teen Torment. These books describe teenage problems that include apathy, violence, suicide, sexual abuse, depression, loss of values, poor mental health, crime, gang involvement, and drug and alcohol addiction.

Naturally, caring parents are worried by all this. Their worry showed in a 2002 national poll in which 76% of parents said that raising children was "a lot harder" than it was when they were growing up ("A Lot Easier Said"). But just as most popular TV shows don't give a realistic view of American teens, these frightening books and statistics do not provide a complete picture of what's going on in families today. The fact is that not all teens and families are lost and without values. While they struggle with problems in our culture like everyone else, successful families are doing what they've always done: finding ways to protect and nurture their children. They are fighting the battle for their families in three ways: by fighting against the loss of quality family time, by fighting against the loss of community, and by fighting against the influence of the media.

Double- space between lines of the text. Leave a one-inch margin all the way around the page. Your name and the page number should be typed one-half inch from the top of the page.

Common knowledge is not documented.

This typical citation shows the source by giving the author's last name or (as here, if no author is provided) the title of the article (and if relevant, a page number). "Works Cited" then provides full information about the source.

Thesis, followed by plan of development.

Philips 2

It's true that these days, parents face more challenges than ever before when it comes to finding quality time to spend with their children. The economist Edward Wolff explains the loss of time:

> Over a thirty-year time span, parental time has declined 13%. The time parents have available for their children has been squeezed by the rapid shift of mothers into the paid labor force, by escalating divorce rates and the subsequent abandonment of children by their fathers, and by an increase in the number of hours required on the job. The average worker is now at work 163 hours a year more than in 1969, which adds up to an extra month of work annually (qtd. in Hewlett and West 48).

As a result, more children are at home alone than ever before. And this situation does leave children vulnerable to getting into trouble. Richardson and others, in their study of five thousand eighth-graders in California, found that children who were home alone after school were twice as likely to experiment with drugs and alcohol as children who had a parent (or another adult) home in the after-school hours.

But creative parents still come up with ways to be there for their kids. For some, it's been a matter of cutting back on working hours and living more simply. For example, in her book <u>The Shelter of Each Other</u>, Mary Pipher tells the story of a couple with three-year-old twin boys. Eduardo worked sixty-hour weeks at a factory. Sabrina supervised checkers at a K-Mart, cared for the boys, and tried to watch over her mother, who had cancer. Money was tight,

Source is identified by name and area of expertise.

Direct quotations of five typed lines or more are indented ten spaces (or one inch) from the left margin. Quotation marks are not used.

The abbreviation *qtd.* means *quoted.* No comma is used between the authors' names and the page number.

When citing a work in general, not part of a work, it is best to include the author's name in the text instead of using a parenthetical citation. No page number is needed, as the citation refers to the findings of the study overall.

especially since day care was expensive and the parents felt they had to keep the twins stylishly dressed and supplied with new toys. The parents were stressed over money problems, their lack of time together, and especially having so little time with their boys. It bothered them that the twins had begun to cry when their parents picked them up at day care, as if they'd rather stay with the day-care workers. Finally, Sabrina and Eduardo made a difficult decision. Sabrina quit her job, and the couple invited her mother (whose illness was in remission) to live with them. With three adults pooling their resources, Sabrina and Eduardo found that they could manage without Sabrina's salary. The family no longer ate out, and they gave up their cable TV. Their sons loved having their grandmother in the house. Sabrina was able to begin doing relaxed, fun projects with the boys. They planted a garden and built a sandbox together. Sabrina observed, "I learned I could get off the merry-go-round" (195). Other parents have "gotten off the merry-go-round" by working at home, even if it means less money than they had previously.

Some parents even home-school their children as a way to be sure they have plenty of time together. Home schooling used to be thought of as a choice made only by very religious people or back-to-nature radicals. Now, teaching children at home is much less unusual. It's estimated that as many as 2 million American children are being home-schooled. Harvard even has an admissions officer whose job it is to review applications from home-schooled kids.

Only the page number is needed, as the author has already been named in the text.

Philips 4

Parents who home-school have different reasons, but, according to a cover story in <u>Newsweek</u>, "Some . . . are looking for a way to reclaim family closeness in an increasingly fast-paced society. . . . Still others worry about unsavory influences in school—drugs, alcohol, sex, violence" (Kantrowitz and Wingert 66). Home schooling is no guarantee that a child will resist those temptations, but some families do believe it's a great way to promote family closeness. One fifteen-year-old, home-schooled since kindergarten, explained why he liked the way he'd been raised and educated. He ended by saying, "Another way I'm different is that I love my family. One guy asked me if I'd been brainwashed. I think it's spooky that liking my family is considered crazy" (Pipher 103).

Many parents can't quit their jobs or teach their children at home. But some parents find a second way to nurture their children, through building community ties. They help their children develop a healthy sense of belonging by creating links with positive, constructive people and activities. In the past, community wasn't so hard to find. In <u>The Way We Really Are</u>, Stephanie Coontz writes, "Right up through the 1940s, ties of work, friendship, neighborhood, ethnicity, extended kin, and voluntary organizations were as important a source of identity for most Americans, and sometimes a <u>more</u> important source of obligation, than marriage and the nuclear family" (37). Even when today's parents were teenagers, neighborhoods were places where kids felt a sense of belonging and responsibility. But today

Ellipses show where the student has omitted material from the original source. The quoted material is not capitalized because the student has blended it into a sentence with an introductory phrase.

"parents . . . mourn the disappearance of neighborhoods where a web of relatives and friends kept a close eye on everyone's kids. And they worry their own children grow up isolated, knowing more about the cast of Friends than the people in surrounding homes" (Donahue D1).

One way that some families are trying to build old-fashioned community is through "intentional community" or "cohousing." Begun in Denmark in 1972, the cohousing movement is modeled after the traditional village. It brings together a number of families who live in separate houses but share some common space. For instance, families might share central meeting rooms, dining areas, gardens, day care, workshops, or office space. They might own tools and lawn mowers together, rather than each household having its own. The point is that they treat their neighbors as extended family, not as strangers. As described by the online site Cohousing.org, cohousing is "a type of collaborative housing that attempts to overcome the alienation of modern subdivisions in which no one knows their neighbors, and there is no sense of community." In its 2004 database, the International Communities website estimates that "several thousand" such communities exist in North America.

Other families turn to religion as a source of community. Michael Medved and Diane Medved, authors of Saving Childhood, are raising their family in a religious Jewish home. Their children attend Jewish schools, go to synagogue, and follow religious

Philips 6

customs. They frequently visit, eat, play with, and are cared for by neighboring Jewish families. The Medveds believe their family is stronger because of their belief "in planting roots—in your home, in your family, in your community. That involves making a commitment, making an investment both physically and emotionally, in your surroundings" (200). Other religious traditions offer families a similar sense of community, purpose, and belonging. Marcus and Tracy Glover are members of the Nation of Islam. They credit the Nation with making their marriage and family strong and breaking a three-generation cycle of single motherhood (Hewlett and West 201–202).

Cited material extends from one page to another, so both page numbers are given.

A third way that families are fighting to protect their children is by controlling the impact of the media and technology. Hewlett and West and Pipher use similar words to describe this impact. As they describe growing up today, Hewlett and West write about children living "without a skin" (xiii), and Pipher writes about "houses without walls" (12). These authors mean that today—unlike in the old days, when children were protected from the outside world while they were in their homes—the home offers little protection. Even in their own living rooms, all children have to do is to turn on a TV, radio, or computer to be hit with a flood of violence, sick humor, and often weird sexuality. Children are growing up watching shows like <u>The Osbournes</u>, a program that celebrates two spoiled, foul-mouthed children and their father—a burnt-out rock star slowed by years of carefree drug abuse. A recent article in <u>Science</u> magazine offered the most damning link yet between TV watching and antisocial behavior. Reporting on the results of its seventeen-year study that followed viewers from youth to adulthood, <u>Science</u> found that the more television a teen watched, the higher the chances he or she would commit violent acts later in life. Of kids who watched an hour or less TV a day, fewer than 6% of teens went on to commit assaults, robberies, or other violent acts as adults. But nearly 28% of teens who watched TV three or more hours a day did commit crimes of violence. Sadly, many parents seem to have given up even trying to protect their growing kids against the flood of televised garbage. They are like the mother quoted in <u>USA Today</u> as saying, "How can I fight five hundred channels on TV?" (Donahue D1).

Fortunately, some parents are still insisting on control over the information and entertainment that comes into their homes. Some subscribe to "The Television Project," an online educational organization that helps parents "understand how television affects their families and community and proposes alternatives that foster positive emotional, cognitive and spiritual development within families and communities." Others ban TV entirely from their homes. More try to find a way to use TV and other electronics as helpful tools, but not allow them to dominate their homes. One family in Nebraska, the Millers, who home-school their children, described to Mary Pipher their attitude toward TV. They hadn't owned a TV for years, but they bought one so that

Philips 8

they could watch the Olympics. The set is now stored in a closet unless a program is on that the family agrees is worthwhile. Some programs the Millers have enjoyed together include the World Cup soccer games, the TV drama Sarah Plain and Tall, and an educational TV course in sign language. Pipher was impressed by the Miller children, and she thought their limited exposure to TV was one reason why. In her words:

> Calm, happy children and relaxed, confident parents are so rare today. Probably most notable were the long attention spans of the children and their willingness to sit and listen to the grown-ups talk. The family had a manageable amount of information to deal with. They weren't stressed by more information than they could assimilate. The kids weren't overstimulated and edgy. Nor were they sexualized in the way most kids now are. (107)

Pipher's words describe children raised by parents who won't give in to the idea that their children are lost. Such parents structure ways to be present in the home, build family ties to a community, and control the impact of the media in their homes. Through their efforts, they succeed in raising nurtured, grounded, successful children. Such parents acknowledge the challenges of raising kids in today's America, but they are up to the job.

The conclusion provides a summary and restates the thesis.

Works Cited

"A Lot Easier Said Than Done: Parents Talk About Raising

Children in Today's America." <u>Public Agenda</u>. Oct. 2002.

4 Oct. 2004 <http://www.publicagenda.org/specials/

parents/parents1.htm>.

Anderson, Craig A., and Brad J. Bushman. "The Effects of Media

Violence on Society." <u>Science</u> 29 Mar. 2002: 2377–79.

Coontz, Stephanie. <u>The Way We Really Are</u>. New York: Basic

Books, 1997.

Donahue, Deirdre. "Struggling to Raise Good Kids in Toxic Times."

<u>USA Today</u> 1 Oct. 1998: D1+.

Hewlett, Sylvia Ann, and Cornel West. <u>The War Against Parents</u>.

Boston: Houghton Mifflin, 1998.

<u>The Intentional Communities Home Page</u>. Fellowship of

Intentional Communities. 2 Sept. 2003 <http://www.ic.org/>.

Kantrowitz, Barbara, and Pat Wingert. "Learning at Home: Does

It Pass the Test?" <u>Newsweek</u> 5 Oct. 1998: 64–70.

Louv, Richard. <u>Childhood's Future</u>. Boston: Houghton Mifflin, 1990.

Medved, Michael, and Diane Medved. <u>Saving Childhood</u>. New

York: HarperCollins, 1998.

Pipher, Mary. <u>The Shelter of Each Other</u>. New York: Putnam, 1996.

<u>The Television Project Home Page</u>. The Television Project.

2 Feb. 2004 <http://www.tvp.org>.

"What Is Cohousing?" <u>Cohousing</u>. The Cohousing Association of

the United States. 10 Sept. 2003: 10 pars. 2 Feb. 2004 <http://

www.cohousing.org/resources/whatis.html>.

Works cited should be double-spaced. Titles of books, magazines, and the like should be underlined.

Include the date you accessed a Web source—in this case, October 4, 2004.

Several of these sources— *Public Agenda, Intentional Communities Home Page,* and the *Television Project*—are online. By going online and typing the letters after *www.* in each citation, you can access any of the sources.

PART FOUR

Handbook of Sentence Skills

23 Subjects and Verbs

The basic building blocks of English sentences are subjects and verbs. Understanding them is an important first step toward mastering a number of sentence skills.

Every sentence has a subject and a verb. Who or what the sentence speaks about is called the *subject;* what the sentence says about the subject is called the *verb.* In the following sentences, the subject is underlined once and the verb twice.

The boy cried.

That fish smells.

Many people applied for the job.

The show is a documentary.

A Simple Way to Find a Subject

To find a subject, ask *who* or *what* the sentence is about. As shown below, your answer is the subject.

Who is the first sentence about? The boy

What is the second sentence about? That fish

Who is the third sentence about? Many people

What is the fourth sentence about? The show

A Simple Way to Find a Verb

14.1c

To find a verb, ask what the sentence *says about* the subject. As shown below, your answer is the verb.

What does the first sentence *say about* the boy? He cried.

What does the second sentence *say about* the fish? It smells.

411

What does the third sentence *say about* the people? They <u>applied</u>.

What does the fourth sentence *say about* the show? It <u>is</u> a documentary.

A second way to find the verb is to put *I, you, he, she, it,* or *they* in front of the word you think is a verb. If the result makes sense, you have a verb. For example, you could put *he* in front of *cried* in the first sentence above, with the result, *he cried,* making sense. Therefore, you know that *cried* is a verb. You could use the same test with the other three verbs as well.

Finally, it helps to remember that most verbs show action. In the sentences already considered, the three action verbs are *cried, smells,* and *applied.* Certain other verbs, known as *linking verbs,* do not show action. They do, however, give information about the subject. In "The show is a documentary," the linking verb *is* joins the subject (*show*) with a word that identifies or describes it (*documentary*). Other common linking verbs include *am, are, was, were, feel, appear, look, become,* and *seem.*

ACTIVITY

In each of the following sentences, draw one line under the subject and two lines under the verb.

1. The ripening <u>tomatoes</u> <u>glistened</u> on the sunny windowsill.
2. <u>Acupuncture</u> <u>reduces</u> the pain of my headaches.
3. <u>Elena</u> <u>twisted</u> a strand of hair around her fingers.
4. My <u>brother</u> <u>built</u> his bookshelves from cinder blocks and wood planks.
5. A <u>jackrabbit</u> <u>bounds</u> up to fifteen feet in one leap.
6. The singer's diamond <u>earrings</u> <u>sparkled</u> in the spotlight.
7. My <u>roommate</u> <u>crashed</u> his car on the icy highway.
8. On St. Patrick's Day, our neighborhood <u>tavern</u> <u>serves</u> green beer.
9. My six-year-old <u>brother</u> <u>survives</u> on a diet of peanut butter and jelly.
10. During my parents' divorce, <u>I</u> <u>felt</u> like a rag doll being torn between two people.

More about Subjects and Verbs

18.1

1   A sentence may have more than one verb, more than one subject, or several subjects and verbs.

The <u>engine</u> <u>coughed</u> and <u>sputtered</u>.

Broken <u>glass</u> and empty <u>cans</u> <u>littered</u> the parking lot.

<u>Marta</u>, <u>Nilsa</u>, and <u>Robert</u> <u>met</u> after class and <u>headed</u> downtown.

2   The subject of the sentence never appears within a prepositional phrase. A *prepositional phrase* is simply a group of words that begins with a preposition. Following is a list of common prepositions.

Prepositions				
about	before	by	inside	over
above	behind	during	into	through
across	below	except	like	to
among	beneath	for	of	toward
around	beside	from	off	under
at	between	in	on, onto	with

Crossing out prepositional phrases will help you find the subject or subjects of a sentence.

A <u>stream</u> ~~of cold air~~ <u>seeps</u> in ~~through the space below the door~~.

<u>Specks</u> ~~of dust~~ <u>dance</u> gently ~~in a ray of sunlight~~.

The <u>people</u> ~~in the apartment above ours~~ <u>fight</u> loudly.

The murky <u>waters</u> ~~of the polluted lake~~ <u>spilled</u> ~~over the dam~~.

The amber <u>lights</u> ~~on its sides~~ <u>outlined</u> the tractor-trailer ~~in the hazy dusk~~.

3   Many verbs consist of more than one word. (The extra verbs are called *auxiliary,* or *helping,* verbs.) Here, for example, are some of the many forms of the verb *work.*

Forms of work		
work	worked	should work
works	were working	will be working
does work	have worked	can work
is working	had worked	could be working
are working	had been working	must have worked

4   Words like *not, just, never, only,* and *always* are not part of the verb, although they may appear within the verb.

Ruby <u>has</u> never <u>liked</u> cold weather.

Our boss <u>will</u> not <u>be singing</u> with the choir this year.

The intersection <u>has</u> not always <u>been</u> this dangerous.

5   A verb preceded by *to* is never the verb of a sentence.

At night, my son <u>likes</u> to read under the covers.

Evelyn <u>decided</u> to separate from her husband.

6   An *-ing* word by itself is never the verb of a sentence. (It may be part of the verb, but it must have a helping verb in front of it.)

They going on a trip this weekend.
(not a sentence, because the verb is not complete)

They <u>are going</u> on a trip this weekend. (a sentence)

ACTIVITY

Draw a single line under subjects and a double line under verbs. Cross out prepositional phrases as necessary to find the subjects.

1. A thick <u>layer</u> ~~of dust~~ <u>covers</u> the top of our refrigerator.
2. In June, sagging Christmas <u>decorations</u> <u>were</u> still <u>hanging</u> in the windows of the abandoned house.
3. The <u>people</u> ~~in the all-night coffee shop~~ <u>seemed</u> weary and lost.
4. Every <u>plant</u> ~~in the dim room~~ <u>bent</u> toward the small window.
5. A glaring <u>headline</u> ~~about the conviction of a local congressman~~ <u>attracted</u> my attention.
6. <u>Two</u> ~~of the biggest stores in the mall~~ <u>are going</u> out of business.
7. The battery tester's tiny red <u>lights</u> suddenly <u>started</u> to flicker.
8. A <u>neighbor</u> ~~of mine~~ <u>does</u> all her work at home and <u>e-mails</u> it to her office.
9. The <u>jar</u> ~~of peppercorns~~ <u>tumbled</u> ~~from the spice shelf~~ and <u>shattered</u> on the floor.
10. The <u>scar</u> ~~in the hollow of Brian's throat~~ <u>is</u> the result of an emergency operation to clear his windpipe.

■ Review Test

Draw a single line under subjects and a double line under verbs. Cross out prepositional phrases as necessary to find the subjects.

1. ~~With one graceful motion~~, the shortstop fielded the grounder and threw to first base.

2. Like human mothers, sheep and goat mothers develop close bonds with their babies.

3. ~~Before class~~, Antonietta and Jorge rushed to the coffee machine in the hall.

4. I shifted uncomfortably on the lumpy mattress before falling into a restless sleep.

5. Waiting ~~in the long ticket line~~, Matt shifted his weight from one foot to the other.

6. Ancient Egyptians were branding cattle more than four thousand years ago.

7. Dogs and cats crowded the veterinarian's office on Monday morning.

8. The driver abruptly halted her Jeep and backed up toward a narrow parking place.

9. ~~During the American Revolution~~, some brides rejected white wedding gowns and wore red as a symbol of rebellion.

10. The little girl's frantic family called a psychic to locate the child.

24 Fragments

15.2

Every sentence must have a subject and a verb and must express a complete thought. A word group that lacks a subject or a verb and does not express a complete thought is a *fragment*. Following are the most common types of fragments that people write:

1   Dependent-word fragments
2   *-ing* and *to* fragments
3   Added-detail fragments
4   Missing-subject fragments

Once you understand what specific kinds of fragments you might write, you should be able to eliminate them from your writing. The following pages explain all four types.

Dependent-Word Fragments

Some word groups that begin with a dependent word are fragments. Following is a list of common dependent words. Whenever you start a sentence with one of these words, you must be careful that a fragment does not result.

Dependent Words		
after	if, even if	when, whenever
although, though	in order that	where, wherever
as	since	whether
because	that, so that	which, whichever
before	unless	while
even though	until	who
how	what, whatever	whose

416

In the example below, the word group beginning with the dependent word *after* is a fragment:

After I cashed my paycheck. I treated myself to dinner.

A *dependent statement*—one starting with a dependent word like *after*—cannot stand alone. It depends on another statement to complete the thought. *After I cashed my paycheck* is a dependent statement. It leaves us hanging. We expect to find out, in the same sentence, *what happened after* the writer cashed the check. When a writer does not follow through and complete a thought, a fragment results.

To correct the fragment, simply follow through and complete the thought:

After I cashed my paycheck, I treated myself to dinner.

Remember, then, that *dependent statements by themselves are fragments.* They must be attached to a statement that makes sense standing alone.

Here are two other examples of dependent-word fragments.

I won't leave the house. Until I hear from you.

Rick finally picked up the socks. That he had thrown on the floor days ago.

Until I hear from you is a fragment; it does not make sense standing by itself. We want to know in the same statement *what cannot happen* until I hear from you. The writer must complete the thought. Likewise, *That he had thrown on the floor days ago* is not in itself a complete thought. We want to know in the same statement what *that* refers to.

How to Correct a Dependent-Word Fragment

In most cases you can correct a dependent-word fragment by attaching it to the sentence that comes after it or the sentence that comes before it:

After I cashed my paycheck, I treated myself to dinner.
(The fragment has been attached to the sentence that comes after it.)

I won't leave the house until I hear from you.
(The fragment has been attached to the sentence that comes before it.)

Rick finally picked up the socks that he had thrown on the floor days ago.
(The fragment has been attached to the sentence that comes before it.)

Another way of correcting a dependent-word fragment is simply to eliminate the dependent word by rewriting the sentence.

I cashed my paycheck and then treated myself to dinner.

I will wait to hear from you.

He had thrown them on the floor days ago.

Notes

a Use a comma if a dependent word group comes at the *beginning* of a sentence (see also page 516):

After I cashed my paycheck, I treated myself to dinner.

However, do not generally use a comma if the dependent word group comes at the *end* of a sentence.

I won't leave the house until I hear from you.

Rick finally picked up the socks that he had thrown on the floor days ago.

b Sometimes the dependent words *who, that, which,* or *where* appear not at the very start but *near* the start of a word group. A fragment often results:

I drove slowly past the old brick house. The place where I grew up.

The place where I grew up is not in itself a complete thought. We want to know in the same statement *where was the place* the writer grew up. The fragment can be corrected by attaching it to the sentence that comes before it:

I drove slowly past the old brick house, the place where I grew up.

ACTIVITY 1

Turn each of the following dependent word groups into a sentence by adding a complete thought. Use a comma after the dependent word group if a dependent word starts the sentence. Note the examples.

EXAMPLES   Although I felt miserable
Although I felt miserable, I tried to smile for the photographer.

The man who found my wallet
The man who found my wallet returned it the next day.

Answers will vary. Examples are shown.

1. If I don't get a raise soon

   If I don't get a raise soon, I'll quit.

2. Because it was raining

   Because it was raining, we canceled the picnic.

3. When I heard the news

   When I heard the news, I cried.

4. Because I couldn't find the car keys

   Because I couldn't find the car keys, I had to walk.

5. The restaurant that we tried

   The restaurant that we tried was disappointing.

ACTIVITY 2

Underline the dependent-word fragment in each item. Then rewrite the items, correcting each fragment by attaching it to the sentence that comes before or the sentence that comes after it—whichever sounds more natural. Use a comma after the dependent word group if it starts the sentence.

1. <u>Whenever I spray deodorant.</u> My cat arches her back. She thinks she is hearing a hissing enemy.

   . . . deodorant, my cat . . .

2. My father, a salesman, was on the road all week. We had a great time playing football in the house. <u>Until he came home for the weekend.</u>

   . . . house until he . . .

3. <u>If Kim takes too long saying good-bye to her boyfriend.</u> Her father will start flicking the porch light. Then he will come out with a flashlight.

   . . . boyfriend, her father . . .

4. Scientists are studying mummified remains. <u>That are thousands of years old.</u>
    Most of the people were killed by parasites.

    . . . remains that are thousands . . .

    _____

    _____

5. <u>After I got to class.</u> I realized my report was still on the kitchen table. I had
    been working there the night before.

    . . . class, I realized . . .

    _____

    _____

-ing and *to* Fragments

When an *-ing* word appears at or near the start of a word group, a fragment may
result. Such fragments often lack a subject and part of the verb. In the items below,
underline the word groups that contain *-ing* words. Each is a fragment.

1. Ellen walked all over the neighborhood yesterday. <u>Trying to find her dog Bo.</u>
    Several people claimed they had seen him only hours before.
2. We sat back to watch the movie. <u>Not expecting anything special.</u> To our
    surprise, we clapped, cheered, and cried for the next two hours.
3. I telephoned the balloon store. <u>It being the day before our wedding anniversary.</u>
    I knew my wife would be surprised to receive a dozen heart-shaped balloons.

People sometimes write *-ing* fragments because they think that the subject of one
sentence will work for the next word group as well. Thus, in item 1 the writer thinks
that the subject *Ellen* in the opening sentence will also serve as the subject for
Trying to find her dog Bo. But the subject must actually be in the same sentence.

How to Correct *-ing* Fragments

1 Attach the fragment to the sentence that comes before it or the sentence that
comes after it, whichever makes sense. Item 1 could read: "Ellen walked all
over the neighborhood yesterday trying to find her dog Bo."

2 Add a subject and change the *-ing* verb part to the correct form of the verb.
Item 2 could read: "We didn't expect anything special."

3 Change *being* to the correct form of the verb *be (am, are, is, was, were)*. Item
3 could read: "It was the day before our wedding anniversary."

How to Correct *to* Fragments

When *to* appears at or near the start of a word group, a fragment sometimes results:

> At the Chinese restaurant, Tim used chopsticks. To impress his date. He spent one hour eating a small bowl of rice.

The second word group is a fragment and can be corrected by adding it to the preceding sentence:

> At the Chinese restaurant, Tim used chopsticks to impress his date.

ACTIVITY 1

Underline the *-ing* fragment in each of the following items. Then correct the item by using the method described in parentheses.

EXAMPLE Stepping hard on the accelerator. Armon tried to beat the truck to the intersection. He lost by a hood.
(Add the fragment to the sentence that comes after it.)

Stepping hard on the accelerator, Armon tried to beat the truck to

the intersection.

1. Marble-sized hailstones fell from the sky. Flattening the young plants in the cornfield. A year's work was lost in an hour.
(Add the fragment to the preceding sentence.)
... sky, flattening ...

2. A noisy fire truck suddenly raced down the street. Coming to a stop at my house. My home security system had sent a false alarm.
(Correct the fragment by adding the subject *it* and changing *coming* to the proper form of the verb, *came*.)
... street. It came to a stop at my house. ...

3. My phone doesn't ring. Instead, a light on it blinks. The reason for this being that I am partially deaf.
(Correct the fragment by changing *being* to the proper form of the verb, *is*.)
The reason for this is that I am ...

ACTIVITY 2

Underline the *-ing* or *to* fragment in each item. Then rewrite each item, correcting the fragment by using one of the three methods described above.

1. Looking at the worm on the table. Shelby groaned. She knew she wouldn't like what the biology teacher said next.

    . . . table, Shelby groaned. . . .

    _____

2. I put a box of baking soda in the freezer. To get rid of the musty smell. However, my ice cubes still taste like old socks.

    . . . freezer to get rid of the musty smell. . . .

    _____

3. Staring at the clock on the far wall. I nervously began my speech. I was afraid to look at any of the people in the room.

    . . . wall, I nervously began my speech. . . .

    _____

4. Jerome sat quietly at his desk. Fantasizing about the upcoming weekend. He might meet the girl of his dreams at Saturday night's party.

    . . . desk, fantasizing about . . .

    _____

5. To get to the bus station from here. You have to walk two blocks out of your way. The sidewalk is torn up because of construction work.

    . . . from here, you have to . . .

    _____

Added-Detail Fragments

Added-detail fragments lack a subject and a verb. They often begin with one of the following words:

also	especially	except	for example	like	including	such as

Underline the one added-detail fragment in each of the following items:

1. Before a race, I eat starchy foods. <u>Such as bread and spaghetti.</u> The carbohydrates provide quick energy.
2. Bob is taking a night course in auto mechanics. <u>Also, one in plumbing.</u> He wants to save money on household repairs.
3. My son keeps several pets in his room. <u>Including hamsters and mice.</u>

People often write added-detail fragments for much the same reason they write *-ing* fragments. They think the subject and verb in one sentence will serve for the next word group. But the subject and verb must be in *each* word group.

How to Correct Added-Detail Fragments

1 Attach the fragment to the complete thought that precedes it. Item 1 could read: "Before a race, I eat starchy foods such as bread and spaghetti."

2 Add a subject and a verb to the fragment to make it a complete sentence. Item 2 could read: "Bob is taking a night course in auto mechanics. Also, he is taking one in plumbing."

3 Insert the fragment within the preceding sentence. Item 3 could read: "My son keeps several pets, including hamsters and mice, in his room."

ACTIVITY 1

Underline the fragment in each of the following items. Then make it a sentence by rewriting it, using the method described in parentheses.

EXAMPLE   My mother likes watching daytime television shows. <u>Especially old movies and soap operas.</u> She says that daytime television is less violent. (Add the fragment to the preceding sentence.)

My mother likes watching daytime television shows, especially old movies and soap operas.

1. Luis works evenings in a video store. He enjoys the fringe benefits. <u>For example, seeing the new movies first.</u>
(Correct the fragment by adding the subject and verb *he sees*.)
. . . For example, he sees the new movies first.

2. Bob's fingernails are ragged from years of working as a mechanic. And his fingertips are always black. <u>Like ink pads.</u>
(Attach the fragment to the preceding sentence.)

  . . . black, like ink pads.

3. Electronic devices keep getting smaller. <u>Such as video cameras and cell phones.</u> Some are so tiny they look like toys.
(Correct the fragment by inserting it in the preceding sentence.)

  Electronic devices, such as video cameras and cell phones, keep getting

  smaller. Some are . . .

ACTIVITY 2

Underline the added-detail fragment in each item. Then rewrite to correct the fragment. Use one of the three methods described above.

Methods of correction may vary.

1. Left-handed students face problems. <u>For example, right-handed desks.</u> Spiral notebooks can also be uncomfortable to use.

  . . . problems. For example, they must sit at right-handed desks. . . .

2. Mrs. Fields always wears her lucky clothes to bingo. <u>Such as a sweater printed with four-leaf clovers.</u> She also carries a rhinestone horseshoe.

  . . . clothes, such as a sweater printed with four-leaf clovers, to bingo. . . .

3. Hundreds of moths were swarming around the stadium lights. <u>Like large flecks of snow.</u> However, I knew they couldn't be snow—it was eighty degrees outside.

  . . . lights like large flecks of snow. . . .

4. Trevor buys and sells paper collectors' items. <u>For instance, comic books and movie posters.</u> He sets up a display at local flea markets and carnivals.

  . . . items. For instance, he buys and sells comic books and movie posters. . . .

5. I wonder now why I had to learn certain subjects. <u>Such as geometry.</u> No one has ever asked me about the hypotenuse of a triangle.

  . . .subjects, such as geometry. No one . . .

Missing-Subject Fragments

In each item below, underline the word group in which the subject is missing:

1. Alicia loved getting wedding presents. <u>But hated writing thank-you notes.</u>
2. Mickey has orange soda and potato chips for breakfast. <u>Then eats more junk food, like root beer and cookies, for lunch.</u>

How to Correct Missing-Subject Fragments

1 Attach the fragment to the preceding sentence. Item 1 could read: "Alicia loved getting wedding presents but hated writing thank-you notes."

2 Add a subject (which can often be a pronoun standing for the subject in the preceding sentence). Item 2 could read: "Then he eats more junk food, like root beer and cookies, for lunch."

ACTIVITY

Underline the missing-subject fragment in each item. Then rewrite that part of the item needed to correct the fragment. Use one of the two methods of correction described above.

Methods of correction may vary.

1. Every other day, Kara runs two miles. <u>Then does fifty sit-ups.</u> She hasn't lost weight, but she looks trimmer and more muscular.
   . . . miles. Then she does . . .
   _____

2. I like all kinds of fresh pizza. <u>But refuse to eat frozen pizza.</u> The sauce is always dried out, and the crust tastes like leather.
   . . . pizza. But I refuse . . .
   _____

3. Many people are allergic to seafood. They break out in hives when they eat it. <u>And can even have trouble breathing.</u>
   . . . they eat it, and they can even . . .
   _____

4. To distract me, the dentist tugged at a corner of my mouth. <u>Then jabbed a needle into my gums and injected a painkiller.</u> I hardly felt it.
   . . . mouth. Then he jabbed a needle . . .
   _____

5. Last semester, I took six courses. <u>And worked part-time in a discount drugstore.</u>
    Now that the term is all over, I don't know how I did it.

    ... courses and worked ...

A Review: How to Check for Sentence Fragments

1 Read your paper aloud from the *last* sentence to the *first*. You will be better able to see and hear whether each word group you read is a complete thought.

2 If you think a word group may be a fragment, ask yourself: Does this contain a subject and a verb and express a complete thought?

3 More specifically, be on the lookout for the most common fragments:

- Dependent-word fragments (starting with words like *after, because, since, when,* and *before*)

- *-ing* and *to* fragments (*-ing* and *to* at or near the start of a word group)

- Added-detail fragments (starting with words like *for example, such as, also,* and *especially*)

- Missing-subject fragments (a verb is present but not the subject)

■ Review Test 1

Each word group in the following student paragraph is numbered. In the space provided, write C if a word group is a complete sentence; write F if it is a fragment. You will find eight fragments in the paragraph.

C	1. ¹I'm starting to think that there is no safe place left. ²To ride a bicycle.
F	2. ³When I try to ride on the highway, in order to go to school. ⁴I feel like a
F	3. rabbit being pursued by predators. ⁵Drivers whip past me at high speeds.
C	4. ⁶And try to see how close they can get to my bike without actually killing
C	5. me. ⁷When they pull onto the shoulder of the road or make a right turn.
F	6. ⁸Drivers completely ignore my vehicle. ⁹On city streets, I feel more like a
F	7. cockroach than a rabbit. ¹⁰Drivers in the city despise bicycles. ¹¹Regardless of
C	8. an approaching bike rider. ¹²Street-side car doors will unexpectedly open.
C	9. ¹³Frustrated drivers who are stuck in traffic will make nasty comments. ¹⁴Or
C	10. shout out obscene propositions. ¹⁵Even pedestrians in the city show their
F	11. disregard for me. ¹⁶While jaywalking across the street. ¹⁷The pedestrian
C	12. will treat me, a law-abiding bicyclist, to a withering look of disdain.
C	13. ¹⁸Pedestrians may even cross my path deliberately. ¹⁹As if to prove their
F	14. higher position in the pecking order of the city streets. ²⁰Today, bicycling
C	15. can be hazardous to the rider's health.
F	16.
C	17.
C	18.
F	19.
C	20.

Now (on separate paper) correct the fragments you have found. Attach the fragments to sentences that come before or after them or make whatever other change is needed to turn each fragment into a sentence.
Answers will vary for this part of the test.

■ Review Test 2

Underline the two fragments in each item below. Then make whatever changes are needed to turn the fragments into sentences.

EXAMPLE   Sharon was going to charge her new suit_x *B*ut then decided to pay cash instead. She remembered her New Year's resolution_x *T*o cut down on her use of credit cards.

1. We both began to tire_x *A*s we passed the halfway mark in the race. But whenever I'd hear Reggie's footsteps behind me_x I would pump my legs faster.

2. I have a few phobias_x *S*uch as fear of heights and fear of dogs. My nightmare is to be trapped in a hot-air balloon_x *W*ith three German shepherds.

3. Punching all the buttons on his radio in sequence_x Phil kept looking for a good song. He was in the mood to cruise down the highway_x *A*nd sing at the top of his voice.

4. My children joke that we celebrate "Hanumas_x" *W*ith our Jewish neighbors. We share Hanukkah and Christmas activities_x *I*ncluding making potato pancakes at their house and decorating our tree.

5. I noticed two cartons of cigarettes_x *S*ticking up out of my neighbor's trash bag. I realized he had made up his mind_x *T*o give up smoking for the fifth time this year.

6. I've decided to leave home_x *A*nd rent an apartment. By being away from home and on my own_x I will get along better with my parents.

7. The alley behind our house was flat_x *E*xcept for a wide groove in the center. We used to sail paper boats down the groove_x *W*henever it rained hard enough to create a "river" there.

8. Don passed the computer school's aptitude test. ~~Which~~ *This* qualifies him for nine months of training. Don kidded that anyone could be accepted_x *I*f he or she had $4,000.

■ **Review Test 3**

Turn each of the following word groups into a complete sentence.

EXAMPLES   With trembling hands

With trembling hands, I headed for the front of the classroom.

As the race wore on

Some runners dropped out as the race wore on.

Answers will vary; examples are given.

1. After the storm passed

. . . passed, the sun came out.

2. Such as fresh fruits and vegetables

I hate any food that's good for me, such as fresh fruits and vegetables.

3. During the mystery movie

. . . movie, I fell asleep.

4. Unless I study harder

. . . harder, I'll flunk out.

5. Enrique, who works at his uncle's restaurant

. . . restaurant, is hoping to become a chef.

6. Knocking over the table

A strong wind suddenly came up, knocking over the table.

7. To get to class on time

. . . on time, Jeannie ran all the way.

8. Hurrying to get dressed

. . . dressed, Dana put his shoes on the wrong feet.

9. Up in the attic

. . . attic is an old violin.

10. Losing my temper

. . . temper, I yelled at the kids.

25 Run-Ons

What Are Run-Ons?

A *run-on* is two complete thoughts that are run together with no adequate sign given to mark the break between them.*

Some run-ons have no punctuation at all to mark the break between the thoughts. Such run-ons are known as *fused sentences:* they are fused, or joined together, as if they were only one thought.

Fused Sentences

The bus stopped suddenly, I spilled coffee all over my shirt.

Mario told everyone in the room to be quiet his favorite show was on.

In other run-ons, known as *comma splices,* a comma is used to connect, or "splice" together, the two complete thoughts. However, a comma alone is *not enough* to connect two complete thoughts. Some stronger connection than a comma alone is needed.

Comma Splices

The bus stopped suddenly. I spilled coffee all over my shirt.

Mario told everyone in the room to be quiet, his favorite show was on.

Comma splices are the most common kind of run-on. Students sense that some kind of connection is needed between two thoughts, and so they often put a comma at the dividing point. But the comma alone is *not sufficient.* A stronger, clearer mark is needed between the two complete thoughts.

Notes:
1. Some instructors regard all run-ons as fused sentences. But for many other instructors, and for our purposes in this book, the term *run-on* applies equally to fused sentences and comma splices. The bottom line is that you do not want either fused sentences or comma splices in your writing.
2. Some instructors refer to each complete thought in a run-on as an *independent clause.* A *clause* is simply a group of words having a subject and a verb. A clause may be *independent* (expressing a complete thought and able to stand alone) or *dependent* (not expressing a complete thought and not able to stand alone). Using this terminology, we'd say that a run-on is two independent clauses run together with no adequate sign given to mark the break between them.

A Warning—Words That Can Lead to Run-Ons   People often write run-ons when the second complete thought begins with one of the following words:

I	we	there	now
you	they	this	then
he, she, it	that	next	

Whenever you use one of these words in writing a paper, remember to be on the alert for run-ons.

How to Correct Run-Ons

Here are three common methods of correcting a run-on:

1   Use a period and a capital letter to break the two complete thoughts into separate sentences:

The bus stopped suddenly. I spilled coffee all over my shirt.
Mario told everyone in the room to be quiet. His favorite show was on.

2   Use a comma plus a joining word (*and, but, for, or, nor, so, yet*) to connect the two complete thoughts:

The bus stopped suddenly, and I spilled coffee all over my shirt.
Mario told everyone in the room to be quiet, for his favorite show was on.

3   Use a semicolon to connect the two complete thoughts:

The bus stopped suddenly; I spilled coffee all over my shirt.
Mario told everyone in the room to be quiet; his favorite show was on.

A fourth method of correcting a run-on is to use *subordination*. The following activities will give you practice in the first three methods. Subordination is described fully on page 115, in the section of the book that deals with sentence variety.

Method 1: Period and a Capital Letter

One way of correcting a run-on is to use a period and a capital letter between the two complete thoughts. Use this method especially if the thoughts are not closely related or if another method would make the sentence too long.

ACTIVITY

In each of the following run-ons, locate the point at which one complete thought ends and another begins. Each is a *fused sentence*—that is, each consists of two sentences fused, or joined together, with no punctuation at all between them. Reading each sentence aloud will help you "hear" where a major break or split between the thoughts occurs. At such a point, your voice will probably drop and pause.

Correct the run-on by putting a period at the end of the first thought and a capital letter at the start of the next thought.

EXAMPLE   Bev's clock radio doesn't work anymore. She spilled a glass of soda on it.

1. The men at the door claimed to have paving material left over from another job. They wanted to pave our driveway for a "bargain price."

2. Linh, a paralegal who speaks Vietnamese, helps other people from her country write wills. She assists others by going with them when they have to appear in court.

3. Vicky has her own unique style of dressing. She wore a man's tuxedo with a red bow tie to her cousin's wedding.

4. In the summer, ants are attracted to water. They will often enter a house through the dishwasher.

5. Humans have managed to adapt to any environment. They can survive in Arctic wastes, tropical jungles, and barren deserts.

6. A five-year-old child knows over six thousand words. He or she has also learned more than one thousand rules of grammar.

7. I rummaged around the crowded drawer looking for a pair of scissors. T̶hen it suddenly stabbed me in the finger.

8. Squirrels like to jump from trees onto our roof. T̶heir footsteps sound like ghosts running around our attic.

9. Today I didn't make good time driving to work. E̶very traffic light along the way was red.

10. Since I started using the Internet, I've sent hundreds of e-mails to my friends. I never write letters by hand anymore.

Method 2: Comma and a Joining Word

Another way of correcting a run-on is to use a comma plus a joining word to connect the two complete thoughts. Joining words (also called *conjunctions*) include *and, but, for, or, nor, so,* and *yet.* Here is what the four most common joining words mean:

and　in addition

> Teresa works full-time for an accounting firm, and she takes evening classes.

(*And* means *in addition:* Teresa works full-time for an accounting firm; *in addition,* she takes evening classes.)

but　however, on the other hand

> I turned to the want ads, but I knew my dream job wouldn't be listed.

(*But* means *however:* I turned to the want ads; *however,* I knew my dream job wouldn't be listed.)

for　because

> Lizards become sluggish at night, for they need the sun's warmth to maintain an active body temperature.

(*For* means *because:* Lizards become sluggish at night *because* they need the sun's warmth to maintain an active body temperature.)

so   as a result, therefore

The canoe touched bottom, so Dave pushed it toward deeper water.

(*So* means *as a result:* The canoe touched bottom; *as a result,* Dave pushed it toward deeper water.)

ACTIVITY 1

Insert the joining word (*and, but, for, so*) that logically connects the two thoughts in each sentence.

1. Napoleon may have been a brave general, _____but_____ he was afraid of cats.

2. The large dog was growling at me, _____and_____ there were white bubbles of foam around its mouth.

3. The library had just closed, _____so_____ I couldn't get any of the reserved books.

4. He checked on the new baby every five minutes, _____for_____ he was afraid that something would happen to her.

5. Kate thought the milk was fresh, _____but_____ it broke up into little sour flakes in her coffee.

6. Elephants have no thumbs, _____so_____ baby elephants suck their trunks.

7. Lonnie heard a noise and looked out the window, _____but_____ the only thing there was his reflection.

8. Although I like most creatures, I am not fond of snakes, _____and_____ I like spiders even less.

9. My sister wants to exercise more and use her car less, _____so_____ she walks to the grocery store.

10. Barry spends hours every day on his computer, _____and_____ he often has the television on at the same time.

ACTIVITY 2

Add a complete and closely related thought to go with each of the following statements. Use a comma plus the indicated joining word when you write the second thought.

EXAMPLE for   I decided to leave school an hour early, _for I had a pounding_
                headache.

Answers will vary; examples are given.

but
1. The corner store is convenient _____
    , but it's not very clean.

for
2. Leo attended night class _____
    , for he had a daytime job.

and
3. Aisha studied for an hour before dinner _____
    , and after dinner she went to the library.

so
4. Paul can't retrieve his e-mail _____
    , so he feels very frustrated.

but
5. I needed a haircut _____
    , but I decided to wait another week.

ACTIVITY 3

Correct each run-on with either (1) a period and a capital letter or (2) a comma and a
logical joining word. Do not use the same method of correction for every sentence.

Some of the run-ons are fused sentences (there is no punctuation between
the two complete thoughts), and some are comma splices (there is only a comma
between the two complete thoughts). One sentence is correct.

EXAMPLE   There was a strange odor in the house, ᐱso Burt called the gas company
            immediately.

Answers may vary; examples are shown.

1. Antonio got a can of soda from the refrigerator, ᐱand then he walked outside to sit
    on the porch steps.

2. Cockroaches adapt to any environment. ᵀthey have even been found living
    inside nuclear reactors.

3. My dog was panting from the heat ᐱ,so I decided to wet him down with the garden
    hose.

4. Our science class is working on a weather project with students from
    Russia. ᵂwe communicate by computer almost every day.

5. The best-selling items in the zoo gift shop are the stuffed pandas and the polar-bear T-shirts, _Tthe profits from these items help support the real animals in the zoo.

6. The bristles of the paintbrushes were very stiff, ^{but} soaking them in turpentine made them soft again.

7. Chen borrows cassettes from the library to listen to on the way to work. ^Ssome are music, and some are recordings of best-selling books.

8. Last week, Rita's two boys chased the baby-sitter out of the house, ^{so} now the sitter won't come back.

9. We knew a power failure had occurred, for all the clocks in the building were forty-seven minutes slow. *Correct*

10. I volunteered to run the "Meals on Wheels" service in our city. ^Wwe deliver hot meals to sick or housebound people.

Method 3: Semicolon

A third method of correcting a run-on is to use a semicolon to mark the break between two thoughts. A *semicolon* (;) looks like a period above a comma and is sometimes called a *strong comma*. A semicolon signals more of a pause than a comma alone but not quite the full pause of a period. When it is used to correct run-ons, the semicolon can be used alone or with a transitional word.

Semicolon Alone Here are some earlier sentences that were connected with a comma plus a joining word. Now they are connected by a semicolon alone. Notice that the semicolon alone—unlike the comma alone—can be used to connect the two complete thoughts in each sentence:

> Lonnie heard a noise and looked out the window; the only thing there was his reflection.
>
> He checked on the new baby every five minutes; he was afraid something would happen to her.
>
> Lizards become sluggish at night; they need the sun's warmth to maintain an active body temperature.

The large dog was growling at me; there were white bubbles of foam around its mouth.

We knew a power failure had occurred; all the clocks in the building were forty-seven minutes slow.

Using semicolons can add to sentence variety. For some people, however, the semicolon is a confusing punctuation mark. Keep in mind that if you are not comfortable using it, you can and should use one of the the first two methods of correcting run-ons.

ACTIVITY

Insert a semicolon where the break occurs between the two complete thoughts in each of the following sentences.

EXAMPLE   The plumber gave me an estimate of $60;I decided to repair the faucet myself.

1. The children stared at the artichokes on their plates;they didn't know how to eat the strange vegetable.
2. I changed that lightbulb just last week;now it's blown again.
3. The Great Wall of China is immense;it's the only man-made structure visible from the Moon.
4. Elaine woke up at 3 A.M. to the smell of sizzling bacon;her husband was having another insomnia attack.
5. Maya curled up under the covers;she tried to get warm by grasping her icy feet with her chilly hands.
6. Three single mothers rent one house;they share bills and help each other out.
7. Ice had formed on the inside edge of our window;Joey scratched a J in it with his finger.
8. Charles peered into the microscope;he saw only his own eyelashes.
9. A man in a bear suit walked slowly down the street;the children stopped their play to stare at him.
10. I angrily punched a hole in the wall with my fist;later I covered the hole with a picture.

Semicolon with a Transitional Word   A semicolon can be used with a transitional word and a comma to join two complete thoughts. Here are some examples:

Larry believes in being prepared for emergencies; therefore, he stockpiles canned goods in his basement.

I tried to cash my paycheck; however, I had forgotten to bring identification.

Athletic shoes must fit perfectly; otherwise, wearers may injure their feet or ankles.

A short nap at the end of the day relaxes me; in addition, it gives me the energy to spend the evening on my homework.

Some zoo animals have not learned how to be good parents; as a result, baby animals are sometimes brought up in zoo nurseries and even in private homes.

People use seventeen muscles when they smile; on the other hand, they use forty-three muscles when they frown.

Following is a list of common transitional words (also known as *adverbial conjunctions*), with brief meanings.

Transitional Word	Meaning
however	but
nevertheless	however
on the other hand	however
instead	as a substitute
meanwhile	in the intervening time
otherwise	under other conditions
indeed	in fact
in addition	also, and
also	in addition
moreover	in addition
furthermore	in addition
as a result	thus, therefore
thus	as a result
consequently	as a result
therefore	as a result

ACTIVITY

For each sentence, choose a logical transitional word from the box above, and write it in the space provided. Use a semicolon *before* the connector and a comma *after* it.

EXAMPLE I dread going to parties; _____*however,*_____ my husband loves meeting new people.

Some answers may vary.

1. Jackie suffers from migraine headaches _____*; therefore,*_____ her doctor has advised her to avoid caffeine and alcohol.

2. Ray's apartment is always neat and clean _____*; on the other hand,*_____ the interior of his car looks like the aftermath of a tornado.

3. I try to attend all my math classes _____*; otherwise,*_____ I'll get too far behind to pass the weekly quizzes.

4. B. J. was singing Aretha Franklin tunes in the shower _____*; meanwhile,*_____ his toast was burning in the kitchen.

5. The reporter was tough and experienced _____*; however,*_____ even he was stunned by the tragic events.

A Note on Subordination

A fourth method of joining related thoughts is to use subordination. *Subordination* is a way of showing that one thought in a sentence is not as important as another thought. (Subordination is explained in full on page 115.) Below are three earlier sentences, recast so that one idea is subordinated to (made less important than) the other idea. In each case, the subordinate (or less important) thought is underlined. Note that each subordinate clause begins with a dependent word.

Because the library had just closed, I couldn't get any of the reserved books.

When the canoe touched bottom, Dave pushed the craft toward deeper water.

I didn't make good time driving to work today because every traffic light along the way was red.

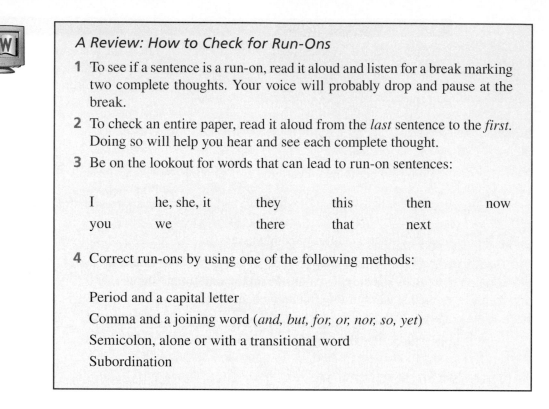

A Review: How to Check for Run-Ons

1 To see if a sentence is a run-on, read it aloud and listen for a break marking two complete thoughts. Your voice will probably drop and pause at the break.

2 To check an entire paper, read it aloud from the *last* sentence to the *first.* Doing so will help you hear and see each complete thought.

3 Be on the lookout for words that can lead to run-on sentences:

I	he, she, it	they	this	then	now
you	we	there	that	next	

4 Correct run-ons by using one of the following methods:

Period and a capital letter

Comma and a joining word (*and, but, for, or, nor, so, yet*)

Semicolon, alone or with a transitional word

Subordination

■ Review Test 1

Correct each run-on with either (1) a period and a capital letter or (2) a comma (if needed) and the joining word *and, but, for,* or *so.* Do not use the same method of correction for every sentence.

Some of the run-ons are fused sentences (there is no punctuation between the two complete thoughts), and some are comma splices (there is only a comma between the two complete thoughts). One sentence is correct.

Some answers may vary.

1. Our boss expects us to work four hours without a break, *but* he wanders off to a vending machine at least once an hour.

2. The children in the next car were making faces at other drivers. *W*hen I made a face back, they giggled and sank out of sight.

3. Chuck bent over and lifted the heavy tray. *T*hen he heard an ominous crack in his back.

4. The branches of the tree were bare *, and* they made a dark feathery pattern against the orange-pink sunset.

5. In the dark alley, the air smelled like rotten garbage *, and* a large rat crept in the shadows.

6. Our class wanted to do something for the earthquake victims, *so* we sent a donation to the Red Cross.

7. My ex-husband hit me just once in our marriage. *F*ive minutes later I was packed and walking out the door.

8. Aunt Jeanne thought a warm dry climate would improve her health *, so* she moved to Arizona.

9. The average American teenager spends thirty-eight hours a week on schoolwork *.* *T*he average Japanese teenager spends about sixty.

10. We stocked our backpacks with high-calorie candy bars, and we also brought bags of dried apricots and peaches. *Correct*

Review Test 2

Correct each run-on by using (1) a period and a capital letter, (2) a comma and a joining word, or (3) a semicolon. Do not use one method exclusively.

Answers may vary.

1. The magazine had lain in the damp mailbox for two days*;* its pages were blurry and swollen.

2. With a groan, Margo pried off her high heels, *and* then she plunged her swollen feet into a bucket of baking soda and hot water.

3. At 2 A.M. the last customer left the diner, *and* a busboy began stacking chairs on the tables for the night.

4. Hypnosis has nothing to do with the occult. *I*t is merely a state of deep relaxation.

5. Many young adults today live at home with their parents ^(, for) this allows them to save money.

6. I waited for the clanking train to clear the intersection ^(, but) rusty boxcars just kept rolling slowly along the rails.

7. Early in life, Thomas Edison suffered with deafness, ^(so) he taught his wife- to-be Morse code while he was courting her.

8. Originally, horses were too small to carry riders very far ^(, so) larger horses had to be bred for use in warfare.

9. The words *month, silver, purple,* and *orange* have something in common ~~,~~ . ^(N)~~n~~o other English words rhyme with them.

10. The broken soda machine dispensed a cup or soda, ^(but) it would not provide both at the same time.

◼ Review Test 3

Locate and correct the five run-ons in the passage that follows.
Corrections may vary.

My worst experience of the week was going home for lunch, rather than eating at work. My children didn't know I was coming, ^(so) they had used most of the bread. All I had to make a sandwich with were two thin, crumpled pieces of crust. I sat there eating my tattered sandwich and trying to relax, ^(but) then the telephone rang. It was for my daughter, who was in the bathroom ~~,~~ ^(;) she called down to me that I should get the person's name and number. As soon as I sat down again, someone knocked on the door ~~,~~ ^(I)~~i~~t was a neatly dressed couple with bright eyes who wanted to talk with me about a higher power in life. I politely got rid of them and went back to finish lunch. I thought I would relax over my coffee ^(, but) I had to break up a fight between my two young sons about which television channel to watch. As a last bit of frustration, my daughter came downstairs and asked me to drive her over to a friend's house before I went back to work.

■ Review Test 4

On separate paper, write quickly for five minutes about what you did this past weekend. Don't worry about spelling, punctuation, finding exact words, or organizing your thoughts. Just focus on writing as many words as you can without stopping.

After you have finished, go back and correct any run-ons in your writing.

26 Regular and Irregular Verbs

Regular Verbs

A Brief Review of Regular Verbs

18.1

Every verb has four principal parts: *present, past, past participle,* and *present participle.* These parts can be used to build all the verb *tenses*—the times shown by verbs.

Most verbs in English are regular. The past and past participle of a regular verb are formed by adding *-d* or *-ed* to the present. The *past participle* is the form of the verb used with the helping verbs *have, has,* or *had* (or some form of *be* with passive verbs). The *present participle* is formed by adding *-ing* to the present.

Here are the principal parts of some regular verbs:

Present	*Past*	*Past Participle*	*Present Participle*
shout	shouted	shouted	shouting
prepare	prepared	prepared	preparing
surprise	surprised	surprised	surprising
tease	teased	teased	teasing
frighten	frightened	frightened	frightening

Nonstandard Forms of Regular Verbs

Many people have grown up in communities where nonstandard forms of regular verbs are used in everyday speech. Instead of saying, for example, "That girl *looks* tired," a person using a community dialect might say, "That girl *look* tired." Instead of saying, "Yesterday I *fixed* the car," a person using a community dialect might say, "Yesterday I *fix* the car." Community dialects have richness and power but are a drawback in college and in the world of work, where regular English verb forms must be used.

The following chart compares the nonstandard and the regular verb forms of the verb *work*.

Nonstandard Verb Form		Regular Verb Form	
(Do *not* use in your writing)		(Use for clear communication)	
Present tense			
~~I works~~	~~we works~~	I work	we work
~~you works~~	~~you works~~	you work	you work
~~he, she, it work~~	~~they works~~	he, she, it works	they work
Past tense			
~~I work~~	~~we work~~	I worked	we worked
~~you work~~	~~you work~~	you worked	you worked
~~he, she, it work~~	~~they work~~	he, she, it worked	they worked

To avoid nonstandard usage, memorize the forms shown above for the regular verb *work*. Then use the activities that follow to help make the inclusion of verb endings a writing habit.

18.2a

Present Tense Endings   The verb ending *-s* or *-es* is needed with a regular verb in the present tense when the subject is *he, she, it,* or any *one person or thing.*

He reads every night.

She watches television every night.

It appears they have little in common.

ACTIVITY

Some verbs in the sentences that follow need *-s* or *-es* endings. Cross out each nonstandard verb form and write the standard form in the space provided.

__wakes__   1. My radio ~~wake~~ me up every morning with soft music.

__clowns__   2. Felix always ~~clown~~ around at the start of the class.

__watches__   3. My wife ~~watch~~ our baby in the morning, and I take over afternoons.

wants   4. Brenda ~~want~~ to go to nursing school next year.

works   5. My brain ~~work~~ much better at night than it does in early morning.

Past Tense Endings   The verb ending -*d* or -*ed* is needed with a regular verb in the past tense.

> This morning I completed my research paper.
>
> The recovering hospital patient walked slowly down the corridor.
>
> Some students hissed when the new assignment was given out.

ACTIVITY

Some verbs in the sentences that follow need -*d* or -*ed* endings. Cross out each nonstandard verb form and write the standard form in the space provided.

cracked   1. One of my teeth ~~crack~~ when I bit on the hard pretzel.

complained   2. The accident victim ~~complain~~ of dizziness right before passing out.

realized   3. We ~~realize~~ a package was missing when we got back from shopping.

burned   4. I ~~burn~~ a hole in my shirt while ironing it.

edged   5. The driver ~~edge~~ her car into the intersection while the light was still red.

Irregular Verbs

Irregular verbs have irregular forms in past tense and past participle. For example, the past tense of the irregular verb *choose* is *chose;* its past participle is *chosen.*

Almost everyone has some degree of trouble with irregular verbs. When you are unsure about the form of a verb, you can check the following list of irregular verbs. (The present participle is not shown on this list because it is formed simply by adding -*ing* to the base form of the verb.) Or you can check a dictionary, which gives the principal parts of irregular verbs.

A List of Irregular Verbs

Present	Past	Past Participle
arise	arose	arisen
awake	awoke *or* awaked	awoken *or* awaked
be (am, are, is)	was (were)	been

Present	Past	Past Participle
become	became	become
begin	began	begun
bend	bent	bent
bite	bit	bitten
blow	blew	blown
break	broke	broken
bring	brought	brought
build	built	built
burst	burst	burst
buy	bought	bought
catch	caught	caught
choose	chose	chosen
come	came	come
cost	cost	cost
cut	cut	cut
do (does)	did	done
draw	drew	drawn
drink	drank	drunk
drive	drove	driven
eat	ate	eaten
fall	fell	fallen
feed	fed	fed
feel	felt	felt
fight	fought	fought
find	found	found
fly	flew	flown
freeze	froze	frozen
get	got	got *or* gotten
give	gave	given
go (goes)	went	gone
grow	grew	grown
have (has)	had	had
hear	heard	heard
hide	hid	hidden
hold	held	held
hurt	hurt	hurt
keep	kept	kept
know	knew	known
lay	laid	laid
lead	led	led

Present	Past	Past Participle
leave	left	left
lend	lent	lent
let	let	let
lie	lay	lain
light	lit	lit
lose	lost	lost
make	made	made
meet	met	met
pay	paid	paid
ride	rode	ridden
ring	rang	rung
run	ran	run
say	said	said
see	saw	seen
sell	sold	sold
send	sent	sent
shake	shook	shaken
shrink	shrank	shrunk
shut	shut	shut
sing	sang	sung
sit	sat	sat
sleep	slept	slept
speak	spoke	spoken
spend	spent	spent
stand	stood	stood
steal	stole	stolen
stick	stuck	stuck
sting	stung	stung
swear	swore	sworn
swim	swam	swum
take	took	taken
teach	taught	taught
tear	tore	torn
tell	told	told
think	thought	thought
wake	woke *or* waked	woke *or* waked
wear	wore	worn
win	won	won
write	wrote	written

ACTIVITY

Cross out the incorrect verb form in each of the following sentences. Then write the correct form of the verb in the space provided.

flown   **EXAMPLE**   After it had ~~flew~~ into the picture window, the dazed bird huddled on the ground.

chosen   1. As graduation neared, Michelle worried about the practicality of the major she'd ~~chose~~.

began   2. Before we could find seats, the theater darkened and the opening credits ~~begun~~ to roll.

drank   3. To be polite, I ~~drunk~~ the slightly sour wine that my grandfather poured from his carefully hoarded supply.

broke   4. With a thunderous crack, the telephone pole ~~breaked~~ in half from the impact of the speeding car.

shrank   5. The inexperienced nurse ~~shrunk~~ from touching the patient's raw, burned skin.

rang   6. After a day on the noisy construction site, Sam's ears ~~rung~~ for hours with a steady hum.

forgotten   7. Sheila had ~~forgot~~ to write her social security number on the test form, so the computer rejected her answer sheet.

gone   8. If I had ~~went~~ to work ten minutes earlier, I would have avoided being caught in the gigantic traffic snarl.

thrown   9. After the bicycle hit a patch of soft sand, the rider was ~~throwed~~ into the thorny bushes along the roadside.

blew   10. Prehistoric people ~~blowed~~ paint over their outstretched hands to stencil their handprints on cave walls.

Nonstandard Forms of Three Common Irregular Verbs

People who use nonstandard forms of regular verbs also tend to use nonstandard forms of three common irregular verbs: *be, have,* and *do.* Instead of saying, for example, "My neighbors *are* nice people," a person using a nonstandard form might say, "My neighbors *be* nice people." Instead of saying, "She doesn't agree," they might say, "She *don't* agree." Instead of saying, "We have tickets," they might say, "We *has* tickets."

The following charts compare the nonstandard and the standard forms of *be*, *have*, and *do*.

Be

Community Dialect		Standard English	
(Do *not* use in your writing)		(Use for clear communication)	
Present tense			
~~I be (*or* is)~~	~~we be~~	I am	we are
you be	you be	you are	you are
~~he, she, it be~~	~~they be~~	he, she, it is	they are
Past tense			
~~I were~~	~~we was~~	I was	we were
you was	you was	you were	you were
~~he, she, it were~~	~~they was~~	he, she, it was	they were

Have

Community Dialect		Standard English	
(Do *not* use in your writing)		(Use for clear communication)	
Present tense			
~~I has~~	~~we has~~	I have	we have
you has	you has	you have	you have
~~he, she, it have~~	~~they has~~	he, she, it has	they have
Past tense			
~~I has~~	~~we has~~	I had	we had
you has	you has	you had	you had
~~he, she, it have~~	~~they has~~	he, she, it had	they had

Do

Community Dialect		*Standard English*	
(Do *not* use in your writing)		(Use for clear communication)	

Present tense

Community Dialect		Standard English	
~~I does~~	~~we do~~	I do	we do
you does	you does	you do	you do
~~he, she, it do~~	they ~~does~~	he, she, it does	they do

Past tense

Community Dialect		Standard English	
~~I done~~	~~we done~~	I did	we did
you done	you done	you did	you did
~~he, she, it done~~	they ~~done~~	he, she, it did	they did

Note   Many people have trouble with one negative form of *do*. They will say, for example, "He don't agree" instead of "He doesn't agree," or they will say "The door don't work" instead of "The door doesn't work." Be careful to avoid the common mistake of using *don't* instead of *doesn't*.

ACTIVITY

Cross out the nonstandard verb form in each sentence. Then write the standard form of *be, have,* or *do* in the space provided.

is	1. My cat, Tugger, ~~be~~ the toughest animal I know.
has	2. He ~~have~~ survived many close calls.
was	3. Three years ago, he ~~were~~ caught inside a car's engine.
had	4. He ~~have~~ one ear torn off and lost the sight in one eye.
were	5. We ~~was~~ surprised that he lived through the accident.
was	6. Within weeks, though, he ~~were~~ back to normal.
were	7. Then, last year, we ~~was~~ worried that we would lose Tugger.
were	8. Lumps that ~~was~~ growing on his back turned out to be cancer.
did	9. But the vet ~~done~~ an operation that saved Tugger's life.
does	10. By now, we know that Tugger really ~~do~~ have nine lives.

■ Review Test 1

Cross out the incorrect verb form in each sentence. Then write the correct form in the space provided.

walked   1. The health inspectors ~~walk~~ into the kitchen as the cook was picking up a hamburger off the floor.

stolen   2. The thieves would have ~~stole~~ my stereo, but I had had it engraved with a special identification number.

chose   3. At the Chinese restaurant, Hollis ~~choose~~ his food by the number.

torn   4. He had ~~tore~~ his girlfriend's picture into little pieces and tossed them out the window.

have   5. Because I ~~has~~ asthma, I carry an inhaler to use when I have trouble breathing.

don't   6. Baked potatoes ~~doesn't~~ have as many calories as I thought.

began   7. The grizzly bear, with the dart dangling from its side, ~~begun~~ to feel the effects of the powerful tranquilizer.

checked   8. Yesterday I ~~check~~ my bank balance and saw that my money was getting low.

have   9. Many childhood diseases ~~has~~ almost vanished in the United States.

stuck   10. Nancy ~~sticked~~ notes on the refrigerator with fruit-shaped magnets.

■ Review Test 2

Write short sentences that use the form requested for the following verbs.

EXAMPLE Past of _grow_ _I grew my own tomatoes last year._
Answers will vary; examples are given.

1. Past of _know_ _I knew I could pass the course, and I did._

2. Present of _take_ _To get to work, Luz takes two buses and a subway._

3. Past participle of _give_ _Mom has always given me good advice._

4. Past participle of _write_ _Have you ever written a narrative essay?_

5. Past of _do_ _As a schoolchild, I never did my homework until the last minute._

6. Past of _talk_ _They talked for an hour before finally hanging up._

7. Present of _begin_ _An opera usually begins with an overture._

8. Past of _go_ _After work, Todd went shopping._

9. Past participle of _see_ _I have not seen my cousin for years._

10. Present of _drive_ _My kids drive me crazy sometimes._

27 Subject-Verb Agreement

17

A verb must agree with its subject in number. A *singular subject* (one person or thing) takes a singular verb. A *plural subject* (more than one person or thing) takes a plural verb. Mistakes in subject-verb agreement are sometimes made in the following situations:

1   When words come between the subject and the verb
2   When a verb comes before the subject
3   With compound subjects
4   With indefinite pronouns

Each of these situations is explained in this chapter.

Words between Subject and Verb

Words that come between the subject and the verb do not change subject-verb agreement. In the sentence

> The sharp <u>fangs</u> in the dog's mouth <u>look</u> scary.

the subject (*fangs*) is plural, and so the verb (*look*) is plural. The words that come between the subject and the verb are a prepositional phrase: *in the dog's mouth.* They do not affect subject-verb agreement. (A list of prepositions can be found on page 413.)

To help find the subject of certain sentences, you should cross out prepositional phrases.

17.5d

> The lumpy <u>salt</u> ~~in the shakers~~ <u>needs</u> to be changed.
> An old <u>chair</u> ~~with broken legs~~ <u>has sat</u> in our basement for years.

ACTIVITY

Underline the subject and lightly cross out any words that come between the subject and the verb. Then double-underline the verb in parentheses that you believe is correct.

1. Some members of the parents' association (want, <u>wants</u>) to ban certain books from the school library.
2. Chung's trench coat, with its big lapels and shoulder flaps, (make, <u>makes</u>) him feel like a tough private eye.
3. Misconceptions about apes like the gorilla (has, <u>have</u>) turned a relatively peaceful animal into a terrifying monster.
4. The rising cost of necessities like food and shelter (force, <u>forces</u>) many elderly people to live in poverty.
5. In my opinion, a few slices of pepperoni pizza (<u>make</u>, makes) a great evening.

Verb before Subject

A verb agrees with its subject even when the verb comes *before* the subject. Words that may precede the subject include *there, here,* and, in questions, *who, which, what,* and *where.*

Here are some examples of sentences in which the verb appears before the subject:

There are wild dogs in our neighborhood.
In the distance was a billow of black smoke.
Here is the newspaper.
Where are the children's coats?

If you are unsure about the subject, ask *who* or *what* of the verb. With the first example above, you might ask, "*What* are in our neighborhood?" The answer, *wild dogs,* is the subject.

ACTIVITY

Write the correct form of each verb in the space provided.

(is, are)   1. There __are__ dozens of frenzied shoppers waiting for the store to open.

(is, are)   2. Here ___are___ the notes from yesterday's anthropology lecture.

(do, does)   3. When ___do___ we take our break?

(was, were)   4. There ___were___ scraps of yellowing paper stuck between the pages of the cookbook.

(was, were)   5. At the very bottom of the grocery list ___was___ an item that meant a trip all the way back to aisle one.

Compound Subjects

ALLWRITE!
17.2

A *compound subject* is two subjects separated by a joining word, such as *and*. Subjects joined by *and* generally take a plural verb.

> A patchwork quilt and a sleeping bag cover my bed in the winter.
> Clark and Lois are a contented couple.

When subjects are joined by *either . . . or, neither . . . nor, not only . . . but also,* the verb agrees with the subject closer to the verb.

> Neither the negotiator nor the union leaders want the strike to continue.

The nearer subject, *leaders*, is plural, and so the verb is plural.

> Neither the union leaders nor the negotiator wants the strike to continue.

In this version, the nearer subject, *negotiator,* is singular, so the verb is singular.

ACTIVITY

Write the correct form of the verb in the space provided.

(sit, sits)   1. A crusty baking pan and a greasy plate ___sit___ on the countertop.

(cover, covers)   2. Spidery cracks and a layer of dust ___cover___ the ivory keys on the old piano.

(know, knows)   3. Not only the assistant managers but also the secretary ___knows___ that the company is folding.

(was, were)   4. In eighteenth-century France, makeup and high heels ___were___ worn by men.

(smell, smells)   5. Either the trash can or those socks ___smell___ horrible.

Indefinite Pronouns

17.5

The following words, known as *indefinite pronouns,* always take singular verbs:

(*-one* words)	(*-body* words)	(*-thing* words)	
one	nobody	nothing	each
anyone	anybody	anything	either
everyone	everybody	everything	neither
someone	somebody	something	

Note   *Both* always takes a plural verb.

ACTIVITY

Write the correct form of the verb in the space provided.

(suit, suits)

1. Neither of those hairstyles ___suits___ the shape of your face.

(mention, mentions)

2. Somebody without much sensitivity always ___mentions___ my birthmark.

(is, are)

3. Both of the puppies ___are___ cute in their own ways.

(enter, enters)

4. Everyone ___enters___ the college kite-flying contest in the spring.

(fall, falls)

5. One of these earrings constantly ___falls___ off my ear.

Review Test 1

In the space provided, write the correct form of the verb shown in the margin.

(is, are)

1. Some wheelchair-bound patients, as a result of a successful experiment, ___are___ using trained monkeys as helpers.

(was, were)

2. Each of their children ___was___ given a name picked at random from a page of the Bible.

(seem, seems)

3. Many of the headlines in the *National Enquirer* ___seem___ hard to believe.

(is, are)   4. Envelopes, file folders, and a telephone book ___are___ jammed into Lupe's kitchen drawers.

(contains, contain)   5. Neither of the main dishes at tonight's dinner ___contains___ any meat.

(damage, damages)   6. The use of metal chains and studded tires ___damages___ roadways because metal and studs chip away at the paved surface.

(was, were)   7. Next to the cash register ___was___ a can for donations to the animal protection society.

(makes, make)   8. A metal grab bar bolted onto the tiles ___makes___ it easier for elderly people to get into and out of the bathtub.

(cleans, clean)   9. In exchange for reduced rent, Karla and James ___clean___ the dentist's office beneath their second-floor apartment.

(is, are)   10. One of the hospital's delivery rooms ___is___ furnished with bright carpets and curtains to resemble a room at home.

■ Review Test 2

Cross out the incorrect verb form in each sentence. In addition, underline the subject or subjects that go with the verb. Then write the correct form of the verb in the space provided.

___are___   1. Why is Martha and her mother digging a hole in their garden so late at night?

___looks___   2. Neither of my children look like me.

___were___   3. Three goats, a potbellied pig, and a duck was among the entrants in the pet parade.

___look___   4. The little balls all over my pink sweater looks like woolen goose bumps.

___are___   5. Here is the low-calorie cola and the double-chocolate cake you ordered.

___interferes___   6. The odor of those perfumed ads interfere with my enjoyment of a magazine.

___is___   7. One of my roommates are always leaving wet towels on the bathroom floor.

___are___   8. A tiny piece of gum and some tape is holding my old glasses together.

___begins___   9. A person in his or her forties often begin to think about making a contribution to the world and not just about himself or herself.

___has___   10. Each of the child's thirty-four stuffed animals have a name and an entire life history.

■ Review Test 3

Complete each of the following sentences using *is, are, was, were, have,* or *has.*
Then underline the subject.

EXAMPLE For me, <u>popcorn</u> at the movies <u>is like coffee at breakfast.</u>
Answers will vary.

1. The <u>magazines</u> under my roommate's bed <u>are collecting dust.</u>

2. The <u>car</u> with the purple fenders <u>is Ken's.</u>

3. My <u>boss</u> and her <u>secretary</u> <u>were both out sick today.</u>

4. <u>Neither</u> of the football players <u>was able to score.</u>

5. Here <u>are the sneakers you</u> were looking for.

28 Additional Information about Verbs

The purpose of this chapter is to provide additional information about verbs. Some people will find the grammatical terms here a helpful reminder of what they've learned earlier, in school, about verbs. For them, the terms will increase their understanding of how verbs function in English. Other people may welcome more detailed information about terms used elsewhere in the text. In either case, remember that the most common mistakes people make with verbs have been treated in previous chapters of the book.

Verb Tense

18.1

Verbs tell us the time of an action. The time that a verb shows is usually called *tense*. The most common tenses are the simple present, past, and future. In addition, there are nine tenses that enable us to express more specific ideas about time than we could with the simple tenses alone. Following are the twelve verb tenses and examples of each tense. Read them over to increase your sense of the many different ways of expressing time in English.

Tenses	*Examples*
Present	I *work.* Tony *works.*
Past	Ellen *worked* on her car.
Future	You *will work* on a new project next week.
Present perfect	He *has worked* on his term paper for a month. They *have worked* out a compromise.
Past perfect	The nurse *had worked* two straight shifts.
Future perfect	Next Monday, I *will have worked* here exactly two years.

continued

Tenses	Examples
Present progressive	I *am working* on my speech for the debate. You *are working* too hard. The tape recorder *is* not *working* properly.
Past progressive	He *was working* in the basement. The contestants *were working* on their talent routines.
Future progressive	My son *will be working* in our store this summer.
Present perfect progressive	Sarah *has been working* late this week.
Past perfect progressive	Until recently, I *had been working* nights.
Future perfect progressive	My mother *will have been working* as a nurse for forty-five years by the time she retires.

ACTIVITY

On a separate paper, write twelve sentences using the twelve verb tenses.
Answers will vary.

Helping Verbs

18.3

There are three common verbs that can either stand alone or combine with (and "help") other verbs. Here are the verbs and their forms:

> be (am, are, is, was, were, being, been)
> have (has, having, had)
> do (does, did)

Here are examples of the helping verbs:

Used Alone	**Used as Helping Verbs**
I *was* angry.	I *was growing* angry.
Sue *has* the key.	Sue *has forgotten* the key.
He *did* well in the test.	He *did fail* the previous test.

There are nine helping verbs (traditionally known as *modals,* or *modal auxiliaries*) that are always used in combination with other verbs. Here are the nine verbs and a sentence example of each:

can	I *can see* the rainbow.
could	I *could* not *find* a seat.
may	The game *may be postponed.*
might	Cindy *might resent* your advice.
shall	I *shall see* you tomorrow.
should	He *should get* his car serviced.
will	Tony *will want* to see you.
would	They *would* not *understand.*
must	You *must visit* us again.

Note from the examples that these verbs have only one form. They do not, for instance, add an *-s* when used with *he, she, it,* or any one person or thing.

ACTIVITY

On separate paper, write nine sentences using the nine helping verbs.
Answers will vary.

Verbals

18.4

Verbals are words formed from verbs. Verbals, like verbs, often express action. They can add variety to your sentences and vigor to your writing style. The three kinds of verbals are *infinitives, participles,* and *gerunds.*

Infinitive

An infinitive is *to* plus the base form of the verb.

> I love *to dance.*
>
> Lina hopes *to write* for a newspaper.
>
> I asked the children *to clean* the kitchen.

Participle

A participle is a verb form used as an adjective (a descriptive word). The present participle ends in *-ing.* The part participle ends in *-ed* or has an irregular ending.

> *Peering* into the cracked mirror, the *crying* woman wiped her eyes.
>
> The *astounded* man stared at his *winning* lottery ticket.
>
> *Swinging* a sharp ax, Omar split the *rotted* beam.

Gerund

A gerund is the *-ing* form of a verb used as a noun.

> *Swimming* is the perfect exercise.
>
> *Eating* junk food is my diet downfall.
>
> Through *doodling,* people express their inner feelings.

ACTIVITY

On separate paper, write three sentences using infinitives, three sentences using participles, and three sentences using gerunds.

Answers will vary.

29 Pronoun Agreement and Reference

Nouns name persons, places, or things. *Pronouns* are words that take the place of nouns. In fact, the word *pronoun* means "for a noun." Pronouns are shortcuts that keep you from unnecessarily repeating words in writing. Here are some examples of pronouns:

> Eddie left *his* camera on the bus.
> (*His* is a pronoun that takes the place of *Eddie's*.)

> Elena drank the coffee even though *it* was cold.
> (*It* replaces *coffee*.)

> As I turned the newspaper's damp pages, *they* disintegrated in my hands.
> (*They* is a pronoun that takes the place of *pages*.)

This chapter presents rules that will help you avoid two common mistakes people make with pronouns. The rules are:

1   A pronoun must agree in number with the word or words it replaces.
2   A pronoun must refer clearly to the word it replaces.

Pronoun Agreement

17.8

A pronoun must agree in number with the word or words it replaces. If the word a pronoun refers to is singular, the pronoun must be singular; if that word is plural, the pronoun must be plural. (Note that the word a pronoun refers to is known as the *antecedent*.)

> Marie showed me (her) antique wedding band.

> Students enrolled in the art class must provide (their) own supplies.

In the first example, the pronoun *her* refers to the singular word *Marie;* in the second example, the pronoun *their* refers to the plural word *Students*.

463

Write the appropriate pronoun (*their, they, them, it*) in the blank space in each of the following sentences.

EXAMPLE   I opened the wet umbrella and put _____*it*_____ in the bathtub to dry.

1. Kate and Omar left for the movies earlier than usual, because _____*they*_____ knew the theater would be packed.

2. The clothes were still damp, but I decided to fold _____*them*_____ anyway.

3. Young adults often face a difficult transition period when _____*they*_____ leave home for the first time.

4. Paul's grandparents renewed _____*their*_____ marriage vows at a huge fiftieth wedding anniversary celebration.

5. The car's steering wheel began to pull to one side, and then _____*it*_____ started to shimmy.

Indefinite Pronouns

17.8

The following words, known as *indefinite pronouns,* are always singular.

(-one words)	*(-body* words)	
one	nobody	each
anyone	anybody	either
everyone	everybody	neither
someone	somebody	

If a pronoun in a sentence refers to one of these singular words, the pronoun should be singular.

Somebody left (her) shoulder bag on the back of a chair.

One of the busboys just called and said (he) would be an hour late.

Everyone in the club must pay (his) dues next week.

Each circled pronoun is singular because it refers to an indefinite pronoun.

Note   There are two important points to remember about indefinite pronouns:

1 In the last example, if everyone in the club was a woman, the pronoun would be *her*. If the club had women and men, the pronoun would be *his or her:*

> Everyone in the club must pay his or her dues next week.

Some writers follow the traditional practice of using *his* to refer to both women and men. Some now use *his or her* to avoid an implied sexual bias. To avoid using *his* or the somewhat awkward *his or her,* a sentence can often be rewritten in the plural:

> Club members must pay their dues next week.

2 In informal spoken English, *plural* pronouns are often used with the indefinite pronouns. Many people would probably not say:

> Everybody has his or her own opinion about the election.

Instead, they would be likely to say:

> Everybody has their own opinion about the election.

Here are other examples:

> Everyone in the choir must buy their robes.
> Everybody in the line has their ticket ready.
> No one in the class remembered to bring their books.

In such cases, the indefinite pronouns are clearly plural in meaning, and using them helps people avoid the awkward *his or her*. In time, the plural pronoun may be accepted in formal speech or writing. Until then, however, you should use the grammatically correct singular form in your writing.

ACTIVITY

Underline the correct pronoun.

1. Neither of the potential buyers had really made up (her, their) mind.
2. Not one of the new cashiers knows what (he, they) should be doing.
3. Each of these computers has (its, their) drawbacks.

4. Anyone trying to reduce (<u>his or her</u>, their) salt intake should avoid canned and processed foods.

5. If anybody calls when I'm out, tell (<u>him</u>, them) I'll return in an hour.

Pronoun Reference

19.5

A sentence may be confusing and unclear if a pronoun appears to refer to more than one word or does not refer to any specific word. Look at this sentence:

Miriam was annoyed when they failed her car for a faulty turn signal.

Who failed her car? There is no specific word that *they* refers to. Be clear:

Miriam was annoyed when the inspectors failed her car for a faulty turn signal.

Here are sentences with other faulty pronoun references. Read the explanations of why they are faulty and look carefully at how they are corrected.

Faulty	Clear
Peter told Alan that his wife was unhappy. (Whose wife is unhappy: Peter's or Alan's? Be clear.)	Peter told Alan, "My wife is unhappy."
Kia is really a shy person, but she keeps it hidden. (There is no specific word that *it* refers to. It would not make sense to say, "Kia keeps shy hidden.")	Kia is really a shy person, but she keeps her shyness hidden.
Marsha attributed her success to her husband's support, which was generous. (Does *which* mean that Marsha's action was generous or that her husband's support was generous?)	Generously, Marsha attributed her success to her husband's support. *Or:* Marsha attributed her success to her husband's generous support.

ACTIVITY

Rewrite each of the following sentences to make clear the vague pronoun reference. Add, change, or omit words as necessary.

EXAMPLE Susan's mother wondered if she was tall enough to be a model.

Susan's mother wondered if Susan was tall enough to be a model.

Answers may vary.

1. Dad spent all day fishing but didn't catch a single one.

   . . . a single fish.

2. At that fast-food restaurant, they give you free glasses with your soft drinks.

   The waiters at that fast-food restaurant give you . . .

3. Ruth told Denise that her bouts of depression were becoming serious.

   Ruth told Denise, "My bouts of depression are becoming serious."

4. Dipping her spoon into the pot of simmering spaghetti sauce, Helen felt it slip out of her hand.

   . . . felt the spoon slip out of her hand.

5. Pete visited the tutoring center because they can help him with his economics course.

   . . . center because its staff can help . . .

Review Test 1

Underline the correct word in parentheses.

1. Each of the little girls may choose one prize for (her, their) own.
2. I asked at the body shop how quickly (they, the shop employees) could fix my car.
3. The coaches told each member of the football team that (his, their) position was the most important in the game.
4. Darlene tried to take notes during the class, but she didn't really understand (it, the subject).
5. When someone has a cold, (they, he or she) should take extra vitamin C and drink a lot of fluids.

Review Test 2

Cross out the pronoun error in each of the following sentences, and write the correction in the space provided at the left. Then circle the letter that correctly describes the type of error that was made.

EXAMPLES

his (or her)

Anyone without a ticket will lose ~~their~~ place in the line.

Mistake in   a. pronoun reference   (b.) pronoun agreement

*Ellen
(or Kim)*

When Ellen takes her daughter Kim to the park, ~~she~~ enjoys herself.

Mistake in   (a.) pronoun reference   b. pronoun agreement

his (or her)

1. Could someone volunteer ~~their~~ services to clean up after the party?

    Mistake in   a. pronoun reference   (b.) pronoun agreement

the players

2. The referee watched the basketball game closely to make sure ~~they~~ didn't commit any fouls.

    Mistake in   (a.) pronoun reference   b. pronoun agreement

they

3. If job-hunters want to make a good impression at an interview, ~~he~~ should be sure to arrive on time.

    Mistake in   a. pronoun reference   (b.) pronoun agreement

her

4. Neither of those girls appreciates ~~their~~ parents' sacrifices.

    Mistake in   a. pronoun reference   (b.) pronoun agreement

the owners

5. There wasn't much to do on Friday nights after ~~they~~ closed the only movie theater in town.

    Mistake in   (a.) pronoun reference   b. pronoun agreement

30 Pronoun Types

This chapter describes some common types of pronouns: subject and object pronouns, possessive pronouns, and demonstrative pronouns.

Subject and Object Pronouns

Most pronouns change their form depending on what place they occupy in a sentence. In the box that follows is a list of subject and object pronouns.

Subject Pronouns	Object Pronouns
I	me
you	you (no change)
he	him
she	her
it	it (no change)
we	us
they	them

Subject Pronouns

Subject pronouns are subjects of verbs.

> He served as a soldier during the war in Iraq. (*He* is the subject of the verb *served.*)

> *They* are moving into our old apartment. (*They* is the subject of the verb *are moving.*)

> *We* students should have a say in the decision. (*We* is the subject of the verb *should have.*)

Following are several rules for using subject pronouns—and several kinds of mistakes people sometimes make with subject pronouns.

Rule 1   Use a subject pronoun when you have a compound subject (more than one subject).

Incorrect	**Correct**
My brother and *me* are Bruce Springsteen fanatics.	My brother and *I* are Bruce Springsteen fanatics.
Him and *me* know the lyrics to all of Bruce's songs.	*He* and *I* know the lyrics to all of Bruce's songs.

Hint for Rule 1   If you are not sure what pronoun to use, try each pronoun by itself in the sentence. The correct pronoun will be the one that sounds right. For example, "Him knows the lyrics to all of Bruce's songs" does not sound right; "He knows the lyrics to all of Bruce's songs" does.

Rule 2   Use a subject pronoun after forms of the verb *be*. Forms of *be* include *am, are, is, was, were, has been, have been,* and others.

> It was *I* who left the light on.
> It may be *they* in that car.
> It is *he*.

The sentences above may sound strange and stilted to you because they are seldom used in conversation. When we speak with one another, forms such as "It was me," "It may be them," and "It is him" are widely accepted. In formal writing, however, the grammatically correct forms are still preferred.

Hint for Rule 2   You can avoid having to use a subject pronoun after *be* by simply rewording a sentence. Here is how the preceding examples could be reworded:

> I was the one who left the light on.
> They may be in that car.
> He is here.

Rule 3 Use subject pronouns after *than* or *as*. The subject pronoun is used because a verb is understood after the pronoun.

> You play better than I (play). (The verb *play* is understood after *I*.)
>
> Jenny is as bored as I (am). (The verb *am* is understood after *I*.)
>
> We don't need the money as much as they (do). (The verb *do* is understood after *they*.)

Hint for Rule 3 Avoid mistakes by mentally adding the "missing" verb at the end of the sentence.

Object Pronouns

Object pronouns (*me, him, her, us, them*) are the objects of verbs or prepositions. (*Prepositions* are connecting words like *for, at, about, to, before, by, with,* and *of.* See also page 413.)

> Tony helped me. (*Me* is the object of the verb *helped*.)
>
> We took *them* to the college. (*Them* is the object of the verb *took*.)
>
> Leave the children with *us.* (*Us* is the object of the preposition *with*.)
>
> I got in line behind *him.* (*Him* is the object of the preposition *behind*.)

People are sometimes uncertain about what pronoun to use when two objects follow a verb.

Incorrect	**Correct**
I gave a gift to Ray and *she*.	I gave a gift to Ray and *her.*
She came to the movie with Bobbie and *I.*	She came to the movie with Bobbie and *me.*

Hint If you are not sure what pronoun to use, try each pronoun by itself in the sentence. The correct pronoun will be the one that sounds right. For example, "I gave a gift to she" does not sound right; "I gave a gift to her" does.

ACTIVITY

Underline the correct subject or object pronoun in each of the following sentences. Then show whether your answer is a subject or object pronoun by circling the S or O in the margin. The first one is done for you as an example.

S Ⓞ   1. The sweaters Mom knitted for Victor and (I, me) are too small.

Ⓢ O   2. The umpire and (he, him) started to argue.

Ⓢ O   3. No one has a quicker temper than (she, her).

Ⓢ O   4. Your grades prove that you worked harder than (they, them).

Ⓢ O   5. (We, Us) runners train indoors when the weather turns cold.

Ⓢ O   6. (She, Her) and Betty never put the cap back on the toothpaste.

Ⓢ O   7. Chris and (he, him) are the most energetic kids in the first grade.

S Ⓞ   8. Arguing over clothes is a favorite pastime for my sister and (I, me).

S Ⓞ   9. The rest of (they, them) will be arriving in about ten minutes.

S Ⓞ   10. The head of the ticket committee asked Melba and (I, me) to help with sales.

Possessive Pronouns

ALLWRITE!
19.2c

Here is a list of possessive pronouns:

my, mine	our, ours
your, yours	your, yours
his	their, theirs
her, hers	
its	

Possessive pronouns show ownership or possession.

> Adam revved up *his* motorcycle and blasted off.
> The keys are *mine.*

Note   A possessive pronoun *never* uses an apostrophe. (See also page 504.)

Incorrect	**Correct**
That coat is *hers'.*	That coat is *hers.*
The card table is *theirs'.*	The card table is *theirs.*

ACTIVITY

Cross out the incorrect pronoun form in each of the sentences below. Write the correct form in the space at the left.

EXAMPLE _____hers_____ Those gloves are ~~hers'~~.

_____its_____ 1. I discovered that my car had somehow lost ~~its'~~ rear license plate.

_____theirs_____ 2. Are those seats ~~theirs'~~?

_____hers_____ 3. I knew that sweater was ~~hers'~~ when I saw the monogram.

_____ours_____ 4. The dog in that cage is ~~our's~~.

_____yours_____ 5. These books are ~~yours'~~ if you want them.

Demonstrative Pronouns

Demonstrative pronouns point to or single out a person or thing. There are four demonstrative pronouns:

this	these
that	those

Generally speaking, *this* and *these* refer to things close at hand; *that* and *those* refer to things farther away. The four demonstrative pronouns are also commonly used as demonstrative adjectives.

Is anyone using *this* spoon?
I am going to throw away *these* magazines.
I just bought *that* black pickup truck at the curb.
Pick up *those* toys in the corner.

Note   Do not use *them, this here, that there, these here,* or *those there* to point out. Use only *this, that, these,* or *those.*

ACTIVITY

Cross out the incorrect form of the demonstrative pronoun, and write the correct form in the space provided.

EXAMPLE ___*Those*___ ~~Them~~ tires look worn.

___This___   1. ~~This here~~ map is out of date.

___those___   2. Leave ~~them~~ keys out on the coffee table.

___those___   3. I've seen ~~them~~ girls somewhere before.

___that___   4. Jack entered ~~that there~~ dog in an obedience contest.

___those___   5. Where are ~~them~~ new knives?

■ Review Test

Underline the correct word in the parentheses.

1. If the contract negotiations are left up to (they, them), we'll have to accept the results.
2. (Them, Those) student crafts projects have won several awards.
3. Our grandmother told David and (I, me) to leave our muddy shoes outside on the porch.
4. The judge decided that the fault was (theirs', theirs) and ordered them to pay the damages.
5. I gave the money to (she, her) and asked her to put it in the bank's night deposit slot.
6. The black-masked raccoon stared at Rudy and (I, me) for an instant and then ran away.
7. When we saw the smashed window, Lynn and (I, me) didn't know whether to enter the house.
8. (This here, This) is my cousin Manuel.
9. This coat can't be (hers, her's); it's too small.
10. Because we weren't wearing shoes, Tara and (I, me) had a hard time walking on the sharp gravel.

31 Adjectives and Adverbs

Adjectives

What Are Adjectives?

ALLWRITE!
20.1

Adjectives describe nouns (names of persons, places, or things) or pronouns.

> Yoko is a *wise* woman. (The adjective *wise* describes the noun *woman*.)
>
> She is also *funny*. (The adjective *funny* describes the pronoun *she*.)
>
> I'll carry the *heavy* bag of groceries. (The adjective *heavy* describes the noun *bag*.)
>
> It is *torn*. (The adjective *torn* describes the pronoun *it*.)

Adjectives usually come before the word they describe (as in *wise* woman and *heavy* bag). But they also come after forms of the verb *be* (*is, are, was, were,* and so on). They also follow verbs such as *look, appear, seem, become, sound, taste,* and *smell*.

> That road is *slippery*. (The adjective *slippery* describes the road.)
>
> The dogs are *noisy*. (The adjective *noisy* describes the dogs.)
>
> Those customers were *impatient*. (The adjective *impatient* describes the customers.)
>
> Your room looks *neat*. (The adjective *neat* describes the room.)

Using Adjectives to Compare

ALLWRITE!
20.4

For all one-syllable adjectives and some two-syllable adjectives, add *-er* when comparing two things and *-est* when comparing three or more things.

> Phil's beard is *longer* than mine, but Lee's is the *longest*.
>
> Meg may be the *quieter* of the two sisters; but that's not saying much, since they're the *loudest* girls in school.

For some two-syllable adjectives and all longer adjectives, use *more* when comparing two things and *most* when comparing three or more things.

> Liza Minnelli is *more famous* than her sister; but their mother, Judy Garland, is still the *most famous* member of the family.

> The red letters on the sign are *more noticeable* than the black ones, but the Day-Glo letters are the *most noticeable*.

You can usually tell when to use *more* and *most* by the sound of a word. For example, you can probably tell by its sound that "carefuller" would be too awkward to say and that *more careful* is thus correct. But there are many words for which both *-er* or *-est* and *more* or *most* are equally correct. For instance, either "a more fair rule" or "a fairer rule" is correct.

To form negative comparisons, use *less* and *least*.

> During my first dance class, I felt *less graceful* than an injured elephant.

> When the teacher came to our house to complain to my parents, I offered her the *least* comfortable chair in the room.

Points to Remember about Comparing

Point 1   Use only one form of comparison at a time. That is, do not use both an *-er* ending and *more* or both an *-est* ending and *most:*

Incorrect	Correct
My mother's suitcase is always *more heavier* than my father's.	My mother's suitcase is always *heavier* than my father's.
Psycho is still the *most frighteningest* movie I've ever seen	*Psycho* is still the *most frightening* movie I've ever seen.

Point 2   Learn the irregular forms of the words shown below.

	Comparative (for comparing two things)	Superlative (for comparing three or more things)
bad	worse	worst
good, well	better	best
little (in amount)	less	least
much, many	more	most

Do not use both *more* and an irregular comparative or *most* and an irregular superlative.

Incorrect	Correct
It is *more better* to give than to receive.	It is *better* to give than to receive.
Last night I got the *most worst* snack attack I ever had.	Last night I got the *worst* snack attack I ever had.

ACTIVITY

Add to each sentence the correct form of the word in the margin.

bad

EXAMPLES The _____worst_____ job I ever had was baby-sitting for spoiled four-year-old twins.

wonderful

The _____most wonderful_____ day of my life was when my child was born.

good

1. The _____best_____ chocolate cake I ever ate had bananas in it.

young

2. Aunt Sonja is the _____youngest_____ of the three sisters.

bad

3. A rain that freezes is _____worse_____ than a snowstorm.

unusual

4. That's the _____most unusual_____ home I've ever seen—it's shaped like a teapot.

little

5. Being painfully shy has made Leon the _____least_____ friendly person I know.

Adverbs

What Are Adverbs?

Adverbs describe verbs, adjectives, or other adverbs. They usually end in *-ly*.

The father *gently* hugged the sick child. (The adverb *gently* describes the verb *hugged*.)

Newborns are *totally* innocent. (The adverb *totally* describes the adjective *innocent*.)

The lecturer spoke so *terribly* fast that I had trouble taking notes. (The adverb *terribly* describes the adverb *fast*.)

A Common Mistake with Adverbs and Adjectives

People often mistakenly use an adjective instead of an adverb after a verb.

Incorrect	Correct
Sam needs a haircut *bad*.	Sam needs a haircut *badly*.
I laugh too *loud* when I'm embarrassed.	I laugh too *loudly* when I'm embarrassed.
You might have won the race if you hadn't run so *slow* at the beginning.	You might have won the race if you hadn't run so *slowly* at the beginning.

ACTIVITY

Underline the adjective or adverb needed. (Remember that adjectives describe nouns, and adverbs describe verbs and other adverbs.)

1. As Mac danced, his earring bounced (rapid, <u>rapidly</u>).
2. A drop of (<u>thick</u>, thickly) pea soup dripped down his chin.
3. I hiccuped (continuous, <u>continuously</u>) for fifteen minutes.
4. The detective opened the door (careful, <u>carefully</u>).
5. All she heard when she answered the phone was (<u>heavy</u>, heavily) breathing.

Well and *Good*

Two words that are often confused are *well* and *good*. *Good* is an adjective; it describes nouns. *Well* is usually an adverb; it describes verbs. But *well* (rather than *good*) is used as an adjective when referring to health.

ACTIVITY

Write *well* or *good* in each of the sentences that follow.

1. If you kids do a _____*good*_____ job of cleaning the garage, I'll take you out for some ice cream.

2. If I organize the office records too _____*well*_____, my bosses may not need me anymore.

3. After eating a pound of peanuts, I didn't feel too _____*well*_____.

4. When Ernie got AIDS, he discovered who his _____*good*_____ friends really were.

5. Just because brothers and sisters fight when they're young doesn't mean they won't get along _____*well*_____ as adults.

Review Test 1

Underline the correct word in parentheses.

1. The waitress poured (littler, <u>less</u>) coffee into my cup than yours.

2. Humid air seems to make Sid's asthma (more worse, <u>worse</u>).

3. The movie is so interesting that the three hours pass (quick, <u>quickly</u>).

4. The talented boy sang as (confident, <u>confidently</u>) as a seasoned performer.

5. Our band played so (good, <u>well</u>) that a local firm hired us for its annual dinner.

6. Tamika is always (<u>truthful</u>, truthfully), even when it might be better to tell a white lie.

7. The driver stopped the bus (sudden, <u>suddenly</u>) and yelled, "Everybody out!"

8. Shirt and pants in the same color make you look (more thin, <u>thinner</u>) than ones in contrasting colors.

9. Your intentions may have been (<u>good</u>, well), but I'd prefer that you ask before arranging a blind date for me.

10. Our cat likes to sit in the (<u>warmest</u>, most warm) spot in any room—by a fireplace, on a windowsill in the sunshine, or on my lap.

Review Test 2

Write a sentence that uses each of the following adjectives and adverbs correctly. *Answers will vary; examples are shown.*

1. careless _It's embarassing to make a careless mistake._

2. angrily _"Get out!" the shop owner shouted angrily to the panhandler._

3. well _If a thing is worth doing, it's worth doing well._

4. most relaxing _A lullaby is one of the most relaxing kinds of music._

5. best _My husband is also my best friend._

32 Misplaced Modifiers

16.2

Misplaced modifiers are words that, because of awkward placement, do not describe what the writer intended them to describe. A misplaced modifier can make a sentence confusing or unintentionally funny. To avoid this, place words as close as possible to what they describe.

Misplaced Words	Correctly Placed Words
George couldn't drive to work in his small sports car *with a broken leg.* (The sports car had a broken leg?)	With a broken leg, George couldn't drive to work in his small sports car. (The words describing George are now placed next to *George.*)
The toaster was sold to us by a charming salesman *with a money-back guarantee.* (The salesman had a money-back guarantee?)	The toaster with a money-back guarantee was sold to us by a charming salesman. (The words describing the toaster are now placed next to it.)
He *nearly* brushed his teeth for twenty minutes every night. (He came close to brushing his teeth but in fact did not brush them at all?)	He brushed his teeth for nearly twenty minutes every night. (The meaning—that he brushed his teeth for a long time—is now clear.)

ACTIVITY

Underline the misplaced word or words in each sentence. Then rewrite the sentence, placing related words together and thereby making the meaning clear.

EXAMPLES Frozen shrimp lay in the steel pans <u>that were thawing rapidly</u>.
Frozen shrimp that were thawing rapidly lay in the steel pans.

The speaker discussed the problem of crowded prisons <u>at the college</u>.
At the college, the speaker discussed the problem of crowded prisons.

480

1. The patient talked about his childhood <u>on the psychiatrist's couch</u>.
   The patient on the psychiatrist's couch talked . . .

2. The crowd watched the tennis players <u>with swiveling heads</u>.
   With swiveling heads, the crowd watched . . .

3. Vonnie put four hamburger patties on the counter <u>which she was cooking for dinner</u>.
   . . . patties, which she was cooking for dinner, on . . .

4. Steve carefully hung the new suit that he would wear to his first job interview <u>in the bedroom closet</u>.
   . . . hung in the bedroom closet the new suit that he . . .

5. Anne ripped the shirt on a car door <u>that she made in sewing class</u>.
   . . . shirt that she made in sewing class on a car door.

6. The latest Denzel Washington movie has <u>almost</u> opened in 2,200 theaters across the country.
   . . . has opened in almost 2,200 theaters . . .

7. The newscaster spoke softly into a microphone <u>wearing a bulletproof vest</u>.
   Wearing a bulletproof vest, the newscaster spoke . . .

8. The tenants left town in a dilapidated old car <u>owing two months' rent</u>.
   Owing two months' rent, the tenants left town . . .

9. The woman picked up a heavy frying pan <u>with arthritis</u>.
   The woman with arthritis picked up a heavy frying pan.

10. I discovered an unusual plant <u>in the greenhouse</u> that oozed a milky juice.
    In the greenhouse, I discovered . . .

■ Review Test 1

Write MM for *misplaced modifier* or C for *correct* in the space provided for each sentence.

MM   1. I nearly napped for twenty minutes during the biology lecture.

C   2. I napped for nearly twenty minutes during the biology lecture.

C   3. Ron paused as the girl he had been following stopped at a shop window.

MM   4. Ron paused as the girl stopped at a shop window he had been following.

MM   5. Marta dropped out of school after taking ten courses on Friday.

_C_   6. On Friday, Marta dropped out of school after taking ten courses.

_C_   7. Under his shirt, the player wore a good luck charm that resembled a tiny elephant.

_MM_   8. The player wore a good luck charm under his shirt that resembled a tiny elephant.

_MM_   9. I ordered a new telephone from the mail-order catalog shaped like a cartoon character.

_C_   10. I ordered from the mail-order catalog a new telephone shaped like a cartoon character.

■ Review Test 2

Make the changes needed to correct the misplaced modifier in each sentence.

1. Henry Wadsworth Longfellow wrote that rainbows are flowers that have died and gone to heaven in a poem.

   In a poem, Henry Wadsworth Longfellow wrote that . . .

   _____

2. Because of the storm, I almost arrived two hours late for my first day on the job.

   Because of the storm, I arrived almost two . . .

   _____

3. The apprentice watched the carpenter expertly fit the door with envious eyes.

   With envious eyes, the apprentice watched . . .

   _____

4. The photographer pointed the camera at the shy deer equipped with a special night-vision scope.

   . . . pointed at the shy deer the camera . . .

   or: . . . scope at the shy deer.

5. The people on the bus stared at the ceiling or read newspapers with tired faces.

   The people with tired faces on the bus stared . . .

   Or: With tired faces, the people . . .

33 Dangling Modifiers

16.4

A modifier that opens a sentence must be followed immediately by the word it is meant to describe. Otherwise, the modifier is said to be dangling, and the sentence takes on an unintended meaning. For example, in the sentence

> While reading the newspaper, my dog sat with me on the front steps.

the unintended meaning is that the *dog* was reading the paper. What the writer meant, of course, was that *he* (or *she*), the writer, was reading the paper. The writer should have said,

> While reading the newspaper, *I* sat with my dog on the front steps.

The dangling modifier could also be corrected by placing the subject within the opening word group:

> While *I* was reading the newspaper, my dog sat with me on the front steps.

Here are other sentences with dangling modifiers. Read the explanations of why they are dangling, and look carefully at how they are corrected.

Dangling	**Correct**
Shaving in front of the steamy mirror, the razor nicked Ed's chin. (*Who* was shaving in front of the mirror? The answer is not *razor* but *Ed*. The subject *Ed* must be added.)	Shaving in front of the steamy mirror, *Ed* nicked his chin with the razor. *Or:* When *Ed* was shaving in front of the steamy mirror, he nicked his chin with the razor.
While turning over the bacon, hot grease splashed my arm. (*Who* is turning over the bacon? The answer is not *hot grease,* as it unintentionally seems to be, but *I.* The subject *I* must be added.)	While *I* was turning over the bacon, hot grease splashed my arm. *Or:* While turning over the bacon, *I* was splashed by hot grease.

Dangling	**Correct**
Taking the exam, the room was so stuffy that Keisha almost fainted. (*Who* took the exam? The answer is not *the room* but *Keisha*. The subject *Keisha* must follow the modifier.)	Taking the exam, *Keisha* found the room so stuffy that she almost fainted. *Or:* When *Keisha* took the exam, the room was so stuffy that she almost fainted.
To impress the interviewer, punctuality is essential. (*Who* is to impress the interviewer? The answer is not *punctuality* but *you*. The subject *you* must be added.)	To impress the interviewer, *you* must be punctual. *Or:* For *you* to impress the interviewer, punctuality is essential.

The examples above show two ways of correcting a dangling modifier. Decide on a logical subject and do one of the following:

1 Place the subject *within* the opening word group:

When *Ed* was shaving in front of the steamy mirror, he nicked his chin.

Note   In some cases, an appropriate subordinating word such as *when* must be added and the verb may have to be changed slightly as well.

2 Place the subject right *after* the opening word group:

Shaving in front of the steamy mirror, *Ed* nicked his chin.

ACTIVITY

Look at the opening words in each sentence and ask, *Who?* The subject that answers the question should be nearby in the sentence. If it is not, provide the logical subject by using either method of correction described above.

EXAMPLE While pitching his tent, a snake bit Tony on the ankle.
While Tony was pitching his tent, a snake bit him on the ankle.

Or: *While pitching his tent, Tony was bitten on the ankle by a snake.*

Note: Some instructors might consider the first example on this page a misplaced modifier since the subject of the phrase *taking the exam*—Keisha—does appear later in the sentence. However, since correcting the error would involve omitting one word (*was*) and changing additional words (*Keisha found the room so stuffy that she*), this type of error is classified as a dangling modifier in *College Writing Skills with Readings*. In general, if a word group is a participial phrase, and if the phrase occurs at the beginning of the sentence but modifies a subject that *does not* appear until later in the sentence, it is called a dangling rather than a misplaced modifier.

Answers may vary.

1. Dancing on their hind legs, the audience cheered wildly as the elephants paraded by.

   The audience cheered wildly as the elephants, dancing on their hind legs, paraded by.

2. Last seen wearing dark glasses and a blond wig, the police spokesperson said the suspect was still being sought.

   The police spokesperson said the suspect, last seen wearing dark glasses and a blond wig, was . . .

3. Pouring out the cereal, a coupon fell into my bowl of milk.

   As I poured out the cereal, a coupon fell . . .

4. Escorted by dozens of police motorcycles, I knew the limousine carried someone important.

   Because it was escorted by dozens of police motorcycles, I knew the limousine . . .

5. Tired and exasperated, the fight we had was inevitable.

   We were tired and exasperated, so the fight we had . . .

6. Packed tightly in a tiny can, Fran had difficulty removing the anchovies.

   . . . removing the anchovies, which were packed tightly . . .

7. Kicked carelessly under the bed, Raquel finally found her sneakers.

   Raquel finally found her sneakers, which were kicked carelessly under the bed.

8. Working at the Xerox machine, the morning dragged on.

   As I worked at the Xerox machine, the morning . . .

9. Sitting at a sidewalk café, all sorts of interesting people passed by.

   As we sat at a sidewalk café, all sorts . . .

10. Though somewhat warped, Uncle Zeke played his records from the forties.

   Though they were somewhat warped, Uncle Zeke played his records from the forties.

Review Test 1

Write DM for *dangling modifier* or C for *correct* in the space provided for each sentence.

DM   1. While riding the bicycle, a vicious-looking German shepherd snapped at Tim's ankles.

C   2. While Tim was riding the bicycle, a vicious-looking German shepherd snapped at his ankles.

C   3. Afraid to look his father in the eye, Howard kept his head bowed.

DM   4. Afraid to look his father in the eye, Howard's head remained bowed.

DM   5. Boring and silly, I turned the TV show off.

C   6. I turned off the boring and silly TV show.

C   7. Munching leaves from a tall tree, the giraffe fascinated the children.

DM   8. Munching leaves from a tall tree, the children were fascinated by the giraffe.

DM   9. At the age of twelve, several colleges had already accepted the boy genius.

C   10. At the age of twelve, the boy genius had already been accepted by several colleges.

Review Test 2

Make the changes needed to correct the dangling modifier in each sentence.
Answers may vary; examples are shown.

1. Not having had much sleep, my concentration during class was weak.

   Since I had not had much sleep, my concentration . . .

   _____

2. Joined at the hip, a team of surgeons successfully separated the Siamese twins.

   . . . separated the Siamese twins, who were joined at the hip.

   _____

3. Wading in the shallow surf, a baby shark brushed past my leg.

   As I was wading in the shallow surf, a baby . . .

   _____

4. While being restrained by federal marshals, the judge sentenced the kidnapper.

The judge sentenced the kidnapper, who was being restrained . . .

5. In a sentimental frame of mind, the music brought tears to Beth's eyes.

Beth was in a sentimental frame of mind, so the music brought tears to

her eyes.

■ Review Test 3

Complete the following sentences. In each case, a logical subject should follow the opening words.

EXAMPLE Looking through the door's peephole, *I couldn't see who rang the*

doorbell.

Answers will vary; examples are shown.

1. Noticing the light turn yellow, *Barry slowed the car down.*

2. Being fragile, *the vase broke when I set it down too hard.*

3. While washing the car, *the kids got soaking wet.*

4. Although very expensive, *the coat did not wear well.*

5. Driving past the cemetery, *Terry had gloomy thoughts of death.*

34 Manuscript Form

When you hand in a paper for any course, it will probably be judged first by its format. It is important, then, to make the paper look attractive, neat, and easy to read. Here is a checklist you should use when preparing a paper for an instructor:

____ • Is the paper full-size, 8$\frac{1}{2}$ by 11 inches?

____ • Are there wide margins (1 to 1$\frac{1}{2}$ inches) all around the paper? In particular, have you been careful not to crowd the right-hand or bottom margin?

____ • If the paper is handwritten, have you

   Used a blue or black pen?

   Been careful not to overlap letters or to make decorative loops on letters?

   Made all your letters distinct, with special attention to *a, e, i, o,* and *u* —five letters that people sometimes write illegibly?

   Kept all your capital letters clearly distinct from small letters?

____ • Have you centered the title of your paper on the first line of page 1? Have you been careful *not* to put quotation marks around the title and *not* to underline it? Have you capitalized all the words in the title except short connecting words like *of, for, the, and, in,* and *to*?

____ • Have you skipped a line between the title and the first line of your paper?

____ • Have you indented the first line of each paragraph about five spaces (half an inch) from the left-hand margin?

____ • Have you made commas, periods, and other punctuation marks firm and clear? If you are typing or keyboarding, have you left a double space after a period?

____ • If you have broken any words at the end of a line, have you been careful to break only between syllables?

____ • Have you put your name, the date, and other information at the end of the paper (or wherever your instructor has specified)?

Also ask yourself these important questions about the title and the first sentence of your paper:

_____ • Is your title made up of several words that tell what the paper is about? (The title should be just several words, not a complete sentence.)

_____ • Does the first sentence of your paper stand independent of the title? (The reader should *not* have to use the words in the title to make sense of the opening sentence.)

ACTIVITY

Use the checklist to locate the seven mistakes in format in the following lines from a student paper. Explain the mistakes in the spaces provided. One mistake is described for you as an example.

	"Being alone"
	This is something that I simply cannot tolerate, and I will predi-
	ctably go to great lengths to prevent it. For example, if I know that

1. Hyphenate only between syllables (predict-ably, not predi-ctably).

2. Right-hand margin should not be crowded.

3. Title should not be in quotation marks.

4. In title, the word "Alone" should be capitalized.

5. A line should be skipped below the title.

6. Paragraph indent is needed.

7. The first sentence should stand independent of the title. (Here, the meaning of "This" depends on the title.)

35 Capital Letters

Main Uses of Capital Letters

25.1

Capital letters are used with

1   First word in a sentence or direct quotation
2   Names of persons and the word *I*
3   Names of particular places
4   Names of days of the week, months, and holidays
5   Names of commercial products
6   Titles of books, magazines, newspapers, articles, stories, poems, films, television shows, songs, papers that you write, and the like
7   Names of companies, associations, unions, clubs, religious and political groups, and other organizations

Each use is illustrated in this chapter.

First Word in a Sentence or Direct Quotation

> The corner grocery was robbed last night.
> The alien said, "Take me to your leader."
> "If you need help," said Teri, "call me. I'll be over in no time."

Note   In the third example above, *If* and *I'll* are capitalized because they start new sentences. But *call* is not capitalized, because it is part of the first sentence.

Names of Persons and the Word *I*

> Last night, I saw a hilarious movie starring Stan Laurel and Oliver Hardy.

Names of Particular Places and Institutions

Although Bill dropped out of Port Charles High School, he eventually earned his degree and got a job with Atlas Realty Company.

But   Use small letters if the specific name is not given.

Although Bill dropped out of high school, he eventually earned his degree and got a job with a real estate company.

Names of Days of the Week, Months, and Holidays

On the last Friday afternoon in May, the day before Memorial Day, my boss is having a barbecue for all the employees.

But   Use small letters for the seasons—summer, fall, winter, spring.

Most people feel more energetic in the spring and fall.

Names of Commercial Products

Keith installed a new Sony stereo and a Motorola cell phone into his old Ford Ranger pickup.

But   Use small letters for the *type* of product (stereo, cell phone, pickup, and so on).

Titles of Books, Magazines, Newspapers, Articles, Stories, Poems, Films, Television Shows, Songs, Papers That You Write, and the Like

We read the book *Hiroshima*, by John Hersey, for our history class.

In the doctor's waiting room, I watched *All My Children*, read an article in *Reader's Digest*, and leafed through the *Miami Herald*.

Names of Companies, Associations, Unions, Clubs, Religious and Political Groups, and Other Organizations

Joe Naples is a Roman Catholic, but his wife is a Methodist.

The Hilldale Square Dancers' Club has won many competitions.

Brian, a member of Bricklayers Local 431 and the Knights of Columbus, works for Ace Construction.

ACTIVITY

Underline the words that need capitals in the following sentences. Then write the capitalized form of each word in the space provided. The number of spaces tells you how many corrections to make in each case.

EXAMPLE   In our biology class, each student must do a report on an article in the magazine *scientific american*.   *Scientific*   *American*

1. Leon's collection of <u>beatles</u> souvenirs includes a pair of tickets from their last concert in <u>candlestick park</u> in San Francisco.

    Beatles   Candlestick   Park

2. Yumi read in *natural health* magazine that <u>abraham lincoln</u> suffered from severe depression.

    Natural   Health   Abraham   Lincoln

3. When <u>i</u> have a cold, I use <u>vick's</u> ointment and chew <u>listerine</u> lozenges.

    I   Vick's   Listerine

4. Since no man volunteered for the job, the <u>boy scouts</u> in <u>springfield, illinois,</u> have a woman troop leader.

    Boy   Scouts   Springfield   Illinois

5. A nature trail for the blind in <u>cape cod, massachusetts,</u> has signs written in Braille that encourage visitors to smell and touch the plants.

    Cape   Cod   Massachusetts

6. Some of the most popular items at a restaurant called <u>big river</u> are <u>chilean</u> sea bass and <u>atlantic</u> clam chowder.

    Big   River   Chilean   Atlantic

7. My father is a confirmed Dallas <u>cowboys</u> fan, though he lives in <u>boston</u>.

    Cowboys   Boston

8. Martha bought a <u>diet pepsi</u> to wash down her <u>hostess twinkie</u>.

    Diet   Pepsi   Hostess   Twinkie

9. Vince listened to a U2 album called *The Joshua Tree* while Donna read an article in *glamour* titled "What Do <u>men</u> Really <u>want</u>?"

    Glamour   Men   Want

10. After having her baby, <u>joan</u> received a card from one of her friends that read, "<u>congratulations</u>, we all knew you had it in you."

    Joan   Congratulations

Other Uses of Capital Letters

Capital letters are also used with

1 Names that show family relationships
2 Titles of persons when used with their names
3 Specific school courses
4 Languages
5 Geographic locations
6 Historical periods and events
7 Races, nations, and nationalities
8 Opening and closing of a letter

Each use is illustrated below.

Names That Show Family Relationships

All his life, Father has been addicted to gadgets.

I browsed through Grandmother's collection of old photographs.

Aunt Florence and Uncle Bill bought a mobile home.

But Do not capitalize words like *mother, father, grandmother, grandfather, uncle, aunt,* and so on when they are preceded by a possessive word (such as *my, your, his, her, our, their*).

All his life, my father has been addicted to gadgets.

I browsed through my grandmother's collection of old photographs.

My aunt and uncle bought a mobile home.

Titles of Persons When Used with Their Names

I contributed to Senator McGrath's campaign fund.

Is Dr. Gomez on vacation?

Professor Adams announced that there would be no tests in the course.

But Use lowercase letters when titles appear by themselves, without specific names.

I contributed to my senator's campaign fund.

Is the doctor on vacation?

The professor announced that there would be no tests in the course.

Specific School Courses

The college offers evening sections of Introductory Psychology I, Abnormal Psychology, Psychology and Statistics, and Educational Psychology.

But   Use lowercase letters for general subject areas.

The college offers evening sections of many psychology courses.

Languages

My grandfather's Polish accent makes his English difficult to understand.

Geographic Locations

He grew up in the Midwest but moved to the South to look for a better job.

But   Use lowercase letters in directions.

Head west for five blocks and then turn south on State Street.

Historical Periods and Events

During the Middle Ages, the Black Death killed over one-quarter of Europe's population.

Races, Nations, and Nationalities

The questionnaire asked if the head of our household was Caucasian, African American, Asian, Latino, or Native American.

Tanya has lived on army bases in Germany, Italy, and Spain.

Denise's beautiful features reflect her Chinese and Mexican parentage.

Opening and Closing of a Letter

Dear Sir: Sincerely yours,

Dear Ms. Henderson: Truly yours,

Note   Capitalize only the first word in a closing.

ACTIVITY

Underline the words that need capitals in the following sentences. Then write the capitalized forms of the words in the spaces provided. The number of spaces tells you how many corrections to make in each case.

1. During world war II, many americans were afraid that the japanese would invade California.

   ___World___   ___War___   ___Americans___   ___Japanese___

2. On their job site in korea, the french, swiss, and chinese coworkers used English to communicate.

   ___Korea___   ___French___   ___Swiss___   ___Chinese___

3. When uncle harvey got the bill from his doctor, he called the American Medical Association to complain.

   ___Uncle___   ___Harvey___

4. Dr. Freeling of the business department is offering a new course called introduction to web design.

   ___Introduction___   ___Web___   ___Design___

5. A new restaurant featuring vietnamese cuisine has just opened on the south side of the city.

   ___Vietnamese___

Unnecessary Use of Capitals

ACTIVITY

Many errors in capitalization are caused by using capitals where they are not needed. Underline the incorrectly capitalized words in the following sentences, and write the correct forms in the spaces provided. The number of spaces tells you how many corrections to make in each sentence.

1. George Washington's Forces starved at Valley Forge because Pennsylvania Farmers preferred to sell food to the British for cash.

   ___forces___   ___farmers___

2. The virus damaged the files on my Brother's Dell Computer.

   ___brother's___   ___computer___

3. The country cheered in the summer of 1998 when Mark McGwire of the St. Louis Cardinals <u>Baseball</u> <u>Team</u> broke the single-season <u>Home</u> <u>Run</u> record set by Roger Maris.

<u>   baseball   </u>   <u>   team   </u>   <u>   home   </u>   <u>   run   </u>

4. In his <u>Book</u> titled *Offbeat Museums,* Saul Rubin tells about various <u>Unusual</u> <u>Museums</u>, such as, <u>Believe</u> it or not, the Kansas Barbed Wire Museum.

<u>   book   </u>   <u>   unusual   </u>   <u>   museums   </u>   <u>   believe   </u>

5. Einstein's theory of relativity, which he developed when he was only twenty-six, led to the invention of the <u>Electron</u> <u>Microscope</u>, <u>Television</u>, and the <u>Atomic</u> bomb.

<u>   electron   </u>   <u>   microscope   </u>   <u>   television   </u>   <u>   atomic   </u>

■ Review Test 1

Add capitals where needed in the following sentences.

EXAMPLE   In an injured tone, Mary demanded, "~~w~~(W)hy wasn't ~~u~~(U)ncle Lou invited to the party?"

1. To keep warm, a homeless old man sits on a steam vent near ~~h~~(H)ampton ~~p~~(P)ark on ~~t~~(T)enth ~~s~~(S)treet.

2. Silent movie stars of the twenties, like ~~c~~(C)harlie ~~c~~(C)haplin and ~~g~~(G)loria ~~s~~(S)wanson, earned more than a million tax-free dollars a year.

3. Insects living in ~~mammoth~~ (M)ammoth ~~c~~(C)ave in ~~k~~(K)entucky include blind crickets, spiders, and flies.

4. When former president Bill Clinton was a boy in ~~a~~(A)rkansas, he was photographed shaking hands with ~~p~~(P)resident John F. Kennedy.

5. In an old movie, an attractive young lady invites ~~g~~(G)roucho ~~m~~(M)arx to join her.

6. "~~w~~(W)hy?" asks ~~g~~(G)roucho. "~~a~~(A)re you coming apart?"

7. I was halfway to the ~~w~~(W)ash & ~~d~~(D)ry Laundromat on ~~e~~(E)lm ~~s~~(S)treet when ~~i~~(I) realized that my box of ~~t~~(T)ide was still home on the kitchen counter.

8. Although I know that ~~mother~~ ^M loves holidays, even I was surprised when she
announced a party in ~~february~~ ^F to celebrate ~~groundhog~~ ^G ~~day~~ ^D.

9. *Rolling ~~stone~~* ^S magazine features an article about plans to remake the Alfred
Hitchcock classic ~~the birds~~ ^{T B} and a review of a new biography about ~~elvis presley~~ ^{E P}.

10. Celebrities have earned big money by endorsing products, including ~~nike~~ ^N shoes,
~~trident~~ ^T gum, and ~~jell-O~~ ^J pudding.

Review Test 2

On separate paper, write

Answers will vary.

1. Seven sentences demonstrating the seven main uses of capital letters.

2. Eight sentences demonstrating the eight other uses of capital letters.

36 Numbers and Abbreviations

Numbers

ALLWRITE!
25.2

Here are three helpful rules for using numbers.

Rule 1   Spell out numbers that take no more than two words. Otherwise, use the numbers themselves.

> In Jody's kitchen is her collection of seventy-two cookbooks.
>
> Jody has a file of 350 recipes.
>
> It will take about two weeks to fix the computer database.
>
> Since a number of people use the database, the company will lose over 150 workdays.
>
> Only twelve students have signed up for the field trip.
>
> Nearly 250 students came to the lecture.

Rule 2   Be consistent when you use a series of numbers. If some numbers in a sentence or paragraph require more than two words, then use numbers for the others, too.

> After the storm, maintenance workers unclogged 46 drains, removed 123 broken tree limbs, and rescued 3 kittens who were stuck in a drainpipe.

Rule 3   Use numbers to show dates, times, addresses, percentages, and chapters of a book.

> The burglary was committed on October 30, 2003, but not discovered until January 2, 2004.
>
> Before I went to bed, I set my alarm for 6:45 A.M. (*But:* Spell out numbers before *o'clock*. For example: I didn't get out of bed until seven o'clock.)
>
> The library is located at 45 West 52nd Street.

When you take the skin off a piece of chicken, you remove about 40 percent of the fat.

The name of the murderer is revealed in Chapter 8 on page 236.

ACTIVITY

Cross out the mistakes in numbers and write the corrections in the spaces provided.

1. The Puerto Rican Pride Parade will begin at ~~three-thirty~~ in front of the newspaper office at ~~one-oh-six~~ South ~~Forty-Second~~ Street.

   _____3:30_____   _____106_____   _____42nd_____

2. It took ~~4~~ hours to proofread all ~~75~~ pages of the manuscript.

   _____four_____   _____seventy-five_____

3. We expect to have ~~fifty~~ percent of the work completed by March ~~tenth~~.

   _____50_____   _____10_____

Abbreviations

Using abbreviations can save you time when you take notes. In formal writing, however, you should avoid most abbreviations. Listed below are some of the few abbreviations that are considered acceptable in compositions. Note that a period is used after most abbreviations.

1   Mr., Mrs., Ms., Jr., Sr., Dr. when used with names:

    Mrs. Johnson   Dr. Garcia   Howard Kelley, Jr.

2   Time references:

    A.M. or a.m.   P.M. or p.m.   B.C., A.D.

3   Initials in a person's name:

    J. Edgar Hoover   John F. Kennedy   Michael J. Fox

4   Organizations, technical words, and company names known primarily by their initials:

    IBM   UNICEF   ABC   IRS   NBA   AIDS

ACTIVITY

Cross out the words that should not be abbreviated, and correct them in the spaces provided.

1. Between mid-~~Nov.~~ and the beginning of ~~Jan.~~, I typically gain about five ~~lbs.~~

   November   _January_   _pounds_

2. I had such a bad headache this ~~aftern.~~ that I called my ~~doc.~~ for an ~~appt.~~

   afternoon   _doctor_   _appointment_

3. I stopped at the ~~p.o.~~ at about twenty ~~min.~~ past ten and bought five ~~dol.~~ worth of stamps.

   post   _office_   _minutes_   _dollars_

■ **Review Test**

Cross out the mistakes in numbers and abbreviations, and correct them in the spaces provided.

1. Sanjay was shocked when he transferred from a small ~~h.s.~~ to one with over ~~5,000~~ students.

   high   _school_   _five_   _thousand_

2. Grandpa lived to be ninety-nine despite smoking ~~3~~ packs of ~~cigs.~~ every day.

   three   _cigarettes_

3. Although the ~~2~~ girls are twins, they have different birthdays: one was born just before midnight on ~~Feb.~~ ~~twenty-fifth~~ and the other a few minutes later, after midnight.

   two   _February_   _25_

4. In their first week of ~~Span.~~ class, students learned to count from ~~1~~ to twenty-one and studied Chapter ~~One~~ in their textbook.

   Spanish   _one_   _1_

5. When I cleaned out the junk drawer in the ~~kitch.~~, I found twelve rubber bands, thirty-seven paper clips, and ~~3~~ used-up batteries.

   kitchen   _three_

37 Apostrophe

ALL WRITE!
24.6

The two main uses of the apostrophe are

1   To show the omission of one or more letters in a contraction
2   To show ownership or possession

Each use is explained in this chapter.

Apostrophe in Contractions

A *contraction* is formed when two words are combined to make one word. An apostrophe is used to show where letters are omitted in forming the contraction. Here are two contractions:

> have + not = haven't (the *o* in *not* has been omitted)
> I + will = I'll (the *wi* in *will* has been omitted)

Following are some other common contractions:

I + am = I'm	it + is = it's
I + have = I've	it + has = it's
I + had = I'd	is + not = isn't
who + is = who's	could + not = couldn't
do + not = don't	I + would = I'd
did + not = didn't	they + are = they're

Note   Will + not has an unusual contraction: won't.

ACTIVITY

Write the contractions for the words in parentheses. One is done for you.

1. (Are not) _Aren't_ the reserve books in the library kept at the circulation desk?

2. If (they are) _they're_ coming over, (I had) _I'd_ better cook more hot dogs.

3. (I am) _I'm_ the kind of student (who is) _who's_ extremely nervous before tests.

4. (We are) _We're_ hoping to find out (who is) _who's_ responsible for this error; (it is) _it's_ important to us to keep our customers happy.

5. I (can not) _can't_ remember if (there is) _there's_ gas in the car or not.

Note   Even though contractions are common in everyday speech and in written dialogue, it is often best to avoid them in formal writing.

Apostrophe to Show Ownership or Possession

To show ownership or possession, we can use such words as *belongs to, possessed by, owned by,* or (most commonly) *of.*

> the umbrella *that belongs to* Mark
>
> the toys *possessed by* children
>
> the tape recorder *owned by* the school
>
> the gentleness *of* my father

But the apostrophe plus *s* (if the word does not end in *s*) is often the quickest and easiest way to show possession. Thus we can say

> Mark's umbrella
>
> children's toys
>
> the school's tape recorder
>
> my father's gentleness

Points to Remember

1   The *'s* goes with the owner or possessor (in the examples given, *Mark, children, the school, my father*). What follows is the person or thing possessed (in the examples given, *the umbrella, the toys, the tape recorder, gentleness*).

2   There should always be a break between the word and *'s*.

Mark's   not   Marks

Yes   No

3   An apostrophe plus *s* is used to show possession with a singular word even if the word already ends in *s*: for example, Doris's purse (the purse belonging to Doris).

ACTIVITY 1

Rewrite the *italicized* part of each of the sentences below, using *'s* to show possession. Remember that the *'s* goes with the owner or possessor.

EXAMPLE   *The wing of the bluejay* was broken.
           The bluejay's wing was broken.

1. *The annoying voice of the comedian* irritated me, so I changed the TV channel.
   The comedian's annoying voice

2. *The performance of the quarterback* is inconsistent.
   The quarterback's performance

3. *The thin hand belonging to the old woman* felt as dry as parchment.
   The old woman's thin hand

4. *In the window of the jewelry store* is a sign reading "Ears Pierced While You Wait."
   In the jewelry store's window

5. A fly flew into *the mouth of the TV weatherperson*.
   the TV weatherperson's mouth

6. *The new denim shirt belonging to Lamont* was as scratchy as sandpaper.
   Lamont's new denim shirt

7. *The hair belonging to Rachel* is usually not green—she colored it for Halloween.

   Rachel's hair

8. *The bowl of cereal belonging to Dennis* refused to snap, crackle, or pop.

   Dennis's bowl of cereal

9. *The Honda owned by Donna* was crammed with boxes and furniture.

   Donna's Honda

10. *The previous tenant of the apartment* had painted all the walls bright green.

    The apartment's previous tenant

ACTIVITY 2

Add *'s* to each of the following words to make it the possessor or owner of something. Then write sentences using the words. The first one is done for you.

Sentences will vary; examples are given.

1. rock star _____ rock star's _____

   The rock star's limousine pulled up to the curb.

2. Felipe _____ Felipe's _____

   Felipe's name is the Spanish version of Philip.

3. pilot _____ pilot's _____

   The pilot's last message was "We're losing altitude!"

4. neighbor _____ neighbor's _____

   Our neighbor's yard is filled with flowers.

5. school _____ school's _____

   The school's enrollment is about five hundred students.

6. gunslinger _____ gunslinger's _____

   The gunslinger's moll is a favorite character in crime movies.

Apostrophe versus Possessive Pronouns

Do not use an apostrophe with possessive pronouns. They already show ownership. Possessive pronouns include *his, hers, its, yours, ours,* and *theirs.*

Incorrect	Correct
The sun warped his' albums.	The sun warped his albums.
The restored Model T is theirs'.	The restored Model T is theirs.
The decision is yours'.	The decision is yours.
The plaid suitcase is ours'.	The plaid suitcase is ours.
The lion charged its' prey.	The lion charged its prey.

Apostrophe versus Simple Plurals

When you want to make a word plural, just add an *s* at the end of the word. Do not add an apostrophe. For example, the plural of the word *movie* is *movies,* not *movie's* or *movies'.*

Look at this sentence:

Tim coveted his roommate's collection of cassette tapes and compact discs.

The words *tapes* and *discs* are simple plurals, meaning more than one tape, more than one disc. The plural is shown by adding *s* only. On the other hand, the *'s* after *roommate* shows possession—that the roommate owns the tapes and discs.

ACTIVITY

Insert an apostrophe where needed to show possession in the following sentences. Write *plural* above words where the *s* ending simply means more than one thing.

                                              plural   plural
EXAMPLE   Arlene's tinted contact lenses protect her eyes from glare.

                                                                    plural
1. Harry grasped his wife's arm as she stood on in-line skates for the first time.

                                                                    plural
2. Vonette's decision to study computer science is based on predictions of good
        plural
   opportunities for women in that field.

                                                            plural
3. The fire's extreme heat had melted the telephones in the office and welded the
        plural
   metal chairs into a twisted heap.

4. At the doctor's request, Lyndon pulled up his shirt and revealed the zipperlike
   plural
   scars from his operation.

                            plural   plural
5. Of all the people's names in all the world's countries, the most common is

   Muhammad.

6. At the end of the day, Hal's shirt and *plural* pants smelled like gasoline, and his *plural* fingernails were rimmed with grease.

7. The *plural* children's shouts of delight grew louder as the clown added eggs, *plural* lightbulbs, *plural* and a bowling ball to the *plural* items he was juggling.

8. Tina's camping handbook suggests that we bring water purification *plural* tablets and nylon ropes. *plural*

9. Carmen's leaky pen had stained her fingers *plural* a deep blue.

10. The rattlesnake's head has a sensitive pit below the eyes, *plural* capable of detecting

the body heat of warm-blooded prey.

Apostrophe with Plurals Ending in -s

Plurals that end in -*s* show possession simply by adding the apostrophe, rather than an apostrophe plus *s*.

the Thompsons' porch

the players' victory

her parents' motor home

the Rolling Stones' last CD

the soldiers' hats

ACTIVITY

Add an apostrophe where needed.

1. Several campers' tents collapsed during the storm.

2. The Murrays' phone bills are often over $100 a month.

3. Many buildings' steep steps make it difficult for wheelchair users to gain access.

4. The twins' habit of dressing alike was started by their mother when they were children.

5. At the crowded intersection, several young men rushed out to wash the cars' windshields.

Review Test

In each sentence, underline the two words that need apostrophes. Then write the words correctly in the spaces provided.

sofa's

chair's

barn's

hayloft's

book's

customer's

Sofia's

writer's

boss's

Charlie's

couldn't

car's

parents'

children's

cat's

dog's

sun's

street's

river's

Hendersons'

1. The sagging <u>sofas</u> stuffing was coming out in several places, and one of the <u>chairs</u> legs was broken.

2. A shaky rope ladder led from the <u>barns</u> wooden floor to the <u>haylofts</u> dusty shadows.

3. The paperback <u>books</u> glaring purple and orange cover was designed to attract a hurrying <u>customers</u> eye.

4. <u>Sofias</u> essay was due in a matter of hours, but she suffered <u>writers</u> block that emptied her brain.

5. While he waited in his <u>bosss</u> office, <u>Charlies</u> nervous fingers shredded a Styrofoam coffee cup into a pile of jagged white flakes.

6. Gregory <u>couldnt</u> remember whether he had left his wallet in his <u>cars</u> glove compartment or at home.

7. Members of the <u>parents</u> association constructed a maze made of old tires for the <u>childrens</u> playground.

8. The <u>cats</u> great green eyes grew even wider as the curious <u>dogs</u> sniffing nose came too close to her.

9. The <u>suns</u> rays beat down until the <u>streets</u> blacktopped surface softened with the heat.

10. The <u>rivers</u> swirling floodwaters lapped against the <u>Hendersons</u> porch.

38 Quotation Marks

24.3

The two main uses of quotation marks are

1 To set off the exact words of a speaker or writer
2 To set off the titles of short works

Each use is explained here.

Quotation Marks to Set Off the Words of a Speaker or Writer

Use quotation marks to show the exact words of a speaker or writer.

"I feel as though I've been here before," Angie murmured to her husband.

(Quotation marks set off the exact words that Angie spoke to her husband.)

Ben Franklin once wrote, "To lengthen thy life, lessen thy meals."

(Quotation marks set off the exact words that Ben Franklin wrote.)

"Did you know," said the nutrition expert, "that it's healthier to be ten pounds overweight?"

(Two pairs of quotation marks are used to enclose the nutrition expert's exact words.)

The biology professor said, "Ants are a lot like human beings. They farm their own food and raise smaller insects as livestock. And, like humans, ants send armies to war."

(Note that the end quotation marks do not come until the end of the biology professor's speech. Place quotation marks before the first quoted word and after the last quoted word. As long as no interruption occurs in the speech, do not use quotation marks for each new sentence.)

Punctuation Hint   In the four examples above, notice that a comma sets the quoted part off from the rest of the sentence. Also, observe that commas and periods at the end of a quotation always go *inside* quotation marks.

Complete the following statements, which explain how capital letters, commas, and periods are used in quotations. Refer to the four examples as guides.

1. Every quotation begins with a _____*capital*_____ letter.

2. When a quotation is split (as in the sentence about the nutrition expert), the second part does not begin with a capital letter unless it is a _____*new*_____ sentence.

3. _____*Commas*_____ are used to separate the quoted part of a sentence from the rest of the sentence.

4. Commas and periods that come at the end of a quotation go _____*inside*_____ the quotation marks.

The answers are *capital, new, Commas,* and *inside.*

ACTIVITY 1

Place quotation marks around the exact words of a speaker or writer in the sentences that follow.

1. Several people have been credited with saying, "The more I see of people, the more I like dogs."

2. Beatrice asked, "Do you give a discount to senior citizens?"

3. "This hamburger is raw!" cried Leon.

4. The bumper sticker on the rear of the battered old car read, "Don't laugh—it's paid for."

5. "I know why Robin Hood robbed only the rich," said the comedian. "The poor don't have any money."

6. "These CDs," proclaimed the television announcer, "are not sold in any store."

7. "When chefs go to great lengths," the woman at the diet center said, "I go to great widths."

8. "If I go with you to the dinner party," my friend said, "you must promise not to discuss politics."

9. On a tombstone in a Maryland cemetery are the words "Here lies an atheist, all dressed up and no place to go."

10. The columnist advised, "Be nice to people on your way up because you'll meet them on your way down."

ACTIVITY 2

1. Write a sentence in which you quote a favorite expression of someone you
    know. In the same sentence, identify the person's relationship to you.

    EXAMPLE *My grandfather loves to say, "It can't be as bad as all that."*

    _____

    _____

    _____

    _____

2. Write a quotation that contains the words *Pablo asked Teresa.* Write a second
    quotation that includes the words *Teresa replied.*

    "What time is it?" Pablo asked Teresa.

    "How should I know?" Teresa replied.

    _____

    _____

    _____

    _____

    _____

3. Quote an interesting sentence or two from a book or magazine. In the same
    sentence, identify the title and author of the work.

    EXAMPLE *In The Dilbert Desk Calendar by Scott Adams, the cartoon
    character Dilbert says, "I can please only one person per day. Today isn't
    your day, and tomorrow isn't looking good either."*

    _____

    _____

    _____

    _____

    _____

    _____

    _____

    _____

Indirect Quotations

An indirect quotation is a rewording of someone else's comments rather than a word-for-word direct quotation. The word *that* often signals an indirect quotation.

Direct Quotation	**Indirect Quotation**
The nurse said, "Some babies cannot tolerate cows' milk."	The nurse said that some babies cannot tolerate cows' milk.
(The nurse's exact spoken words are given, so quotation marks are used.)	(We learn the nurse's words indirectly, so no quotation marks are used.)
Vicky's note to Dan read, "I'll be home by 7:30."	Vicky left a note for Dan saying that she would be home by 7:30.
(The exact words that Vicky wrote in the note are given, so quotation marks are used.)	(We learn Vicky's words indirectly, so no quotation marks are used.)

ACTIVITY

Rewrite the following sentences, changing words as necessary to convert the sentences into direct quotations. The first one has been done for you as an example.

1. Teddy asked Margie if she wanted to see his spider collection.

   Teddy asked Margie, "Do you want to see my spider collection?"

2. Sonya said that her uncle looks just like a large basset hound.

   Sonya said, "My uncle looks just like a large basset hound."

3. Angelo said that he wanted a box of the extra-crispy chicken.

   Angelo said, "I want a box of the extra-crispy chicken."

4. My boss told me that I could make mistakes as long as I didn't repeat them.

   My boss told me, "You can make mistakes as long as you don't repeat them."

5. The instructor announced that Thursday's test had been canceled.

   The instructor announced, "Thursday's test has been canceled."

Quotation Marks to Set Off Titles of Short Works

24.3c

Titles of short works are usually set off by quotation marks, while titles of long works are underlined. Use quotation marks to set off titles of such short works as articles in books, newspapers, or magazines; chapters in a book; short stories; poems; and songs. But you should underline titles of books, newspapers, magazines, plays, movies, CDs, and television shows. Following are some examples.

Quotation Marks	**Underlines**
the essay "On Self-Respect"	in the book Slouching Towards Bethlehem
the article "The Problem of Acid Rain"	in the newspaper The New York Times
the article "Living with Inflation"	in the magazine Newsweek
the chapter "Chinese Religion"	in the book Paths of Faith
the story "Hands"	in the book Winesburg, Ohio
the poem "When I Have Fears"	in the book Complete Poems of John Keats
the song "Ziggy Stardust"	in the CD Changes
	the television show 60 Minutes
	the movie High Noon

Note   In printed works, including papers that are prepared on a computer, italic type—slanted type that looks *like this*—is used instead of underlining.

ACTIVITY

Use quotation marks or underlines as needed.

1. In her short story "A Sea Worry," Maxine Hong Kingston describes a group of teenage surfers and a mother who tries to understand them.

2. I bought the National Enquirer to read an article titled "Painful Beauty Secrets of the Stars."

3. We read the chapter "Pulling Up Roots" in Gail Sheehy's book Passages.

4. Jamila used an article titled "Winter Blues" from Time magazine in her research paper about seasonal depression.

5. The movie <u>Casablanca</u>, which starred Humphrey Bogart, was originally cast with Ronald Reagan in the leading role.

6. One of my grandfather's favorite old TV shows was <u>Thriller</u>, a horror series hosted by Boris Karloff, the man who starred in the 1931 movie <u>Frankenstein</u>.

7. When the Beatles' movie <u>A Hard Day's Night</u> was first shown, fans screamed so much that no one could hear the songs or the dialogue.

8. On my father's wall is a framed front page of <u>The New York Times</u> of February 25, 1940—the day he was born.

9. The sociology test will cover the first two chapters: "Culture and Diversity" and "Social Stratification."

10. An article in <u>Consumer Reports</u> called "Which Cereal for Breakfast?" claims that children can learn to like low-sugar cereals like Cheerios and Wheaties.

Other Uses of Quotation Marks

Quotation marks are also used as follows:

1   To set off special words or phrases from the rest of a sentence:

In grade school, we were taught a little jingle about the spelling rule "*i* before *e*."

What is the difference between "it's" and "its"?

(In this book, *italics* are often used instead of quotation marks to set off words.)

24.3a

2   To mark off a quotation within a quotation:

The physics professor said, "For class on Friday, do the problems at the end of the chapter titled 'Work and Energy.'"

Brendan remarked, "Did you know that Humphrey Bogart never actually said, 'Play it again, Sam' in the movie *Casablanca*?"

Note   A quotation within a quotation is indicated by *single* quotation marks, as shown above.

Review Test 1

Insert quotation marks where needed in the sentences that follow.

1. The psychology class read a short story called "Silent Snow, Secret Snow," about a young boy who creates his own fantasy world.

2. While filming the movie *Vertigo,* the actress Kim Novak was agonizing over how to play a particular scene until the director, Alfred Hitchcock, reminded her, "Kim, it's only a movie!"

3. "I'm against grade school students' using pocket calculators," said Fred. "I spent three years learning long division, and so should they."

4. The composer George Gershwin wrote many hundreds of hit songs, including classics like "Summertime" and "Somebody Loves Me."

5. When I gagged while taking a foul-tasting medicine, my wife said, "Put an ice cube on your tongue first, and then you won't taste it."

6. I looked twice at the newspaper headline that read, "Man in River Had Drinking Problem."

7. To learn more about the stock market for his business class, Jared began reading the column by Pablo Galarza in *Money* magazine called "MarketRap."

8. When a guest at the wedding was asked what he was giving the couple, he replied, "About six months."

9. Theodore Roosevelt, a pioneer in conservation, once said, "When I hear of the destruction of a species, I feel as if all the works of some great writer had perished."

10. "If you're ever in trouble," said the police officer, "you'll have a better chance of attracting aid if you shout 'Fire' instead of 'Help.'"

Review Test 2

Go through the comics section of a newspaper to find a comic strip that amuses you. Be sure to choose a strip where two or more characters are speaking to each other. Write a full description that will enable people who have not read the comic strip to visualize it clearly and appreciate its humor. Describe the setting and action in each panel, and enclose the words of the speakers in quotation marks.

Answers will vary.

39 Comma

Six Main Uses of the Comma

23.2

Commas are used mainly as follows:

1   To separate items in a series
2   To set off introductory material
3   On both sides of words that interrupt the flow of thought in a sentence
4   Between two complete thoughts connected by *and, but, for, or, nor, so, yet*
5   To set off a direct quotation from the rest of a sentence
6   For certain everyday material

You may find it helpful to remember that the comma often marks a slight pause or break in a sentence. Read aloud the sentence examples given for each rule, and listen for the minor pauses or breaks that are signaled by commas.

1 Comma between Items in a Series

Use commas to separate items in a series.

> The street vendor sold watches, necklaces, and earrings.
> The pitcher adjusted his cap, pawed the ground, and peered over his shoulder.
> The exercise instructor told us to inhale, exhale, and relax.
> Joe peered into the hot, still-smoking engine.

Notes

a   The final comma in a series is optional, but it is often used.
b   A comma is used between two descriptive words in a series only if *and* inserted between the words sounds natural. You could say:

> Joe peered into the hot *and* still-smoking engine.

But notice in the following sentence that the descriptive words do not sound natural when *and* is inserted between them. In such cases, no comma is used.

Tony wore a pale green tuxedo. (A pale *and* green tuxedo does not sound right, so no comma is used.)

ACTIVITY

Place commas between items in a series.

1. The old kitchen cabinets were littered with dead insects, crumbs, and dust balls.
2. Rudy stretched out on the swaying hammock, popped open a frosty can of soda, and balanced it carefully on his stomach.
3. The children splashed through the warm, deep, swirling rainwater that flooded the street.
4. The police officer's warm brown eyes, relaxed manner, and pleasant smile made her easy to talk to.
5. The musty, shadowy cellar with the crumbling cement floor was our favorite playground.

2 Comma after Introductory Material

Use a comma to set off introductory material.

Just in time, Sherry applied the brakes and avoided a car accident.

Muttering under his breath, Hassan reviewed the terms he had memorized.

In a wolf pack, the dominant male holds his tail higher than the other pack members.

Although he had been first in the checkout line, Deion let an elderly woman go ahead of him.

After the fire, we slogged through the ashes of the burned-out house.

Note   If the introductory material is brief, the comma is sometimes omitted. In the activities here, you should include the comma.

ACTIVITY

Place commas after introductory material.

1. As Patty struggled with the stuck window, gusts of cold rain blew in her face.

2. His heart pounding wildly, Jesse opened the letter that would tell him whether or not he had been accepted at college.

3. Along the once-pretty river, people had dumped old tires and loads of household trash.

4. When the band hadn't taken the stage forty-five minutes after the concert was supposed to begin, the audience members started shouting and stamping their feet.

5. Setting down a smudged glass of murky water, the waitress tossed Darren a greasy menu and asked if he'd care to order.

3 Comma around Words Interrupting the Flow of Thought

Use a comma on both sides of words or phrases that interrupt the flow of thought in a sentence.

The vinyl car seat, sticky from the heat, clung to my skin.

Marty's computer, which his wife got him as a birthday gift, occupies all of his spare time.

The hallway, dingy and dark, was illuminated by a bare bulb hanging from a wire.

Usually, by reading a sentence aloud, you can "hear" words that interrupt the flow of thought. In cases where you are not sure if certain words are interrupters, remove them from the sentence. If it still makes sense without the words, you know that the words are interrupters and that the information they give is nonessential. *Such nonessential or extra information is set off with commas.*

In the sentence

Sue Dodd, who goes to aerobics class with me, was in a serious car accident.

the words *who goes to aerobics class with me* are extra information not needed to identify the subject of the sentence, *Sue Dodd*. Commas go around such nonessential information. On the other hand, in the sentence

The woman who goes to aerobics class with me was in a serious accident.

the words *who goes to aerobics class with me* supply essential information—information needed for us to identify the woman being spoken of. If the words were removed from the sentence, we would no longer know exactly who was in the accident: "The woman was in a serious accident." Here is another example:

> *Watership Down,* a novel by Richard Adams, is the most thrilling adventure story I've ever read.

Here the words *a novel by Richard Adams* could be left out, and we would still know the basic meaning of the sentence. Commas are placed around such nonessential material. But in the sentence

> Richard Adams's novel *Watership Down* is the most thrilling adventure story I've ever read.

the title of the novel is essential. Without it the sentence would read, "Richard Adams's novel is the most thrilling adventure story I've ever read." We would not know which of Richard Adams's novels was so thrilling. Commas are not used around the title, because it provides essential information.

Most of the time you will be able to "hear" words that interrupt the flow of thought in a sentence and will not have to think about whether the words are essential or nonessential.

ACTIVITY

Use commas to set off interrupting words.

1. A slight breeze,hot and damp,ruffled the bedroom curtains.
2. The defrosting chickens,loosely wrapped in plastic,left a pool on the counter.
3. Lenny's wallet,which he kept in his front pants pocket,was linked to his belt with a metal chain.
4. Mr. Delgado,who is an avid Yankees fan,remembers the grand days of Mickey Mantle and Yogi Berra.
5. The fleet of tall ships,a majestic sight,made its way into the harbor.

4 Comma between Complete Thoughts

Use a comma between two complete thoughts connected by *and, but, for, or, nor, so, yet.*

> Sam closed all the windows, but the predicted thunderstorm never arrived.
>
> I like wearing comfortable clothing, so I buy oversize shirts and sweaters.
>
> Peggy doesn't envy the skinny models in magazines, for she is happy with her own well-rounded body.

Notes

a The comma is optional when the complete thoughts are short.

> The Ferris wheel started and Wilson closed his eyes.
> Many people left but the band played on.
> I made a wrong turn so I doubled back.

b Be careful not to use a comma to separate two verbs that belong to one subject. The comma is used only in sentences made up of two complete thoughts (two subjects and two verbs). In the sentence

> The doctor stared over his bifocals and lectured me about smoking.

there is only one subject (*doctor*) and a double verb (*stared* and *lectured*). No comma is needed. Likewise, the sentence

> Dean switched the lamp on and off and then tapped it with his fingers.

has only one subject (*Dean*) and a double verb (*switched* and *tapped*); therefore, no comma is needed.

ACTIVITY

Place a comma before a joining word that connects two complete thoughts (two subjects and two verbs). Remember, do *not* place a comma within a sentence that has only one subject and a double verb. (Some items may be correct as given.)

1. The television sitcom was interrupted for a special news bulletin, and I poked my head out of the kitchen to listen to the announcement.
2. The puppy was beaten by its former owner and cringes at the sound of a loud voice. *Correct*
3. The eccentric woman brought all her own clips and rollers to the beauty parlor, for she was afraid to use the ones there.
4. The tuna sandwich in my lunch is crushed, and the cream-filled cupcake is plastered to the bottom of the bag.
5. The landlord promised repeatedly to come and fix the leaking shower, but three months later he hasn't done a thing.
6. Ruth was tired of summer reruns, so she visited the town library to pick up some interesting books.

7. You can spend hours driving all over town to look for a particular type of camera,or you can telephone a few stores to find it quickly.

8. Many people strolled among the exhibits at the comic book collectors' convention and stopped to look at a rare first edition of *Superman*. *Correct*

9. Our neighborhood crime patrol escorts elderly people to the local bank and installs free dead-bolt locks on their apartment doors. *Correct*

10. Brendan tapped the small geraniums out of their pots and carefully planted them on his grandfather's grave. *Correct*

5 Comma with Direct Quotations

Use a comma to set off a direct quotation from the rest of a sentence.

The carnival barker cried, "Step right up and win a prize!"

"Now is the time to yield to temptation," my horoscope read.

"I'm sorry," said the restaurant hostess. "You'll have to wait."

"For my first writing assignment," said Scott, "I have to turn in a five-hundred-word description of a stone."

Note   Commas and periods at the end of a quotation go inside quotation marks. See also page 509.

ACTIVITY

Use commas to set off direct quotations from the rest of the sentence.

1. The coach announced,"In order to measure your lung capacity, you're going to attempt to blow up a plastic bag with one breath."

2. "A grapefruit," said the comedian,"is a lemon that had a chance and took advantage of it."

3. My father asked,"Did you know that the family moving next door has thirteen children?"

4. "Speak louder," a man in the back row said to the guest speaker. "I paid five dollars to hear you talk, not whisper."

5. The zookeeper explained to the visitors,"We can't tell the sex of a giant tortoise for almost ten years after its birth."

6 Comma with Everyday Material

Use a comma with certain everyday material.

Persons Spoken To

If you're the last to leave, Paul, please switch off the lights.

Fred, I think we're on the wrong road.

Did you see the playoff game, Lisa?

Dates

June 30, 2008, is the day I make the last payment on my car.

Addresses

I buy discount children's clothing from Isaacs Baby Wear Factory, Box 900, Chicago, Illinois 60614.

Note   No comma is used before a zip code.

Openings and Closings of Letters

Dear Santa,   Sincerely yours,

Dear Roberto,   Truly yours,

Note   In formal letters, a colon is used after the opening:
Dear Sir: *or* Dear Madam: *or* Dear Allan: *or* Dear Ms. Mohr:

Numbers

The insurance agent sold me a $50,000 term life insurance policy.

ACTIVITY

Place commas where needed.

1. Would you mind,George,if we borrowed your picnic cooler this weekend?

2. The enchiladas served at Los Amigos,5607 Pacific Boulevard,are the best in town.

3. An estimated 875,000 African American men participated in the Million Man March on Washington on October 16,1995.

4. The mileage chart shows,Elaine,that we'll have to drive 1,231 miles to get to Sarasota,Florida.

5. The coupon refund address is 2120 Industrial Highway,Great Plains,Minnesota 55455.

■ Review Test 1

Insert commas where needed. In the space provided below each sentence, summarize briefly the rule that explains the comma or commas used.

Wording of rules may vary.

1. "Kleenex tissues," said the history professor, "were first used as gas mask filters in World War I."

   comma with direct quotation

2. Dee ordered a sundae with three scoops of vanilla ice cream, miniature marsh-mallows, and raspberry sauce.

   comma with items in a series

3. While waiting to enter the movie theater, we studied the faces of the people just leaving to see if they had liked the show.

   comma after introductory material

4. I had left my wallet on the store counter, but the clerk called me at home to say that it was safe.

   comma between two complete thoughts

5. The demonstrators protesting nuclear arms carried signs reading, "Humans have never invented a weapon that they haven't used."

   comma to set off a direct quotation

6. Large cactus plants, which now sell for very high prices, are being stolen from national parks and protected desert areas.

   comma with words interrupting the flow of thought

7. At the age of twenty-one, Tiger Woods won the 1997 Masters Tournament with the highest margin of victory in the golfing tournament's history.

   comma after introductory material

8. The talk-show guest, a former child star, said that one director threatened to shoot her dog if she didn't cry on cue.

   comma with words interrupting the flow of thought

9. Tom watched nervously as the dentist assembled drills, mirrors, clamps, picks, and cylinders of cotton on a tray next to the reclining chair.

   comma with items in a series

10. Cats and dogs, like most animals, love the taste of salt and will lick humans' hands to get it.

    comma with words interrupting the flow of thought

■ Review Test 2

Insert commas where needed. Mark the one sentence that is correct with a C.

1. Before leaving for the gym,Nikki added extra socks and a tube of shampoo to the gear in her duffel bag.

2. My father said,"Golf isn't for me. I can't afford to buy lots of expensive sticks so that I can lose lots of expensive white balls."

3. Clogged with soggy birds' nests,the chimney had allowed dangerous gases to accumulate in our house.

4. Oscar took a time-exposure photo of the busy highway,so the cars' taillights appeared in the developed print as winding red ribbons.

5. On May 16,2003,my older brother got married,and exactly a year later he got divorced.

6. During the summer graduation ceremony, students fanned themselves with commencement programs,and parents hid in the shade of trees.

7. Leaving eight astronauts dead,the space shuttle *Columbia* broke apart as it returned to Earth on February 1,2003.

8. "When I was little," said Ernie,"my brother told me it was illegal to kill praying mantises. I still don't know if that's true or not."

9. A huge side of beef,its red flesh marbled with streaks of creamy fat,hung from a razor-sharp steel hook.

10. A line of dancing numerals on *Sesame Street* kicked across the screen like a chorus line. *Correct*

■ Review Test 3

In the following passage, there are ten missing commas. Add the commas where needed. The types of mistakes to look for are shown in the box below.

> 2 commas missing between items in a series
> 1 comma missing after introductory material
> 4 commas missing around interrupting words
> 2 commas missing between complete thoughts
> 1 comma missing with a direct quotation

When I was about ten years old, I developed several schemes to avoid eating liver, a food I despise. My first scheme involved my little brother. Timmy, too young to realize what a horrible food liver is, always ate every bit of his portion. On liver nights, I used to sit next to Tim and slide my slab of meat onto his plate when my parents weren't paying attention. This strategy worked until, older and wiser, Tim decided to reject his liver along with the rest of us. Another liver-disposal method I used was hiding the meat right on the plate. I'd cut the liver into tiny squares half the size of postage stamps, and then I would carefully hide the pieces. I'd put them inside the skin of my baked potato, beneath some mashed peas, or under a crumpled paper napkin. This strategy worked perfectly only if my mother didn't look too closely as she scraped the dishes. Once she said to me, "Do you know you left a lot of liver on your plate?" My best liver trick was to hide the disgusting stuff on a three-inch-wide wooden ledge that ran under our dining-room table. I'd put little pieces of liver on the ledge when Mom wasn't looking; I would sneak the dried-up scraps into the garbage early the next day. Our dog would sometimes smell the liver, try to get at it, and bang his head noisily against the bottom of the table. These strategies seemed like a lot of work, but I never hesitated to take whatever steps I could. Anything was better than eating a piece of meat that tasted like old socks soaked in mud.

■ Review Test 4

On separate paper, write six sentences, one illustrating each of the six main comma rules.
Answers will vary.

40 Other Punctuation Marks

Colon (:)

24.2

Use the colon at the end of a complete statement to introduce a list, a long quotation, or an explanation.

1   List:

The store will close at noon on the following dates: November 26, December 24, and December 31.

2   Quotation:

In his book *Life Lines,* Forrest Church maintains that people should cry more: "Life is difficult. Some people pretend that it is not, that we should be able to breeze through. Yet hardly a week passes in which most of us don't have something worth crying about."

3   Explanation:

Here's a temporary solution to a dripping faucet: tie a string to it, and let the drops slide down the string to the sink.

ACTIVITY

Place colons where needed in the sentences below:

1. Bring these items to registration:a ballpoint pen, your student ID card, and a check made out to the college.
2. The road was closed because of an emergency:an enormous tree had fallen and blocked both lanes.

525

3. Willa Cather, the American author, had an insightful comment about plots: "There are only two or three human stories, and they go on repeating themselves as fiercely as if they had never happened before."

Semicolon (;)

24.1

The main use of the semicolon is to mark a break between two complete thoughts, as explained on pages 436–439. Another use is to mark off items in a series when the items themselves contain commas. Here are some examples:

Maya's children are named Melantha, which means "black flower"; Yonina, which means "dove"; and Cynthia, which means "moon goddess."

My parents' favorite albums are *Rubber Soul,* by the Beatles; *Songs in the Key of Life,* by Stevie Wonder; and *Bridge over Troubled Water,* by Simon and Garfunkel.

ACTIVITY

Place semicolons where needed in the sentences below.

1. Strange things happen at very low temperatures; a rose will shatter like glass.
2. My sister had a profitable summer: by mowing lawns, she earned $125; by washing cars, $85; and by walking the neighbors' dogs, $110.
3. The children who starred in the play were Kari Rosoff, nine years old; Flora Junco, twelve years old; and Ezra Johnson, three years old.

Dash (—)

24.4

A dash signals a pause longer than a comma but not as complete as a period. Use a dash to set off words for dramatic effect:

I was so exhausted that I fell asleep within seconds—standing up.

He had many good qualities—sincerity, honesty, and thoughtfulness—yet he had few friends.

The pardon from the governor finally arrived—too late.

Notes

    a A dash can be formed on a keyboard by striking the hyphen twice (--). Computer software also has a symbol for the dash. In handwriting, a dash is as long as two letters would be.

    b Be careful not to overuse dashes.

ACTIVITY

Place dashes where needed in the following sentences.

1. The victim's leg broken in three places lay twisted at an odd angle on the pavement.
2. The wallet was found in a trash can minus the cash.
3. After nine days of hiking in the wilderness, sleeping under the stars, and communing with nature, I could think of only one thing a hot shower.

Parentheses ( )

ALLWRITE!
24.5

Parentheses are used to set off extra or incidental information from the rest of a sentence:

In 1913, the tax on an annual income of $4,000 (a comfortable wage at that time) was one penny.

Arthur C. Clarke, author of science fiction books (including *2001: A Space Odyssey*), was inspired as a young man by the magazine *Astounding Stories*.

Note   Do not use parentheses too often in your writing.

ACTIVITY

Add parentheses where needed.

1. Though the first *Star Trek* series originally ran for only three seasons (1965–1968), it gave rise to a number of spinoff shows which remain popular to this day.
2. Whenever Jack has too much to drink (even one drink is sometimes too much), he becomes loud and abusive.
3. When I opened the textbook, I discovered that many pages (mostly in the first chapter) were completely blank.

Hyphen (-)

26.2

1 Use a hyphen with two or more words that act as a single unit describing a noun.

The light-footed burglar silently slipped open the sliding glass door.

While being interviewed on the late-night talk show, the quarterback announced his intention to retire.

With a needle, Rich punctured the fluid-filled blister on his toe.

2 Use a hyphen to divide a word at the end of a line of writing or typing. When you need to divide a word at the end of a line, divide it between syllables. Use your dictionary to be sure of correct syllable divisions.

Selena's first year at college was a time filled with numerous new pressures and responsibilities.

Notes

a Do not divide words of one syllable.

b Do not divide a word if you can avoid dividing it.

ACTIVITY

Place hyphens where needed.

1. The blood-red moon hanging low on the horizon made a picture-perfect atmosphere for Halloween night.

2. My father, who grew up in a poverty-stricken household, remembers putting cardboard in his shoes when the soles wore out.

3. The well-written article in *Newsweek* described the nerve-racking experiences of a journalist who infiltrated the mob.

■ Review Test

At the appropriate spot, place the punctuation mark shown in the margin.

—

1. A bad case of flu, a burglary, the death of an uncle it was not what you would call a pleasant week.

( )   2. My grandfather(who will be ninety in May)says that hard work and a glass of wine every day are the secrets of a long life.

:   3. Mark Twain offered this advice to writers:"The difference between the right word and the nearly right word is the difference between lightning and the lightning bug."

-   4. The passengers in the glass-bottomed boat stared at the colorful fish in the water below.

( )   5. Ellen's birthday(December 27)falls so close to Christmas that she gets only one set of presents.

;   6. The dog-show winners included Freckles, a springer spaniel;King Leo, a German shepherd;and Big Guy, a miniature schnauzer.

—   7. I feel I have two chances of winning the lottery slim and none.

-   8. Cold-hearted stepmothers are a fixture in many famous fairy tales.

;   9. Some people need absolute quiet in order to study;they can't concentrate with the soft sounds of a radio, air conditioner, or television in the background.

:   10. A critic reviewing a bad play wrote, "I saw the play under the worst possible circumstances:the curtain was up."

Spelling Improvement

Poor spelling often results from bad habits developed in the early school years. With work, such habits can be corrected. If you can write your name without misspelling it, there is no reason why you cannot do the same with almost any word in the English language. Following are steps you can take to improve your spelling.

Step 1: Use the Dictionary

26.1

Get into the habit of using the dictionary. When you write a paper, allow yourself time to look up the spelling of all those words you are unsure about. Do not overlook the value of this step just because it is such a simple one. By using the dictionary, you can probably make yourself a 95 percent better speller.

Step 2: Keep a Personal Spelling List

Keep a list of words you misspell and study the words regularly. Write the list on the back page of a frequently used notebook or on a separate sheet of paper titled "Personal Spelling List."

To master the words on your personal spelling list, do the following:

1   Write down any hint that will help you remember the spelling of a word. For example, you might want to note that *occasion* is spelled with two *c*'s or that *all right* is two words, not one word.

2   Study a word by looking at it, saying it, and spelling it. You may also want to write out the word one or more times, or "air write" it with your finger in large, exaggerated motions.

3   When you have trouble spelling a long word, try to break the word into syllables and see whether you can spell the syllables. For example, *inadvertent* can be spelled easily if you can hear and spell in turn its four syllables: *in ad ver tent.* The word *consternation* can be spelled easily if you hear and spell its four

syllables in turn: *con ster na tion*. Remember, then: Try to see, hear, and spell long words in terms of their syllables.

4   Keep in mind that review and repeated self-testing are keys to effective learning. When you are learning a series of words, go back after studying each new word and review all the preceding ones.

Step 3: Master Commonly Confused Words

Master the meanings and spellings of the commonly confused words on pages 535–543. Your instructor may assign twenty words for you to study at a time and give you a series of quizzes until you have mastered the words.

Step 4: Learn Key Words in Major Subjects

Make up and master lists of words central to the vocabulary of your major subjects. For example, a list of key words in business might include *economics, management, resources, scarcity, capitalism, decentralization, productivity, enterprise,* and so on; in psychology, *behavior, investigation, experimentation, frustration, cognition, stimulus, response, organism,* and so on. Set aside a specific portion of your various course notebooks to be used only for such lists, and study them using the methods described above for learning words.

Step 5: Study a Basic Word List

Following is a list of 250 English words that are often misspelled. Study their spellings. Your instructor may assign 25 or 50 words for you to study at a time and give you a series of quizzes until you have mastered the entire list.

250 Basic
Words

absence	comfortable	harass
ache	committed	height
achieve	completely	hospital
acknowledge	conceit	hundred
advice	conscience	husband
aisle	conscious	imitation
all right	conversation	incredible
already	cruelty	independent
amateur	50 daughter	instant
answer	deceit	instead
anxious	definite	intelligence
appearance	deposit	interest
appetite	dictionary	interfere
attempt	disastrous	interrupt
attendance	disease	irresistible
autumn	distance	January
awful	doctor	kindergarten
bachelor	doubt	100 leisure
balance	efficient	library
bargain	eighth	lightning
basically	either	likely
beautiful	emphasize	livelihood
believe	entrance	loneliness
beneficial	environment	loose
25 bottom	exaggerate	magazine
breathe	examine	making
brilliant	existence	maintain
bureau	familiar	marriage
business	fascinate	material
cafeteria	February	mathematics
calendar	financial	medicine
candidate	foreign	minute
category	forty	mortgage
ceiling	75 friend	muscle
cemetery	furniture	naturally
chief	government	necessary
choose	grammar	neither
cigarette	grieve	nickel
citizen	guidance	niece
college	hammer	ninety
column	handkerchief	noise

obedience
125 obstacle
occasion
occur
occurrence
omission
opinion
opportunity
optimist
ounce
outrageous
pageant
pamphlet
people
perform
persistent
physically
picnic
plausible
pleasant
policeman
possible
precede
prefer
preference
prejudice
150 prescription
probably
psychology
pursue
quantity
quarter
quiet
quiz
raise
really
recede
receive
recognize
recommend
reference
region
reign

relieve
religion
representative
resistance
restaurant
rhythm
ridiculous
right
175 safety
said
salary
scarcely
scholastic
science
scissors
secretary
seize
separate
sergeant
several
severely
shriek
siege
similar
sincerely
sophomore
straight
succeed
suppress
telephone
temperature
tenant
tendency
200 tenth
than
theater
though
thousand
through
tomorrow
tongue
tonight

tournament
toward
transferred
trousers
truly
twelfth
unanimous
until
unusual
usage
used
usual
usually
vacuum
valuable
variety
225 vegetable
vengeance
view
villain
vision
visitor
voice
Washington
wear
weather
Wednesday
weight
weird
welcome
whether
which
woman
women
won't
writing
written
wrong
yesterday
yolk
your
250 you're

Step 6: Use Electronic Aids

There are several electronic aids that can help your spelling. First, most *electronic typewriters* can be set to beep automatically when you misspell a word. They include built-in dictionaries that will then give you the correct spelling. Second, *electronic spell-checks* are pocket-size devices that look much like the pocket calculators you may use in math class. Electronic spellers can be found in almost any electronics store. The checker includes a tiny keyboard. You type out the word the way you think it is spelled, and the checker quickly provides you with the correct spelling of related words. Finally, *a computer with a spell-checker* as part of its word-processing program will identify incorrect words and suggest correct spellings. If you know how to write on the computer, you will have little trouble learning how to use the spell-check feature.

42 Commonly Confused Words

Homonyms

Some words are commonly confused because they have the same sounds but different meanings and spellings; such words are known as *homonyms*. Following are a number of homonyms. Complete the activity for each set of words, and check off and study the words that give you trouble.

all ready   completely prepared
already   previously; before

It was *already* four o'clock by the time I thought about lunch.

My report was *all ready,* but the class was canceled.

Fill in the blanks: Tyrone was ___all ready___ to sign up for the course when he discovered that it had ___already___ closed.

brake   stop
break   come apart

The mechanic advised me to add *brake* fluid to my car.

During a commercial *break,* Marie lay on the floor and did fifty sit-ups.

Fill in the blanks: Tim, a poor driver, would always ___brake___ at the last minute and would usually ___break___ the speed limit as well.

course   part of a meal; a school subject; direction
coarse   rough

At the movies, I tried to decide on a *course* of action that would put an end to the *coarse* language of the man behind me.

Fill in the blanks: Over the _____course_____ of time, jagged, _____coarse_____ rocks will be polished to smoothness by the pounding waves.

hear   perceive with the ear
here   in this place

I can *hear* the performers so well from *here* that I don't want to change my seat.

Fill in the blanks: The chairperson explained that the meeting was being held _____here_____ in the auditorium to enable everyone to _____hear_____ the debate.

hole   an empty spot
whole   entire

A *hole* in the crumbling brick mortar made a convenient home for a small bird and its *whole* family.

Fill in the blanks: The _____hole_____ in Dave's argument wouldn't exist if he put his _____whole_____ concentration into his thinking.

its   belonging to it
it's   shortened form of "it is" or "it has"

The tall giraffe lowered *its* head (the head belonging to the giraffe) to the level of the car window and peered in at us.

It's (it is) too late to sign up for the theater trip to New York.

Fill in the blanks: I decided not to take the course because _____it's_____ too easy; _____its_____ content offers no challenge whatever.

knew   past form of *know*
new   not old

No one *knew* our *new* phone number, but the obscene calls continued.

Fill in the blanks: Even people who _____*knew*_____ Charlie well didn't recognize him with his _____*new*_____ beard.

know   to understand
no   a negative

By the time students complete that course, they *know* two computer languages and have *no* trouble writing their own programs.

Fill in the blanks: Dogs and cats usually _____*know*_____ by the tone of the speaker's voice when they are being told " _____*no*_____ ."

passed   went by; succeeded in; handed to
past   a time before the present; by, as in "I drove past the house"

As Yvonne *passed* exit six on the interstate, she knew she had gone *past* the correct turnoff.

Fill in the blanks: Lewis asked for a meeting with his boss to learn why he had been _____*passed*_____ over for promotion twice in the _____*past*_____ year.

peace   calm
piece   a part

The best *piece* of advice she ever received was to maintain her own inner *peace*.

Fill in the blanks: Upon hearing that _____*piece*_____ of music, my angry mood was gradually replaced by one of _____*peace*_____ .

plain   simple
plane   aircraft

The *plain* box contained a very expensive model *plane* kit.

Fill in the blanks: After unsuccessfully trying to overcome her fear, Selena finally admitted the _____plain_____ truth: she was terrified of flying in a _____plane_____.

principal   main; a person in charge of a school
principle   a law or standard

If the *principal* ingredient in this stew is octopus, I'll abandon my *principle* of trying everything at least once.

Fill in the blanks: Our _____principal_____ insists that all students adhere to every school _____principle_____ regarding dress, tardiness, and smoking.

right   correct; opposite of "left"
write   to put words on paper

Without the *right* amount of advance planning, it is difficult to *write* a good research paper.

Fill in the blanks: Connie wanted to send for the CDs offered on TV, but she could not _____write_____ fast enough to get all the _____right_____ information down before the commercial ended.

than   (thăn)   used in comparisons
then   (thĕn)   at that time

I made more money *then,* but I've never been happier *than* I am now.

Fill in the blanks: When I was in high school, I wanted a racy two-seater convertible more _____than_____ anything else; but _____then_____ my friends pointed out that only one person would be able to ride with me.

their   belonging to them

there   at that place; a neutral word used with verbs like *is, are, was, were, have,* and *had*

they're   shortened form of "they are"

    The tenants *there* are complaining because *they're* being cheated by *their* landlord.

Fill in the blanks: The tomatoes I planted _____*there*_____ in the back of the garden are finally ripening, but _____*their*_____ bright red color will attract hungry raccoons, and I fear ___ *they're* ___ going to be eaten.

threw   past form of *throw*

through   from one side to the other; finished

    As the inexperienced pizza-maker *threw* the pie into the air, he punched a hole *through* its thin crust.

Fill in the blanks: As the president moved slowly _____*through*_____ the cheering crowd, the Secret Service agent suddenly _____*threw*_____ himself at a man waving a small metal object.

to   verb part, as in *to smile;* toward, as in "I'm going *to* heaven"

too   overly, as in "The pizza was *too* hot"; also, as in "The coffee was hot, *too.*"

two   the number 2

    I ran *to* the car *to* roll up the windows. (The first *to* means "toward"; the second *to* is a verb part that goes with *roll.*)

    That amusement park is *too* far away; I hear that it's expensive, *too.* (The first *too* means "overly"; the second *too* means "also.")

    The *two* players (2 players) jumped up to tap the basketball away.

Fill in the blanks: The _____*two*_____ of them have been dating for a year, but lately they seem _____*to*_____ be arguing _____*too*_____ often to pretend nothing is wrong.

wear   to have on
where   in what place

Where I will *wear* a purple feather boa is not the point; I just want to buy it.

Fill in the blanks: _____Where_____ were we going the night I refused to _____wear_____ a tie?

weather   atmospheric conditions
whether   if it happens that; in case; if

Although meteorologists are *weather* specialists, even they can't predict *whether* a hurricane will change course.

Fill in the blanks: The gloomy _____weather_____ report in the paper this morning ended all discussion of _____whether_____ to pack a picnic lunch for later.

whose   belonging to whom
who's   shortened form of "who is" and "who has"

"*Who's* the patient *whose* filling fell out?" the dentist's assistant asked.

Fill in the blanks: _____Who's_____ the salesperson _____whose_____ customers are always complaining about his high-pressure tactics?

your   belonging to you
you're   shortened form of "you are"

You're making a fool of yourself; *your* Elvis imitation isn't funny.

Fill in the blanks: If _____you're_____ having trouble filling out _____your_____ tax return, why don't you call the IRS's toll-free hot line?

Other Words Frequently Confused

Not all frequently confused words are homonyms. Here is a list of other words that people often confuse. Complete the activities for each set of words, and check off and study the words that give you trouble.

a   Both *a* and *an* are used before other words to mean, approximately, "one."
an

Generally you should use *an* before words starting with a vowel (*a, e, i, o, u*):

     an orange   an umbrella   an indication   an ape   an effort

Generally you should use *a* before words starting with a consonant (all other letters):

     a genius   a movie   a speech   a study   a typewriter

Fill in the blanks: The morning after the party, I had _____*a*_____ pounding headache and _____*an*_____ upset stomach.

accept   (ăk sĕpt′)   to receive; agree to
except   (ĕk sĕpt′)   excluding; but

     It was easy to *accept* the book's plot, *except* for one unlikely coincidence at the very end.

Fill in the blanks: Ved would _____*accept*_____ the position, _____*except*_____ that it would add twenty minutes to his daily commute.

advice   (ăd vīs′)   noun meaning "an opinion"
advise   (ăd vīz′)   verb meaning "to counsel, to give advice"

     I have learned not to take my sister's *advice* on straightening out my life.
     A counselor can *advise* you about the courses you'll need next year.

Fill in the blanks: Karen is so troubled about losing her job that I will _____*advise*_____ her to seek the _____*advice*_____ of a professional counselor.

affect   (uh fĕkt′)   verb meaning "to influence"
effect   (ĭ fĕkt′)   verb meaning "to cause something"; noun meaning "result"

> The bad weather will definitely *affect* the outcome of the election.
>
> If we can *effect* a change in George's attitude, he may do better in his courses.
>
> One *effect* of the strike will be dwindling supplies in the supermarkets.

Fill in the blanks: Scientists have studied the _____*effect*_____ of large quantities of saccharine on lab animals but have yet to learn how similar amounts _____*affect*_____ human beings.

among   implies three or more
between   implies only two

> After the team of surgeons consulted *among* themselves, they decided that the bullet was lodged *between* two of the patient's ribs.

Fill in the blanks: _____*Between*_____ halves, one enthusiastic fan stood up _____*among*_____ his equally fanatic friends and took off his coat and shirt.

beside   along the side of
besides   in addition to

> *Besides* doing daily inventories, I have to stand *beside* the cashier whenever the store gets crowded.

Fill in the blanks: _____*Besides*_____ those books on the table, I plan to use these magazines stacked _____*beside*_____ me while doing my research paper.

fewer   used with things that can be counted
less   refers to amount, value, or degree

> I've taken *fewer* classes this semester, so I hope to have *less* trouble finding time to study.

Fill in the blanks: This beer advertises that it has _____*fewer*_____ calories and is _____*less*_____ filling.

former   refers to the first of two items named
latter   refers to the second of two items named

> Sue yelled at her sons, Greg and John, when she got home; the *former* (Greg) had left the refrigerator open and the *latter* (John) had left wet towels all over the bathroom.

Fill in the blanks: Eddy collects coupons and parking tickets: the _____*former*_____ save him money and the _____*latter*_____ are going to cost him a great deal of money some day.

learn   to gain knowledge
teach   to give knowledge

> I can't *learn* a new skill unless someone with lots of patience *teaches* me.

Fill in the blanks: Because she is quick to _____*learn*_____ new things, Mandy has offered to _____*teach*_____ me how to play the latest video games.

loose   (lōōs)   not fastened; not tight-fitting
lose   (lōōz)   to misplace; fail to win

> In this strong wind, the house may *lose* some of its *loose* roof shingles.

Fill in the blanks: A _____*loose*_____ wire in the television set was causing us to _____*lose*_____ the picture.

quiet   (kwī′ĭt)   peaceful
quite   (kwīt)   entirely; really; rather

> Jennifer seems *quiet* and demure, but she has *quite* a temper at times.

Fill in the blanks: Most people think the library is _____*quite*_____ a good place to study, but I find the extreme _____*quiet*_____ distracting.

ACTIVITY

These sentences check your understanding of *its, it's; there, their, they're; to, too, two;* and *your, you're.* Underline the two incorrect spellings in each sentence. Then spell the words correctly in the spaces provided.

_It's_

your

1. "Its not a very good idea," yelled Alexandra's boss, "to tell you're customer that the striped dress she plans to buy makes her look like a pregnant tiger."

Your

_it's_

2. You're long skirt got stuck in the car door, and now its sweeping the highway.

you're

there

3. When your young, their is a tendency to confuse a crush with true love.

two

too

4. After too hours of typing, Lin was to tired to type any longer.

its

its

5. It is unusual for a restaurant to lose it's license, but this one had more mice in its' kitchen than cooks.

_to_

their

6. The vampires bought a knife sharpener in order too sharpen there teeth.

You're

your

7. Your sometimes surprised by who you're friends turn out to be in difficult times.

too

they're

8. When the children get to quiet, Clare knows their getting into trouble.

Their

they're

9. There friendship developed into love as the years passed, and now, in midlife, their newlyweds.

two

_It's_

10. There is no reason to panic if you get a bad grade or too. Its well known that many successful people were not great students.

■ Review Test 1

Underline the correct word in the parentheses. Rather than guessing, look back at the explanations of the words when necessary.

1. I (know, no) that several of the tenants have decided (to, too, two) take (their, there, they're) case to court.

2. (Whose, <u>Who's</u>) the author of that book about the (affects, <u>effects</u>) of eating (to, <u>too</u>, two) much protein?

3. In our supermarket is a counter (<u>where</u>, wear) (your, <u>you're</u>) welcome to sit down and have free coffee and doughnuts.

4. (Its, <u>It's</u>) possible to (loose, <u>lose</u>) friends by constantly giving out unwanted (<u>advice</u>, advise).

5. For a long time, I couldn't (<u>accept</u>, except) the fact that my husband wanted a divorce; (<u>then</u>, than) I decided to stop being angry and get on with life.

6. I spent the (hole, <u>whole</u>) day browsing (threw, <u>through</u>) the chapters in my business textbook, but I didn't really study them.

7. The newly appointed (<u>principal</u>, principle) is (<u>quite</u>, quiet) familiar with the problems (hear, <u>here</u>) at our school.

8. I found that our cat had (all ready, <u>already</u>) had her kittens (<u>among</u>, between) the weeds (<u>beside</u>, besides) the porch.

9. I (advice, <u>advise</u>) you not to take children to that movie; the special (affects, <u>effects</u>) are (to, <u>too</u>, two) frightening.

10. It seems that nobody will ever be able to (learn, <u>teach</u>) Mario to take (<u>fewer</u>, less) chances with his car.

■ Review Test 2

On separate paper, write short sentences using the ten words shown below.
Answers will vary.

1. accept
2. its
3. you're
4. too
5. then
6. principal
7. their
8. passed
9. fewer
10. who's

43 Effective Word Choice

Choose your words carefully when you write. Always take the time to think about your word choices rather than simply use the first word that comes to mind. You want to develop the habit of selecting words that are precise and appropriate for your purpose. One way you can show sensitivity to language is by avoiding slang, clichés, and pretentious words.

Slang

We often use slang expressions when we talk because they are so vivid and colorful. However, slang is usually out of place in formal writing. Here are some examples of slang:

> Someone *ripped off* Ken's new Adidas running shoes from his locker.
>
> After the game, we *stuffed our faces* at the diner.
>
> I finally told my parents to *get off my case.*
>
> The movie really *grossed me out.*

Slang expressions have a number of drawbacks. They go out of date quickly, they become tiresome if used excessively in writing, and they may communicate clearly to some readers but not to others. Also, the use of slang can be an evasion of the specific details that are often needed to make one's meaning clear in writing. For example, in "The movie really grossed me out," the writer has not provided the specific details about the movie necessary for us to clearly understand the statement. Was it acting, special effects, or violent scenes that the writer found so disgusting? In general, then, you should avoid slang in your writing. If you are in doubt about whether an expression is slang, it may help to check a recently published hardbound dictionary.

ACTIVITY

Rewrite the following sentences, replacing the italicized slang words with more formal ones.

EXAMPLE   When we told the neighbors to *can the noise,* they *freaked out.*

 When we told the neighbors to be quiet, they got upset.

Answers may vary.

1. I didn't realize how *messed up* Joey was until he stole some money from his parents and *split* for a month.

   . . . troubled . . . left

2. Greg was so *bummed out* the day he got fired that he didn't do anything except *veg out* in front of the TV.

   . . . depressed. . . relax.

3. Theo was so *wiped out* after his workout at the gym that he couldn't *get it together* to defrost a frozen dinner.

   . . . tired . . . find the energy . . .

4. When Rick tried to *put the move on* Lola at the school party, she told him to *shove off.*

   . . . flirt with . . . leave.

5. The entire town was *psyched* that the corrupt mayor *got busted.*

   . . . thrilled (or: excited) . . . was arrested.

Clichés

21.5

A *cliché* is an expression that has been worn out through constant use. Here are some typical clichés:

short but sweet	last but not least
drop in the bucket	work like a dog
had a hard time of it	all work and no play
word to the wise	it goes without saying
it dawned on me	at a loss for words
sigh of relief	taking a big chance
too little, too late	took a turn for the worse
singing the blues	easier said than done
in the nick of time	on top of the world
too close for comfort	time and time again
saw the light	make ends meet

Clichés are common in speech but make your writing seem tired and stale. Also, they are often an evasion of the specific details that you must work to provide in your writing. You should, then, avoid clichés and try to express your meaning in fresh, original ways.

ACTIVITY 1

Underline the cliché in each of the following sentences. Then substitute specific, fresh words for the trite expression.

EXAMPLE   My boyfriend has stuck with me <u>through thick and thin</u>.
          through good times and bad

Rewritten passages may vary.
  1. As the only girl in an otherwise all-boy family, I <u>got away with murder</u>.
     . . . was spoiled. (or: . . . could do anything I wanted.)

2. When I realized I'd lost my textbook, I knew I was <u>up the creek without a paddle</u>.

   . . . in serious trouble.

3. My suggestion is just <u>a shot in the dark</u>, but it's better than nothing.

   . . . just a guess . . .

4. Janice got <u>more than she bargained for</u> when she offered to help Larry with his math homework.

   . . . more work than she expected . . .

5. Bob is <u>pushing his luck</u> by driving a car with bald tires.

   . . . taking a risk . . .

6. On a hot, sticky midsummer day, iced tea or any frosty drink <u>really hits the spot</u>.

   . . . is really refreshing. (or: is really satisfying.)

7. Nadia <u>thanks her lucky stars</u> that she was born with brains, beauty, and humility.

   . . . is grateful . . .

8. Anything that involves mathematical ability has always been <u>right up my alley</u>.

   . . . easy for me. (or: I've always done well at anything that . . .)

9. Your chance of buying a good used car from that dealer is <u>one in a million</u>.

   . . . slim.

10. Even when we are <u>up to our eyeballs in work</u>, our boss wonders if we have enough to do.

    . . . overloaded with work . . . (or: . . . very busy . . . ; or: . . . overworked . . .)

ACTIVITY 2

Write a short paragraph describing the kind of day you had. Try to put as many clichés as possible into it. For example, "I got up at the crack of dawn, ready to take on the world. I grabbed a bite to eat. . . ." By making yourself aware of clichés in this way, you should lessen the chance that they will appear in your writing.

Answers will vary.

Pretentious Words

Some people feel that they can improve their writing by using fancy, elevated words rather than simple, natural words. They use artificial, stilted language that more often obscures their meaning than communicates it clearly. Here are some unnatural-sounding sentences:

It was a splendid opportunity to get some slumber.

We relished the delicious repast.

The officer apprehended the intoxicated operator of the vehicle.

This establishment sells women's apparel and children's garments.

The same thoughts can be expressed more clearly and effectively by using plain, natural language, as below:

It was a good chance to get some sleep.

We enjoyed the delicious meal.

The officer arrested the drunken driver.

This store sells women's and children's clothes.

Here are some other inflated words and simpler words that could replace them:

Inflated Words	Simpler Words
subsequent to	after
finalize	finish
transmit	send
facilitate	help
component	part
initiate	begin
delineate	describe
manifested	shown
to endeavor	to try

ACTIVITY

Cross out the inflated words in each sentence. Then substitute clear, simple language for the inflated words.

EXAMPLE The ~~conflagration~~ was ~~initiated~~ by an arsonist.

The fire was started by an arsonist.

Rewritten versions may vary.

1. Rico and his brother do not ~~interrelate in a harmonious manner.~~

   . . . get along well.

2. The meaning of the movie's ~~conclusion eluded my comprehension.~~

   I didn't understand the end of the movie.

3. The ~~departmental conference~~ will ~~commence~~ promptly at two o'clock.

   . . . department meeting will begin . . .

4. A man dressed in odd ~~attire accosted~~ me on the street.

   . . . clothing stopped . . .

5. When my ~~writing implement malfunctioned,~~ I asked the professor for another.

   . . . pen (or pencil) broke . . .

Review Test

Certain words are italicized in the following sentences. In the space provided at the left, identify the words as slang (S), a cliché (C), or pretentious words (PW). Then replace the words with more effective diction.

Rewritten versions may differ.

C   1. Losing weight is *easier said than done* for someone who loves sweets.

     . . . difficult . . . (or: not easy)

PW   2. After dinner, we washed the *culinary utensils* and wrapped the *excess* food.

     . . . dishes . . . leftover

C   3. Bruce is so stubborn that talking to him is like *talking to a brick wall.*

     useless (or: hopeless; or: futile)

S   4. Michelle spent the summer *watching the tube* and *catching rays.*

     . . . watching television and sunbathing.

S   5. The fans, *all fired up* after the game, *peeled out* of the parking lot and honked their horns.

     . . . excited (or: elated) . . . drove quickly . . .

_____C_____   6. The stew I made contained *everything but the kitchen sink.*
         . . . many ingredients.

_____S_____   7. That *guy* isn't really a criminal; he's just gotten a *bum rap.*
         . . . man . . . an unjust sentence (or: unfair treatment)

_____PW_____   8. A company cannot *implement changes and attain growth* without *input from its personnel.*
         . . . change and grow . . . feedback from its workers.

_____C_____   9. I failed the test, and to *add insult to injury,* I got a low grade on my paper.
         . . . and to make matters worse, . . .

_____PW_____   10. I *perused* several *periodicals* while I waited for the doctor.
         . . . read . . . magazines . . .

Editing Tests

The twelve editing tests in this chapter will give you practice in revising to correct sentence-skills mistakes. Remember that if you don't edit carefully, you run the risk of sabotaging much of the work you have put into a paper. If readers see too many surface flaws, they may assume that you don't place much value on what you have to say, and they may not give your ideas a fair hearing. Revising to eliminate sentence-skills errors is a basic part of clear, effective writing.

In five of the tests, the spots where errors occur have been underlined; your job is to identify and correct each error. In the rest of the tests, you must locate as well as identify and correct the errors.

Editing Hints

1.1d

Here are hints that can help you edit the next-to-final draft of a paper for sentence-skills mistakes:

1   Have at hand two essential tools: a good dictionary and a sentence-skills handbook (you can use Chapter 5 and Part Four of this book).

2   Use a sheet of paper to cover your essay so that you will expose only one sentence at a time. Look for errors in grammar, spelling, and typing. It may help to read each sentence out loud. If a sentence does not read clearly and smoothly, chances are something is wrong.

3   Pay special attention to the kinds of errors you yourself tend to make. For example, if you tend to write run-ons or fragments, be especially on the lookout for those errors.

4   Proofreading symbols that may be of particular help are the following:

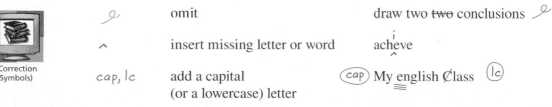

(Correction Symbols)

ℯ	omit	draw two ~~two~~ conclusions ℯ
^	insert missing letter or word	achéve ^
cap, lc	add a capital (or a lowercase letter)	(cap) My english Class (lc)

■ Editing Test 1

In the spaces at the bottom, write the numbers of the ten word groups that contain fragments or run-ons. Then, in the spaces between the lines and in the margin, edit by making the necessary corrections.

[margin: *e*] ¹I remember my childhood as being generally happy and can recall experiencing some of the most carefree times of my life. ²But I can also remember, even more vividly, other moments,

[margin: (lc)] ³When I was deeply frightened. ⁴As a child, I was truly terrified of the dark and of getting lost.

[margin: ;] ⁵These fears were very real, they caused me some extremely uncomfortable moments.

[margin: *e*] ⁶Maybe it was the strange way things looked and sounded in my familiar room at night,

[margin: (lc)] ⁷That scared me so much. ⁸The streetlight outside or passing car lights would create shadows

[margin: took] in my room. ⁹As a result, clothes hung over a chair ~~taking~~ on the shape of an unknown beast.

¹⁰Out of the corner of my eye, I saw curtains move when there was no breeze. ¹¹A tiny creak

[margin: and] in the floor would sound a hundred times louder than in daylight, my imagination would take

[margin: ;/(lc)] over, ¹²Creating burglars and monsters on the prowl. ¹³Because darkness always made me feel

[margin: ;] so helpless, ¹⁴I would lie there motionless so that the "enemy" would not discover me.

[margin: ;/(lc)] ¹⁵Another of my childhood fears was that I would get lost, ¹⁶Especially on the way home

[margin: when] from school. ¹⁷After school, all the buses lined up along the curb, I was terrified that I'd get on

[margin: ;] the wrong one. ¹⁸Scanning the bus windows for the faces of my friends, ¹⁹I'd also look to make

sure that the bus driver was the same one I had in the morning.

1. __3__   3. __7__   5. __11__   7. __13__   9. __17__

2. __5__   4. __9__   6. __12__   8. __16__   10. __18__

■ Editing Test 2

Identify the five mistakes in essay format in the student paper that follows. From the box below, choose the letters that describe the five mistakes and write those letters in the spaces provided. Then correct each mistake.

---

a. Title should not be underlined.
b. Title should not be set off in quotation marks.
c. There should not be a period at the end of a title.
d. All major words in a title should be capitalized.
e. Title should be a phrase, not a complete sentence.
f. First line of a paper should stand independent of the title.
g. One line should be skipped between title and first line of the paper.
h. First line of a paragraph should be indented.
i. Right-hand margin should not be crowded.
j. Hyphenation should occur only between syllables.

"eating in fast-food restaurants"

Doing so doesn't have to be terrible for your health. Although I often stop at Wendy's or Burger King, I find ways to make healthful choices there. For one thing, I order sandwiches that are as plain as possible. A broiled hamburger or fish sandwich isn't so bad for you, as long as it isn't covered with melted cheese, fatty sauces, bacon, or other "extras" that pile on the fat and calories. Another health-conscious choice is to skip deep-fat-fried potatoes loaded with salt and heavy with cholesterol; instead, I'll order a plain baked potato from Wendy's and add just a bit of butter and salt for taste. In addition, I take advantage of healthy items on menus. For example, most fast-food places now offer green salads and low-fat chicken choices. And finally, I order a sensible beverage—ice water or a diet soda—instead of soda or a milk shake.

1. _b_   2. _d_   3. _f_   4. _g_   5. _h_

■ Editing Test 3

Identify the ten sentence-skills mistakes at the underlined spots in the student paper that follows. From the box below, choose the letter that describes each mistake and write that letter in the space provided. (The same kind of mistake may appear more than once.) Then, in the spaces between the lines, edit and correct each mistake.

a. fragment	d. dangling modifier
b. run-on	e. missing comma
c. inconsistent verb tense	f. spelling mistake

Corrections may vary.

                        winter. I

I had a strange experience last <u>winter, I</u> was shopping for Christmas presents when I came
                      ₁

                                      by, until

to a small clothing shop. I was going to pass it by. <u>Until I saw a beautiful purple robe on a</u>
                                               ₂

                          When I stopped to look at it,

<u>mannequin in the window.</u> <u>Stopping to look at it,</u> the mannequin seemed to wink at me. I was
                               ₃

              ;   *head,*

really <u>startled, I</u> looked around to see if anyone else was watching. Shaking my <u>head I</u> stepped
      ₄   ₅

                                                sanity. It

closer to the window. Then I really began to question my <u>sanity, it</u> looked as if the mannequin
                                                              ₆

     its   *smiled and*

moved <u>it's</u> legs. My face must have shown alarm because the mannequin then <u>smiles.</u> <u>And even</u>
     ₇   ₈   ₉

                              relief. It

<u>waved her arm.</u> I sighed with <u>relief, it</u> was a human model after all.
                            ₁₀

1. _b_   3. _d_   5. _e_   7. _f_   9. _a_

2. _a_   4. _b_   6. _b_   8. _c_   10. _b_

Editing Test 4

Identify the ten sentence-skills mistakes at the underlined spots in the student paper that follows. From the box below, choose the letter that describes each mistake and write that letter in the space provided. (The same kind of mistake may appear more than once.) Then, in the spaces between the lines, edit and correct each mistake.

<table>
<tr><td>a. run-on</td><td>d. missing quotation marks</td></tr>
<tr><td>b. mistake in subject-verb agreement</td><td>e. wordiness</td></tr>
<tr><td>c. faulty parallelism</td><td>f. slang</td></tr>
<tr><td></td><td>g. missing comma</td></tr>
</table>

Corrections may vary.

               I think
      <u>It is this writer's opinion that</u> smokers should quit smoking for the sake of those who
                     1

are around them. Perhaps the most helpless creatures that suffer from being near a smoker

are   babies. Onc
<u>is</u> unborn babies, <u>one</u> study suggests that the risk of having an undersized baby is doubled if
2   3

pregnant women are exposed to cigarette smoke for about two hours a day. Pregnant women

                   should avoid
should refrain from smoking and <u>to avoid</u> smoke-filled rooms. Spouses of smokers are also
                        4

  at risk.
<u>in big trouble.</u> They are more likely than spouses of nonsmokers to die of heart disease and
   5

      to develop
the <u>development of</u> fatal cancers. Office workers are a final group that can be harmed by a
    6

                              said,
smoke-filled environment. The U.S. Surgeon General has <u>said</u> "Workers who smoke are a
                                 7

        coworkers."
health risk to their <u>coworkers.</u> While <u>~~it is undoubtedly true that~~</u> one can argue that smokers have
          8   9

       themselves, they
the right to hurt <u>themselves they</u> do not have the right to hurt others. Smokers should abandon
       10

their deadly habit for the health of others at home and at work.

1. _e_   3. _a_   5. _f_   7. _g_   9. _e_

2. _b_   4. _c_   6. _c_   8. _d_   10. _g_

■ Editing Test 5

Identify the ten sentence-skills mistakes at the underlined spots in the student paper that follows. From the box below, choose the letter that describes each mistake and write that letter in the space provided. (The same kind of mistake may appear more than once.) Then, in the spaces between the lines, edit and correct each mistake.

a. fragment	e. dangling modifier
b. run-on	f. missing comma
c. mistake in subject-verb agreement	g. wordiness
d. misplaced modifier	h. slang

Corrections may vary.

society, but

The United States will never be a drug-free <u>society but</u> we could eliminate many of our
                                                         1

If drugs were legal, they

drug-related problems by legalizing drugs. ~~Drugs~~ would be sold by companies and not criminals
                                                    ^

business, freeing

~~if they were legal~~. The drug trade would then take place like any <u>business freeing</u> the police
          2   3

price,

and courts to devote their time to other problems. Lawful drugs would be sold at a fair <u>price,</u>
                                                                                              4

so   *we would deprive*   *of one of*

<u>no</u> one would need to steal in order to buy them. <u>By legalizing drugs,</u> organized crime ~~would~~
                                                                5   ^

We

~~lose one of~~ its major sources of revenue. <u>It goes without saying that we</u> would, instead, create
                                                            6

were

important tax revenues for the government. Finally, if drugs <u>was</u> sold through legal outlets,
                                                                 7

we could reduce drug problems among our young people. It would be illegal to sell drugs to

age, just

people under a certain <u>age. Just as is the case now with alcohol.</u> And because the profits on
                              8

be so high,

drugs would no longer <u>be out of sight</u>, there would be little incentive for drug pushers to sell to
                              9

solution to

young people. Decriminalizing drugs, in short, could be a <u>solution. To many of the problems</u>
                                                                                    10

<u>that result from the illegal drug trade.</u>

1. __f__   3. __f__   5. __e__   7. __c__   9. __h__
2. __d__   4. __b__   6. __g__   8. __a__   10. __a__

■ Editing Test 6

Identify the ten sentence-skills mistakes at the underlined spots in the student paper that follows. From the box below, choose the letter that describes each mistake and write that letter in the space provided. (The same kind of mistake may appear more than once.) Then, in the spaces between the lines, edit and correct each mistake.

---

a. fragment	e. mistake with quotation marks
b. run-on	f. mistake in pronoun point of view
c. mistake in subject-verb agreement	
d. mistake in verb tense	g. spelling error
	h. missing comma

Corrections may vary.

         uninterrupted

One reason that I enjoy the commute to school is that the drive gives me <u>uninterupted</u>
           ₁

          are

time to myself. The classes and socializing at college <u>is</u> great, and so is the time I spend with
                                    ₂
                                      me

my family, but sometimes all this togetherness keeps <u>you</u> from being able to think. In fact, I
                                        ₃

          alone, for

look forward to the time I have <u>alone, it</u> gives me a chance to plan what I'll accomplish in the
                           ₄

                                           announced

day ahead. For example, one Tuesday afternoon my history professor <u>announces</u> that a rough
                                                ₅

                         Fortunately,   *reading,*

outline for our semester report was due that Friday. <u>Fortunatly,</u> I had already done some <u>reading</u>
                                        ₆   ₇

and

<u>and</u> I had checked my proposed topic with her the week before. <u>Therefore, on the way home in</u>
                                                        ₈

      evening, I

<u>the car that evening</u> I planned the entire history report in my mind. Then all I had to do when I

got home was quickly jot it down before I forgot it. <u>When I handed the professor the outline at</u>
                                                   ₉

      morning, she

<u>8:30 Wednesday morning.</u> She asked me "if I had stayed up all night working on it." She was
                                        <u>if I had stayed up all night working on it.</u>
                                                    ₁₀

amazed when I told her that I owed it all to commuting.

---

1. *g*   3. *f*   5. *d*   7. *h*   9. *a*

2. *c*   4. *b*   6. *g*   8. *a*   10. *e*

■ Editing Test 7

Identify the ten sentence-skills mistakes at the underlined spots in the student paper that follows. From the box below, choose the letter that describes each mistake and write that letter in the space provided. (The same kind of mistake may appear more than once.) Then, in the spaces between the lines, edit and correct each mistake.

a. fragment	f. dangling modifier
b. run-on	g. homonym mistake
c. mistake in subject-verb agreement	h. missing apostrophe
d. missing comma	i. cliché
e. missing capital letter	

Corrections may vary.

                                                                    all, the
          Cars can destroy your ego. First of all the kind of car you drive can make you feel like
                                                                        1

a second-class citizen. If you can't afford a new, expensive car and are forced to drive an old
                                                                        2
     clunker, you'll
clunker. You'll be the object of pitying stares and nasty sneers. Drivers of newer-model cars just

    don't   Buick
doesn't appreciate it when an '83 buick with terminal body rust lurches into the next parking
    3   4
                                     their
slot. You may even find that drivers go out of there way not to park near you. Breakdowns, too,
                                     5
                                                                  foreman, but
can damage your self-respect. You may be an assistant bank manager or a job foreman, you'll
                                                                        6
          inferior   you're
still feel like two cents when your sitting on the side of the road. As the other cars whiz past,
          7   8
                    car's
you'll stare helplessly at your cars open hood or steaming radiator. In cases like this, you may
                    9
                                                  As you shuffle
even be turned into that lowest of creatures, the pedestrian. Shuffling humbly along the highway
                                                                        10

to the nearest pay phone, your car has delivered another staggering blow to your self-esteem.

1. __d__   3. __c__   5. __g__   7. __i__   9. __h__

2. __a__   4. __e__   6. __b__   8. __g__   10. __f__

■ Editing Test 8

Locate the ten sentence-skills mistakes in the following passage. The mistakes are listed in the box below. As you locate each mistake, write the number of the word group in the space provided. Then, in the space between the lines, edit and correct each mistake.

---

1 fragment ___2___   1 missing comma after

1 run-on ___9___   introductory material ___7___

1 mistake in verb tense ___11___   2 missing quotation marks
                                      ___5___   ___6___
1 nonparallel structure ___3___
                                   1 missing apostrophe ___7___
1 dangling modifier ___5___

1 mistake in pronoun point of
  view ___12___

Corrections may vary.

                                               technology, beginning

¹The greatest of my everyday fears is technology. ²Beginning when I couldn't master bike

riding and extending to the present day. ³Fear kept me from learning to operate a jigsaw, start
                            use   *When*

an outboard motor, or even using a simple tape recorder. ⁴I almost didn't learn to drive a car. ⁵At
I was

age sixteen, Dad lifted the hood of our Chevy and said, "All right, you're going to start learning

to drive. ⁶Now, this is the distributor. . ."⁷When my eyes glazed over he shouted, "Well, I'm not
                              you're

going to bother if youre not interested!" ⁸Fortunately, the friend who later taught me to drive
                                                                          camera. I

skipped what goes on under the hood. ⁹My most recent frustration is the digital camera, I would

love to take professional-quality pictures, but all the buttons and tiny electronic menus confuse

me. ¹⁰As a result, my unused camera is hidden away on a shelf in my closet. ¹¹Just last week, my
I   *gave*

sister gives me a beautiful digital watch for my birthday. ¹²I may have to put it on the shelf with
                                                     I

the camera—the alarm keeps going off, and you can't figure out how to stop it.

■ Editing Test 9

Locate the ten sentence-skills mistakes in the following passage. The mistakes are listed in the box below. As you locate each mistake, write the number of the word group in the space provided. Then, in the space between the lines, edit and correct each mistake.

---

1 fragment ___7___

1 run-on ___10___

1 missing comma around an
  interrupter ___13___

2 apostrophe mistakes
  ___2___ ___10___

1 mistake in subject-verb
  agreement ___13___

2 missing quotation marks
  ___3___ ___3___

1 dangling modifier ___1___

1 nonparallel structure ___12___

Corrections may vary.

                                                                    I was
¹I was six years old when, one day, my dog was struck by a car while ^getting ready for

                                                            brakes.
school. ²My mother and I heard the terrifying sound of squealing brake's. ³In a low voice, she

said,"Oh, my God—Rusty."⁴I remember trailing her out the door and seeing a car filled with

teenagers and a spreading pool of bright blood on our cobblestoned street. ⁵To me, it seemed

only a matter of seconds until a police car pulled up. ⁶The officer glanced at the crumpled dog
                    car and
under the car. ⁷And drew his gun. ⁸My mother shouted "No!" ⁹She crawled halfway under the

car and took the dog, like a sack of flour, out from under the wheels. ¹⁰Her housedress was
                    blood. She
splashed with blood, she cradled the limp dog in her arms and ordered the officers to drive her
        vet's
to the vets office. ¹¹It was only then that she remembered me, I think. ¹²She patted my head,
        told
was telling me to walk up to school, and reassured me that Rusty would be all right. ¹³The rest
        story,   is
of the story including Rusty's slow recovery and few more years of life, are fuzzy and vague

now. ¹⁴But the sights and sounds of those few moments are as vivid to me now as they were

twenty-five years ago.

■ Editing Test 10

Locate the ten sentence-skills mistakes in the following passage. The mistakes are listed in the box below. As you locate each mistake, write the number of the word group in the space provided. Then, in the space between the lines, edit and correct each mistake.

2 fragments __9__ __12__	2 apostrophe mistakes	
1 run-on __1__	__1__ __2__	
1 mistake in subject-verb agreement __6__	3 missing commas __2__ __3__ __5__	
1 nonparallel structure __6__		

Corrections may vary.

                                                                    sex, but
[1]Most products have little or nothing to do with sex a person would never know that by

                    ℓ   example,
looking at ads. [2]A television ad for a headache remedy, for example shows the product being

                    woman's   say,
useful because it ends a womans throbbing head pain just in time for sex. [3]Now she will not say

"Not tonight, Honey." [4]Another ad features a detergent that helps a single woman meet a man

                                                                    appeal,
in a laundry room. [5]When it comes to products that do relate to sex appeal advertisers often

                                                                    makes
present more obvious sexuality. [6]A recent magazine ad for women's clothing, for instance, make

                    or comfort of
no reference to the quality of or how comfortable are the company's clothes. [7]Instead, the ad

features a picture of a woman wearing a low-cut sleeveless T-shirt and a very short skirt. [8]Her

                    hair and
eyes are partially covered by semi-wild hair. [9]And stare seductively at the reader. [10]A recent

television ad for perfume goes even further. [11]In this ad, a boy not older than twelve reaches out

                    woman who is sexily
to a beautiful woman. [12]Sexily dressed in a dark room filled with sensuous music. [13]With such

ads, it is no wonder that young people seem preoccupied with sex.

■ Editing Test 11

Locate the ten sentence-skills mistakes in the following passage. The mistakes are listed in the box below. As you locate each mistake, write the number of the word group in the space provided. Then, in the space between the lines, edit and correct each mistake.

1 fragment __6__	2 missing apostrophes __5__
1 run-on __9__	__9__
1 mistake in subject-verb agreement __8__	1 nonparallel structure __2__
	1 dangling modifier __3__
2 missing commas after introductory material __7__ __9__	1 mistake in pronoun point of view __10__

Corrections may vary.

¹Being a waitress is an often underrated job. ²A waitress needs the tact of a diplomat,

the organization of   *She serves*

she must be as organized as a business executive, and the ability of an acrobat. ³Serving as

;

the link between customers and kitchen, the most demanding diners must be satisfied, and the

often-temperamental kitchen help must be kept tamed. ⁴Both groups tend to blame the waitress

whenever anything goes wrong. ⁵Somehow, she is held responsible by the customer for any

kitchen's   *dessert,*

delay (even if it's the kitchens fault), for an overcooked steak, or for an unavailable dessert.

while

⁶While the kitchen automatically blames her for the diners who change their orders or return

addition,

those burned steaks. ⁷In addition she must simultaneously keep straight who ordered what at

each table, who is yelling for the check, and whether the new arrivals want cocktails or not. ⁸She

must be sure empty tables are cleared, everyone has refills of coffee, and no one is scowling

is

because a request for more rolls are going unheard. ⁹Finally the waitress must travel a hazardous

;   *diner's*

route between the busy kitchen and the crowded dining room, she has to dodge a diners leg

she

in the aisle or a swinging kitchen door. ¹⁰And you must do this while balancing a tray heaped

with steaming platters. ¹¹The hardest task of the waitress, though, is trying to maintain a decent

imitation of a smile on her face—most of the time.

■ Editing Test 12

Locate the ten sentence-skills mistakes in the following passage. The mistakes are listed in the box below. As you locate each mistake, write the number of the word group in the space provided. Then, in the space between the lines, edit and correct each mistake.

2 fragments ___6___ ___16___	2 missing capital letters ___2___
1 run-on ___10___	___2___
2 mistakes in irregular verbs	1 mistake in pronoun point of
___2___ ___9___	view ___4___
1 misplaced modifier ___12___	1 mistake in a subject pronoun
	___7___

Corrections may vary.

¹The thirtieth anniversary party of my uncle and aunt was the worst family gathering I've

Saturday   July   drove

ever attended. ²On a hot saturday morning in july, Mom and I drived out into the country to

Uncle Ted's house. ³It had already rained heavily, and the only place left to park was in a muddy

we

field. ⁴Then, you could not believe the crowd. ⁵There must have been two hundred people in

Uncle Ted's small yard, including his five daughters with their husbands and children, all the

other relatives, all the neighbors, and the entire congregation of their church. ⁶Since the ground

falling, |

was soaked and light rain was falling. ⁷Mom and me went under the big rented canopy with

everybody else. ⁸We couldn't move between the tables, and the humidity fogged my glasses.

saw

⁹After wiping my glasses, I seen that there was a lot of food. ¹⁰It was mainly cold chicken and

;

potato and macaroni salads, I ate a lot just because there was nothing else to do. ¹¹We were

Staggering with exhaustion, they

surprised that Uncle Ted and his wife were doing all the work themselves. ¹²They ran back

.

and forth with trays of food and gathered trash into plastic bags staggering with exhaustion.

¹³It didn't seem like much of a way to celebrate. ¹⁴Mom was upset that she didn't get to speak

|

with them. ¹⁵When we left, I was hot, sticky, and sick to my stomach from overeating. ¹⁶But

^

quickly pushed our car out of the mud and got us on the road. ¹⁷I have never been happier to

leave a party.

ESL Pointers

This section covers rules that most native speakers of English take for granted but that are useful for speakers of English as a second language (ESL).

Articles with Count and Noncount Nouns

Articles are noun markers—they signal that a noun will follow. (A noun is a word used to name something—a person, place, thing, or idea.) The indefinite articles are *a* and *an*. (Use *a* before a word that begins with a consonant sound: **a c**ar, **a p**iano, **a u**niform—the *u* in *uniform* sounds like the consonant *y* plus *u*. Use *an* before a word beginning with a vowel sound: **an e**gg, **an o**ffice, **an h**onor—the *h* in *honor* is silent.) The definite article is *the*. An article may immediately precede a noun: **a** smile, **the** reason. Or it may be separated from the noun by modifiers: **a** slight smile, **the** very best reason.

To know whether to use an article with a noun and which article to use, you must recognize count and noncount nouns.

Count nouns name people, places, things, or ideas that can be counted and made into plurals, such as *teacher, restroom*, and *joke* (*one teacher, two restrooms, three jokes*).

Noncount nouns refer to things or ideas that cannot be counted, such as *flour, history,* and *truth.* The following box lists and illustrates common types of noncount nouns.

Note   There are various other noun markers besides articles, including quantity words (*some, several, a lot of*), numerals (*one, ten, 120*), demonstrative adjectives (*this, these*), possessive adjectives (*my, your, our*), and possessive nouns (*Jaime's, the school's*).

Common Noncount Nouns

Abstractions and emotions: anger, bravery, health, pride, truth

Activities: baseball, jogging, reading, teaching, travel

Foods: bread, broccoli, chocolate, cheese, flour

Gases and vapors: air, helium, oxygen, smoke, steam

Languages and areas of study: Korean, Spanish, algebra, history, physics

Liquids: blood, gasoline, lemonade, tea, water

Materials that come in bulk form: aluminum, cloth, dust, sand, soap

Natural occurrences: magnetism, moonlight, rain, snow, thunder

Other things that cannot be counted: clothing, furniture, homework, machinery, money, news, transportation, vocabulary, work

The quantity of a noncount noun can be expressed with a word or words called a **qualifier**, such as *some, a lot of, a unit of,* and so on. (In the following two examples, the qualifiers are shown in *italic* type, and the noncount nouns are shown in **boldface** type.)

Please have *some* **patience.**

We need to buy *two bags of* **flour** today.

Some words can be either count or noncount nouns, depending on whether they refer to one or more individual items or to something in general.

Certain **cheeses** give some people a headache.
(This sentence refers to individual cheeses; *cheese* in this case is a count noun.)

Cheese is made in almost every country where milk is produced.
(This sentence refers to cheese in general; in this case, *cheese* is a noncount noun.)

Using *a* or *an* with Nonspecific Singular Count Nouns

Use *a* or *an* with singular nouns that are nonspecific. A noun is nonspecific when the reader doesn't know its specific identity.

A left-hander faces special challenges with right-handed tools.
(The sentence refers to any left-hander, not a specific one.)

Today, our cat proudly brought **a** baby bird into the house.
(The reader isn't familiar with the bird. This is the first time it is mentioned.)

Using *the* with Specific Nouns

In general, use *the* with all specific nouns—specific singular, plural, and noncount nouns. Certain conditions make a noun specific and therefore require the article *the*.
A noun is specific in the following cases:

- When it has already been mentioned once

    Today, our cat proudly brought a baby bird into the house. Luckily, **the** bird was still alive.
    (The is used with the second mention of *bird.)*

- When it is identified by a word or phrase in the sentence

    The pockets in the boy's pants are often filled with sand and dirt.
    (Pockets is identified by the words *in the boy's pants.)*

- When its identity is suggested by the general context

    At Willy's Diner last night, **the** service was terrible and **the** food was worse.
    (The reader can conclude that the service and food being discussed were at Willy's Diner.)

- When it is unique

    There will be an eclipse of **the** moon tonight.
    (Earth has only one moon.)

- When it is preceded by a superlative adjective (*best, biggest, wisest*)

    The best way to store broccoli is to refrigerate it in an open plastic bag.

Omitting Articles

Omit articles with nonspecific plurals and noncount nouns. Plurals and noncount nouns are nonspecific when they refer to something in general.

Pockets didn't exist until the end of the 1700s.
Service is as important as **food** to a restaurant's success.
Iris serves her children homemade **lemonade**.

Using *the* with Proper Nouns

Proper nouns name particular people, places, things, or ideas and are always capitalized. Most proper nouns do not require articles; those that do, however, require *the*. Following are general guidelines about when and when not to use *the*.

1 Do not use *the* for most singular proper nouns, including names of the following:

- *People and animals* (Benjamin Franklin, Fido)
- *Continents, states, cities, streets, and parks* (North America, Illinois, Chicago, First Avenue, Washington Square)
- *Most countries* (France, Mexico, Russia)
- *Individual bodies of water, islands, and mountains* (Lake Erie, Long Island, Mount Everest)

2 Use *the* for the following types of proper nouns:

- *Plural proper nouns* (the Turners, the United States, the Great Lakes, the Rocky Mountains)
- *Names of large geographic areas, deserts, oceans, seas, and rivers* (the South, the Gobi Desert, the Atlantic Ocean, the Black Sea, the Mississippi River)
- *Names with the format* the _____ of _____ (the Fourth of July, the People's Republic of China, the University of California)

ACTIVITY 1

Underline the correct form of the noun in parentheses.

1. (A library, Library) is a valuable addition to a town.
2. This morning, the mail carrier brought me (a letter, the letter) from my cousin.
3. As I read (a letter, the letter), I began to laugh at what my cousin wrote.
4. Every night we have to do lots of (homework, homeworks).
5. We are going to visit our friends in (the Oregon, Oregon) next week.
6. Children should treat their parents with (the respect, respect).
7. The soldiers in battle showed a great deal of (courage, courages).
8. A famous sight in Arizona is (Grand Canyon, the Grand Canyon).
9. My son would like to eat (the spaghetti, spaghetti) at every meal.
10. It is dangerous to stare directly at (the sun, sun).

ACTIVITY 2

Underline the correct form of the noun in parentheses.

1. Last night, I went to (a restaurant, the restaurant) with my best friend.
2. (The restaurant, A restaurant) was a more expensive place than we had expected.
3. (The accident, Accident) was caused by ice on the highway.
4. A newspaper reporter is supposed to write a story with (the honesty, honesty).
5. My neighbor's son attends college in (the Chicago, Chicago).
6. Long-distance runners need lots of (determination, determinations) to succeed.
7. A hurricane crossed (Atlantic Ocean, the Atlantic Ocean) before it hit the United States.
8. As the hurricane approached, residents felt a great deal of (fears, fear).
9. (Jupiter, The Jupiter) is the largest planet in our solar system.
10. Computers have been programmed to play (the chess, chess) and can now beat most human players.

Subjects and Verbs

Avoiding Repeated Subjects

In English, a particular subject can be used only once in a clause. Don't repeat a subject in the same clause by following a noun with a pronoun.

> Incorrect: The *manager he* asked Dmitri to lock up tonight.
> Correct: The **manager** asked Dmitri to lock up tonight.
> Correct: **He** asked Dmitri to lock up tonight.

Even when the subject and verb are separated by a long word group, the subject cannot be repeated in the same clause.

> Incorrect: The *girl* who danced with you *she is* my cousin.
> Correct: The **girl** who danced with you **is** my cousin.

Including Pronoun Subjects and Linking Verbs

Some languages may omit a pronoun as a subject, but in English, every clause other than a command must have a subject. In a command, the subject *you* is understood: (**You**) Hand in your papers now.

Incorrect: The Grand Canyon is in Arizona. *Is* 217 miles long.

Correct: The Grand Canyon is in Arizona. **It is** 217 miles long.

Every English clause must also have a verb, even when the meaning of the clause is clear without the verb.

Incorrect: Angelita's piano teacher very patient.

Correct: Angelita's piano teacher **is** very patient.

Including *There* and *Here* at the Beginning of Clauses

Some English sentences begin with *there* or *here* plus a linking verb (usually a form of *to be: is, are,* and so on). In such sentences, the verb comes before the subject.

There are masks in every culture on Earth.

The subject is the plural noun *masks,* so the plural verb *are* is used.

Here is your driver's license.

The subject is the singular noun *license,* so the singular verb *is* is used.

In sentences like those above, remember not to omit *there* or *here*.

Incorrect: *Are* several chickens in the Bensons' yard.

Correct: **There are** several chickens in the Bensons' yard.

Not Using the Progressive Tense of Certain Verbs

ALLWRITE!
18.2e

The progressive tenses are made up of forms of *be* plus the *-ing* form of the main verb. They express actions or conditions still in progress at a particular time.

George **will be taking** classes this summer.

However, verbs for mental states, the senses, possession, and inclusion are normally not used in the progressive tense.

Incorrect: All during the movie they *were hearing* whispers behind them.

Correct: All during the movie they **heard** whispers behind them.

Incorrect: That box *is containing* a surprise for Pedro.

Correct: That box **contains** a surprise for Pedro.

Common verbs not generally used in the progressive tense are listed in the following box.

Common Verbs Not Generally Used in the Progressive

Thoughts, attitudes and desires: agree, believe, imagine, know, like, love, prefer, think, understand, want, wish

Sense perceptions: hear, see, smell, taste

Appearances: appear, seem

Possession: belong, have, own, possess

Inclusion: contain, include

Using Only Transitive Verbs for the Passive Voice

Only transitive verbs—verbs that need direct objects to complete their meaning—can have a passive form (one in which the subject receives the action instead of performing it). Intransitive verbs cannot be used in the passive voice.

Incorrect: If you don't fix those brakes, an accident *may be happened.*
(*Happen* is an intransitive verb—no object is needed to complete its meaning.)

Correct: If you don't fix those brakes, an accident **may happen.**

If you aren't sure whether a verb is transitive or intransitive, check your dictionary. Transitive verbs are indicated with an abbreviation such as *tr. v.* or *v. t.* Intransitive verbs are indicated with an abbreviation such as *intr. v.* or *v. i.*

Using Gerunds and Infinitives after Verbs

ALLWRITE!
18.4,
ESL

A gerund is the *-ing* form of a verb that is used as a noun: For Walter, **eating** is a daylong activity. An infinitive is *to* plus the basic form of the verb (the form in which the verb is listed in the dictionary): **to eat.** The infinitive can function as an adverb, an adjective, or a noun. Some verbs can be followed by only a gerund or only an infinitive; other verbs can be followed by either. Examples are given in the following lists. There are many others; watch for them in your reading.

Verb + gerund (*admit + stealing*)
Verb + preposition + gerund (*apologize + for + yelling*)

Some verbs can be followed by a gerund but not by an infinitive. In many cases, there is a preposition (such as *for, in,* or *of*) between the verb and the gerund. Following are some verbs and verb/preposition combinations that can be followed by gerunds but not by infinitives:

admit	deny	look forward to
apologize for	discuss	postpone
appreciate	dislike	practice
approve of	enjoy	suspect of
avoid	feel like	talk about
be used to	finish	thank for
believe in	insist on	think about

Incorrect: He must *avoid to jog* until his knee heals.

Correct: He must **avoid jogging** until his knee heals.

Incorrect: The instructor *apologized for to be* late to class.

Correct: The instructor **apologized for being** late to class.

Verb + infinitive (*agree + to leave*)

Following are common verbs that can be followed by an infinitive but not by a gerund:

agree	decide	plan
arrange	have	refuse
claim	manage	wait

Incorrect: The children *want going* to the beach.

Correct: The children **want to go** to the beach.

Verb + noun or pronoun + infinitive (*cause + them + to flee*)

Below are common verbs that are followed first by a noun or pronoun and then by an infinitive (not a gerund):

cause	force	remind
command	persuade	warn

Incorrect: The coach *persuaded Yasmin studying* harder.

Correct: The coach **persuaded Yasmin to study** harder.

Following are common verbs that can be followed either by an infinitive alone or by a noun or pronoun and an infinitive:

ask	need	want
expect	promise	would like

Dena asked to have a day off next week.

Her boss asked her to work on Saturday.

Verb + gerund or infinitive (*begin + packing* or *begin + to pack*)

Following are verbs that can be followed by either a gerund or an infinitive:

begin	hate	prefer
continue	love	start

The meaning of each of the above verbs remains the same or almost the same whether a gerund or an infinitive is used.

Faith hates **being** late.

Faith hates **to be** late.

With the verbs below, the gerunds and the infinitives have very different meanings.

forget	remember	stop

Esta **stopped to call** home.
(She interrupted something to call home.)

Esta **stopped calling** home.
(She discontinued calling home.)

ACTIVITY 1

Underline the correct form in parentheses.

1. The doctor (<u>asked me</u>, she asked me) if I smoked.
2. The coffee is very fresh. (Is, <u>It is</u>) strong and delicious.
3. (Are mice, <u>There are mice</u>) living in our kitchen.
4. The box (is containing, <u>contains</u>) a beautiful necklace.
5. Unless you take your foot off the brake, the car will not (be gone, <u>go</u>).
6. Most basketball players (very tall, <u>are very tall</u>).
7. Many people (enjoy to spend, <u>enjoy spending</u>) a day in the city.
8. The teacher (plans taking, <u>plans to take</u>) us on a field trip tomorrow.
9. Some old men in my neighborhood (<u>play cards</u>, they play cards) every afternoon.
10. When I am happy, I feel like (to sing, <u>singing</u>).

ACTIVITY 2

Underline the correct form in parentheses.

1. My grandparents (<u>are</u>, they are) in their nineties.
2. The pizza is two days old. (Is, <u>It is</u>) dry and stale.
3. (Was money, <u>There was money</u>) stolen from the convenience store last night.
4. The manager (<u>owns</u>, is owning) two SUVs: a Honda and a Ford.
5. The package will not (be arrived, <u>arrive</u>) until Friday morning.
6. After a twelve-hour shift, the employees (very tired, <u>were very tired</u>).

7. Most adults need (to sleep, sleeping) at least seven hours each night.

8. Our new puppy (wants to be chewing, wants to chew) all the furniture in our apartment.

9. The library's computer (broke down, it broke down) when I tried to use it.

10. Whenever she hears music, Sara feels like (to dance, dancing).

Adjectives

Following the Order of Adjectives in English

Adjectives modify nouns and pronouns. In English, an adjective usually comes directly before the word it describes or after a linking verb (a form of *be* or a "sense" verb such as *look, seem,* and *taste*), in which case it modifies the subject. In each of the following two sentences, the adjective is **boldfaced** and the noun it describes is *italicized*.

That is a **false** *story*.

The *story* is **false**.

When more than one adjective modifies the same noun, the adjectives are usually stated in a certain order, though there are often exceptions. Following is the typical order of English adjectives:

Typical Order of Adjectives in a Series

1 **Article or other noun marker:** a, an, the, Lee's, this, three, your

2 **Opinion adjective:** dull, handsome, unfair, useful

3 **Size:** big, huge, little, tiny

4 **Shape:** long, short, round, square

5 **Age:** ancient, medieval, old, new, young

6 **Color:** blue, green, scarlet, white

7 **Nationality:** Italian, Korean, Mexican, Vietnamese

8 **Religion:** Buddhist, Catholic, Jewish, Muslim

9 **Material:** cardboard, gold, marble, silk

10 **Noun used as an adjective:** house (as in *house call*), tea (as in *tea bag*), wall (as in *wall hanging*)

Here are some examples of the above order:

a long cotton scarf

the beautiful little silver cup

your new lavender evening gown

Ana's sweet Mexican grandmother

In general, use no more than two or three adjectives after the article or another noun marker. Numerous adjectives in a series can be awkward: **the beautiful big new blue cotton** sweater.

Using the Present and Past Participles as Adjectives

20.5,
ESL

The present participle ends in *-ing*. Past participles of regular verbs end in *-ed* or *-d;* a list of the past participles of many common irregular verbs appears on pages 446–448. Both types of participles may be used as adjectives. A participle used as an adjective may precede the word it describes: That was an **exciting** *ball game.* It may also follow a linking verb and describe the subject of the sentence: The *ball game* was **exciting**.

While both present and past participles of a particular verb may be used as adjectives, their meanings differ. Use the present participle to describe whoever or whatever causes a feeling: an **embarrassing** *incident* (the incident is what causes the embarrassment). Use the past participle to describe whoever or whatever experiences the feeling: the **embarrassed** *parents* (the parents are the ones who are embarrassed).

The long day of holiday shopping was **tiring**.

The shoppers were **tired**.

Following are pairs of present and past participles with similar distinctions:

annoying / annoyed   exhausting / exhausted

boring / bored   fascinating / fascinated

confusing / confused   frightening / frightened

depressing / depressed   surprising / surprised

exciting / excited

ACTIVITY 1

Underline the correct form in parentheses.

1. The Johnsons live in a (stone big, <u>big stone</u>) house.
2. Mr. Kim runs a (<u>popular Korean</u>, Korean popular) restaurant.
3. For her party, the little girl asked if her mother would buy her a (<u>beautiful long velvet</u>, beautiful velvet long) dress.
4. When their son didn't come home by bedtime, Mr. and Mrs. Singh became (<u>worried</u>, worrying).
5. In the center of the city is a church with (<u>three enormous colorful stained-glass</u>, three stained-glass colorful enormous) windows.

ACTIVITY 2

Underline the correct form in parentheses.

1. The candies came in a (<u>little red cardboard</u>, cardboard red little) box.
2. The creek is spanned by (<u>an old wooden</u>, a wooden old) bridge.
3. A gunshot left (<u>a tiny round</u>, a round tiny) hole in the car's rear windshield.
4. Many people find public speaking a (<u>terrifying</u>, terrified) experience.
5. The museum acquired (<u>an ancient marble</u>, a marble ancient) statue from Greece.

Prepositions Used for Time and Place

The use of prepositions in English is often idiomatic—a word that means "peculiar to a certain language"—and there are many exceptions to general rules. Therefore, correct preposition use must be learned gradually through experience. Following is a chart showing how three of the most common prepositions are used in some customary references to time and place:

Use of *On*, *In*, and *At* to Refer to Time and Place

Time

***On** a specific day:* on Monday, on January 1, on your anniversary

***In** a part of a day:* in the morning, in the daytime (but at night)

***In** a month or a year:* in December, in 1776

In *a period of time:* in an hour, in a few days, in a while

At *a specific time:* at 10:00 A.M., at midnight, at sunset, at dinnertime

Place

On *a surface:* on the desk, on the counter, on a ceiling

In *a place that is enclosed:* in my room, in the office, in the box

At *a specific location:* at the mall, at his house, at the ballpark

ACTIVITY 1

Underline the correct preposition in parentheses.

1. Can you baby-sit for my children (<u>on</u>, at) Thursday?
2. Please come to my office (on, <u>at</u>) 3:00.
3. You will find some computer disks (<u>in</u>, on) the desk drawer.
4. Miguel will begin his new job (<u>in</u>, at) two weeks.
5. A fight broke out between two groups of friends (on, <u>at</u>) the park.

ACTIVITY 2

Underline the correct preposition in parentheses.

1. Tina's husband always sends her flowers (<u>on</u>, at) her birthday.
2. The patients (at, <u>in</u>) the waiting room at the dentist's office all looked uneasy.
3. Let's meet (on, <u>at</u>) the coffee shop after work.
4. The bank is open (in, <u>on</u>) Thursday evenings, but only until six.
5. The Great Depression began when the stock market crashed (<u>in</u>, at) 1929.

Review Test 1

Underline the correct form in parentheses.

1. During the storm, I was startled by the loud (<u>thunder</u>, thunders).
2. (Is, <u>Here is</u>) your new textbook.
3. The ending of the movie was very (surprised, <u>surprising</u>).
4. Many animals that sleep all day are active (<u>at</u>, in) night.

5. (The people, People) in the photograph are my mother's relatives.

6. The city streets were full of (big yellow, yellow big) taxis.

7. My friend and I (are usually agreeing, usually agree) with each other.

8. In the West, New Year's Day is celebrated (in, on) January 1.

9. If the weather is nice tomorrow, let's (think about to go, think about going) to the city ourselves.

10. Most (cheese, cheeses) are made from cow's milk, but others are made from the milk of sheep or goats.

■ **Review Test 2**

Underline the correct form in parentheses.

1. Volunteers who gave (bloods, blood) were served coffee and cookies afterward.

2. (Were, There were) only two donuts left in the box.

3. The instructions for the new computer were very (confused, confusing).

4. The snow began to fall (in, at) dawn and continued all day.

5. I stopped at a newsstand to buy (the magazine, a magazine) to read on the train.

6. A (large hairy, hairy large) spider crawled across the basement floor.

7. Susan agreed (marrying, to marry) her boyfriend but then changed her mind.

8. In the United States, Halloween is celebrated (on, in) October 31.

9. After we finished dinner, we (decided to go, decided to be going) to the movies.

10. Most (homes, home) in that neighborhood were affected by the blackout.

PART FIVE

Readings for Writing

Introduction to the Readings

The nineteen reading selections in Part Five will help you find topics for writing. (Note that there are also nine professional essays in Part Two.) These selections deal in various ways with interesting, often thought-provoking concerns or experiences of contemporary life. Subjects of the essays include the value of expressing appreciation; the shame of poverty; the violence of professional sports; the power of family; basic life goals; practical advice on surviving the first year of college; problems with the college lecture system; ways the media influence our attitudes; and the shocks and challenges of everyday life. The varied subjects should inspire lively class discussions as well as serious individual thought. The selections should also provide a continuing source of high-interest material for a wide range of writing assignments.

The selections serve another purpose as well. They will help develop reading skills, with direct benefits to you as a writer. One benefit is that, through close reading, you will learn how to recognize the thesis in a selection and to identify and evaluate the supporting material that develops the thesis. In your own writing, you will aim to achieve the same essential structure: an overall thesis followed by detailed, valid support for that thesis. A second benefit is that close reading will also help you explore a selection and its possibilities thoroughly. The more you understand about what is said in a piece, the more ideas and feelings you may have about writing on an assigned topic or a related topic of your own. A third benefit of close reading is that you will become more aware of authors' stylistic devices—for example, their introductions and conclusions, their ways of presenting and developing a point, their use of transitions, their choice of language to achieve a particular tone. Recognizing these devices in other people's writing will help you enlarge your own range of ideas and writing techniques.

The Format of Each Selection

Each selection begins with a short overview that gives helpful background information as well as a brief idea of the topic of the reading. The selection is followed by three sets of questions:

- First, there are ten "Reading Comprehension" questions to help you measure your understanding of the material. These questions involve several important reading skills: understanding vocabulary in context, recognizing a subject or topic, determining a thesis or main idea, identifying key supporting points, and making inferences. Answering the questions will enable you and your instructor to check your basic understanding of a selection quickly. More significantly, as you move from one selection to the next, you will sharpen your reading skills as well as strengthen your thinking skills—two key factors in making you a better writer.

- Following the comprehension questions are four questions on "Structure and Technique" that focus on aspects of a writer's craft, and four questions on "Critical Reading and Discussion" that involve you in reading carefully and thinking actively about a writer's ideas.

Finally, several writing assignments accompany each selection. The assignments range from personal narratives to expository and persuasive essays about issues in the world at large. Many assignments provide detailed guidelines on how to proceed, including suggestions for prewriting and appropriate methods of development. When writing your essay responses to the readings, you will have opportunities to apply all the methods of development presented in Part Two of this book.

How to Read Well: Four General Steps

Skillful reading is an important part of becoming a skillful writer. Following is a series of four steps that will make you a better reader—both of the selections here and in your reading at large.

1. Concentrate As You Read

To improve your concentration, follow these tips:

- First, read in a place where you can be quiet and alone. Don't choose a spot where there is a TV or stereo on or where friends or family are talking nearby.

- Next, sit upright when you read. If your body is in a completely relaxed position, sprawled across a bed or nestled in an easy chair, your mind is also going to be completely relaxed. The light muscular tension that comes from sitting in a straight chair promotes concentration and keeps your mind ready to work.

- Third, consider using your index finger (or a pen) as a pacer while you read. Lightly underline each line of print with your index finger as you read down a page. Hold your hand slightly above the page and move your finger at a speed that is a little too fast for comfort. This pacing with your index finger, like sitting upright in a chair, creates a slight physical tension that will keep your body and mind focused and alert.

2. Skim Material before You Read It

In skimming, you spend about two minutes rapidly surveying a selection, looking for important points and skipping secondary material. Follow this sequence when skimming:

- Begin by reading the overview that precedes the selection.
- Then study the title of the selection for a few moments. A good title is the shortest possible summary of a selection; it often tells you in several words—or even a single word—just what a selection is about. For example, the title "Shame" suggests that you're going to read about a deeply embarrassing condition or incident in a person's life.
- Next, form a question (or questions) based on the title. For instance, for the selection titled "Shame," you might ask, "What exactly is the shame?" "What caused the shame?" "What is the result of the shame?" Using a title to form questions is often a key to locating a writer's thesis, your next concern in skimming.
- Read the first and last couple of paragraphs in the selection. Very often a writer's thesis, *if* it is directly stated, will appear in one of these places and will relate to the title. For instance, in "Why Are Students Turned Off?" the author says in his second paragraph that "many students are turned off because they have little power and responsibility for their own education."
- Finally, look quickly at the rest of the selection for other clues to important points. Are there any subheads you can relate in some way to the title? Are there any words the author has decided to emphasize by setting them off in *italic* or **boldface** type? Are there any major lists of items signaled by words such as *first, second, also, another,* and so on?

3. Read the Selection Straight Through with a Pen in Hand

Read the selection without slowing down or turning back; just aim to understand as much as you can the first time through. Write a check or star beside answers to basic questions you formed from the title, and beside other ideas that seem important. Number lists of important points: 1, 2, 3, ... Circle words you don't understand. Write question marks in the margins next to passages that are unclear and that you will want to reread.

4. Work with the Material

Go back and reread passages that were not clear the first time through. Look up words that block your understanding of ideas and write their meanings in the margin. Also, reread carefully the areas you identified as most important; doing so will enlarge your understanding of the material. Now that you have a sense of the whole, prepare a short written outline of the selection by answering these questions:

- What is the thesis?
- What key points support the thesis?
- What seem to be other important ideas in the selection?

By working with the material in this way, you will significantly increase your understanding of a selection. Effective reading, just like effective writing, does not happen all at once. Rather, it must be worked on. Often you begin with a general impression of what something means, and then, by working at it, you move to a deeper level of understanding.

How to Answer the Comprehension Questions: Specific Hints

The ten reading comprehension questions that follow each selection involve several important reading skills:

- Understanding vocabulary in context
- Summarizing the selection in a title
- Determining the main idea
- Recognizing key supporting details
- Making inferences

The following hints will help you apply each of these reading skills:

- *Vocabulary in context.* To decide on the meaning of an unfamiliar word, consider its context. Ask yourself, "Are there any clues in the sentence that suggest what this word means?"
- *Subject or title.* Remember that the title should accurately describe the *entire* selection. It should be neither too broad nor too narrow for the material in the

selection. It should answer the question "What is this about?" as specifically as possible. Note that you may at times find it easier to answer the title question *after* the main-idea question.

- *Main idea.* Choose the statement that you think best expresses the main idea—also known as the *central point* or *thesis*—of the entire selection. Remember that the title will often help you focus on the main idea. Then ask yourself, "Does most of the material in the selection support this statement?" If you can answer "yes," you have found the thesis.

- *Key details.* If you were asked to give a two-minute summary of a selection, the key, or major, details are the ones you would include in that summary. To determine the key details, ask yourself, "What are the major supporting points for the thesis?"

- *Inferences.* Answer these questions by drawing upon the evidence presented in the selection and your own common sense. Ask yourself, "What reasonable judgments can I make on the basis of the information in the selection?"

On page 725 is a chart on which you can keep track of your performance as you answer the ten comprehension questions for each selection. The chart will help you identify reading skills you may need to strengthen.

Looking Inward

Three Passions

Bertrand Russell

(Links)

Bertrand Russell (1872–1970), a philosopher and mathematician, was a controversial figure on the world stage. He was imprisoned twice, first in 1918 for his outspoken criticism of British involvement in World War I, and again in 1961 for "inciting civil disobedience" while campaigning for nuclear disarmament. His writings on social, political, and educational issues led to his winning the Nobel Prize for Literature in 1950. "Three Passions" is taken from the prologue to his autobiography.

1   Three passions, simple but overwhelmingly strong, have governed my life: the longing for love, the search for knowledge, and unbearable pity for the suffering of mankind. These passions, like great winds, have blown me hither and thither, in a wayward course, over a deep ocean of anguish, reaching to the very verge of despair.

2   I have sought love, first, because it brings ecstasy—ecstasy so great that I would often have sacrificed all the rest of life for a few hours of this joy. I have sought it, next, because it relieves loneliness—that terrible loneliness in which one shivering consciousness looks over the rim of the world into the cold unfathomable lifeless abyss. I have sought it, finally, because in the union of love I have seen, in a mystic miniature, the prefiguring vision of the heaven that saints and poets have imagined. This is what I sought, and though it might seem too good for human life, this is what—at last—I have found.

3   With equal passion I have sought knowledge. I have wished to understand the hearts of men. I have wished to know why the stars shine. And I have tried to apprehend the Pythagorean power by which number holds sway above the flux. A little of this, but not much, I have achieved.

4   Love and knowledge, so far as they were possible, led upward toward the heavens. But always pity brought me back to earth. Echoes of cries of pain reverberate in my heart. Children in famine, victims tortured by oppressors, helpless old people a hated burden to their sons, and the whole world of loneliness, poverty, and pain make a mockery of what human life should be. I long to alleviate the evil, but I cannot, and I too suffer.

5   This has been my life. I have found it worth living, and would gladly live it again if the chance were offered me.

■ Reading Comprehension

1. The word *alleviate* in "I long to alleviate the evil, but I cannot, and I too suffer" means
   a. increase.
   b. tolerate.
   c. enjoy.
   (d.) relieve.

2. Which of the following would be a good alternative title for this selection?
   (a.) The Forces Driving Me
   b. The Truth about Love
   c. The Anguish of Life
   d. The Power of Knowledge

3. What sentence best expresses the main idea of the selection?
   a. People's inhumanity to other humans has been a source of great pain in the author's life.
   b. The author wishes he had his life to live over again.
   c. The author sees his life driven by three passions.
   (d.) The author has found life's struggle to be painful, but ultimately rewarding.

4. Russell compares his life's passions to
   (a.) great winds.
   b. the stars.
   c. a bottomless abyss.
   d. a boundless ocean.

5. Which of the following is *not* a reason that Russell sought love?
   a. It relieves loneliness.
   (b.) It leads to marriage.
   c. It brings ecstacy.
   d. It provides a glimpse of heaven.

6. *True or false?* _False_ Russell believes that he has gained considerable knowledge in life.

7. When Russell uses the metaphor of a "deep ocean" to describe his anguish, he implies that it is
   a. cold.
   b. without life.
   (c.) almost bottomless.
   d. lacking in color.

8. Russell implies that loneliness, at its core, is

   a. a self-defeating impulse.

   b. impossible to avoid.

   c. a sign of selfishness.

   d. a fear of death.

9. Russell implies that life for him has been

   a. passionately complex.

   b. simpler than he would have imagined.

   c. so troubled that it has increased his faith in God.

   d. more materialistic than he would have wished.

10. We can conclude that the author would agree with which statement?

    a. He regrets that he could not free himself of pity.

    b. Human love is ultimately disappointing.

    c. Heaven is merely a poetic invention.

    d. A loving person naturally wants to relieve the suffering of others.

Structure and Technique

1. Does this essay follow the traditional one-three-one essay model of introduction, support, and conclusion? How would you outline the essay?

2. This essay primarily is organized in terms of three causes and their overall effect. What is the effect and what are the causes? The essay can also be seen as an examples essay. What examples does the author provide to help the reader understand each of his lifelong passions?

3. What kind of transitional signals—time, space, or addition—does Russell employ in the second paragraph? List the transitions you find there.

4. Russell is a master of the use of metaphorical language. For instance, as has already been seen, he compares his anguish to an "ocean." What other examples of metaphorical language can you find? Why do you think Russell chose to use such imaginative language, rather than write in plain-spoken terms?

Critical Reading and Discussion

1. Can you identify one or two passions—or at least strong influences—that have, in Russell's words, governed your life? What examples can you provide of how those passions have affected you?

2. Do think that many people are influenced by the same passions as Russell: love, knowledge, then pity? Or do you feel that many people spend their lives

influenced by other factors? What other passions or influences do people live by, in your experience?

3. Russell writes, "[I]n the union of love I have seen, in a mystic miniature, the prefiguring vision of the heaven that saints and poets have imagined" (paragraph 2). Most people, whether they believe in heaven in a religious sense or not, have a concept of an ideal place of perfect love and harmony. What on earth—perhaps a place, a relationship, an individual, or a situation—comes closest to giving you a "prefiguring vision" of heaven? What is it about that place, person, or thing that seems heavenly to you?

4. Overall, do you find Russell's statement an uplifting or a saddening one? What elements of each do you find within it? What makes one element outweigh the other, in your mind?

Writing Assignments

Assignment 1

Write an essay in which you identify three passions that have strongly influenced your life. Like Russell, explain why each of them has been so important to you, and provide examples of how those passions have played out in your life.

Alternatively, select one particular passion, and write about three areas of your life in which this passion has influenced you.

If you choose the first alternative, your thesis statement might be something like this:

The love of family, a rebellious streak, and affection for the outdoors are three passions that have governed my life.

If you choose the second alternative, this is how your thesis might look:

My rebellious streak has strongly influenced my family life, my performance in school, and my choice of career.

Assignment 2

Write an essay in which you describe three earthly things you've observed or experienced that have given you something like Russell's "prefiguring vision of heaven." In other words, they have given you a sense of something ideal, pure, perfect, and beautiful. Describe your observations or experiences in rich detail so that your reader will understand why you found them so special, and explain what effect they have had on you. Here is a sample thesis for such an essay:

In the faces of my newborn niece, my elderly grandmother, and a seriously ill friend, I have glimpsed something like Russell's "prefiguring vision of heaven."

Assignment 3

Clearly, "love" is a multifaceted emotion. People might say they love their spouses, love their children, love their friends, and love humankind in general, but they mean quite different things in each case. Write an essay in which you divide and classify three types of love. Give detailed examples that illustrate how each type of love is demonstrated.

Thank You

Alex Haley

(Links)

Alex Haley, the author of *Roots,* served in the Coast Guard during World War II. On an especially lonely day at sea—Thanksgiving—he began to give serious thought to a holiday that has become, for most of us, a day of overeating and watching endless games of football. Haley decided to celebrate the true meaning of Thanksgiving, not by remembering the Pilgrims and their turkey dinner, but by writing three very special letters.

It was 1943, during World War II, and I was a young U.S. coast-guardsman, serial number 212-548, a number we never seem to forget. My ship, the USS *Murzim*, had been under way for several days. Most of her holds contained thousands of cartons of canned or dried foods. The other holds were loaded with five-hundred-pound bombs packed delicately in padded racks. Our destination was a big base on the island of Tulagi in the South Pacific.   1

I was one of the *Murzim*'s several cooks and, quite the same as for folk ashore, this Thanksgiving morning had seen us busily preparing a traditional dinner featuring roast turkey.   2

Well, as any cook knows, it's a lot of hard work to cook and serve a big meal, and clean up and put everything away. But finally, around sundown, with our whole galley crew just bushed, we finished at last and were free to go flop into our bunks in the fo'c'sle.[1]   3

But I decided first to go out on the *Murzim*'s afterdeck for a breath of open air. I made my way out there, breathing in great, deep draughts while walking slowly about, still wearing my white cook's hat and the long apron, my feet sensing the big ship's vibrations from the deep-set turbine diesels and my ears hearing that slightly hissing sound the sea makes in resisting the skin of a ship.   4

[1]*fo'c'sle:* contraction of *forecastle,* the part of the upper deck of a ship located in the bow (front), where the crew is usually housed.

I got to thinking about Thanksgiving. In reflex, my thoughts registered the 5 historic imagery of the Pilgrims, Indians, wild turkeys, pumpkins, corn on the cob, and the rest.

Yet my mind seemed to be questing for something else—some way that I could 6 personally apply to the waning Thanksgiving. It must have taken me a half hour to sense that maybe some key to an answer could result from reversing the word "Thanksgiving"—at least that suggested a verbal direction, "Giving thanks."

Giving thanks—as in praying, thanking God, I thought. Yes, of course. Certainly. 7

Yet my mind continued nagging me. Fine. But something else. 8

After a while, like a dawn's brightening, a further answer did come—that 9 there were *people* to thank, people who had done so much for me that I could never possibly repay them. The embarrassing truth was I'd always just accepted what they'd done, taken all of it for granted. Not one time had I ever bothered to express to any of them so much as a simple, sincere "Thank you."

At least seven people had been particularly and indelibly helpful to me. I real- 10 ized, with a gulp, that about half of them had since died—so they were forever beyond any possible expression of gratitude from me. The more I thought about it, the more ashamed I became. Then I pictured the three who were still alive and, within minutes, I was down in the fo'c'sle.

Sitting at a mess table with writing paper and memories of things each 11 had done, I tried composing genuine statements of heartfelt appreciation and gratitude to my dad, Simon A. Haley, a professor at the old AMNC (Agricultural Mechanical Normal College) in Pine Bluff, Ark., now a branch of the University of Arkansas; to my grandma, Cynthia Palmer, back in our little hometown of Henning, Tenn.; and to the Rev. Lonual Nelson, my grammar school principal, retired and living in Ripley, six miles north of Henning.

I couldn't even be certain if they would recall some of their acts of years past, 12 acts that I vividly remembered and saw now as having given me vital training, or inspiration, or directions, if not all of these desirables rolled into one.

The texts of my letters began something like, "Here, this Thanksgiving at 13 sea, I find my thoughts upon how much you have done for me, but I have never stopped and said to you how much I feel the need to thank you—" And briefly I recalled for each of them specific acts performed on my behalf.

For instance, something uppermost about my father was how he had im- 14 pressed upon me from boyhood to love books and reading. In fact, this graduated into a family habit of after-dinner quizzes at the table about books read most recently and new words learned. My love of books never diminished and later led me toward writing books myself. So many times I have felt a sadness when exposed to modern children so immersed in the electronic media that they have little to no awareness of the wondrous world to be discovered in books.

I reminded the Reverend Nelson how each morning he would open our little 15 country town's grammar school with a prayer over his assembled students. I told him that whatever positive things I had done since had been influenced at least in part by his morning school prayers.

In the letter to my grandmother, I reminded her of a dozen ways she used to 16
teach me how to tell the truth, to be thrifty, to share, and to be forgiving and con-
siderate of others. (My reminders included how she'd make me pull switches from
a peach tree for my needed lesson.) I thanked her for the years of eating her good
cooking, the equal of which I had not found since. (By now, though, I've reflected
that those peerless dishes are most gloriously flavored with a pinch of nostalgia.)
Finally, I thanked her simply for having sprinkled my life with stardust.

Before I slept, my three letters went into our ship's office mail sack. They got 17
mailed when we reached Tulagi Island.

We unloaded cargo, reloaded with something else, then again we put to sea 18
in the routine familiar to us, and as the days became weeks, my little personal experience receded. Sometimes, when we were at sea, a mail ship would rendezvous[2]
and bring us mail from home, which, of course, we accorded topmost priority.

Every time the ship's loudspeaker rasped, "Attention! Mail call!" two-hundred- 19
odd shipmates came pounding up on deck and clustered about the raised hatch
atop which two yeomen, standing by those precious bulging gray sacks, were
alternately pulling out fistfuls of letters and barking successive names of sailors
who were, in turn, hollering "Here! Here!" amid the jostling.

One "mail call" brought me responses from Grandma, Dad, and the Reverend 20
Nelson—and my reading of their letters left me not only astounded but more
humbled than before.

Rather than saying they would forgive that I hadn't previously thanked them, 21
instead, for Pete's sake, they were thanking *me*—for having remembered, for having considered they had done anything so exceptional.

Always the college professor, my dad had carefully avoided anything he con- 22
sidered too sentimental, so I knew how moved he was to write me that, after having helped educate many young people, he now felt that his best results included
his own son.

The Reverend Nelson wrote that his decades as a "simple, old-fashioned prin- 23
cipal" had ended with grammar schools undergoing such swift changes that he
had retired in self-doubt. "I heard more of what I had done wrong than what I did
right," he said, adding that my letter had brought him welcome reassurance that
his career had been appreciated.

A glance at Grandma's familiar handwriting brought back in a flash memories 24
of standing alongside her white wicker rocking chair, watching her "settin' down"
some letter to relatives. Frequently touching her pencil's tip to pursed lips, character by character, each followed by a short, soft grunt, Grandma would slowly accomplish one word, then the next, so that a finished page would consume hours.
I wept over the page representing my Grandma's recent hours invested in expressing her loving gratefulness to *me*—whom she used to diaper!

Much later, retired from the Coast Guard and trying to make a living as a 25
writer, I never forgot how those three "thank you" letters gave me an insight into

[2]*rendezvous:* meet at a prearranged time and place.

something nigh[3] mystical in human beings, most of whom go about yearning in secret for more of their fellows to express appreciation for their efforts.

I discovered in time that, even in the business world, probably no two words 26 are more valued than "thank you," especially among people at stores, airlines, utilities and others that directly serve the public.

Late one night, I was one of a half-dozen passengers who straggled weary 27 and grumbling off a plane that had been forced to land at the huge Dallas/Fort Worth Airport. Suddenly, a buoyant, cheerful, red-jacketed airline man waved us away from the regular waiting room seats, saying, "You sure look bushed. I know a big empty office where you can stretch out while you wait." And we surely did. When the weather improved enough for us to leave, "Gene Erickson" was in my notebook and, back home, I wrote the president of that airline describing his sensitivity and his courtesy. And I received a thank you!

I travel a good deal on lecture tours and I urge students especially to tell their 28 parents, grandparents, and other living elders simply "thank you" for all they have done to make possible the lives they now enjoy. Many students have told me they found themselves moved by the response. It is not really surprising, if one only reflects how it must feel to be thanked after you have given for years.

Now, approaching Thanksgiving of 1982, I have asked myself what will I wish for 29 all who are reading this, for our nation, indeed for our whole world—since, quoting a good and wise friend of mine, "In the end we are mightily and merely people, each with similar needs." First, I wish for us, of course, the simple common sense to achieve world peace, that being paramount for the very survival of our kind.

And there is something else I wish—so strongly that I have had this line print- 30 ed across the bottom of all my stationery: *"Find the good—and praise it."*

Reading Comprehension

1. The word *indelibly* in "seven people had been particularly and indelibly helpful to me" (paragraph 10) means

   a. partially.

   b. temporarily.

   (c.) unforgettably.

   d. unhappily.

2. The word *immersed* in "modern children so immersed in the electronic media" (paragraph 14) means

   a. ignorant.

   (b.) absorbed.

   c. frightened.

   d. misled.

[3]*nigh:* nearly.

3. Which of the following would be a good alternative title for this selection?

    a. The Importance of Showing Gratitude

    b. The Three Most Important People in My Life

    c. A Lonely Time

    d. Why Letters Are Important

4. Which of the following sentences best expresses the main idea of the selection?

    a. The author took the people he loved for granted.

    b. The author felt grateful to arrive home safely from the war.

    c. The author's father, grandmother, and grammar school principal were delighted to receive letters of thanks.

    d. Writing letters of thanks to the important people in his life taught the author the value of showing appreciation.

5. During World War II, the author served

    a. on a cargo ship.

    b. in the Navy.

    c. on an Army base.

    d. on an aircraft carrier.

6. The author encourages his lecture audiences to

    a. make Thanksgiving a special day.

    b. write to company presidents.

    c. thank their elders.

    d. work for world peace.

7. *True or false?* __True__ The author's father taught him to love books and reading.

8. In paragraph 14, the author implies that

    a. children should watch less television.

    b. he resented his father's after-dinner quizzes.

    c. he dislikes children.

    d. his father disapproved of his choice to be a writer.

9. The author implies that

    a. his father was not openly emotional.

    b. the Reverend Lonual Nelson's teaching methods were ineffective.

    c. he never achieved success as a professional writer.

    d. he regrets the years he spent in the Coast Guard.

10. The author assumed that the people he wrote to

    a. would be angry that he had not expressed thanks much sooner.

    b. would not reply.

    (c.) might have forgotten the incidents he referred to.

    d. would brag about his letters.

▇ Structure and Technique

1. Which pattern or patterns of development does Haley use in his essay? Explain.

2. Paragraph 4 contains a vivid description of part of Haley's Thanksgiving night on the *Murzim*. What sensory details (sight, smell, hearing, taste, and/or touch) does he provide? What is the effect of all these details?

3. Most of Haley's essay is about the three thank-you letters he wrote. Why do you think he included the anecdote about the helpful man at the airport? How is it related to his point about giving thanks?

4. Writers' most common purposes are to inform, to entertain, and to persuade. Which purpose—or purposes—do you think Haley has in mind?

▇ Critical Reading and Discussion

1. Before Haley decides to write to his loved ones, what thoughts and images go through his mind as he reflects on the meaning of Thanksgiving? What is the connection between these traditional images and what Haley finally realizes?

2. Alex Haley was far from home when he decided to thank the important people in his life. If he had remained at home, do you think he would still have thanked these people? Why or why not?

3. How does Haley feel about the three responses to his thank-you letters? What conclusions about human nature does he draw from these responses?

4. Haley is a world-renowned writer. Who might have influenced his decision to be a writer? What made these people such powerful role models in his life? In general, what would you say are the qualities of a good role model?

▇ Writing Assignments

Assignment 1

There's an old Chinese proverb: "Give me a fish, and I will eat for a day. Teach me to fish, and I will eat for a lifetime." Think of someone in your life who taught you something important that you have used (or benefited from) ever since. Write a thank-you letter to this person, telling him or her exactly how you have gained or what you have learned as a result. The person might be a parent, a relative, a family friend, a favorite teacher, an employer, a coach, or a favorite sports hero or movie star.

Organize your letter in the form of a five-paragraph essay. In your introduction, you might mention how you know this person or why you were prompted to write the letter. In your thesis, state that this person has been especially important to you because you learned something important from him or her—and tell what that "something" is. In each of your supporting paragraphs, show one way in which this knowledge or skill has made a difference in your life.

Alternatively, write about three different people, each of whom has taught you something important.

Assignment 2

Pretend that it is Thanksgiving, and one of the members of your family, who is not in a very good mood, says, "I don't have anything to be thankful for this year." Persuade this person that there are some things to be thankful for. Think of at least three and develop each with specific details. Here are some areas you could consider:

Jobs or job opportunities

Educational opportunities

Loved ones

A recent success or triumph in the family

Something beautiful

Recovery from an accident or illness

A prayer that was, or seemed to be, answered

Being together

Sharing a meaningful experience

Learning a valuable lesson

Assignment 3

At the end of his essay, Alex Haley says we should "Find the good—and praise it." Think of three kinds of people who do important work yet receive little praise. Such people might include

Teachers

Nurses

Garbage collectors

Police officers

Fathers or mothers

School maintenance workers

People who keep essential services going

Write an essay about three of these groups, giving specific reasons why each deserves to be praised for good work. Alternatively, write an essay about one of these groups, discussing three specific areas in which it deserves praise.

Shame

Dick Gregory

(Links)

In this selection, Dick Gregory—the comedian and social critic—narrates two painful experiences from his boyhood. Although the incidents show graphically what it can be like to grow up black and poor, the essay also deals with universal emotions: shame, embarrassment, and the burning desire to hold on to one's self-respect.

I never learned hate at home, or shame. I had to go to school for that. I was about seven years old when I got my first big lesson. I was in love with a little girl named Helene Tucker, a light-complexioned little girl with pigtails and nice manners. She was always clean and she was smart in school. I think I went to school then mostly to look at her. I brushed my hair and even got me a little old handkerchief. It was a lady's handkerchief, but I didn't want Helene to see me wipe my nose on my hand. The pipes were frozen again, there was no water in the house, but I washed my socks and shirt every night. I'd get a pot, and go over to Mister Ben's grocery store, and stick my pot down into his soda machine. Scoop out some chopped ice. By evening the ice melted to water for washing. I got sick a lot that winter because the fire would go out at night before the clothes were dry. In the morning I'd put them on, wet or dry, because they were the only clothes I had.

Everybody's got a Helene Tucker, a symbol of everything you want. I loved her for her goodness, her cleanness, her popularity. She'd walk down my street and my brothers and sisters would yell, "Here comes Helene," and I'd rub my tennis sneakers on the back of my pants and wish my hair wasn't so nappy and the white folks' shirt fit me better. I'd run out on the street. If I knew my place and didn't come too close, she'd wink at me and say hello. That was a good feeling. Sometimes I'd follow her all the way home, and shovel the snow off her walk and try to

1

2

make friends with her Momma and her aunts. I'd drop money on her stoop late at night on my way back from shining shoes in the taverns. And she had a Daddy, and he had a good job. He was a paper hanger.

I guess I would have gotten over Helene by summertime, but something happened in that classroom that made her face hang in front of me for the next twenty-two years. When I played the drums in high school it was for Helene and when I broke track records in college it was for Helene and when I started standing behind microphones and heard applause I wished Helene could hear it, too. It wasn't until I was twenty-nine years old and married and making money that I finally got her out of my system. Helene was sitting in that classroom when I learned to be ashamed of myself.

It was on a Thursday. I was sitting in the back of the room, in a seat with a chalk circle drawn around it. The idiot's seat, the troublemaker's seat.

The teacher thought I was stupid. Couldn't spell, couldn't read, couldn't do arithmetic. Just stupid. Teachers were never interested in finding out that you couldn't concentrate because you were so hungry, because you hadn't had any breakfast. All you could think about was noontime, would it ever come? Maybe you could sneak into the cloakroom and steal a bite of some kid's lunch out of a coat pocket. A bite of something. Paste. You can't really make a meal of paste, or put it on bread for a sandwich, but sometimes I'd scoop a few spoonfuls out of the big paste jar in the back of the room. Pregnant people get strange tastes. I was pregnant with poverty. Pregnant with dirt and pregnant with smells that made people turn away, pregnant with cold and pregnant with shoes that were never bought for me, pregnant with five other people in my bed and no Daddy in the next room, and pregnant with hunger. Paste doesn't taste too bad when you're hungry.

The teacher thought I was a troublemaker. All she saw from the front of the room was a little black boy who squirmed in his idiot's seat and made noises and poked the kids around him. I guess she couldn't see a kid who made noises because he wanted someone to know he was there.

It was on a Thursday, the day before the Negro payday. The eagle always flew on Friday. The teacher was asking each student how much his father would give to the Community Chest. On Friday night, each kid would get the money from his father, and on Monday he would bring it to the school. I decided I was going to buy a Daddy right then. I had money in my pocket from shining shoes and selling papers, and whatever Helene Tucker pledged for her Daddy I was going to top it. And I'd hand the money right in. I wasn't going to wait until Monday to buy me a Daddy.

I was shaking, scared to death. The teacher opened her book and started calling out names alphabetically.

"Helene Tucker?"

"My Daddy said he'd give two dollars and fifty cents."

"That's very nice, Helene. Very, very nice indeed."

That made me feel pretty good. It wouldn't take too much to top that. I had almost three dollars in dimes and quarters in my pocket. I stuck my hand in my pocket and held on to the money, waiting for her to call my name. But the teacher closed her book after she called everybody else in the class.

I stood up and raised my hand.   13

"What is it now?"   14

"You forgot me?"   15

She turned toward the blackboard. "I don't have time to be playing with you, Richard."   16

"My Daddy said he'd . . ."   17

"Sit down, Richard, you're disturbing the class."   18

"My Daddy said he'd give . . . fifteen dollars."   19

She turned around and looked mad. "We are collecting this money for you and your kind, Richard Gregory. If your Daddy can give fifteen dollars you have no business being on relief."   20

"I got it right now, I got it right now, my Daddy gave it to me to turn in today, my Daddy said . . ."   21

"And furthermore," she said, looking right at me, her nostrils getting big and her lips getting thin and her eyes opening wide, "we know you don't have a Daddy."   22

Helene Tucker turned around, her eyes full of tears. She felt sorry for me. Then I couldn't see her too well because I was crying, too.   23

"Sit down, Richard."   24

And I always thought the teacher kind of liked me. She always picked me to wash the blackboard on Friday, after school. That was a big thrill; it made me feel important. If I didn't wash it, come Monday the school might not function right. 25

"Where are you going, Richard!"   26

I walked out of school that day, and for a long time I didn't go back very often. There was shame there.   27

Now there was shame everywhere. It seemed like the whole world had been inside that classroom, everyone had heard what the teacher had said, everyone had turned around and felt sorry for me. There was shame in going to the Worthy Boys Annual Christmas Dinner for you and your kind, because everybody knew what a worthy boy was. Why couldn't they just call it the Boys Annual Dinner—why'd they have to give it a name? There was shame in wearing the brown and orange and white plaid mackinaw[1] the welfare gave to three thousand boys. Why'd it have to be the same for everybody so when you walked down the street the people could see you were on relief? It was a nice warm mackinaw and it had a hood, and my Momma beat me and called me a little rat when she found out I stuffed it in the bottom of a pail full of garbage way over on Cottage Street. There was shame in running over to Mister Ben's at the end of the day and asking for his rotten peaches, there was shame in asking Mrs. Simmons for a spoonful of sugar, there was shame in running out to meet the relief truck. I hated that truck, full of food for you and your kind. I ran into the house and hid when it came. And then I started to sneak through alleys, to take the long way home so the people going 28

---

[1]*mackinaw:* a short, heavy woolen coat, usually plaid and double-breasted.

into White's Eat Shop wouldn't see me. Yeah, the whole world heard the teacher that day—we all know you don't have a Daddy.

It lasted for a while, this kind of numbness. I spent a lot of time feeling sorry 29 for myself. And then one day I met this wino in a restaurant. I'd been out hustling all day, shining shoes, selling newspapers, and I had googobs of money in my pocket. Bought me a bowl of chili for fifteen cents, and a cheeseburger for fifteen cents, and a Pepsi for five cents, and a piece of chocolate cake for ten cents. That was a good meal. I was eating when this old wino came in. I love winos because they never hurt anyone but themselves.

The old wino sat down at the counter and ordered twenty-six cents worth of 30 food. He ate it like he really enjoyed it. When the owner, Mister Williams, asked him to pay the check, the old wino didn't lie or go through his pocket like he suddenly found a hole.

He just said: "Don't have no money."   31

The owner yelled: "Why in hell did you come in here and eat my food if you 32 don't have no money? That food cost me money."

Mister Williams jumped over the counter and knocked the wino off his stool 33 and beat him over the head with a pop bottle. Then he stepped back and watched the wino bleed. Then he kicked him. And he kicked him again.

I looked at the wino with blood all over his face and I went over. "Leave him 34 alone, Mister Williams. I'll pay the twenty-six cents."

The wino got up, slowly, pulling himself up to the stool, then up to the coun- 35 ter, holding on for a minute until his legs stopped shaking so bad. He looked at me with pure hate. "Keep your twenty-six cents. You don't have to pay, not now. I just finished paying for it."

He started to walk out, and as he passed me, he reached down and touched my 36 shoulder. "Thanks, sonny, but it's too late now. Why didn't you pay it before?"

I was pretty sick about that. I waited too long to help another man.   37

■ Reading Comprehension

1. The words *pregnant with* in "pregnant with poverty" (paragraph 5) mean
   a. full of.
   b. empty of.
   c. sick of.
   d. satisfied with.

2. The word *hustling* in "I'd been out hustling all day" (paragraph 29) means
   a. learning.
   b. stealing.
   c. making friends.
   d. working hard.

3. Which of the following would be a good alternative title for this selection?
   a. Helene Tucker
   (b.) The Pain of Being Poor
   c. Losing a Father
   d. Mr. Williams and the Wino

4. Which sentence best expresses the main idea of the selection?
   (a.) Richard felt that being poor was humiliating.
   b. Richard liked Helene Tucker very much.
   c. Richard had to work hard as a child.
   d. The wino refused Richard's money.

5. The teacher disliked Richard because he
   a. was dirty.
   b. liked Helene.
   (c.) was a troublemaker.
   d. ate paste.

6. *True or false?* __True__ Helene Tucker felt sorry for Richard when the teacher embarrassed him.

7. Richard had trouble concentrating and learning in school because he was
   (a.) poor and hungry.
   b. distracted by Helene.
   c. lonely.
   d. unable to read.

8. Gregory implies that in his youth, he
   a. was not intelligent.
   (b.) was proud.
   c. had many friends.
   d. and Helene became friends.

9. The author implies that
   a. Mr. Williams felt sorry for the wino.
   (b.) Richard's teacher was insensitive.
   c. Richard liked people to feel sorry for him.
   d. Richard's father was dead.

10. The author implies that

   a. the mackinaws were poorly made.

   b. Helene was a sensitive girl.

   c. Helene disliked Richard.

   d. the wino was ashamed of his poverty.

Structure and Technique

1. In paragraphs 1 and 2, Gregory mentions several steps he took to impress Helene Tucker. What were they? Why does he include them in his essay?

2. A metaphor is a suggested comparison. What metaphor does Gregory use in paragraph 5, and what is its purpose? What metaphor does he use in the second sentence of paragraph 7, and what does it mean?

3. In narrating the incidents in the classroom and in the restaurant, Gregory chooses to provide actual dialogue rather than merely to tell what happened. Why?

4. At the end of the essay, Gregory shifts his focus from the classroom to the scene involving the wino at the restaurant. What is the connection between this closing scene and the rest of the essay?

Critical Reading and Discussion

1. When Gregory writes, "I never learned hate at home, or shame. I had to go to school for that" (paragraph 1), he is using irony—an inconsistency between what is expected and what actually occurs. What does he mean by these two statements? What is the effect of his irony?

2. What are Gregory's feelings about his teacher? What were your feelings about her as you read this essay? What could the teacher have done or said that would *not* have made Gregory feel ashamed?

3. Gregory shows how a childhood incident taught him shame. What other important lessons does Gregory learn in this essay? Explain.

4. At the end of his essay, Gregory says, "I waited too long to help another man." Why do you think he waited so long to assist the wino? What are some reasons people do not always help others who are in need (for example, ignoring a homeless person seated on the sidewalk)?

Writing Assignments

Assignment 1

Dick Gregory tells us in "Shame" that he was ashamed of his poverty and of being on welfare—to the point that he threw away the warm hooded mackinaw he had been given simply because it was obvious proof that he and his family were on relief. Do you think Gregory was justified in feeling so ashamed of his situation? How about other people who are on welfare? Are they justified if they feel ashamed? Choose either of the following thesis statements and develop it in an essay of several paragraphs:

> People on welfare are justified in feeling ashamed.
>
> People on welfare should not feel ashamed.

Then develop your thesis by thinking of several reasons to support the statement you have chosen. You might think along the following lines:

> Availability of jobs
>
> Education or lack of education
>
> Number of young children at home requiring care
>
> Illness, physical disability
>
> Psychological factors—depression, work habits, expectations, mental illness
>
> Society's attitude toward people on welfare

Assignment 2

At some time in your life, you probably had an experience like Dick Gregory's in "Shame"—something that happened in a classroom, a group of friends or peers, or a family situation that proved to be both embarrassing and educational. At the time, the experience hurt you very much, but you learned from it. Write a narrative essay in which you retell this experience. Try to include vivid details and plenty of conversation so that the incident will come to life.

Assignment 3

Write an essay about three basic things that people must have in order to feel self-respect. In your thesis statement, name these three necessities and state that a person must possess them in order to feel self-respect. Here are some ideas to consider:

> A certain number of material possessions
>
> A job
>
> A loving family or a special person
>
> A clear conscience
>
> A feeling of belonging
>
> Freedom from addictions

In your supporting paragraphs, discuss the factors you have chosen, showing specifically why each is so important. In order to avoid falling into the trap of writing generalities, you may want to give examples of people who lack these necessities and show how such people lose self-respect. Your examples may be drawn from personal experience, or they may be hypothetical.

I Became Her Target

Roger Wilkins

(Links)

Any newcomer in school often has an awkward time breaking the ice with classmates. For Roger Wilkins, being the only black student in his new school made the situation considerably worse. He could easily have become the focus of the other students' prejudice and fear. Instead, help came in the form of a teacher who quickly made it clear how she saw him—as a class member with something to contribute.

My favorite teacher's name was "Deadeye" Bean. Her real   1
name was Dorothy. She taught American history to eighth-graders in the junior high section of Creston, the high school that served the north end of Grand Rapids, Michigan. It was the fall of 1944. Franklin D. Roosevelt was president; American troops were battling their way across France; Joe DiMaggio was still in the service; the Montgomery bus boycott was more than a decade away, and I was a twelve-year-old black newcomer in a school that was otherwise all white.

My mother, who had been a widow in New York, had married my stepfather,   2
a Grand Rapids physician, the year before, and he had bought the best house he could afford for his new family. The problem for our new neighbors was that their neighborhood had previously been pristine[1] (in their terms) and that they were ignorant about black people. The prevailing wisdom in the neighborhood was that we were spoiling it and that we ought to go back where we belonged (or alternatively, ought not intrude where we were not wanted). There was a lot of angry talk among the adults, but nothing much came of it.

But some of the kids, those first few weeks, were quite nasty. They threw   3
stones at me, chased me home when I was on foot and spat on my bike seat when I was in class. For a time, I was a pretty lonely, friendless and sometimes frightened kid. I was just transplanted from Harlem, and here in Grand Rapids, the dominant

[1]*pristine:* pure.

culture was speaking to me insistently. I can see now that those youngsters were bullying and culturally disadvantaged. I knew then that they were bigoted, but the culture spoke to me more powerfully than my mind and I felt ashamed for being different—a nonstandard person.

I now know that Dorothy Bean understood most of that and deplored it. So 4
things began to change when I walked into her classroom. She was a pleasant-looking single woman, who looked old and wrinkled to me at the time, but who was probably about forty. Whereas my other teachers approached the problem of easing in their new black pupil by ignoring him for the first few weeks, Miss Bean went right at me. On the morning after having read our first assignment, she asked me the first question. I later came to know that in Grand Rapids, she was viewed as a very liberal person who believed, among other things, that Negroes were equal.

I gulped and answered her question and the follow-up. They weren't brilliant 5
answers, but they did establish the facts that I had read the assignment and that I could speak English. Later in the hour, when one of my classmates had bungled an answer, Miss Bean came back to me with a question that required me to clean up the girl's mess and established me as a smart person.

Thus, the teacher began to give me human dimensions, though not perfect 6
ones for an eighth-grader. It was somewhat better to be an incipient[2] teacher's pet than merely a dark presence in the back of the room onto whose silent form my classmates could fit all the stereotypes they carried in their heads.

A few days later, Miss Bean became the first teacher ever to require me to 7
think. She asked my opinion about something Jefferson had done. In those days, all my opinions were derivative.[3] I was for Roosevelt because my parents were, and I was for the Yankees because my older buddy from Harlem was a Yankee fan. Besides, we didn't have opinions about historical figures like Jefferson. Like our high school building or old Mayor Welch, he just was.

After I had stared at her for a few seconds, she said: "Well, should he have 8
bought Louisiana or not?"

"I guess so," I replied tentatively.   9

"Why?" she asked.   10

Why! What kind of question was that, I groused silently. But I ventured an an- 11
swer. Day after day, she kept doing that to me, and my answers became stronger and more confident. She was the first teacher to give me the sense that thinking was part of education and that I could form opinions that had some value.

Her final service to me came on a day when my mind was wandering and I 12
was idly digging my pencil into the writing surface on the arm of my chair. Miss Bean impulsively threw a hunk of gum eraser at me. By amazing chance, it hit my hand and sent the pencil flying. She gasped, and I crept mortified after my pencil as the class roared. That was the icebreaker. Afterward, kids came up to me to laugh about "Old Deadeye Bean." The incident became a legend, and I, a part of that story, became a person to talk to. So that's how I became just another kid in school and Dorothy Bean became "Old Deadeye."

---

[2]*incipient:* about to become.
[3]*derivative:* not original.

■ Reading Comprehension

1. The word *deplored* in "But some of the kids, those first few weeks, were quite nasty. . . . Dorothy Bean understood most of that and deplored it" (paragraphs 3–4) means

   a. supported.

   b. imitated.

   c. often taught.

   (d.) disapproved of.

2. The word *groused* in "Why! What kind of question was that, I groused silently" (paragraph 11) means

   (a.) complained.

   b. agreed.

   c. answered.

   d. yelled.

3. Which of the following would be a good alternative title for this selection?

   a. Education in the Forties

   b. A True Teacher's Pet

   c. Eighth Grade

   (d.) A Teacher's Help

4. Which of the following sentences best expresses the main idea of the selection?

   a. After moving from Harlem to Grand Rapids, Michigan, the author had numerous adjustments to make.

   b. Eighth grade can be a challenging time for a new student.

   c. Using unusual methods, Miss Bean helped her eighth-grade students learn to think for themselves.

   (d.) A teacher helped the first black student in school to be accepted and to learn to think for himself.

5. After moving to Grand Rapids, Wilkins felt ashamed of

   a. having a stepfather.

   b. being smart.

   c. having lived in Harlem.

   (d.) being different.

6. By involving Wilkins in class discussion, Miss Bean helped the other students see him as more than a

   (a.) stereotype.

   b. liberal.

   c. legend.

   d. bigot.

7. Wilkins writes that before entering Miss Bean's class, he held

   a. no opinions.

   (b.) no original opinions.

   c. opinions based on careful thought.

   d. opinions on various historical figures.

8. The author implies that some of the bigotry in Grand Rapids was the result of

   a. anger about the war.

   (b.) ignorance about black people.

   c. his youth.

   d. ignorance about physicians.

9. In stating "the teacher began to give me human dimensions, though not perfect ones for an eighth-grader" (paragraph 6), the imperfection that Wilkins refers to is his

   a. different race.

   b. inadequate answers.

   (c.) becoming a teacher's pet.

   d. coming from another state.

10. We can conclude that Dorothy Bean threw an eraser at the author because she

    a. knew the event would become an icebreaker for him.

    b. wanted to knock the pencil from his hand.

    c. wanted to ask his opinion about something.

    (d.) wanted him to pay attention in class.

■ Structure and Technique

1. Which pattern of development— comparison, narration, or description—does Wilkins use in most of his essay? Explain.

2. Which kind of transition signal—addition, time, or space—does Wilkins use to move his essay smoothly from one event to the next? Find at least four different words that are examples of this signal.

3. In the first paragraph, Wilkins chooses to provide some historical background for his story. Why do you think he chose the specific details mentioned there? What might have been lost if these details had been excluded from the essay?

4. A title can offer interesting insights into an essay, especially if the title acquires unexpected meanings. Before reading this essay, what did you think the title "I Became Her Target" might refer to? What additional meanings do you think Wilkins intended?

■ Critical Reading and Discussion

1. What does Wilkins mean by the term *nonstandard person* (paragraph 3)? Do you think he later felt more like a "standard" person? Why or why not?

2. Wilkins mentions several ways in which Miss Bean treated him differently from the way he was treated by the other teachers at Creston. How did her approach differ from theirs? What does this approach reveal about Miss Bean—as a teacher and as a person?

3. Wilkins says that initially he was Miss Bean's "incipient teacher's pet" (paragraph 6). But how did Miss Bean's behavior toward him go beyond mere favoritism? In what way did her treatment of Wilkins affect how his peers regarded him?

4. In paragraph 7, Wilkins says, "Miss Bean became the first teacher ever to require me to think." Before Miss Bean's class, what do you suspect Wilkins—and his classmates—were being taught to do in school? Describe a teacher who gave you "the sense that thinking was part of education." In your opinion, what can teachers do to get students to think?

■ Writing Assignments

Assignment 1

Dorothy Bean, Wilkins's favorite teacher, obviously had an important influence on him in more ways than one. She helped him become accepted by the other students, she strengthened his self-image, and she helped him learn to think for himself. Write an essay on one of your favorite teachers and the ways in which he or she influenced you.

Like Wilkins, dramatize specific incidents to show how this teacher affected you. Provide whatever background is necessary to put the teacher's influence into perspective. Your thesis will be a general statement that summarizes the teacher's impact on your life, such as this one: "Mrs. Croson, my sixth-grade teacher, helped me in ways that strengthened all of the rest of my education." Then go on in your introduction to list three specific ways in which the teacher influenced you. An example of such a plan of development is: "She gave me confidence and taught me the joys of reading and writing."

Alternatively, write an essay on three of your favorite teachers. Your thesis might be about the characteristics the three teachers shared or how they influenced you.

Assignment 2

Wilkins suggests that the students in his new school misjudged him because at first they saw him only as a stereotype, a stranger with no particular personal characteristics. Perhaps we are all subject to prejudging people, if not because of their race, then for another reason. Did a person who made a good impression on you ever turn out to be boring and mean? Did a boss you thought was overly strict ever turn out to be supportive and teach you a lot? Write an essay about someone who was really quite different from what you initially thought he or she would be. You may wish to consider the following characteristics, which often lead people to prejudge each other:

Age

Gender

Race

Sexual preference

Size

Clothing

Job

Begin your essay by explaining in vivid detail your first impression and what caused it. Then go on to narrate some experiences you had with the person and how these experiences changed your mind about him or her.

Alternatively, write about an individual or individuals who have prejudged you. Explain what those people thought of you and why, and describe how they treated you. If they came to change their minds, explain why and how your relationship changed.

Assignment 3

Write an essay in which you contrast your best teacher and your worst teacher. Make a list of the qualities that made one teacher excellent and the other ineffective or worse. Focus on three pairs of contrasting qualities, using either a *one-side-at-a-time* or a *point-by-point* method of development (see pages 264–266). Following are some elements of teaching to consider as you plan your essay:

Grasp of the subject

Ability to communicate

Ability to motivate

Interest in students

Classroom presentation

Sense of humor

In addition, consider what you or other students learned or did not learn, such as the following:

Subject matter

Ways to learn

Ways to think

Self-confidence

Methods of cooperation

Smash Thy Neighbor

John McMurtry

(Links)

We think of football as one of those all-American things, like baseball or apple pie. Children are encouraged to play football from middle school through college. Hundreds of hours of network TV are devoted to football coverage. And *Monday Night Football* is almost a patriotic ritual. In this selection, however, a former football player says that football games are cruel contests that injure players and bring out the worst in fans.

A few months ago my neck got a hard crick in it. I couldn't turn my head; to look   1
left or right I had to turn my whole body. But I'd had cricks in my neck since I
started playing grade-school football and hockey, so I just ignored it. Then I began
to notice that when I reached for any sort of large book (which I do pretty often as
a philosophy teacher at the University of Guelph), I had trouble lifting it with one
hand. I was losing the strength in my left arm, and I had such a steady pain in my
back that I often had to stretch out on the floor to relieve the pressure.

Several weeks after my problems with book-lifting, I mentioned to my brother,   2
an orthopedic surgeon, that I'd lost the power in my arm since my neck began to

hurt. Twenty-four hours later I was in a Toronto hospital, not sure whether I might end up with a wasted upper limb. Apparently the steady pounding I had received playing college and professional football in the late fifties and early sixties had driven my head into my backbone so that the disks had crumpled together at the neck—"acute herniation"—and had cut the nerves to my left arm like a pinched telephone wire (without nerve stimulation, of course, the muscles atrophy, leaving the arm crippled). So I spent my Christmas holidays in the hospital in heavy traction, and much of the next three months with my neck in a brace. Today most of the pain is gone, and I've recovered most of the strength in my arm. But from time to time I still have to don the brace, and surgery remains a possibility.

3   Not much of this will surprise anyone who knows football. It is a sport in which body wreckage is one of the leading conventions. A few days after I went into the hospital for that crick in my neck, another brother, an outstanding football player in college, was undergoing spinal surgery in the same hospital two floors above me. In his case it was a lower, more massive herniation, which every now and again buckled him so that he was unable to lift himself off his back for days. By the time he entered the hospital for surgery he had already spent several months in bed. The operation was successful, but, as in all such cases, it will take him a year to recover fully.

4   These aren't isolated experiences. Just about anybody who has ever played football for any length of time, in high school, college, or one of the professional leagues, has suffered for it later.

5   Indeed, it is arguable that body shattering is the very *point* of football, as killing and maiming are of war. (In the United States, for example, the game results in fifteen to twenty deaths a year and about fifty thousand major operations on knees alone.) To grasp some of the more conspicuous similarities between football and war, it is instructive to listen to the imperatives most frequently issued to the players by their coaches, teammates, and fans. "Hurt 'em!" "Level 'em!" "Kill 'em!" "Take 'em apart!" Or watch for the plays that are most enthusiastically applauded by the fans, where someone is "smeared," "knocked silly," "creamed," "nailed," "broken in two," or even "crucified." (One of my coaches when I played corner linebacker with the Calgary Stampeders in 1961 elaborated, often very inventively, on this language of destruction: admonishing us to "unjoin" the opponent, "make 'im remember you," and "stomp 'im like a bug."). Just as in hockey, where a fight will bring fans to their feet more often than a skillful play, so in football the mouth waters most of all for the really crippling block or tackle. For the kill. Thus the good teams are "hungry," the best players are "mean," and "casualties" are as much a part of the game as they are of a war.

6   The family resemblance between football and war is, indeed, striking. Their languages are similar: "field general," "long bomb," "blitz," "take a shot," "front line," "pursuit," "good hit," "the draft," and so on. Their principles and practices are alike: mass hysteria, the art of intimidation, absolute command and total obedience, territorial aggression, censorship, inflated insignia and propaganda, blackboard maneuvers and strategies, drills, uniforms, formations, marching bands, and training camps. And the virtues they celebrate are almost identical: hyperaggressiveness, coolness under fire, and suicidal bravery.

One difference between war and football, though, is that there is little or no   7
protest against football. Perhaps the most extraordinary thing about the game is
that the systematic infliction of injuries excites in people not concern, as would
be the case if they were sustained at, say, a rock festival, but a collective rejoicing
and euphoria. Players and fans alike revel in the spectacle of a combatant felled
into semiconsciousness, "blindsided," "clotheslined," or "decapitated." I can remember, in fact, being chided by a coach in pro ball for not "getting my hat"
injuriously into a player who was lying helpless on the ground.

After every game, of course, the papers are full of reports on the day's injuries, a   8
sort of post-battle "body count," and the respective teams go to work with doctors
and trainers, tape, whirlpool baths, cortisone, and morphine to patch and deaden
the wounds before the next game. Then the whole drama is reenacted—injured
athletes held together by adhesive, braces, and drugs—and the days following it
are filled with even more feverish activity to put on the show yet again at the end
of the week. (I remember being so taped up in college that I earned the nickname
"Mummy.") The team that survives this merry-go-round spectacle of skilled masochism with the fewest incapacitating injuries usually wins. It is a sort of victory by
ordeal: "We hurt them more than they hurt us."

My own initiation into this brutal circus was typical. I loved the game from   9
the moment I could run with a ball. Played shoeless on a green, open field with
no one keeping score and in a spirit of reckless abandon and laughter, it's a very
different sport. Almost no one gets hurt, and it's rugged, open, and exciting (it still
is for me). But, like everything else, it starts to be regulated and institutionalized
by adult authorities. And the fun is over.

So it was as I began the long march through organized football. Now there   10
were a coach and elders to make it clear by their behavior that beating other people was the only thing to celebrate and that trying to shake someone up every play
was the only thing to be really proud of. Now there were severe rule enforcers,
audiences, formally recorded victors and losers, and heavy equipment to permit
crippling bodily moves and collisions (according to one survey, more than 80 percent of all football injuries occur to fully equipped players). And now there was the
official "given" that the only way to keep playing was to wear suffocating armor,
to play to defeat, to follow orders silently, and to renounce spontaneity in favor of
joyless drill. The game has been, in short, ruined. But because I loved to play, and
play skillfully, I stayed. And progressively and inexorably, as I moved through high
school, college, and pro leagues, my body was dismantled. Piece by piece.

I started off with torn ligaments in my knee at thirteen. Then, as the organ-   11
ization and the competition increased, the injuries came faster and harder. Broken
nose (three times), broken jaw (fractured in the first half and dismissed as a "bad
wisdom tooth," so I played with it for the rest of the game), ripped knee ligaments
again. Torn ligaments in one ankle and a fracture in the other (which I remember
feeling relieved about because it meant I could honorably stop drill-blocking a
270-pound defensive end). Repeated rib fractures and cartilage tears (usually carried, again, through the remainder of the game). More dislocations of the left
shoulder than I can remember (the last one I played with because, as the Calgary

Stampeders' doctor said, it "couldn't be damaged any more"). Occasionally broken or dislocated fingers and toes. Chronically hurt lower back (I still can't lift with it or change a tire without worrying about folding). Separated right shoulder (as with many other injuries, like badly bruised hips and legs, needled with morphine for the games). And so on. The last pro game I played—against the Winnipeg Blue Bombers in the Western finals in 1961—I had a recently dislocated left shoulder, a more recently wrenched right shoulder, and a chronic pain center in one leg. I was so tied up with soreness that I couldn't drive to the airport. But it never occurred to me that I should miss a play as a corner linebacker.

By the end of my football career, I had learned that physical injury—giving it 12 and taking it—is the real currency of the sport. And that in the final analysis, the "winner" is the man who can hit to kill even if only half his limbs are working. In brief, a warrior game with a warrior ethos[1] into which (like almost everyone I played with) my original boyish enthusiasm had been relentlessly conditioned.

In thinking back on how all this happened, though, I can pick out no villains. 13 As with the social system as a whole, the game has a life of its own. Everyone grows up inside it, accepts it, and fulfills its dictates as obediently as Helots[2]. Far from questioning the principles of the activity, most men simply concentrate on executing these principles more aggressively than anybody else. The result is a group of people who, as the leagues become of a higher and higher class, are progressively insensitive to the possibility that things could be otherwise. Thus, in football, anyone who might question the wisdom or enjoyment of putting on heavy equipment on a hot day and running full speed at someone else with the intention of knocking him senseless would be regarded as not really a devoted athlete and probably "chicken." The choice is made straightforward. Either you, too, do your very utmost to smash efficiently and be smashed, or you admit incompetence or cowardice and quit. Since neither of these admissions is very pleasant, people generally keep any doubts they have to themselves, and carry on.

Of course, it would be a mistake to suppose that there is more blind acceptance 14 of brutal practices in organized football than elsewhere. On the contrary, a recent Harvard study argues that football's characteristics of "impersonal acceptance of inflicted injury," an overriding "organization goal," the "ability to turn oneself on and off," and being, above all, "out to win" are prized by ambitious executives in many large corporations. Clearly, football is no sicker than the rest of our society. Even its organized destruction of physical well-being is not anomalous.[3] A very large part of our wealth, work, and time is, after all, spent in systematically destroying and harming human life; manufacturing, selling, and using weapons that tear opponents to pieces; making ever bigger and faster predator-named cars with which to kill and injure one another by the millions every year; and devoting our very lives to outgunning one another for power in an ever-more-destructive rat race. Yet all these practices are accepted without question by most people, even zealously defended and honored. Competitive, organized injuring is integral

[1]*ethos:* set of values.
[2]*Helots:* in ancient Greece, people of slave-like status.
[3]*anomalous:* abnormal.

to our way of life, and football is one of the more intelligible mirrors of the whole process: a sort of colorful morality play showing us how exciting and rewarding it is to Smash Thy Neighbor.

Now, it is fashionable to rationalize our collaboration in all this by arguing   15
that, well, men *like* to fight and injure their fellows, and such games as football should be encouraged to discharge this original-sin[4] urge into less harmful channels than, say, war. Public-show football, this line goes, plays the same sort of cathartic role as Aristotle said stage tragedy does: without real blood (or not much), it releases players and audience from unhealthy feelings stored up inside them.

As an ex-player in this seasonal coast-to-coast drama, I see little to recommend   16
such a view. What organized football did to me was make me *suppress* my natural urges and reexpress them in alienating, vicious form. Spontaneous desires for free bodily exuberance and fraternization with competitors were shamed and forced under ("If it ain't hurtin', it ain't helpin'"), and in their place were demanded armored, mechanical moves, and cool hatred of all opposition. Endless authoritarian drill and dressing-room harangues (ever wonder why competing teams can't prepare for a game in the same dressing room?) were the kinds of mechanisms employed to reconstruct joyful energies into mean and alien shapes. I am quite certain that everyone else around me was being similarly forced into this heavily equipped military precision and angry antagonism, because there was always a mutinous attitude about full-dress practices, and everybody (the pros included) had to concentrate incredibly hard for days to whip himself into just one hour's hostility a week against another club. The players never speak of these things, of course, because everyone is anxious to appear tough.

The claim that men like seriously to battle one another to some sort of finish   17
is a myth. It endures only because it wears one of the oldest and most propagandized of masks—the romantic combatant. I sometimes wonder whether the violence all around us doesn't depend for its survival on the existence and preservation of this tough-guy disguise.

As for the effect of organized football on the spectator, the fans are not so   18
much released from supposed feelings of violent aggression by watching their athletic heroes perform it as they are encouraged in the view that people-smashing is an admirable mode of self-expression. The most savage attackers, after all, are, by general agreement, the most efficient and worthy players of all (the biggest applause I ever received as a football player occurred when I ran over people or slammed them so hard that they couldn't get up). . . . Watching well-advertised strong men knock other people around, make them hurt, is in the end like other tastes. It does not weaken with feeding and variation in form. It grows.

I got out of football in 1962. In a preseason intersquad game, I ripped the   19
cartilage in my ribs on the hardest block I'd ever thrown. I had trouble breathing, and I had to shuffle-walk with my torso on a tilt. The doctor in the local hospital said three weeks rest; the coach said scrimmage in two days. Three days later I was back home reading philosophy.

---

[4]*original-sin:* referring to the Christian belief that all humans are in a sinful state because of Adam's disobedience in the Garden of Eden.

■ Reading Comprehension

1. The word *atrophy* in "without nerve stimulation, of course, the muscles atrophy, leaving the arm crippled" (paragraph 2) means

   a. get stronger.

   b. flex.

   c. weaken.

   d. are unaffected.

2. The word *imperatives* in "It is instructive to listen to the imperatives most frequently issued to the players. . . . 'Hurt 'em!' 'Level 'em!' 'Kill 'em!'" (paragraph 5) means

   a. insults.

   b. commands.

   c. compliments.

   d. questions.

3. Which of the following would be a good alternative title for this selection?

   a. The Violence of Football

   b. Football in the United States

   c. A Man Who Played Football

   d. Football and Corporate Competition

4. Which sentence best expresses the main idea of the selection?

   a. Playing football has caused the author much physical pain.

   b. Most football coaches try to make the game less violent.

   c. Football's popularity is a reflection of some negative aspects of society.

   d. Violence is a central part of organized football both for the teams and for the fans.

5. The author says that organized football is like

   a. all other sports.

   b. philosophy.

   c. war.

   d. football played without coaches and rules.

6. For the author, football was ruined by

   a. people who play without equipment.

   b. adult authorities.

   c. people who dislike its violence.

   d. ambitious executives.

7. According to the author, watching football makes people

   a. believe that "smashing thy neighbor" is good.

   b. realize that football is too violent.

   c. feel a great release from their own violent feelings.

   d. escape from the anxieties of their jobs.

8. The author implies that

   a. society is much less brutally competitive than football.

   b. football players never have doubts about the brutality of the game.

   c. the brutal values of football exist in other parts of society.

   d. many people question the violence in football.

9. The author implies that fans

   a. get rid of unhealthy feelings when watching football.

   b. encourage the violence in football.

   c. are unaware of the violence in football.

   d. discourage the really savage attacks in football.

10. In the last paragraph, the author implies that

   a. his injuries were mild.

   b. the doctor exaggerated the extent of his injuries.

   c. the coach thought that his injuries were mild.

   d. the coach cared more about winning than about his players' injuries.

Structure and Technique

1. McMurtry uses several patterns of development in his essay: comparison and contrast, cause-and-effect, description, narration, and argumentation. Where does he use each of those patterns?

2. McMurtry uses terms such as "body wreckage," "body shattering," and "skilled masochism" to describe organized football. Find three other phrases the author uses to describe football (beginning with paragraph 9). What effect does McMurtry hope this language will have on the reader?

3. In paragraph 11, McMurtry provides a series of details about the injuries he has sustained playing football. List some of these details. Why do you think he includes these personal details in his essay?

4. In "Smash Thy Neighbor," McMurtry repeatedly describes his own personal experiences with football. What do these anecdotes contribute to the essay? How do they relate to the larger point he is trying to make?

Critical Reading and Discussion

1. What is McMurtry's current profession? How might his present position have influenced his opinions about football?

2. The author makes a comparison between war and football. Do you think this is a fair comparison? Why or why not?

3. According to McMurtry, what qualities of our society are reflected in football? What is your opinion of his analysis?

4. In paragraphs 15–18, McMurtry points out— and then rebuts—the belief that football benefits society. Do you believe that football and sports in general are harmful or helpful to society? Explain.

Writing Assignments

Assignment 1

Imagine that you are a professional football coach (or, if you prefer, the head coach of your school's football team). You have just read "Smash Thy Neighbor" in a national magazine, and you feel angered and hurt by McMurtry's opinion of football. How would you answer his accusations about the sport? Write a letter to the editor of the magazine in which you give three reasons why John McMurtry is wrong about football and its effects on people. You might want to get started with this thesis statement:

I feel John McMurtry is wrong about football for several reasons.

Then continue your letter, describing each reason in detail. Write a separate paragraph for each detail.

Alternatively, imagine that, as a coach, you agree with McMurtry, and write a letter in which you detail three reasons for agreeing.

Assignment 2

Write a narrative essay about a bad experience you had with sports. Among the topics you might write about are

An injury

Not being chosen for a team

Missing an important point or goal

Being pressured by a parent or coach

Being the clumsiest person in gym class

Being embarrassed while trying to learn a sport

You could begin the essay with a sentence or two about your experience with sports in general—whether sports have been an area of pain or pleasure for you. Your thesis should name the particular experience you will write about and tell your readers that this experience was bad (or embarrassing, or humiliating, or disillusioning, or any other word that seems appropriate).

Then organize your supporting paragraphs by dividing your experience into two or three time phases. First, you may want to review Chapter 9, on the narrative essay (pages 191–206).

Assignment 3

Write an essay about a sport you feel is a good one. In each of your supporting paragraphs, give one reason why this sport is good for either players or spectators.

A Hanging

George Orwell

(Links)

You are about to attend an execution. In this essay, George Orwell (author of *Animal Farm* and *1984*) recalls a hanging he witnessed when he was an English police officer stationed in Burma. Orwell's sensitivity and vividly descriptive writing will make you see and feel what it is like to take the seemingly endless walk from cell to gallows. You will share the guards' uneasiness and the prisoner's terror. And, after you finish the selection, you may also share Orwell's views on capital punishment.

It was in Burma, a sodden morning of the rains. A sickly light, like yellow tinfoil, was slanting over the high walls into the jail yard. We were waiting outside the condemned cells, a row of sheds fronted with double bars, like small animal cages. Each cell measured about ten feet by ten and was quite bare within except for a plank bed and a pot of drinking water. In some of them brown silent men were squatting at the inner bars, with their blankets draped round them. These were the condemned men, due to be hanged within the next week or two.   1

One prisoner had been brought out of his cell. He was a Hindu, a puny wisp of   2
a man, with a shaven head and vague liquid eyes. He had a thick, sprouting moustache, absurdly too big for his body, rather like the moustache of a comic man on the films. Six tall Indian warders were guarding him and getting him ready for the gallows. Two of them stood by with rifles with fixed bayonets, while the

others handcuffed him, passed a chain through his handcuffs and fixed it to their belts, and lashed his arms tight to his sides. They crowded very close about him, with their hands always on him in a careful, caressing grip, as though all the while feeling him to make sure he was there. It was like men handling a fish which is still alive and may jump back into the water. But he stood quite unresisting, yielding his arms limply to the ropes, as though he hardly noticed what was happening.

Eight o'clock struck and a bugle call, desolately thin in the wet air, floated from the distant barracks. The superintendent of the jail, who was standing apart from the rest of us, moodily prodding the gravel with his stick, raised his head at the sound. He was an army doctor, with a grey toothbrush moustache and a gruff voice. "For God's sake hurry up, Francis," he said irritably. "The man ought to have been dead by this time. Aren't you ready yet?" 3

Francis, the head jailer, a fat Dravidian in a white drill suit and gold spectacles, waved his black hand. "Yes sir, yes sir," he bubbled. "All iss satisfactorily prepared. The hangman iss waiting. We shall proceed." 4

"Well, quick march, then. The prisoners can't get their breakfast till this job's over." 5

We set out for the gallows. Two warders marched on either side of the prisoner, with their files at the slope; two others marched close against him, gripping him by arm and shoulder, as though at once pushing and supporting him. The rest of us, magistrates and the like, followed behind. Suddenly, when we had gone ten yards, the procession stopped short without any order or warning. A dreadful thing had happened—a dog, come goodness knows whence, had appeared in the yard. It came bounding among us with a loud volley of barks, and leapt round us wagging its whole body, wild with glee at finding so many human beings together. It was a large woolly dog, half Airedale, half pariah. For a moment it pranced round us, and then, before anyone could stop it, it had made a dash for the prisoner, and jumping up tried to lick his face. Everyone stood aghast, too taken aback even to grab at the dog. 6

"Who let that bloody brute in here?" said the superintendent angrily. "Catch it, someone!" 7

A warden, detached from the escort, charged clumsily after the dog, but it danced and gambolled just out of his reach, taking everything as part of the game. A young Eurasian jailer picked up a handful of gravel and tried to stone the dog away, but it dodged the stones and came after us again. Its yaps echoed from the jail walls. The prisoner, in the grasp of the two warders, looked on incuriously, as though this was another formality of the hanging. It was several minutes before someone managed to catch the dog. Then we put my handkerchief through its collar and moved off once more, with the dog still straining and whimpering. 8

It was about forty yards to the gallows. I watched the bare brown back of the prisoner marching in front of me. He walked clumsily with his bound arms, but quite steadily, with that bobbing gait of the Indian who never straightens his knees. At each step his muscles slid neatly into place, the lock of hair on his scalp danced up and down, his feet printed themselves on the wet gravel. And once, in spite of the men who gripped him by each shoulder, he stepped slightly aside to avoid a puddle on the path. 9

It is curious, but till that moment I had never realised what it means to destroy   10
a healthy, conscious man. When I saw the prisoner step aside to avoid the puddle,
I saw the mystery, the unspeakable wrongness, of cutting a life short when it is
in full tide. This man was not dying; he was alive just as we were alive. All the
organs of his body were working—bowels digesting food, skin renewing itself,
nails growing, tissues forming—all toiling away in solemn foolery. His nails would
still be growing when he stood on the drop, when he was falling through the air
with a tenth of a second to live. His eyes saw the yellow gravel and the grey walls,
and his brain still remembered, foresaw, reasoned—reasoned even about puddles.
He and we were a party of men walking together, seeing, hearing, feeling, understanding the same world; and in two minutes, with a sudden snap, one of us
would be gone—one mind less, one world less.

The gallows stood in a small yard, separate from the main grounds of the   11
prison, and overgrown with tall prickly weeds. It was a brick erection like three
sides of a shed, with planking on top, and above that two beams and a crossbar
with the rope dangling. The hangman, a grey-haired convict in the white uniform
of the prison, was waiting beside his machine. He greeted us with a servile crouch
as we entered. At a word from Francis the two warders, gripping the prisoner
more closely than ever, half led, half pushed him to the gallows and helped him
clumsily up the ladder. Then the hangman climbed up and fixed the rope round
the prisoner's neck.

We stood waiting, five yards away. The warders had formed in a rough circle   12
round the gallows. And then, when the noose was fixed, the prisoner began crying
out to his god. It was a high, reiterated cry of "Ram! Ram! Ram! Ram!" not urgent
and fearful like a prayer or a cry for help, but steady, rhythmical, almost like the
tolling of a bell. The dog answered the sound with a whine. The hangman, still
standing on the gallows, produced a small cotton bag like a flour bag and drew it
down over the prisoner's face. But the sound, muffled by the cloth, still persisted,
over and over again: "Ram! Ram! Ram! Ram! Ram!"

The hangman climbed down and stood ready, holding the lever. Minutes   13
seemed to pass. The steady, muffled crying from the prisoner went on and on,
"Ram! Ram! Ram!" never faltering for an instant. The superintendent, his head
on his chest, was slowly poking the ground with his stick; perhaps he was counting
the cries, allowing the prisoner a fixed number—fifty, perhaps, or a hundred. Everyone had changed colour. The Indians had gone grey like bad coffee, and one or
two of the bayonets were wavering. We looked at the lashed, hooded man on the
drop, and listened to his cries—each cry another second of life; the same thought
was in all our minds: oh, kill him quickly, get it over, stop that abominable noise!

Suddenly the superintendent made up his mind. Throwing up his head he   14
made a swift motion with his stick. "Chalo!" he shouted almost fiercely.

There was a clanking noise, and then dead silence. The prisoner had vanished,   15
and the rope was twisting on itself. I let go of the dog, and it galloped immediately to the back of the gallows; but when it got there it stopped short, barked,
and then retreated into a corner of the yard, where it stood among the weeds,
looking timorously out at us. We went round the gallows to inspect the prisoner's

body. He was dangling with his toes pointed straight downwards, very slowly re-volving, as dead as a stone.

The superintendent reached out with his stick and poked the bare body; it 16 oscillated,[1] slightly. "*He's* all right," said the superintendent. He backed out from under the gallows, and blew out a deep breath. The moody look had gone out of his face quite suddenly. He glanced at his wristwatch. "Eight minutes past eight. Well, that's all for this morning, thank God."

The warders unfixed bayonets and marched away. The dog, sobered and 17 conscious of having misbehaved itself, slipped after them. We walked out of the gallows yard, past the condemned cells with their waiting prisoners, into the big central yard of the prison. The convicts, under the command of warders armed with lathis,[2] were already receiving their breakfast. They squatted in long rows, each man holding a tin pannikin,[3] while two warders with buckets marched round ladling out rice; it seemed quite a homely, jolly scene, after the hanging. An enor-mous relief had come upon us now that the job was done. One felt an impulse to sing, to break into a run, to snicker. All at once everyone began chattering gaily.

The Eurasian boy walking beside me nodded towards the way we had come, 18 with a knowing smile: "Do you know, sir, our friend (he meant the dead man), when he heard his appeal had been dismissed, he pissed on the floor of his cell. From fright.—Kindly take one of my cigarettes, sir. Do you not admire my new silver case, sir? From the boxwallah,[4] two rupees eight annas. Classy European style."

Several people laughed—at what, nobody seemed certain. 19

Francis was walking by the superintendent, talking garrulously: "Well, sir, all 20 hass passed off with the utmost satisfactoriness. It wass all finished—flick! like that. It iss not always so –oah, no! I have known cases where the doctor wass obliged to go beneath the gallows and pull the prisoner's legs to ensure deccase. Most disagreeable!"

"Wriggling about, eh? That's bad," said the superintendent. 21

"Ach, sir, it iss worse when they become refractory! One man, I recall, clung 22 to the bars of hiss cage when we went to take him out. You will scarcely credit, sir, that it took six warders to dislodge him, three pulling at each leg. We reasoned with him. 'My dear fellow,' we said, 'think of all the pain and trouble you are caus-ing to us!' But no, he would not listen! Ach, he wass very troublesome!"

I found that I was laughing quite loudly. Everyone was laughing. Even the super- 23 intendent grinned in a tolerant way. "You'd better all come out and have a drink," he said quite genially. "I've got a bottle of whisky in the car. We could do with it."

We went through the big double gates of the prison, into the road. "Pull- 24 ing at his legs!" exclaimed a Burmese magistrate suddenly, and burst into a loud chuckling. We all began laughing again. At that moment Francis's anecdote seemed extraordinarily funny. We all had a drink together, native and European alike, quite amicably. The dead man was a hundred yards away.

---

[1]*oscillated:* swung back and forth.
[2]*lathis:* long, heavy sticks, usually of bamboo and bound with iron.
[3]*pannikin:* small metal (usually tinned iron) drinking vessel.
[4]*boxwallah:* expert box-maker.

■ **Reading Comprehension**

1. The word *gambolled* in "[the dog] danced and gambolled just out of his reach" (paragraph 8) means

   a. crawled.

   b. limped.

   (c.) leaped.

   d. stood.

2. The word *amicably* in "We all had a drink together, . . . quite amicably" (paragraph 24) means

   a. with hostility.

   b. unnecessarily.

   c. quietly.

   (d.) in a friendly way.

3. Which of the following would be a good alternative title for this selection?

   a. A Burmese Prisoner

   b. Methods of Capital Punishment

   c. The Necessity of Execution

   (d.) The Difficulty of Taking a Life

4. Which sentence best expresses the main idea of the selection?

   a. Capital punishment is unpleasant to carry out, but it is necessary in some cases.

   b. Executions in Burma were done in an inefficient and amateurish way.

   (c.) Taking another person's life is morally wrong.

   d. No one cared about the Burmese prisoner who was hanged.

5. Just before he was executed, the prisoner

   a. protested his innocence.

   (b.) cried out to his god.

   c. tried to escape from the gallows.

   d. said a quiet prayer.

6. *True or false?* _False_ The author says that the prisoner had been convicted of murder.

7. After the execution, the author and the other officials

   (a.) felt relief.

   b. became very depressed.

    c. chased away the dog.

    d. couldn't speak for a long while.

8. The author implies that

    a. the dog that interrupted the march to the gallows belonged to the prisoner.

    (b.) no one has the right to take another person's life.

    c. the authorities knew the prisoner was innocent.

    d. other methods of execution are more humane than hanging.

9. The author implies that

    a. the prisoner would have escaped if he had not been so heavily guarded.

    b. the prisoner did not die immediately.

    c. the hangman had volunteered for the job.

    (d.) the superintendent of the jail was nervous and upset about the hanging.

10. The author implies

    (a.) the people who witnessed the hanging later laughed and joked to cover up the uneasiness they felt.

    b. the native people and the Europeans felt differently about the hanging.

    c. he had become friends with the prisoner before the execution.

    d. Burmese officials were corrupt.

Structure and Technique

1. Paragraphs 1, 2, and 3 contain vivid descriptions of the people and things surrounding the author on the morning of the execution. What details does he use that appeal to the readers' senses of sight, hearing, and touch? What is the effect of all these details?

2. "A Hanging" takes place in Burma, and Orwell occasionally uses regional terms such as *lathis* and *boxwallah* in the course of his essay. Why do you think Orwell chose to include these foreign terms rather than translate them into English?

3. In part, Orwell uses dialogue to tell his story, giving the actual words of numerous individuals. What does the essay gain or lose from this technique? Explain.

4. In paragraph 10, Orwell provides a series of details about the bodily organs of the condemned man. List these details. How do they relate to Orwell's larger point in "A Hanging"?

Critical Reading and Discussion

1. Why does everyone stand "aghast" when the stray dog licks the prisoner's face? Why is this incident important?

2. The author has a moment of understanding when the prisoner steps "slightly aside to avoid a puddle on the path" (paragraph 9). What realization does Orwell come to? How is this insight related to the small incident of avoiding a puddle?

3. The character of the superintendent evolves in the course of this narrative. How do the words he speaks (and the tone of voice he speaks them in) reflect the emotional changes he goes through?

4. The author's thesis is most clearly stated in paragraph 10: "When I saw the prisoner step aside to avoid the puddle, I saw the mystery, the unspeakable wrongness, of cutting a life short when it is in full tide." Do you agree that capital punishment is always wrong? Explain your answer.

Writing Assignments

Assignment 1

Use examples and details from "A Hanging" to support the following thesis statement:

In "A Hanging," George Orwell constantly contrasts death with life in order to show us how wrong it is to kill another human being.

You might organize your paragraphs by showing how death is contrasted with life (1) on the way to the gallows, (2) at the gallows, and (3) after the hanging.

To get started, reread the selection closely, noting words and incidents that seem to be closely related to either death or life. For example, in paragraph 2, Orwell describes the prisoner as "quite unresisting, yielding his arms limply to the ropes." It is as if the prisoner is already dead. In contrast, the guards are filled with life and action: they handcuff the prisoner, lash his arms, and keep a "careful, caressing grip" on him. At many other points in the story, this strong contrast between death and life is described.

Use a point-by-point method of contrast in developing your essay. You may want to look first at the example of this method on pages 265–266.

Assignment 2

Find out (1) if capital punishment is legal in your state, and, if so, (2) which method of execution is used. (You could find this information by calling your city or county library.) Then imagine that a statewide vote will soon be taken to find out if voters want to change this law. Decide if you would (or would not) change the law. Give reasons for your decision. For example, if your state does have capital punishment, and you would vote not to change the law, you might give the reasons in the following essay outline:

> <u>Thesis:</u> Our state law allows a jury to vote for "death by lethal injection" for convicted criminals, and I would not vote to change this law.
>
> <u>Topic sentences:</u>
> (a) First of all, the death penalty saves thousands of tax dollars that would be spent to keep criminals in prison for life.
> (b) In addition, the punishment acts as a deterrent to other criminals.
> (c) Most important, death is an appropriate punishment for someone who commits a terrible crime.

In order to avoid writing in vague, general terms, you may want to use specific examples of cases or crimes currently being discussed in the news. You may also need facts and statistics. You can find these by doing a Google search on your computer using "capital punishment law" and the name of your state.

Assignment 3

On the basis of the knowledge you have gained by reading this selection, write an essay with *either* of the thesis statements below:

> Executions today are as brutal as the one described in "A Hanging."
>
> Executions today are humane compared with the one described in "A Hanging."

In your supporting paragraphs, you may want to write about each of the following:

> Methods of execution and atmosphere in which executions are conducted
> Kinds of people who are executed
> Fairness of the trials and judges

In My Day

Russell Baker

"Other people can become frail and break, but not parents." In the essay that follows, Russell Baker describes how he comes to see the error of that statement. Watching his ill mother drift further and further away in time, he recognizes ways in which we are linked to and isolated from our parents and our children.

At the age of eighty my mother had her last bad fall, and after that her mind wandered free through time. Some days she went to weddings and funerals that had taken place half a century earlier. On others she presided over family dinners cooked on Sunday afternoons for children who were now gray with age. Through all this she lay in bed but moved across time, traveling among the dead decades with a speed and ease beyond the gift of physical science. 1

"Where's Russell?" she asked one day when I came to visit at the nursing home. 2

"I'm Russell," I said. 3

She gazed at this improbably overgrown figure out of an inconceivable future and promptly dismissed it. 4

"Russell's only this big," she said, holding her hand, palm down, two feet from the floor. That day she was a young country wife with chickens in the backyard and a view of hazy blue Virginia mountains behind the apple orchard, and I was a stranger old enough to be her father. 5

Early one morning she phoned me in New York. "Are you coming to my funeral today?" she asked. 6

It was an awkward question with which to be awakened. "What are you talking about, for God's sake?" was the best reply I could manage. 7

"I'm being buried today," she declared briskly, as though announcing an important social event. 8

"I'll phone you back," I said and hung up, and when I did phone back she was all right, although she wasn't all right, of course, and we all knew she wasn't. 9

She had always been a small woman—short, light-boned, delicately structured—but now, under the white hospital sheet, she was becoming tiny. I thought of a doll with huge, fierce eyes. There had always been a fierceness in her. It showed in that angry, challenging thrust of the chin when she issued an opinion, and a great one she had always been for issuing opinions. 10

"I tell people exactly what's on my mind," she had been fond of boasting. "I tell them what I think, whether they like it or not." Often they had not liked it. She could be sarcastic to people in whom she detected evidence of the ignoramus or the fool. 11

"It's not always good policy to tell people exactly what's on your mind," I used   12
to caution her.

"If they don't like it, that's too bad," was her customary reply, "because that's   13
the way I am."

And so she was. A formidable woman. Determined to speak her mind, deter-   14
mined to have her way, determined to bend those who opposed her. In that time
when I had known her best, my mother had hurled herself at life with chin thrust
forward, eyes blazing, and an energy that made her seem always on the run.

She ran after squawking chickens, an axe in her hand, determined on a be-   15
heading that would put dinner in the pot. She ran when she made the beds, ran
when she set the table. One Thanksgiving she burned herself badly when, running
up from the cellar oven with the ceremonial turkey, she tripped on the stairs and
tumbled back down, ending at the bottom in the debris of giblets, hot gravy,
and battered turkey. Life was combat, and victory was not to the lazy, the timid,
the slugabed, the drugstore cowboy,[1] the libertine,[2] the mushmouth afraid to tell
people exactly what was on his mind whether people liked it or not. She ran.

But now the running was over. For a time I could not accept the inevitable. As   16
I sat by her bed, my impulse was to argue her back to reality. On my first visit to
the hospital in Baltimore, she asked who I was.

"Russell," I said.   17

"Russell's way out west," she advised me.   18

"No, I'm right here."   19

"Guess where I came from today?" was her response.   20

"Where?"   21

"All the way from New Jersey."   22

"When?"   23

"Tonight."   24

"No. You've been in the hospital for three days," I insisted.   25

"I suggest the thing to do is calm down a little bit," she replied. "Go over to   26
the house and shut the door."

Now she was years deep into the past, living in the neighborhood where she   27
had settled forty years earlier, and she had just been talking with Mrs. Hoffman, a
neighbor across the street.

"It's like Mrs. Hoffman said today: The children always wander back to where   28
they come from," she remarked.

"Mrs. Hoffman has been dead for fifteen years."   29

"Russ got married today," she replied.   30

"I got married in 1950," I said, which was the fact.   31

"The house is unlocked," she said.   32

So it went until a doctor came by to give one of those oral quizzes that medi-   33
cal men apply in such cases. She failed catastrophically, giving wrong answers or
none at all to "What day is this?" "Do you know where you are?" "How old are
you?" and so on. Then, a surprise.

---

[1]*drugstore cowboy:* someone who is all talk and no action.
[2]*libertine:* someone who acts without moral restraint.

"When is your birthday?" he asked.   34

"November 5, 1897," she said. Correct. Absolutely correct.   35

"How do you remember that?" the doctor asked.   36

"Because I was born on Guy Fawkes Day," she said.   37

"Guy Fawkes?" asked the doctor, "Who is Guy Fawkes?"   38

She replied with a rhyme I had heard her recite time and again over the years   39
when the subject of her birth date arose:

> "Please to remember the Fifth of November,
> Gunpowder treason and plot.
> I see no reason why gunpowder treason
> Should ever be forgot."

Then she glared at this young doctor so ill informed about Guy Fawkes's failed
scheme to blow King James off his throne with barrels of gunpowder in 1605. She
had been a schoolteacher, after all, and knew how to glare at a dolt. "You may
know a lot about medicine, but you obviously don't know any history," she said.
Having told him exactly what was on her mind, she left us again.

The doctors diagnosed a hopeless senility. Not unusual, they said. "Hardening   40
of the arteries" was the explanation for laymen. I thought it was more complicated
than that. For ten years or more the ferocity with which she had once attacked life
had been turning to a rage against the weakness, the boredom, and the absence
of love that too much age had brought her. Now, after the last bad fall, she seemed
to have broken chains that imprisoned her in a life she had come to hate and to return to a time inhabited by people who loved her, a time in which she was needed.
Gradually I understood. It was the first time in years I had seen her happy.

She had written a letter three years earlier which explained more than "hard-   41
ening of the arteries." I had gone down from New York to Baltimore, where she
lived, for one of my infrequent visits and, afterwards, had written her with some
banal advice to look for the silver lining, to count her blessings instead of burdening
others with her miseries. I suppose what it really amounted to was a threat that if
she was not more cheerful during my visits I would not come to see her very often.
Sons are capable of such letters. This one was written out of a childish faith in the
eternal strength of parents, a naive belief that age and wear could be overcome
by an effort of will, that all she needed was a good pep talk to recharge a flagging
spirit. It was such a foolish, innocent idea, but one thinks of parents differently
from other people. Other people can become frail and break, but not parents.

She wrote back in an unusually cheery vein intended to demonstrate, I sup-   42
pose, that she was mending her ways. She was never a woman to apologize, but
for one moment with a pen in her hand she came very close. Referring to my visit,
she wrote: "If I seemed unhappy to you at times—" Here she drew back, reconsid-
ered, and said something quite different:

"If I seemed unhappy to you at times, I am, but there's really nothing anyone   43
can do about it, because I'm just so very tired and lonely that I'll just go to sleep
and forget it." She was then seventy-eight.

Now, three years later, after the last bad fall, she had managed to forget the 44
fatigue and loneliness and, in these freewheeling excursions back through time,
to recapture happiness. I soon stopped trying to wrest her back to what I considered the real world and tried to travel along with her on those fantastic swoops
into the past. One day when I arrived at her bedside she was radiant.

"Feeling good today," I said. 45

"Why shouldn't I feel good?" she asked. "Papa's going to take me up to Bal- 46
timore on the boat today."

At that moment she was a young girl standing on a wharf at Merry Point, 47
Virginia, waiting for the Chesapeake Bay steamer with her father, who had been
dead sixty-one years. William Howard Taft was in the White House, Europe still
drowsed in the dusk of the great century of peace, America was a young country, and the future stretched before it in beams of crystal sunlight. "The greatest
country on God's green earth," her father might have said, if I had been able to
step into my mother's time machine and join him on the wharf with the satchels
packed for Baltimore.

I could imagine her there quite clearly. She was wearing a blue dress with big 48
puffy sleeves and long black stockings. There was a ribbon in her hair and a big
bow tied on the side of her head. There had been a childhood photograph in her
bedroom which showed all this, although the colors of course had been added
years later by a restorer who tinted the picture.

About her father, my grandfather, I could only guess, and indeed, about the 49
girl on the wharf with the bow in her hair, I was merely sentimentalizing. Of my
mother's childhood and her people, of their time and place, I knew very little. A
world had lived and died, and though it was part of my blood and bone I knew
little more about it than I know of the world of the pharaohs. It was useless now
to ask for help from my mother. The orbits of her mind rarely touched present
interrogators for more than a moment.

Sitting at her bedside, forever out of touch with her, I wondered about my 50
own children, and their children, and children in general, and about the discon-
nections between children and parents that prevent them from knowing each
other. Children rarely want to know who their parents were before they were
parents, and when age finally stirs their curiosity there is no parent left to tell
them. If a parent does lift the curtain a bit, it is often only to stun the young with
some exemplary tale of how much harder life was in the old days.

I had been guilty of this when my children were small in the early 1960s and 51
living the affluent life. It galled me that their childhoods should be, as I thought,
so easy when my own had been, as I thought, so hard. I had developed the habit,
when they complained about the steak being overcooked or the television being
cut off, of lecturing them on the harshness of life in my day.

"In my day all we got for dinner was macaroni and cheese, and we were glad 52
to get it."

"In my day we didn't have any television." 53

"In my day . . ." 54

"In my day . . ." 55

At dinner one evening a son had offended me with an inadequate report card, 56
and as I leaned back and cleared my throat to lecture, he gazed at me with an expression of unutterable resignation and said, "Tell me how it was in your day, Dad."

I was angry at him for that, but angrier with myself for having become one of 57
those ancient bores whose highly selective memories of the past become transparently dishonest even to small children. I tried to break the habit, but must have failed. A few years later my son was referring to me when I was out of earshot as "the old-timer." Between us there was a dispute about time. He looked upon the time that had been my future in a disturbing way. My future was his past, and being young, he was indifferent to the past.

As I hovered over my mother's bed listening for muffled signals from her child- 58
hood, I realized that this same dispute had existed between her and me. When she was young, with life ahead of her, I had been her future and resented it. Instinctively, I wanted to break free, cease being a creature defined by her time, consign her future to the past, and create my own. Well, I had finally done that, and then with my own children I had seen my exciting future become their boring past.

These hopeless end-of-line visits with my mother made me wish I had not 59
thrown off my own past so carelessly. We all come from the past, and children ought to know what it was that went into their making, to know that life is a braided cord of humanity stretching up from time long gone, and that it cannot be defined by the span of a single journey from diaper to shroud.

■ Reading Comprehension

1. The word *formidable* in "And so she was. A formidable woman. Determined to speak her mind, determined to have her way, determined to bend those who opposed her" (paragraph 14) means

    a. gentle.

    b. forgetful.

    c. difficult and demanding.

    d. mean and violent.

2. The word *dolt* in "she had been a schoolteacher . . . and knew how to glare at a dolt. '. . . you obviously don't know any history,' she said" (paragraph 39) means

    a. stupid person.

    b. spot on the wall.

    c. genius.

    d. son.

3. Which of the following would be a good alternative title for this selection?

    a. Bringing Up Children

    b. Losing Touch with Our Past

    c. Mom's Childhood Memories

    d. A Woman's Life

4. Which sentence best expresses the main idea of the selection?

    a. A bad fall led to the mental deterioration of the author's mother.

    b. Aging parents are a problem for adult children.

    (c.) Children ought to know their family's past and know that they are connected to a series of generations.

    d. There is often conflict within a family.

5. *True or false?* __True__ Baker's mother had been unhappy before her senility set in.

6. Toward the end of her life, Baker's mother

    a. remained physically strong.

    b. frequently repeated the saying "In my day . . . ."

    (c.) mentally wandered through her past.

    d. refused to go to the hospital.

7. Eventually, Baker decided

    a. to stop visiting his mother.

    b. to move to Baltimore.

    c. that he was right to lecture his children on the harshness of life in his day.

    (d.) to try to join his mother on her mental journeys to the past.

8. From the reading, we can conclude that Baker's mother

    a. would recover.

    (b.) believed she was really living the events she was remembering.

    c. actually predicted the day of her own funeral.

    d. had been unhappy most of her life.

9. From the details Baker selects to describe his mother, we can conclude that his description of her is

    a. overly sentimental.

    b. without insight.

    (c.) realistic.

    d. totally unsympathetic.

10. *True or false?* __False__ The author implies that parents and children tend to understand each other well.

■ Structure and Technique

1. The author's thesis is a general point that he derives from his personal family experiences. Where does he first mention this thesis? Why do you think he chose to state his thesis at this point in the piece?

2. Baker uses repetition and parallel wording—phrases with the same grammatical form—in three places: paragraphs 14, 15, and 52–55. Find the instances of these two techniques. What does Baker achieve by using these stylistic elements?

3. Throughout "In My Day," Baker uses dialogue to narrate conversations that he had with his mother. Locate at least two of these dialogues. What is gained by including these conversations in this essay?

4. In paragraph 15, Baker presents a series of details about his mother. What do these details illustrate about his mother? How does this description relate to Baker's main point?

■ Critical Reading and Discussion

1. In both his own words and those of his mother, the author reveals that she was unhappy during most of the last years of her life. According to the selection, what were the reasons for her unhappiness?

2. When his mother's mind began to wander, Baker's first impulse was to "argue her back to reality" (paragraph 16). Later, he instead "tried to travel along with her on those fantastic swoops into the past" (paragraph 44). What does the reading suggest about why he wanted to bring his mother back to reality? And why did he later change his mind?

3. Does Baker believe he has been a good son to his mother? A good father to his children? In your opinion, what does it mean to be a "good son" or a "good father"?

4. In paragraph 41, Baker says that "one thinks of parents differently from other people. Other people can become frail and break, but not parents." What does he mean? Would this view strengthen—or weaken—people's relationships with their parents or guardians?

■ Writing Assignments

Assignment 1

Is there an elderly person in your life of whom you could say, "When I grow old, I hope I do it just like him, or her?" Write an essay describing that person, using details and anecdotes to make your points dramatically and colorfully. It will be helpful to review the explanation of descriptive essays on page 170.

Assignment 2

Baker provides us with a sharp picture of his mother at several stages of her life. Choose a member of your own family and write about him or her at one particular time of life. Your essay might be about "my grandfather in his eighties," "my sister at fifteen," or "my mother after her children had all left home." Select the most significant details you can to create a vivid word portrait of that person. Incorporate one of more of these elements used by Baker:

Physical description

Anecdotes

Dialogue

First-person point of view

Repetition for emphasis and dramatic effect

Stating the thesis *after* providing the evidence

Assignment 3

Crises such as a family member's illness or death have significant effects, as they did in Baker's case. Write an essay about a crisis in your family's life in which you explore the effects the crisis had on individual family members, on the family as a unit, or on both. Common family crises include illness, death, loss of a job, and disasters such as fires, floods, and earthquakes.

An example of a thesis statement for this essay is "My grandfather's death was a significant experience for me in several ways." Support for this thesis would be a few ways in which the experience was significant: for example, seeing a grieving parent in a different light—as a child, not a parent; personally realizing the finality of death; and learning significant pieces of family history from the family's reminiscing about the grandfather.

Here are two more possible thesis statements for this assignment:

My father's heart disease has changed our family's lifestyle.

Although having our house burn down was a terrible event, it had several surprisingly positive effects.

Alternatively, you can write about the influence of an important *positive* event in your family's life, perhaps a wedding or birth.

Observing Others

A Legendary Moment

Haven Kimmel

Probably every family preserves the memory of at least one noteworthy argument. Few such arguments, though, are as vividly recorded as the one that appears below. Taken from a widely acclaimed memoir, *A Girl Named Zippy* by Haven Kimmel, it tells of an unforgettable confrontation between two strong personalities.

(Links)

My mom and dad never fought, not really, which was a good thing, because my dad had a wicked, wicked bad temper, and if he'd married a woman who fought him they probably would have killed each other. There was a great, legendary moment between them, though, which I'd heard about all my life.

One of the architectural marvels that was in my house in Mooreland was my parents' bedroom door, which was solid wood and heavy, and had a porcelain doorknob. It opened into the bedroom. At a forty-five-degree angle from the bedroom door was the closet door, which was solid wood and heavy, and had a porcelain doorknob. It also opened into the bedroom. If the closet door was open, the bedroom door could not be; if they were both halfway open the doorknobs clinked together like little figurines in a rummage sale. It was possible, I had discovered through much trial and error, to get the doorknobs stuck together with neither door open enough to accommodate a grown person. Blocking the door in such a creative way was part of my mental plan for when and if the vampires came.

My mom was nine months pregnant with me, and hugely so, and she and my father were having an actual, vocal argument in their bedroom. My sister's friend Terri was visiting, and the two of them and my brother were all in the living room. The argument reached some critical phase and Mom walked out of the bedroom at the same moment that Dad decided to go in the closet, which caused the bedroom door to smack my mother in the back. She became so instantly enraged (she claimed it was pregnancy that did it) that she waited just a moment until she was sure Dad was halfway into the closet, and then she threw the bedroom door open, which sent my father flying headfirst into the closet about sixty-four miles an hour, all the way back to where we kept the paint cans. My sister said they could

636

hear him tumbling against the cans, and could actually discern the thick moment when he gathered himself up and prepared to face my mother.

He came out of the bedroom like a bullet, red-faced and with his eyebrows 4 riding up his forehead. Mother was standing in the middle of the living room with her hands on her former hips, waiting for him. Melinda and Danny and Terri fled so quickly, and in so many different directions, that Mom later claimed they must have evaporated into the walls. Dad finally came to a stop right in Mother's face, nose to nose, panting like a bull, with his fists clenched.

"Are you going to *hit* me?!?" my mother asked, pressing her forehead more 5 aggressively into his. And before he could answer, she arced out her own arm and slapped his right cheek, hard. He pulled away from her slightly, stunned.

"I said, are you going to hit me?!" and she raised her left arm, and got him 6 on the other cheek, like a good Christian.

Miraculously, he walked away from her. Looking no less deranged *or* murder- 7 ous, he backed out of the house without taking his eyes off her, got in his truck and drove away.

It became one of the touchstone moments of their marriage, and afterward, 8 there was never a threat of violence between them again. Mom told me, when I was old enough to ask, that she had learned the lesson from Mom Mary, Dad's mother, who took her future daughter-in-law aside and told her that a woman has got to make herself absolutely clear, and early on. In Mom Mary's own case, she waited until she and my grandfather Anthel were just home from their honeymoon, and then sat him down and told him this: "Honey, I know you like to take a drink, and that's all right, but be forewarned that I ain't your maid and I ain't your punching bag, and if you ever raise your hand to me you'd best kill me. Because otherwise I'll wait till you're asleep; sew you into the bed; and beat you to death with a frying pan." Until he died, I am told, my grandfather was a gentle man.

Reading Comprehension

1. The word *discern* in "[they] could actually discern the thick moment when he gathered himself up and prepared to face my mother" (paragraph 3) means
   a. ignore.
   b. laugh at.
   c. detect.
   d. be mistaken about.

2. The word *deranged* in "Looking no less deranged *or* murderous" (paragraph 7) means
   a. calm.
   b. sad.
   c. amused.
   d. crazed.

3. Which of the following would be a good alternative title for this selection?

   a. Fighting

   (b.) Mother Makes It Clear

   c. Family Memories

   d. Physical Violence in the Home

4. Which sentence best expresses the main idea of the selection?

   a. Because her parents fought so rarely, the author vividly remembers a time that they did.

   b. The author's father had a terrible temper and could have been capable of violence.

   c. The author's mother and grandmother had dealt with the same issue in similar ways.

   (d.) An argument between the author's parents made it clear that her mother would not be intimidated.

5. True or false? _False_ The author had personally witnessed this argument between her mother and father.

6. When the bedroom door hit the author's mother in the back, she

   a. slapped her husband.

   (b.) became instantly enraged.

   c. began to cry.

   d. left the house.

7. The author's mother had been given advice about dealing with her husband by

   (a.) her husband's mother.

   b. her own mother.

   c. her daughter.

   d. her husband's father.

8. The phrase "when and if the vampires came" implies that, as a child, Kimmel

   (a.) believed in supernatural beings.

   b. thought that her parents were evil, like vampires.

   c. played a vampire game with other children.

   d. enjoyed reading about vampires.

9. The sentence "Mother was standing in the middle of the living room with her hands on her former hips, waiting for him" suggests that the author's mother

a. was badly frightened.

b. was ready to confront her husband.

c. felt apologetic.

d. thought the situation was amusing.

10. A reasonable conclusion we can draw from the reading is that

a. the author was deeply disturbed by the argument between her parents.

b. the author considers her mother and grandmother to be abused women.

c. the author thought her mother had gone too far in the argument with her father.

d. the author admired her mother's spirit in standing up to her father.

Structure and Technique

1. Find instances in the reading where Kimmel uses (or quotes someone as using) exaggeration. Why might a writer choose to exaggerate? What effect does Kimmel's exaggeration have?

2. What method of introduction—anecdote, question, or broad-to-narrow—does Kimmel use? Why do you think she chose this way to begin her essay?

3. Using Kimmel's description as a guide, draw a sketch that shows what happened if her parents' bedroom door and closet door were opened at the same time. Why does she go into such detail in order to describe the relationship between the two doors?

4. Kimmel never mentions the subject of her parents' original "actual, vocal argument." Why do you think she chose not to? Would the story have been stronger if she had explained what that argument was about?

Critical Reading and Discussion

1. You might expect a memoir about an author's parents fighting to have a dark, threatening, unhappy tone. But Haven Kimmel presents this incident in quite a different light. How does she seem to feel about what happened? What words or phrases give you clues to her viewpoint?

2. Do you think Kimmel's opinion about what happened between her parents would have been different if her father had slapped her mother? Would your opinion change? Explain your answer.

3. Kimmel uses figurative language to compare her father, first, to a bullet, and later, to a bull. What characteristics of a bullet and a bull does she suggest he shares? Later, why does she say that her mother acted "like a good Christian"? Is that comparison meant seriously or humorously?

4. The author describes this incident as "a great, legendary moment" that she had heard about all her life. Why do you think the incident was so important to the family? Do you have any family stories that people tell over and over again? Why do you think they are important to your family?

Writing Assignments

Assignment 1

Most families tell and retell certain stories that, for some reason, have become meaningful to them. Write a narrative essay in which you tell of such a memorable incident that occurred in your family.

You might begin your essay with a bit of background about your family—indicating, perhaps, whether the incident you are going to describe was in character or out of the ordinary for the people involved. Your thesis should indicate how you feel about the incident—whether it was, for example, frightening, amusing, touching, or sad.

If appropriate, use bits of dialogue to make the scene come alive for your reader. Add your own comments about why, in your opinion, the story is significant to your family.

Assignment 2

Kimmel refers to her father's "wicked bad temper." Select a person you know who has a very strong personal characteristic—perhaps a bad temper, a great sense of humor, a jealous streak, an optimistic attitude, or some other quality. Write an essay in which you describe three incidents in which the person demonstrated that characteristic. Alternatively, describe three areas of the person's life in which this characteristic is evident.

Your thesis might look like one of these:

My sister's generosity most memorably stands out for me on three particular occasions.

Whether he's at work, at school, or at home, my friend Hal always believes the worst is going to happen.

Assignment 3

Unfortunately, most stories concerning a partner hitting another one are not as lighthearted as Kimmel's. Still, many people remain with abusive partners for many years. Write an essay in which you explore three reasons why a man or a woman might stay with a partner who physically abused her or him. Your reasons might be based on personal experience, observation of people around you, or stories you've heard or read through the media.

Here is a possible thesis statement for this assignment:

A person might stay with a physically abusive partner for one of several reasons.

The Professor Is a Dropout

Beth Johnson

(Links)

After being mistakenly labeled "retarded" and humiliated into dropping out of first grade, Lupe Quintanilla knew she wanted nothing more to do with formal education. Life as a wife and mother would satisfy her . . . and it did, until she saw her own children being pushed aside as "slow learners." Driven to help them succeed, Lupe took steps that dramatically changed her life.

1. Guadalupe Quintanilla is an assistant professor at the University of Houston. She is president of her own communications company. She trains law enforcement officers all over the country. She was nominated to serve as the U.S. Attorney General. She's been a representative to the United Nations.

2. That's a pretty impressive string of accomplishments. It's all the more impressive when you consider this: "Lupe" Quintanilla is a first-grade dropout. Her school records state that she is retarded, that her IQ is so low she can't learn much of anything.

3. How did Lupe Quintanilla, "retarded" nonlearner, become Dr. Quintanilla, respected educator? Her remarkable journey began in the town of Nogales, Mexico, just below the Arizona border. That's where Lupe first lived with her grandparents. (Her parents had divorced.) Then an uncle who had just finished medical school made her grandparents a generous offer. If they wanted to live with him, he would support the family as he began his medical practice.

4. Lupe, her grandparents, and her uncle all moved hundreds of miles to a town in southern Mexico that didn't even have paved roads, let alone any schools. There, Lupe grew up helping her grandfather run his little pharmacy and her grandmother keep house. She remembers the time happily. "My grandparents were wonderful," she said. "Oh, my grandfather was stern, authoritarian, as Mexican culture demanded, but they were also very kind to me." When the chores were done, her grandfather taught Lupe to read and write Spanish and do basic arithmetic.

5. When Lupe was 12, her grandfather became blind. The family left Mexico and went to Brownsville, Texas, with the hope that doctors there could restore his sight. Once they arrived in Brownsville, Lupe was enrolled in school. Although she understood no English, she was given an IQ test in that language. Not surprisingly, she didn't do very well.

Lupe even remembers her score. "I scored a sixty-four, which classified me as seri- 6
ously retarded, not even teachable," she said. "I was put into first grade with a class
of six-year-olds. My duties were to take the little kids to the bathroom and to cut
out pictures." The classroom activities were a total mystery to Lupe—they were all
conducted in English. And she was humiliated by the other children, who teased her
for being "so much older and so much dumber" than they were.

After four months in first grade, an incident occurred that Lupe still does not 7
fully understand. As she stood in the doorway of the classroom waiting to escort
a little girl to the bathroom, a man approached her. He asked her, in Spanish, how
to find the principal's office. Lupe was delighted. "Finally someone in this school
had spoken to me with words I could understand, in the
language of my soul, the language of my grandmother,"
she said. Eagerly, she answered his question in Spanish. Instantly her teacher swooped down on her, grabbing her arm
and scolding her. She pulled Lupe along to the principal's
office. There, the teacher and the principal both shouted at
her, obviously very angry. Lupe was frightened and embarrassed, but also bewildered. She didn't understand a word
they were saying.

"Why were they so angry? I don't know," said Lupe.   8
"Was it because I spoke Spanish at school? Or that I spoke
to the man at all? I really don't know. All I know is how   Guadalupe
humiliated I was."   Quintanilla today

When she got home that day, she cried miserably, begging her grandfather 9
not to make her return to school. Finally he agreed.

From that time on, Lupe stayed at home, serving as her blind grandfather's 10
"eyes." She was a fluent reader in Spanish, and the older man loved to have her
read newspapers, poetry, and novels aloud to him for hours.

Lupe's own love of reading flourished during these years. Her vocabulary 11
was enriched and her imagination fired by the novels she read—novels which she
learned later were classics of Spanish literature. She read *Don Quixote,* the famous
story of the noble, impractical knight who fought against windmills. She read
thrilling accounts of the Mexican revolution. She read *La Prensa,* the local Spanish-
language paper, and *Selecciones,* the Spanish-language version of *Reader's Digest.*

When she was just 16, Lupe married a young Mexican-American dental tech- 12
nician. Within five years, she had given birth to her three children, Victor, Mario,
and Martha. Lupe's grandparents lived with the young family. Lupe was quite
happy with her life. "I cooked, sewed, cleaned, and cared for everybody," she said.
"I listened to my grandmother when she told me what made a good wife. In the
morning I would actually put on my husband's shoes and tie the laces—anything
to make his life easier. Living with my grandparents for so long, I was one generation behind in my ideas of what a woman could do and be."

Lupe's contentment ended when her children started school. When they 13
brought home their report cards, she struggled to understand them. She could
read enough English to know that what they said was not good. Her children had
been put into a group called "Yellow Birds." It was a group for slow learners.

At night in bed, Lupe cried and blamed herself. It was obvious—not only was 14 she retarded, but her children had taken after her. Now they, too, would never be able to learn like other children.

But in time, a thought began to break through Lupe's despair: Her children 15 didn't seem like slow learners to her. At home, they learned everything she taught them, quickly and easily. She read to them constantly, from the books that she herself had loved as a child. *Aesop's Fables* and stories from *1,001 Arabian Nights* were family favorites. The children filled the house with the sounds of the songs, prayers, games, and rhymes they had learned from their parents and grandparents. They were smart children, eager to learn. They learned quickly—in Spanish.

A radical idea began to form in Lupe's mind. Maybe the school was wrong 16 about her children. And if the school system could be wrong about her children— maybe it had been wrong about her, too.

Lupe visited her children's school, a daring action for her. "Many Hispanic par- 17 ents would not dream of going to the classroom," she said. "In Hispanic culture, the teacher is regarded as a third parent, as an ultimate authority. To question her would seem most disrespectful, as though you were saying that she didn't know her job." That was one reason Lupe's grandparents had not interfered when Lupe was classified as retarded. "Anglo teachers often misunderstand Hispanic parents, believing that they aren't concerned about their children's education because they don't come visit the schools," Lupe said. "It's not a lack of concern at all. It's a mark of respect for the teacher's authority."

At her children's school, Lupe spoke to three different teachers. Two of them told 18 her the same thing: "Your children are just slow. Sorry, but they can't learn." A third offered a glimmer of hope. He said, "They don't know how to function in English. It's possible that if you spoke English at home they would be able to do better."

Lupe pounced on that idea. "Where can I learn English?" she asked. The 19 teacher shrugged. At that time there were no local English-language programs for adults. Finally he suggested that Lupe visit the local high school. Maybe she would be permitted to sit in the back of a classroom and pick up some English that way.

Lupe made an appointment with a counselor at the high school. But when 20 the two women met, the counselor shook her head. "Your test scores show that you are retarded," she told Lupe. "You'd just be taking space in the classroom away from someone who could learn."

Lupe's next stop was the hospital where she had served for years as a volun- 21 teer. Could she sit in on some of the nursing classes held there? No, she was told, not without a diploma. Still undeterred, she went on to Texas Southmost College in Brownsville. Could she sit in on a class? No; no high-school diploma. Finally she went to the telephone company, where she knew operators were being trained. Could she listen in on the classes? No, only high-school graduates were permitted.

That day, leaving the telephone company, Lupe felt she had hit bottom. She 22 had been terrified in the first place to try to find an English class. Meeting with rejection after rejection nearly destroyed what little self-confidence she had. She walked home in the rain, crying. "I felt like a big barrier had fallen across my path," she said. "I couldn't go over it; I couldn't go under it; I couldn't go around it."

But the next day Lupe woke with fresh determination. "I was motivated by   23
love of my kids," she said. "I was not going to quit." She got up; made breakfast for
her kids, husband, and grandparents; saw her children and husband off for the day;
and started out again. "I remember walking to the bus stop, past a dog that always
scared me to death, and heading back to the college. The lady I spoke to said, 'I told
you, we can't do anything for you without a high-school degree.' But as I left the
building, I went up to the first Spanish-speaking student I saw. His name was Gabito.
I said, 'Who really makes the decisions around here?' He said, 'The registrar.'" Since
she hadn't had any luck in the office building, Lupe decided to take a more direct
approach. She asked Gabito to point out the registrar's car in the parking lot. For
the next two hours she waited beside it until its owner showed up.

Impressed by Lupe's persistence, the registrar listened to her story. But instead   24
of giving her permission to sit in on a class and learn more English, he insisted

Lupe enjoys a story with
(left to right) her twin
grandchildren, Alyssa
and Christian, and a
visiting friend.

that she sign up for a full college load. Before she knew it, she was
enrolled in four classes: basic math, basic English, psychology, and
typing. The registrar's parting words to her were, "Don't come back
if you don't make it through."

With that "encouragement," Lupe began a semester that was   25
part nightmare, part dream come true. Every day she got her husband and children off to school, took the bus to campus, came home
to make lunch for her husband and grandparents, went back to campus, and was home in time to greet Victor, Mario, and Martha when
they got home from school. In the evenings she cooked, cleaned, did
laundry, and got the children to bed. Then she would study, often
until three in the morning.

"Sometimes in class I would feel sick with the stress of it," she   26
said. "I'd go to the bathroom and talk to myself in the mirror. Sometimes I'd say, 'What are you doing here? Why don't you go home and
watch *I Love Lucy*?'"

But she didn't go home. Instead, she studied furiously, using her Spanish-   27
English dictionary, constantly making lists of new words she wanted to understand. "I still do that today," she said. "When I come across a word I don't know, I
write it down, look it up, and write sentences using it until I own that word."

Although so much of the language and subject matter was new to Lupe,   28
one part of the college experience was not. That was the key skill of reading, a
skill Lupe possessed. As she struggled with English, she found the reading speed,
comprehension, and vocabulary that she had developed in Spanish carrying over
into her new language. "Reading," she said, "reading was the vehicle. Although I
didn't know it at the time, when I was a girl learning to love to read, I was laying
the foundation for academic success."

She gives credit, too, to her Hispanic fellow students. "At first, they didn't   29
know what to make of me. They were eighteen years old, and at that time it
was very unfashionable for an older person to be in college. But once they decided I wasn't a 'plant' from the administration, they were my greatest help."
The younger students spent hours helping Lupe, explaining unfamiliar words and
terms, coaching her, and answering her questions.

That first semester passed in a fog of exhaustion. Many mornings, Lupe   30
doubted she could get out of bed, much less care for her family and tackle her
classes. But when she thought of her children and what was at stake for them,
she forced herself on. She remembers well what those days were like. "Just a day
at a time.That was all I could think about. I could make myself get up one more
day, study one more day, cook and clean one more day. And those days eventually
turned into a semester."

To her own amazement perhaps as much as anyone's, Lupe discovered that   31
she was far from retarded. Although she sweated blood over many assignments,
she completed them. She turned them in on time. And, remarkably, she made the
dean's list her very first semester.

After that, there was no stopping Lupe Quintanilla. She soon realized that   32
the associate's degree offered by Texas Southmost College would not satisfy her.
Continuing her Monday, Wednesday, and Friday schedule at Southmost, she enrolled for Tuesday and Thursday courses at Pan American University, a school 140
miles from Brownsville. Within three years, she had earned both her junior-college
degree and a bachelor's degree in biology. She then won a fellowship that took
her to graduate school at the University of Houston, where she earned a master's
degree in Spanish literature. When she graduated, the university offered her a job
as director of the Mexican-American studies program. While in that position, she
earned a doctoral degree in education.

How did she do it all? Lupe herself isn't sure. "I hardly know. When I think   33
back to those years, it seems like a life that someone else lived." It was a rich and
exciting but also very challenging period for Lupe and her family. On the one
hand, Lupe was motivated by the desire to set an example for her children, to
prove to them that they could succeed in the English-speaking academic world. On
the other hand, she worried about neglecting her family. She tried hard to attend
important activities, such as parents' meetings at school and her children's sport-
ing events. But things didn't always work out. Lupe still remembers attending a
baseball game that her older son, Victor, was playing in. When Victor came to bat,
he hit a home run. But as the crowd cheered and Victor glanced proudly over at
his mother in the stands, he saw she was studying a textbook. "I hadn't seen the
home run," Lupe admitted. "That sort of thing was hard for everyone to take."

Although Lupe worried that her children would resent her busy schedule, she   34
also saw her success reflected in them as they blossomed in school. She forced herself
to speak English at home, and their language skills improved quickly. She read to
them in English instead of Spanish—gulping down her pride as their pronunciation
became better than hers and they began correcting her. (Once the children were in
high school and fluent in English, Lupe switched back to Spanish at home, so that
the children would be fully comfortable in both languages.) "I saw the change in
them almost immediately," she said. "After I helped them with their homework,
they would see me pulling out my own books and going to work. In the morning, I
would show them the papers I had written. As I gained confidence, so did they." By
the next year, the children had been promoted out of the Yellow Birds.

Even though Victor, Mario, and Martha all did well academically, Lupe re-   35
alized she could not assume that they would face no more obstacles in school.

When Mario was in high school, for instance, he wanted to sign up for a debate class. Instead, he was assigned to woodworking. She visited the school to ask why. Mario's teacher told her, "He's good with his hands. He'll be a great carpenter, and that's a good thing for a Mexican to be." Controlling her temper, Lupe responded, "I'm glad you think he's good with his hands. He'll be a great physician someday, and he is going to be in the debate class."

Two members of the Houston police department learn job-specific Spanish phrases from Lupe. Lupe also trains the officers in cultural awareness.

Today, Lupe Quintanilla teaches at the University of Houston, 36 where she has developed several dozen courses concerning Hispanic literature and culture. Her cross-cultural training for law enforcement officers, which helps bring police and firefighters and local Hispanic communities closer together, is renowned throughout the country. Former President Ronald Reagan named her to a national board that keeps the White House informed of new programs in law enforcement. She has received numerous awards for teaching excellence, and there is even a scholarship named in her honor. Her name appears in the Hispanic Hall of Fame, and she has been co-chair of the White House Commission on Hispanic Education.

The love of reading that her grandfather instilled in Lupe is still 37 alive. She thinks of him every year when she introduces to her students one of his favorite poets, Amado Nervo. She requires them to memorize these lines from one of Nervo's poems: "When I got to the end of my long journey in life, I realized that I was the architect of my own destiny." Of these lines, Lupe says, "That is something that I deeply believe, and I want my students to learn it before the end of their long journey. We create our own destiny."

Her love of reading and learning has helped Lupe create a distinguished destiny. But none of the honors she has received means more to her than the success of her own children, the reason she made that frightening journey to seek classes in English years ago. Today Mario is a physician. Victor and Martha are lawyers, both having earned doctor of law degrees. And so today, Lupe likes to say, "When someone calls the house and asks for 'Dr. Quintanilla,' I have to ask, 'Which one?' There are four of us—one retarded and three slow learners."

Lupe surrounded by her children: Martha, Victor, and Mario.

■ Reading Comprehension

1. The word *flourished* in "Lupe's own love of reading flourished during these years. Her vocabulary was enriched and her imagination fired by the novels she read "(paragraph 11) means

   a. grew.

   b. stood still.

   c. was lost.

   d. remained.

2. The word *instilled* in "The love of reading that Lupe grandfather instilled in Lupe is still alive" (paragraph 37) means

   a. frightened.

   (b) established.

   c. forced.

   d. forgot.

3. Which of the following would be a good alternative title for this selection?

   a. Difficulties Facing Spanish-Speaking Students

   b. Unfair Labeling

   c. Balancing School and Family

   (d) A Courageous Mother's Triumph

4. Which sentence best expresses the main idea of the selection?

   a. Lupe, a first-grade dropout, eventually earned a doctoral degree and created a professional career.

   b. Lupe Quintanilla's experience proves that the educational system must be set up to accommodate non-English-speaking children.

   (c) Through hard work and persistence combined with a love of reading and learning, Lupe has created a distinguished career and helped her children become professionals.

   d. In school, Spanish-speaking students may experience obstacles as they aim for professional careers.

5. Lupe realized that her children were not retarded when

   a. they got good grades at school.

   (b) she saw how quickly they learned at home.

   c. they were put in the group called "Yellow Birds."

   d. they read newspapers, poetry, and novels to her.

6. Lupe's training for law enforcement officers

   a. teaches them to speak Spanish.

   b. teaches Hispanic literature and culture.

   c. offers a scholarship named in her honor.

   (d) brings police, firefighters, and local Hispanic communities together.

7. According to Lupe, Hispanic parents rarely visit their children's schools because they

   a. do not consider schoolwork important.

   (b) think doing so would be disrespectful to the teacher.

c. are ashamed of their English language skills.

d. are usually working during school visitation hours.

8. "Once they arrived in Brownsville, Lupe was enrolled in school. Although she understood no English, she was given an IQ test in that language. Not surprisingly, she didn't do very well" (paragraph 5). From these sentences, we might conclude that

a. an IQ test in a language that the person tested doesn't know is useless.

b. although Lupe was not very intelligent at first, she became more intelligent once she learned English.

c. Lupe really did know English.

d. there are no IQ tests in Spanish.

9. We might conclude from the reading that

a. a school system's judgment about an individual is always accurate.

b. it is often better for a child to stay home rather than attend school.

c. by paying attention and speaking up, parents may remove obstacles to their children's education.

d. working parents should accept the fact that they cannot attend important events in their children's lives.

10. The last line of the reading suggests that

a. retarded people can become successful professionals.

b. people should not blindly accept other people's opinions of them.

c. Lupe's children are smarter than she is.

d. all of the above

■ Structure and Technique

1. Johnson begins the essay by listing Lupe Quintanilla's accomplishments, then revealing that Quintanilla was once classified as retarded. What introductory technique is Johnson employing? Why is it effective here?

2. Paragraphs 3–11 are devoted to the first fifteen years of Lupe's life. But the next decade or so is covered in only two paragraphs (12–13). Why might Johnson have presented Lupe's earlier life in so much more detail? Do you agree with her decision?

3. In paragraph 2, Johnson writes that "[Lupe's] school records state that she is retarded. . . ." But in the next sentence, she writes, "How did Lupe Quintanilla, 'retarded' nonlearner, become Dr. Quintanilla, respected educator?" Why does Johnson put the word "retarded" in quotation marks in the second sentence,

but not in the first? What is she implying? Can you find another place where Johnson makes similar use of quotation marks?

4. At one point, Johnson switches from the topic of Lupe's success in college to the topic of the challenges that continued to face her children in school. In what paragraph does she make that switch? What transitional words does she use to alert the reader to her new direction?

Critical Reading and Discussion

1. In the course of the essay, what characteristics and attitudes does Lupe suggest are typical of Hispanic culture? Does she seem sympathetic, critical, or neutral about those qualities or attitudes? How has she dealt with cultural expectations in her own life?

2. How has Lupe handled the question of what language to use with her children? If you grew up in a two-language household, how did your family deal with the issue? How would you approach the issue with children of your own?

3. Do you think Lupe's grandfather was right in allowing her to quit school? What factors do you imagine might have gone into his decision?

4. Lupe credits her fellow Hispanic students with giving her valuable support in college. Is there anyone in your life—a teacher, family member, or friend—who has helped you through challenging times in your education? Explain what obstacles you faced and how this person helped you overcome them.

Writing Assignments

Assignment 1

Write an essay that takes as its thesis one of the following statements:

Schools need to be prepared to help non-English-speaking students catch up with other students at their grade level.

The responsibility for catching non-English-speaking students up to their grade level rests solely with the students and their families.

Support your thesis with several points, each developed in its own paragraph.

Assignment 2

Lupe Quintanilla is an outstanding example of someone who has taken charge of her life. She has been, to echo the poet whose work she teaches, the architect of her own destiny. Choose a person you know who, in your opinion, has done a fine job of taking charge of his or her own destiny. Write an essay about this person. You might describe three areas of life in which the person has taken control. Alternatively, you might narrate three incidents from the person's life that illustrate his or her admirable self-determination.

Assignment 3

Lupe had to struggle in order to balance her school responsibilities with her duties as a wife and mother. Write an essay in which you identify aspects of your life that you need to juggle along with your responsibilities as a student. They may include a job, a spouse or significant other, children, housekeeping duties, pets, extracurricular activities, a difficult living situation, or anything else that poses a challenge to your academics. Provide vivid, real-life illustrations of how each of those responsibilities sometimes conflicts with your studies.

The Monster

Deems Taylor

(Links)

You're about to be introduced to someone you won't like at all. By standards too numerous to count, this individual deserves dislike, disrespect, and dishonor. And yet you will be invited to admire him and overlook his many faults. Can you? Should you? This essay by Deems Taylor, a noted American composer of operas, may challenge your perceptions in suggesting that extraordinary people can't be measured by ordinary yardsticks.

He was an undersized little man, with a head too big for his body—a sickly little   1
man. His nerves were bad. He had skin trouble. It was agony for him to wear anything next to his skin coarser than silk. And he had delusions of grandeur.

He was a monster of conceit. Never for one minute did he look at the world   2
or at people, except in relation to himself. He was not only the most important person in the world, to himself; in his own eyes he was the only person who existed. He believed himself to be one of the greatest dramatists in the world, one of the greatest thinkers, and one of the greatest composers. To hear him talk, he was Shakespeare, and Beethoven, and Plato, rolled into one. And you would have had no difficulty in hearing him talk. He was one of the most exhausting conversationalists that ever lived. An evening with him was an evening spent in listening to a monologue. Sometimes he was brilliant; sometimes he was maddeningly tiresome. But whether he was being brilliant or dull, he had one sole topic of conversation: himself—what *he* thought and what *he* did.

He had a mania for being in the right. The slightest hint of disagreement, 3
from anyone, on the most trivial point, was enough to set him off on a harangue
that might last for hours, in which he proved himself right in so many ways, and
with such exhausting volubility,[1] that in the end his hearer, stunned and deafened,
would agree with him, for the sake of peace.

It never occurred to him that he and his doings were not of the most intense 4
and fascinating interest to anyone with whom he came in contact. He had theories about almost any subject under the sun, including vegetarianism, the drama,
politics, and music; and in support of these theories he wrote pamphlets, letters,
books . . . thousands upon thousands of words, hundreds and hundreds of pages.
He not only wrote these things, and published them—usually at somebody else's
expense—but he would sit and read them aloud, for hours, to his friends and his
family.

He wrote operas; and no sooner did he have the synopsis of a story, but he 5
would invite—or rather summon—a crowd of his friends to his house and read
it aloud to them: not for criticism; for applause. When the complete poem was
written, the friends had to come again, and hear *that* read aloud. Then he would
publish the poem, sometimes years before the music that went with it was written. He played the piano like a composer, in the worst sense of what that implies,
and he would sit down at the piano before parties that included some of the fin-
est pianists of his time, and play for them, by the hour, his own music, needless to
say. He had a composer's voice. And he would invite eminent vocalists to his house
and sing them his operas, taking all the parts.

He had the emotional stability of a six-year-old child. When he felt out of 6
sorts, he would rave and stamp, or sink into suicidal gloom and talk darkly of
going to the East to end his days as a Buddhist monk. Ten minutes later, when
something pleased him, he would rush out of doors and run around the garden,
or jump up and down on the sofa, or stand on his head. He could be grief-stricken
over the death of a pet dog, and he could be callous and heartless to a degree that
would have made a Roman emperor shudder.

He was almost innocent of any sense of responsibility. Not only did he seem 7
incapable of supporting himself, but it never occurred to him that he was under
any obligation to do so. He was convinced that the world owed him a living. In
support of this belief, he borrowed money from everybody who was good for a
loan—men, women, friends, or strangers. He wrote begging letters by the score,
sometimes groveling without shame, in others loftily offering his intended benefactor the privilege of contributing to his support, and being mortally offended
if the recipient declined the honor. I have found no record of his ever paying or
repaying money to anyone who did not have a legal claim upon it.

What money he could lay his hands on he spent like an Indian rajah.[2] The 8
mere prospect of a performance of one of his operas was enough to set him to
running up bills amounting to ten times the amount of his prospective royalties.

[1]*volubility:* excessive talking.
[2]*rajah:* prince in India.

On an income that would reduce a more scrupulous man to doing his own laundry, he would keep two servants. Without enough money in his pocket to pay his rent, he would have the walls and ceiling of his study lined with pink silk. No one will ever know—certainly he never knew—how much money he owed. We do know that his greatest benefactor gave him $6,000 to pay the most pressing of his debts in one city, and a year later had to give him $16,000 to enable him to live in another city without being thrown into jail for debt.

He was equally unscrupulous in other ways. An endless procession of women   9 marched through his life. His first wife spent twenty years enduring and forgiving his infidelities. His second wife had been the wife of his most devoted friend and admirer, from whom he stole her. And even while he was trying to persuade her to leave her first husband he was writing to a friend to inquire whether he could suggest some wealthy woman—*any* wealthy woman—whom he could marry for her money.

He was completely selfish in his other personal relationships. His liking for   10 his friends was measured solely by the completeness of their devotion to him, or by their usefulness to him, whether financial or artistic. The minute they failed him—even by so much as refusing a dinner invitation—or began to lessen in usefulness, he cast them off without a second thought. At the end of his life he had exactly one friend left whom he had known even in middle age.

He had a genius for making enemies. He would insult a man who disagreed   11 with him about the weather. He would pull endless wires in order to meet some man who admired his work and was able and anxious to be of use to him—and would proceed to make a mortal enemy of him with some idiotic and wholly uncalled-for exhibition of arrogance and bad manners. A character in one of his operas was a caricature of one of the most powerful music critics of his day. Not content with burlesquing[3] him, he invited the critic to his house and read him the libretto[4] aloud in front of his friends.

The name of this monster was Richard Wagner. Everything that I have said   12 about him you can find on record—in newspapers, in police reports, in the testimony of people who knew him, in his own letters, between the lines of his autobiography. And the curious thing about this record is that it doesn't matter in the least.

Because this undersized, sickly, disagreeable, fascinating little man was right   13 all the time. The joke was on us. He *was* one of the world's great dramatists; he *was* a great thinker; he *was* one of the most stupendous musical geniuses that, up to now, the world has ever seen. The world did owe him a living. People couldn't know those things at the time, I suppose; and yet to us, who know his music, it does seem as though they should have known. What if he did talk about himself all the time? If he had talked about himself for twenty-four hours every day for the span of his life, he would not have uttered half the number of words that other men have spoken and written about him since his death.

---

[3]*burlesquing:* mocking.
[4]*libretto:* opera text.

When you consider what he wrote—thirteen operas and music dramas, elev- 14
en of them still holding the stage, eight of them unquestionably worth ranking
among the world's great musico-dramatic masterpieces—when you listen to what
he wrote, the debts and heartaches that people had to endure from him don't
seem much of a price. Eduard Hanslick, the critic whom he caricatured in *Die Meistersinger* and who hated him ever after, now lives only because he was caricatured
in *Die Meistersinger*. The women whose hearts he broke are long since dead; and
the man who could never love anyone but himself has made deathless atonement,
I think, with *Tristan und Isolde*. Think of the luxury with which for a time, at least,
fate rewarded Napoleon, the man who ruined France and looted Europe; and
then perhaps you will agree that a few thousand dollars' worth of debts were not
too heavy a price to pay for the *Ring* trilogy.

What if he was faithless to his friends and to his wives? He had one mistress to 15
whom he was faithful to the day of his death: Music. Not for a single moment did
he ever compromise with what he believed, with what he dreamed. There is not
a line of his music that could have been conceived by a little mind. Even when he
is dull, or downright bad, he is dull in the grand manner. There is greatness about
his worst mistakes. Listening to his music, one does not forgive him for what he
may or may not have been. It is not a matter of forgiveness. It is a matter of being
dumb with wonder that his poor brain and body didn't burst under the torment of
the demon of creative energy that lived inside him, struggling, clawing, scratching
to be released; tearing, shrieking at him to write the music that was in him. The
miracle is that what he did in the little space of seventy years could have been done
at all, even by a great genius. Is it any wonder that he had no time to be a man?

▪ Reading Comprehension

1. The word *harangue* in "The slightest hint of disagreement, from anyone, on
   the most trivial point, was enough to set him off on a harangue that might last
   for hours, in which he proved himself right" (paragraph 3) means

   a. sarcastic joke.

   b. offended silence.

   c. arrogant speech.

   d. state of depression.

2. The word *caricature* in "A character in one of his operas was a caricature of
   one of the most powerful music critics of his day. Not content with burlesquing
   him, he invited the critic to his house and read him the libretto aloud in front
   of his friends" (paragraph 11) means

   a. mistake.

   b. friend.

   c. flattering description.

   d. exaggerated, mocking portrayal.

3. Which of the following would be a good alternative title for this selection?

   a. Wagner: His Personal Life

   b. Operas and Their Composers

   (c.) A Selfish Man Who Gave Much

   d. Wagner: A Musical Genius

4. Which sentence best expresses the main idea of this selection?

   (a.) Wagner's personal failings are less important than the great works he produced.

   b. Although Wagner was famous during his lifetime, very few of his operas are still performed.

   c. Wagner was an unfaithful lover as well as a spendthrift who borrowed money he never intended to repay.

   d. Wagner's operas are still considered among the greatest ever composed.

5. While trying to persuade his best friend's wife to leave her husband, Wagner was

   a. writing *Tristan und Isolde*.

   b. still married to his first wife.

   (c.) searching for a rich woman to marry.

   d. borrowing money from the husband.

6. *True or false?* __False__ Wagner was once thrown into jail for debt.

7. In paragraph 14, the author implies that

   a. the *Ring* trilogy is one of Wagner's less successful works.

   b. Hanslick came to enjoy the character based on him in *Die Meistersinger*.

   (c.) *Tristan und Isolde* is a magnificent love story.

   d. Wagner had stopped writing music years before his death.

8. The author implies that Wagner

   (a.) was often able to get the money he desired from others.

   b. neglected the dogs that belonged to him.

   c. despised vegetarians.

   d. was self-conscious about his odd appearance.

9. The author implies that

   a. no one recognized Wagner's talent during his own lifetime.

   b. Wagner was embarrassed to ask others for money.

   (c.) Wagner thrived on attention.

   d. Wagner may have suffered from a brain disorder.

10. The author implies that Wagner

   a. respected those people who would argue energetically with him.

   b. was chronically depressed, unable to feel pleasure.

   c. was genuinely brilliant about nonmusical subjects as well as musical ones.

   d. profoundly regretted, at the end of his life, his loss of friends.

Structure and Technique

1. Taylor avoids revealing the name of his subject until paragraph 12. Why do you think he made this choice? And why does he wait until paragraph 14 to balance the negative information about Wagner's behavior with positive comments about his musical works?

2. Why do you think Taylor chose to title his essay "The Monster"?

3. What wording in paragraph 2 is echoed in paragraph 13? How has it been changed when used the second time? What is the effect of this change?

4. Taylor uses unexpected wording in some of his descriptions. What is surprising about the wording in the following excerpts, and how is the meaning affected by that wording?

   "He was almost innocent of any sense of responsibility." (Paragraph 7)

   "He had a genius for making enemies." (Paragraph 11)

   "There is greatness about his worst mistakes." (Paragraph 15)

Critical Reading and Discussion

1. When Taylor writes in paragraph 5, "He had a composer's voice," what is he implying about Wagner's singing? What makes you think so?

2. In what ways, according to Taylor, was Wagner like a six-year-old child (paragraph 6)? Like an Indian rajah (paragraph 8)?

3. From what sources does Taylor imply that he gathered his negative information about Wagner? Why does the author include information about those sources?

4. Do you agree with Taylor's conclusion that Wagner's failings should be overlooked? Do unusually gifted people deserve to be held to different standards from the rest of us? Can you think of any gifted people of our time who are held to different standards?

■ Writing Assignments

Assignment 1

Write an essay about a person in your life toward whom you have mixed feelings. Perhaps you enjoy this person's company but do not fully trust him or her. Or you admire the person's family values but find him or her narrow-minded. In your thesis, state both sides of your feelings, as in the following sample thesis statement:

> While Mimi is often caring and generous, she can also be too critical.

Then fully describe one side of your subject's personality before you begin describing the other. Throughout your essay, illustrate your points with specific revealing comments and incidents.

Assignment 2

Describe a person you know who has managed to alienate nearly everyone in his or her life. Divide your essay into three sections. Those sections could be about *individuals* the person has alienated, such as any of these:

> A parent
> A former spouse
> A former best friend
> A coworker

Alternatively, divide your essay into *categories* of people the person has alienated, such as any of the following:

> Family members
> Neighbors
> Coworkers
> Classmates

Describe in what ways your subject has made enemies of these people (or at least lost their friendship). Your thesis statement for this assignment might be like this one:

> By being extremely self-centered and unkind, _____ has managed to alienate several people in his life.

Assignment 3

Wagner was a person who had no qualms about taking advantage of the people in his life—by insisting that they listen to him, endlessly borrowing money he never repaid, or having careless affairs. Although most people are not as manipulative as Wagner, most of us know what it's like to have someone take advantage of us for selfish reasons. Write an essay about how it feels to be taken advantage of. Select several specific instances in your life when you felt that someone else was "using" you. In your essay, devote each supporting paragraph to one such anecdote, describing what happened and how you responded. Below is an outline of such a paper.

> <u>Thesis</u>: When I was younger, I was taken advantage of by several important people in my life.
>
> <u>Topic sentences</u>:
> (a) My sister often borrowed my things and then carelessly damaged or lost them.
> (b) A good friend of mine in junior high school took advantage of our friendship to spend time with my brother, whom she had a crush on.
> (c) My boss at a shoe store took advantage of the fact that I needed the job by forcing me to do some of his work.

Why Are Students Turned Off?

Casey Banas

(Links)

A teacher pretends to be a student and sits in on several classes. What does she find in the typical class? Boredom. Routine. Apathy. Manipulation. Discouragement. If this depressing list sounds familiar, you will be interested in the following analysis of why classes often seem to be more about killing time than about learning.

Ellen Glanz lied to her teacher about why she hadn't done her homework; but, of course, many students have lied to their teachers. The difference is that Ellen Glanz was a twenty-eight-year-old high school social studies teacher who was a student for six months to improve her teaching by gaining a fresh perspective of her school.   1

She found many classes boring, students doing as little as necessary to pass 2 tests and get good grades, students using ruses to avoid assignments, and students manipulating teachers to do the work for them. She concluded that many students are turned off because they have little power and responsibility for their own education.

Ellen Glanz found herself doing the same things as the students. There was 3 the day when Glanz wanted to join her husband in helping friends celebrate the purchase of a house, but she had homework for a math class. For the first time, she knew how teenagers feel when they think something is more important than homework.

She found a way out and confided: "I considered my options: Confess openly 4 to the teacher, copy someone else's sheet, or make up an excuse." Glanz chose the third option—the one most widely used—and told the teacher that the pages needed to complete the assignment had been ripped from the book. The teacher accepted the story, never checking the book. In class, nobody else did the homework; and student after student mumbled responses when called on.

"Finally," Glanz said, "the teacher, thinking that the assignment must have 5 been difficult, went over each question at the board while students copied the problems at their seats. The teacher had 'covered' the material and the students had listened to the explanation. But had anything been learned? I don't think so."

Glanz found this kind of thing common. "In many cases," she said, "people 6 simply didn't do the work assignment, but copied from someone else or manipulated the teacher into doing the work for them."

"The system encourages incredible passivity," Glanz said. "In most classes one 7 sits and listens. A teacher, whose role is activity, simply cannot understand the passivity of the student's role," she said. "When I taught," Glanz recalled, "my mind was going constantly—figuring out how to best present an idea, thinking about whom to call on, whom to draw out, whom to shut up; how to get students involved, how to make my point clearer, how to respond; when to be funny, when serious. As a student, I experienced little of this. Everything was done to me."

Class methods promote the feeling that students have little control over or 8 responsibility for their own education because the agenda is the teacher's, Glanz said. The teacher is convinced the subject matter is worth knowing, but the student may not agree. Many students, Glanz said, are not convinced they need to know what teachers teach; but they believe good grades are needed to get into college.

Students, obsessed with getting good grades to help qualify for the college 9 of their choice, believe the primary responsibility for their achievement rests with the teacher, Glanz said. "It was his responsibility to teach well rather than their responsibility to learn carefully."

Teachers were regarded by students, Glanz said, not as "people," but as "role- 10 players" who dispensed information needed to pass a test. "I often heard students describing teachers as drips, bores, and numerous varieties of idiots," she said. "Yet I knew that many of the same people had traveled the world over, conducted fascinating experiments or learned three languages, or were accomplished musicians, artists, or athletes."

But the sad reality, Glanz said, is the failure of teachers to recognize their 11
tremendous communications gap with students. Some students, she explained,
believe that effort has little value. After seeing political corruption they conclude
that honesty takes a back seat to getting ahead any way one can, she said. "I
sometimes estimated that half to two-thirds of a class cheated on a given test,"
Glanz said. "Worse, I've encountered students who feel no remorse about cheating but are annoyed that a teacher has confronted them on their actions."

Glanz has since returned to teaching at Lincoln-Sudbury. Before her stint as 12
a student, she would worry that perhaps she was demanding too much. "Now I
know I should have demanded more," she said. Before, she was quick to accept
the excuses of students who came to class unprepared. Now she says, "You are
responsible for learning it." But a crackdown is only a small part of the solution.

The larger issue, Glanz said, is that educators must recognize that teachers and 13
students, though physically in the same school, are in separate worlds and have
an ongoing power struggle. "A first step toward ending this battle is to convince
students that what we attempt to teach them is genuinely worth knowing," Glanz
said. "We must be sure, ourselves, that what we are teaching is worth knowing."
No longer, she emphasized, do students assume that "teacher knows best."

■ Reading Comprehension

1. The word *ruses* in "students using ruses to avoid assignments" (paragraph 2)
   means

   a. questions.

   b. sicknesses.

   c. parents.

   d. tricks.

2. The word *agenda* in "the agenda is the teacher's" (paragraph 8) means

   a. program.

   b. boredom.

   c. happiness.

   d. book.

3. Which of the following would be a good alternative title for this selection?

   a. How to Get Good Grades

   b. Why Students Dislike School

   c. Cheating in Our School System

   d. Students Who Manipulate Teachers

4. Which sentence best expresses the main idea of the selection?

    a. Ellen Glanz is a burned-out teacher.

    b. Ellen Glanz lied to her math teacher.

    c. Students need good grades to get into college.

    (d.) Teachers and students feel differently about schooling.

5. How much of a class, according to the author's estimate, would often cheat on a test?

    a. One-quarter or less

    b. One-half

    (c.) One-half to two-thirds

    d. Almost everyone

6. *True or false?* _False_ As a result of her experience, Glanz now accepts more of her students' excuses.

7. Glanz found that the school system encourages an incredible amount of

    a. enthusiasm.

    (b.) passivity.

    c. violence.

    d. creativity.

8. The author implies that

    a. few students cheat on tests.

    b. most students enjoy schoolwork.

    (c.) classroom teaching methods should be changed.

    d. Glanz had a lazy math teacher.

9. The author implies that

    a. Glanz should not have become a student again.

    (b.) Glanz is a better teacher than she was before.

    c. Glanz later told her math teacher that she lied.

    d. social studies is an unimportant subject.

10. The author implies that

    a. most students who cheat on tests are caught by their teachers.

    (b.) most teachers demand too little of their students.

    c. students who get good grades in high school also do so in college.

    d. students never question what teachers say.

Structure and Technique

1. Which method of introduction—broad-to-narrow, anecdote, or questions—does Banas use in his essay? Why do you think he chose this approach?

2. List the time transitions that Banas uses in paragraph 12. How do they help Banas make his point?

3. Throughout "Why Are Students Turned Off?" Banas shifts between summarizing Ellen Glanz's words and quoting Glanz directly. Find an instance in the essay in which both direct and indirect quotations are used in the same paragraph. What does Banas gain or lose from using this technique? (Refer to pages 508–511 for definitions and examples of direct and indirect quotations.)

4. Parallel structures are often used to emphasize similar information. They can create a smooth, readable style. For example, note the series of *-ing* verbs in the following sentence from paragraph 2: "... students **doing** as little as necessary to pass tests and get good grades, students **using** ruses to avoid assignments, and students **manipulating** teachers to do the work for them." Find two other uses of parallelism, one in paragraph 4 and one in paragraph 7.

Critical Reading and Discussion

1. After reading this essay, what do you think Glanz's attitude is? Is she pro- or anti-teacher? Pro- or anti-student? Provide evidence for your position.

2. Banas suggests that many students are in school to get good grades—not to learn. Explain whether or not you agree with this assessment. Do you find that getting a good grade isn't always the same as really learning?

3. The author ends with Glanz's view of "the larger issue": "We must be sure, ourselves, that what we are teaching is worth knowing." What was taught in your high school classes that you feel is worth knowing or not worth knowing? Explain why. Also, what is being taught in your college classes that you feel is worth knowing or not worth knowing, and why?

4. Much of this essay contrasts the behavior of students with that of teachers. In what ways does Glanz see their behavior and views differing? What do you think each group should be doing differently?

Writing Assignments

Assignment 1

Play the role of student observer in one of your college classes. Then write an essay with *either* of the following theses:

In my _____ class, students are turned off.

In my _____ class, students are active and interested.

In each supporting paragraph, state and detail one reason why the atmosphere in that particular class is either boring or interesting. You might want to consider areas such as these:

Instructor: presentation, tone of voice, level of interest and enthusiasm, teaching aids used, ability to handle questions, sense of humor, and so on

Students: level of enthusiasm, participation in class, attitude (as shown by body language and other actions), and so on

Other factors: conditions of classroom, length of class period, noise level in classroom, and so on

Assignment 2

Glanz says that students like to describe their teachers as "drips, bores, and numerous varieties of idiots." Write a description of one of your high school teachers or college instructors who either *does* or *does not* fit that description. Show, in your essay, that your teacher or instructor was weak, boring, and idiotic—or just the opposite (dynamic, creative, and bright). In either case, your focus should be on providing specific details that *enable your readers to see for themselves* that your thesis is valid.

Assignment 3

How does the classroom situation Ellen Glanz describes compare with a classroom situation with which you are familiar—either one from the high school you attended or one from the school in which you are presently enrolled? Select one class you were or are a part of, and write an essay in which you compare or contrast your class with the ones Ellen Glanz describes. Here are some areas you might wish to include in your essay:

How interesting the class was

How many of the students did their assignments

What the teaching methods were

How much was actually learned

How active the teacher or instructor was

How passive the students were

What the students thought of the teacher or instructor

Choose any three of the above areas or three other areas. Then decide which method of development you will use: *one side at a time* or *point by point* (see pages 264–266).

Propaganda Techniques in Today's Advertising

Ann McClintock

(Links)

Advertisers want your business, and they will use a variety of clever ad slogans to get it. If you've ever responded to ads, you have been swayed by the effective use of propaganda. You may associate the word *propaganda* with the tactics used by strong-arm governments. But Ann McClintock provides evidence that we are the targets of propaganda every day and that it shapes many of our opinions and decisions.

Americans, adults and children alike, are being seduced. They are being brain- 1
washed. And few of us protest. Why? Because the seducers and the brainwashers
are the advertisers we willingly invite into our homes. We are victims, content—
even eager—to be victimized. We read advertisers' propaganda messages in newspapers and magazines; we watch their alluring images on television. We absorb
their messages and images into our subconscious. We all do it—even those of us
who claim to see through advertisers' tricks and therefore feel immune to advertising's charm. Advertisers lean heavily on propaganda to sell products, whether
the "products" are a brand of toothpaste, a candidate for office, or a particular
political viewpoint.

Propaganda is a systematic effort to influence people's opinions, to win them 2
over to a certain view or side. Propaganda is not necessarily concerned with what
is true or false, good or bad. Propagandists simply want people to believe the
messages being sent. Often, propagandists will use outright lies or more subtle
deceptions to sway people's opinions. In a propaganda war, any tactic is considered
fair.

When we hear the word "propaganda," we usually think of a foreign menace: 3
anti-American radio programs broadcast by a totalitarian regime or brainwashing
tactics practiced on hostages. Although propaganda may seem relevant only in
the political arena, the concept can be applied fruitfully to the way products and
ideas are sold in advertising. Indeed, the vast majority of us are targets in advertisers' propaganda war. Every day, we are bombarded with slogans, print and Internet pop-up ads, commercials, packaging claims, billboards, trademarks, logos, and
designer brands—all forms of propaganda. One study reports that each of us, during an average day, is exposed to over *five hundred* advertising claims of various
types. This saturation may even increase in the future, since current trends include
ads on movie screens, shopping carts, videocassettes, and even public television.

What kind of propaganda techniques do advertisers use? There are seven   4
basic types:

1. Name Calling.   Name calling is a propaganda tactic in which negatively charged   5
names are hurled against the opposing side or competitor. By using such names,
propagandists try to arouse feelings of mistrust, fear, and hate in their audiences.
For example, a political advertisement may label an opposing candidate a "loser,"
"fence-sitter," or "warmonger." Depending on the advertiser's target market,
labels such as "a friend of big business" or "a dues-paying member of the party in
power" can be the epithets that damage an opponent. Ads for products may also
use name calling. An American manufacturer may refer, for instance, to a "foreign
car" in its commercial—not an "imported" one. The label of foreignness will have
unpleasant connotations in many people's minds. A childhood rhyme claims that
"names can never hurt me," but name calling is an effective way to damage the
opposition, whether it is another car maker or a congressional candidate.

2. Glittering Generalities.   Using glittering generalities is the opposite of name   6
calling. In this case, advertisers surround their products with attractive—and slippery—
words and phrases. They use vague terms that are difficult to define and that may
have different meanings to different people: *freedom, democratic, all-American,
progressive, Christian,* and *justice.* Many such words have strong affirmative over-
tones. This kind of language stirs positive feelings in people, feelings that may spill
over to the product or idea being pitched. As with name calling, the emotional
response may overwhelm logic. Target audiences accept the product without
thinking very much about what the glittering generalities mean—or whether they
even apply to the product. After all, how can anyone oppose "truth, justice, and
the American way"?

The ads for politicians and political causes often use glittering generalities   7
because such "buzzwords" can influence votes. Election slogans include high-
sounding but basically empty phrases like the following:

"He cares about people." (That's nice, but is he a better candidate than his
opponent?)

"Vote for progress." (Progress by *whose* standards?)

"They'll make this country great again." (What does "great" mean? Does
"great" mean the same thing to others as it does to me?)

"Vote for the future." (What kind of future?)

"If you love America, vote for Phyllis Smith." (If I don't vote for Smith, does
that mean I don't love America?)

Ads for consumer goods are also sprinkled with glittering generalities. Product   8
names, for instance, are supposed to evoke good feelings: *Luvs* diapers, *Stayfree*
feminine hygiene products, *Joy* liquid detergent, *Loving Care* hair color, *Almost*

Home cookies, *Yankee Doodle* pastries. Product slogans lean heavily on vague but comforting phrases: . . . General Electric "brings good things to life," and Dow Chemical "lets you do great things." Chevrolet, we are told, is the "heartbeat of America," and Chrysler boasts cars that are "built by Americans for Americans."

3. Transfer. In transfer, advertisers try to improve the image of a product by 9 associating it with a symbol most people respect, like the American flag or Uncle Sam. The advertisers hope that the prestige attached to the symbol will carry over to the product. Many companies use transfer devices to identify their products: Lincoln Insurance shows a profile of the President; Continental Insurance portrays a Revolutionary War minuteman; Amtrak's logo is red, white, and blue; Liberty Mutual's corporate symbol is the Statue of Liberty; Allstate's name is cradled by a pair of protective, fatherly hands.

Corporations also use the transfer technique when they sponsor prestigious 10 shows on radio and television. These shows function as symbols of dignity and class. Kraft Corporation, for instance, sponsored a "Leonard Bernstein Conducts Beethoven" concert, while Gulf Oil is the sponsor of *National Geographic* specials and Mobil supports public television's *Masterpiece Theater.* In this way, corporations can reach an educated, influential audience and, perhaps, improve their public image by associating themselves with quality programming.

Political ads, of course, practically wrap themselves in the flag. Ads for a political 11 candidate often show either the Washington Monument, a Fourth of July parade, the Stars and Stripes, a bald eagle soaring over the mountains, or a white-steepled church on the village green. The national anthem or "America the Beautiful" may play in the background. Such appeals to Americans' love of country can surround the candidate with an aura of patriotism and integrity.

4. Testimonial. The testimonial is one of advertisers' most-loved and most-used 12 propaganda techniques. Similar to the transfer device, the testimonial capitalizes on the admiration people have for a celebrity to make the product shine more brightly—even though the celebrity is not an expert on the product being sold.

Print and television ads offer a nonstop parade of testimonials: here's William 13 Shatner for Priceline.com; here's basketball star Michael Jordan eating Wheaties; a slew of well-known people (including pop star Madonna) advertise clothing from the Gap; and Jerry Seinfeld assures us he never goes anywhere without his American Express card. Testimonials can sell movies, too; newspaper ads for films often feature favorable comments by well-known reviewers. And, in recent years, testimonials have played an important role in pitching books; the backs of paperbacks frequently list complimentary blurbs by celebrities.

Political candidates, as well as their ad agencies, know the value of testimo- 14 nials. Barbra Streisand lent her star appeal to the presidential campaign of Bill Clinton, while Arnold Schwarzenegger endorsed George Bush. Even controversial social issues are debated by celebrities. The nuclear freeze, for instance, starred Paul Newman for the pro side and Charlton Heston for the con.

As illogical as testimonials sometimes are (Pepsi's Michael Jackson, for in- 15
stance, is a health-food adherent who does not drink soft drinks), they are effective propaganda. We like the *person* so much that we like the *product* too.

5. Plain Folks.   The plain folks approach says, in effect, "Buy me or vote for me. 16
I'm just like you." Regular folks will surely like Bob Evans's Down on the Farm Country Sausage or good old-fashioned Countrytime Lemonade. Some ads emphasize
the idea that "we're all in the same boat." We see people making long-distance
calls for just the reasons we do—to put the baby on the phone to Grandma or to
tell Mom we love her. And how do these folksy, warmhearted (usually saccharine)
scenes affect us? They're supposed to make us feel that AT&T—the multinational
corporate giant—has the same values we do. Similarly, we are introduced to the
little people at Ford, the ordinary folks who work on the assembly line, not to
bigwigs in their executive offices. What's the purpose of such an approach? To
encourage us to buy a car built by these honest, hardworking "everyday Joes"
who care about quality as much as we do.

Political advertisements make almost as much use of the "plain folks" ap- 17
peal as they do of transfer devices. Candidates wear hard hats, farmers' caps, and
assembly-line coveralls. They jog around the block and carry their own luggage
through the airport. The idea is to convince voters that the candidates are average
people, not the elite—not wealthy lawyers or executives but common citizens.

6. Card Stacking.   When people say that "the cards were stacked against me," 18
they mean that they were never given a fair chance. Applied to propaganda, card
stacking means that one side may suppress or distort evidence, tell half-truths,
oversimplify the facts, or set up a "straw man"—a false target—to divert attention
from the issue at hand. Card stacking is a difficult form of propaganda both to
detect and to combat. When a candidate claims that an opponent has "changed
his mind five times on this important issue," we tend to accept the claim without
investigating whether the candidate had good reasons for changing his mind.
Many people are simply swayed by the distorted claim that the candidate is "waf-
fling" on the issue.

Advertisers often stack the cards in favor of the products they are pushing. 19
They may, for instance, use what are called "weasel words." These are small words
that usually slip right past us, but that make the difference between reality and
illusion. The weasel words are underlined in the following claims:

> "Helps control dandruff symptoms." (The audience usually interprets this as
> *stops* dandruff.)

> "Most dentists surveyed recommend sugarless gum for their patients who
> chew gum." (We hear the "most dentist" and "for their patients," but we
> don't think about how many were surveyed or whether or not the dentists
> first recommended that the patients not chew gum at all.)

> "Sticker price $1,000 lower than most comparable cars." (How many is "most"?
> What car does the advertiser consider "comparable"?)

Advertisers also use a card stacking trick when they make an unfinished claim. 20 For example, they will say that their product has "twice as much pain reliever." We are left with a favorable impression. We don't usually ask, "Twice as much pain reliever as what?" Or advertisers may make extremely vague claims that sound alluring but have no substance: Toyota's "Oh, what a feeling!"; Vantage cigarettes' "the taste of success"; "The spirit of Marlboro"; Coke's "the real thing." Another way to stack the cards in favor of a certain product is to use scientific-sounding claims that are not supported by sound research. When Ford claimed that its LTD model was "400% quieter," many people assumed that its LTD must be quieter than all other cars. When taken to court, however, Ford admitted that the phrase referred to the difference between the noise level inside and outside the LTD. Other scientific-sounding claims use mysterious ingredients that are never explained as selling points: Retsyn, "special whitening agents," "the ingredient doctors recommend."

7. Bandwagon.   In the bandwagon technique, advertisers pressure, "Everyone's 21 doing it. Why don't you?" This kind of propaganda often succeeds because many people have a deep desire not to be different. Political ads tell us to vote for the "winning candidate." The advertisers know we tend to feel comfortable doing what others do; we want to be on the winning team. Or ads show a series of people proclaiming, "I'm voting for the Senator. I don't know why anyone wouldn't." Again, the audience feels under pressure to conform.

In the marketplace, the bandwagon approach lures buyers. Ads tell us that 22 "nobody doesn't like Sara Lee" (the message is that you must be weird if you don't). They tell us that "most people prefer Brand X two to one over other leading brands" (to be like the majority, we should buy Brand X). If we don't drink Pepsi, we're left out of "the Pepsi generation." To take part in "America's favorite health kick," the National Dairy Council asks us, "Got Milk?" And Honda motorcycle ads, praising the virtues of being a follower, tell us, "Follow the leader. He's on a Honda."

Why do these propaganda techniques work? Why do so many of us buy the 23 products, viewpoints, and candidates urged on us by propaganda messages? They work because they appeal to our emotions, not to our minds. Often, in fact, they capitalize on our prejudices and biases. For example, if we are convinced that environmentalists are radicals who want to destroy America's record of industrial growth and progress, then we will applaud the candidate who refers to them as "treehuggers." Clear thinking requires hard work: analyzing a claim, researching the facts, examining both sides of an issue, using logic to see the flaws in an argument. Many of us would rather let the propagandists do our thinking for us.

Because propaganda is so effective, it is important to detect it and understand 24 how it is used. We may conclude, after close examination, that some propaganda sends a truthful, worthwhile message. Some advertising, for instance, urges us not to drive drunk, to become volunteers, to contribute to charity. Even so, we must be aware that propaganda is being used. Otherwise, we have consented to handing over to others our independence of thought and action.

■ Reading Comprehension

1. The word *epithets* in "labels such as 'a friend of big business' or 'a dues-paying member of the party in power' can be the epithets that damage an opponent" (paragraph 5) means

   a. courtesies.

   (b.) descriptive labels.

   c. assurances.

   d. delays.

2. The words *capitalizes on* in "the testimonial capitalizes on the admiration people have for a celebrity" (paragraph 12) mean

   a. reports about.

   b. ignores.

   c. cuts back on.

   (d.) takes advantage of.

3. Which of the following would be a good alternative title for this selection?

   a. The World of Advertising

   (b.) Common Persuasion Techniques in Advertising

   c. Propaganda in Politics

   d. Common Advertising Techniques on Television

4. Which sentence best expresses the main idea of the selection?

   a. Americans may be exposed daily to over five hundred advertising claims of some sort.

   b. The testimonial takes advantage of the admiration people have for celebrities, even though they have no expertise on the product being sold.

   (c.) People should detect and understand common propaganda techniques, which appeal to the emotions rather than to logic.

   d. Americans need to understand that advertising, a huge industry, affects their lives in numerous ways.

5. The propaganda technique in which a product is associated with a symbol or image most people admire and respect is

   a. glittering generalities.

   (b.) transfer.

   c. testimonials.

   d. bandwagon.

6. The technique in which evidence is withheld or distorted is called

   a. glittering generalities.

   b. bandwagon.

   c. plain folks.

   (d.) card stacking.

7. The technique that makes a political candidate seem to be just like the people an ad is aimed at is

   a. glittering generalities.

   b. bandwagon.

   (c.) plain folks.

   d. card stacking.

8. A way to avoid being taken in by propaganda is to use

   a. our emotions.

   b. name calling.

   (c.) clear thinking.

   d. our subconscious.

9. The author implies in paragraph 16 that

   a. most Americans do not frequently call their grandmothers.

   (b.) multinational corporations do not have the same values as average citizens.

   c. Bob Evans is an American celebrity.

   d. executives at AT&T and Ford are hardworking and honest.

10. From paragraphs 23 and 24, we can conclude that the author feels

   (a.) we are unlikely to analyze advertising logically unless we recognize it as propaganda.

   b. propaganda should not be allowed.

   c. if we don't want to hand over to others our independence, we should ignore all propaganda.

   d. we should not support the "products, viewpoints, and candidates urged on us by propaganda messages."

■ Structure and Technique

1. In paragraph 1, McClintock's choice of words reveals her attitudes toward both propagandists and the public. What specific words reveal her attitudes, and what attitudes do they represent?

2. What key term does McClintock define in paragraph 2? Why does she define it here? Where else in the essay does she use the technique of definition?

3. McClintock uses parentheses in two lists, the ones in paragraphs 7 and 19. What purpose do these parentheses serve?

4 . McClintock provides abundant examples throughout her essay. Why does she provide so many examples? What does she accomplish with this technique?

Critical Reading and Discussion

1. Some of the propaganda techniques listed in the selection have contrasting appeals. How do name-calling and glittering generalities contrast with each other? Testimonials and plain folks?

2. Why are ads that use the bandwagon approach so effective? What ads have you seen recently that use that approach?

3. The author states, "Americans, adults and children alike, are being seduced." What might be the differences between the ways adults and children react to the seductions of advertising?

4. McClintock states, "We are victims, content—even eager—to be victimized" (paragraph 1). Do you agree? Is this article likely to change how you view ads in the future? Why or why not?

Writing Assignments

Assignment 1

Choose three ads currently appearing on television or in print. Show that each ad uses one or more of the propaganda techniques McClintock discusses. Be specific about product names, what the ad looks like, kinds of characters in the ad, and so on. Don't forget that all your specific details should back up your point that each ad uses a certain propaganda technique (or techniques) to sell a product. Your thesis will make some overall statement about the three ads, such as either of these:

Beer advertisements use a variety of propaganda techniques.

Glittering generalities are used to sell very different types of products.

Assignment 2

Imagine that you work for an ad agency and have been asked to come up with at least three possible campaigns for a new product (for example, a car, a perfume, a detergent, jeans, beer, a toothpaste, a deodorant, or an appliance). Write an essay in which you describe three different propaganda techniques that might be used to sell the product and how these claims could persuade the public to buy. Be specific about the general looks, the character, and the wording of your ads and about how they fit in with the techniques you suggest.

Assignment 3

Do some informal "market research" on why people buy the products they do. Begin by asking at least ten people why they bought a particular brand-name item. You might question them about something they're wearing (designer jeans, for example). Or you might ask them what toothpaste they use, what car they drive, what pain reliever they take, or what chicken they eat—or ask about any other product people use. Take notes on the reasons people give for their purchases.

Then write an essay with the thesis "My research suggests that people often buy products for three reasons." Include in your introductory paragraph your plan of development—a list of the three reasons that were mentioned most often by the people you interviewed. Develop your supporting paragraphs with examples drawn from the interviews. As part of your support, use quotations from the people you spoke with.

Confronting Problems

Bombs Bursting in Air

Beth Johnson

(Links)

Nobody looks forward to the "bombs" of life, to the shocks and even tragedies that blindside us all eventually. After a frightening incident, Beth Johnson muses over the responses that are open to us in the wake of such unwelcome experiences. Is it possible to protect ourselves from the grief and pain that life sends our way? Is it desirable? This essay explores some possible answers.

It's Friday night and we're at the Olympics—the Junior Olympics, that is. My son is on a relay-race team competing against fourth-graders from all over the school district. His little sister and I sit high in the stands, trying to pick Isaac out from the crowd of figures milling around on the field during these moments of pre-game confusion. The public address system sputters to life and summons our attention. "And now," the tinny voice rings out, "please join together in the singing of our national anthem."

"Oh saaay can you seeeeee," we begin. My arm rests around Maddie's shoulders. I am touching her a lot today, and she notices. "Mom, you're *squishing* me," she chides, wriggling from my grip. I content myself with stroking her hair. News that reached me today makes me need to feel her near. We pipe along, squeaking out the impossibly high note of "land of the freeeeeeeee." Maddie clowns, half-singing, half-shouting the lyrics, hitting the "b's" explosively on "bombs bursting in air."

Bombs indeed, I think, replaying the sound of my friend's voice over the phone that afternoon: ". . . bumped her head sledding. We took her in for an X ray, you know, just to make sure. There was something strange, so they did more tests . . . a brain tumor . . . Children's Hospital in Boston Tuesday . . . surgery, yes, right away . . ." Maddie's playmate Shannon, only five years old. We'd last seen her at Halloween, dressed in her blue princess costume, and talked of Furby and Scooby-Doo and Tootsie Rolls. Now her parents were hurriedly learning a new vocabulary—CAT scans and pediatric neurosurgery and frontal lobe. A bomb had exploded in their midst, and, like troops under attack, they were rallying in response.

1

2

3

The games over, the children and I edge our way out of the school parking 4 lot, bumper to bumper with other parents ferrying their families home. I tell the kids as casually as I can about Shannon. "She'll have to have an operation. It's lucky, really, that they found it by accident this way while it's small."

"I want to send her a present," Maddie announces. "That'd be nice," I say, glad 5 to keep the conversation on a positive note.

But my older son is with us now. Sam, who is thirteen, says, "She'll be OK, 6 though, right?" he says. It's not a question, really; it's a statement that I must either agree with or contradict. I want to say yes. I want to say of course she'll be all right. I want them to inhabit a world where five-year-olds do not develop silent, mysterious growths in their brains, where "malignancy" and "seizure" are words for *New York Times* crossword puzzles, not for little girls. They would accept my assurance; they would believe me and sleep well tonight. But I can't; the bomb that exploded in Shannon's home has sent splinters of shrapnel into ours as well, and they cannot be ignored or lied away. "We hope she'll be just fine," I finally say. "She has very good doctors. She has wonderful parents who are doing everything they can. The tumor is small. Shannon's strong and healthy."

"*She'll* be OK," says Maddie matter-of-factly. "In school we read about a little 7 boy who had something wrong with his leg and he had an operation and got better. Can we go to Dairy Queen?"

Bombs on the horizon don't faze Maddie. Not yet. I can just barely remem- 8 ber from my own childhood the sense that still surrounds her, that feeling of being cocooned within reassuring walls of security and order. Back then, Mondays meant gym, Tuesdays were pizza in the cafeteria, Wednesdays brought clarinet lessons. Teachers stood in their familiar spots in the classrooms, telling us with reassuring simplicity that World War II happened because Hitler, a very bad man, invaded Poland. Midterms and report cards, summer vacations and new note-books in September gave a steady rhythm to the world. It wasn't all necessarily happy—through the years there were poor grades, grouchy teachers, exclusion from the desired social group, dateless weekends when it seemed the rest of the world was paired off—but it was familiar territory where we felt walled off from the really bad things that happened to other people.

There were hints of them, though, even then. Looking back, I recall the tiny 9 shock waves, the tremors from far-off explosions that occasionally rattled our shelter. There was the little girl who was absent for a week and when she returned wasn't living with her mother and stepfather anymore. There was the big girl who threw up in the bathroom every morning and then disappeared from school. A playful, friendly custodian was suddenly fired, and it had something to do with an angry parent. A teacher's husband had a heart attack and died. These were inter-esting tidbits to report to our families over dinner, mostly out of morbid interest in seeing our parents bite their lips and exchange glances.

As we got older, the bombs dropped closer. A friend's sister was arrested for 10 selling drugs; we saw her mother in tears at church that Sunday. A boy I thought I knew, a school clown with a sweet crooked grin, shot himself in the woods behind his house. A car full of senior boys, going home from a dance where I'd been sent into ecstasy when the cutest of them all greeted me by name, rounded a curve too fast and crashed, killing them. We wept and hugged each other in the halls. Our teachers listened to us grieve and tried to comfort us, but their words came out impatient and almost angry. I realize now that what sounded like anger was helplessness—the inability to teach us lessons we were still too young or too ignorant to learn. For although our sorrow was real, we still had some sense of a protective curtain between us and the bombs. If only, we said. If only she hadn't used drugs. If only he'd told someone how depressed he was. If only they'd been more careful. *We* weren't like them; we were careful. Like magical incantations, we recited the things that we would or wouldn't do in order to protect ourselves from such sad, unnecessary fates.

When my best friend, a beautiful girl of sixteen, went to sleep one January 11
night and never woke up, I found myself shaken to the core of my being. My grief at the loss of my vibrant, laughing friend was great. But what really tilted my universe was the nakedness of my realization that there was no "if only." There were no drugs, no careless actions, no crimes, no accidents, nothing I could focus on to explain away what had happened. She had simply died. This could only mean that there was no magic barrier separating me and my loved ones from the bombs. We were as vulnerable as everyone else. For months the shock stayed with me. I sat in class watching my teachers draw diagrams of Saturn, talk about Watergate, and multiply fractions, and I wondered at their apparent cheer and normality. Didn't they *know* we were all doomed? Didn't they know it was only a matter of time until one of us took a direct hit? What was the point of anything?

But time moved on, and of course I moved with it. College came and went, 12
graduate school, adulthood, middle age. My heightened sense of vulnerability began to subside, though I could never again slip fully into the soothing security of my younger days. I became more aware of the intertwining threads of joy, pain, and occasional tragedy that weave through all our lives. College was stimulating, exciting, full of friendship and challenge. I fell in love for the first time, reveled in its sweetness, then learned the painful lesson that love comes with no guarantee. A beloved professor lost two children to leukemia, but continued with skill and passion to introduce students to the riches of literature. My father fell ill, but the last day of his life, when I sat by his bed holding his hand, remains one of my sweetest memories. The marriage I'd entered into with optimism ended in bitter divorce but produced three children whose existence is my daily delight. At every step along the way, I've seen that the most rewarding chapters of my life have contained parts that I not only would not have chosen, but would have given much to avoid. But selecting just the good parts is not an option we are given.

The price of allowing ourselves to truly live, to love and be loved, is (and it's 13
the ultimate irony) the knowledge that the greater our investment in life, the larger the target we create. Of course, it is within our power to refuse friendship, shrink from love, live in isolation, and thus create for ourselves a nearly impenetrable bomb shelter. There are those among us who choose such an existence,

the price of intimacy being too high. Looking about me, however, I see few such examples. Instead, I am moved by the courage with which most of us, ordinary folks, continue soldiering on. We fall in love, we bring our children into the world, we forge our friendships, we give our hearts, knowing with increasing certainty that we do so at our own risk. Still we move ahead with open arms, saying yes, yes to life.

Shannon's surgery is behind her; the prognosis is good. Her mother reports   14
that the family members are returning to their normal routines, laughing again and talking of ordinary things, even while they step more gently, speak more quietly, are more aware of the precious fragility of life and of the blessing of every day that passes without explosion.

Bombs bursting in air. They can blind us, like fireworks at the moment of   15
explosion. If we close our eyes and turn away, all we see is their fiery image. But if we have the courage to keep our eyes open and welcoming, even bombs finally fade against the vastness of the starry sky.

■ Reading Comprehension

1. The word *faze* in "'*She'll* be OK,' says Maddie matter-of-factly. '. . . Can we go to Dairy Queen?' Bombs on the horizon don't faze Maddie" (paragraphs 7–8) means

   a. surprise.

   b. relieve.

   c. please.

   d. upset.

2. The word *impenetrable* in "it is within our power to refuse friendships, shrink from love . . . and thus create for ourselves a nearly impenetrable bomb shelter" (paragraph 13) means

   a. flimsy.

   b. unable to be entered.

   c. dangerous.

   d. invisible.

3. Which of the following would be a good alternative title for this selection?

   a. Pediatric Tumors

   b. Childhood Tragedies

   c. Life's Lessons

   d. Shannon's Story

4. Which sentence best expresses the main idea of the selection?

    a. Despite all our precautions, sad events will eventually occur in our lives.

    b. Although Shannon's condition was frightening, it turned out well in the end.

    c. The author has experienced a number of unhappy events in her life.

    (d.) It is worth being truly open to life's joys even though that also means experiencing its sorrows.

5. Shannon's brain tumor was discovered

    a. after she experienced severe headaches.

    b. when she began having seizures.

    (c.) after she had bumped her head sledding.

    d. during surgery for another condition.

6. The author's best friend had died

    a. after taking an overdose of drugs.

    (b.) in her sleep.

    c. in a car crash.

    d. as a result of suicide.

7. *True or false?* __False__ The author's daughter was alarmed at news of Shannon's illness.

8. The author implies that

    a. most brain tumors prove to be harmless.

    (b.) her son realized Shannon's condition could be serious.

    c. she had suspected at Halloween that Shannon was ill.

    d. her daughter did not care what happened to Shannon.

9. We can conclude from paragraph 11 that

    a. the author really did know why her best friend died.

    b. the author's teachers didn't care much about her friend's death.

    c. the author's depression led her to take drugs.

    (d.) her friend's death made the author pessimistic for months.

10. The reader can conclude that the author

    a. thinks her life has been unusually difficult.

    (b.) believes that the sorrows of life are outweighed by the joys.

    c. thinks people should protect themselves better against pain.

    d. never recovered from the shock of her best friend's death.

Structure and Technique

1. Johnson begins her essay with a narrative of an evening at her son's sports event. At what point does she make the transition into the body of her essay? Which words or phrases does she use to make this transition?

2. Foreshadowing is a technique an author sometimes uses to hint at something that has not yet been revealed. Find an example of foreshadowing in paragraph 2. Where, later in the essay, does she return to this subject? What is the effect of this foreshadowing?

3. Why do you think the author delays telling about the outcome of Shannon's surgery until the end of the essay? How would the essay be different if she had revealed early on that the surgery was successful?

4. Note the parallel phrasing in paragraph 3: "We'd . . . talked of Furby and Scooby-Doo and Tootsie Rolls. Now her parents were hurriedly learning a new vocabulary—CAT scans and pediatric neurosurgery and frontal lobe." Why might the author have used parallel structure here? What is the effect?

Critical Reading and Discussion

1. The author mentions bombs in the introduction and then uses *bomb* symbolically in other parts of the essay. What are some of the places in which she uses that symbol, and what does she intend it to mean? Do you think it is an effective symbol?

2. In paragraph 12, Johnson mentions incidents involving her first love, a professor, her father, and her marriage. What do these examples have in common? Why do you think Johnson included them?

3. Judging from the rest of the essay, what does Johnson mean by saying that "the greater our investment in life, the larger the target we create" (paragraph 13)?

4. Adults sometimes sentimentally think of childhood as a time of happy, carefree innocence, as the author suggests in paragraph 8. Yet, during childhood, most of us witnessed events that began to make us aware that life was not always happy or fair. What such events do you remember? What impression did they make on you?

Writing Assignments

Assignment 1

Johnson writes, "I can just barely remember from my own childhood the sense that still surrounds her [Maddie], that feeling of being cocooned within reassuring walls of security and order."

As a child, what provided you with a sense of security? You might think in terms of people (a grandparent, teacher, pastor), places (your school, the corner store), or situations (lying in bed at night hearing your parents talk) in your life that seemed—at the time, anyway—to be unshakable.

The thesis of your essay might be similar to this:

> The sense of security I felt as a child was in large part due to a few important people in my life.

A supporting paragraph about your grandmother, for instance, might begin, "My grandmother's calm personality always made me feel safe and secure. For example, when I broke a dish at her house, she didn't get angry. Instead, she hugged me and said it didn't matter."

Assignment 2

Describe three events in your own life that forced you to recognize the existence of grief and even tragedy. In each case, provide details about how the incident affected you and your outlook on life. You might choose incidents similar to the ones Johnson mentions (there are many examples in paragraphs 9–12) or others.

A topic sentence about one such incident might be something like this:

> My cousin's death at an early age made me realize that adults could not always protect their children.

You would continue by describing the circumstances of the death and how it made you regard the power of adults differently.

Alternatively, write about only one significant tragedy in your life. In your essay, narrate the key events and tell how they affected you and, perhaps, others involved.

Assignment 3

Johnson writes about how her childhood feeling of security eventually changed, first to a "heightened sense of vulnerability" and then to an awareness "of the intertwining threads of joy, pain, and occasional tragedy that weave through all our lives."

Write an essay about a few things that changed for you, or ways that you changed, as you made the transition from childhood to adulthood. For example, after having loved school at first, you might have grown to look down on education and then finally come to realize the importance of education. Below are a few other things toward which people's attitudes often change as they mature.

Birthdays

Family relationships

Relationships with teachers

Career choices

Household responsibilities

Choice of friends

One's own sense of confidence

You might use a thesis statement such as the following for your essay:

> As I made the transition from childhood to adulthood, some of my basic attitudes changed.

Support your topic sentences by contrasting your earlier views with your current views. Consider using examples, narration, and descriptions to help your readers understand the changes you discuss.

An alternative is to write an essay about only one thing in your life that changed. For instance, changes in your relationship with one or more siblings might merit an essay of their own.

Here's to Your Health

Joan Dunayer

(Links)

Joan Dunayer contrasts the glamorous "myth" about alcohol, as presented in advertising and popular culture, with the reality—which is often far less appealing. After reading her essay, you will be more aware of how we are encouraged to think of alcohol as being tied to happiness and success. You may also become a more critical observer of images presented by advertisers.

As the only freshman on his high school's varsity wrestling team, Tod was anxious to fit in with his older teammates. One night after a match, he was offered a tequila bottle on the ride home. Tod felt he had to accept, or he would seem like a sissy. He took a swallow, and every time the bottle was passed back to him, he took another swallow. After seven swallows, he passed out. His terrified teammates carried him into his home, and

1

his mother then rushed him to the hospital. After his stomach was pumped, Tod learned that his blood alcohol level had been so high that he was lucky not to be in a coma or dead.

Unfortunately, drinking is not unusual among high-school students or, for that matter, in any other segment of our society. And that's no accident. There are numerous influences in our society urging people to drink, not the least of which is advertising. Who can recall a televised baseball or basketball game without a beer commercial? Furthermore, alcohol ads appear with pounding frequency in magazines, on billboards, and in college newspapers. According to industry estimates, brewers spend more than $600 million a year on radio and TV commercials and another $90 million on print ads. In addition, the liquor industry spends about $230 million a year on print advertising, and since 1966 it has greatly expanded its presence on cable and independent broadcast stations. Just recently, NBC became the first network station to accept hard liquor ads for broadcast. 2

To top it all off, this aggressive advertising of alcohol fosters a harmful myth about drinking. 3

Part of the myth is that liquor signals professional success. In a slick men's magazine, one full-page ad for Scotch whiskey shows two men seated in an elegant restaurant. Both are in their thirties, perfectly groomed, and wearing expensive-looking gray suits. The windows are draped with velvet, the table with spotless white linen. Each place-setting consists of a long-stemmed water goblet, silver utensils, and thick silver plates. On each plate is a half-empty cocktail glass. The two men are grinning and shaking hands, as if they've just concluded a business deal. The caption reads, "The taste of success." 4

Contrary to what the liquor company would have us believe, drinking is more closely related to lack of success than to achievement. Among students, the heaviest drinkers have the lowest grades. In the work force, alcoholics are frequently late or absent, tend to perform poorly, and often get fired. Although alcohol abuse occurs in all economic classes, it remains most prevalent among the poor. 5

Another part of the alcohol myth is that drinking makes you more attractive to the opposite sex. "Hot, hot, hot," one commercial's soundtrack begins, as the camera scans a crowd of college-age beachgoers. Next it follows the curve of a woman's leg up to her bare hip and lingers there. She is young, beautiful, wearing a bikini. A young guy, carrying an ice chest, positions himself near to where she sits. He is tan, muscular. She doesn't show much interest—until he opens the chest and takes out a beer. Now she smiles over at him. He raises his eyebrows and, invitingly, holds up another can. She joins him. This beer, the song concludes, "attracts like no other." 6

Beer doesn't make anyone sexier. Like all alcohol, it lowers the levels of male hormones in men and of female hormones in women—even when taken in small amounts. In substantial amounts, alcohol can cause infertility in women and impotence in men. Some alcoholic men even develop enlarged breasts. 7

The alcohol myth also creates the illusion that beer and athletics are a perfect combination. One billboard features three high-action images: a sprinter running 8 at top speed, a surfer riding a wave, and a basketball player leaping to make a dunk shot. A particular light beer, the billboard promises, "won't slow you down."

"Slow you down" is exactly what alcohol does. Drinking plays a role in over 9 six million injuries each year—not counting automobile accidents. Even in small amounts, alcohol dulls the brain, reducing muscle coordination and slowing reaction time. It also interferes with the ability to focus the eyes and adjust to a sudden change in brightness—such as the flash of a car's headlights. Drinking and driving, responsible for over half of all automobile deaths, is the leading cause of death among teenagers. Continued alcohol abuse can physically change the brain, permanently impairing learning and memory. Long-term drinking is related to malnutrition, weakening of the bones, and ulcers. It increases the risk of liver failure, heart disease, and stomach cancer.

Finally, according to the myth, alcohol is the magic ingredient for social suc- 10 cess. Hundreds of TV and radio ads have echoed this message in recent years. In one commercial, for instance, an overweight man sits alone in his drab living room. He reaches into a cooler, pulls out a bottle of beer, and twists off the bottle cap. Instantly dance music erupts, and dozens of attractive young adults appear in a shower of party streamers and confetti. "Where the party begins," a voice says. The once lonely man, now a popular guy with lots of male and female friends, has found the answer to his social problems—beer.

Relationships based on alcohol are unlikely to lead to social success and true 11 friendships. Indeed, studies show that when alcohol becomes the center of a social gathering, it may lead to public drunkenness and violence. The ad's image of the man's new friends ignores an undeniable reality: that alcohol ruins—not creates—relationships. In addition to fighting and simple assault, drinking is linked to two-thirds of domestic violence incidents. Rather than leading to healthy social connections, alcohol leads to loneliness, despair, and mental illness. Over a fourth of the patients in state and county mental hospitals have alcohol problems; more than half of all violent crimes are alcohol-related; the rate of suicide among alcoholics is fifteen times higher than among the general population.

Advertisers would have us believe the myth that alcohol is part of being suc- 12 cessful, sexy, healthy, and happy; but those who have suffered from it—directly or indirectly—know otherwise. For alcohol's victims, "Here's to your health" rings with a terrible irony when it is accompanied by the clink of liquor glasses.

■ **Reading Comprehension**

1. The word *impairing* in "Continued alcohol abuse can physically alter the brain, permanently impairing learning and memory" (paragraph 9) means

   a. postponing.

   b. doubling.

   (c.) damaging.

   d. teaching.

2. The word *fosters* in "this aggressive advertising of alcohol fosters a harmful myth about drinking" (paragraph 3) means

   a. avoids.

   b. delays.

   (c.) promotes.

   d. discourages.

3. Which one of the following would be a good alternative title for this selection?

   a. The Taste of Success

   b. Alcohol and Your Social Life

   c. Too Much Tequila

   (d.) Alcohol: Image and Reality

4. Which sentence best expresses the main idea of the selection?

   a. Sports and alcohol don't mix.

   b. The media and our culture promote false images about success and happiness.

   (c.) The media and our culture promote false beliefs about alcohol.

   d. Liquor companies should not be allowed to use misleading ads.

5. According to the selection, drinking can

   a. actually unify a family.

   (b.) lower hormone levels.

   c. temporarily improve performance in sports.

   d. increase the likelihood of pregnancy.

6. *True or false?* __False__ Alcohol abuse is most severe among middle-class people.

7. *True or false?* __True__ The leading cause of death among teenagers is drinking and driving.

8. From the first paragraph of the essay, we can conclude that

   (a.) even one encounter with alcohol can lead to death.

   b. tequila is the worst type of alcohol to drink.

   c. wrestlers tend to drink more than other athletes.

   d. by the time students reach high school, peer pressure doesn't influence them.

9. *True or false?* __False__ The author implies that one or two drinks a day are probably harmless.

10. The author implies that heavy drinking can lead to

   a. poor grades.

   b. getting fired.

   c. heart disease.

   d. all of the above.

Structure and Technique

1. What method of introduction does Dunayer use? What effect do you think she hoped to achieve with this introduction?

2. Dunayer begins her criticism of alcohol with "Part of the myth is . . . ." (See the first sentence of paragraph 4.) What addition transitions does she use to introduce each of the three other parts of the myth (in the first sentences of paragraphs 6, 8, and 10)? What is gained by the use of these transitions?

3. The body of Dunayer's essay is made up of four pairs of paragraphs (paragraphs 4 and 5; 6 and 7; 8 and 9; 10 and 11). What is the relationship between the paragraphs in each pair? In which of the two paragraphs does Dunayer present her own perspective? Why do you think she puts her own perspective in that paragraph?

4. In her essay, Dunayer provides vivid descriptions of alcohol advertisements, particularly in paragraphs 4 and 6. What vivid details does she provide? How do these details support her main point?

Critical Reading and Discussion

1. Dunayer presents and then rebuts four "myths" about alcohol. What are these four myths? According to Dunayer, what is the reality behind each myth?

2. Dunayer concludes, "'Here's to your health' rings with a terrible irony when it is accompanied by the clink of liquor glasses" (paragraph 12). What is the "terrible irony" she refers to? How does this irony—already signaled in her essay's title—relate to her main point?

3. Do you think Dunayer's essay is one-sided or balanced? Explain. What additional points could be used to support her point or to rebut it?

4. Advertisers often create myths or use false ideas to get people to buy their products. Besides alcohol ads, what are some other examples of manipulative or deceptive advertising? Do you think advertisers should be permitted to use such tactics to sell products?

■ Writing Assignments

Assignment 1

Describe and analyze several recent advertisements for wine, beer, or liquor on television or radio, in newspapers or magazines, or on billboards. Argue whether the ads are socially responsible or irresponsible in the way that they portray drinking. Your thesis might be something like one of the following examples:

> In three recent ads, ad agencies and liquor companies have acted irresponsibly in their portrayal of alcohol.

> In three recent ads, ad agencies and liquor companies have acted with a measure of responsibility in their portrayal of alcohol.

Alternatively, write about what you consider responsible or irresponsible advertising for some other product or service. Cigarettes, weight loss, and cosmetics are possibilities to consider.

Assignment 2

If you have a friend, relative, or classmate who drinks a lot, write a letter warning him or her about the dangers of alcohol. If appropriate, use information from Dunayer's essay. Remember that since your purpose is to get someone you care about to control or break a dangerous habit, you should make your writing very personal. Don't bother explaining how alcoholism affects people in general. Instead, focus directly on what you see it doing to your reader.

Divide your argument into at least three supporting paragraphs. You might, for instance, talk about how your reader is jeopardizing his or her relationship with three of the following: family, friends, boss and coworkers, instructors and classmates.

Assignment 3

Dunayer describes how alcohol advertisements promote false beliefs, such as the idea that alcohol will make you successful. Imagine that you work for a public service ad agency given the job of presenting the negative side of alcohol. What images would you choose to include in your ads?

Write a report to your boss in which you propose in detail three anti-alcohol ads. Choose from among the following:

> Ad counteracting the idea that alcohol leads to success

> Ad counteracting the idea that alcohol is sexy

> Ad counteracting the idea that alcohol goes well with athletics

> Ad counteracting the idea that alcohol makes for happy families

How to Make It in College, Now That You're Here

Brian O'Keeney

(Links)

The author of this selection presents a compact guide to being a successful student. He will show you how to pass tests, how to avoid becoming a student zombie, how to find time to fit in everything you want to do, and how to deal with personal problems while keeping up with your studies. These and other helpful tips have been culled from the author's own experience and his candid interviews with fellow students.

Today is your first day on campus. You were a high school senior three months ago. Or maybe you've been at home with your children for the last ten years. Or maybe you work full time and you're coming to school to start the process that leads to a better job. Whatever your background is, you're probably not too concerned today with staying in college. After all, you just got over the hurdle (and the paperwork) of applying to this place and organizing your life so that you could attend. And today, you're confused and tired. Everything is a hassle, from finding the classrooms to standing in line at the bookstore. But read my advice anyway. And if you don't read it today, clip and save this article. You might want to look at it a little further down the road. 1

By the way, if this isn't your very first day, don't skip this article. Maybe you haven't been doing as well in your studies as you'd hoped. Or perhaps you've had problems juggling your work schedule, your class schedule, and your social life. If so, read on. You're about to get the inside story on making it in college. On the basis of my own experience as a final-year student, and after dozens of interviews with successful students, I've worked out a no-fail system for coping with college. These are the inside tips every students needs to do well in school. I've put myself in your place, and I'm going to answer the questions that will cross (or have already crossed) your mind during your stay here. 2

What's the Secret of Getting Good Grades?

It all comes down to getting those grades, doesn't it? After all, you came here for some reason, and you're going to need passing grades to get the credits or degree you want. Many of us never did much studying in high school; most of the learning we did took place in the classroom. College, however, is a lot different. You're really on your own when it comes to passing courses. In fact, sometimes 3 you'll feel as if nobody cares if you make it or not. Therefore, you've got to figure out a study system that gets results. Sooner or later, you'll be alone with those books. After that, you'll be sitting in a classroom with an exam sheet on your desk. Whether you stare at that exam with a queasy stomach or whip through it fairly confidently depends on your study techniques. Most of the successful students I talked to agreed that the following eight study tips deliver solid results.

1. Set Up a Study Place.   Those students you see "studying" in the cafeteria or 4
game room aren't learning much. You just can't learn when you're distracted by people and noise. Even the library can be a bad place to study if you constantly find yourself watching the clouds outside or the students walking through the stacks. It takes guts to sit, alone, in a quiet place in order to study. But you have to do it. Find a room at home or a spot in the library that's relatively quiet—and boring. When you sit there, you won't have much to do except study.

2. Get into a Study Frame of Mind.   When you sit down, do it with the attitude 5
that you're going to get this studying done. You're not going to doodle in your notebook or make a list for the supermarket. Decide that you are going to study and learn *now,* so that you can move on to more interesting things as soon as possible.

3. Give Yourself Rewards.   If you sweat out a block of study time, and do a 6
good job on it, treat yourself. You deserve it. You can "psych" yourself up for studying by promising to reward yourself afterward. A present for yourself can be anything from a favorite TV show to a relaxing bath to a dish of double chocolate ice cream.

4. Skim the Textbook First.   Lots of students sit down with an assignment like 7
"Read chapter five, pages 125–150" and do just that. They turn to page 125 and start to read. After a while, they find that they have no idea what they just read. For the last ten minutes, they've been thinking about their five-year-old or what they're going to eat for dinner. Eventually, they plod through all the pages but don't remember much afterward.

In order to prevent this problem, skim the textbook chapter first. This means: 8
look at the title, the subtitles, the headings, the pictures, the first and last paragraphs. Try to find out what the person who wrote the book had in mind when he or she organized the chapter. What was important enough to set off as a title or in bold type? After skimming, you should be able to explain to yourself what the main points of the chapter are. Unless you're the kind of person who would step into an empty elevator shaft without looking first, you'll soon discover the value of skimming.

5. Take Notes on What You're Studying.   This sounds like a hassle, but it works. 9
Go back over the material after you've read it, and jot down key words and phrases in the margins. When you review the chapter for a test, you'll have handy little

things like "definition of rationalization" or "example of assimilation" in the margins. If the material is especially tough, organize a separate sheet of notes. Write down definitions, examples, lists, and main ideas. The idea is to have a single sheet that boils the entire chapter down to a digestible lump.

6. Review After You've Read and Taken Notes.   Some people swear that talking to yourself works. Tell yourself about the most important points in the chapter. Once you've said them out loud, they seem to stick better in your mind. If you can't talk to yourself about the material after reading it, that's a sure sign you don't really know it.   10

7. Give Up.   This may sound contradictory, but give up when you've had enough. You should try to make it through at least an hour, though. Ten minutes here and there are useless. When your head starts to pound and your eyes develop spidery red lines, quit. You won't do much learning when you're exhausted.   11

8. Take a College Skills Course If You Need It.   Don't hesitate or feel embarrassed about enrolling in a study skills course. Many students say they wouldn't have made it without one.   12

How Can I Keep Up with All My Responsibilities Without Going Crazy?

You've got a class schedule. You're supposed to study. You've got a family. You've got a husband, wife, boyfriend, girlfriend, child. You've got a job. How are you possibly going to cover all the bases in your life and maintain your sanity? This is one of the toughest problems students face. Even if they start the semester with the best of intentions, they eventually find themselves tearing their hair out trying to do everything they're supposed to do. Believe it or not, though, it is possible to meet all your responsibilities. And you don't have to turn into a hermit or give up your loved ones to do it.   13

The secret here is to organize your time. But don't just sit around half the semester planning to get everything together soon. Before you know it, you'll be confronted with midterms, papers, family, and work all at once. Don't let yourself reach that breaking point. Instead, try these three tactics.   14

1. Monthly Calendar.   Get one of those calendars with big blocks around the dates. Give yourself an overview of the whole term by marking down the due dates for papers and projects. Circle test and exam days. This way those days don't sneak up on you unexpectedly.   15

2. Study Schedule.   Sit down during the first few days of this semester and make up a sheet listing the days and hours of the week. Fill in your work and class hours first. Then try to block out some study hours. It's better to study a little every   16 day than to create a huge once-or-twice-a-week marathon session. Schedule study hours for your hardest classes for the times when you feel most energetic. For example, I battled my tax law textbook in the mornings; when I looked at it after 7:00 P.M., I might as well have been reading Chinese. The usual proportion, by the way, is one hour of study time for every class hour.

In case you're one of those people who get carried away, remember to leave blocks of free time, too. You won't be any good to yourself or anyone else if you don't relax and pack in the studying once in a while.   17

3. "To Do" List.   This is the secret that, more than any other, got me through college. Once a week (or every day if you want to), write a list of what you have to do. Write down everything from "write English paper" to "buy cold cuts for lunch." The best thing about a "to do" list is that it seems to tame all those stray "I have to" thoughts that nag at your mind. Just making the list seems to make the tasks "doable." After you finish something on the list, cross it off. Don't be compulsive about finishing everything; you're not Superman or Wonder Woman. Get the important things done first. The secondary things you don't finish can simply be moved to your next "to do" list.   18

What Can I Do If Personal Problems Get in the Way of My Studies?

One student, Roger, told me this story: 19

> Everything was going OK for me until the middle of the spring semester. I went through a terrible time when I broke up with my girlfriend and started seeing her best friend. I was trying to deal with my ex-girlfriend's hurt and anger, my new girlfriend's guilt, and my own worries and anxieties at the same time. In addition to this, my mother was sick and on a medication that made her really irritable. I hated to go home because the atmosphere was so uncomfortable. Soon, I started missing classes because I couldn't deal with the academic pressures as well as my own personal problems. It seemed easier to hang around my girlfriend's apartment than to face all my problems at home and at school.

Another student, Marian, told me: 20

> I'd been married for eight years and the relationship wasn't going too well. I saw the handwriting on the wall, and I decided to prepare for the future. I enrolled in college, because I knew I'd need a decent job to support myself. Well, my husband had a fit because I was going to school. We were arguing a lot anyway, and he made it almost impossible for me to study at home. I think he was angry and almost jealous because I was drawing away from him. It got so bad that I thought

about quitting college for a while. I wasn't getting any support at home, and it was just too hard to go on.

Personal troubles like these are overwhelming when you're going through 21 them. School seems like the least important thing in your life. The two students above are perfect examples of this. But if you think about it, quitting or failing school would be the worst thing for these two students. Roger's problems, at least with his girlfriends, would simmer down eventually, and then he'd regret having left school. Marian had to finish college if she wanted to be able to live independently. Sometimes, you've just got to hang tough.

But what do you do while you're trying to live through a lousy time? First 22 of all, do something difficult. Ask yourself, honestly, if you're exaggerating small problems as an excuse to avoid classes and studying. It takes strength to admit this, but there's no sense in kidding yourself. If your problems are serious, and real, try to make some human contacts at school. Lots of students hide inside a miserable shell made of their own troubles and feel isolated and lonely. Believe me, there are plenty of students with problems. Not everyone is getting A's and having a fabulous social and home life at the same time. As you go through the term, you'll pick up some vibrations about the students in your classes. Perhaps someone strikes you as a compatible person. Why not speak to that person after class? Share a cup of coffee in the cafeteria or walk to the parking lot together. You're not looking for a best friend or the love of your life. You just want to build a little network of support for yourself. Sharing your difficulties, questions, and complaints with a friendly person on campus can make a world of difference in how you feel.

Finally, if your problems are overwhelming, get some professional help. Why 23 do you think colleges spend countless dollars on counseling departments and campus psychiatric services? More than ever, students all over the country are taking advantage of the help offered by support groups and therapy sessions. There's no shame attached to asking for help, either; in fact, almost 40 percent of college students (according to one survey) will use counseling services during their time in school. Just walk into a student center or counseling office and ask for an appointment. You wouldn't think twice about asking a dentist to help you get rid of your toothache. Counselors are paid—and want—to help you with your problems.

Why Do Some People Make It and Some Drop Out?

Anyone who spends at least one semester in college notices that some students 24 give up on their classes. The person who sits behind you in accounting, for example, begins to miss a lot of class meetings and eventually vanishes. Or another student comes to class without the assignment, doodles in a notebook during the lecture, and leaves during the break. What's the difference between students like this and the ones who succeed in school? My survey may be nonscientific, but everyone I asked said the same thing: attitude. A positive attitude is the key to everything else—good study habits, smart time scheduling, and coping with personal difficulties.

What does "a positive attitude" mean? Well, for one thing, it means avoiding 25 the zombie syndrome. It means not only showing up for your classes, but also do- ing something while you're there. Really listen. Take notes. Ask a question if you want to. Don't just walk into a class, put your mind in neutral, and drift away to never-never land.

Having a positive attitude goes deeper than this, though. It means being ma- 26 ture about college as an institution. Too many students approach college classes like six-year-olds who expect first grade to be as much fun as *Sesame Street.* First grade, as we all know, isn't as much fun as *Sesame Street.* And college classes can sometimes be downright dull. If you let a boring class discourage you so much that you want to leave school, you'll lose in the long run. Look at your priorities. You want a degree, or a certificate, or a career. If you have to, you can make it through a less-than-interesting class in order to achieve what you want. Get whatever you can out of every class. But if you simply can't stand a certain class, be determined to fulfill its requirements and be done with it once and for all.

After the initial high of starting school, you have to settle in for the long haul. 27 If you follow the advice here, you'll be prepared to face the academic crunch. You'll also live through the semester without giving up your family, your job, or *Monday Night Football.* Finally, going to college can be an exciting time. You do learn. And when you learn things, the world becomes a more interesting place.

◼ Reading Comprehension

1. The word *queasy* in "with a queasy stomach" (paragraph 3) means
   a. strong.
   b. healthy.
   c. full.
   (d.) nervous.

2. The word *tactics* in "try these three tactics" (paragraph 14) means
   a. proofs.
   b. problems.
   (c.) methods.
   d. questions.

3. Which of the following would be a good alternative title for this selection?
   a. Your First Day on Campus
   (b.) Coping with College
   c. How to Budget Your Time
   d. The Benefits of College Skills Courses

4. Which sentence expresses the main idea of the selection?

    a. In high school, most of us did little homework.

    b. You should give yourself rewards for studying well.

    c. Sometimes personal problems interfere with studying.

    (d.) You can succeed in college by following certain guidelines.

5. According to the author, "making it" in college means

    a. studying whenever you have any free time.

    b. getting a degree by barely passing your courses.

    c. quitting school until you solve your personal problems.

    (d.) getting good grades without making your life miserable.

6. If your personal problems seem overwhelming, you should

    a. drop out for a while.

    b. exaggerate them to teachers.

    c. avoid talking about them.

    (d.) get help from a professional.

7. Which of the following is *not* described by the author as a means of time control?

    a. Monthly calendar

    b. To-do list

    c. Study schedule

    (d.) Flexible job hours

8. We can infer that the writer of this essay

    (a.) cares about college students and their success.

    b. dropped out of college.

    c. is very disorganized.

    d. is an A student.

9. From the selection we can conclude that

    a. college textbooks are very expensive.

    (b.) it is a good practice to write notes in your textbook.

    c. taking notes on your reading takes too much time.

    d. a student should never mark up an expensive book.

10. The author implies that

   a. fewer people than before are attending college.

   b. most college students experience no problems during their first year.

   c. all college students experience overwhelming problems.

   d. coping with college is difficult.

Structure and Technique

1. O'Keeney uses a highly structured format in his essay. What are some of the features of this format? Why do you think O'Keeney structured his essay in this way?

2. Does the author clearly state his thesis? If so, where is it stated, and how?

3. What method of introduction does the author use in the section on personal problems (starting with paragraph 19)? What is the value of using this method?

4. Throughout his essay, O'Keeney addresses his audience in the second person— using the word *you*. How does such a technique advance his main point?

Critical Reading and Discussion

1. What, according to O'Keeney, is the secret of getting good grades? Have you used any of O'Keeney's study methods? If so, how useful do you think they have been for you? Are there any that you haven't used, but might try? Explain your answer.

2. What does O'Keeney recommend students do in order to manage their time and responsibilities more effectively? Which of these suggestions are you most likely to use? Which are you least likely to use? Why?

3. What is the secret the author says got him through college? What do you think is the most helpful or important suggestion the author makes in the selection? Give reasons for your choice.

4. Do you agree with the author that Roger and Marian should stay in school? Are there any situations in which it would be better for students to quit school or leave, at least temporarily? Explain, giving examples to support your answer.

Writing Assignments

Assignment 1

Write a process essay similar to the one you've just read that explains how to succeed in some other field—for example, a job, a sport, marriage, child rearing. First, brainstorm three or four problem areas a newcomer to this experience might encounter. Then, under each area you have listed, jot down some helpful hints and techniques for overcoming these problems. For example, a process paper on "How to Succeed as a Waitress" might describe the following problem areas in this kind of job:

Developing a good memory

Learning to do tasks quickly

Coping with troublesome customers

Each supporting paragraph in this paper would discuss specific techniques for dealing with these problems. Be sure that the advice you give is detailed and specific enough to really help a person in such a situation.

You may find it helpful to look over the process essays in Chapter 11.

Assignment 2

Write a letter to Roger or Marian, giving advice on how to deal with the personal problem mentioned in the article. You could recommend any or all of the following:

Face the problem realistically. (By doing what?)

Make other contacts at school. (How? Where?)

See a counselor. (Where? What should this person be told?)

Realize that the problem is not so serious. (Why not?)

Ignore the problem. (How? By doing what instead?)

In your introductory paragraph, explain why you are writing the letter. Include a thesis statement that says what plan of action you are recommending. Then, in the rest of the paper, explain the plan of action in detail.

Assignment 3

Write an essay contrasting college *as you thought it would be* with college *as it is*. You can organize the essay by focusing on three specific things that are different from what you expected. Or you can cover three areas of difference. For instance, you may decide to contrast your expectations about (1) a college dorm room, (2) your roommate, and (3) dining-hall food with reality. Or you could contrast your expectations about (1) fellow students, (2) college professors, and (3) college courses with reality.

Refer to the section in Chapter 13 on methods of developing comparison and contrast essays to review point-by-point and one-side-at-a-time development. Be sure to make an outline of your essay before you begin to write.

College Lectures: Is Anybody Listening?

David Daniels

(Links)

College students are doodling in their notebooks or gazing off into space as their instructor lectures for fifty minutes. What is wrong with this picture? Many would say that what is wrong is the students. However, the educator and author David Daniels would say that the lecture itself is the problem. As you read this article, see if you agree with Daniels's analysis of lectures and their place in a college education.

A former teacher of mine, Robert A. Fowkes of New York University, likes to tell the story of a class he took in Old Welsh while studying in Germany during the 1930s. On the first day the professor strode up to the podium, shuffled his notes, coughed, and began, "*Guten Tag, Meine Damen und Herren*" ("Good day, ladies and gentlemen"). Fowkes glanced around uneasily. He was the only student in the course.   1

Toward the middle of the semester, Fowkes fell ill and missed a class. When he returned, the professor nodded vaguely and, to Fowkes's astonishment, began to deliver not the next lecture in the sequence but the one after. Had he, in fact, lectured to an empty hall in the absence of his solitary student? Fowkes thought it perfectly possible.   2

Today, American colleges and universities (originally modeled on German ones) are under strong attack from many quarters. Teachers, it is charged, are not doing a good job of teaching, and students are not doing a good job of learning. American businesses and industries suffer from unenterprising, uncreative executives educated not to think for themselves but to mouth outdated truisms[1] the rest of the world has long discarded. College graduates lack both basic skills and general culture. Studies are conducted and reports are issued on the status of higher education, but any changes that result either are largely cosmetic or make a bad situation worse.   3

One aspect of American education too seldom challenged is the lecture system. Professors continue to lecture and students to take notes much as they did in the thirteenth century, when books were so scarce and expensive that few students could own them. The time is long overdue for us to abandon the lecture system and turn to methods that really work.   4

---

[1]*truisms:* self-evident truths.

To understand the inadequacy of the present system, it is enough to follow 5
a single imaginary first-year student—let's call her Mary—through a term of lectures on, say, introductory psychology (although any other subject would do as
well). She arrives on the first day and looks around the huge lecture hall, taken
a little aback to see how large the class is. Once the hundred or more students
enrolled in the course discover that the professor never takes attendance (how
can he?—calling the role would take far too much time), the class shrinks to a less
imposing size.

Some days Mary sits in the front row, from where she can watch the professor 6
read from a stack of yellowed notes that seem nearly as old as he is. She is bored
by the lectures, and so are most of the other students, to judge by the way they are
nodding off or doodling in their notebooks. Gradually she realizes the professor is
as bored as his audience. At the end of each lecture he asks, "Are there any questions?" in a tone of voice that makes it plain he would much rather there weren't.
He needn't worry—the students are as relieved as he is that the class is over.

Mary knows very well she should read an assignment before every lecture. 7
However, as the professor gives no quizzes and asks no questions, she soon realizes she needn't prepare. At the end of the term she catches up by skimming her
notes and memorizing a list of facts and dates. After the final exam, she promptly
forgets much of what she has memorized. Some of her fellow students, disappointed at the impersonality of it all, drop out of college altogether. Others, like
Mary, stick it out, grow resigned to the system and await better days when, as
juniors and seniors, they will attend smaller classes and at last get the kind of
personal attention real learning requires.

I admit this picture is overdrawn—most universities supplement lecture cours- 8
es with discussion groups, usually led by graduate students; and some classes, such
as first-year English, are always relatively small. Nevertheless, far too many courses
rely principally or entirely on lectures, an arrangement much loved by faculty and
administrators but scarcely designed to benefit the students.

One problem with lectures is that listening intelligently is hard work. Reading 9
the same material in a textbook is a more efficient way to learn because students
can proceed as slowly as they need to until the subject matter becomes clear to
them. Even simply paying attention is very difficult; people can listen at a rate of
four hundred to six hundred words a minute, while the most impassioned[2] professor talks at scarcely a third of that speed. This time lag between speech and
comprehension leads to daydreaming. Many students believe years of watching
television have sabotaged their attention span, but their real problem is that listening attentively is much harder than they think.

Worse still, attending lectures is passive learning, at least for inexperienced 10
listeners. Active learning, in which students write essays or perform experiments
and then have their work evaluated by an instructor, is far more beneficial for
those who have not yet fully learned how to learn. While it's true that techniques
of active listening, such as trying to anticipate the speaker's next point or taking

[2]*impassioned:* enthusiastic.

notes selectively, can enhance the value of a lecture, few students possess such skills at the beginning of their college careers. More commonly, students try to write everything down and even bring tape recorders to class in a clumsy effort to capture every word.

Students need to question their professors and to have their ideas taken 11 seriously. Only then will they develop the analytical skills required to think intelligently and creatively. Most students learn best by engaging in frequent and even heated debate, not by scribbling down a professor's often unsatisfactory summary of complicated issues. They need small discussion classes that demand the common labors of teacher and students rather than classes in which one person, however learned, propounds his or her own ideas.

The lecture system ultimately harms professors as well. It reduces feedback to 12 a minimum, so that the lecturer can neither judge how well students understand the material nor benefit from their questions or comments. Questions that require the speaker to clarify obscure points and comments that challenge sloppily constructed arguments are indispensable to scholarship. Without them, the liveliest mind can atrophy. Undergraduates may not be able to make telling contributions very often, but lecturing insulates a professor even from the beginner's naive question that could have triggered a fruitful line of thought.

If lectures make so little sense, why have they been allowed to continue? Ad- 13 ministrators love them, of course. They can cram far more students into a lecture hall than into a discussion class, and for many administrators that is almost the end of the story. But the truth is that faculty members, and even students, conspire with them to keep the lecture system alive and well. Lectures are easier on everyone than debates. Professors can pretend to teach by lecturing just as students can pretend to learn by attending lectures, with no one the wiser, including the participants. Moreover, if lectures afford some students an opportunity to sit back and let the professor run the show, they offer some professors an irresistible forum for showing off. In a classroom where everyone contributes, students are less able to hide and professors less tempted to engage in intellectual exhibitionism.

Smaller classes in which students are required to involve themselves in discus- 14 sion put an end to students' passivity. Students become actively involved when forced to question their own ideas as well as their instructor's. Their listening skills improve dramatically in the excitement of intellectual give-and-take with their instructors and fellow students. Such interchanges help professors do their job better because they allow them to discover who knows what—before final exams, not after. When exams are given in this type of course, they can require analysis and synthesis from the students, not empty memorization. Classes like this require energy, imagination, and commitment from professors, all of which can be exhausting. But they compel students to share responsibility for their own intellectual growth.

Lectures will never entirely disappear from the university scene both because 15 they seem to be economically necessary and because they spring from a long tradition in a setting that values tradition for its own sake. But the lectures too frequently come at the wrong end of the students' educational careers—during the first two years, when they most need close, even individual, instruction. If lecture classes were restricted to junior and senior undergraduates and to graduate students, who are less in need of scholarly nurturing and more able to prepare work on their own, they would be far less destructive of students' interests and enthusiasms than the present system. After all, students must learn to listen before they can listen to learn.

Reading Comprehension

1. The word *enhance* in "techniques of active listening . . . can enhance the value of a lecture" (paragraph 10) means

   a. ruin.

   b. ignore.

   (c.) increase.

   d. claim.

2. The word *atrophy* in "Without [questions and comments], the liveliest mind can atrophy" (paragraph 12) means

   (a.) waste away.

   b. be unchanged.

   c. compete.

   d. strengthen.

3. Which of the following would be a good alternative title for this selection?

   a. How to Benefit from Lecture Classes

   b. The Necessity of Classroom Lecturing

   (c.) Problems with Lecture Classes

   d. College Lectures: An Inspirational Tradition

4. Which sentence best expresses the main idea of the selection?

   a. American colleges and universities are being attacked from many sides.

   (b.) Colleges and universities should offer interactive, not lecture, classes to first-year and second-year students.

   c. College graduates lack basic skills and general culture.

   d. American colleges and universities are modeled on German ones.

5. According to the author, the lecture system

   a. encourages efficient learning.

   b. encourages students to ask questions.

   c. helps professors teach better.

   (d.) discourages students' attendance and preparation.

6. An example of passive learning is
   a. attending lectures.
   b. writing essays.
   c. doing experiments.
   d. debating a point.

7. To develop their thinking skills, students, do *not* need to
   a. bring tape recorders to class.
   b. question professors.
   c. debate.
   d. attend small discussion classes.

8. The author implies that large lecture classes
   a. require students to have well-developed listening skills.
   b. encourage participation.
   c. are more harmful for juniors and seniors than for first-year students.
   d. are a modern invention.

9. *True or false?* __True__ Daniels suggests that small classes demand greater effort from both faculty and students.

10. The author implies that administrators love lectures because
    a. students learn better in lectures.
    b. professors teach better through lecturing.
    c. schools make more money on lecture classes.
    d. professors can show off in lectures.

■ Structure and Technique

1. Daniels begins his essay with an anecdote about a former teacher of his. How does this introduction relate to his thesis?

2. Does Daniels directly state his thesis? If so, where is it stated?

3. In describing Mary's classroom experience (paragraphs 5–7), Daniels provides numerous details. What are some of these details? How do they relate to the essay's main idea?

4. Daniels's essay is an argument against the lecture system of education. What argumentation techniques does he employ? (See pages 319–322 for information on argumentation.)

▪ Critical Reading and Discussion

1. Daniels states that "listening intelligently is hard work" (paragraph 9) and "Active learning . . . is far more beneficial for those who have not yet fully learned how to learn" (paragraph 10). Why might Daniels feel that listening is so hard? And why does he feel that active learning is so good?

2. In paragraph 8, Daniels acknowledges that he has exaggerated Mary's negative classroom experience, saying, "I admit this picture is overdrawn." Does this admission strengthen or weaken his argument? Explain.

3. According to Daniels, the lecture system harms professors by reducing feedback from students to a minimum. What is useful about feedback from students?

4. How do your experiences in both lecture classes *and* smaller classes compare with Daniels's descriptions? As a student, which type of class do you prefer? Why? If you were an instructor, which type of class would you prefer to teach? Why?

▪ Writing Assignments

Assignment 1

Write an essay in which you contrast a lecture class with a smaller, more interactive class. First make a list of the differences between the two classes. Following are some possible areas of difference you might consider:

> Interest level
>
> Demands on students
>
> Opportunities for asking questions
>
> Opportunities for discussions
>
> Quality of feedback from the instructor

Choose three of the differences you found, and then decide which class you learned more in. You will then have the basis for a thesis statement and three supporting topic sentences. An example of a thesis statement for this essay is

> Because of the different approaches to students' questions, class discussion, and feedback from the instructor in grading papers, I learned a lot more in my first-year English class than in my business lecture class.

That thesis statement could be shortened to

> I learned a lot more in my first-year English class than in my business lecture class.

The three supporting points for this thesis statement are about

> Different approaches to students' questions
> Class discussion
> Personal feedback on assignments

Change each of the points listed above into a sentence, and you have your three topic sentences. A topic sentence based on the last point above might be "While my English instructor gave me a lot of useful feedback on my assignments, my business instructor put only a grade on papers." Use specific details from your experience to develop your supporting paragraphs.

Here is another possible thesis for this assignment:

> While my business principles class was a large lecture class, I learned a lot more in it than in my American literature class because of the quality of the instructor's presentations, time set aside for attention to individual students, and use of audiovisual and computer materials.

> If you haven't as yet taken any lecture classes, compare any two classes in college or high school.

Assignment 2

In this selection, Daniels has given some disadvantages of lectures. Write an essay on the advantages of lectures. To support your points, use examples from your personal experience and the experiences of others. Begin by jotting down a list of advantages. Then choose the advantages you have the most to say about and develop those in your essay.

Assignment 3

Which teachers or instructors have you had who were not in a rut, who conducted classes that made you glad to learn? Write a description of your idea of a very good teacher or instructor. Your description may be of someone who actually taught you, or it may be of a fictional person who combines all the traits you have enjoyed (or missed) in your teachers and instructors through the years. Be sure to include plenty of specific examples of classroom activities and their effects on students. Here is a list of various aspects of teaching that you may wish to use in your description:

> Mastery of subject matter
> Ability to excite students about subject

Seven Ways to Keep the Peace at Home

Daniel A. Sugarman

(Links)

We like to think of our homes as havens of peace and security, but they more often resemble battlegrounds. Living together in close quarters, family members must cope with each other's moods, problems, worries, and pressures. The author of this selection presents several helpful suggestions for defusing tense situations in the home. You may discover the underlying reasons for some of your own recurring family quarrels.

Not long ago, the parents of a seven-year-old girl consulted me because their daughter was on her way to becoming a full-fledged hypochondriac.[1] The girl's father was a physician, and both parents were busy, involved people. During an early session with the family, the reasons behind the girl's problems became clear. Dad arrived late and was preoccupied and worried. He started to speak to me when his daughter interrupted: "My throat hurts a lot. I feel sick." Automatically he produced a tongue depressor and looked into her throat. As he reassured her about her health, I realized the girl's complaints represented the *only* way that she could engage her father's full attention.   1

When I pointed out that it was *he* who was unconsciously turning his daughter into a chronic complainer, the father altered his behavior. He began giving her more attention when she was *not* complaining about her health, and treating her physical complaints very lightly when they did occur. The girl began to improve. Soon, she hardly complained about her health at all.   2

In the course of my clinical practice, I have seen hundreds of families in conflict, and I am astounded at how frequently families unwittingly perpetuate   3

---

[1] *hypochondriac:* someone who is actually healthy but is convinced he or she is sick.

tension-causing behavior. Explosions just seem to happen again and again, until family members can be helped to understand their interactions and learn to meet their mutual needs in less destructive ways.

Although conflicts may be so ingrained for some families that outside profes- 4 sional help is needed, certain principles of Family First Aid can go a long way in reducing friction for most families. Here are seven steps that I have found to be helpful for diminishing family tension.

1. Give Up the Myth of the Perfect Family

A couple of years ago, an unhappy teenager came to my office with her family 5 and announced, "Well, here we are! The *Shady,* not the *Brady,* Bunch!" I find that many people, like this girl, resent their own families for not living up to some romanticized notion of family life that can be found only on television. In contrast to TV, *real* families go through periods of crisis that strain everyone's nerves. During these trying times, most families' feelings and actions bear little resemblance to the sanitized, prepackaged half-hour comedy routines on TV.

Some months ago, for example, Grace and Lew Martin[2] brought their sixteen- 6 year-old son to me. Frank was an angry, sullen boy who had been doing poorly in school and been caught smoking pot there. When Frank took his father's car out and was caught speeding at ninety miles per hour, his parents insisted he come for treatment.

During our first session, it became evident that Frank's problem was certainly 7 not the only one in the family. Mr. Martin had been consistently passed over for promotion at work. Mrs. Martin worked long hours trying to sell real estate, but because of high mortgage rates she was having little success. Frank's fourteen-year-old sister had fractured her leg the previous winter, and several operations had been required before it was set properly. Mr. Martin had become angry and withdrawn, and he was criticizing Mrs. Martin's ability to manage the household. She, in turn, spent more time away from home and began to drink heavily. Family fights became more and more frequent. Everyone tried to bolster his or her own tottering sense of self-esteem by shattering the self-esteem of a loved one.

As I listened to this troubled family, I became aware that it wasn't the real 8 problems that were about to do them in. It was their self-hate. Mr. Martin was furious at himself for not having gotten his promotion and because his wife had to work. Mrs. Martin was furious with herself because she wasn't selling houses and because she couldn't stay at home and care for her daughter. Frank was angry at them all, and so guilty about his angry feelings that I suspect his ninety-mile-per-hour ride partially represented an attempt at self-execution.

Once the Martin family understood how they were punishing themselves for 9 not being a perfect family, they began to show compassion toward themselves. They rapidly began to solve the real problems.

---

[2]All names in this article have been changed to protect patients' privacy.

The idea of the typical happy family is becoming an anachronism. As the na- 10
tional divorce rate approaches 50 percent, increasing numbers of people will live
in single-parent families. Should these people hate themselves because they aren't
part of a typical family? Unfortunately, too many do just that. As high interest rates
nibble away at the American dream of owning one's own home, should people
hate themselves because they don't have a "typical" single-family dwelling—or
because everyone in the family has to work to support this home? Unfortunately,
too many do that, too.

I often wonder if the perfect American family ever did exist. If it did, I haven't 11
met it often in the past few years. As a matter of fact, research suggests that
growing up in a perfectly happy family is not as important as psychologists once
thought. In one continuing study of 248 children, Jean Macfarlane at the University of California Institute of Human Development has found that children who
grew up in troubled homes do *not* necessarily grow up to be troubled adults.
Children who grew up in happy homes are *not* necessarily better adjusted by the
age of thirty.

When you give up the myth of the perfect family and deal with your real 12
problems in a spirit of compassion, psychological growth begins to take place.

2. Tell It Like You Feel It

Have you heard the story of the fifteen-year-old boy who had never said a word in 13
his whole life? He came to breakfast one day and suddenly yelled, "This oatmeal
is cold!" His astounded mother replied, "You can *talk!* Why haven't you spoken
before?" The boy shrugged and said, "Before this, everything was OK."

Funny story. Not so funny when situations like this occur in real families. And 14
they do. All too frequently I encounter people in families who, for one reason or
another, feel they must hide their feelings.

A few months ago, I saw an unhappy couple. Mrs. Raymond was almost al- 15
ways depressed. Sometimes she couldn't even take care of her home and children.
Mr. Raymond was quite protective of his wife—but at the same time he was having an affair.

Together in my office, the Raymonds had little to say to each other. Each was 16
very solicitous, but wary of saying something that might upset the other. By not
saying what they felt, they managed to upset each other more than if they had
communicated their feelings directly.

It's odd how many people believe that when they stop verbalizing, communi- 17
cation ceases. Nothing, of course, is further from the truth, because communication consists of much more than words. Angry silence, sighs, headaches, impotence,
and arrests for drunken driving can often be forms of distorted communication.

For his vacation, Mr. Raymond made plans to take his family on a two-week 18
camping trip. Mrs. Raymond told me she *dreaded* the idea of camping. When I
urged her to express her displeasure so a mutually satisfying vacation could be arranged, she replied, "But he works so hard. He deserves to go where he wants for

vacation." Once at the campsite, she developed headaches and nausea. After two days of misery, she went to a local doctor, who failed to find any physical reason for her discomfort. During the rest of the vacation she tortured both herself and her husband with her physical complaints. It would have been much kinder had she told him how she felt before they left home.

Each time we conceal something from someone close to us, the relationship becomes poorer. So, if you want to reduce family tensions, one of the most important ways to start is to send honest communications to those you love.   19

3. Don't Play Telephone

Do you remember the game "Telephone"? A message gets passed from person to person, and everyone laughs at how distorted it becomes. As a game, telephone can be fun. In real life, sending messages through third parties fouls things up. It's important for family members who have "business" with other family members to take it up *directly*.   20

When tension mounts in a relationship between two people, a frequent way of dealing with this is to send messages through a third person. Family therapists refer to the process as "triangulation." Following a spat, a mother may say to her son, "Tell your father to pass the salt," which may be answered by, "Tell your mother to get her own salt." In many chronic cases of triangulation, the middleman becomes severely disturbed.   21

Two years ago, Ruth and Ralph Gordon brought their seventeen-year-old daughter for treatment. Lucille was not doing well in school, using drugs heavily and becoming blatantly promiscuous. When I began to work with her, she was uncommunicative and hostile. After some time, however, she opened up and told me her parents rarely talked to each other—but both used her as a confidante. Mrs. Gordon was sexually unsatisfied and suggested to Lucille that she ask her father to go for marital counseling. Mr. Gordon told Lucille that he was seeing another woman, and he urged Lucille to speak to her mother about improving her grooming. Caught in this tangle of feelings, Lucille became more and more troubled. It wasn't until she refused to play middleman that she began to improve. When either parent began to send a message through her, she learned to say, "Tell him/her yourself!"   22

You'll find that when family members learn to dial each other directly, there's rarely a busy signal or wrong number. With direct dialing, a sense of freshness is engendered.[3]   23

4. Make Your Blueprints Flexible

Almost all parents have a secret master plan for their children. Sometimes this calls for a child to grow up exactly like a parent—or, more often, for the child to become an improved version of the parent. In our culture, with its emphasis on   24

---

[3]*engendered:* created.

getting ahead and self-fulfillment, it's tempting to hope that our children will realize many of our own desires. Whether we like it or not, though, children have a habit of spinning their own dreams. When a child's plans become different from his parents' blueprint, the family is on a collision course that can be avoided only by understanding and flexibility.

Most parents don't even realize how much they push and pull. I think you would be surprised, too, at how frequently children will say things to their parents only to placate[4] them.   25

One teenage girl assured her parents that she was going to study harder and prepare for college. This girl told me, "I don't plan to go to college, but I can't tell them yet. They are disappointed enough, and I don't want to rip up any more of their dreams for me." Caught in a web of parental expectations, this girl was miserable, and didn't feel free enough to explore her own potential and channel her abilities into realistic vocational goals.   26

An experienced parent knows that different children require different handling. When we become wise and willing enough to revise our blueprints so that they incorporate the child's realistic needs and aptitudes, we are on the road to a less tension-filled family life.   27

5. Learn to Use Contracts

Psychologists say that when two people marry, they agree to a contract. Sometimes couples have a strong emotional investment in keeping the not-so-pretty clauses of the contract hidden from everyone—including themselves. Gina and Tom Butler were married twenty-five years before their hidden contract caused problems.   28

When Tom met Gina, he was a skinny kid from a poor family who had a burning desire to become financially successful. He was, under his bravado,[5] painfully anxious, and he felt very inadequate. Gina was the prettiest girl in town. She was also desperately unhappy at home and couldn't wait to get away from the constant bickering there. When she was sixteen, she had an abortion. At seventeen, she met Tom. As they dated, they unwittingly began to draft their contract. Gina, unconsciously, agreed to make Tom feel adequate to reduce his anxieties. Tom, for his part, agreed never to discuss Gina's abortion, and to remove her from her hostile home situation by marrying her.   29

For many years their contract worked well. Gina massaged Tom's ego. She encouraged, reassured, supported him. When the children went off to college, however, she felt she needed to grow. She attended a local college, graduated with honors, and accepted a position with a well-known company. As Gina became successful, Tom became irritable and angry. He accused her of not being interested in the family. Eventually, he accused her of having a lover and of being "a tramp, like you were when I met you and like you'll always be." With these words, their contract was breached, and both sought the services of attorneys.   30

---

[4]*placate:* please.
[5]*bravado:* false show of courage.

Fortunately, Gina's lawyer suggested counseling before divorce. In treatment, the hidden aspects of Gina and Tom's contract were uncovered, and they negotiated a more mature contract based upon mutual respect.

Many family contracts, like the Butlers', tend to disintegrate when one member of the family begins to grow. And that's really all right, if the family can use the anxiety that inevitably results as a catalyst to promote healthy mutual growth.   31

I find it helps a lot if you can face up to your hidden contracts and then update them. It's also fruitful when you set clear provisions for the many minor vicissitudes of daily living that can vex the family. Coats not hung up in the closet, hedges left untrimmed—these are the raw materials that fuel family explosions. Frequently, an annoying, persistent source of tension can be cleared away by drafting a new contract, whose terms are clearly understood by all parties.   32

One teenager agreed to wash the dishes in exchange for transportation to cheerleading practice. One husband agreed not to smoke when he was with his wife, in exchange for her maintaining her weight loss. In these cases, all involved felt they had gotten a good deal, and niggling sources of family tension were eliminated by negotiation.   33

6. Stop the "Good Guy"–"Bad Guy" Routine

Sometimes, the greatest problems in families arise when people classify children as Good Guys and Bad Guys. These families tend to make a scapegoat of one of their members, who from that point on becomes "it" in a never-ending game of tag.   34

The Freemonts had four children. Brett, the third child, resembled Mrs. Freemont's uncle Mark, who was serving time for embezzlement. "He's just like Uncle Mark," the Freemonts proclaimed when Brett came home from nursery school with a toy giraffe that he had taken, and again when Brett was eight and got into a fight with another third-grader. By the time Brett was fifteen, he had far more serious problems. "I'm just like my uncle Mark," he told me: the label had become a self-fulfilling prophecy. Brett felt doomed to replicate his uncle's life. But once you realize that no two people are exactly alike, you can free members of your family to be themselves.   35

Curiously, sometimes the Bad Guy of the family really serves to hold that family together. I once worked with an eighteen-year-old girl who was constantly involved in mischief. As I began to understand her family situation, I realized that this girl's parents were emotionally estranged and the constant turmoil her behavior produced was an attempt to get her parents to form a united front. Indeed, she was partially successful. Her bizarre antics were at times so extreme that her parents barely had time to examine their own problems.   36

The next time you're in the midst of a family problem, resist your natural urge to think in terms of *right* and *wrong*. Rather, ask yourself, "What is going on here and why?" In our era of no-fault car insurance and no-fault divorce, it makes increasing sense to have no-fault (or all-fault) family problems.   37

7. Get Rid of Old Emotional Baggage

When people enter into any new relationship, they come to the new with a lot of 38
old fears and unhealed emotional wounds. Unless you look at your own history
honestly, you're likely to unwittingly re-create the same unhappy mess that gave
you so much pain in the past.

Rachel Dorton grew up in an unhappy household in which her father fre- 39
quently had affairs. When *she* married, with fidelity her top priority, Rachel chose
Mal, a hardworking, earnest accountant. For a time, all went well. After several
months of marriage, however, Rachel became increasingly suspicious when Mal
did audits in distant cities. She made his life miserable with constant suspicion and
pleas for reassurance. After several sessions of counseling, Rachel came to realize
that, without conscious intent, she was re-creating the very experiences she had
hated so much as a child. As she faced her feelings squarely, she was able to become less provocative, and she came to understand that *some* men—particularly
Mal—could indeed be trusted.

During periods of severe stress, it's astounding how people may treat others 40
the same way they were treated by their parents. Ed Richardson had had a tough
childhood. His father, a hardworking train conductor, would often take abuse
from passengers and arrive home irritable and tense. Sometimes he would beat
Ed severely. "You're no good," his father would proclaim. "You're a nothing."

Ed resolved that he would never hit his own children or call them names. For 41
years his resolve held, but then Ed's company went bankrupt and he was forced
to take a job he despised. The family had to retrench and move to a smaller
home. During this crisis, Ed's oldest boy cut school and was caught shoplifting.
Ed brought the boy home and began to beat him. To his horror he found himself
yelling, "You're no good . . . you're a nothing." Shaken by this experience, Ed got
professional help. It took him a while to put things back together, but it helped
when he realized that, when the chips are down, most people do unto others
what has been done unto them.

At its best, a nourishing family serves as a safe haven enclosed by invisible 42
walls of love and concern. In such a family, individuals can replenish diminished
feelings of self-esteem.

At its worst, a family can become a red-hot crucible in which ancient con- 43
flicts brew and boil and are reenacted again and again. Most frequently, however,
families just seem to bumble along with little emotional insight into how the family itself may be responsible for intensifying or perpetuating a family member's
problem.

Solving family problems has never been easy. As a practicing psychologist, I 44
know that good intentions alone are usually not enough. Effective action most
often follows accurate understanding. With a little practice, care and use of these
seven steps, the chances are good that you'll be able to lower the tension level in
the best family of all—your own.

■ **Reading Comprehension**

1. The word *anachronism* in "The idea of the typical happy family is becoming an anachronism. As the national divorce rate approaches 50 percent, increasing numbers of people will live in single-parent families" (paragraph 10) means

    a. an ideal.

    b. an injustice.

    c. a disease.

    (d.) something out of its time.

2. The word *catalyst* in "the family can use the anxiety . . . as a catalyst to promote healthy mutual growth" (paragraph 31) means

    (a.) something that helps bring about change.

    b. an unfortunate accident.

    c. criticism.

    d. a form of destruction.

3. Which of the following would be a good alternative title for this selection?

    a. Creating Family Blueprints

    (b.) How to Reduce Family Tension

    c. Hidden Contracts

    d. American Families

4. Which sentence best expresses the main idea of the selection?

    a. Believing myths about the perfect family can cause problems.

    b. When people marry, they agree to a contract.

    (c.) Following certain steps can help keep peace in a family.

    d. Family members play psychological games with each other.

5. The way for a family to stop playing "telephone" is to

    a. get rid of old emotional baggage.

    b. negotiate better contracts.

    (c.) communicate directly.

    d. create flexible blueprints.

6. *True or false?* __True__ Children who grow up in happy homes are not necessarily better adjusted as adults.

7. The "Good Guy"–"Bad Guy" routine means that

    a. family members feel they must be perfect.

    b. family members refuse to communicate with each other directly.

c. families make scapegoats of one of their members.

d. parents create secret master plans for their children.

8. The author implies that

a. "triangulation" can be a helpful way for family members to communicate.

b. making a scapegoat of a family member can unite a family.

c. people need to identify their problems before they can act to help themselves.

d. fidelity is essential in marriage.

9. The author implies that

a. the perfect American family existed until fairly recently.

b. creating family contracts inevitably leads to problems.

c. how a parent treats a child can affect the following generations.

d. families need "middlemen" to pass along communications.

10. *True or false?* _False_ The author implies that all families need professional help at times.

Structure and Technique

1. For the essay as a whole, what method of introduction—broad-to-narrow, anecdote, or questions—does the author use? What method does he use to begin section 1? Section 2? Section 3?

2. Sugarman supports his main points in several ways. One way is with examples. What examples does he use to support his first step, "Give Up the Myth of the Perfect Family"? How much space is given to each of those examples? What other type of support is used in paragraph 11?

3. How does Sugarman organize and present his main supporting details? What do his methods achieve?

4. Throughout his essay, Sugarman alternates between quoting people directly and reporting indirectly what they said. Should he have used only direct quotations? Should he have used only indirect quotations? Why or why not?

Critical Reading and Discussion

1. According to Sugarman, who is more to blame for family problems: parents or children? Give examples from the selection to support your point.

2. In section 4, what does Sugarman mean by the term "blueprint"? What does he suggest is the way to avoid "a collision course" between parents with a blueprint and a child with different plans for himself or herself? What blueprint did your parents have for you, and how does it compare with your own goals for yourself?

3. Sugarman states that people often "feel they must hide their feelings" from family members. Why do you think it is sometimes difficult for family members to be honest with one another? Do you agree with Sugarman that an important way of reducing family tensions is "to send honest communication"? Or are there times when it is best not to be totally honest? Explain.

4. In section 5, Sugarman discusses family contracts. What does he mean by the word "contract"? Describe any contracts that exist between members of families you're familiar with.

■ Writing Assignments

Assignment 1

Write about the three ways that would be most appropriate for keeping peace at your home. Following are examples of how the three supporting paragraphs in your essay might begin.

First supporting paragraph:

> One way our family would benefit is if we would stop playing the game of telephone. All too often, one family member uses another to . . .

Second supporting paragraph:

> Another step our family should take is "Tell it like you feel it." My mother, for example, sometimes hides her true feelings about . . .

Third supporting paragraph:

> Perhaps most important, our family needs to stop the "Good-Guy"–"Bad-Guy" routine. Two people in my family seem to have been cast in these roles . . .

Develop the ways you choose with specific examples that actually involve the members of your family.

Assignment 2

Sugarman tells us seven ways to keep the peace at home. However, there are other places where it is important to keep the peace—for instance, at school, at the workplace, in the dormitory room. Choose one of these other places and write your own guide to how to keep the peace there. Use three of the rules discussed in the article or think of other rules, and develop each paragraph by giving specific examples of the rule you are suggesting. Try to include appropriate stories, as Sugarman does, to show what you mean.

Assignment 3

Write an essay-length summary of the selection. Your goal is to write a shortened and condensed—but accurate—version of the selection in about five hundred words. To do this, you should do the following:

In each supporting paragraph of your summary, cover two or three of the peacekeeping methods.

Include only *key* ideas.

Shorten examples (or eliminate extra examples).

Eliminate dialogue and repeated ideas.

Most important, remember that a summary should be *in your own words*, not the original author's. Therefore, don't simply copy material from the selection. You should, instead, put the author's ideas into your own words.

Below is an introduction that you can use to begin your summary:

A Summary of "Seven Ways to Keep the Peace at Home"

Family is a word associated with warmth, affection, caring, love, and peace. In reality, though, family life can be very different. Tension, anger, and frustration take over, at times, in almost every household. In his article "Seven Ways to Keep the Peace at Home," Daniel A. Sugarman describes several techniques people can use to prevent or resolve family conflicts.

In Praise of the F Word

Mary Sherry

(Links)

What does it take to get by in high school? Too little, according to the author, a teacher in an "educational-repair shop." In this article, which originally appeared in *Newsweek*, Mary Sherry describes the ways she sees students being cheated by their schools and proposes a remedy you may find surprising.

1

Tens of thousands of eighteen-year-olds will graduate this year and be handed meaningless diplomas. These diplomas won't look any different from those awarded to their luckier classmates. Their validity will be questioned only when their employers discover that these graduates are semiliterate.

Eventually a fortunate few will find their way into educational-repair shops— adult-literacy programs, such as the one where I teach basic grammar and writing. There, high school graduates and high school dropouts pursuing graduate-equivalency certificates will learn the skills they should have learned in school. They will also discover that they have been cheated by our educational system. 2

As I teach, I learn a lot about our schools. Early in each session I ask my students to write about an unpleasant experience they had in school. No writer's block here! "I wish someone had made me stop doing drugs and made me study." "I liked to party, and no one seemed to care." "I was a good kid and didn't cause any trouble, so they just passed me along even though I didn't read well and couldn't write." And so on. 3

I am your basic do-gooder, and prior to teaching this class I blamed the poor academic skills our kids have today on drugs, divorce, and other impediments to the concentration necessary for doing well in school. But, as I rediscover each time I walk into the classroom, before a teacher can expect students to concentrate, he has to get their attention, no matter what distractions may be at hand. There are many ways to do this, and they have much to do with teaching style. However, if style alone won't do it, there is another way to show who holds the winning hand in the classroom. That is to reveal the trump card[1] of failure. 4

I will never forget a teacher who played that card to get the attention of one of my children. Our youngest, a world-class charmer, did little to develop his intellectual talents but always got by—until Mrs. Stifter. 5

Our son was a high school senior when he had her for English. "He sits in the back of the room talking to his friends," she told me. "Why don't you move him to the front row?" I urged, believing the embarrassment would get him to settle down. Mrs. Stifter looked at me steely-eyed over her glasses. "I don't move seniors," she said. "I flunk them." I was flustered. Our son's academic life flashed before my eyes. No teacher had ever threatened him with that before. I regained my composure and managed to say that I thought she was right. By the time I got home I was feeling pretty good about this. It was a radical approach for these times, but, well, why not? "She's going to flunk you," I told my son. I did not discuss it any further. Suddenly English became a priority in his life. He finished out the semester with an A. 6

I know one example doesn't make a case, but at night I see a parade of students who are angry and resentful for having been passed along until they could no longer even pretend to keep up. Of average intelligence or better, they eventually quit school, concluding that they were too dumb to finish. "I should have been held back," is a comment I hear frequently. Even sadder are those students who are high school graduates who say to me after a few weeks of class, "I don't know how I ever got a high school diploma." 7

---

[1]*trump card:* in bridge, a card of the suit that ranks highest; thus, something powerful, often held in reserve to be used as the right moment.

Passing students who have not mastered the work cheats them and the em- 8 ployers who expect graduates to have basic skills. We excuse this dishonest behavior by saying kids can't learn if they come from terrible environments. No one seems to stop to think that—no matter what environments they come from—most kids don't put school first on their list unless they perceive that something is at stake. They'd rather be sailing.

Many students I see at night could give expert testimony on unemployment, 9 chemical dependency, abusive relationships. In spite of these difficulties, they have decided to make education a priority. They are motivated by the desire for a better job or the need to hang on to the one they've got. They have a healthy fear of failure.

People of all ages can rise above their problems, but they need to have a rea- 10 son to do so. Young people generally don't have the maturity to value education in the same way my adult students value it. But fear of failure, whether economic or academic, can motivate both.

Flunking as a regular policy has just as much merit today as it did two genera- 11 tions ago. We must review the threat of flunking and see it as it really is—a positive teaching tool. It is an expression of confidence by both teachers and parents that the students have the ability to learn the material presented to them. However, making it work again would take a dedicated, caring conspiracy between teachers and parents. It would mean facing the tough reality that passing kids who haven't learned the material—while it might save them grief for the short term—dooms them to long-term illiteracy. It would mean that teachers would have to follow through on their threats, and parents would have to stand behind them, knowing their children's best interests are indeed at stake. This means no more doing Scott's assignments for him because he might fail. No more passing Jodi because she's such a nice kid.

This is a policy that worked in the past and can work today. A wise teacher, 12 with the support of his parents, gave our son the opportunity to succeed—or fail. It's time we returned this choice to all students.

Reading Comprehension

1. The word *validity* in "[The diplomas'] validity will be questioned only when . . . employers discover that these graduates are semiliterate" (paragraph 1) means

   a. soundness.

   b. dates.

   c. age.

   d. supply.

2. The word *impediments* in "I blamed the poor academic skills our kids have today on drugs, divorce, and other impediments to concentration" (paragraph 4) means

   a. questions.

   b. paths.

   c. skills.

   (d.) obstacles.

3. Which of the following would be a good alternative title for this selection?

   a. Learning to Concentrate in School

   b. Teaching English Skills

   (c.) A Useful Tool for Motivating Students

   d. Adult-Literacy Programs

4. Which sentence best expresses the main idea of the selection?

   a. Many adults cannot read or write well.

   b. English skills can be learned through adult-literacy programs.

   (c.) Schools should include flunking students as part of their regular policy.

   d. Before students will concentrate, the teacher must get their attention.

5. Sherry's night students are

   a. usually unemployed.

   b. poor students.

   (c.) motivated to learn.

   d. doing drugs.

6. According to the author, many students who get "passed along"

   a. are lucky.

   b. never find a job.

   c. don't get into trouble.

   (d.) eventually feel angry and resentful.

7. Sherry feels that to succeed, flunking students as a regular policy requires

   a. adult-literacy programs.

   b. graduate-equivalency certificates.

   (c.) the total cooperation of teachers and parents.

   d. a strong teaching style.

8. The author implies that our present educational system is

   a. the best in the world.

   b. doing the best that it can.

   c. very short of teachers.

   (d.) not demanding enough of students.

9. *True or false?* __True__ Sherry implies that high school students often don't realize the value of academic skills.

10. From the selection, we may conclude that the author based her opinion on

    a. statistics.

    b. educational research.

    (c.) her personal and professional experiences.

    d. expert professional testimony.

Structure and Technique

1. In current vocabulary, "the F word" usually refers to something other than "fail." Why do you think Mary Sherry used the term in her title, rather than simply using "fail" or "failure"? What effect does her title have on the reader?

2. In which paragraph does the author first mention her thesis? What is her main method of development, and how is it related to that thesis? Where does she use narration to support her thesis?

3. What contrast transition is used in the first sentence of paragraph 10? What ideas are being contrasted within that sentence?

4. In paragraph 11, how many times does Sherry use "mean" or "means"? What might her purpose be for repeating this word so frequently?

Critical Reading and Discussion

1. Sherry writes that "before a teacher can expect students to concentrate, he has to get their attention, no matter what distractions may be at hand" (paragraph 4). What examples of distractions does Sherry mention? Find several in her essay. Can you think of others—perhaps ones that existed in your own high school?

2. What does Sherry mean by calling the program she teaches in an "educational-repair shop"? What does the term tell us about Sherry's attitude toward high schools?

3. Sherry writes, "Young people generally don't have the maturity to value education in the same way my adult students value it." Do you agree or disagree? Support your view with details and observations from your own experience.

4. Do you feel your high school teachers made an honest effort to give you the skills you need—and to make you aware of the importance of those skills? If not, what should your school have done that it did not do?

■ Writing Assignments

Assignment 1

Write an essay that has as its thesis *one* of the following statements:

> In my opinion, students have no one to blame but themselves if they leave school without having learned basic skills.
>
> When students graduate or quit school lacking basic skills, they are the victims of an inadequate educational system.
>
> Flunking students has more disadvantages than advantages.

Support your thesis with several points, each developed in its own paragraph.

Assignment 2

Sherry proposes using "flunking as a regular policy" as a way to encourage students to work harder. What else might school systems do to help students? Write an essay in which you suggest a few policies for our public schools and give the reasons you think those changes will be beneficial. Following are some policies you may wish to consider:

> More writing in all classes
>
> Shorter summer vacations
>
> Less emphasis on memorization and more on thinking skills
>
> A language requirement
>
> A daily quiet reading session in elementary grades

Assignment 3

Here are two letters sent to *Newsweek* by teachers in response to Sherry's article:

Letter 1

Mary Sherry's essay advocating the use of flunking as a teaching tool was well intentioned but naive. In the first place, my local school district—and I doubt it's unique—discourages the practice by compiling teachers' failure rates for comparison. (Would you want to rank first?) More important, though, F's don't even register on many kids' Richter scales. When your spirit has been numbed—as some of my students' spirits have—by physical, sexual, and psychological abuse, it's hard to notice an F. Walk a mile in one of my kids' shoes. Real fear has little to do with school.

Kay Keglovits
Arlington, Texas

Letter 2

Sherry is right: flunking poor students makes sense. But, as she notes, "making it work again would take a dedicated, caring conspiracy between teachers and parents." I once failed a high school junior for the year. I received a furious call from the student's mother. I was called to a meeting with the school superintendent, the principal, the mother, and the student. There it was decided that I would tutor the student for four months so that the F could be replaced with a passing grade. This was a total sham; the student did nothing during this remedial work, but she was given a passing grade. No wonder education is in the condition that we find it today.

Arthur J. Hochhalter
Minot, North Dakota

These letters suggest that if schools want to try flunking as a regular policy, they will have to plan carefully. Write an essay in which you discuss ways to make failing poor students work as a regular policy. Your thesis statement can be something like this: "In order for a policy of flunking to work, certain policies and attitudes would need to be changed in many schools." As support in your essay, use the ideas in these letters, Sherry's ideas, and any other ideas you have heard or thought of. Describe your supporting ideas in detail and explain why each is necessary or useful.

Is Sex All That Matters?

Joyce Garity

(Links)

From the skimpy clothing in ads to the suggestive themes in many of today's TV comedies, our young people are bombarded with sexuality. How does the constant stream of sexual images influence their behavior and dreams? In considering that question, social worker Joyce Garity focuses on one young woman named Elaine, alone and pregnant with her second child.

A few years ago, a young girl lived with me, my husband, and our children for   1
several months. The circumstances of Elaine's coming to us don't matter here;
suffice it to say that she was troubled and nearly alone in the world. She was also
pregnant—hugely, clumsily pregnant with her second child. Elaine was seventeen.
Her pregnancy, she said, was an accident; she also said she wasn't sure who had
fathered her child. There had been several sex partners and no contraception. Yet,
she repeated blandly, gazing at me with clear blue eyes, the pregnancy was an
accident, and one she would certainly never repeat.

Eventually I asked Elaine, after we had grown to know each other well enough   2
for such conversations, why neither she nor her lovers had used birth control. She
blushed—porcelain-skinned girl with one child in foster care and another swelling
the bib of her fashionably faded overalls—stammered, and blushed some more. Birth
control, she finally got out, was "embarrassing." It wasn't "romantic." You couldn't
be really passionate, she explained, and worry about birth control at the same time.

I haven't seen Elaine for quite a long time. I think about her often, though. I   3
think of her as I page through teen fashion magazines in the salon where I have
my hair cut. Although mainstream and relatively wholesome, these magazines
trumpet sexuality page after leering page. On the inside front cover, an advertisement for Guess jeans features junior fashion models in snug denim dresses, their
legs bared to just below the crotch. An advertisement for Liz Claiborne fragrances
shows a barely clad young couple sprawled on a bed, him painting her toenails.
An advertisement for Obsession cologne displays a waif-thin girl draped stomach-
down across a couch, naked, her startled expression suggesting helplessness in the
face of an unseen yet approaching threat.

I think of Elaine because I know she would love these ads. "They're so beauti-   4
ful," she would croon, and of course they are. The faces and bodies they show are
lovely. The lighting is superb. The hair and makeup are faultless. In the Claiborne
ad, the laughing girl whose toenails are being painted by her handsome lover is
obviously having the time of her life. She stretches luxuriously on a bed heaped
with clean white linen and fluffy pillows. Beyond the sheer blowing curtains of her
room, we can glimpse a graceful wrought-iron balcony. Looking at the ad, Elaine
could only want to be her. Any girl would want to be her. Heck, *I* want to be her.

But my momentary desire to move into the Claiborne picture, to trade lives   5
with the exquisite young creature pictured there, is just that—momentary. I've
lived long enough to know that what I see is a marketing invention. A moment
after the photo session was over, the beautiful room was dismantled, and the
models moved on to their next job. Later, the technicians took over the task of
doctoring the photograph until it reached full-blown fantasy proportions.

Not so Elaine. After months of living together and countless hours of watch-   6
ing her yearn after magazine images, soap-opera heroines, and rock goddesses,
I have a pretty good idea of why she looks at ads like Claiborne's. She sees the
way life—her life—is supposed to be. She sees a world characterized by sexual
spontaneity, playfulness, and abandon. She sees people who don't worry about
such unsexy details as birth control. Nor, apparently, do they spend much time
thinking about such pedestrian topics as commitment or whether they should act
on their sexual impulses. Their clean sunlit rooms are never invaded by the fear

of AIDS, of unwanted pregnancy, of shattered lives. For all her apparent lack of defense, the girl on the couch in the Obsession ad will surely never experience the brutality of rape.

Years of exposure to this media-invented, sex-saturated universe have done   7
their work on Elaine. She is, I'm sure, completely unaware of the irony in her situation: She melts over images from a sexual Shangri-la,[1] never realizing that her attempts to mirror those images left her pregnant, abandoned, living in the spare bedroom of a stranger's house, relying on charity for rides to the welfare office and supervised visits with her toddler daughter.

Of course, Elaine is not the first to be suckered by the cynical practice of using   8
sex to sell underwear, rock groups, or sneakers. Using sex as a sales tool is hardly new. At the beginning of this century, British actress Lily Langtry shocked her contemporaries by posing, clothed somewhat scantily, with a bar of Pear's soap. The advertisers have always known that the masses are susceptible to the notion that a particular product will make them more sexually attractive. In the past, however, ads used euphemisms, claiming that certain products would make people "more lovable" or "more popular." What is a recent development is the abandonment of any such polite double-talk. Advertising today leaves no question about what is being sold along with the roasted peanuts or artificial sweetener. "Tell us about your first time," coyly invites the innuendo[2]-filled magazine advertisement for Campari liquor. A billboard for Levi's shows two jeans-clad young men on the beach, hoisting a girl in the air. The boys' perfect, tan bodies are matched by hers, although we see a lot more of hers: bare midriff, short shorts, cleavage. She caresses their hair; they stroke her legs. A jolly fantasy where sex exists without consequences.

But this fantasy is a lie—one which preys on young people. Studies show that   9
by the age of twenty, 75 percent of Americans have lost their virginity. In many high schools—and an increasing number of junior highs—virginity is regarded as an embarrassing vestige of childhood, to be disposed of as quickly as possible. Young people are immersed from their earliest days in a culture that parades sexuality at every turn and makes heroes of the advocates of sexual excess. Girls, from toddlerhood on up, shop in stores packed with clothing once thought suitable only for streetwalkers—lace leggings, crop tops, and wedge-heeled boots. Parents drop their children off at concerts featuring simulated on-stage masturbation or pretended acts of copulation. Young boys idolize sports stars like the late Wilt Chamberlain, who claimed to have bedded 20,000 women. And when the "Spur Posse," eight California high school athletes, were charged with systematically raping girls as young as ten as part of a "scoring" ritual, the beefy young jocks were rewarded with a publicity tour of talk shows, while one father boasted to reporters about his son's "manhood."

In a late, lame attempt to counterbalance this sexual overload, most schools   10
offer sex education as part of their curriculums. (In 1993, forty-seven states recommended or required such courses.) But sex ed classes are heavy on the mechanics of fertilization and birth control—sperm, eggs, and condoms—and light on any

---

[1]*Shangri-la:* an imaginary paradise on earth (the name of a beautiful faraway place in the novel *Lost Horizon*).
[2]*innuendo:* subtle suggestion.

discussion of sexuality as only one part of a well-balanced life. There is passing reference to abstinence as a method of contraception, but little discussion of abstinence as an emotionally or spiritually satisfying option. Promiscuity is discussed for its role in spreading sexually transmitted diseases. But the concept of rejecting casual sex in favor of reserving sex for an emotionally intimate, exclusive, trusting relationship—much less any mention of waiting until marriage—is foreign to most public school settings. "Love and stuff like that really wasn't discussed" is the way one Spur Posse member remembers his high school sex education class.

Surely teenagers need the factual information provided by sex education   11
courses. But where is "love and stuff like that" talked about? Where can they turn for a more balanced view of sexuality? Who is telling young people like Elaine, my former houseguest, that sex is not an adequate basis for a healthy, respectful relationship? Along with warnings to keep condoms on hand, is anyone teaching kids that they have a right to be valued for something other than their sexuality? Madison Avenue, Hollywood, and the TV, music, and fashion industries won't tell them that. Who will?

No one has told Elaine—at least, not in a way she comprehends. I haven't seen   12
her for a long time, but I hear of her occasionally. The baby boy she bore while living in my house is in a foster home, a few miles from his older half-sister, who is also in foster care. Elaine herself is working in a local convenience store—and she is pregnant again. This time, I understand, she is carrying twins.

■ Reading Comprehension

1. The word *dismantled* in "A moment after the photo session was over, the beautiful room was dismantled, and the models moved on to their next job" (paragraph 5) means

   a. used.

   b. photographed.

   (c.) taken apart.

   d. perfected.

2. The word *vestige* in "In many high schools—and an increasing number of junior highs—virginity is regarded as an embarrassing vestige of childhood" (paragraph 9) means

   a. reversal.

   b. activity.

   (c.) remainder.

   d. error.

3. Which of the following would be a good alternative title for this selection?

   a. Teens and Birth Control

   b. The Use of Sex to Sell Products

c. An Unbalanced View of Sexuality

d. The Advantages of Casual Sex

4. Which sentence best expresses the main idea of the selection?

a. Sexual images have helped our society become more open and understanding about a natural part of life.

b. We live in a society ruled by Madison Avenue, Hollywood, and the TV, music, and fashion industries.

c. Sex education courses, required in most states, have not done enough to teach our children about sexuality and responsible behavior.

d. Nothing, not even sex education, is counteracting the numerous sexual images in our society that encourage irresponsible, casual sex.

5. According to the author, Elaine probably likes to look at sexy magazine ads because

a. she doesn't have high moral standards.

b. she wishes she could afford the products being advertised.

c. they portray the kind of life she'd like to lead.

d. they remind her of her life before she had children.

6. In contrast to Elaine, the author

a. understands that most ads portray an unreal world.

b. finds ads like the Claiborne ad distasteful.

c. never looks at fashion magazines.

d. does not have children.

7. Elaine

a. wanted to become pregnant.

b. thinks birth control isn't romantic.

c. never finished high school.

d. has a healthy fear of AIDS.

8. We can conclude the author believes that

a. sex is a private matter that should not be discussed.

b. many young people view sex as an adequate basis for a relationship.

c. Madison Avenue, Hollywood, and the TV, music, and fashion industries have completely destroyed all morality in America.

d. virginity is an embarrassing vestige of childhood.

9. The author implies that

   a. sexy ads should be illegal.

   b. schools should teach contraception at an earlier age.

   (c.) sex should be reserved for an exclusive, loving relationship.

   d. casual sex is sometimes, though not always, a good idea.

10. The author suggests that sex education classes

   a. are a major cause of casual, unprotected sex.

   (b.) should include the role of sex in a meaningful relationship.

   c. should not include the mechanics of fertilization and birth control.

   d. have taken over a role that rightfully belongs to parents.

▪ Structure and Technique

1. To support her views about sexuality in popular culture, Garity presents the case of Elaine. Why has the author chosen to focus so much of her essay on Elaine? What would have been lost if Garity had omitted Elaine?

2. List the details that Garity provides as she describes the Claiborne ad. Why does she go to such lengths to describe it? Why might she think it important for the reader to see it so clearly?

3. Garity uses a number of examples to support her claim about the prevalence of sex in popular culture. Cite some of these examples and explain how they support her argument.

4. Throughout paragraph 11, Garity poses a series of questions. What does she gain by using this technique?

▪ Critical Reading and Discussion

1. How do you think Garity felt about Elaine? Affectionate? Scornful? Resentful? Disapproving? Pitying? Explain your answer, pointing out evidence from Garity's text.

2. In paragraph 7, the author says that Elaine is "completely unaware of the irony in her situation." In an ironic situation, there is an inconsistency between what might be expected and what actually happens. What about Elaine's situation is ironic?

3. The author lists numerous examples to illustrate and support her claim that "young people are immersed from their earliest days in a culture that parades sexuality at every turn and makes heroes of advocates of sexual excess." What examples can you think of to add to her list? Describe and explain them.

4. In arguing against the emphasis on sexuality in our culture, Garity focuses on potential dangers to young women. How do you think this highly sexualized culture affects young men? Are they also at risk? Explain.

Writing Assignments

Assignment 1

Garity accuses the advertising, film, TV, music, and fashion industries of contributing to our sex-saturated society by parading "sexuality at every turn." Choose one industry from that list, and write your own essay about how it portrays sexuality.

There is more than one way you can approach this assignment. In an essay on the fashion industry, for instance, you could focus on types of clothing being promoted, ads in print, and ads on TV. In an essay on the music industry, you might discuss three musicians and how their lyrics and their performances promote a particular view of sex. Whatever your choice, include specific, colorful descriptions, as Garity does when discussing ads and fashions. (See, for example, paragraphs 3 and 8.)

Assignment 2

Garity suggests that sex education courses should include more than the "mechanics of fertilization and birth control" (paragraph 10). Write an essay describing several ways you feel sex education classes could incorporate "love and stuff like that." Begin by selecting three general approaches that could be used in a sex education class to get students to think about what a rich, balanced romantic relationship is made of. For example, you might focus on three of the following:

Discussion of what students seek in a relationship

Discussion of a fictional relationship, such as that of Romeo and Juliet or two characters on a TV show

Discussion of the lyrics of a popular song

Bringing into class a psychologist who deals with problems in relationships

Bringing into class one or more couples who have been together for many years

Discuss each method you choose in a separate paragraph. Describe in detail how the method would work, using hypothetical examples to illustrate your points.

Assignment 3

Advertisements represent many elements of our society. Choose an element other than sexuality, and analyze the way ads of any kind (in magazines and newspapers, on billboards and buses, on TV and radio and the Internet) portray that subject. Following are some areas of our lives that are commonly represented in ads:

Family life

Women's roles

Men's roles

Possessions

Looks

Health

In analyzing an ad, consider what images and words are used, how they are intended to appeal to the audience, and what values they promote. Use the conclusion you come to as the thesis of your essay. For example, an essay on men's roles might make this point: "Many of today's TV ads promote participation of fathers in domestic activities."

Support your conclusion with colorful descriptions of several ads. Make your descriptions detailed enough so that your readers can "see" the elements of ads you refer to. Be sure to focus on the parts of the ads that support the point you are trying to make. You could organize your essay by devoting a paragraph each to three significant ads. Or you could devote each supporting paragraph to one of several important points about the subject you've chosen. For instance, an essay about fathers helping at home might discuss child care, cleaning, and cooking. A paragraph on each of those topics might refer to two or more ads.

Reading Comprehension Chart

Write an X through the numbers of any questions you missed while answering the comprehension questions for each selection in Part Five, Readings for Writing. Then write in your comprehension score. If you repeatedly miss questions in any particular skill, the chart will make that clear. Then you can pay special attention to that skill in the future.

Selection	Vocabulary in Context	Title and Main Idea	Key Details	Inferences	Comprehension Score
Russell	1	2 3	4 5 6	7 8 9 10	%
Haley	1 2	3 4	5 6 7	8 9 10	%
Gregory	1 2	3 4	5 6 7	8 9 10	%
Wilkins	1 2	3 4	5 6 7	8 9 10	%
McMurtry	1 2	3 4	5 6 7	8 9 10	%
Orwell	1 2	3 4	5 6 7	8 9 10	%
Baker	1 2	3 4	5 6 7	8 9 10	%
Kimmel	1 2	3 4	5 6 7	8 9 10	%
Johnson	1 2	3 4	5 6 7	8 9 10	%
Taylor	1 2	3 4	5 6	7 8 9 10	%
Banas	1 2	3 4	5 6 7	8 9 10	%
McClintock	1 2	3 4	5 6 7 8	9 10	%
Johnson	1 2	3 4	5 6 7	8 9 10	%
Dunayer	1 2	3 4	5 6 7	8 9 10	%
O'Keeney	1 2	3 4	5 6 7	8 9 10	%
Daniels	1 2	3 4	5 6 7	8 9 10	%
Sugarman	1 2	3 4	5 6 7	8 9 10	%
Sherry	1 2	3 4	5 6 7	8 9 10	%
Garity	1 2	3 4	5 6 7	8 9 10	%

Credits

Text credits:

Baker, Russell. "In My Day" from *Growing Up* by Russell Baker. Copyright © 1985. Used with permission of NTC/Contemporary Publishing Group.

Banas, Casey. "Why Are Students Turned Off?" from *The Chicago Tribune*, August 5, 1979. Copyright © 1979 by the Chicago Tribune. Used with permission.

Bodett, Tom. "Wait Divisions" from *Small Comforts* by Tom Bodett. Copyright © 1987 by Tom Bodett. Reprinted by permission of Perseus Books PLC, a member of Perseus Books, L.L.C.

Daniels, David. "College Lectures: Is Anybody Listening?" Reprinted by permission of the author.

Davidson, Anne. "Taming the Anger Monster." Reprinted with permission from the author.

Davis, Glenda. "How to Do Well on a Job Interview." Reprinted by permission of the author.

Dunayer, Joan. "Here's To Your Health." Reprinted by permission of Townsend Press.

Garity, Joyce. "Is Sex All That Matters?" Reprinted by permission of the author.

Google Search Results. Screen Shot courtesy of Google Inc. Internet Explorer frame reprinted by permission of Microsoft Corporation.

Gregory, Dick. "Shame," from *Nigger: An Autobiography* by Dick Gregory. Copyright © 1964 by Dick Gregory Enterprises, Inc. Used by permission of Dutton, a division of Penguin Group (USA) Inc.

Haley, Alex. "Thank You" by Alex Haley, published November 21, 1982 by *Parade Magazine*. Copyright © 1982 by Alex Haley. Reprinted by permission of John Hawkins & Associates, Inc.

Hamill, Pete. "The Yellow Ribbon." Copyright © by Pete Hamill. Reprinted by permission of International Creative Management, Inc.

Ivins, Molly. "Ban the Things, Ban Them All." First appeared in *The Washington Post*, March 16, 1993. Reprinted by permission of POM-INC.

Johnson, Beth. "The Professor Is a Dropout" and "Bombs Bursting in Air." Reprinted with permission from the author.

Beth Johnson lives in Lederach, PA.

Kimmel, Haven. "A Legendary Moment" from *A Girl Named Zippy* by Haven Kimmel. Copyright © 2001 by Haven Kimmel. Used by permission of Doubleday, a division of Random House, Inc.

Lewis, Camille. "Born To Be Different?" Reprinted with permission from the author.

Photo Credits:

Index

Instructor's Guide

Note   An *Instructor's Manual and Test Bank,* providing thirty-two supplementary activities and tests along with the materials in this Instructor's Guide and a full answer key, is available separately for instructors who use *College Writing Skills with Readings* as a classroom text. It can be downloaded from the Online Learning Center for the text (www.mhhe.com/langan). It is also available on the Instructor's CD-ROM (0-07-287134-2).

Suggested Approaches and Techniques

On the following pages, I describe briefly some approaches and techniques I have found helpful while using the materials in *College Writing Skills with Readings*.

Beginning the Course

Here are three brief activities—"Getting Acquainted," "Prewriting," and "Outlining"— that, right at the start of the course, will get students working together, writing, and thinking.

Getting Acquainted

An excellent way to get a class started is to leave it. I tell students that I'm going to go out of the classroom for about ten minutes and that during that time I want them to learn each other's first names. I explain that on returning, I want to be able to ask any one of them to introduce me to all the people in the room. I don't tell them how to learn each other's first names; I let them work out their own method. A current of nervous energy and excitement is invariably flowing as I walk out the door, and it is still there when I return. I then ask for a volunteer to introduce me to everyone else. I remind the class that they won't be shot on the spot if they miss a name. I say that they're not expected to remember every name (though in fact they usually do). Someone always volunteers, and as the introductions proceed, I shake everyone's hand. It's a little corny, but everyone enjoys it, and providing this personal touch at the start of a semester seems like a good thing to do. I often have about five other volunteers go through the names as well (though I dispense with the handshaking for these subsequent rounds). It's a good way for me and the students to begin to learn everyone's name. I congratulate the class afterward on their impressive performance and say I hope they'll all be around so that I can shake their hands at the end of the course.

Prewriting

2.3b

Freewriting   To get students writing from the very beginning of the course, I say something like this:

"Often, people don't like to write because they feel they have nothing to write about. I'm now going to introduce you to a technique that will help you get words and ideas down on paper. It's called *freewriting*. Freewriting means trying to write on a specific subject for ten minutes. You write whatever comes into your head about the subject, and you *don't* worry about making mistakes in spelling, punctuation, or grammar. Mistakes don't matter; all that matters is getting thoughts and information down on paper.

"The subject that I want you to write about is *movies*. Everyone goes to the movies at times; some people go a lot. I want you to write about why you like going to movies or about why you dislike going to movies. See if you can write for ten minutes about why you like or don't like going to the movies. If you run out of things to say, just write *I am looking for something to say* until something comes. Remember not to worry about errors; they don't count. And don't worry about putting things in logical order; that doesn't count either. Try to keep your pen moving. Write all the details you can think of about why you like going to movies or don't like going to movies."

After the ten minutes are up, I say something like this:

"It looks as though you did a good job with the freewriting. You'll find that this can be a good way of getting started whenever you have an assignment to write. Freewriting helps you think about and explore a topic as you get words on paper. It helps you accumulate some raw material that you can then work with and shape in writing the assignment."

List-Making   I next introduce list-making, or brainstorming:

ALLWRITE!
2.3a

"Let's suppose that you're going to write about why you dislike going to the movies. I'm going to write on the board the sentence, *There are several reasons why I don't like going to the movies.* Let's *brainstorm* this sentence. Brainstorming, much like freewriting, can help us generate ideas and details. We'll work together and think of as many reasons as possible why people might not like going to the movies. Reasons might include things like the high cost of tickets or the behavior of some moviegoers."

The students and I brainstorm a list of reasons. I write down all of their ideas under the topic sentence on the board. After we have a long list, we talk about items that overlap. We also talk a little (in what serves as an informal introduction to organizing details) about how some items fit under other items (that is, how some items are reasons and other items are supporting details for those reasons), and about how we might narrow the list down to three main reasons and supporting details for each of those reasons.

Outlining

4.1

I next explain that, even more than freewriting and list making, outlining is a key to effective writing. I pass out copies of pages 4–8 of the text (which students may not yet have bought). We read and outline the paragraph on moviegoing. I emphasize the basic structure: that a *point* is made and followed by *support* for that point. Then I draw the following diagram across the entire front blackboard to dramatize visually the essential structure of a paragraph:

We then read and outline the essay on moviegoing. I talk a bit about the difference between a paragraph and an essay, and about the reasons for writing essays. I then change the diagram on the board so that it becomes

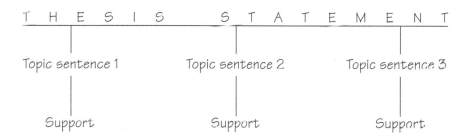

Students are thus introduced immediately to the fundamentals of sound essay writing. All the essays in *College Writing Skills with Readings* go on to reinforce the same relentlessly logical three-part structure. The result is that by the end of the semester, if not before, students have internalized the clear thinking process needed to write an effective paper—whether the paper is a five-hundred-word essay or some more specialized type of writing.

If there is time left in a class after the above introduction to writing essays, I hand out copies of the mastery test titled "General Outlining Activities" (in the *Instructor's Manual and Test Bank*), and the students and I go through the activities together. This early attention to the logic involved in good writing strikes the right note for the unfolding semester.

Teaching with the Text: Using the Activities

College Writing Skills with Readings is designed as a core text; a course can easily be built around it by instructors using a traditional classroom approach. For instance, an instructor could begin by explaining step 1 in essay writing on page 48. (Alternatively, the instructor could have a student read this section aloud in class.) Then, after looking at the examples of narrowed subjects, the class could work through the activity on pages 49–50. The book follows this sequence throughout: explanation and illustration of a skill, followed by hands-on experience in learning that skill.

For the sake of variety, I approach the activities in the book in several different ways:

1   Instructor and class work together on an activity. When a student figures out an answer, he or she raises a hand and volunteers the answer to the class.

2   Students work individually in class. The instructor goes around, looks over people's shoulders, offers suggestions, and confirms correct answers.

3   Students work in groups of three or four. The class then comes together, with the instructor calling on a spokesperson for each group to give answers. Often some lively group competition is possible here. The spokesperson for each group goes to the board and records that group's answers. When all the answers for all the groups are on the board, they can be compared and used as a basis for class discussion. For example, each group could decide on supporting points needed to complete the ten informal outlines on pages 55–56. After answers are written on the board, the instructor and class can decide whether all the answers logically fit. Or the group can put the answers to the activity on page 58 on the board. The answers—and especially differences in answers—can serve as the basis for a class discussion of what constitutes *specific* evidence.

4   Students work on activities at home. The activities are then discussed in class or collected and graded by the instructor. An effective strategy here is *not* to let students know in advance whether you will or will not collect and grade an assignment.

5   Students work on activities independently, on the basis of their individual needs. They are then given copies of the appropriate answer pages (these appear in the *Instructor's Manual and Test Bank*) so that they can evaluate their work. The instructor thus has more time to spend conferring with students about their work.

The activities in *College Writing Skills with Readings* lend themselves to all of these approaches.

Evaluating Students' Papers

Students' papers are generally evaluated in terms of both form and content.

I always insist that students present papers in correct manuscript *form,* including wide margins. I cover Chapter 34, "Manuscript Form," in class early in the semester and reinforce it thereafter. A neat paper represents a minimal, initial kind of organization that some students need to learn.

With regard to *content,* papers can be evaluated for their effectiveness in terms of the four bases in Chapter 6. I introduce a grading scale after I have covered the chapters in Part One. As my model syllabus suggests, this may be about the fifth week of the semester, because I have not gone straight through Part One but have included material from Part Two as well. Students know at this point that a paper should achieve all four of the bases summarized on the inside front cover of the book.

I explain that in grading I give a maximum of one point for each base that is fully realized in a paper. Thus, for each base there is a scale of 0 to 1. For example, if a paper is unified—if it has a clear thesis statement and its supporting topic sentences and details are on target in backing up the thesis statement—it receives 1 for *unity.* On the other hand, if the paper lacks, say, one or more clear supporting topic sentences, it might receive 0.7. If a paper is fully supported, it receives 1 for *support.* If more details are needed, it may receive, for example, 0.6. A fully coherent paper receives 1 for *coherence;* a paper without a clear method of organization or without helpful transitions may get 0.2. A paper with no sentence-skills mistakes earns 1 for *sentence skills;* two run-ons, say, may result in 0.8.

The following grading scale results:

3.5–4 points	=	A
2.8–3.4 points	=	B
2–2.7 points	=	C
Less than 2 points	=	R (rewrite)

For example, a given paper might be graded as follows:

Unity	0.7
Support	0.6
Coherence	0.2
Sentence skills	0.8
Total	2.3 = grade of C

Notes on Evaluating Papers

1   I do not always supply a numerical breakdown of the four bases. Often, I simply give a letter grade along with comments on how the paper stands in light of the four bases.

2   I explain to my class that I reserve the right to grade a paper *S* (for *satisfactory*) rather than give a letter grade. *S* seems more appropriate when, say, the writing is especially personal (at no time is a grading system more unnatural).

3   Rather than marking a very ineffective paper *U,* for *unsatisfactory,* I simply indicate with an *R* that it needs to be *rewritten.*

4   Some teachers may want to include a fifth base, "style." This may mean, variously, imagination, originality, flair, or interest level. I prefer to emphasize basic clarity and logic. If students achieve these things, I feel they have done enough to merit a high grade.

5   To show students how the four bases can make grading a more objective process, I periodically have people discuss and grade papers in small groups. (The papers can be either shown with an overhead projector or reproduced on a copying machine.) Students use the "Form for Peer Review" on page IG-12 as a guideline. A spokesperson for each group goes to the board and records the agreed-upon grade for each paper. Class discussion follows, in which the groups support their grading decisions by indicating how the paper specifically does or does not realize each of the four bases. After several such sessions, groups come surprisingly close to agreement on the exact grade any given paper deserves.

Class consideration of individual papers is also an excellent way to teach the art of revision. Students whose papers have been discussed know exactly what areas they must work on to improve an essay.

Individual Conferences and Rewriting

Individual conferences with students and the rewriting that often follows such conferences are two of the most important techniques in teaching students to write effectively. One of the main reasons I have provided so many activities in *College Writing Skills with Readings* is that they free me to spend more time in conferences with students. To teach a skill, five minutes of personal discussion about a paper may do more than an entire page of written comments.

Here are some approaches I find helpful in individual conferences.

Comments and Corrections

Positive comments should balance negative comments. Some words of praise are essential—"You have a good specific detail here." "Nicely written topic sentence." "This is a good transition." "This paper shows a definite improvement in your writing." "I like your touch of humor here." "This is real; it's honest, and it's often hard to be honest." "This paper is going in the right direction." Without some positive feedback, students may lack the incentive (or the belief in their own ability) needed to improve their writing.

Corrections in any single conference should be limited in number. After skimming a paper, an instructor may decide to focus on the central logic of a paragraph; if so, he or she should resist the urge to correct spelling, fix run-ons, cross out an incorrect apostrophe, and so on. (On the other hand, the instructor may enter some corrections without commenting on them in the conference so that the student won't repeat them when rewriting.) No one, especially a student with unhappy past experiences in writing, can effectively absorb and profit from a great deal of negative feedback at one time. At the end of the conference, the instructor should list specific skills for the student to concentrate on in rewriting. The instructor may also want to list one or more related activities in the text for the student to complete.

"Mini-Outlines"

Very often, the first thing I do in a conference is to ask a student to write a "mini-outline" of a paper. For instance, a mini-outline of the moviegoing essay on pages 7–8 of the text would be

> Moviegoing presents problems.
> 1. Getting there
> 2. Theater itself
> 3. Other moviegoers

The mini-outline enables me to quickly check and discuss the fundamental logic of the student's essay. Such an outline is also an indispensable guide when I'm helping a student plan an essay. A student with a clear mini-outline is ready to start working on the more detailed "Diagram of an Essay" on page 11 of the text.

Self-Evaluation and Peer Review

I sometimes precede a conference with a student by asking the student to evaluate his or her own paper and to have a fellow student evaluate it also. Specifically, I ask the student to fill in the "Form for Self-Evaluation" on page IG-11 and the "peer" to fill in the "Form for Peer Review" on page IG-12.

Note   For a larger version of either evaluation sheet, see the *Instructor's Manual and Test Bank*.

At times, I also ask students to check the logic of each other's paragraphs. Each student prepares a mini-outline of his or her own paragraph. This outline is referred to as the paper is read. The students then decide if the logic is (1) very clear, (2) clear, (3) fair, (4) doubtful, or (5) absent.

I may also ask the two students to proofread each other's essays. To do this, they sit alongside (not facing) each other so that they can both see the paper clearly. One reads his or her paper aloud to the other, and both look and listen for awkwardly written sentences that are difficult to read smoothly and clearly, and for sentence-skills mistakes such as fragments, run-ons, incorrect verbs, incorrect pronouns, and so on. The writer of the paper must correct all such mistakes (rewriting the paper if more than five errors have been found) before conferring with the instructor.

FORM FOR SELF-EVALUATION:
FOUR BASES FOR REVISING ESSAYS

Title of your paper: _____

Your name: _____

Base 1: Unity

- Is there a clear opening statement of the thesis of the paper?
- Does all the material in the paper support the thesis statement?

Your comments:

Score (up to 1 point): _____

Base 2: Support

- *Specific* evidence?
- Plenty of it?

Your comments:

Score (up to 1 point): _____

Base 3: Coherence

- Clear method of organization? (List of items or time order?)
- Use of transitions to connect sentences and ideas?

Your comments:

Score (up to 1 point): _____

Base 4: Sentence Skills

- Are there any rough spots where the sentences do not flow smoothly and clearly?

Your comments:

Score (up to 1 point): _____

Total score (up to 4 points): _____

Less than 2 points = rewrite   2 to 2.7 = C   2.8 to 3.4 = B   3.5 to 4 = A

FORM FOR PEER REVIEW:
FOUR BASES FOR REVISING ESSAYS

Title of paper being evaluated: _____

Author of paper: _____

Evaluator of paper: _____

Base 1: Unity

- Is there a clear opening statement of the thesis of the paper?
- Does all the material in the paper support the thesis statement?

Your comments:

Score (up to 1 point): _____

Base 2: Support

- *Specific* evidence?
- Plenty of it?

Your comments:

Score (up to 1 point): _____

Base 3: Coherence

- Clear method of organization? (List of items or time order?)
- Use of transitions to connect sentences and ideas?

Your comments:

Score (up to 1 point): _____

Base 4: Sentence Skills

- Are there any rough spots where the sentences do not flow smoothly and clearly?

Your comments:

Score (up to 1 point): _____

Total score (up to 4 points): _____

Less than 2 points = rewrite   2 to 2.7 = C   2.8 to 3.4 = B   3.5 to 4 = A

Conference Record-Keeping

For conferences, I use the kind of record sheet shown below. The student keeps it in a folder with his or her papers.

RECORD OF CONFERENCES

Name _____ _____ Section _____

1 Date _____ Paper or skill discussed: ___ _____
   Comments:

2 Date _____ Paper or skill discussed: ___ _____
   Comments:

3 Date _____ Paper or skill discussed: ___ _____
   Comments:

4 Date _____ Paper or skill discussed: _____ ____
   Comments:

5 Date _____ Paper or skill discussed: _____
   Comments:

6 Date _____ Paper or skill discussed: _____
   Comments:

7 Date _____ Paper or skill discussed: ___ _____
   Comments:

8 Date _____ Paper or skill discussed: _____
   Comments:

Papers Completed

1. _____   5. _____
2. _____   6. _____
3. _____   7. _____
4. _____   8. _____

Improving Spelling

Instead of spending all-too-limited class time on spelling rules (which, in any case, work for some students but not for others), I emphasize the techniques in Chapter 41 of the text. Also, I ask students to keep track of their spelling mistakes in a personal spelling list, as shown on pages 531–533. As spelling mistakes accumulate on the list, patterns of errors or repeated errors can be discovered and pointed out to the student.

Developing Vocabulary

I work on vocabulary development in the following way. I ask students to collect unfamiliar words from their leisure reading (no matter what the source), television, other students' papers, and other courses. I also periodically write five or so words on the board and hold students responsible for those words, as well as for the words in their personal collections. Students must collect and master five words a week, so that by the end of the semester they have added about seventy-five words (more when derivations are included) to their vocabulary.

The number of words involved is modest. The intention is to get students into the habit of following through on puzzling words and to make them believe that unknown words need not be ignored: these words can be looked up and mastered.

Using the Twenty-Eight Reading Selections

To Improve Reading Skills

Ten reading comprehension questions follow each of the twenty-eight reading selections in the book. The questions help ensure that students understand what they have read; they also give students a chance to apply—and so improve—important reading skills. The questions emphasize such key comprehension skills as finding main ideas, identifying key details, and making inferences. Research studies clearly indicate that sustained practice in such skills turns people into stronger readers.

I always assign the ten questions at the same time that I assign a reading. The answers can be reviewed quickly in class, and they provide a good starting point for the discussion questions that follow. To check that students do the work, I sometimes collect and attach a grade to the ten questions.

In my experience, almost all students need work in improving their reading skills. To give them the practice they need, I assign most of the readings in the book, varying the number of readings depending on what else needs to be done in a particular session. Even though I cannot cover all these selections closely in class, I provide the answers and have students keep track of their reading performance in the chart on page 725.

Students enjoy the challenge of bettering their score from one selection to the next; they also learn to pay special attention to the skills they need to work on. Most students appreciate that reading skills are important to their college and career success, and they welcome the opportunity that the course offers to improve their reading skills at the same time as their writing skills.

I encourage students to take advantage of an extra-credit option, in which they earn bonus points by reading and turning in the answers for all twenty-eight selections. The extra credit can mean the difference between a B+ and an A–, or a C+ and a B–.

To Improve Writing Skills

I use the readings discussed in class to emphasize two essential writing principles presented in the book: that every effective communication *makes a point* and then *supports that point.* In the course of going over the comprehension and discussion questions, I always ask specifically:

1   What is the thesis of this selection?
2   What is the support for the thesis?

These two questions provide a vital link between the writing principles in Parts One to Three of the book and the reading selections in Parts Two and Five. (Asking students to answer the two questions by preparing a brief outline of each selection is an excellent homework assignment.)

The discussion questions after each selection in Part Five are divided into two parts. The questions under "Structure and Technique" will remind students of important points made in earlier parts of the book about organization, transitions, and connecting devices. In addition, they will make students aware of devices that can be part of a writer's craft and of ways that a writer can express his or her attitude toward the subject matter. And the questions under "Critical Reading and Discussion" should extend and deepen the understanding of the selection provided by the ten comprehension questions as well as give students an opportunity to react to issues raised by the selection. Suggested answers for the two questions appear in the answer key provided for each selection, starting on page IG–24. The answers make no claim to being definitive. At the least, they should provide students with a basis for clarifying their own thoughts on matters relating to a reading. I always encourage students to advance their own individual responses and the reasoning, the textual evidence, or both to support those responses.

Following each selection are three writing assignments; the three choices help ensure that every student will find a topic about which he or she will want to write—or that teachers will have a topic appropriate for their students. The assignments are detailed enough to help students avoid some of the more obvious errors that can occur in creating a five-paragraph essay.

Aids for Teaching and Learning

Several aids for teaching and learning are part of *College Writing Skills with Readings* or accompany it.

1   Two visual aids will help students in the process of writing a paragraph. Students stand an excellent chance of writing solid papers if they refer to the "Checklist of the Four Steps in Writing an Effective Essay" (on the inside front cover) and complete the "Diagram of an Essay" (on page 11 and also provided in the *Instructor's Manual*).

2   The separate *Instructor's Manual and Test Bank* contains a detailed answer key and also contains thirty-two additional activities and tests that can serve as supplemental learning aids. These activities and tests can be easily duplicated on a photocopying machine.

A Model Syllabus

The following syllabus serves as a general guide for *College Writing Skills with Readings*. It is based on a three-hour class meeting once a week for fifteen weeks. (For classes that meet in shorter time blocks, the syllabus can, of course, be adjusted accordingly.) It also assumes that time is allowed in class for discussion of papers and for review of homework activities or matters covered in previous class sessions. Rarely do I cover everything that is on the syllabus; instead, I select whatever is most appropriate for the individual needs of the students.

Instructors will note that I do *not* suggest teaching the book straight through. Because parts and chapters are self-contained, they can be taught easily in any order, depending on the preferences of the instructor and the needs of the class. I suggest that at the same time Part One is being covered, instructors start assigning essays from Part Two and reading selections from Part Five. And the skills in Parts Three and Four may be taken up as needed as the class proceeds through the semester. Varying the mix of writing activities in the five parts of the book will sustain student interest more effectively.

Class I

- Business matters.
- Introduction to each other (see page IG-3).
- Introduction to the instructor (personal anecdotes) and to the course. This includes the material in Chapter 1, "An Introduction to Writing."
- In-class prewriting and outlining activities (see pages IG-3 to IG-5).
- Homework assignments:

  Get the book, read "An Introduction to Writing" (Chapter 1), and prepare for an objective test on the chapter.

  Read the "Introduction to the Readings" on pages 583–587 and "How to Make It in College, Now That You're Here" on pages 685–690. Answer the questions that follow the selection on pages 690–693.

Class 2

- Mastery test on Chapter 1, "An Introduction to Writing." (*Note*: Mastery tests are provided in the separate *Instructor's Manual and Test Bank*.)
- Read and work through Chapter 2, "The Writing Process."

- Discuss "How to Make It in College, Now That You're Here," going over the questions on pages 690–692.
- Read and work through selected parts of Chapter 3, "The First and Second Steps in Essay Writing."
- Homework assignments:

  Continue work on "The First and Second Steps in Essay Writing," and prepare for an objective test on "The Writing Process."

  Read and answer the questions following "Thank You" on pages 592–599 and "Bombs Bursting in Air" on pages 672–679.

Class 3

- Mastery test on "The Writing Process."
- Do selected activities in "The First and Second Steps in Essay Writing" on pages 60–75.
- Discuss "Thank You" as an examples piece and go over the questions on pages 595–599. If time allows, do the same for "Bombs Bursting in Air" as well.
- Work through "Use Parallelism" in Chapter 5. (This is a skill needed to write a balanced thesis statement.)
- Read Chapter 7, "Introduction to Essay Development." Go over Chapter 34, "Manuscript Form."
- Cover the "Examples" essays in Chapter 10, reading the student essays and the professional essay in class and then discussing the ten questions that follow the essays. If there is time, do the prewriting activity on page 221.
- Homework assignments:

  Prepare for a mastery test on "The First and Second Steps in Essay Writing."

  Continue work on the above areas not completed in class.

  Write the examples essay on pages 220–221. Instructors of more advanced students may want to substitute one of the less structured assignments on pages 223–224.

Class 4

- Mastery test on "The First and Second Steps in Essay Writing."
- Read and discuss selected example essays turned in by students.

Note   I suggest you refuse to accept any papers that appear to be written in a careless, last-minute way. Instead, return the papers, telling students they are not being fair to themselves or to you, and ask them to rewrite the paper and resubmit it in the following class.

- Read and work through selected parts of Chapters 4 and 5, on the third and fourth steps in essay writing.
- Review Chapter 24, "Fragments"; and Chapter 25, "Run-Ons."
- Homework assignments:

  Do selected activities on pages 93–100 and 122–134, and prepare for an objective test on these chapters.

  Continue review of fragments and run-ons, and prepare for an objective test on these skills.

  Rewrite the examples essay as needed.

Class 5

- Mastery tests on Chapters 4 and 5 and on fragments and run-ons.

Note   Here and in later classes, other mastery tests can be used for in-class exercises, extra-credit work, and homework assignments. For example, "Outlining an Essay II," "Writing a Thesis Statement," and "Evaluating an Essay for Coherence" all serve to review important skills in essay writing.

- Review the activities on pages 93–100 and 122–134 done at home, and work through other activities on these pages.
- Read and work through Chapter 6, "Four Bases for Revising Essays."
- Review other sentence skills as needed: Chapter 39, "Comma," and skills relating to verbs (Chapters 26–28).
- Homework assignments:

  Continue review of sentence skills and prepare for an objective test on these skills.

  Read and answer the questions on "Seven Ways to Keep the Peace at Home," pages 701–710.

Class 6

- Mastery tests on comma and verb skills as needed.
- Discuss "Seven Ways to Keep the Peace at Home" as a process piece, and go over the questions on pages 708–711.

- Cover the process essays in Chapter 11, reading the student essays and the professional essay in class and then discussing the ten questions that follow the essays. If there is time, do the prewriting activity on pages 239–240.
- Homework assignments:

  Continue work on the above areas not completed in class.

  Write one of the process essays on pages 239–244.

Class 7

- Read and discuss selected process essays turned in by students.
- Review Chapter 37, "Apostrophe"; Chapter 38, "Quotation Marks"; and Chapter 43, "Effective Word Choice," as needed.
- Cover the cause-and-effect essays in Chapter 12, reading the student essays and the professional essay in class and then discussing the ten questions that follow the essays. Also do the scratch-outline activity under "Writing Assignment 1" on pages 259–260.
- Homework assignments:

  Continue review of sentence skills and prepare for an objective test on these skills.

  Rewrite the process essay as needed.

  Read and answer the questions on "Why Are Students Turned Off?" on pages 657–662 and "The Professor Is a Dropout" on pages 641–649. (Alternatively, assign two of the other cause-and-effect essays listed on page xiii.)

Class 8

- Mastery tests on apostrophe, quotation marks, and effective word choice, as needed.
- Discuss "Why Are Students Turned Off?" and "The Professor Is a Dropout" as cause-and-effect pieces, and go over the questions on pages 659–662 and 646–649.
- Cover one or more "Special Skills" appropriate for students in the class (such as Chapter 17, "Taking Essay Exams"; Chapter 19, "Writing a Report"; and Chapter 21, "Using the Library and the Internet").
- Homework assignment:

  Write the cause-and-effect essay on pages 259–260. For more advanced students, the instructor may want to substitute one of the cause-and-effect essays on pages 260–263.

knowledge of psychology comes in handy. Offer her a choice of staying up until 7:30 with you or going upstairs and playing until 8:00. Since she gets to make the choice, she does not feel so powerless and will not resist. Psychology is also useful in rewarding a child for a job well done. Instead of telling your ten-year-old son what a good boy he is when he makes his own bed, tell him how neat it looks, how happy you are to see it, and how proud of him you are for doing it by himself. The psychology books will tell you that being a good boy is much harder to live up to than doing one job well.

Pronouns

Pronouns (*he, she, it, you, they, this, that,* and others) are another way to connect ideas. Also, using pronouns in place of other words can help you avoid needless repetition. (Note, however, that pronouns should be used with care to avoid the problems described on pages 463–465.) Here is a selection that makes good use of pronouns:

Another way for people to economize at an amusement park is to bring their own food. If they pack a nourishing, well-balanced lunch of cold chicken, carrot sticks, and fruit, they will avoid having to pay high prices for hamburgers and hot dogs. They will also save on calories. Also, instead of filling up on soft drinks, they should bring a thermos of iced tea. Iced tea is more refreshing than soda, and it is a great deal cheaper. Every dollar that is not spent at a refreshment stand is one that can be spent on another ride.

Synonyms

Synonyms are words alike in meaning. Using synonyms can also help move the reader easily from one thought to the next. In addition, the use of synonyms increases variety and interest by avoiding needless repetition. Note the synonyms for *method* in the following selection:

There are several methods of fund-raising that work well with small organizations. One technique is to hold an auction, with everyone either contributing an item from home or obtaining a donation from a sympathetic local merchant. Because all the merchandise and the services of the auctioneer have been donated, the entire proceeds can be placed in the organization's treasury. A second fund-raising procedure is a car wash. Club members and their children get together on a Saturday and wash all the cars in the neighborhood for a few dollars apiece. A third, time-tested way to raise money is to hold a bake sale, with each family contributing homemade cookies, brownies, layer cakes, or cupcakes. Sold by the piece words needed to complete the second

m my parents are the importance
good education.

members should stick

rtance of   *family support*

                              ,

   hard work

vork   ,

od education

nnecting words that
rds, *pronouns*, and

elves in writing.
ught in a paper.
a.

ith your
hen you want
" A little

Class 12

- Discuss the three assigned readings as narrative pieces, and go over the activities for each. (If the students read descriptive essays, discuss the readings as descriptive pieces and go over the activities for each.)
- Cover the narration essays in Chapter 9 (or the description essays in Chapter 8), reading the student essays and the professional essay in class and then discussing the ten questions that follow the essays. Also do the activities on page 202 (or, alternatively, do those on pages 184–187).
- Write and complete a narrative (or a descriptive) essay in class, choosing one of the assignments on pages 202–206 or 187–190.
- Homework assignment:
  Read "College Lectures: Is Anybody Listening?" (pages 694–701), "Here's to Your Health" (679–684), and "In Praise of the F Word" (711–716). Answer the questions for all three selections.

Class 13

- Discuss the three assigned readings as argumentative pieces and go over the activities for each.
- Cover the argumentation essays in Chapter 16, reading the student essays and the professional essay in class and then discussing the ten questions that follow the essays.
- In class, do some of the prewriting for an argumentation paper, using either the prewriting activity on pages 334–335 or the one on pages 336–337.
- Homework assignments:
  Read "Smash Thy Neighbor" (612–619) and "Is Sex All That Matters?" (717–724).
  Answer the questions for both selections.
  Write one of the argumentation essays on pages 334–338.

Class 14

- Discuss the two assigned readings as argumentative pieces and go over the activities for each.
- Read and discuss selected argumentation and persuasion essays turned in by students.
- In-class rewriting of an earlier essay in light of the four bases of effective writing.

- Homework assignment:

  Complete the rewriting of earlier essays as needed so that at the last class of the semester they can be turned in as part of a "Collected Works" folder.

Class 15

- Final exam: Write in class an essay on one of the "Essay Writing Assignments I" (included in the *Instructor's Manual*).

  Alternatively, write an essay based on one of other writing assignments in the argumentation chapter.

- Hand in to the instructor a "Collected Works" folder of completed essays.

Suggested Answers to the Discussion Questions in Part Five

Bertrand Russell, "Three Passions"

Structure and Technique

1 *Does this essay follow the traditional one-three-one essay model of introduction, support, and conclusion? How would you outline the essay?*

Answer: It does follow the traditional pattern, although it is unusually brief.

Introduction: paragraph 1

Support: paragraphs 2–4

Conclusion: paragraph 5

2 *This essay primarily is organized in terms of three causes and their overall effect. What is the effect and what are the causes? The essay can also be seen as an examples essay. What examples does the author provide to help the reader understand each of his lifelong passions?*

Answer

Effect: How Russell has lived his life

Causes: His seeking of love, his seeking of knowledge, and his pity for humankind

Examples of love's power: It brings ecstasy; it relieves loneliness; it provides a glimpse of heaven.

Examples of the power of knowledge: It provides insight into the hearts of men; it reveals why the stars shine; it allows us to understand the universe in terms of mathematics.

Examples of situations that evoke pity: children suffering famine; victims of oppression; elderly people abused by their children

3   *What kind of transitional signals—time, space, or addition—does Russell employ in the second paragraph? List the transitions you find there.*

Answer: He uses addition signals: first, next, finally, at last.

4   *Russell is a master of the use of metaphorical language. For instance, as has already been seen, he compares his anguish to an "ocean." What other examples of metaphorical language can you find? Why do you think Russell chose to use such imaginative language, rather than write in plain-spoken terms?*

Answer: Other metaphors are

His passions have blown him about like "great winds." (Paragraph 1) [Figures of speech using *like* or *as* are known as similes.]

"[O]ne shivering consciousness looks over the rim of the world into the cold unfathomable lifeless abyss." (Paragraph 2)

"Love and knowledge . . . led upward toward the heavens." (Paragraph 4)

Answers to the second part of the question will vary, but Russell was trying to express ideas that were outside of ordinary, daily experience. In order to communicate the deeply felt nature of his passions, he turned to extraordinary, figurative language.

Critical Reading and Discussion

1   *Can you identify one or two passions—or at least strong influences—that have, in Russell's words, governed your life? What examples can you provide of how those passions have affected you?*

Answer: Answers will vary. In order to identify their passions, students may need to examine the forces that were behind important decisions they have made.

2   *Do you think that many people are influenced by the same passions as Russell: love, knowledge, then pity? Or do you feel that many people spend their lives influenced by other factors? What other passions or influences do people live by, in your experience?*

Answer: Answers will vary. Certainly other factors, such as greed, fear, jealousy, anger, optimism, or hope, could be powerful influences in people's lives.

3   *Russell writes, "[I]n the union of love I have seen, in a mystic miniature, the prefiguring vision of the heaven that saints and poets have imagined" (paragraph 2). Most people, whether they believe in heaven in a religious sense or not, have a concept of an ideal place of perfect love and harmony. What on*

earth—perhaps a place, a relationship, an individual, or a situation—comes closest to giving you a "prefiguring vision" of heaven? What is it about that place, person, or thing that seems heavenly to you?

Answer: Answers will vary, but most people will probably identify a person, place, or thing that inspires strong feelings of love or awe. It might be a relationship with a romantic partner, a spouse, or a family member. It could be a place of great natural beauty. It could be an example they have seen of a person's loving or self-sacrificing behavior.

4   *Overall, do you find Russell's statement an uplifting or a saddening one? What elements of each do you find within it? What makes one element outweigh the other, in your mind?*

Answer: The fact that Russell concludes by saying that his life has been "worth living" and that he would be "glad" to live it again suggests that he sees his statement as an uplifting one. However, his references to life's loneliness and to the tragedies of the world—children going hungry, old people being unloved—certainly imply that life has its share of sadness. He seems to say that it is our love and pity for one another that ultimately makes life a good experience.

Alex Haley, "Thank You"

Structure and Technique

1   *Which pattern or patterns of development does Haley use in his essay? Explain.*

Answer: Much of "Thank You" is a *narration* of the story of Haley's letters. As is usually the case with narration, that story also includes *description* (especially in paragraphs 1, 4, and 19). However, Haley's conclusion reveals that his essay is meant to be an *argument* for saying "thank you." In paragraphs 28–30, he writes of encouraging students to say thank you. And to readers—of letters written on his stationery and of this reading—he addresses words that summarize his argument: "Find the good—and praise it."

2   *Paragraph 4 contains a vivid description of part of Haley's Thanksgiving night on the* Murzim. *What sensory details (sight, smell, hearing, taste, and/or touch) does he provide? What is the effect of all these details?*

Answer: Haley provides details that appeal to three senses. First, he appeals to the sense of *touch* when he writes of the "great, deep draughts" he breathed in and the feeling in his feet of "vibrations from the deep-set, turbine diesels." He appeals to the sense of *sight* with the images of the "white cook's hat and the long apron" and of the movement of water "resisting the skin of a ship."

And he appeals to the sense of *hearing* with the words "that slightly hissing sound the sea makes."

The effect of the descriptive details is a peaceful scene that sets the mood for Haley's thoughts about Thanksgiving and the people he should thank.

3   *Most of Haley's essay is about the three thank-you letters he wrote. Why do you think he included the anecdote about the helpful man at the airport? How is it related to his point about giving thanks?*

Answer: By including the anecdote about the helpful airline man, Haley shows that he feels it is important to give thanks to people in everyday situations, not just to our elders.

This anecdote provides a transition from his first three letters of thanks (which apply only to the author) to his implied argument that we *all* should remember to thank others.

4   *Writers' most common purposes are to inform, to entertain, and to persuade. Which purpose—or purposes—do you think Haley has in mind?*

Answer: The information about Haley's experiences and conclusions supports his central purpose, which is to persuade readers of the importance of giving thanks (28 and 30).

Critical Reading and Discussion

1   *Before Haley decides to write to his loved ones, what thoughts and images go through his mind as he reflects on the meaning of Thanksgiving? What is the connection between these traditional images and what Haley finally realizes?*

Answer: After having cooked dinner on the ship, Haley first thinks about "the historic . . . Pilgrims, Indians" and the foods typically associated with Thanksgiving (5). Yet this conventional imagery is inadequate, and Haley seeks a way to "personally apply" the holiday (6). He then thinks about giving thanks through prayer to God (6–7) but again feels dissatisfied with this approach (8). Finally, Haley comes up with a more concrete and personal way to celebrate Thanksgiving: to thank the people in his life for all they have done for him (9). By going beyond the images of the holiday, Haley expands the traditional meaning of Thanksgiving to include a personal one.

2   *Alex Haley was far from home when he decided to thank the important people in his life. If he had remained at home, do you think he would still have thanked these people? Why or why not?*

Answer: Answers will vary. Some students may say that Haley would probably have continued to take the important people in his life for granted if he had not been far away. They might reasonably argue that he needed time and distance to really appreciate what they had done for him.

3   *How does Haley feel about the three responses to his thank-you letters? What conclusions about human nature does he draw from these responses?*

Answer: All three letters left Haley "not only astounded, but more humbled than before" (20). The fact that his father was "moved" to answer his letter showed Haley how profoundly the thank-you letter had affected his father (22). By quoting parts of Reverend Nelson's letter, Haley implies that it brought him great satisfaction to have given the minister "welcome reassurance that his career had been appreciated" (23). Grandma's letter evoked tears from Haley, who is moved by the gratitude that would cause her to spend hours responding to him (24).

The three responses reveal something almost "mystical in human beings," which Haley identifies as the secret "yearning . . . for more of their fellows to express appreciation for their efforts" (25).

4   *Haley is a world-renowned writer. Who might have influenced his decision to be a writer? What made these people such powerful role models in his life? In general, what would you say are the qualities of a good role model?*

Answer: Answers may vary, although one reasonable response is that all three people Haley thanked—as well as the other four who had died (10)—helped shape the person he has become and therefore influenced his decision to be a writer. The father's insistence on the value and beauty of reading probably influenced Haley most profoundly (14). But Haley is also indebted to Reverend Nelson and Grandma, who trained him to be a good and moral human being with positive aspirations.

Answers to the final question may vary, but students might cite, as qualities of a good role model, integrity, persistence, resilience, sensitivity, compassion, and the like.

Dick Gregory, "Shame"

Structure and Technique

1   *In paragraphs 1 and 2, Gregory mentions several steps he took to impress Helene Tucker. What were they? Why does he include them in his essay?*

Answer: In order to impress Helene, Gregory brushed his hair, got a handkerchief, washed his socks and shirt every night, shoveled the snow off her walk, tried to make friends with her mother and aunts, and left money on her stoop. He describes those steps in detail because, besides demonstrating his devotion to Helene, they give a clear picture of Gregory's poverty.

2   *A metaphor is a suggested comparison. What metaphor does Gregory use in paragraph 5, and what is its purpose? What metaphor does he use in the second sentence of paragraph 7, and what does it mean?*

Answer: In paragraph 5, Gregory uses the metaphor that he was pregnant to suggest the effects poverty had on him—it gave him strange tastes, which pregnant women get. It also filled him (as pregnancy fills someone), but with negative things: poverty, dirt, "smells that made people turn away," and so on.

In the second sentence of paragraph 7, Gregory uses the metaphor of a flying eagle to represent the movement of money. (A picture of an eagle is engraved on one side of a quarter).

3   *In narrating the incidents in the classroom and in the restaurant, Gregory chooses to provide actual dialogue rather than merely to tell what happened. Why?*

Answer: By using the exact words spoken by Helene, the teacher, and himself, Gregory gives a very clear picture of what happened and allows the reader to "experience" it, rather than simply hear a general summary. The dialogue between Helene and the teacher shows Helene as an ideal little student who received approval from the teacher. The dialogue between Gregory and the teacher, however, clearly demonstrates Gregory's eagerness to impress Helene and his unsuccessful, embarrassing attempt to gain the teacher's approval. If Gregory had merely described what had happened, we would have a much less vivid impression of the characters involved.

4   *At the end of the essay, Gregory shifts his focus from the classroom to the scene involving the wino at the restaurant. What is the connection between this closing scene and the rest of the essay?*

Answer: In the body of the essay, Gregory is narrating a time when he was shamed publicly and no one came to his defense. In the closing scene, Gregory realizes that he has done the same thing—that he, too, has witnessed a person being shamed without assisting him. He feels a new kind of "shame," that of having failed to help another man in need.

Critical Reading and Discussion

1   *When Gregory writes, "I never learned hate at home, or shame. I had to go to school for that" (paragraph 1), he is using irony—an inconsistency between what is expected and what actually occurs. What does he mean by these two statements? What is the effect of his irony?*

Answer: Gregory means that although his home life was one of poverty and want, his home was not a place of inhumane values, such as hatred and shame. But at school, which on its surface was a more positive place, he was made to feel hatred and shame. The ironic statement intrigues the reader and makes him or her want to know more about what Gregory means.

2 *What are Gregory's feelings about his teacher? What were your feelings about her as you read this essay? What could the teacher have done or said that would* not *have made Gregory feel ashamed?*

Answer: Gregory seems sad and resentful that the teacher did not understand why he misbehaved in class and that she assumed he was stupid and a troublemaker. But he also badly wanted her approval, as is seen by the Community Chest incident and the fact that he got a "big thrill" out of being chosen to clean the blackboard. Students' suggestions about the teacher will vary. One possibility: She could have merely thanked Gregory in class and then spoken to him privately later if she doubted that he could contribute to Community Chest.

3 *Gregory shows how a childhood incident taught him shame. What other important lessons does Gregory learn in this essay? Explain.*

Answer: From paragraph 3, in which Gregory talks about his accomplishments later in life, we can conclude that he learned he could boost his self-esteem through his own efforts. Paragraph 5 shows that from his own experiences, he learned that children who are hungry and poor may feel invisible and so behave in ways that attract attention. From his experience with the wino, he learned that in order to feel good about himself, he would have to start standing up for other people who were shamed.

4 *At the end of his essay, Gregory says, "I waited too long to help another man." Why do you think he waited so long to assist the wino? What are some reasons people do not always help others who are in need (for example, ignoring a homeless person seated on the sidewalk)?*

Answer: Gregory probably had many reasons for not helping the wino sooner: embarrassment at drawing attention to himself, reluctance to part with his hard-earned money, not wanting to get into trouble with Mr. Williams, not knowing the wino and thus feeling the affair wasn't his business, and so on. People have similar reasons for not helping others in need. In addition, people who ignore a homeless man may feel that the man's problems—maybe including substance abuse or mental illness—are so big and deep-rooted that they are not qualified to help him in any effective way.

Roger Wilkins, "I Became Her Target"

Structure and Technique

1 *Which pattern of development—comparison, narration, or description—does Wilkins use in most of his essay? Explain.*

Answer: Wilkins primarily uses narration. Although description is woven throughout, he is generally telling the story of his family's move to Grand Rapids and a series of events that occurred there.

2   *Which kind of transition signal—addition, time, or space—does Wilkins use to move his essay smoothly from one event to the next? Find at least four different words that are examples of this signal.*

Answer: Wilkins uses time signals, including "before" (paragraph 2), "later" (7), "after" (8), "final" (12), and "afterward" (12). Time signals are often used in narratives to clarify the time relationships between events.

3   *In the first paragraph, Wilkins chooses to provide some historical background for his story. Why do you think he chose the specific details mentioned there? What might have been lost if these details had been excluded from the essay?*

Answer: The historical events Wilkins lists provide helpful context for the story he is about to tell. By telling readers that he is writing about the World War II era, when the symbolic beginning of the civil rights movement was more than ten years away, he helps readers understand how unusual it was in those days for a single black student to enroll in a formerly all-white school. If Wilkins had not included the details and readers had assumed the story happened more recently, they would have been surprised to read of an all-white school where blacks were considered a novelty.

4   *A title can offer interesting insights into an essay, especially if the title acquires unexpected meanings. Before reading this essay, what did you think the title "I Became Her Target" might refer to? What additional meanings do you think Wilkins intended?*

Answer: The first impression most readers are likely to get of the title is that someone "targeted" Wilkins in an unpleasant way, as in "targeted for criticism." Wilkins's real meaning seems to be twofold: that Miss Bean made him a "target" for her attention because she wanted to force other students to recognize him as a colleague, and later he became the literal "target" of the eraser she threw.

Critical Reading and Discussion

1   *What does Wilkins mean by the term* nonstandard person *(paragraph 3)? Do you think he later felt more like a "standard" person? Why or why not?*

Answer: At first, it seemed that "standard" in the Grand Rapids school could only mean white. As a nonwhite student, Wilkins was made to feel less than normal, adequate, or accepted. By saying in paragraph 12 that he became "just another kid in school," Wilkins indicates that he came to feel more "standard."

2   *Wilkins mentions several ways in which Miss Bean treated him differently from the way he was treated by the other teachers at Creston. How did her approach differ from theirs? What does this approach reveal about Miss Bean—as a teacher and as a person?*

Answer: Unlike Wilkins's other teachers, who chose to ease him in by ignoring him for a while, Miss Bean made him talk in class immediately. She also asked him questions that required him to do his own thinking, not merely give the "correct" answer. Her approach reveals that she was an effective teacher: she realized that if she did not take the lead, the other students would isolate Wilkins. Also, she knew the value of encouraging students to think for themselves and express their own opinions. In addition, her approach reveals that she was a sensitive person, concerned about Wilkins's success in his new school.

3   *Wilkins says that initially he was Miss Bean's "incipient teacher's pet" (paragraph 6). But how did Miss Bean's behavior toward him go beyond mere favoritism? In what way did her treatment of Wilkins affect how his peers regarded him?*

Answer: Through her attention to Wilkins, Miss Bean was inviting him to demonstrate to the class that he was an intelligent, normal kid. By forcing him to give answers, to "clean up [another student's] mess," and to present his opinions, she made it more likely that other students would see him as a person rather than as a "dark presence."

4   *In paragraph 7, Wilkins says, "Miss Bean became the first teacher ever to require me to think." Before Miss Bean's class, what do you suspect Wilkins— and his classmates—were being taught to do in school? Describe a teacher who gave you "the sense that thinking was part of education." In your opinion, what can teachers do to get students to think?*

Answer: Wilkins's comment suggests that his other teachers had primarily required him to memorize material and parrot it back. Answers to the rest of the question will vary.

John McMurtry, "Smash Thy Neighbor"

Structure and Technique

1   *McMurtry uses several patterns of development in his essay: comparison and contrast, cause-and-effect, description, narration, and argumentation. Where does he use each of those patterns?*

Answer: McMurtry uses comparison and contrast in paragraphs 5–8, where he compares football and war; and 9–10, where he contrasts his early joy in football with what the game became. He uses cause-and-effect in paragraphs 15 and 17–18 and talking about the game's effect on players and audience. Description is found in numerous places, such as paragraph 11, in which he describes his injuries. Narration occurs in paragraph 2, where McMurtry tells the story of his injury and hospitalization. The entire piece is argumentation—everything the author says is meant to support his argument that football in its present state is too violent. In addition to supporting his case forcefully throughout, he uses two specific argumentation strategies: (1) in paragraph 15, he states an opposing view of football, and (2) he then rebuts that view in paragraphs 16–18.

2   *McMurtry uses terms such as "body wreckage," "body shattering," and "skilled masochism" to describe organized football. Find three other phrases the author uses to describe football (beginning with paragraph 9). What effect does McMurtry hope this language will have on the reader?*

Answer: "Brutal circus," "crippling bodily moves," "joyless drill," "people-smashing," and "angry antagonism" are among the descriptive phrases McMurtry uses. He wants the reader to conclude that football in its present form causes too much harm.

3   *In paragraph 11, McMurtry provides a series of details about the injuries he has sustained playing football. List some of these details. Why do you think he includes these personal details in his essay?*

Answer: The details McMurtry provides include torn knee ligaments, broken nose, broken jaw, torn ankle ligaments, fractured ankle, fractured ribs, torn cartilage, dislocated fingers and toes, and dislocated shoulder. McMurtry includes such details to give a powerful picture of the toll football has taken on his body and also to show that he is writing about a topic with which he has had considerable experience.

4   *In "Smash Thy Neighbor," McMurtry repeatedly describes his own personal experiences with football. What do these anecdotes contribute to the essay? How do they relate to the larger point he is trying to make?*

Answer: The anecdotes make it clear that even a thoughtful, intelligent man like McMurtry could become nearly irrational in his attitude toward football: that he would do things to his opponents that he never would in his other life; that he would play despite injuries that threatened his health; that he became vicious and inhumane. By sharing his own experiences, he makes a persuasive point that organized football has very negative effects.

Critical Reading and Discussion

1   *What is McMurtry's current profession? How might his present position have influenced his opinions about football?*

Answer: In paragraph 1, McMurtry says he is a university philosophy teacher. As a scholar and philosopher, McMurtry has probably spent a good deal of time thinking about his former life as a professional athlete. As a philosopher, he would know the works of Aristotle (cited in paragraph 15) and be capable of seeing the difference between the role of stage tragedy and bloody athletic contests.

2   *The author makes a comparison between war and football. Do you think this is a fair comparison? Why or why not?*

Answer: Answers will vary.

3   *According to McMurtry, what qualities of our society are reflected in football? What is your opinion of his analysis?*

Answer: In paragraph 14, McMurtry cites a Harvard study that says such qualities as "impersonal acceptance of inflicted injury," the devotion of "organizational goals," the "ability to turn oneself on and off," and the desire to win are prized by our society, especially in business. Students' opinion of the analysis will vary.

4   *In paragraphs 15–18, McMurtry points out—and then rebuts—the belief that football benefits society. Do you believe that football and sports in general are harmful or helpful to society? Explain.*

Answer: Answers will vary.

George Orwell, "A Hanging"

Structure and Technique

1   *Paragraphs 1, 2, and 3 contain vivid descriptions of the people and things surrounding the author on the morning of the execution. What details does he use that appeal to the readers' senses of sight, hearing, and touch? What is the effect of all these details?*

Answer: A few of Orwell's many sight details include "sickly light," "high walls," cells "like small animal cages," the condemned man being a "puny wisp of a man, with a shaven head and vague liquid eyes." Hearing details include "a bugle call, desolately thin" and the "gruff voice" of the superintendent. Touch details include the humid feeling of the "sodden morning of the rains" and the "wet air," and the guards holding the condemned man, "their hands always on him in a careful, caressing grip, as though all the while feeling him to make sure he was there . . . like men handling a fish." The many rich details give readers a vivid sense of the morning and the moments before the execution. In addition, some of the details—a "sickly light, like yellow tinfoil," sheds "like small animal cages," "a bugle call, desolately thin"—set an appropriate mood for the story, one of gloomy sadness.

2   *"A Hanging" takes place in Burma, and Orwell occasionally uses regional terms such as* lathis *and* boxwallah *in the course of his essay. Why do you think Orwell chose to include these foreign terms rather than translate them into English?*

Answer: By using the occasional regional term, Orwell gives some local flavor to the story, emphasizing the story's location and making the story more realistic.

3   *In part, Orwell uses dialogue to tell his story, giving the actual words of numerous individuals. What does the essay gain or lose from this technique? Explain.*

Answer: The superintendent, the jailer, the prisoner, and the Eurasian boy all have distinct personalities that are best communicated by allowing the reader to hear their own words. The direct quotations help us form a much more complete picture of each person involved and his response to the events of the morning. For example, the head jailer's comment in paragraph 4—"Yes sir, yes sir. . . . All iss satisfactorily prepared. The hangman iss waiting. We shall proceed"—shows in a more interesting way than a summary would that his focus is on following orders and pleasing his boss, the superintendent.

4   *In paragraph 10, Orwell provides a series of details about the bodily organs of the condemned man. List these details. How do they relate to Orwell's larger point in "A Hanging"?*

Answer: Orwell points out that the man's bowels were digesting food; that his skin, hair, and nails were all growing; that his eyes perceived the yellow gravel. By emphasizing how alive the man was, Orwell heightens the horror that in a few more moments he will be dead.

Critical Reading and Discussion

1   *Why does everyone stand "aghast" when the stray dog licks the prisoner's face? Why is this incident important?*

Answer: The people are aghast because of the painful contrast between the condemned man on his death march and the ordinary playfulness of the lively dog. The incident is important because it points up the humanity of the prisoner (the dog licks him) and emphasizes the joy, freedom, and life he is losing.

2   *The author has a moment of understanding when the prisoner steps "slightly aside to avoid a puddle on the path" (paragraph 9). What realization does Orwell come to? How is this insight related to the small incident of avoiding a puddle?*

Answer: Orwell realizes that the man is as fully alive as any of the other people in the group and that what they are about to do is horrible. Prior to seeing the man step around the puddle, Orwell was apparently able to think of him merely as "the condemned prisoner" instead of as a fellow living human being who is still concerned about details as mundane as not getting his feet wet.

3   *The character of the superintendent evolves in the course of this narrative. How do the words he speaks (and the tone of voice he speaks them in) reflect the emotional changes he goes through?*

Answer: At first the superintendent is clearly tense, gruffly ordering the head jailer to hurry up with the preparations. His anger at the appearance of the dog also reveals his tension. The superintendent waits with his eyes on the ground as the prisoner cries out his prayer and then "almost fiercely" shouts out the command to hang him. Once the prisoner is dead, however, the superintendent shows how difficult the event was for him by commenting, "Well, that's all for this morning, thank God." Then he becomes almost jolly, clearly relieved that the task is over. He is "genial," asking the other men to join him in a drink of whiskey, and then acknowledges again the horror of the morning by saying, "We could do with [a drink]."

4   *The author's thesis is most clearly stated in paragraph 10: "When I saw the prisoner step aside to avoid the puddle, I saw the mystery, the unspeakable wrongness, of cutting a life short when it is in full tide." Do you agree that capital punishment is always wrong? Explain your answer.*

Answer: Answers will vary.

Russell Baker, "In My Day"

Structure and Technique

1   *The author's thesis is a general point that he derives from his personal family experiences. Where does he first mention this thesis? Why do you think he chose to state his thesis at this point in the piece?*

Answer: Baker states his thesis—that children should recognize their link to the past—in the final paragraph of the essay. Perhaps he does so to allow readers to experience events in the order in which they occurred: he had to first live through the experiences with his mother and his children to come to the conclusion that is his thesis. He may also have saved his thesis for the end to emphasize that he came to this realization too late in his own life, when he was already "forever out of touch" with his mother.

2 *Baker uses repetition and parallel wording—phrases with the same grammatical pattern—in three places: paragraphs 14, 15, and 52–55. Find the instances of these two techniques. What does Baker achieve by using these stylistic elements?*

Answer: In paragraph 14, Baker uses both repetition and parallel wording when he writes, "Determined to speak her mind, determined to have her way, determined to bend those who opposed her." In paragraph 15, he repeats the word "ran" four times and the phrase "she ran" three times. He uses parallel structure as well in paragraph 15 when he writes, "She ran when she made the beds, ran when she set the table," and "victory was not to the lazy, the timid, the slugabed, the drugstore cowboy, the libertine." Finally, in paragraphs 52–55 he repeats the phrase "In my day" four times.

   The author uses parallelism and repetition to emphasize repeated behavior and continuing attitudes: his mother's aggressive determination, her constant activity, and her continuing view of those less active than she, as well as the author's frequent "lectures" to his children comparing his youth and that of his children.

3 *Throughout "In My Day," Baker uses dialogue to narrate conversations that he had with his mother. Locate at least two of these dialogues. What is gained by including these conversations in this essay?*

Answer: Baker quotes conversations with his mother in paragraphs 2–9, 11–13, 16–26, 28–32, and 45–46. Dialogue shows readers what happened by allowing them to witness the conversations. It is thus a more direct and often more interesting method of narration than description. Compare, for example, the following:

- *Dialogue:* "Where's Russell?" she asked one day when I came to visit at the nursing home.

   "I'm Russell," I said.

- *Description:* One day when I visited my mother at the nursing home, she didn't recognize me and asked where I was.

4 *In paragraph 15, Baker presents a series of details about his mother. What do these details illustrate about his mother? How does this description relate to Baker's main point?*

Answer: The details make it clear that she was not only physically energetic but also disapproving of people whom she saw as less hardworking and outspoken than she. This image is the one Baker had as he grew up, the one that formed his long-held opinions of his mother. It relates to his thesis in that it contrasts with the mother he would have known if he had had a better idea of what she and her family were like before he knew her.

Critical Reading and Discussion

1   *In both his own words and those of his mother, the author reveals that she was unhappy during most of the last years of her life. According to the selection, what were the reasons for her unhappiness?*

Answer: In paragraph 40, Baker explains that his mother has a "rage against the weakness, the boredom, and the absence of love that too much age had brought her," some of which she communicates in the letter quoted in paragraph 43 ("I'm just so very tired and lonely").

2   *When his mother's mind began to wander, Baker's first impulse was to "argue her back to reality" (paragraph 16). Later, he instead "tried to travel along with her on those fantastic swoops into the past" (paragraph 44). What does the reading suggest about why he wanted to bring his mother back to reality? And why did he later change his mind?*

Answer: Baker's initial desire to "argue her back to reality" is probably related to his admission that "one thinks of parents differently from other people. Other people can become frail and break, but not parents." He felt a need for his mother to be healthy and strong because he found it hard to admit she was changing and weakening—he states in paragraph 16, "For a time I could not accept the inevitable." He later changed his mind because he realized that her "swoops into the past" brought her more peace and happiness than reality did.

3   *Does Baker believe he has been a good son to his mother? A good father to his children? In your opinion, what does it mean to be a "good son" or a "good father"?*

Answer: Baker is critical of himself both as a son and as a father. His reference to his "infrequent visits" to his mother and his comment that his pep-talk letter to his mother was really "a threat" suggest that he feels guilty that he was not more supportive of her. Likewise, his references to his lecturing of his children and to himself as an "ancient bore" imply that he thinks he could have done a better job of parenting. Students' answers to the last question will vary.

4   *In paragraph 41, Baker says that "one thinks of parents differently from other people. Other people can become frail and break, but not parents." What does he mean? Would this view strengthen—or weaken—people's relationships with their parents or guardians?*

Answer: Answers will vary, but following are some common views on the topics in question 4: For most of us, parents play an extremely powerful role in our lives as we are growing up. As a result, it is easy for us to form the impression, as illogical as it may be, that they are invulnerable. Even when we resent them, we expect them always to be there and be strong. Many of us find it threatening when our parents show weakness, whether because of age, illness, or adversity. We don't know how to cope when our parents need us to become their caretakers instead of the other way around. If adult children cannot accept their parents' frailty, they are likely to withdraw from a parent in his or her time of need.

Haven Kimmel, "A Legendary Moment"

Structure and Technique

1   *Find instances in the essay where Kimmel uses (or quotes someone as using) exaggeration. Why might a writer choose to exaggerate? What effect does Kimmel's exaggeration have?*

Answer: Examples of exaggeration are

"[I]f he'd married a woman who fought him they probably would have killed each other." (Paragraph 1)

"[The bedroom door] sent my father flying headfirst into the closet about sixty-four miles an hour." (Paragraph 3)

"Mom later claimed they must have evaporated into the walls." (Paragraph 4)

"Because otherwise I'll wait till you're asleep; sew you into the bed; and beat you to death with a frying pan." (Paragraph 8)

Writers use exaggeration for effect. The effect is often humorous as well as descriptive. While Kimmel could have written, "The door knocked my father into the closet," the sentence "The door sent my father flying headfirst into the closet about sixty-four miles an hour" more strongly expresses the idea that the door hit him very forcefully. The exaggerated idea that he was flying "sixty-four miles an hour" helps explain his very angry and indignant response.

2   *What method of introduction—anecdote, question, or broad-to-narrow—does Kimmel use? Why do you think she chose this way to begin her essay?*

Answer: Broad-to-narrow. Kimmel begins with a broad idea—that her parents rarely fought—and narrows the topic to a particular time that they did fight. Beginning this way helps the reader understand that this episode was particularly memorable because it was so unusual.

3   *Using Kimmel's description as a guide, draw a sketch that shows what happened if her parents' bedroom door and closet door were opened at the same time. Why does she go into such detail in order to describe the relationship between the two doors?*

Answer: Kimmel wants the reader to be able to vividly picture the incident, which occurred only because the doors were inconveniently close to one another. Understanding the relationship of the doors allows the reader to see that getting hit in the back with a door was a constant potential problem in the room—and one that could understandably irritate the victim.

4   *Kimmel never mentions the subject of her parents' original "actual, vocal argument." Why do you think she chose not to? Would the story have been stronger if she had explained what that argument was about?*

Answer: The subject of the original argument was overshadowed by what happened next. It became relatively unimportant. To have gone into detail about the original argument would have shifted the focus away from the story Kimmel really wanted to tell.

Critical Reading and Discussion

1   *You might expect a memoir about an author's parents fighting to have a dark, threatening, unhappy tone. But Haven Kimmel presents this incident in quite a different light. How does she seem to feel about what happened? What words or phrases give you clues to her viewpoint?*

Answers: Kimmel seems to regard the incident as interesting, amusing, and even admirable, certainly not as traumatic or disturbing. Her first reference to it as a "great, legendary moment" indicates how she regards it. Her humorous touches, such as referring to her pregnant mother's "former hips" and her mother hitting her father on both cheeks, "like a good Christian," also indicate her attitude.

2   *Do you think Kimmel's opinion about what happened between her parents would have been different if her father had slapped her mother? Would your opinion change? Explain your answer.*

Answer: One suspects that Kimmel would have been more critical if her father, who she describes as having a "wicked bad temper," had slapped her mother. While there are certainly physically violent women, the great majority of domestic violence cases involve a man hitting a woman, and such violence is usually part of a pattern of abuse and intimidation. In contrast, Kimmel describes this incident as a highly unusual one, not part of a pattern; she says that "afterward, there was never a threat of violence between them again" (paragraph 8).

Answers to the second part of the question will vary. Students may be critical of the story, saying that a woman striking a man is just as unacceptable as a man hitting a woman.

3   *Kimmel uses figurative language to compare her father, first, to a bullet, and later, to a bull. What characteristics of a bullet and a bull does she suggest he shares? Later, why does she say that her mother acted "like a good Christian"? Is that comparison meant seriously or humorously?*

Answer: Kimmel suggests that her father shot out of the closet with the speed of a bullet. Later, she suggests that he seems as angry and aggressive as a bull, a notoriously dangerous animal.

The mention of her mother acting "like a good Christian" is intended humorously. It refers to a biblical passage in which Jesus says, "But if any one strikes you on the right cheek, turn to him the other also." Jesus was telling his followers to *receive* blows on both cheeks, not to inflict them.

4 *The author describes this incident as "a great, legendary moment" that she had heard about all her life. Why do you think the incident was so important to the family? Do you have any family stories that people tell over and over again? Why do you think they are important to your family?*

Answer: The incident was important in Kimmel's family because it was so unusual and dramatic. It also, as she writes, was "a touchstone moment" in her parents' marriage, which established that her mother would not be intimidated. Answers to the second part of the question will vary.

Beth Johnson, "The Professor Is a Dropout"

Structure and Technique

1 *Johnson begins the essay by listing Lupe Quintanilla's accomplishments, then revealing that Quintanilla was once classified as retarded. What introductory technique is Johnson employing? Why is it effective here?*

Answer: Johnson is starting with a situation (Lupe's many accomplishments) that is the opposite of what she then reveals (that Lupe was once labeled as retarded). It is a particularly effective technique here because the revelation that Lupe was thought to be retarded is such a surprising one.

2 *Paragraphs 3–11 are devoted to the first fifteen years of Lupe's life. But the next decade or so is covered in only two paragraphs (12–13). Why might Johnson have presented Lupe's earlier life in so much more detail? Do you agree with her decision?*

Answer: The first fifteen years of Lupe's life are described in some detail because it was during that time period that several significant events occurred. Those events set Lupe on what seemed to be her permanent path in life—as a traditional, old-fashioned Mexican girl without formal education who could speak only Spanish. During the next decade or so, nothing occurred to vary that pattern, so it could be described quite briefly. Answers to the final part of the question will vary.

3 *In paragraph 2, Johnson writes that "[Lupe's] school records state that she is retarded. . . ." But in the next sentence, she writes, "How did Lupe Quintanilla, 'retarded' nonlearner, become Dr. Quintanilla, respected educator?" Why does Johnson put the word "retarded" in quotation marks in the second sentence, but not in the first? What is she implying? Can you find another place where Johnson makes similar use of quotation marks?*

Answer: In the first instance, Johnson is simply reporting what Lupe's school records say. But in the second, she is herself using the word "retarded" to refer to Lupe. Because she knows that Lupe is not in fact retarded, she puts the word in quotation marks to call attention to the fact that she is using the word ironically—that she knows it is inaccurate.

In paragraph 25, after describing how the college registrar told Lupe she had to manage a full course load or not come back, Johnson writes: "With that 'encouragement,' Lupe began a semester that was part nightmare, part dream come true." Again, Johnson puts "encouragement" in quotation marks to make it clear that the registrar's words were not, in fact, encouraging at all.

4 *At one point, Johnson switches from the topic of Lupe's success in college to the topic of the challenges that continued to face her children in school. In what paragraph does she make that switch? What transitional words does she use to alert the reader to her new direction?*

Answer: The switch occurs in paragraph 35. She uses the transitional words "Even though."

Critical Reading and Discussion

1 *In the course of the essay, what characteristics and attitudes does Lupe suggest are typical of Hispanic culture? Does she seem sympathetic, critical, or neutral about those qualities or attitudes? How has she dealt with cultural expectations in her own life?*

Answer: Lupe makes several references to Hispanic, and particularly Mexican, characteristics and attitudes. She describes her grandfather as "stern and authoritarian, as Mexican culture demanded" but also says that her grandparents were extremely kind to her. After she married, she followed her grandmother's example in being a very traditional Mexican wife, devoting herself to her husband's and children's welfare. She describes Hispanic parents as traditionally being reluctant to interfere with their children's schooling, believing that such interference would be disrespectful of the teacher.

Lupe seems to regard such traditional Hispanic attitudes with affection and sympathy. For instance, despite her course load at school, she continued to carry out what she saw as her traditional wifely and motherly duties, coming home to prepare her husband's and grandparents' meals, and doing all the housework. At the same time, though, she seems to support working around such expectations when they interfere with a person's growth and development. She has taken a number of very bold and nontraditional steps, beginning with going to talk with her children's teachers, persevering in her search for a way to learn English, enrolling in college, disputing a teacher's decision to put her son in woodworking class, and so on.

2   *How has Lupe handled the question of what language to use with her children? If you grew up in a two-language household, how did your family deal with the issue? How would you approach the issue with children of your own?*

Answer: When Lupe was concerned about her children's ability to function in English, she spoke only English with them in order to encourage their development in that language. Once they were fluent in English, she reverted to Spanish at home so that they would not forget their first language. Answers to the second part of the question will vary.

3   *Do you think Lupe's grandfather was right in allowing her to quit school? What factors do you imagine might have gone into his decision?*

Answer: Answers will vary. From the perspective of a modern-day North American, it might seem irresponsible to allow a twelve-year-old to quit school. But her grandfather was an elderly man with traditional Mexican values. In all likelihood, he did not see education as being essential to a woman; he probably expected her to be content being a wife and mother.

4   *Lupe credits her fellow Hispanic students with giving her valuable support in college. Is there anyone in your life—a teacher, family member, or friend— who has helped you through challenging times in your education? Explain what obstacles you faced and how this person helped you overcome them.*

Answer: Answers will vary.

Deems Taylor, "The Monster"

Structure and Technique

1   *Taylor avoids revealing the name of his subject until paragraph 12. Why do you think he made this choice? And why does he wait until paragraph 14 to balance the negative information about Wagner's behavior with positive comments about his musical works?*

Answer: By withholding his subject's name, the author strengthens readers' interest: The strong picture of a nameless monstrous person makes us more and more curious about who the monster is. In addition, by at first causing readers to despise the "monster," only to tell them their conclusion is wrong, the author adds drama that emphasizes his thesis.

2   *Why do you think Taylor chose to title his essay "The Monster"?*

Answer: The answer lies in his final sentence, in which he implies that Wagner was hardly a human being at all. By the usual standards of human behavior, Wagner was monstrous. But Taylor suggests that only a superhuman "monster" could accomplish all that Wagner did as a composer.

3   *What wording in paragraph 2 is echoed in paragraph 13? How has it been changed when used the second time? What is the effect of this change?*

Answer: The wording in paragraph 2 is this: "He believed himself to be one of the greatest dramatists in the world, one of the greatest thinkers, and one of the greatest composers." This wording causes the reader to strongly doubt the man's opinion of himself. In paragraph 13, the wording is this: "He *was* one of the world's great dramatists; he *was* a great thinker; he *was* one of the most stupendous musical geniuses. . . ." The effect is to let the reader know, in a startling and emphatic fashion, that Wagner's very high opinion of himself was, after all, justified.

4   *Taylor uses unexpected wording in some of his descriptions. What is surprising about the wording in the following excerpts, and how is the meaning affected by that wording?*

"He was almost innocent of any sense of responsibility." (Paragraph 7)

"He had a genius for making enemies." (Paragraph 11)

"There is greatness about his worst mistakes." (Paragraph 15)

Answer: We usually think of "innocent" as referring to a harmless, childlike quality, so it is an unusual word to describe a person's lack of responsibility. The use of the word makes us think of Wagner less as an irresponsible adult than as a sort of overgrown child who can be forgiven for shortcomings. "Genius" usually has the positive connotations of a great gift or talent; so to speak of Wagner's "genius for making enemies" is surprising. It suggests again that Wagner was such an unusual man that normal standards of behavior were beyond him. And the idea that even his mistakes were "great" suggests that no matter what Wagner did, he was incapable of writing mediocre music.

Critical Reading and Discussion

1   *When Taylor writes in paragraph 5, "He had a composer's voice," what is he implying about Wagner's singing? What makes you think so?*

Answer: Taylor is implying that Wagner sang poorly. We can conclude this from Taylor's previous statement that Wagner "played the piano like a composer, in the worst sense of what that implied." In other words, the author is reminding us that a composer's talent is composing, not necessarily playing the piano or singing.

2   *In what ways, according to Taylor, was Wagner like a six-year-old child (paragraph 6)? Like an Indian rajah (paragraph 8)?*

Answer: Wagner was like a child in his sudden, self-absorbed mood changes. He was like an Indian rajah in his grand lifestyle. The word "rajah" not only emphasizes Wagner's lifestyle; it also underscores the contrast between a rajah's income and Wagner's.

3   *From what sources does Taylor imply that he gathered his negative information about Wagner? Why does the author include information about those sources?*

Answer: The author suggests in paragraph 12 that he consulted newspapers, police reports, the testimony of people who knew Wagner, Wagner's own letters, and Wagner's autobiography. By naming those sources, the author answers any doubts readers might have about the hard-to-believe details of Wagner's behavior.

4   *Do you agree with Taylor's conclusion that Wagner's failings should be overlooked? Do unusually gifted people deserve to be held to different standards from the rest of us? Can you think of any gifted people of our time who are held to different standards?*

Answer: Answers will vary. However, in thinking about their answers, students might consider sports and entertainment stars.

Casey Banas, "Why Are Students Turned Off?"

Structure and Technique

1   *Which method of introduction—broad-to-narrow, anecdote, or questions— does Banas use in his essay? Why do you think she chose this approach?*

Answer: Banas begins with a brief anecdote about Ellen Glanz lying about her homework. He uses the anecdote to draw his readers in by making them curious about who Ellen is and why she lied.

2   *List the time transitions that Banas uses in paragraph 12. How do they help Banas make his point?*

Answer: He uses the transitions "since," "before," "now," "before," and "now." They help make clear the contrast in Glanz's attitudes before and after her time as a student. That contrast, in turn, supports the author's main idea: "teachers and students . . . are in separate worlds and have an ongoing power struggle."

3   *Throughout "Why Are Students Turned Off?" Banas shifts between summarizing Ellen Glanz's words and quoting Glanz directly. Find an instance in the essay in which both direct and indirect quotations are used in the same paragraph. What does Banas gain or lose from using this technique? (Refer to pages 508–511 for definitions and examples of direct and indirect quotations.)*

Answer: In paragraph 11, for instance, Banas both paraphrases Glanz and quotes her directly. Paraphrasing allows Banas to express Glanz's thoughts concisely, while the occasional direct quotation lets the reader hear Glanz's own voice when she expresses herself especially clearly or memorably.

4   *Parallel structures are often used to emphasize similar information. They can create a smooth, readable style. For example, note the series of -ing verbs in the following sentence from paragraph 2: " . . . students **doing** as little as necessary to pass tests and get good grades, students **using** ruses to avoid assignments, and students **manipulating** teachers to do the work for them." Find two other uses of parallelism, one in paragraph 4 and one in paragraph 7.*

Answer: Paragraph 4: "I considered my options: Confess openly to the teacher, copy someone else's sheet, or make up an excuse." (Each phrase begins with a verb in the same tense).

Paragraph 7: " . . . figuring out how to best present an idea, thinking about whom to call on, whom to draw out, whom to shut up; how to get students involved, how to make my point clearer, how to respond . . ." (The first series of parallel phrases begins with an *-ing* verb, the second with "whom to . . . ," and the third with "how to . . . .")

Critical Reading and Discussion

1   *After reading this essay, what do you think Glanz's attitude is? Is she pro- or anti-teacher? Pro- or anti-student? Provide evidence for your position.*

Answer: Student answers will vary, but it is apparent that Glanz wants to be supportive of both teachers and students. She sees an educational system that has evolved in forms that damage both the teachers' ability to teach and the students' ability to learn.

2   *Banas suggests that many students are in school to get good grades—not to learn. Explain whether or not you agree with this assessment. Do you find that getting a good grade isn't always the same as really learning?*

Answer: Answers will vary.

3   *The author ends with Glanz's view of "the larger issue": "We must be sure, ourselves, that what we are teaching is worth knowing." What was taught in your high school classes that you feel is worth knowing or not worth knowing?*

Explain why. Also, what is being taught in your college classes that you feel is worth knowing or not worth knowing, and why?

Answer: Answers will vary.

4 *Much of this essay contrasts the behavior of students with that of teachers. In what ways does Glanz see their behavior and views differing? What do you think each group should be doing differently?*

Answer: Glanz sees students avoiding assignments and teachers then doing the work for them in class. She sees students sitting passively in class while teachers are active. She sees students regarding their teachers as boring, while the teachers are (in their own lives) very interesting. She sees students avoiding responsibility for their own learning and teachers assuming they are demanding too much. And she sees students doing only what they feel is necessary to get a good grade, including cheating, and teachers unaware of the big gap between them and students. Students will have their own opinions about what each group should be doing differently.

Ann McClintock, "Propaganda Techniques in Today's Advertising"

Structure and Technique

1 *In paragraph 1, McClintock's choice of words reveals her attitudes toward both propagandists and the public. What specific words reveal her attitudes, and what attitudes do they represent?*

Answer: McClintock describes propagandists as "seducers" and "brainwashers." She refers to their "alluring images," their "tricks," and their "charm." She describes the public as "content" and "eager . . . victims." Her choice of words makes it clear that she thinks propagandists are untrustworthy and interested in taking unfair advantage of a too-trusting public.

2 *What key term does McClintock define in paragraph 2? Why does she define it here? Where else in the essay does she use the technique of definition?*

Answer: She defines the term "propaganda." She places the definition close to the beginning because it is so essential to the reader's understanding of the rest of her essay. Other points at which McClintock uses definition are in paragraphs 5, 6, 9, 12, 16, 18, and 21. In each of those paragraphs, she defines a particular propaganda technique.

3 *McClintock uses parentheses in two lists, the ones in paragraphs 7 and 19. What purpose do these parentheses serve?*

Answer: Paragraph 7 lists "high-sounding but basically empty phrases." The author uses parentheses to add comments that reveal the emptiness of those listed phrases. Paragraph 19 lists claims that include "weasel words." The author uses parentheses to show just how insubstantial those weasel words are.

4 *McClintock provides abundant examples throughout her essay. Why does she provide so many examples? What does she accomplish with this technique?*

Answer: McClintock's many examples, drawn from the television and print ads we all see every day, clarify her definitions and demonstrate that propaganda techniques are truly a factor in everyday life. The examples make the reader more aware of the effects of propaganda on decisions he or she makes.

Critical Reading and Discussion

1 *Some of the propaganda techniques listed in the selection have contrasting appeals. How do name-calling and glittering generalities contrast with each other? Testimonials and plain folks?*

Answer: Name-calling appeals to the instincts of fear, anger, and mistrust. Name-calling propaganda encourages the public to reject something or someone. Glittering generalities, on the other hand, appeal to the public's positive emotions: love, attraction, patriotism. The public is asked to accept the thing or person advertised by associating it with those emotions.

Testimonials depend on the public's interest in or affection for celebrities—people ordinary viewers don't know but admire and see as bigger and more important than themselves. By contrast, plain folks advertising is based on the idea that members of the public like to see ordinary people—people like themselves—in the products and services they buy.

2 *Why are ads that use the bandwagon approach so effective? What ads have you seen recently that use that approach?*

Answer: The bandwagon technique is effective because of the human need to be part of a group. We feel safe and secure when we are surrounded by people who agree with us about something—even something as trivial as what frozen coffee cake is best ("Nobody doesn't like Sara Lee"). Answers to the second question will vary.

3 *The author states, "Americans, adults and children alike, are being seduce" (paragraph 1). What might be the differences between the ways adults and children react to the seductions of advertising?*

Answer: Answers will vary.

4 *McClintock states, "We are victims, content—even eager—to be victimized" (paragraph 1). Do you agree? Is this article likely to change how you view ads in the future? Why or why not?*

Answer: Answers will vary.

Beth Johnson, "Bombs Bursting in Air"

Structure and Technique

1 *Johnson begins her essay with a narrative of an evening at her son's sports event. At what point does she make the transition into the body of her essay? Which words or phrases does she use to make this transition?*

Answer: The transition occurs at the beginning of paragraph 3. There, Johnson uses the words "Bombs indeed" to make the transition from the "bombs" mentioned in the lyrics of the national anthem to "bombs" of another kind.

2 *Foreshadowing is a technique an author sometimes uses to hint at something that has not yet been revealed. Find an example of foreshadowing in paragraph 2. Where, later in the essay, does she return to this subject? What is the effect of this foreshadowing?*

Answer: The author foreshadows by writing of "[n]ews that reached me today" without revealing what that news was. In the following paragraph (3), she reveals the news and how it was conveyed. The foreshadowing heightens the readers' interest—we read on, curious to learn about the "news."

3 *Why do you think the author delays telling about the outcome of Shannon's surgery until the end of the essay? How would the essay be different if she had revealed early on that the surgery was successful?*

Answer: By saving the results of Shannon's surgery for the end, Johnson accomplishes several things. She creates a balanced structure for the essay, beginning and ending it with Shannon's story. She helps the reader experience a little of the suspense and worry that Shannon's friends and family went through as they awaited the results of the surgery. If Johnson had immediately told the outcome of the surgery, the way Shannon's illness qualified as a "bomb" in people's lives would have been less evident.

4 *Note the parallel phrasing in paragraph 3: "We'd . . . talked of Furby and Scooby-Doo and Tootsie Rolls. Now her parents were hurriedly learning a new vocabulary—CAT scans and pediatric neurosurgery and frontal lobe." Why might the author have used parallel structure here? What is the effect?*

Answer: By balancing pleasant childish words against frightening medical terminology, Johnson heightens the contrast between a child's everyday world and Shannon's situation. The effect of this contrast is to give the reader a sense of the frightening shift in concerns that Shannon's parents had to make.

Critical Reading and Discussion

1 *The author mentions bombs in the introduction and then uses bomb symbolically in other parts of the essay. What are some of the places in which* *she uses that symbol, and what does she intend it to mean? Do you think it is an effective symbol?*

Answer: Johnson uses the word "bomb" and bomb-related imagery (tremors, shock waves, explosions, shrapnel, bomb shelter) frequently—for example, in paragraphs 3, 6, 9, 10, 11, 13, and 15. The symbol represents those upsetting and even tragic incidents that occur unavoidably in every life. Answers will vary as to its effectiveness, but students may feel it is a fitting symbol for incidents which shake us badly and whose aftereffects can be far-reaching.

2   *In paragraph 12, Johnson mentions incidents involving her first love, a professor, her father, and her marriage. What do these examples have in common? Why do you think Johnson included them?*

Answer: Each example is of a life incident that has both sweet and sad memories for the author. She includes the examples to demonstrate that life is filled with experiences that are not simply "good" or "bad" but a mixture of both.

3   *Judging from the rest of the essay, what does Johnson mean by saying that "the greater our investment in life, the larger the target we create" (paragraph 13)?*

Answer: Johnson focuses on relationships with others, so we can deduce that she uses "investment in life" to mean an emotional commitment to others. Once we are committed to people, they may hurt us, or we may feel sad when they experience misfortune. Therefore, the more people we care about and the deeper our caring, the greater a "target" we are for such painful experiences.

4   *Adults sometimes sentimentally think of childhood as a time of happy, carefree innocence, as the author suggests in paragraph 8. Yet, during childhood, most of us witnessed events that began to make us aware that life was not always happy or fair. What such events do you remember? What impression did they make on you?*

Answer: Answers will vary according to students' experience.

Joan Dunayer, "Here's to Your Health"

Structure and Technique

1   *What method of introduction does Dunayer use? What effect do you think she hoped to achieve with this introduction?*

Answer: She uses an anecdote. By telling a brief story about Tod's experience, she puts a human face on the larger idea that alcohol abuse is linked to societal pressure. The anecdote also sets the tone for Dunayer's thesis by showing the potential danger of even small amounts of alcohol.

2 *Dunayer begins her criticism of alcohol with "Part of the myth is . . . ." (See the first sentence of paragraph 4.) What addition transitions does she use to introduce each of the three other parts of the myth (in the first sentences of paragraphs 6, 8, and 10)? What is gained by the use of these transitions?*

Answer: The three addition transitions are "another," "also," and "finally." Each transition makes the reader aware that one element of the myth is being introduced.

3 *The body of Dunayer's essay is made up of four pairs of paragraphs (paragraphs 4 and 5; 6 and 7; 8 and 9; 10 and 11). What is the relationship between the paragraphs in each pair? In which of the two paragraphs does Dunayer present her own perspective? Why do you think she puts her own perspective in that paragraph?*

Answer: In the first paragraph of each pair, Dunayer presents one part of the alcohol myth. She begins each second paragraph with a topic sentence that represents her perspective. She then goes on to support her topic sentence with a series of facts. For example, below is the topic sentence of paragraph 5; it represents her perspective, which contradicts what the ad in paragraph 4 suggests about whiskey.

Contrary to what the liquor company would have us believe, drinking is more closely related to lack of success than to achievements.

She then follows that sentence with supporting facts.

By presenting her perspective *after* describing each part of the myth, Dunayer makes her points more dramatically: She sets up an appealing image in the first paragraph of each pair only to knock it down with force in the second one.

4 *In her essay, Dunayer provides vivid descriptions of alcohol advertisements, particularly in paragraphs 4 and 6. What vivid details does she provide? How do these details support her main point?*

Answer: In paragraph 4, she describes in detail the print ad showing two prosperous-looking businessmen in a restaurant, surrounded by fine crystal, velvet draperies, and spotless linen. In paragraph 6, she provides details about a beach scene: a young, beautiful, sexy woman; a young muscular man enticing her with a cold beer. By providing such detailed description, Dunayer makes the reader very much aware of the premise (alcohol will make you successful; alcohol will make you sexually attractive) behind such ads.

Critical Reading and Discussion

1 *Dunayer presents and then rebuts four "myths" about alcohol. What are these four myths? According to Dunayer, what is the reality behind each myth?*

Answer: (1) Alcohol will make you professionally successful. In fact, says Dunayer, alcohol is frequently tied to low achievement and poverty. (2) Alcohol will make you sexually attractive. Dunayer says that alcohol actually lowers one's hormones and can lead to impotence and infertility. (3) Alcohol and sports mix well. Dunayer points out that alcohol slows the reflexes, interferes with the eyes' ability to focus, and increases the likelihood of various serious diseases. (4) Alcohol brings families closer together. In fact, Dunayer writes, alcohol is frequently involved in domestic violence, suicide, and birth defects.

2   *Dunayer concludes, "'Here's to your health' rings with a terrible irony when it is accompanied by the clink of liquor glasses" (paragraph 12). What is the "terrible irony" she refers to? How does this irony—already signaled in her essay's title—relate to her main point?*

Answer: The irony is that alcohol, rather than promoting one's health, is often tied to illness and misery. The irony is also implied in her main point—that while advertising myths promise us that alcohol will improve our lives, it is far more likely to have destructive effects.

3   *Do you think Dunayer's essay is one-sided or balanced? Explain. What additional points could be used to support her point or to rebut it?*

Answer: The essay is one-sided in the sense that Dunayer does not include opinions from people who disagree with her. Other points she might have used to support her argument include the widespread idea among young people that using alcohol makes them seem more adult. Rebuttals of Dunayer's argument could include the ideas that many people use alcohol responsibly and that the problem is not with the product itself but with irresponsible people's misuse of it.

4   *Advertisers often create myths or use false ideas to get people to buy their products. Besides alcohol ads, what are some other examples of manipulative or deceptive advertising? Do you think advertisers should be permitted to use such tactics to sell products?*

Answer: Answers will vary.

Brian O'Keeney, "How to Make It in College, Now That You're Here"

Structure and Technique

1   *O'Keeney uses a highly structured format in his essay. What are some of the features of this format? Why do you think O'Keeney structured his essay in this way?*

Answer: O'Keeney divides the body of his essay into four sections; each section begins with a boldfaced question that might be asked by a college student, followed by the author's answer or answers to the question. His answers to two of the questions take the form of a numbered list. He uses such a structure in order to give students very specific, easy-to-remember advice.

2   *Does the author clearly state his thesis? If so, where is it stated, and how?*

Answer: The thesis is found in paragraph 2: "On the basis of my own experience as a final-year student, and after dozens of interviews with successful students, I've worked out a no-fail system for coping with college."

3   *What method of introduction does the author use in the section on personal problems (starting with paragraph 19)? What is the value of using this method?*

Answer: O'Keeney begins the section with two anecdotes, the stories of Roger and Marian. The value of such anecdotes is that they vividly illustrate the kinds of personal problems a student might have and the toll those problems might take on him or her.

4   *Throughout his essay, O'Keeney addresses his audience in the second person— using the word* you. *How does such a technique advance his main point?*

Answer: In using the second person, the author makes it clear that his "no-fail system for coping with college" was written for students to read, emphasizing that to succeed, students must take his advice personally.

Critical Reading and Discussion

1   *What, according to O'Keeney, is the secret of getting good grades? Have you used any of O'Keeney's study methods? If so, how useful do you think they have been for you? Are there any that you haven't used, but might try? Explain your answer.*

Answer: O'Keeney says the key to good grades is effective study techniques. He provides eight tips for effective studying: (1) Set up a study place; (2) get into a studious frame of mind; (3) reward yourself; (4) skim textbook readings first; (5) take notes; (6) review by "talking to yourself"; (7) take a break before you're exhausted; and (8) take a skills course if you need it. Answers to the last three questions will vary.

2   *What does O'Keeney recommend students do in order to manage their time and responsibilities more effectively? Which of these suggestions are you most likely to use? Which are you least likely to use? Why?*

Answer: O'Keeney's recommendations include keeping a monthly calendar, establishing a study schedule, and making to-do lists. Students' answers will vary as to the techniques they might use and why.

3 *What is the secret the author says got him through college? What do you think is the most helpful or important suggestion the author makes in the selection? Give reasons for your choice.*

Answer: The author cites "to-do lists" as the technique that was most important for him. Students' answers to the rest of the question will vary.

4 *Do you agree with the author that Roger and Marian should stay in school? Are there any situations in which it would be better for students to quit school or leave, at least temporarily? Explain, giving examples to support your answer.*

Answer: Answers will vary.

David Daniels, "College Lectures: Is Anybody Listening?"

Structure and Technique

1 *Daniels begins his essay with an anecdote about a former teacher of his. How does this introduction relate to his thesis?*

Answer: The anecdote is an extreme example of a college teacher who seemed unaware of whether his students were listening to him or not. The professor serves as a caricature of the type of teaching Daniels is criticizing.

2 *Does Daniels directly state his thesis? If so, where is it stated?*

Answer: Daniels states his thesis at the end of paragraph 4: "The time is long overdue for us to abandon the lecture system and turn to methods that really work."

3 *In describing Mary's classroom experience (paragraphs 5–7), Daniels provides numerous details. What are some of these details? How do they relate to the essay's main idea?*

Answer: Some of the details provided are the huge class size, the lack of a roll call, the professor's ancient notes, the lack of opportunity for student feedback, and the absence of quizzes. The details all contribute to the idea that lecture-heavy classes do a poor job of involving the student in the subject and stimulating his or her thinking.

4 *Daniels's essay is an argument against the lecture system of education. What argumentation techniques does he employ? (See pages 319–322 for information on argumentation.)*

Answer: Daniels uses four of the argumentation techniques explained in Chapter 16, "Argumentation," pages 319–338:

(1) *Point out common ground.* Daniels points out common ground between him and schools that support lectures. In paragraph 8, he admits that many schools supplement lectures with discussion groups and that some classes, such as first-year English, are relatively small.

(2) *Acknowledge differing viewpoints.* Daniels acknowledges (but does not support) viewpoints that differ from his. In paragraph 13, he states that administrators like lectures because they "can cram far more students into a lecture hall than into a discussion class." He adds in the same paragraph that teachers and students find lectures easier because students can sit back and be passive and teachers can "engage in intellectual exhibitionism."

(3) *Grant the merits of differing viewpoints when appropriate.* Daniels grants the merits of opposing views in paragraph 15, where he states that lectures are "economically necessary" and also "spring from a tradition in a setting that rightly values tradition for its own sake."

(4) *Rebut differing views.* Daniels rebuts the support for lecture classes for first- and second-year students by stating the virtues of smaller classes, which are listed in paragraph 14: smaller classes force students to become more active, students' listening skills improve, professors do a better job, and tests demand analysis and synthesis instead of "empty memorization." And while Daniels supports the tradition of lectures in paragraph 15, he immediately argues against their use in the first two years of college.

Critical Reading and Discussion

1   *Daniels states that "listening intelligently is hard work" (paragraph 9) and "Active learning . . . is far more beneficial for those who have not yet fully learned how to learn" (paragraph 10). Why might Daniels feel that listening is so hard? And why does he feel that active learning is so good?*

Answer: In paragraph 10, Daniels mentions that listening actively involves special techniques, including these two: "trying to anticipate the speaker's next point" or "taking notes selectively." We can assume that he feels it takes time and practice to learn such techniques. In discussing active learning in paragraph 10, Daniels mentions several types: writing essays, performing experiments, and having work evaluated by an instructor. He obviously feels that these types of active work involve students in ways they are not ready to be involved in as listeners.

2   *In paragraph 8, Daniels acknowledges that he has exaggerated Mary's negative classroom experience, saying, "I admit this picture is overdrawn." Does this admission strengthen or weaken his argument? Explain.*

Answer: The case could be made that the admission strengthens Daniels's argument. By admitting that he is exaggerating slightly, Daniels can point out that many classes do have most if not all of the negative aspects of Mary's class. It is also psychologically sound to admit a shortcoming of one's argument, as it helps establish the writer as a reasonable person.

3   *According to Daniels, the lecture system harms professors by reducing feedback from students to a minimum. What is useful about feedback from students?*

Answer: If students' comments indicate they don't understand something, the teacher can then do something to help students improve their understanding. Students' comments may also help teachers decide which activities and materials are effective and ineffective. Also, the knowledge that their view counts in class may motivate students to get involved with class work.

4   *How do your experiences in both lecture classes and smaller classes compare with Daniels's descriptions? As a student, which type of class do you prefer? Why? If you were an instructor, which type of class would you prefer to teach? Why?*

Answer: Answers will vary.

Daniel A. Sugarman, "Seven Ways to Keep the Peace at Home"

Structure and Technique

1   *For the essay as a whole, what method of introduction—broad-to-narrow, anecdote, or questions—does the author use? What method does he use to begin section 1? Section 2? Section 3?*

Answer: He begins the essay with an anecdote. Sections 1 and 2 also begin with anecdotes; section 3 begins with a question.

2   *Sugarman supports his main points in several ways. One way is with examples. What examples does he use to support his first step, "Give Up the Myth of the Perfect Family"? How much space is given to each of those examples? What other type of support is used in paragraph 11?*

Answer: The first example for "Give Up the Myth of the Perfect Family" is the unhappy teenager, whom Sugarman describes in just two sentences. He uses the teenager as an introduction to the false idea of a "perfect family." The second example is of the Martin family, a more detailed account covering four paragraphs. The Martin family shows how destructive it is to expect oneself or others to be perfect family members.

In paragraph 11, Sugarman supports his point about the perfect family with expert testimony showing that "happy homes" aren't as important as people may think, and "troubled homes" aren't as bad as people may think.

3   *How does Sugarman organize and present his main supporting details? What do his methods achieve?*

Answer: Sugarman organizes his main supporting details by presenting them as numbered steps in boldface. This has the effect of helping the reader to remember (and easily review) his points—while the selection is several pages long, there are only seven main supporting points to remember. To further help the reader understand and remember his points, Sugarman provides a brief summary of each point before going on to the next one. For instance, before presenting his second step, he reviews point 1 in a single sentence that makes up paragraph 12.

4   *Throughout his essay, Sugarman alternates between quoting people directly and reporting indirectly what they said. Should he have used only direct quotations? Should he have used only indirect quotations? Why or why not?*

Answer: Student opinions will vary, but in general a mix of direct and indirect quotations is desirable. Direct quotations are called for when a speaker's words are particularly memorable or to the point. Indirect quotations are preferable when an author's paraphrase can get the point across more meaningfully than the speaker's own words.

Critical Reading and Discussion

1   *According to Sugarman, who is more to blame for family problems: parents or children? Give examples from the selection to support your point.*

Answer: Sugarman implies that children's bad behavior is often a response to parents' unresolved tensions or issues. Some examples: The little girl became a hypochondriac in response to her parents' busyness. Frank Martin was acting out because of his parents' self-hatred. Lucille was using drugs and sex to escape from her parents' use of her as a middleman.

2   *In section 4, what does Sugarman mean by the term "blueprint"? What does he suggest is the way to avoid "a collision course" between parents with a blueprint and a child with different plans for himself or herself? What blueprint did your parents have for you, and how does it compare with your own goals for yourself?*

Answer: A blueprint is a "secret master plan" parents have for a child's life. Sugarman states that avoiding a clash with their children over those blueprints requires "understanding and flexibility," the wisdom to revise their blueprints "so that they incorporate the child's realistic needs and aptitudes." Students' reports on their parents' blueprints will, of course, vary.

3   *Sugarman states that people often "feel they must hide their feelings" from family members. Why do you think it is sometimes difficult for family members to be honest with one another? Do you agree with Sugarman that an important way of reducing family tensions is "to send honest communication"? Or are there times when it is best not to be totally honest? Explain.*

Answer: Answers will vary, but here are some reasons family members might hide their feelings from one another: They are confused about their own feelings and so unable to express them clearly; they are afraid their real feelings will anger or hurt someone else; or they wish to hurt another person by refusing to share their feelings.

4   *In section 5, Sugarman discusses family contracts. What does he mean by the word "contract"? Describe any contracts that exist between members of families you're familiar with.*

Answer: Sugarman uses the word "contract" to refer to an unspoken, unrecognized agreement (as between Tom and Gina in their early years) or an agreement between people who are aware of it (as with the husband and wife in paragraph 33). Students will have various answers about families they're familiar with.

Mary Sherry, "In Praise of the F Word"

Structure and Technique

1   *In current vocabulary, "the F word" usually refers to something other than "fail." Why do you think Mary Sherry used the term in her title, rather than simply using "fail" or "failure"? What effect does her title have on the reader?*

Answer: "The F word" usually refers to a common obscenity. The title intrigues readers, who probably initially think Sherry will somehow be praising that obscenity. Her choice to use "the F word" rather than "fail" or "failure" immediately gains the reader's interest and implies the wry point that for many teachers and students, "failure" is actually as objectionable a word as the obscenity.

2   *In which paragraph does the author first mention her thesis? What is her main method of development, and how is it related to that thesis? Where does she use narration to support her thesis?*

Answer: Sherry first mentions her thesis at the end of paragraph 4, when she speaks approvingly of "the trump card of failure." Her essay is primarily an argument piece, in which she hopes to persuade the reader that failure is a useful educational tool. She narrates the incident about Mrs. Stifter and her son to demonstrate how the threat of failure worked in that case.

3   *What contrast transition is used in the first sentence of paragraph 10? What ideas are being contrasted within that sentence?*

Answer: The transition is "but." Sherry is contrasting the ideas that (1) people can rise above their problems and (2) they need a reason to do so. She is emphasizing that people don't necessarily do what they *can* do—they need a compelling motivation.

4   *In paragraph 11, how many times does Sherry use "mean" or "means"? What might her purpose be for repeating this word so frequently?*

Answer: She uses the words three times. Her point is to drive home the idea that bringing failing back into the classroom would require participation from various parties—parents *and* teachers.

Critical Reading and Discussion

1   *Sherry writes that "before a teacher can expect students to concentrate, he has to get their attention, no matter what distractions may be at hand" (paragraph 4). What examples of distractions does Sherry mention? Find several in her essay. Can you think of others—perhaps ones that existed in your own high school?*

Answer: Sherry mentions the "distractions" of drugs and divorce. Her own son was "distracted" by talking to his friends. She mentions her own students who are dealing with unemployment, chemical dependency, and abusive relationships. Students may contribute other "distractions."

2   *What does Sherry mean by calling the program she teaches in an "educational-repair shop"? What does the term tell us about Sherry's attitude toward high schools?*

Answer: The words "repair shop" suggest that the program she teaches in must repair damage done in high school, where the skills she teaches should have been taught. Sherry clearly believes high schools are doing an inadequate job.

3   *Sherry writes, "Young people generally don't have the maturity to value education in the same way my adult students value it." Do you agree or disagree? Support your view with details and observations from your own experience.*

Answer: Answers will vary.

4   *Do you feel your high school teachers made an honest effort to give you the skills you need—and to make you aware of the importance of those skills? If not, what should your teachers and school have done that they did not do?*

Answer: Answers will vary.

Joyce Garity, "Is Sex All That Matters?"

Structure and Technique

1   *To support her views about sexuality in popular culture, Garity presents the case of Elaine. Why has the author chosen to focus so much of her essay on Elaine? What would have been lost if Garity had omitted Elaine?*

Answer: Elaine serves as a real-life example of a young girl whose life has been deeply damaged by her embracing of popular culture's view of sexuality. If Elaine had been omitted, the essay would have lacked the persuasiveness of a fully drawn case, leaving the reader with only a series of generalities, facts, and brief examples.

2   *List the details that Garity provides as she describes the Claiborne ad. Why does she go to such lengths to describe it? Why might she think it important for the reader to see it so clearly?*

Answer: Garity describes the Claiborne ad as including a nearly naked couple on a bed, with the man painting the woman's toenails. The woman laughs; the bed is heaped with clean white linen and pillows. There are sheer curtains at the window, and a wrought-iron balcony is visible. Garity describes the ad in such detail in order to make the reader understand what a highly attractive and seductive scene it is, especially to impressionable young readers.

3   *Garity uses a number of examples to support her claim about the prevalence of sex in popular culture. Cite some of these examples and explain how they support her argument.*

Answer: Garity mentions numerous magazine advertisements, billboards, children's fashions, and sexually promiscuous celebrities. Taken together, the examples make a persuasive case for her claim that sexually suggestive messages are everywhere young people look.

4   *Throughout paragraph 11, Garity poses a series of questions. What does she gain by using this technique?*

Answer: By asking questions, she hopes to provoke the reader into realizing the answer: that there are few voices in our society presenting an alternative to the perspective presented by much of popular culture.

Critical Reading and Discussion

1 *How do you think Garity felt about Elaine? Affectionate? Scornful? Resentful? Disapproving? Pitying? Explain your answer, pointing out evidence from Garity's text.*

Answer: Garity's attitude toward Elaine might be described as fond, concerned, and somewhat exasperated. The fact that Elaine lived with Garity's family for some time and that the two had intimate conversations suggests that Garity felt affection for her. Her hosting of Elaine makes it clear, too, that she was concerned about what would become of Elaine and her children. In addition, Elaine's unrealistic attitude toward her own situation—her "yearn[ing] after magazine images, soap-opera heroines, and rock goddesses" even while she carries yet another child she is not equipped emotionally or financially to bring up—seems to exasperate Garity.

2 *In paragraph 7, the author says that Elaine is "completely unaware of the irony of her situation." In an ironic situation, there is an inconsistency between what might be expected and what actually happens. What about Elaine's situation is ironic?*

Answer: The irony lies in the fact that while Elaine wanted a glamorous life of passion, romance, and sexual spontaneity, she actually has a life of poverty, unwed teen motherhood, and reliance on charity.

3 *The author lists numerous examples to illustrate and support her claim that "young people are immersed from their earliest days in a culture that parades sexuality at every turn and makes heroes of advocates of sexual excess." What examples can you think of to add to her list? Describe and explain them.*

Answer: Answers will vary.

4 *In arguing against the emphasis on sexuality in our culture, Garity focuses on potential dangers to young women. How do you think this highly sexualized culture affects young men? Are they also at risk? Explain.*

Answer: Answers will vary, but students might realize that, like the members of the "Spur Posse" mentioned in paragraph 9, young men may receive the message from popular culture that their "manhood" is determined primarily by their ability to "score" sexually.

Diagnostic Tests

Notes to Instructors:

1. These diagnostic tests are also available online at www.mhhe.com/langan/ diagnostics. Students who take these tests online will automatically receive their scores with recommendations for areas they need to work on, but they will not receive question-by-question feedback. Instructors who wish to receive detailed feedback on individual students' performances must supply students with an e-mail address, to which a detailed evaluation will be sent.

2. Diagnostic Test C consists of questions drawn from Tests A and B.

3. These diagnostics and the *Instructor's Manual* that accompanies *College Writing Skills* are available to instructors online in the Instructor's Center of the Online Learning Center (www.mhhe.com/langan). To access this material, you will need to use the following user ID and password: **langan/skills.**

Diagnostic Test A (40 Questions)

1. Which of the following sentences should end in a question mark?
   a. I would like to use your telephone
   b. I need to use your telephone
   c. May I use your telephone
   d. I wonder if I can use your telephone

2. Which of the following has the correct form for a title on the top line of a school paper?
   a. "Creating a Business Plan"
   b. Creating a Business Plan
   c. Creating a business plan
   d. Creating a Business Plan.

3. The jewels are safely hidden in a velvet box.
   In the sentence above, the word JEWELS is a(n)
   a. noun.   c. adjective.
   b. preposition.   d. adverb.

4. The jewels are safely hidden in a velvet box.
   In the sentence above, the word VELVET is a(n)
   a. noun.   c. adjective.
   b. preposition.   d. adverb.

5. The jewels are safely hidden in a velvet box.
   In the sentence above, the word SAFELY is a(n)
   a. noun.   c. adjective.
   b. preposition.   d. adverb.

6. The green stripes in that shirt match your eyes perfectly.
   In the sentence above, the subject is
   a. stripes.   c. eyes.
   b. shirt.   d. perfectly.

7. The green stripes in that shirt match your eyes perfectly.
   In the sentence above, the verb is
   a. stripes.   c. match.
   b. in.   d. perfectly.

8. The mysterious visitor to the president's office must have entered through a side door.
   In the sentence above, the subject is
   a. mysterious.   c. office.
   b. visitor.   d. door.

9. The famous violinist _____ last night.
   Which word should fill the blank in the sentence above?
   a. plays   c. is playing
   b. played   d. to play

10. Every time the phone rings, the cat JUMPED.

    In the sentence above, the capitalized part should be written:

    a. jumped   c. jumps

    b. jump   d. had jumped

11. The painter finished one wall and then stepped back and ADMIRES his work.

    In the sentence above, the capitalized part should be written:

    a. admires   c. is admiring

    b. admire   d. admired

12. When the teacher caught two students cheating, she MAKED them stay after school.

    In the sentence above, the capitalized part should be written:

    a. maked   c. make

    b. maded   d. made

13. Over the summer, Jaime TEACHED crafts at a camp for teenagers.

    In the sentence above, the capitalized part should be written:

    a. teached   c. teach

    b. taught   d. taughted

14. At the motel, we used the exercise room and SWAM in the outdoor pool.

    In the sentence above, the capitalized part should be written:

    a. swam   c. swimmed

    b. swum   d. swammed

15. That carton of eggs ARE outdated.

    In the sentence above, the capitalized part should be written:

    a. are   b. is

16. Deep inside the woods WAS several camping spots.

    In the sentence above, the capitalized part should be written:

    a. was   b. were

17. Neither of those science courses LOOK easy.

    In the sentence above, the capitalized part should be written:

    a. look   b. looks

18. Those cows will always eat. Whether they are hungry or not.

    One correct way to write the above is:

    a. Those cows will always eat. Whether they are hungry or not.

    b. Those cows will always eat; whether they are hungry or not.

    c. Those cows will always eat whether they are hungry or not.

    d. Those cows will always eat, whether they are hungry or not.

19. My sister wakes up an hour earlier each day. To have more time for studying.

    One correct way to write the above is:

    a. My sister wakes up an hour earlier each day. To have more time for studying.

    b. My sister wakes up an hour earlier each day; to have more time for studying.

    c. My sister wakes up an hour earlier each day. She wants to have more time for studying.

    d. My sister, wakes up an hour earlier each day, to have more time for studying.

20. When I dropped the book. A ten-dollar bill fell out of the back.

    One correct way to write the above is:

    a. When I dropped the book. A ten-dollar bill fell out of the back.

    b. When I dropped the book, a ten-dollar bill fell out of the back.

    c. When I dropped the book; a ten-dollar bill fell out of the back.

    d. When I dropped the book a ten-dollar bill fell out; of the back.

21. That tree should be sprayed, it also needs trimming.

    One correct way to write the above is:

    a. That tree should be sprayed, it also needs trimming.

    b. That tree should be sprayed it also needs trimming.

    c. That tree should be sprayed; and it also needs trimming.

    d. That tree should be sprayed, and it also needs trimming.

22. The two sisters hadn't seen each other for months, so they planned a weekend together.

    One correct way to write the above is:

    a. The two sisters hadn't seen each other for months, so they planned a weekend together.

    b. The two sisters hadn't seen each other for months, they planned a weekend together.

    c. The two sisters hadn't seen each other for months; so they planned a weekend together.

    d. The two sisters hadn't seen each other for months so they planned a weekend together.

23. Kareem got in late on Friday night he slept till noon on Saturday.

    One correct way to write the above is:

    a. Kareem got in late on Friday night he slept till noon on Saturday.

    b. Kareem got in late on Friday. He slept till noon on Saturday.

    c. Kareem got in late on Friday night; he slept till noon on Saturday.

    d. Both b and c are correct.

24. One can get into the basketball game if THEY LINE up for a ticket.

    In the sentence above, the capitalized part should be written:

    a. one lines   b. he lines   c. they line

25. At the end of a hard day, I like to soak in a hot bathtub and forget all YOUR troubles.

    In the sentence above, the capitalized part should be written:

    a. your   b. one's   c. my

26. Horatio went to the movies with Franklin and ME.

    The capitalized part of the above sentence should be written:

    a. me.   b. I.

27. Our spanish teacher at valley college never eats meat or fish.

    The correct way to write the above sentence is:

    a. Our Spanish teacher at Valley College never eats meat or fish.

    b. Our spanish teacher at Valley College never eats meat or fish.

    c. Our Spanish teacher at Valley college never eats meat or fish.

    d. Our Spanish Teacher at Valley College never eats meat or fish.

28. Jane said, "ON SUNDAYS, MOM would make us pancakes shaped like our initials."

In the sentence above, the capitalized part should be written:

a. "On Sundays, Mom   c. "on Sundays, mom

b. "on sundays, mom   d. "On Sundays, mom

29. The panda, a native of China, was my Aunt's favorite animal at the zoo.

The correct way to write the above sentence is:

a. The panda, a native of China, was my Aunt's favorite animal at the zoo.

b. The panda, a native of china, was my aunt's favorite animal at the zoo.

c. The panda, a native of China, was my aunt's favorite animal at the zoo.

d. The panda, a native of China, was my aunt's favorite animal at the Zoo.

30. The magician NEEDS A WATCH A RING AND A VOLUNTEER FROM THE AUDIENCE for his next trick.

In the sentence above, the capitalized part should be written:

a. needs a watch a ring and a volunteer from the audience

b. needs a watch a ring, and a volunteer from the audience

c. needs a watch, a ring, and a volunteer from the audience

d. needs, a watch a ring, and a volunteer from the audience

31. The principal announced "The snow is heavy so we will dismiss school early today."

The correct way to write the above sentence is:

a. The principal announced "The snow is heavy so we will dismiss school early today."

b. The principal announced, "The snow is heavy so we will dismiss school early today."

c. The principal announced "The snow is heavy so we will dismiss school, early today."

d. The principal announced, "The snow is heavy, so we will dismiss school early today."

32. These BOOT'S look great, but they ARENT comfortable.

In the sentence above, the capitalized parts should be written:

a. boot's . . . arent   c. boots . . . arent

b. boots . . . aren't   d. boot's . . . aren't

33. A horn PLAYERS most valued possession is his LIPS.

In the sentence above, the capitalized parts should be written:

a. players . . . lips   c. players . . . lip's

b. player's . . . lips   d. player's . . . lip's

34. My HUSBAND'S brother volunteered to coach our CHURCH'S softball team this year.

In the sentence above, the capitalized parts should be written:

a. husband's . . . church's   c. husband's . . . churchs

b. husbands . . . church's   d. husbands . . . churchs

35. "The candidate ended his long speech by asking, Can I count on your vote?"

The sentence above should be written:

a. "The candidate ended his long speech by asking, Can I count on your vote?"

b. The candidate ended his long speech by asking, "Can I count on your vote"?

c. The candidate ended his long speech by asking, Can I count on your vote?

d. The candidate ended his long speech by asking, "Can I count on your vote?"

36. My greatest challenge, Rick said, is balancing my personal life and my career.

    The sentence above should be written:

    a. My greatest challenge, Rick said, is balancing my personal life and my career.

    b. "My greatest challenge," Rick said, "is balancing my personal life and my career."

    c. "My greatest challenge," Rick said, "is balancing my personal life and my career".

    d. "My greatest challenge", Rick said, "is balancing my personal life and my career."

37. I didn't think I could be hypnotized. However, I quickly went into a trance, Felice explained to Joe.

    The correct way to write the above sentence is:

    a. I didn't think I could be hypnotized. However, I quickly went into a trance, Felice explained to Joe.

    b. "I didn't think I could be hypnotized." "However, I quickly went into a trance," Felice explained to Joe.

    c. "I didn't think I could be hypnotized. However, I quickly went into a trance," Felice explained to Joe.

    d. "I didn't think I could be hypnotized. However, I quickly went into a trance", Felice explained to Joe.

38. IT'S true that many people can speak better THEN they can write.

    In the sentence above, the capitalized parts should be written:

    a. It's . . . then   c. Its . . . than

    b. It's . . . than   d. Its . . . then

39. Although the BREAKS in the car were KNEW, they failed and caused an accident.

    In the sentence above, the capitalized parts should be written:

    a. breaks . . . knew   c. breaks . . . new

    b. brakes . . . knew   d. brakes . . . new

40. I don't believe YOU'RE cut-off jeans are the RIGHT clothes for the wedding.

    In the sentence above, the capitalized parts should be written:

    a. you're . . . right   c. your . . . right

    b. you're . . . write   d. your . . . write

SCORING KEY, Diagnostic Test A:

1. c (Basic Punctuation and Paper Format)
2. b (Basic Punctuation and Paper Format)
3. a (Parts of Speech)
4. c (Parts of Speech)
5. d (Parts of Speech)
6. a (Subjects and Verbs)
7. c (Subjects and Verbs)
8. b (Subjects and Verbs)
9. b (Verb Tenses)
10. c (Verb Tenses)
11. d (Verb Tenses)
12. d (Irregular Verbs)
13. b (Irregular Verbs)
14. a (Irregular Verbs)
15. b (Subject-Verb Agreement)
16. b (Subject-Verb Agreement)
17. b (Subject-Verb Agreement)
18. d (Sentence Fragments)
19. c (Sentence Fragments)
20. b (Sentence Fragments)

21. d (Run-Ons and Comma Splices)
22. a (Run-Ons and Comma Splices)
23. d (Run-Ons and Comma Splices)
24. a (Pronouns)
25. c (Pronouns)
26. a (Pronouns)
27. a (Capital Letters)
28. a (Capital Letters)
29. c (Capital Letters)
30. c (Commas)
31. d (Commas)
32. b (Apostrophes)
33. b (Apostrophes)
34. a (Apostrophes)
35. d (Quotation Marks)
36. b (Quotation Marks)
37. c (Quotation Marks)
38. b (Homonyms)
39. d (Homonyms)
40. c (Homonyms)

If a student got one of these questions wrong:	She or he needs help with . . .	Coverage of this topic is available here:	
		College Writing Skills:	AllWrite! 2.0:
1 or 2	Basic Punctuation and Paper Format	Chapter 34	Chapter 23
3, 4, or 5	Parts of Speech	Chapters 23 and 29	Chapter 14.1
6, 7, or 8	Subjects and Verbs	Chapter 23	Chapter 18.1
9, 10, or 11	Verb Tenses	Chapter 28	Chapter 18.2
12, 13, or 14	Irregular Verbs	Chapter 26	Chapter 18
15, 16, or 17	Subject-Verb Agreement	Chapter 27	Chapter 17
18, 19, or 20	Sentence Fragments	Chapter 24	Chapter 15.2
21, 22, or 23	Run-Ons and Comma Splices	Chapter 25	Chapter 15.3, 15.4
24, 25, or 26	Pronouns	Chapters 29 and 30	Chapter 19
27, 28, or 29	Capital Letters	Chapter 35	Chapter 25.1
30 or 31	Commas	Chapter 39	Chapter 23.2
32, 33, or 34	Apostrophes	Chapter 37	Chapter 24.6
35, 36, or 37	Quotation Marks	Chapter 38	Chapter 24.3
38, 39, or 40	Homonyms	Chapter 42	

Diagnostic Test B (40 Questions)

1. Which of the following sentences should end in a question mark?
   a. I need a flashlight
   b. I wonder if I could borrow your flashlight
   c. Do you have a flashlight that I could borrow
   d. You may have a flashlight that I could borrow

2. Which of the following has the correct form for a title on the top line of a school paper?
   a. "My Career Goals"   c. My Career Goals.
   b. My Career Goals   d. my career goals

3. The college president read the names of the graduates in a loud, clear voice.
   In the sentence above, the word NAMES is a(n)
   a. noun.   c. adjective.
   b. adverb.   d. preposition.

4. The college president read the names of the graduates in a loud, clear voice.
   In the sentence above, the word CLEAR is a(n)
   a. noun.   c. adjective.
   b. adverb.   d. preposition.

5. The college president read the names of the graduates in a loud, clear voice.
   In the sentence above, the word OF is a(n)
   a. noun.   c. adjective.
   b. adverb   d. preposition.

6. The bananas in this store cost far too much.
   In the sentence above, the subject is
   a. bananas.   c. cost.
   b. store.   d. much.

7. I always read the newspaper on Sundays.
   In the sentence above, the verb is
   a. read.   c. Sundays.
   b. the.   d. newspaper.

8. The bananas in this store cost far too much.
   In the sentence above, the verb is
   a. bananas.   c. cost.
   b. in this store.   d. cost far too much.

9. In many cases, medicine should be taken along with some food.
   In the sentence above, the subject is
   a. cases.   c. should be.
   b. medicine.   d. food.

10. Once a week, Lydia steams her face and PLACED cucumber slices over her eyes.
    In the sentence above, the capitalized part should be written:
    a. placed   c. places
    b. will place   d. place

11. The boy spotted an ice-cream truck and YELL for it to stop.

In the sentence above, the capitalized part should be written:

a. yell   c. will have yelled

b. yells   d. yelled

12. The puddles in the driveway FREEZED solid overnight.

In the sentence above, the capitalized part should be written:

a. freezed   c. frozen

b. frozed   d. froze

13. More people in the cafeteria CHOOSED pizza than macaroni and cheese.

In the sentence above, the capitalized part should be written:

a. choosed   c. chosen

b. chose   d. chosed

14. As the final buzzer rang, O'Neal THREW the basketball from the far end of the court.

In the sentence above, the capitalized part should be written:

a. threw   c. throwed

b. threwed   d. thrown

15. The man in the apartment next door STAY there for days at a time.

In the sentence above, the capitalized part should be written:

a. stay   b. stays

16. There IS two reasons I can't come to the party.

In the sentence above, the capitalized part should be written:

a. is   b. are

17. Nobody in this family SING well.

In the sentence above, the capitalized part should be written:

a. sing   b. sings

18. Until the race began. The horses waited at the starting line.

One correct way to write the above is:

a. Until the race began. The horses waited at the starting line.

b. Until the race began, the horses waited. At the starting line.

c. Until the race began, the horses waited; at the starting line.

d. Until the race began, the horses waited at the starting line.

19. The children stood quietly on the street corner. Waiting for the light to turn green.

One correct way to write the above is:

a. The children stood quietly on the street corner. Waiting for the light to turn green.

b. The children stood quietly on the street corner, waiting for the light to turn green.

c. The children stood quietly on the street corner. They were waiting for the light to turn green.

d. Both b and c are correct.

20. Nothing appeals to me right now. Except a nap.

One correct way to write the above is:

a. Nothing appeals to me right now. Except a nap.

b. Nothing appeals to me right now except a nap.

c. Nothing appeals to me right now; except a nap.

d. Nothing appeals to me right now. Except for taking a nap.

21. Tennis is fun, it is also good exercise.

One correct way to write the above is:

a. Tennis is fun, it is also good exercise.

b. Tennis is fun it is also good exercise.

c. Tennis is fun. It is also good exercise.

d. Tennis is fun; and it is also good exercise.

22. It is only three o'clock, but the sky is very dark.

One correct way to write the above is:

a. It is only three o'clock, but the sky is very dark.

b. It is only three o'clock; the sky is very dark.

c. It is only three o'clock but, the sky is very dark.

d. Both a and b are correct.

23. There is a long line for the roller coaster the Ferris wheel is broken.

One correct way to write the above is:

a. There is a long line for the roller coaster the Ferris wheel is broken.

b. There is a long line for the roller coaster. Because the Ferris wheel is broken.

c. There is a long line for the roller coaster, the Ferris wheel is broken.

d. There is a long line for the roller coaster because the Ferris wheel is broken.

24. Neither of my brothers WANTS to be a salesman like our father.

In the sentence above, the capitalized part should be written:

a. wants   b. want

25. One should never hand in a paper unless THEY CHECK it over first.

In the sentence above, the capitalized part should be written:

a. they check   b. you check   c. one checks

26. Someone left THEIR shoes on my bed.

In the sentence above, the capitalized part should be written:

a. their   b. his or her   c. one's

27. EVERY JUNE, THE METHODISTS IN TOWN host a big strawberry festival.

In the sentence above, the capitalized part should be written:

a. Every june, the methodists in town

b. Every june, the Methodists in town

c. Every June, the Methodists in town

d. Every June, the Methodists in Town

28. That man holding the can of Cola is an English teacher at Highland College.

The sentence above should be written:

a. That man holding the can of cola is an English teacher at Highland College.

b. That man holding the can of cola is an english teacher at Highland college.

c. That man holding the can of Cola is an English teacher at Highland College.

d. That man holding the can of Cola is an english teacher at Highland College.

29. For his entire life, Uncle Henry has said that his favorite book is the Bible.

   The correct way to write the above sentence is:

   a. For his entire life, Uncle Henry has said that his favorite book is the Bible.

   b. For his entire life, Uncle Henry has said that his favorite book is the bible.

   c. For his entire life, uncle Henry has said that his favorite book is the Bible.

   d. For his entire life, uncle Henry has said that his favorite book is the bible.

30. My grandfather a sweet man with a quiet voice was a terrific storyteller.

   The correct way to write the above sentence is:

   a. My grandfather a sweet man with a quiet voice was a terrific storyteller.

   b. My grandfather, a sweet man with a quiet voice was a terrific storyteller.

   c. My grandfather, a sweet man with a quiet voice, was a terrific storyteller.

   d. My grandfather a sweet man with a quiet voice, was a terrific storyteller.

31. "This action is a disgrace" said the mayor angrily.

   The correct way to write the above sentence is:

   a. "This action is a disgrace" said the mayor angrily.

   b. "This action is a disgrace, said the mayor angrily.

   c. "This action is a disgrace", said the mayor angrily.

   d. "This action is a disgrace," said the mayor angrily.

32. Jose lives in a green house which was built in the forties.

   One correct way to write this sentence is:

   a. Jose lives in a green house which was built in the forties.

   b. Jose lives in a green house that was built in the forties.

   c. Jose lives in a green house, which was built in the forties.

   d. Both b and c are correct.

33. It is lovely to watch those HORSE'S MANES blow in the wind.

   In the sentence above, the capitalized part should be written:

   a. horse's manes   c. horses manes

   b. horses' mane's   d. horses' manes

34. Because of a storm, I COULDN'T make it to my SISTER'S wedding.

   In the sentence above, the capitalized parts should be written:

   a. couldn't . . . sister's   c. couldnt . . . sisters

   b. couldn't . . . sisters   d. couldnt . . . sister's

35. "The waitress explained, We're out of every kind of pie but blueberry."

   The correct way to write the above sentence is:

   a. "The waitress explained, We're out of every kind of pie but blueberry."

   b. The waitress explained, "We're out of every kind of pie but blueberry".

   c. The waitress explained, We're out of every kind of pie but blueberry.

   d. The waitress explained, "We're out of every kind of pie but blueberry."

36. If you ask me, snapped the marriage counselor, "you're both wrong."
    The correct way to write the above sentence is:
    a. If you ask me, snapped the marriage counselor, "you're both wrong."
    b. "If you ask me," snapped the marriage counselor, "you're both wrong."
    c. "If you ask me, snapped the marriage counselor, you're both wrong."
    d. "If you ask me, snapped the marriage counselor," you're both wrong.

37. Terry exclaimed, I can't believe it! I passed my chemistry test!
    The correct way to write the above sentence is:
    a. Terry exclaimed, I can't believe it! I passed my chemistry test!
    b. "Terry exclaimed, I can't believe it! I passed my chemistry test!"
    c. Terry exclaimed, "I can't believe it! I passed my chemistry test!"
    d. Terry exclaimed, "I can't believe it! I passed my chemistry test"!

38. The children claim they don't KNOW where that WHOLE in the carpet came from.
    In the sentence above, the capitalized parts should be written:
    a. know . . . whole   c. no . . . whole
    b. know . . . hole   d. no . . . hole

39. Only one PEACE of YOU'RE birthday cake is left.
    In the sentence above, the capitalized parts should be written:
    a. peace . . . you're   c. piece . . . you're
    b. peace . . . your   d. piece . . . your

40. I don't know WHO'S jeans these are, but they are TOO big for me.
    In the sentence above, the capitalized parts should be written:
    a. who's . . . too   c. whose . . . too
    b. who's . . . to   d. whose . . . to

SCORING KEY, Diagnostic Test B:

1. c (Basic Punctuation and Paper Format)
2. b (Basic Punctuation and Paper Format)
3. a (Parts of Speech)
4. c (Parts of Speech)
5. d (Parts of Speech)
6. a (Subjects and Verbs)
7. a (Subjects and Verbs)
8. c (Subjects and Verbs)
9. b (Subjects and Verbs)
10. c (Verb Tenses)
11. d (Verb Tenses)
12. d (Irregular Verbs)
13. b (Irregular Verbs)
14. a (Irregular Verbs)
15. b (Subject-Verb Agreement)
16. b (Subject-Verb Agreement)
17. b (Subject-Verb Agreement)
18. d (Sentence Fragments)
19. d (Sentence Fragments)
20. b (Sentence Fragments)
21. c (Run-Ons and Comma Splices)
22. d (Run-Ons and Comma Splices)
23. d (Run-Ons and Comma Splices)
24. a (Pronouns)
25. c (Pronouns)
26. b (Pronouns)
27. c (Capital Letters)
28. a (Capital Letters)
29. a (Capital Letters)
30. c (Commas)
31. d (Commas)
32. d (Commas)
33. d (Apostrophes)
34. a (Apostrophes)
35. d (Quotation Marks)
36. b (Quotation Marks)
37. c (Quotation Marks)
38. b (Homonyms)
39. d (Homonyms)
40. c (Homonyms)

If a student got one of these questions wrong:	She or he needs help with . . .	Coverage of this topic is available here:	
		College Writing Skills:	AllWrite! 2.0:
1 or 2	Basic Punctuation and Paper Format	Chapter 34	Chapter 23
3, 4, or 5	Parts of Speech	Chapters 23 and 29	Chapter 14.1
6, 7, 8, or 9	Subjects and Verbs	Chapter 23	Chapter 18.1
10 or 11	Verb Tenses	Chapter 28	Chapter 18.2
12, 13, or 14	Irregular Verbs	Chapter 26	Chapter 18
15, 16, or 17	Subject-Verb Agreement	Chapter 27	Chapter 17
18, 19, or 20	Sentence Fragments	Chapter 24	Chapter 15.2
21, 22, or 23	Run-Ons and Comma Splices	Chapter 25	Chapter 15.3, 15.4
24, 25, or 26	Pronouns	Chapters 29 and 30	Chapter 19
27, 28, or 29	Capital Letters	Chapter 35	Chapter 25.1
30, 31, or 32	Commas	Chapter 39	Chapter 23.2
33 or 34	Apostrophes	Chapter 37	Chapter 24.6
35, 36, or 37	Quotation Marks	Chapter 38	Chapter 24.3
38, 39, or 40	Homonyms	Chapter 42	

Diagnostic Test C (60 Questions)

1. Which of the following sentences should end in a question mark?
   a. I would like to use your telephone
   b. I need to use your telephone
   c. May I use your telephone
   d. I wonder if I can use your telephone

2. Which of the following has the correct form for a title on the top line of a school paper?
   a. "Creating a Business Plan"
   b. Creating a Business Plan
   c. Creating a business plan
   d. Creating a Business Plan.

3. The jewels are safely hidden in a velvet box.
   In the sentence above, the word JEWELS is a(n)
   a. noun.
   b. preposition.
   c. adjective.
   d. adverb.

4. The jewels are safely hidden in a velvet box.
   In the sentence above, the word VELVET is a(n)
   a. noun.
   b. preposition.
   c. adjective.
   d. adverb.

5. The jewels are safely hidden in a velvet box.
   In the sentence above, the word SAFELY is a(n)
   a. noun.
   b. preposition.
   c. adjective.
   d. adverb.

6. The green stripes in that shirt match your eyes perfectly.
   In the sentence above, the subject is
   a. stripes.
   b. shirt.
   c. eyes.
   d. perfectly.

7. The green stripes in that shirt match your eyes perfectly.
   In the sentence above, the verb is
   a. stripes.
   b. in.
   c. match.
   d. perfectly.

8. The mysterious visitor to the president's office must have entered through a side door.
   In the sentence above, the subject is
   a. mysterious.
   b. visitor.
   c. office.
   d. door.

9. The famous violinist _____ last night.
   Which word should fill the blank in the sentence above?
   a. plays
   b. played
   c. is playing
   d. to play

10. Every time the phone rings, the cat JUMPED.
    In the sentence above, the capitalized part should be written:
    a. jumped
    b. jump
    c. jumps
    d. had jumped

11. The painter finished one wall and then stepped back and ADMIRES his work.

    In the sentence above, the capitalized part should be written:

    a. admires   c. is admiring

    b. admire   d. admired

12. When the teacher caught two students cheating, she MAKED them stay after school.

    In the sentence above, the capitalized part should be written:

    a. maked   c. make

    b. maded   d. made

13. Over the summer, Jaime TEACHED crafts at a camp for teenagers.

    In the sentence above, the capitalized part should be written:

    a. teached   c. teach

    b. taught   d. taughted

14. At the motel, we used the exercise room and SWAM in the outdoor pool.

    In the sentence above, the capitalized part should be written:

    a. swam   c. swimmed

    b. swum   d. swammed

15. That carton of eggs ARE outdated.

    In the sentence above, the capitalized part should be written:

    a. are   b. is

16. Deep inside the woods WAS several camping spots.

    In the sentence above, the capitalized part should be written:

    a. was   b. were

17. Neither of those science courses LOOK easy.

    In the sentence above, the capitalized part should be written:

    a. look   b. looks

18. Those cows will always eat. Whether they are hungry or not.

    One correct way to write the above is:

    a. Those cows will always eat. Whether they are hungry or not.

    b. Those cows will always eat; whether they are hungry or not.

    c. Those cows will always eat whether they are hungry or not.

    d. Those cows will always eat, whether they are hungry or not.

19. My sister wakes up an hour earlier each day. To have more time for studying.

    One correct way to write the above is:

    a. My sister wakes up an hour earlier each day. To have more time for studying.

    b. My sister wakes up an hour earlier each day; to have more time for studying.

    c. My sister wakes up an hour earlier each day. She wants to have more time for studying.

    d. My sister, wakes up an hour earlier each day, to have more time for studying.

20. When I dropped the book. A ten-dollar bill fell out of the back.

    One correct way to write the above is:

    a. When I dropped the book. A ten-dollar bill fell out of the back.

    b. When I dropped the book, a ten-dollar bill fell out of the back.

c. When I dropped the book; a ten-dollar bill fell out of the back.

d. When I dropped the book a ten-dollar bill fell out; of the back.

21. That tree should be sprayed, it also needs trimming.

One correct way to write the above is:

a. That tree should be sprayed, it also needs trimming.

b. That tree should be sprayed it also needs trimming.

c. That tree should be sprayed, and it also needs trimming.

d. That tree should be sprayed, and it also needs trimming.

22. The two sisters hadn't seen each other for months, so they planned a weekend together.

One correct way to write the above is:

a. The two sisters hadn't seen each other for months, so they planned a weekend together.

b. The two sisters hadn't seen each other for months, they planned a weekend together.

c. The two sisters hadn't seen each other for months; so they planned a weekend together.

d. The two sisters hadn't seen each other for months so they planned a weekend together.

23. Kareem got in late on Friday night he slept till noon on Saturday.

One correct way to write the above is:

a. Kareem got in late on Friday night he slept till noon on Saturday.

b. Kareem got in late on Friday. He slept till noon on Saturday.

c. Kareem got in late on Friday night; he slept till noon on Saturday.

d. Both b and c are correct.

24. One can get into the basketball game if THEY LINE up for a ticket.

In the sentence above, the capitalized part should be written:

a. one lines   b. he lines   c. they line

25. At the end of a hard day, I like to soak in a hot bathtub and forget all YOUR troubles.

In the sentence above, the capitalized part should be written:

a. your   b. one's   c. my

26. My sister took a train to savannah, georgia, to visit aunt Melba.

The sentence above should be written:

a. My sister took a train to savannah, georgia, to visit aunt Melba.

b. My Sister took a train to Savannah, Georgia, to visit Aunt Melba.

c. My sister took a train to Savannah, Georgia, to visit aunt Melba.

d. My sister took a train to Savannah, Georgia, to visit Aunt Melba.

27. Our spanish teacher at valley college never eats meat or fish.

The correct way to write the above sentence is:

a. Our Spanish teacher at Valley College never eats meat or fish.

b. Our spanish teacher at Valley College never eats meat or fish.

c. Our Spanish teacher at Valley college never eats meat or fish.

d. Our Spanish Teacher at Valley College never eats meat or fish.

28. Jane said, "ON SUNDAYS, MOM would make us pancakes shaped like our initials."

In the sentence above, the capitalized part should be written:

a. "On Sundays, Mom   c. "on Sundays, mom

b. "on sundays, mom   d. "On Sundays, mom

29. The panda, a native of China, was my Aunt's favorite animal at the zoo.

    The correct way to write the above sentence is:

    a. The panda, a native of China, was my Aunt's favorite animal at the zoo.

    b. The panda, a native of china, was my aunt's favorite animal at the zoo.

    c. The panda, a native of China, was my aunt's favorite animal at the zoo.

    d. The panda, a native of China, was my aunt's favorite animal at the Zoo.

30. The magician NEEDS A WATCH A RING AND A VOLUNTEER FROM THE AUDIENCE for his next trick.

    In the sentence above, the capitalized part should be written:

    a. needs a watch a ring and a volunteer from the audience

    b. needs a watch a ring, and a volunteer from the audience

    c. needs a watch, a ring, and a volunteer from the audience

    d. needs, a watch a ring, and a volunteer from the audience

31. The principal announced "The snow is heavy so we will dismiss school early today."

    The correct way to write the above sentence is:

    a. The principal announced "The snow is heavy so we will dismiss school early today."

    b. The principal announced, "The snow is heavy so we will dismiss school early today."

    c. The principal announced "The snow is heavy so we will dismiss school, early today."

    d. The principal announced, "The snow is heavy, so we will dismiss school early today."

32. These BOOT'S look great, but they ARENT comfortable.

    In the sentence above, the capitalized parts should be written:

    a. boot's . . . arent   c. boots . . . arent

    b. boots . . . aren't   d. boot's . . . aren't

33. A horn PLAYERS most valued possession is his LIPS.

    In the sentence above, the capitalized parts should be written:

    a. players . . . lips   c. players . . . lip's

    b. player's . . . lips   d. player's . . . lip's

34. My HUSBAND'S brother volunteered to coach our CHURCH'S softball team this year.

    In the sentence above, the capitalized parts should be written:

    a. husband's . . . church's   c. husband's . . . churchs

    b. husbands . . . church's   d. husbands . . . churchs

35. "The candidate ended his long speech by asking, Can I count on your vote?"

    The sentence above should be written:

    a. "The candidate ended his long speech by asking, Can I count on your vote?"

    b. The candidate ended his long speech by asking, "Can I count on your vote"?

    c. The candidate ended his long speech by asking, Can I count on your vote?

    d. The candidate ended his long speech by asking, "Can I count on your vote?"

36. My greatest challenge, Rick said, is balancing my personal life and my career.

    The sentence above should be written:

    a. My greatest challenge, Rick said, is balancing my personal life and my career.

    b. "My greatest challenge," Rick said, "is balancing my personal life and my career."

c. "My greatest challenge," Rick said, is balancing my personal life and my career".

d. "My greatest challenge", Rick said, "is balancing my personal life and my career."

37. I didn't think I could be hypnotized. However, I quickly went into a trance, Felice explained to Joe.

The correct way to write the above sentence is:

a. I didn't think I could be hypnotized. However, I quickly went into a trance, Felice explained to Joe.

b. "I didn't think I could be hypnotized." "However, I quickly went into a trance," Felice explained to Joe.

c. "I didn't think I could be hypnotized. However, I quickly went into a trance," Felice explained to Joe.

d. "I didn't think I could be hypnotized. However, I quickly went into a trance", Felice explained to Joe.

38. IT'S true that many people can speak better THEN they can write.

In the sentence above, the capitalized parts should be written:

a. It's . . . then   c. Its . . . than

b. It's . . . than   d. Its . . . then

39. Although the BREAKS in the car were KNEW, they failed and caused an accident.

In the sentence above, the capitalized parts should be written:

a. breaks . . . knew   c. breaks . . . new

b. brakes . . . knew   d. brakes . . . new

40. I don't believe YOU'RE cut-off jeans are the RIGHT clothes for the wedding.

In the sentence above, the capitalized parts should be written:

a. you're . . . right   c. your . . . right

b. you're . . . write   d. your . . . write

41. In which of the following sentences are modifiers used correctly?

a. The first time Sharla baked cookies with her friends, most of them were burned to a crisp.

b. The first time Sharla and her friends baked cookies, most of them were burned to a crisp.

42. In which of the following sentences are modifiers used correctly?

a. The girls were exhausted because they'd stayed up nearly all night talking.

b. The girls were exhausted because they'd nearly stayed up all night talking.

43. In which of the following sentences are modifiers used correctly?

a. Phil wore a handsome suit to the dance that had belonged to his grandfather.

b. Phil wore a handsome suit that had belonged to his grandfather to the dance.

44. Which of the following sentences should end in a question mark?

a. I need a flashlight

b. I wonder if I could borrow your flashlight

c. Do you have a flashlight that I could borrow

d. You may have a flashlight that I could borrow

45. Which of the following has the correct form for a title of a school paper?

a. "My Career Goals"   c. My Career Goals.

b. My Career Goals   d. my career goals

46. The college president read the names of the graduates in a loud, clear voice.

    In the sentence above, the word OF is a(n)

    a. noun.   c. adjective.

    b. adverb.   d. preposition.

47. The bananas in this store cost far too much.

    In the sentence above, the subject is

    a. bananas.   c. cost.

    b. store.   d. much.

48. In the next several days, Geoff will _____ whether or not he will run for student council.

    Which of the following words should fill in the blank above?

    a. decided   c. decide

    b. decides   d. deciding

49. The puddles in the driveway FREEZED solid overnight.

    In the sentence above, the capitalized part should be written:

    a. freezed   c. frozen

    b. frozed   d. froze

50. There IS two reasons I can't come to the party.

    In the sentence above, the capitalized part should be written:

    a. is   b. are

51. Nothing appeals to me right now. Except a nap.

    One correct way to write the above is:

    a. Nothing appeals to me right now. Except a nap.

    b. Nothing appeals to me right now except a nap.

    c. Nothing appeals to me. Right now. Except a nap.

    d. Nothing appeals to me right now. Except for taking a nap.

52. There is a long line for the roller coaster the Ferris wheel is broken.

    One correct way to write the above is:

    a. There is a long line for the roller coaster the Ferris wheel is broken.

    b. There is a long line for the roller coaster. the Ferris wheel is broken.

    c. There is a long line for the roller coaster, the Ferris wheel is broken.

    d. There is a long line for the roller coaster because the Ferris wheel is broken.

53. Horatio went to the movies with Franklin and ME.

    The capitalized part of the above sentence should be written:

    a. me.   b. I.

54. Neither of my brothers WANTS to be a salesman like our father.

    In the sentence above, the capitalized part should be written:

    a. wants   b. want

55. "Didn't you know I was at work? Fred asked."

The correct form of the sentence above is:

   a. "Didn't you know I was at work, Fred asked."

   b. "Didn't you know I was at work? Fred asked.

   c. "Didn't you know I was at work"? Fred asked.

   d. "Didn't you know I was at work?" Fred asked.

56. After coughing nervously, Linda began her speech.

The correct way to write the above sentence is:

   a. After coughing nervously, Linda began her speech.

   b. After coughing nervously Linda began her speech.

   c. After coughing nervously, Linda, began her speech.

   d. none of the above

57. My grandfather a sweet man with a quiet voice was a terrific storyteller.

The correct way to write the above sentence is:

   a. My grandfather a sweet man with a quiet voice was a terrific storyteller.

   b. My grandfather, a sweet man with a quiet voice was a terrific storyteller.

   c. My grandfather, a sweet man with a quiet voice, was a terrific storyteller.

   d. My grandfather a sweet man with a quiet voice, was a terrific storyteller.

58. One of TONYS DREAMS is to become a major league baseball player.

In the sentence above, the capitalized part should be written:

   a. Tonys dreams   c. Tony's dream's

   b. Tony's dreams   d. Tonys' dreams

59. The PRINCIPLE asked the students where THERE parents were.

In the sentence above, the capitalized parts should be written:

   a. principle, their   c. principal, there

   b. principle, they're   d. principal, their

60. In which of the following sentences are modifiers used correctly?

   a. Dave found his favorite T-shirt hanging from a hook on the closet door.

   b. Hanging from a hook on the closet door, Dave found his favorite T-shirt.

SCORING KEY, Diagnostic Test C:

1. c (Basic Punctuation and Paper Format)
2. b (Basic Punctuation and Paper Format)
3. a (Parts of Speech)
4. c (Parts of Speech)
5. d (Parts of Speech)
6. a (Subjects and Verbs)
7. c (Subjects and Verbs)
8. b (Subjects and Verbs)
9. b (Verb Tenses)
10. c (Verb Tenses)
11. d (Verb Tenses)
12. d (Irregular Verbs)
13. b (Irregular Verbs)
14. a (Irregular Verbs)
15. b (Subject-Verb Agreement)
16. b (Subject-Verb Agreement)
17. b (Subject-Verb Agreement)
18. d (Sentence Fragments)
19. c (Sentence Fragments)
20. b (Sentence Fragments)
21. d (Run-Ons and Comma Splices)
22. a (Run-Ons and Comma Splices)
23. d (Run-Ons and Comma Splices)
24. a (Pronouns)
25. c (Pronouns)
26. d (Capital Letters)
27. a (Capital Letters)
28. a (Capital Letters)
29. c (Capital Letters)
30. c (Commas)

31. d (Commas)
32. b (Apostrophes)
33. b (Apostrophes)
34. a (Apostrophes)
35. d (Quotation Marks)
36. b (Quotation Marks)
37. c (Quotation Marks)
38. b (Homonyms)
39. d (Homonyms)
40. c (Homonyms)
41. b (Misplaced and Dangling Modifiers)
42. a (Misplaced and Dangling Modifiers)
43. b (Misplaced and Dangling Modifiers)
44. c (Basic Punctuation and Paper Format)
45. b (Basic Punctuation and Paper Format)
46. d (Parts of Speech)
47. a (Subjects and Verbs)
48. c (Verb Tenses)
49. d (Irregular Verbs)
50. b (Subject-Verb Agreement)
51. b (Sentence Fragments)
52. d (Run-Ons and Comma Splices)
53. a (Pronouns)
54. a (Pronouns)
55. d (Quotation Marks)
56. a (Commas)
57. c (Commas)
58. b (Apostrophes)
59. d (Homonyms)
60. a (Misplaced and Dangling Modifiers)

If a student got one of these questions wrong:	She or he needs help with . . .	Coverage of this topic is available here:	
		College Writing Skills:	AllWrite! 2.0:
1, 2, 44, or 45	Basic Punctuation and Paper Format	Chapter 34	Chapter 23
3, 4, 5, or 46	Parts of Speech	Chapters 23 and 29	Chapter 14.1
6, 7, 8, or 47	Subjects and Verbs	Chapter 23	Chapter 18.1
9, 10, 11, or 48	Verb Tenses	Chapter 28	Chapter 18.2
12, 13, 14, or 49	Irregular Verbs	Chapter 26	Chapter 18
15, 16, 17, or 50	Subject-Verb Agreement	Chapter 27	Chapter 17
18, 19, 20, or 51	Sentence Fragments	Chapter 24	Chapter 15.2
21, 22, 23, or 52	Run-Ons and Comma Splices	Chapter 25	Chapter 15.3, 15.4
24, 25, 53, or 54	Pronouns	Chapters 29 and 30	Chapter 19
26, 27, 28, or 29	Capital Letters	Chapter 35	Chapter 25.1
30, 31, 56, or 57	Commas	Chapter 39	Chapter 23.2
32, 33, 34, or 58	Apostrophes	Chapter 37	Chapter 24.6
35, 36, 37, or 55	Quotation Marks	Chapter 38	Chapter 24.3
38, 39, 40, or 59	Homonyms	Chapter 42	
41, 42, 43, or 60	Dangling and Misplaced Modifiers	Chapters 32 and 33	Chapter 16.2–16.4